Verdict of Three Decades

VERDICT

OF THREE

DECADES

FROM THE LITERATURE OF INDIVIDUAL
REVOLT AGAINST SOVIET COMMUNISM: 1917-1950

EDITED BY JULIEN STEINBERG

DUELL, SLOAN AND PEARCE • NEW YORK

I

For permission to include material in this book, acknowledgment is made to authors, magazines, publishers, and others:

Allen & Unwin, Ltd., and The Macmillan Company, distributors of *The Practice and Theory of Bolshevism* by Bertrand Russell, copyright, 1920, for the selection from that book; *The American Mercury*, for selection by Sidney Hook, copyright, 1949; Geoffrey Bles, Ltd., for extracts from *Out of the Deep*; Charles T. Branford Co., for material from *I Speak for the Silent* by Vladimir V. Tchernavin, copyright, 1935; William Henry Chamberlin, for selection from *Russia's Iron Age*, Little, Brown, copyright, 1934; Crown Publishers for permission to use selection from *Whose Revolution?* by Granville Hicks, copyright, 1941; Duell, Sloan & Pearce, Inc., for material from *Men and Politics* by Louis Fischer, copyright, 1941, 1946; The Gresham Press, Inc., for material from *Tell the West* by Jerzy Gliksman, copyright, 1948; Harcourt, Brace and Co., Inc., for permission to use selection from *Assignment in Utopia* by Eugene Lyons, copyright, 1937; "Integer," for selection from *The State and the Socialist Revolution* by Julius Martov, translated by "Integer," copyright, 1938; International Labor Relations Committee of the American Federation of Labor for selection by Solomon M. Schwarz; International Rescue Committee, Inc., 103 Park Avenue, New York 17, N. Y., David Martin, for the text of "The Eight Fallacies of the Left Babbitt," speech delivered by Arthur Koestler on March 26, 1948, copyright, 1948; Alfred A. Knopf, Inc., for permission to use material reprinted from *Return from the U. S. S. R.* by André Gide, translated by Dorothy Bussy, copyright, 1937; Mrs. Walter G. Krivitsky, for selection from *In Stalin's Secret Service*, Harper, copyright, 1939; *Modern Review*, for selections by Rudolf Hilferding and Bertram D. Wolfe, copyright, 1947; *The New Leader*, for selections by Victor Chernov, Sergei Eisenstein, and Kirill Alexeiev; Pioneer Press, 116 University Place, New York 3, N. Y., for selection from *The Revolution Betrayed* by Leon Trotsky, copyright, 1937, 1945; *Politics*, for selections by Victor Serge, copyright, 1944, 1946, and Peter Meyer, copyright, 1946; Rand School of Social Science for selection from *Social Democracy versus Communism* by Karl Kautsky, copyright, 1946; *The Saturday Review of Literature*, for selection by H. J. Muller, copyright, 1948; Ignazio Silone for "The End of a Concordat," copyright, 1950; Simon and Schuster, Inc., for permission to reprint selection from *Heroes I Have Known* by Max Eastman, copyright, 1942; Boris Souvarine, for "The Cult of Lenin"; Stanford University Press and the authors for permission to use a quotation by Maxim Gorky, reprinted from *The Bolshevik Revolution: 1917–18* by James Bunyan and H. H. Fisher; Whittlesey House, for material reprinted from *This Is My Story* by Louis F. Budenz, copyright, 1947; Bertram D. Wolfe, for selection from Rosa Luxemburg's *The Russian Revolution*, translated by Mr. Wolfe; Yale University Press, for selection from *The Real Soviet Russia* by David J. Dallin, copyright, 1944.

PRINTED IN THE UNITED STATES OF AMERICA

CONTENTS

I. The First Decade: The Revolutionary Aftermath (1917-1927)

II. The Second Decade: From Dictatorship to Totalitarian Society (1928-1939)

III. The Third Decade: The End Product (1940-1950)

PREFACE

This book represents an attempt to depict the progress of the Soviet state from infancy to maturity as reflected in the literature of three decades of individual revolt against Soviet Communism.

In these pages each contributor tells a part of the Soviet story, one that he knows especially well; together they furnish the reader with more than a glimpse into the whole. Many of the contributors are former Communists and sympathizers, others are not. All are in revolt against despotism.

The reader, as he becomes familiar with these writers, will rapidly understand that it is in no way the purpose of this book to derogate the quest for social progress. On the contrary, it is our very concern with human and cultural values that is the *raison d'être* for this book. The indictment of the democratic world against Soviet Communism is not that it is "liberal" or "radical"—it is neither—but that it shares with Nazi totalitarianism the distinction of being the most reactionary system ever known to mankind.

For three decades the Western democracies have observed the Soviet state grow until at present it is one of the two most powerful nations in the world. The present extent of its "influence," armed and otherwise, is the tale of the grim daily headline. The final battle that Lenin so confidently predicted, and that Stalin has so diligently made possible, is now perhaps upon the world.

Our guiding belief then is that after three decades a verdict is more than in order. This book hopes to show that at this late date it does not need to be rendered; it merely asks to be recognized.

ACKNOWLEDGMENTS

I have been fortunate in receiving the cooperation of a number of persons in the preparation of this book and should like to name some here. Aid received runs the gamut from personal permission to include material, or facilitation of its use, to furnishing of information, allowing me the use of materials of various kinds, and other assistance. I should especially like to thank Solomon M. Schwarz, Bertram D. Wolfe, Raphael Abramovitch, S. M. Levitas, Granville Hicks, Mrs. Walter G. Krivitsky, Louis Waldman, Theodore Shapiro, Sidney Hook, Max Eastman, Peter Meyer, Boris Souvarine, William Henry Chamberlin, Eugene Lyons, Ignazio Silone, Irving Talmadge, Daniel Seligman, and Esther Scher. It would be impossible to record my very great debt to my wife, Joanna. It would require a long list to give proper credit to all who have conveniently arranged and printed biographical material on the contributors of the name-place-date variety, and I shall have to express my debt here generally, although in some cases I have drawn heavily on such accounts. None of the above-mentioned persons is, of course, responsible for any opinions expressed in this book—except, in the case of contributors, his own.

—J. S.

I. The First Decade

THE REVOLUTIONARY AFTERMATH

(1917-1927)

Part One

MYTH the first: that the Communists made the Russian Revolution. Of the many absurdities of belief that have been cultivated in the past three decades this notion is surely a prime contender for distinction. The fiction exists in two forms. The first, of more recent origin than the second, barely merits explicit refutation. It is sufficient to state that the view that the Bolsheviks overthrew the Tsar would have greatly amused the Russian people in 1917, that is, should anyone have been foolish enough to utter it. The Russian Revolution suddenly erupted in March, 1917. Rather than being freed from absolutism by the tiny Bolshevik group, the Russian people freed *them* and all political prisoners of Tsarism. The celebrated Bolshevik leaders were not even in Russia during the Revolution. Lenin returned in the middle of April, 1917, and Leon Trotsky one month later, the latter not yet even a member of the Bolsheviks. The period from March to November, 1917 (or February to October, according to the old calendar), was the democratic Russian Revolution, an auspicious period that the passing years, aided by the educational apparatus of the present Russian regime, have obscured with the carbuncles of mythology. In the second formulation of the myth, the Communists have diligently attempted to encourage the belief that the March, 1917, Revolution, the democratic period ushered in by the fall of the Tsar, was merely a "prologue" to

5

the Bolshevik *coup* of November of that year. The purpose of this formulation is evident. It leads one to believe that under the guidance of the Bolsheviks the preceding acts were no more than preparations for the logical succession to power of Lenin's minority group of "professional revolutionaries," and that this course represented the natural development and implementation of the revolutionary feelings aroused in the Russian people.

To state the actual facts is not to be guilty of historical peevishness. This is so because Lenin's seizure of power did not represent a continuity of the revolutionary development; rather, it marked its betrayal.

Who did make the Revolution?

> "This revolution is unique," said Professor Eugene Trubetskoy, a moderate liberal, in a now familiar statement. "There have been bourgeois revolutions and proletarian revolutions, but I doubt that there has ever been a revolution so truly national in the widest sense of the term, as the present Russian one. Every one 'made' this revolution, every one took part in it—the proletariat, the soldiers, the bourgeoisie, even the nobility—all the social forces of the land."

The despised tsarism had fallen. The desires, the fervent hopes, of successive waves of rebels were to become actualities in a magic and joyous moment of history. The Russian people desired ardently that which had been most denied them by a long history of despotism. Freedom of speech, of press, of elections, an abolition of restrictions, an equitable and decent way of life, economically, socially and politically. They wanted a Constituent Assembly, the dream of generations, elected by universal suffrage, by secret ballot, a free parliament to implement the victories of the Revolution.

The prisons were opened, jailed socialists and other revolutionary opponents of the Tsar were freed. Publications of all sorts, and of all views, proclaimed the principles of the new life that was to appear. The news of the revolution coursed through the countries of the world, and fired the imaginations of millions of people. The Tsar had fallen! Freedom in Russia was no longer merely a slogan. There was work to do, work such as had faced all countries during a birth of freedom, revolutionary France, revolutionary America. The specter of Russian absolutism was no more. Free Russia had joined the free nations of the world.

When the Revolution burst upon the world, Lenin was in exile in Switzerland.

* * *

Let us recall voices. How has that birth of Russian democracy been remembered?

> "The February Revolution to its very end," Alexander Kerensky, the socialist who was to become Prime Minister of the Provisional Government in the course of the democratic Revolution, has said, "was animated by its will to national unity; by love and not by hatred; by forgiveness and not by vengeance; asserting liberty for every one and not universal oppression. It was in freedom, in the will to freedom that lay the inspiration of the February Revolution. It set forth many aims—political, social and international—but it would countenance nothing without freedom. And how could it be otherwise? February 27, 1917, marked the end of a long and painful trail, from pure absolutism to absolute democracy. That which only the day before appeared as a distant dream came true so suddenly and so very completely. . . . The people themselves were in power, the people themselves were the owners of Russia."

There were those, of course, to whom the new developments were unpleasant. They were those who found a vision of restoration of privilege more glorious than the liberation of a people; but they take on importance only in retrospect, they were powerless against the united will of the nation. The great mass of the country, socialists, middle class liberals, even the small Bolshevik group, foresaw a Constituent Assembly embracing the elected representatives of all the people. When Lenin returned to Russia, his party's paper, *Pravda,* edited by Stalin and two other Bolsheviks, had a conciliatory line towards the other socialist parties, an editorial position that Lenin found distasteful and which soon was reversed. Then began to appear a pattern which was to repeat itself tragically in a number of countries in the next three decades, notably in Germany. Minority extremists, representing opposite political poles, centered their energies on the same objective: the destruction of the democratic middle. If Kerensky later was to remember the first burst of Russian freedom, the bitter memory of its extinction was also unforgettable:

> "What I want to emphasize about the position in Russia in 1917," he said, countering a prevalent Communist myth, "is this: there were no 'class' proletarian reasons for a civil war, because the proletariat itself, the peasantry and the radical middle class were already in power. I want to stress the fact that the Bolshevik uprising in October was strictly an internecine act within the Russian democracy. . . . The chief object of my policy in the Provisional Government was precisely the prevention by every means in my power, of the transformation of the revolution into a civil war. Only with the help of the extremists of the Right and only late in the autumn did Lenin succeed in torpedoing the democracy and fighting his way to a dictatorship." (Both Kerensky quotations will be found in his *The Crucifixion of Liberty.*)

The extremists of the right and left had little affection for one another; they had even less for the democratic center. What was it that the Provisional Government achieved in the few months of its existence that was so distasteful, for "different" reasons, to both extreme viewpoints? The problems of the successive cabinets of the Provisional Government were considerable. The Government, let it be said, made mistakes, it might have done a number of things in a more efficient fashion. Mostly, it might have protected itself with more vigor. But it is only in the light of three decades of history that we have been furnished with a measuring rod to appraise what was done.

Here is a partial list of accomplishments: a full political amnesty was immediately proclaimed, imprisoned revolutionaries and other victims of tsarism returned to their homes; all national, religious and class restrictions were outlawed; unjust courts were abolished and trial by jury was decreed as the only recognized procedure for the administration of justice; a complete system of equal rights for women was established; exile, that most dreaded punishment of tsarism, was banned as a punitive measure; unconditional liberty of press, organization and assembly was proclaimed, with full recognition of the inviolability of the individual; new provisions were drawn up for the election of urban and rural local authorities, based on universal suffrage and proportional representation; discriminatory measures against the peasantry were rescinded; the principle of self-government was extended to the smallest administrative unit; abrogated were all infringements on the integrity of the judiciary; the independence of Poland was proclaimed. These together with a large number of other measures—political and economic—were the first fruits of the Russian Revolution.

It was *this* Russia that Lenin on April 20, 1917, called the "freest country in the world." It was also in *this* Russia that he came to power by a *coup d'état* in November, 1917.

                        *   *   *

So fervent were Lenin's pro-democratic pronouncements, prior to his taking of power, that he found the accomplishments of the Provisional Government wholly inadequate. The Provisional Government, according to his assertion, was the main obstacle to the full liberation of the Russian people. So he and his followers declaimed publicly. He revised his program to include the most advanced, and admirable, democratic slogans. This blueprint for the new Russian Communist state makes for extremely interesting reading in the light of the diametrically opposed policies he instituted once in power, and, of course, in the light of three decades of Russian history since then.

> "The party of the proletariat cannot rest content with a bourgeois parliamentary democratic republic . . . The Party fights for a more democratic workers' and peasants' republic, in which the police and the standing army will be completely abolished and replaced by the universally armed people, by a universal militia; all official persons will be not only elective, but also subject to recall at any time upon the demand of a majority of the electors; all official persons, without exception, will be paid at a rate not exceeding the average wage of a competent worker . . . ," etc. (*From the Bourgeois to the Proletarian Revolution,* volume six of Lenin's *Selected Works,* pp. 116-17.)

This was Lenin's *announced* program. He made preparations for the insurrection.

* 　 * 　 *

There could be no postponement of the taking of power, he insisted in the inner Bolshevik circle. One day before his *coup* he wrote to the Bolshevik leaders:

> "The situation is critical in the extreme. It is absolutely clear that to delay the insurrection now will veritably

be fatal. I exhort my comrades with all my heart and
strength to realize that everything now hangs on a
thread; that we are being confronted by problems that
can be solved not by conferences or congresses (even
Congresses of Soviets), but exclusively by the people,
by the masses, by the struggle of the armed masses. . . .
We must not wait! We may lose everything! . . . The
matter must be decided unconditionally this very evening, or this very night. History will not forgive revolutionaries for procrastinating when they can be victorious today (will certainly be victorious today), while
they risk losing much, in fact, everything, tomorrow. If
we seize power today, we seize it not in opposition to the
Soviets but on their behalf. The seizure of power is a
matter of insurrection; its political purpose will be clear
after the seizure. . . . The people have the right and
the duty to decide such questions not by a vote, but
by force . . ." (Ibid., pp. 334-35.)

The call for the *coup* was in the name of the "people," the
"masses." The circumstances, however, were far from reassuring. If the Bolsheviks represented the "people," there was
available to them an irrefutable way of demonstrating that fact.
They need only have waited for the elections to the All Russian
Constituent Assembly, the dream of generations. Lenin had
often asserted that the Provisional Government had willfully
delayed the elections; now they were set for November 25, why
not wait? Lenin said that his party spoke for the "masses"; why
not wait until the electoral voice of the united masses was
heard? The answer to these questions was provided when the
elections did take place, *after* Lenin took power. Scheduled by
the Provisional Government, *held under the Bolsheviks,* Lenin's
party received only one fourth of the thirty six million votes
cast. The Constituent Assembly met in January, 1918. This first
and last free representative assembly in Russia's history met

for one day and was dissolved by the bayonets of Lenin's regime.

But if the Bolsheviks (formally renamed Communists early in 1918) did not represent a majority of the country, it is insufficiently known that there was considerable dissent against Lenin's policies within his inner circle, both in the days immediately before and *after* he took power by insurrection. Five members of Lenin's *Central Committee* (Zinoviev, Kamenev, Rykov, Miliutin, Nogin) resigned:

> "We cannot accept the responsibility for the disastrous policy of the Central Committee," they declared publicly, "carried on against the will of an enormous majority of the proletariat and soldiers, who are eager to see the rapid end of the bloodshed between the different political parties of the democracy. . . . We renounce our title as members of the Central Committee, in order to be able to say openly our opinions to the masses of workers and soldiers. . . . We leave the Central Committee at the moment of victory; we cannot calmly look on while the policy of the chiefs of the Central Committee leads toward the loss of the fruits of victory and the crushing of the proletariat. . . ."

In addition, opposition to Lenin embraced *eleven out of fifteen* of the Council of People's Commissars. Five (Nogin, Rykov, Miliutin, Theodorovich, Shliapnikov) resigned outright, the other six (Riazanov, Derbychev, Arbuzov, Yureniev, Feodorov, Larin) signed the dissenting declaration. Let us recall those voices:

> "We are in favor of a Socialist government," read the declaration, "composed of all the parties in the Soviets. We consider that only the creation of such a Government can possibly guarantee the results of the heroic

struggle of the working class and the revolutionary army. Outside of that, there remains only one way: the constitution of a purely Bolshevik Government by means of political terrorism. This last is the road taken by the Council of People's Commissars. We cannot and we will not follow it. We see that this leads directly to the elimination from political life of many proletarian organizations, to the establishment of an irresponsible regime, and to the destruction of the Revolution and the country. We cannot take the responsibility for such a policy . . ." (The above two statements will be found in John Reed's *Ten Days That Shook the World*.)

"The answer of the Leninites was swift and ruthless," John Reed wrote in his famed account. Kamenev was stripped of his powers as President of the *Tsay-ee-kah*, or All Russian Central Executive Committee of the Soviets; Zinoviev was deposed as President of the Petrograd Soviet. Lenin subjected his close associates to a prolonged and abusive tirade, labeling them "deserters" and "strikebreakers," and uninhibitedly aroused a mob spirit against them. "The insurgents," reported John Reed, "never got a chance to 'say openly their opinion to the masses of workers and soldiers.'" So the denouement was uneventful. The dissenters submissively accepted Lenin's leadership and the rule of the Bolsheviks, Lenin forgave them their defection —and they aided in the task of inflicting on the Russian people precisely what they had warned against. But in remembering the prescient voices of 1917, it is well to recall the words of those leading Bolsheviks.

✻   ✻   ✻

There are other voices that speak to us now across time from the year 1917, many voices. But they were soon to be silenced. The March Revolution had come to an end; Russian democracy had died in the throes of birth. In November, 1917, began the reign that has not yet ceased, a regime that installed itself by force and that has ruled by compulsion since. Indeed, as Lenin had said, "The seizure of power is a matter of insurrection; its political purpose will be clear after the seizure."

Rosa Luxemburg

THE RUSSIAN REVOLUTION

Editor's Note

FEW persons realized at the time of the writing of Rosa Luxemburg's pamphlet, "The Russian Revolution," how much stature it was to gain with time. In the fifty-odd pages of this unfinished work—written in the difficult environment of prison—the author at the very start had clearly foreseen in many respects what was to become of the Russian Revolution if continued on the base that had been instituted by the Bolsheviks after their ascension to power. The pamphlet was not written to disparage the possible achievements of the Bolshevik Revolution; on the contrary, after having devoted her life to the revolutionary cause—indeed, she lost it in that cause—Luxemburg wanted, most of all, to have achievements solidified, made increasingly better and more secure. Written from such a point of view, her perceptive criticisms become that much more remarkable.

She was born in 1870 in a small town in Russian Poland. Her family was wealthy and well educated; she was one of five children. Interested in political activities she was ultimately forced to flee to Zurich. She studied botany and zoology at first and later law and economics. This latter study converted her to Marxism. In 1893 she assisted in the founding of the Social Democratic Party of Poland and Lithuania, as a section of the Marxian Russian Social Democracy. Arriving in Germany three years later, she rapidly gained recognition as one of the notable economic theorists of the Social Democracy. (Her major economic work, written in 1913, is *Die Akkumulation des Kapitals*.) This preoccupation with theory, however, did not cause her to forsake her revolutionary activity. In Warsaw she played an active role in the revolution of 1905-06, and in time found herself on the extreme revolutionary left. In Stuttgart, at an international socialist congress in 1907, she joined Lenin in composing the resolution which stressed the strategy of the revolutionary overthrow of capitalism during wartime. She differed, however, with Lenin regarding many revolutionary policies, including the formation of a new International, which she opposed, and on the need for democracy in organizational matters, which she stressed. About the latter she said: "It is the mission of the proletariat on attaining power to substitute for bourgeois democracy a socialist democracy, not to destroy all democracy." And again: "Socialism by its nature cannot be imposed, cannot be established by ukase." After World War I began, she attacked the German Social Democracy for supporting the war effort, and, implementing her stand, she and famed revolutionary Karl Liebknecht founded the *Spartakusbund* to build anti-war feeling. She spent the years from 1915 until the end of the war almost uninterruptedly in prison.

During this period her influence on the revolutionary movement continued to grow. Her writings were smuggled out of prison and widely circulated. In 1918 she played an important role in organizing the Communist Party of Germany. When the Berlin workers' uprising broke out she participated in it despite her conviction that it was premature. This led to her arrest by the Ebert Government. In January, 1919, she and Karl Liebknecht were murdered by the "soldiers" in whose custody they had been placed. Later, Rosa Luxemburg's body was found floating in the Landwehr Canal.

Her 1918 pamphlet "The Russian Revolution," from which we extract several pages, was originally written as an article for the underground publication, *Spartacus Letters*, when she was in Breslau prison for her opposition to the First World War. Pressure was exerted by friends urging that she withhold it from publication. Their argument: the time was not ripe, the Russian revolutionary cause would be injured. Her attitude, by contrast, was that honest criticism was always in order.

#

The Russian Revolution by Rosa Luxemburg

LENIN says: the bourgeois state is an instrument of oppression of the working class; the socialist state, of the bourgeoisie. To a certain extent, he says, it is only the capitalist state stood on its head. This simplified view misses the most essential thing: bourgeois class rule has no need of the political training and education of the entire mass of the people, at least not beyond certain narrow limits. But for the proletarian dictatorship that is the life element, the very air without which it is not able to exist.

"Thanks to the open and direct struggle for governmental power," writes Trotsky, "the laboring masses accumulate in the shortest time a considerable amount of political experience and advance quickly from one stage to another of their development."

Here Trotsky refutes himself and his own friends. Just because this is so, they have blocked up the fountain of political experience and the source of this rising development by their suppression of public life! Or else we would have to assume that experience and development were necessary up to the seizure of power by the Bolsheviks, and then, having reached their highest peak, became superfluous thereafter. (Lenin's speech: Russia is won for socialism!!!)

In reality, the opposite is true! It is the very giant tasks which the Bolsheviks have undertaken with courage and determination that demand the most intensive political training of the masses and the accumulation of experience.

Freedom only for the supporters of the government, only for the members of one party—however numerous they may be—is no freedom at all. Freedom is always and exclusively freedom for the one who thinks differently. Not because of any fanatical concept of "justice" but because all that is instructive, wholesome and purifying in political freedom depends on this essential characteristic, and its effectiveness vanishes when "freedom" becomes a special privilege.

The Bolsheviks themselves will not want, with hand on heart, to deny that, step by step, they have to feel out the ground, try out, experiment, test now one way, now another, and that a good many of their measures do not represent priceless pearls of wisdom. Thus it must and will be with all of us when we get to the same point—even if the same difficult circumstances may not prevail everywhere.

The tacit assumption underlying the Lenin-Trotsky theory of the dictatorship is this: that the socialist transformation is something for which a ready-made formula lies completed in the pocket of the revolutionary party, which needs only to be carried out energetically in practice. This is, unfortunately—or perhaps fortunately—not the case. Far from being a sum of ready-made prescriptions which have only to be applied, the practical realization of socialism as an economic, social and juridical system is something which lies completely hidden in the mists of the future. What we possess in our program is nothing but a few main signposts which indicate the general direction in which to look for the necessary measures, and the indications are mainly negative in character at that. Thus we know more or less what we must eliminate at the outset in order to free the road for a socialist economy. But when it comes to the nature of the thousand concrete, practical measures, large and small, necessary to introduce socialist principles into economy, law and all social relationships, there is no key in any socialist party program or textbook. That is not a shortcoming but rather the very thing that makes scientific socialism superior to the utopian varieties. The socialist system of society should only be, and can only be, an historical product, born out of the school of its own experiences, born in the course of its realization, as a result of the developments of living history, which—just like organic nature of which, in the last analysis, it forms a part—has the fine habit of always producing along with any real social need the means to its satisfaction, along with the task simultaneously the solution. However, if such is the case, then it is clear that socialism by its very nature cannot be decreed or introduced by *ukase*. It has as its prerequisite a number of measures of force—against property, etc. The negative, the tearing down, can be decreed; the building up, the positive, cannot. New territory. A thousand problems. Only experience is capable of correcting and opening new ways. Only unobstructed, effervescing life falls into a thousand new forms and improvisations, brings to light creative force, itself corrects all mistaken attempts. The public life of countries with limited freedom is so poverty-stricken, so miserable, so rigid, so unfruitful, precisely because, through the exclusion of democracy, it cuts off the living sources of all spiritual riches and progress. . . .

Public control is indispensably necessary. Otherwise the exchange of experiences remains only with the closed circle of the officials of the new regime. Corruption becomes inevitable. (Lenin's words, Bulletin No. 29) Socialism in life demands a complete spiritual transformation in the masses degraded by centuries of bourgeois class rule. Social instincts in place of egotistical ones, mass initiative in place of inertia, idealism which conquers all suffering, etc., etc. No one knows this better, describes it more penetratingly, repeats it more stubbornly than Lenin. But he is completely mistaken in the means he employs. Decree, dictatorial force of the factory overseer, draconic penalties, rule by terror—all these things are but palliatives. The only way to a rebirth is the school of public life itself, the most unlimited, the broadest democracy and public opinion. It is rule by terror which demoralizes.

When all this is eliminated, what really remains? In place of the representative bodies created by general, popular elections, Lenin and Trotsky have laid down the soviets as the only true representation of the laboring masses. But with the repression of political life in the land as a whole, life in the soviets must also become more and more crippled. Without general elections, without unrestricted freedom of press and assembly, without a free struggle of opinion, life dies out in every public institution, becomes a mere semblance of life, in which only the bureaucracy remains as the active element. Public life gradually falls asleep, a few dozen party leaders of inexhaustible energy and boundless experience direct and rule. Among them, in reality only a dozen outstanding heads do the leading and an elite of the working class is invited from time to time to meetings where they are to applaud the speeches of the leaders, and to approve proposed resolutions unanimously—at bottom, then, a clique affair—a dictatorship, to be sure, not the dictatorship of the proletariat, however, but only the dictatorship of a handful of politicians, that is a dictatorship in the bourgeois sense, in the sense of the rule of the Jacobins (the postponement of the Soviet Congress from three-month periods to six-month period!) Yes, we can go even further: such conditions must inevitably cause a brutalization of public life: attempted assassinations, shooting of hostages, etc. . . .

Karl Kautsky

THE NEW THEORY

Editor's Note

OPPOSITION to the Bolsheviks, the Communists explain simply, came from "counter-revolutionary" elements. In our present day many persons have painfully learned to recognize the manner in which "counter-revolutionary" is defined by the Communists, *i.e.*, anyone who is in opposition to the regime. Thus, in the latter half of the 1930s the most famous Russian Communist leaders were indicted in the Moscow Trials and subsequently executed as counter-revolutionaries. In view of this fact, it is not at all surprising that liberals, socialists, all should regularly be termed "counter-revolutionaries." What still manages, however, to escape sufficient notice is that this technique is not a new one. Historically, this convenient depiction of opponents was a basis of practice for the Communists from the moment they took power in 1917. Our concern here, therefore, is with the prime myth: that all opposition to the Bolsheviks at the very start, as the Communists are fond of maintaining, can truthfully be characterized *per se* as counter-revolutionary.

It is of no small importance that this subject be examined for the Communists have intermittently braved criticism with the defense that they represent The Revolution. By interpreting the phrase in a most general and variable way they have impressed many liberal audiences—precisely those whom they have dealt with most ruthlessly in Russia, and elsewhere—with their role as the chief defenders of liberalism in our time. This is unfortunate, for few ruling classes in history have been more open to the charge of reaction. It is particularly instructive to observe in the present context, as an introduction to this selection, that the person almost universally recognized as the most authoritative exponent of socialist thought in our day, a role he held for half a century, should have termed the Communist ruling class as counter-revolutionary. That man was Karl Kautsky.

He wrote very fully on Russian problems both before and after the 1917 Revolution. As early as the year following their *coup d'état,* he warned the Bolsheviks of what they were creating when they sought dictatorial power. In notable succession he wrote two remarkable books, *Dictatorship of the Proletariat* (1918), and *Terrorism and Communism* (1919), which have since become political classics. Giving the Bolsheviks the benefit of every doubt, Kautsky taught that the revolution—and the great hopes it heralded—could be saved, and an era of extreme fruitfulness inaugurated, but the *sine qua non* of such a development was the replacement of dictatorial methods by democracy. The warning was ignored and Kautsky's name subjected to considerable abuse; for a sample of this treatment, see Lenin's *The Proletarian Revolution and the Renegade Kautsky.*

Before acquainting ourselves further with Kautsky, it is interesting to note, in passing, that even in Lenin's above mentioned tirade against the socialist leader, he is compelled, for all his vituperation, to accept Kautsky's stature, his eminence in the field of Marxist theory, a political heritage which Lenin now claimed to serve in his new role of official prime prophet. Thus, Lenin sneeringly (and significantly) feels obliged to advise his readers: "It must not be forgotten that Kautsky knows Marx almost by heart, and judging by all he has written, he has in his desk, or in his head, a number of pigeon-holes in which all that was ever written by Marx is carefully distributed. . . ." In another place, he omits the qualification "almost" and refers to "Kautsky, who knows Marx and Engels by heart." Since the "point" at issue was that of the "dictatorship of the proletariat," and Lenin's interpretation and advocacy of it as a *dictatorial governmental form* by reference to the teachings of Marx, it will be understood that Kautsky's democratic dissent could not be dismissed merely as uninformed. In a shabby performance, Lenin utilized all his talents, and these were great, of invective and misrepresentation.

The overall "justification" of the more candid Communists for the callous suppression of all opposition soon after they took power was that history left them no alternative; all they did was necessary, a contention that continues to sway the uninformed. As popularly understood, the argument hinges on the choice between the Communist dictatorship or the restoration of the tsarist autocracy. These, as we shall see, were not the only two possible roads. There was a third, and the Communists renounced it, and forcibly suppressed all those who advocated it. As a principle, the argument of necessity has continued to be espoused by the Soviet Union in defence of all its policies and decisions. Thus, the Moscow Trials were "necessary," the recurrent purges were "necessary," the Nazi-Soviet Pact was "necessary." The extreme relevance and significance of Karl Kautsky's views is reflected on two levels. First, as he pointed out immediately after the revolution, dictatorship was advocated and utilized by the Communists as an ideology and not as a temporary measure, a charge no doubt regarded as fanciful by many who were certain that in time the dictatorial apparatus would fade from sight. Had not Lenin himself declared, in keeping with Marxian tradition, that the *state* itself would wither and die? The passing years, however, have witnessed only a steady expansion and tightening of the structures of dictatorship, and Kautsky's early charge has unfortunately been fully established. More than anyone else, Kautsky would have wished to be proven wrong; he was only too correct. Second, he taught that the dictatorial methods that the Communists chose were not "necessary." A democratic alternative was not only possible but vastly preferable to the method of dictatorship; its acceptance was mandatory if the aims of the revolution were to be converted into humanistic achievement. That this should have been recognized and put forward by Karl Kautsky is, again, most damaging to the Communist myth, for he could not be said to advocate a return to tsarism, which he despised, but, on the contrary, insisted on the Bolsheviks implementing the slogans of their announced democratic political program which they had publicized in their rise to power, a program they betrayed in every essential immediately *after* taking power.

Writing about Karl Kautsky, in an introduction to the collection of essays we mention below, Sidney Hook has phrased the matter excellently; his immediate point was rebuttal of Harold Laski's latter-day "discovery" that the Communists had no alternative and therefore were compelled to have acted as they did, a history-made-us-be-dictators kind of justification.

> It should be noted [wrote Professor Hook] that Karl Kautsky meets squarely Laski's newly made discovery that Russia's political and cultural terror is historically justifiable in the sense that no other alternatives were open. As a matter of fact, clear alternatives existed to every major measure of domestic and foreign policy adopted by the Communists from 1918, when they bayoneted out of existence the democratically elected Constituent Assembly (whose convocation they had advocated in the hope they would win a majority), to the Stalin-Nazi Pact of 1939 which secured Hitler against a second front and gave him the green light to unleash a world war. At the time these events occurred Laski condemned them as well as the terror with which they were accompanied. Kautsky discusses with plausible detail what the evolution of Russia and the history

of Europe would have been if the Constituent Assembly had not been dispersed. If one denies that there are major alternatives in history, and makes his moral judgment completely dependent on historical fact, not only must he believe that Stalinism and Hitlerism were inevitable but that whoever wins is right.

From the very start, Kautsky's writings established how unnecessary was the Communist course of action, how it represented from 1917 onwards a betrayal of the democratic aspirations of the Russian people, and made impossible for them the achievement of a democratic way of life, the ideal which gave them encouragement and enthusiasm in their hard years of struggle against pre-revolutionary autocracy. It is essential that this early period be understood if the reader is to recognize the basic continuity—we do not say *identity*—between Lenin's Russia and Stalin's Russia, a subject we shall be recurrently concerned with in this book. Although Stalinism was not yet on the scene—it was to appear, however, soon after Lenin's death—the way for it was being paved, an erection of sturdy dictatorial foundations without which the giant prison of Stalinism could not have been constructed. Therefore, more than "history" is at stake; among other considerations, an understanding of the origins of the Soviet dictatorship is of paramount importance for an understanding of its totalitarian manifestations today.

In 1931, in his *Bolshevism at a Deadlock,* Kautsky reflected on his thinking regarding Communist rule in Russia since its inception. He recalled his conviction during the last few weeks of 1917 and early in 1918 that the "methods of Soviet Russian Communism must achieve exactly the opposite result from the one promised." Remembering the pro-Bolshevik enthusiasm of many of his political friends, he observed: "How willingly would I have joined them!" He waited, and hoped, for his doubts to be dispelled. "Although doubtful I still watched the first steps of Bolshevism with friendly eyes." His hopes were soon shattered. "Sadly I saw, ever more clearly, that the Bolsheviks completely misunderstood the situation; that they thoughtlessly set themselves a task for the fulfillment of which all the necessary conditions were lacking, and that in their endeavor to achieve the impossible by brute force they were employing means which, instead of improving the economic, intellectual and moral position of the working masses, were undermining it more than Tsarism and the War had already done. I considered it my duty to warn the Bolsheviks emphatically not to continue this policy." This he did in the summer of 1918, and from that time until his death, Kautsky was to write on Soviet Communism with especially impressive insight. To quote Professor Hook again: "Next to Karl Marx and Frederick Engels, none can speak on Socialism and Communism with greater intellectual authority than Karl Kautsky."

In order to place before the reader basic strands of Karl Kautsky's clear-sighted and prescient insights at the time of the inception of the Communist dictatorship, and of his later retrospective summation, when time had tragically vindicated his criticisms, this selection is composed of two parts. The first, "The New Theory," is the last chapter of his 1918 work, *Dictatorship of the Proletariat*; the second, "The Russian Revolution of 1917," is from his *Social Democracy versus Communism* (1946), a collection of Kautsky's writings during the years 1932-37. Together, they furnish a key to his central views, and an understanding of the crucial beginning period of the Communist dictatorship that the years, and continuing Soviet propaganda, have obscured.

Karl Kautsky was born in Prague on October 16, 1854. He was early involved in political study and later came to be recognized as Marx' foremost interpreter. When his *The Moving Forces of the Russian Revolution,* published in 1906, was translated into Russian, it carried a preface by Lenin in which the father of Bolshevism paid tribute to Kautsky as the only analyst among western European socialists who truly understood Russia. This accolade Kautsky continued to justify by his later writings but in a way that Lenin was ultimately no longer able to appreciate.

In 1883 Kautsky founded the socialist publication *Die Neue Zeit* and his reputation began to grow. Later he assumed the lead in the fight against the revision of Karl Marx which was waged by Eduard Bernstein and others. In 1914 he adopted a pacifist attitude and three years later helped organize the Independent Social Democratic Party. He declined, however, to follow his party into the United German Communist Party, and later rejoined the Social Democratic Party. He continued to write many essays and books against the theories of Lenin and Trotsky, and later, against Stalin's Russia. He became a citizen of Czechoslovakia in 1934 and escaped to that country from Vienna when the Nazis marched into Austria. Some months later when the Germans were about to absorb the Sudetenland, he fled to Amsterdam. Here he died in modest circumstances in 1938. His works: *Democracy and Dictatorship; From Democracy to State Slavery; The Labor Revolution; The Proletarian Revolution; Bolshevism at a Deadlock; Soviet Russia and the Socialist International; The Limitations of Force;* as well as other books and numerous articles have been translated into many languages. Between 1927 and 1937 he published a several volume work on socialism which was hailed throughout Europe as the most important writings in the socialist literature since the publication of the famed works by Karl Marx.

Kautsky was that rare kind of political leader who was capable of winning respect even from his opponents. He could always be counted upon, whatever the intensity of his feelings, to fight for democracy, for the right of all to be heard. In this connection, one notes with especial interest the high praise accorded him several years ago by Bishop G. Bromley Oxnam, President of the Federal Council of the Churches of Christ in America, who wrote: "The ablest criticism of the entire concept of dictatorship has come from leading socialists, such as Karl Kautsky, whose little volume *The Dictatorship of the Proletar-*

iat was a devastating analysis of the doctrines of dictatorship. Parliamentary socialism has been attacked by the communists with the utmost ferocity; it has been ridiculed as utopian and has been castigated as counter-revolutionary." (*Labor and Tomorrow's World,* 1945.)

#

The New Theory by Karl Kautsky

THE method of dictatorship does not promise good results for the proletariat, either from the standpoint of theory or from that of special Russian conditions; nevertheless, it is understandable only in the light of those conditions.

The fight against Czarism was for a long time a fight against a system of government which had ceased to be based on the conditions prevailing, but was only maintained by naked force, and only by force was to be overthrown. This fact would easily lead to a cult of force even among the revolutionaries, and to over-estimating what could be done by the powers over them, which did not repose on the economic conditions, but on special circumstances. Accordingly, the struggle against Czarism was carried on secretly, and the method of conspiracy created the manners and the habits proper to dictatorship, and not to democracy.

The operation of these factors was, however, crossed by another consequence of the struggle against Absolutism. We have already referred to the fact that, in contradistinction to democracy, which awakens an interest for wider relations and greater objects side by side with its constant preoccupations with momentary ends, Absolutism arouses theoretical interest. There is to-day, however, only one revolutionary theory of society, that of Karl Marx.

This became the theory of Russian Socialism. Now what this theory teaches is that our desires and capabilities are limited by the material conditions, and it shows how powerless is the strongest will which would rise superior to them. It conflicted sharply with the cult of mere force, and caused the Social Democrats to recognise that definite boundaries were set to their participation in the coming Revolution, which, owing to the economic backwardness of Russia, could only be a middle-class one.

Then the second Revolution came, and suddenly brought a measure of power to the Socialists which surprised them, for this Revolution led to the complete demobilisation of the Army, which was the strongest support of property and middle class order. And at the same time as the physical support collapsed, the moral support of this order went to pieces, neither the Church nor the Intellectuals being able to maintain their pretensions. The rule devolved on the lower classes in the State, the workers and peasants, but the peasants do not form a class which is able itself to govern. They willingly permitted themselves to be led by a Proletarian Party, which promised them immediate peace, at whatever price, and immediate satisfaction of their land hunger. The masses of the proletariat rallied to the same party, which promised them peace and bread.

Thus the Bolshevist Party gained the strength which enabled it to seize political power. Did this not mean that at length the prerequisite was obtained which Marx and Engels had postulated for the coming of Socialism, viz., the conquest of political power by the proletariat? In truth, economic theory discountenanced the idea that Socialist production was realisable at once under the social conditions of Russia, and not less unfavourable to it was the practical confirmation of this theory, that the new regime in no way signified the sole rule of the proletariat, but the rule of a coalition of proletarian and peasant elements, which left each section free to behave as it liked on its own territory. The proletariat put nothing in the way of the peasants as regards the land, and the peasants put no obstacle in the way of the proletariat as regards the factories. None the less, a Socialist Party had become the ruler in a great State, for the first time in the world's history. Certainly a colossal and, for the fighting proletariat, a glorious event.

But for what can a Socialist Party use its power except to bring about Socialism? It must at once proceed to do so, and, without thought or regard, clear out of the way all obstacles which confront it. If democracy thereby comes in conflict with the new regime, which, in spite of the great popularity which it so quickly won, cannot dispose of a majority of the votes in the Empire, then so much the worse for democracy. Then it must be replaced by dictatorship, which is all the easier to accomplish, as the people's freedom is quite a new thing in Russia, and as yet has struck no deep roots amongst the masses of the people. It was now the task of dictatorship to bring about Socialism. This object lesson must not only suffice for the elements in its own country which are still in opposition, but must also compel the proletariat of other capitalist countries to imitation, and provoke them to Revolution.

This was assuredly a train of thought of outstanding boldness and fascinating glamour for every proletarian and every Socialist. What we have struggled for during half a century, what we have so often thought ourselves to be near, what has always again evaded us, is at length going to be accomplished. No wonder that the proletarians of all countries have hailed Bolshevism. The reality of proletarian rule weighs heavier in the scale than theoretical considerations. And that consciousness of victory is still more strengthened by mutual ignorance of the conditions of the neighbour. It is only possible for a few to study foreign countries, and the majority believe that in foreign countries it is at bottom the same as with us, and when this is not believed, very fantastic ideas about foreigners are entertained.

Consequently, we have the convenient conception that everywhere the same Imperialism prevails, and also the conviction of the Russian Socialists that the political revolution is as near to the peoples of Western Europe as it is in Russia, and, on the other hand, the belief that the conditions necessary for Socialism exist in Russia as they do in Western Europe.

What happened, once the Army had been dissolved and the Assembly had been proscribed, was only the consequence of the step that had been taken.

All this is very understandable, if not exactly encouraging. On the other hand, it is not so conceivable why our Bolshevist comrades do not explain their measures on the ground of the peculiar situation in Russia, and justify them in the light of the pressure of the special circumstances, which, according to their notions, left no choice but dictatorship or abdication. They went beyond this by formulating quite a new theory, on which they based their measures, and for which they claimed universal application.

For us the explanation of this is to be found in one of their characteristics, for which we should have great sympathy, viz., their great interest in theory.

The Bolshevists are Marxists, and have inspired the proletarian sections coming under their influence with great enthusiasm for Marxism. Their dictatorship, however, is in contradiction to the Marxist teaching that no people can overcome the obstacles offered by the successive phases of their development by a jump, or by legal enactment. How is it that they find a Marxist foundation for their proceedings?

They remembered opportunely the expression, "the dictatorship of the proletariat," which Marx used in a letter written in 1875. In so doing he had, indeed, only intended to describe a political *condition,* and not a *form of government.* Now this expression is hastily employed to designate the latter, especially as manifested in the rule of the Soviets.

Now if Marx had somewhere said that under certain circumstances things might come to a dictatorship of the proletariat, he has described this condition as one unavoidable for the transition to Socialism. In fact, as he declared, almost at the same time that in countries like England and America a peaceful transition to Socialism was possible, which would only be on the basis of democracy and not of dictatorship, he has also shown that he did not mean by dictatorship the suspension of democracy. Yet this does not disconcert the champions of dictatorship. As Marx once stated that the dictatorship of the proletariat might be unavoidable, so they announce that the Soviet Constitution, and the disfranchising of its opponents, was recognised by Marx himself as the form of government corresponding to the nature of the proletariat, and indissolubly bound up with its rule. As such it must last as long as the rule of the proletariat itself, and until Socialism is generally accomplished and all class distinctions have disappeared.

In this sense dictatorship does not appear to be a transitory emergency measure, which, so soon as calmer times have set in, will again give place to democracy, but as a condition for the long duration of which we must adapt ourselves.

This interpretation is confirmed by Theses 9 and 10 respecting the Social Revolution,* which state:

> (9) Hitherto, the necessity of the Dictatorship of the Proletariat was taught, without enquiring as to the form it would take. The Russian Socialist Revolution has discovered this form. It is the form of the Soviet Republic as the type of the permanent Dictatorship of the Proletariat and (in Russia) of the poorer classes of peasants. It is therefore necessary to make the following remarks. We are speaking now, not of a passing phenomenon, in the narrower sense of the word, but of a particular form of the State during the whole historical epoch. What needs now to be done is to organise a new form of the State, and this is not to be confused with special measures directed against the middle class, which are only functions of a special State organisation appropriate to the colossal tasks and struggle.
>
> (10) The proletarian dictatorship accordingly con-

* ["Theses on the Socialist Revolution and the Tasks of the Proletariat During Its Dictatorship in Russia," written by Bukharin in the summer of 1918.—Ed.]

sists, so to speak, in a permanent state of war against the middle class. It is also quite clear that all those who cry out about the violence of the Communists completely forget what dictatorship really is. The Revolution itself is an act of naked force. The word dictatorship signifies in all languages nothing less than government by force. The class meaning of force is here important, for it furnishes the historical justification of revolutionary force. It is also quite obvious that the more difficult the situation of the Revolution becomes, the sharper the dictatorship must be.

From the above it is also apparent that Dictatorship as a form of government is not only to be a permanent thing, but will also arise in all countries.

If in Russia now the newly-acquired general freedom is put an end to again, this must also happen after the victory of the proletariat in countries where the people's freedom is already deeply rooted, where it has existed for half a century and longer, and where the people have won it and maintained it in frequent bloody revolutions. The new theory asserts this in all earnestness. And stranger still it finds support not only amongst the workers of Russia, who still remember the yoke of the old Czardom, and now rejoice to be able to turn the handle for once, even as apprentices when they become journeymen rejoice when they may give the apprentices who come after them the drubbing they used to receive themselves—no, the new theory finds support even in old democracies like Switzerland.

Yet something stranger still and even less understandable is to come.

A complete democracy is to be found nowhere, and everywhere we have to strive after modifications and improvements. Even in Switzerland there is an agitation for the extension of the legislative powers of the people, for proportional representation and for woman suffrage. In America the power and mode of selection of the highest judges need to be very severely restricted. Far greater are the demands that should be put forward by us in the great bureaucratic and militarist States in the interests of democracy. And in the midst of these struggles, the most extreme fighters raise their heads, and say to the opponents: That which we demand for the protection of minorities, the opposition, we only want so long as we ourselves are the opposition, and in the minority. As soon as we have become the majority, and gained the power of government, our first act will be to abolish as far as you are concerned all that we formerly demanded for ourselves, viz., franchise, freedom of Press and of organisation, etc.

The Theses respecting the Socialist Revolution are quite unequivocal on this point:

(17) The former demands for a democratic republic, and general freedom (that is freedom for the middle classes as well) were quite correct in the epoch that is now passed, the epoch of preparation and gathering of strength. The worker needed freedom for his Press, while the middle-class Press was noxious to him, but he could not at this time put forward a demand for the suppression of the middle-class Press. Consequently, the proletariat demanded general freedom, even freedom for reactionary assemblies, for black labour organisations.

(18) Now we are in the period of the direct attack on capital, the direct overthrow and destruction of the imperialist robber State, and the direct suppression of the middle class. It is therefore absolutely clear that in the present epoch the principle of defending general freedom (that is also for the counter-revolutionary middle class) is not only superfluous, but directly dangerous.

(19) This also holds good for the Press, and the leading organisations of the social traitors. The latter have been unmasked as the active elements of the counter-revolution. They even attack with weapons the

proletarian Government. Supported by former officers
and the money bags of the defeated finance capital, they
appear on the scene as the most energetic organisations
for various conspiracies. The proletariat dictatorship is
their deadly enemy. Therefore, they must be dealt with
in a corresponding manner.

(20) As regards the working class and the poor peasants, these possess the fullest freedom.

Do they really possess the fullest freedom?
The "Social Traitors" * are proletarians and Socialists, too, but
they offer opposition, and are therefore to be deprived of rights
like the middle-class opposition. Would we not display the live-
liest anger, and fight with all our strength in any case where a
middle-class government endeavoured to employ similar measures against its opposition?
Certainly we should have to do so, but our efforts would
only have a laughable result if the middle-class government
could refer to Socialist precepts like the foregoing, and a practice corresponding with them.
How often have we reproached the Liberals that they are
different in Government from what they are in opposition, and
that then they abandon all their democratic pretensions. Now
the Liberals are at least sufficiently prudent to refrain from
the formal abandonment of any of their democratic demands.
They act according to the maxim; one does this, but does not
say so.
The authors of the Theses are undeniably more honourable;
whether they are wiser may be doubted. What would be
thought of the wisdom of the German Social Democrats, if they
openly announced that the democracy, for which they fight today, would be abandoned the day after victory. That they have
perverted their democratic principles to their opposites, or that
they have no democratic principles at all; that democracy is

* [A Communist epithet for democratic socialists.—*Ed.*]

merely a ladder for them, up which to climb to governmental omnipotence, a ladder they will no longer need, and will push away, as soon as they have reached the top, that, in a word, they are revolutionary opportunists.

Even for the Russian revolutionaries it is a short-sighted policy of expediency, if they adopt the method of dictatorship, in order to gain power, not to save the jeopardised democracy, but in order to maintain themselves in spite of it. This is quite obvious.

On the other hand, it is less obvious why some German Social Democrats who are not yet in power, who furthermore only at the moment represent a weak opposition, accept this theory. Instead of seeing something which should be generally condemned in the method of dictatorship, and the disfranchising of large sections of the people, which at the most is only defensible as a product of the exceptional conditions prevailing in Russia, they go out of their way to praise this method as a condition which the German Social Democracy should also strive to realise.

This assertion is not only thoroughly false, it is in the highest degree destructive. If generally accepted, it would paralyse the propagandist strength of our party to the utmost, for, with the exception of a small handful of sectarian fanatics, the entire German, as also the whole proletariat of the world, is attached to the principle of general democracy. The proletariat would angrily repudiate every thought of beginning its rule with a new privileged class, and a new disfranchised class. It would repudiate every suggestion of coupling its demand for general rights for the whole people with a mental reservation, and in reality only strive for privileges for itself. And not less would it repudiate the comic insinuation of solemnly declaring now that its demand for democracy is a mere deceit.

Dictatorship as a form of government in Russia is as understandable as the former anarchism of Bakunin. But to understand it does not mean that we should recognize it; we must reject the former as decisively as the latter. The dictatorship does not reveal itself as a resource of a Socialist Party to secure itself in the sovereignty which has been gained in opposition to the majority of the people, but only as a means of grappling with tasks which are beyond its strength, and the solution of which exhausts and wears it; in doing which it only too easily compromises the ideas of Socialism itself, the progress of which it impedes rather than assists.

Happily, the failure of the dictatorship is not synonymous with a collapse of the Revolution. It would be so only if the Bolshevist dictatorship was the mere prelude to a middle-class dictatorship. The essential achievements of the Revolution will be saved, if dictatorship is opportunely replaced by democracy.

The Russian Revolution of 1917

The Russian Revolution of March 1917 occurred under circumstances which could not possibly have been more favorable for the socialist parties, even though not for the immediate introduction of Socialism. The czarist govermental machinery was in ruins, the obsolete nobility lay helpless, while the capitalist class, its capital largely of foreign origin, showed itself impotent. All-powerful were only the workers and intellectuals in combination with the peasantry. Among these the Socialists were in overwhelming majority—the Social Revolutionists among the peasants; the Social Democrats, Mensheviks as well as Bolsheviks, among the wage earners and intellectuals.

After the fall of Czarism it appeared self-evident that the various Socialist parties, the Social Democrats and Social Revolutionists would work together in the Soviets, and that the cooperation would embrace both wings of the Social Democracy, Mensheviks and Bolsheviks. And why not? Did not all of them have a common aim: establishment of a democratic republic, the eight hour day, confiscation of the land?

But Lenin disliked intensely any such cooperation with the Socialists. Long before the revolution he had formed his own organization within the Social Democracy. This dual organization was built on military lines and within this organization Lenin had established his own dictatorship.* For this reason he had brought about a split in the Russian Social Democracy in 1903 and declared war against all Social Democrats who had refused to pay blind obedience to his leadership.

After the split of 1903 and as late as July, 1914, shortly before the outbreak of the war, Lenin fought bitterly against unity with the Mensheviks. During the war he continued to preach the idea of split not only in the Russian Social Democracy but in the entire Socialist International. For this reason he fought bitterly against any united front of the workers when such a united front became possible after the revolution of 1917.

Lenin was in Switzerland when the revolution of March, 1917, occurred in Russia. He returned to Russia a month after the revolution and found a situation which made him very bitter. Shortly before his arrival there was held an all-Russian conference of Soviets which revealed a very great measure of agreement between the Mensheviks and Bolsheviks.

There followed at the conclusion of the conference a joint meeting of the Mensheviks and Bolsheviks to discuss unity of both factions. These negotiations were stopped through the arrival of Lenin, who succeeded in turning sharply the wheel of Bolshevist policy, al-

* ["Lenin's ideas," wrote Rosa Luxemburg in 1904, "are calculated principally to promote control of party activity and not its development, to foster the limitation rather than the growth, the strangulation rather than the solidarity and expansion of the movement." Even more remarkable is Leon Trotsky's prescient 1904 judgment of Lenin: "In Lenin's scheme, the party takes the place of the working class. The party organization displaces the party. The Central Committee displaces the party organization, and finally the Dictator displaces the Central Committee."—Ed.]

though not without stubborn opposition of many influential Bolsheviks.*

Lenin's aim in the Russian Revolution was to destroy not only all organs of self-administration, but also all other parties and social organizations, except his own.

To this end he employed falsehood, slander and brutal force against all opponents, among whom he counted all Socialists, except those who were willing to obey his commands. He finally succeeded in smashing all his opponents through his *coup d'état* of November 7, 1917.

Nevertheless, efforts were continued by some to bring about a government of all Socialist parties.

> At this time Zinoviev, Kamenev, Rykov, Rjazanov, Lozowski and other prominent Bolsheviks demanded the formation of a Socialist government composed of all Soviet parties. They declared that formation of a purely Bolshevist government would lead to a regime of terror and to the destruction of the revolution and the country.**

But again Lenin won his point in the Bolshevist Party. He hoped that the elections to the All Russian Constituent Assembly, which were then in progress, would bring him a majority.

Until 1917 the Bolshevist Party regarded the dictatorship within its organization as a means of struggle for democracy in the state, and Lenin's fight for democracy in the state proceeded along the line of the other socialist parties. Like the latter, as late as 1917, he demanded the convocation of a Constituent Assembly on the basis of universal suffrage.

The elections to the Constituent Assembly revealed that the Bolshevist Party had far from a majority in the Constituent As-

---

* *Theodore Dan*, in his Continuation of Martov's "History of the Russian Social Democracy."
** *Ibid.*

sembly. But the Socialist parties—Mensheviks, Bolsheviks and Social Revolutionists—constituted an overwhelming majority in the Assembly.* Once more the Bolsheviks had an opportunity to take part in a Socialist united front, which could be the basis of a government supported by the overwhelming majority of the people. A government founded on such a basis and having virtually the entire people behind it would have been in a position to crush without any difficulty any attempt at counter-revolution. In fact, any such attempt would have been nipped in the bud.

Had the Bolsheviks at that time agreed to a united front, Russia would have been spared the three years of civil war and the consequent horrible misery. Peace and freedom would have made possible rapid economic recovery and with it a speedy development of the working class, which in turn, would have promoted the realization of a large measure of Socialist economy and its successful administration. *All this would have been possible without dictatorship, without terror, through the democracy of the workers and peasants.* To be sure, we cannot say with certainty that this would have actually come to pass, but this was the only road that offered a possibility of obtaining for the people through the revolution as great a measure of liberty and welfare as existing circumstances permitted. But this would have been possible only through the establishment of a revolutionary government supported by the overwhelming majority of the population. Such a government could have been set up only on the basis of a united front of all Socialist parties.

This united front was rendered impossible by the insatiable yearning for power on the part of Lenin and other leaders of the Bolsheviks. They dissolved the Constituent Assembly, which they themselves had previously so passionately championed, and with the help of the politically inexperienced and ignorant soldiery drawn from the disorganized army, whose support they had won by limitless and irresponsible promises, they succeeded in seizing power, by means of which they strength-

---

* [Electoral figures in the latter part of this selection—*Ed.*]

ened their own party, organized on militarist lines, and crushed completely all their opponents.

The Bolsheviks attained power and have been ruling ever since not through the confidence and support of the majority of the people.

There were two roads open: the road of a Socialist united front or the road of power for the Bolsheviks alone over all other Socialists. It was the Bolsheviks who utilized a favorable combination of circumstances to render impossible any united front in order that they might establish their own dictatorship.

Having established this dictatorship, they inevitably created a situation in which only the mailed fist, unconcerned too much with intellectual and moral restraints, can be victorious.

To emphasize their differentiation from the Social Democracy the Bolsheviks have called themselves Communists since 1918.

Upon the ruins of democracy, for which Lenin had fought until 1917, he erected his political power. Upon these ruins he set up a new militarist-bureaucratic police machinery of state, a new autocracy. This gave him weapons against the other Socialists even more potent than shameless lies. He now had in his hands all the instruments of repression which czarism had used, adding to these weapons also those instruments of oppression which the capitalist, as the owner of the means of production, uses against wage slaves. Lenin now commanded all the means of production, utilizing his state power for the erection of his state capitalism.*

---

* [For an extended statement of Lenin's views on state capitalism see his *'Left-Wing' Childishness and Petty-Bourgeois Mentality*, May, 1918, in which he states "Our task is to study the state capitalism of the Germans, to spare *no effort* in copying it and not shrink from adopting *dictatorial* methods to hasten the copying of it. Our task is to do this even more thoroughly than Peter (Peter the Great—*Ed.*) hastened the copying of Western culture by barbarian Russia, and he did not hesitate to use barbarous methods in fighting against barbarism." (Lenin's italics.) Also, same source: "If we introduced state capitalism in approximately six months' time, we would achieve a great success and a sure guarantee that within a year socialism will have gained a permanently firm hold and will have become invincible in our country." Four years later, he added these words: "Not a single book has been written about the state capitalism that

No form of capitalism makes the workers so absolutely dependent upon it as centralized state capitalism in a state without an effective democracy. And no political police is so powerful and omnipresent as the Cheka or G. P. U., created by men who had spent many years in fighting the czarist police, and knowing its methods as well as its weaknesses and shortcomings, knew also how to improve upon them.

It would have been absolutely unnecessary to resort to any of these instruments of repression had Lenin agreed to form a coalition with the Mensheviks and Social Revolutionists in 1917. These parties commanded the support of the overwhelming majority of the population, as the elections to the Constituent Assembly had shown. Everything of a truly progressive nature which the Bolsheviks sought at that time to realize was also part of the program of the other Socialist parties and would have been carried out by them, for the people had empowered them to do so. The confiscation of the big landed estates had also been planned by the Social Revolutionists and Mensheviks —they actually put it into effect in Georgia. Abolition of illiteracy, marriage law reform, social welfare measures, children's homes, public hospitals, shop councils, unemployment insurance and laws for the protection of labor, about all of which such a big-to-do is being made in Soviet Russia, have been attained to a much greater and more perfect degree in capitalist countries where the democracy of labor has won any considerable power. The socialization of heavy industry, insofar as this would have appeared economically advantageous, would likewise have been approved by the majority of the Constituent Assembly.

All the innovations in the domain of social welfare in which the Communists take so much pride and which so greatly impress tourists would have been introduced by the majority of

---

exists under Communism. It did not even occur to Marx to write a word about this subject; and he died without leaving a single precise quotation or irrefutable instruction on it. That is why we must get out of the difficulty entirely by our own efforts." (*Lenin's Report of the Central Committee to the Eleventh Congress of the Russian Communist Party*, March 27, 1922.)—*Ed.*]

the Constituent Assembly, and in much better fashion than the dictatorship has been able to do, because the country's economic condition would have been immeasurably better. All the social welfare measures in force in Russia suffer from lack of resources, the hasty and ill-prepared manner in which they have been introduced, as well as from the methods of brutal force used by the dictators even in instances where abstention from force would have been more advantageous. Many workers were thereby embittered against the new regime when their willing cooperation was possible and necessary.

How disgusting and unnecessary, for example, have been the forms of struggle against religion in Soviet Russia. The dictatorship does not seek to find a substitute for religion by promoting independent critical thinking and knowledge—such methods are not in the nature of dictatorship. Religious services and institutions, sacred to the devout, are subject to the coarsest insults and humiliations. Without the slightest necessity, harmless, devout folk are embittered and made to suffer while simultaneously the free thinkers themselves are degraded by such low forms of anti-religious propaganda.

All such difficulties of social change as arise from lack of means, undue haste, opposition of the population, would have largely been averted if these changes had been the work of the Constituent Assembly. They were accomplished directly or indirectly through the civil war, which was the inevitable consequence of Lenin's dissolution of the Constituent Assembly by the hands of his sailors in January 1918.

The majority behind the Constituent Assembly was so overwhelming that not a single one of the czarist generals dared move against it. Had any one of them ventured to do so he would have had no following. These generals were emboldened to counter-revolutionary mutiny only *after* Lenin had dissolved the Constituent Assembly and enabled them to put forward the pretense of seeking to restore the rights of the Assembly.

Had Lenin not dissolved the Constituent Assembly, Russia would have been spared the civil war with all its horrors, cruel-

ties and destruction. How much richer the country would have
been, how much greater the good of the social transformation!
All the enormous expenditures of the military bureaucratic
police apparatus, insofar as it has been devoted to purposes of
repression, could have been spared. These expenditures could
have been applied to productive purposes for the promotion
of the general welfare.

The population should have been accorded the greatest possible measure of freedom, freedom of the press, of assembly, of
organization, of self-government. Under such conditions the
masses would have speedily developed economically, physically, intellectually. All this stimulation of independent thinking and mutual confidence among the workers, peasants and
intellectuals would have genuinely enhanced the development
of socialist production, of a nation of liberty, equality, fraternity.

This noble development was halted on the day when Lenin
ordered his military bands to make an end of the Constituent
Assembly.

Certainly, the fact that it proved easy to dissolve it indicates
the high degree of political immaturity of the elements who
dominated Petrograd at that time—quite ignorant soldiery who
had but one wish, immediate peace, and who sensed that
Lenin's dictatorship was the one infallible instrument to bring it
about.

Not the confidence of the majority of the working class but
the complication of the revolution by the war brought Bolshevism to power. And because it did not possess this confidence it was compelled, once in power, to maintain itself by terrorism, which it is employing to this day without the slightest
prospect of its mitigation.

It is often said that terror belongs to the nature of revolution,
that revolutions are not made with rose water or silk gloves,
and that this has ever been so.

It is, indeed, a peculiar revolutionism which asserts that what
has always been must ever be so. Moreover, it is not true that

there never were revolutions without terror. The great French Revolution began in 1789, but the terror did not come until September 1792, and only as a consequence of war. Not the revolution but war brought about the terror as well as the dictatorship. Revolutions resort to terror only when they are driven to civil war.

This was absolutely unnecessary in Russia in 1917. Democracy had been achieved. The workers and peasants were in power. The demands of labor could have been satisfied by democratic methods, insofar as these demands were compatible with the interests of the peasantry and with the material resources available.

The rule of the overwhelming majority in the interest of the overwhelming majority does not require the use of brutal force in a democratic state in order to assert itself.

In the election to the Constituent Assembly 36,000,000 votes were cast, of which only 4,000,000 were polled by the bourgeois parties and 32,000,000 by the socialist parties. The Assembly was in no way threatened from the right. It was in a position to proceed undisturbed, with full hope of success, with the task of the regeneration of Russia and preparation for Socialism.

As the Bolsheviks saw it, it had but one great fault: they had failed to obtain a majority in it. The Bolsheviks received 9,000-000, while 23,000,000 votes were cast for the other Socialist parties. This was an intolerable situation for any brave Bolshevik. The Constituent Assembly would have carried out everything in the interests of labor that was at all realizable, and in more rational, more successful manner than the Bolsheviks acting alone have been able to do. But this would have required the Bolsheviks to act merely as equals and not as a party of dictatorship issuing orders from above.

Against any such democratic procedure the Bolsheviks struggled with all their might, and they utilized a favorable situation to dissolve the Constituent Assembly. *This blow they struck not against a czarist, aristocratic, bourgeois or "white guardist" counter revolution but against the other Socialist*

parties, who had been more successful than the Bolsheviks in
the struggle for the soul of the workers and peasants.

Hence, the abolition of all democratic rights of masses, ergo
the terror. It was the necessary consequence of the rule of a
minority over the great majority of the people. Hence, the
fact that the terror has been indispensable for the Bolsheviks
not only in the civil war but throughout the years after its conclusion. They resort to terror not only as a means of repelling
counter-revolution but as an instrument of holding down and
destroying all revolutionists among the workers and peasants
who refuse to submit without protest to the whip of the new
Red czar and his Communist cossacks. . . .

Victor Chernov

RUSSIA'S ONE DAY PARLIAMENT

Editor's Note

IN THE latter half of the last
selection, Karl Kautsky discusses the significance of the Communist dispersal of Russia's first and last freely elected and
democratic parliament, the Constituent Assembly. Having
called continuously for its convocation, using the demand for
its meeting as a major slogan in their rise to power, the Communists forcibly dissolved it after they had failed to receive a
majority of delegates in the elections. There are those who
pride themselves on tracing the "degeneration" of Communist
rule in Russia to the Nazi-Soviet Pact, others to the Moscow
Trials, still others to Lenin's death in 1924. It would seem
instructive for those persons to note that the snuffing out of this
expression of Russian democracy, its only free parliament, occurred *less than three months* after the Communist *coup d'état!*
The date of the convocation of the Constituent Assembly, and
the date of its dissolution, is January 18, 1918.

In this selection, we are provided with a short and graphic
account of the dispersal by a man eminently equipped to describe it, Victor Chernov, the elected chairman of the Russian
Constituent Assembly of 1918, the co-founder of the Socialist
Revolutionary Party in 1901 and Minister of Agriculture in the
Provisional Government from May–September, 1917. His books
include: *Constructive Socialism; Memoirs;* and *The Great Russian Revolution.* In 1941, he came to New York. In this note of

47

memoir, which appeared in *The New Leader* in January, 1948, he recounts for a new generation the once better known, now largely unknown and forgotten story of the death of Russian democracy. The tactic of dispersal became more familiar in later years in the hands of the Nazis and, in varied versions, as applied by the Communists in countries under their "influence."

Before turning to this selection, however, it might be well to draw attention to how a very well known Russian character- ized Communist policy and behavior at the time. We are re- ferring to Maxim Gorky. The later career of the famed Russian novelist and writer is one of the tragedies of the Russian ex- perience; it has many unexplained facets. He opposed the Bol- sheviks in 1917, and shortly after even left the country after his paper, *Novaya Zhizn*, had been suppressed by the Commu- nists. Later, he returned and, inexplicably, became a kind of of- ficial "front" for the regime, which shamelessly exploited his reputation to keep knowledge of some of its worst atrocities from the world. No one has yet come forward with a definitive explanation for Gorky's conversion. Universally respected for his deep humanism, as well as his considerable talent, it is be- lieved by many that the author of *The Lower Depths* thought that he might be able to ameliorate the dictatorship if he de- clared his loyalty to it. In 1936 his death was announced. In 1938, Henry Yagoda, head of the GPU for many years, recipient of Stalin's "Order of Lenin" in 1933, was suddenly charged with conspiracy to overthrow Stalin! Among other crimes, he was also found guilty of poisoning Gorky! Yagoda was executed in 1938 and Yezhov became the new chief of the secret police; in time the successor also was purged for similar alleged crimes. The real crimes of both men, and they are incalculable, were committed on orders from their superior, Joseph Stalin. One of the peculiarities of Soviet rule, one that fellow travelers are determined to ignore, is why the heads of the secret police, under whose regimes great numbers of Rus- sians are sentenced and executed for "crimes against the state," are successively found guilty themselves of having com-

mitted similar "crimes"? If the absurd charges are to be taken
as true: What kind of state is it in which the J. Edgar Hoov-
ers, General Marshalls and General Eisenhowers, not to speak
of General Washingtons, are all found to be guilty of conspiring for its overthrow? Gorky's end, therefore, remains a Soviet
mystery. Its surrounding circumstances reflect anything but
glory on the Communist regime.

Two weeks after the Bolshevik *coup* in 1917, Gorky wrote in
Novaya Zhizn, as follows:

> The working class cannot fail to realize that Lenin is
> experimenting with its blood, and trying to strain the
> revolutionary mood of the proletariat to the limit to see
> what the outcome will be. . . . The workingman must
> know that there really are no miracles, and that he will
> have to confront hunger, complete disorganization of
> industry and transportation, prolonged and bloody an-
> archy followed by reaction no less sanguinary and dark.
> That is where the proletariat is being led by its present
> leader and one must understand that Lenin is not an
> all-powerful magician, but a deliberate juggler, who has
> no feeling either for the lives or the honor of the pro-
> letariat. The working class must not allow adventurers
> and madmen to thrust upon the proletariat the respon-
> sibility for the disgraceful, senseless, and bloody crimes
> for which not Lenin, but the proletariat will have to
> account. (Quoted in David Shub's *Lenin.*)

On January 22, 1918, days after the dissolution of the
Constituent Assembly, Gorky wrote in *Novaya Zhizn,* what
now reads like the "funeral dirge" of the Russian Revolution:

> When on January 22, 1905, the . . . soldiers, in
> obedience to the orders of the Tsar's government, fired
> on the defenseless and peaceful crowd of workers . . .
> members of the intelligentsia, and laborers rushed up
> to the soldiers shouting: "What are you doing . . . ?

Whom are you killing? They are your brothers; they are without arms; they bear you no malice; they are on the way to ask the Tsar to look into their needs. They are not demanding but merely petitioning . . . Think of what you are doing, you idiots!" . . . But the reply of the soldiers was: "We have orders." And like machines they fired . . . perhaps unwillingly, but they fired nevertheless.

On January 18, 1918, the unarmed Petersburg democracy, workers and employees, came out to celebrate in honor of the Constituent Assembly. For nearly a century the best of the Russians have dreamed of this day. They visualized the Constituent Assembly as a political organ capable of giving the Russian democracy an opportunity of freely expressing its will. Thousands of the intelligentsia, tens of thousands of workers and peasants have died in prison and exile, have been hanged and shot for this dream. Rivers of blood have been shed for this sacred idea. And now that this goal has been reached and the democracy has come out to rejoice, the "People's Commissars" have given orders to shoot. It should not be forgotten that in the course of their lives some of these "People's Commissars" have impressed upon the toiling masses the necessity of fighting for the Constituent Assembly.

Pravda lies when it says that the demonstration of January 18 was organized by the bourgeoisie, by the bankers. . . . *Pravda* lied, for it knows that the "burzhui" have no reason for celebrating the opening of the Constituent Assembly. What is there for them to do among 246 Socialists [-Revolutionists] and 140 Bolsheviks? *Pravada* knows that those in line were workers of factories and that these workers were shot. No matter how much *Pravda* lies, the disgraceful facts remain.

It is possible that the "burzhui" rejoiced to see the soldiers and Red Guards snatch the revolutionary banners from the hands of workers, and drag them through the mud and burn them. But it is also possible that this picture made the "burzhui" sad, for among them are honest men who truly love their country and the people. One of these was Andrei Ivanovich Shingarev, foully murdered by some kind of savages. . . .

Just as on January 22, 1905, so on January 18, 1918, there are people who . . . ask those who fired: "Idiots, what are you doing? These are your own brothers. Can't you see the red banners? There is not a single banner hostile to the working class, or to you."

Now, just as then, the soldiers reply: "We have orders to shoot." . . .

I ask the "People's Commissars," among whom there should be honest and sensible men, if they understand that in putting the halter on their necks they are crushing the Russian democracy, destroying the conquests of the revolution?

Do they understand this? Or do they think: Ourselves or no one, even if it leads to destruction? (Quoted in *The Bolshevik Revolution: 1917-1918*, edited by James Bunyan and H. H. Fischer, a highly valuable collection of documents and source materials, Stanford University Press, 1934.)

#

Russia's One Day Parliament by Victor Chernov

WHEN we, the newly elected members of the Constituent Assembly, entered the Tauride Palace, the seat of the Assembly in Petrograd, on January 18, 1918, we found that the corridors were full of armed guards. They were masters of the building, crude and brazen. At first they did not address us directly, and only exchanged casual observations to the effect that "This guy should get a bayonet between his ribs" or "It wouldn't be bad to put some lead into this one." When we entered the large hall, it was still empty. The Bolshevik deputies had not yet appeared.

A tank division billeted in Petrograd remained faithful to the Assembly. It intended to demostrate this faithfulness by participating in the march to the Palace which was to pass on its way the barracks of the Preobrazhenski and Seminovski Regiments, the two best units of the Petrograd garrison. At the meetings held by these regiments, resolutions were invariably adopted demanding the transfer of state power to the Constituent Assembly. Thus a prospect was open for the consolidation of democratic forces.

But the Bolsheviks were not caught off guard. They attacked the columns of demonstrators converging on the Tauride Palace from various parts of Petrograd. Whenever the unarmed crowd could not be dispersed immediately, the street was blocked by troops or Bolshevik units would shoot into the crowd. The demonstrators threw themselves on the pavement and waited until the rattle of machine guns quieted down; then they would jump up and continue their march, leaving behind the dead and wounded until they were stopped by a new volley. Or the crowd would be bayoneted by enraged Bolshevik outfits, which would get hold of the banners and placards carried by the demonstrators and tear them into scraps.

The Assembly hall was gradually filled by the deputies. Near the dais were placed armed guards. The public gallery was crowded to overflowing. Here and there glittered rifle muzzles. Admission tickets for the public were distributed by the notorious Uritski. He did his job well.

❊   ❊   ❊

At last all the deputies had gathered in a tense atmosphere. The left sector was evidently waiting for something. From our benches rose Deputy Lordkapanidze who said in a calm, businesslike voice that, according to an old parliamentary custom, the first sitting should be presided over by the senior deputy. The senior was S. P. Shvetsov, an old Socialist Revolutionary (SR).

As soon as Shvetsov's imposing figure appeared on the dais, somebody gave a signal, and a deafening uproar broke out. The stamping of feet, hammering on the desks and howling made an infernal noise. The public in the gallery and the Bolshevik allies, the Left Socialist Revolutionaries, joined in the tumult. The guards clapped their rifle butts on the floor. From various sides guns were trained on Shvetsov. He took the President's bell, but the tinkling was drowned in the noise. He put it back on the table, and somebody immediately grabbed it and handed it over, like a trophy, to the representative of the Sovnarkom (Soviet of Commissars), Sverdlov. Taking advantage of a moment of comparative silence, Shvetsov managed to pronounce the sacramental phrase: "The session of the Constituent Assembly is open." These words evoked a new din of protest. Shvetsov slowly left the dais and joined us. He was replaced by Sverdlov, who opened the session for the second time, but now in the name of the Soviets, and presented its "platform." This was an ultimatum: we had just to vote Aye or No.

In the election of the Assembly's President, the Bolsheviks presented no candidate of their own. They voted for Maria Spiridonova, nominated by the Left SRs. Later they threw Spiridonova into jail and tormented her until she was on the verge of insanity. But at this moment they wanted to take full advantage of her popularity and reputation as a martyr in the struggle against Tsarism. My nomination as candidate for the Presidency received even greater support than had been expected. Some leftist peasants evidently could not bring themselves to oppose their own "muzhik minister." I obtained 244 votes against 150.

I delivered my inauguration address, making vigorous efforts to keep self-control. Every sentence of my speech was met with outcries, some ironical, others spiteful, often buttressed by the brandishing of guns. Bolshevik deputies surged forward to the dais. Conscious that the stronger nerves would win, I was determined not to yield to provocation. I said that the nation had made its choice, that the composition of the Assembly was a living testimony to the people's yearning for Socialism, and that its convention marked the end of the hazy transition period. Land reform, I went on, was a foregone conclusion: the land would be equally accessible to all who wished to till it. The Assembly, I said, would inaugurate an era of active foreign policy directed toward peace.

* * *

I finished my speech amidst a cross-fire of interruptions and cries. It was now the turn of the Bolshevik speakers—Skvortsov and Bukharin. During their delivery, our sector was a model of restraint and self-discipline. We maintained a cold, dignified silence. The Bolshevik speeches, as usual, were shrill, clamorous, provocative and rude, but they could not break the icy silence of our majority. As President, I was bound in duty to call them to order for abusive statements. But I knew that this was precisely what they expected. Since the armed guards were under their orders, they wanted clashes, incidents and perhaps a brawl. So I remained silent.

The Social Democrat Tseretelli rose to answer the Bolsheviks. They tried to "scare" him by levelling at him a rifle from the gallery and brandishing a gun in front of his face. I had to restore order—but how? Appeals to maintain the dignity of the Constituent Assembly evoked an even greater noise, at times turning into a raving fury. Dybenko and other demagogues called for more and more assaults. Lenin, in the government box, demonstrated his contempt for the Assembly by lounging in his chair and putting on the air of a man who was bored to death. I threatened to clear the gallery of the yelling public. Though this was an empty threat, since the guards were only waiting for the order to "clear" us out of the hall, it proved temporarily effective. Tseretelli's calm and dignified manner helped to restore peace.

There was a grim significance in the outburst that broke loose when a middle-of-the-road deputy, Severtsov-Odoievski, started to speak Ukrainian. In the Assembly the Bolsheviks did not want to hear any language except Russian. I was compelled to state emphatically that in the new Russia, each nationality had the right to use its own language whenever it pleased.

When it appeared that we refused to vote the Soviet "platform" without discussion, the Bolsheviks walked out of the sitting in a body. They returned to read a declaration charging us with counter-revolution and stating that our fate would be decided by organs which were in charge of such things. Soon after that the Left SRs also made up their minds. Just before the discussion of the land reform started, their representative, I. Z. Steinberg, declared that they were in disagreement with the majority, and left the Assembly.

We knew that the Bolsheviks were in conference, discussing what to do next. I felt sure that we would be arrested. But it was of utmost importance for us to have a chance to say the last word. I declared that the next point on the agenda was the land reform. At this moment somebody pulled at my sleeve.

"You have to finish now. There are orders from the People's Commissar."

Behind me stood a stocky sailor, accompanied by his armed comrades.

"What People's Commissar?"

"We have orders. Anyway, you cannot stay here any longer. The lights will be turned out in a minute. And the guards are tired."

"The members of the Assembly are also tired but cannot rest

until they have fulfilled the task entrusted to them by the people—to decide on the land reform and the future form of government."

And leaving the guards no time to collect themselves, I proceeded to read the main paragraphs of the Land Bill, which our party had prepared long ago. But time was running short. Reports and debates had to be omitted. Upon my proposal, the Assembly voted six basic points of the bill. It provided that all land was to be turned into common property, with every tiller possessing equal rights to use it. Amidst incessant shouts: "That's enough! Stop it now! Clear the hall!" the other points of the bill were voted.

Fearing that the lights would be extinguished, somebody managed to procure candles. It was essential that the future form of government be voted upon immediately. Otherwise the Bolsheviks would not fail to charge the Assembly with having left the door open for the restoration of the monarchy. The motion for a republican form of government was carried unanimously.

In the dawn of a foggy and murky morning I declared a recess until noon.

At the exit a palefaced man pushed his way to me and beseeched me in a trembling voice not to use my official car. A bunch of murderers, he said, was waiting for me. He admitted that he was a Bolshevik, but his conscience revolted against this plot.

I left the building, surrounded by a few friends. We saw several men in sailor's uniforms loitering near my car. We decided to walk. We had a long distance to go, and when I arrived home I learned that rumors were in circulation that the Constituent Assembly had been dispersed, and that Chernov and Tseretelli had been shot.

At noon several members of the Assembly were sent on reconnaissance. They reported that the door of the Tauride Palace was sealed and guarded by a patrol with machine guns and two pieces of field artillery. Later in the day a decree of the Sovnarkom was published by which the Constituent Assembly was "dissolved."

Thus ended Russia's first and last democratic parliament.

Julius Martov

THE IDEOLOGY OF "SOVIETISM"

Editor's Note

THEY were two young, idealistic Russian revolutionists. "Together they had formed the Petersburg League of Struggle, together gone to prison, together planned *Iskra* . . . together they toured the underground on *Iskra's* behalf, together edited it abroad." One the world knows as Lenin, the other the world has forgotten. One became the dictator of the Soviet state, the other his great adversary and one of the most brilliant of all the early critics of Bolshevism. "Between them," writes Bertram D. Wolfe in his *Three Who Made a Revolution*, which we quoted above, "there had been a closer political partnership and intimacy than Lenin was ever to form with any man again, even with Trotsky in the crucial year of their common assault on the heights of power."

Let us listen to Julius Martov: The Soviet state "has not done away with social hierarchy in production. It has not lessened the total subjection of the local community to the power of the state. On the contrary, in proportion to its evolution, the Soviet state shows a tendency in the opposite direction. It shows a tendency toward intensified centralism of the State, a tendency toward the utmost possible strengthening of the principles of hierarchy and compulsion." A man who could speak to us like that in 1919 obviously has a great deal to tell us today. His criticisms penetrated deep beneath the surface, he was able to sense in a remarkable manner long-range developments in the

58

supposed temporary mechanisms of the moment. At a time when, throughout the world, "soviet" was a magical word, a word to confound logic and rational appraisal, he stripped the screen from this "ideology." His analytic and prophetic brilliance is not apt to be disputed by many, nor the bite of his sharp prose style not be felt.

Julius Martov, one of the most distinguished representatives of Russian socialism, writer, historian, was born Yuly Osipovich Zederbaum in 1873. He had turned revolutionist by 1891 and was exiled two years later. He founded the League of Struggle for the Emancipation of the Working Class with Lenin, and three years of exile in Siberia were to follow. Martov then went abroad and with Lenin, and others, collaborated on the publication *Iskra*. ("Spark"—"the spark will kindle a flame.") In 1903 he played what was to become known as an historic role at the second congress of the Russian Social Democratic Labor Party. Here he led the fight against Lenin and the idea of a dictatorially structured party, and thus the cleavage became manifest that was to gain importance as the start of the split between the Bolshevik and Menshevik factions. During World War I, Martov was a leader of the socialist "internationalists," those who opposed the war stands of the majority European socialist parties. Returning to Russia some months after the March Revolution he led the wing of the Menshevik Internationalists in a call for a coalition government of all the socialist parties, including the Bolsheviks. He strongly opposed the Bolshevik seizure of power and still sought to bring about a socialist coalition government, which, had he succeeded, might have changed the fate of Russia and the world. But Lenin and Trotsky were sharply against this proposal. Martov's penetrating criticism of the bases of the Soviet ideology becomes even more impressive when it is realized that he not only opposed armed resistance to the Bolsheviks, fearing reactionary consequences, but called for labor opponents of Lenin's government to join the Red Army against the "whites" and foreign intervention.

Lenin's attitude toward Martov was a curious one. As David

Shub has said in his *Lenin:* "To discredit his enemies in the eyes of the Russian people everything was permissible. Martov was branded as a 'traitor' and 'renegade,' and yet shortly before his death Lenin complained to Gorky: 'What a pity Martov is not with us. What a wonderful comrade he is! He is without peer! . . . What a wise man Martov is.'" Souvarine in his *Stalin* states: "Krupskaya [Lenin's wife] in her *Recollections* testified to the great esteem which Lenin always had for him, even in the midst of the fiercest factional disputes." Krupskaya wrote that "Lenin renewed relations with him whenever he came into line at all."

Martov's view, as a Marxist, was that economically Russia was not yet at a stage at which genuine socialism could be established. He therefore understood the Russian Revolution to be a progressive national upheaval which could help the country make great strides toward ridding itself of its general backwardness. He believed that the assertion of "socialism" being built in conditions vastly different from those anticipated by Marx would lead to vastly different results from those desired. Martov did not mistake the dictatorship of the Bolsheviks for the "dictatorship of the proletariat." "Little by little," he wrote in 1919, observing what was occurring, "the 'power of the soviets' is being replaced with the power of a certain party. Little by little the party becomes the essential State institution, the framework and axis of the entire system of 'soviet republics.'"

As 1920 drew to a close, the "power of the soviets" had been, as Martov had foreseen, completely supplanted by the power of the Communist Party. Terrorism increased and the dictatorship tightened. A man like Martov was an anachronism in Lenin's "liberated" Russia. He had not endeared himself to the regime by denouncing the Bolshevik reestablishment of the death penalty, trials without jury, and similar policies. Although personally unharmed, he was, writes Edmund Wilson in *To the Finland Station,* "requested by the police to leave." In November, 1920, he went abroad, his passport granted to him on Lenin's personal order. In his last years Martov was active in the Socialist International and as editor of the *Socialist Courier*. He died in Germany in 1923, tubercular and in dire circumstances.

This selection is composed of excerpts from an article that originally appeared in the publication *Mysl* in Kharkov, early in 1919.

\#

The Ideology of "Sovietism" by Julius Martov

THE Revolutionary movement that is tinged with Bolshevism recognizes soviets as the form of political organization (even the sole form) by which the emancipation of the proletariat can be realized.

According to this viewpoint, the soviet State structure—said to be a phase in the progressive abolition of the State itself in its role as an instrument of social oppression—is the historically motivated product of a long evolution, arising in the midst of class antagonisms when these have reached great acuteness under imperialism. It is described as the perfect embodiment of the dictatorship of the proletariat. Appearing at a time when "bourgeois" democracy is said to have lost all content, the soviet régime is pictured as the perfect expression of real democracy.

However, every perfection has this dangerous feature. Persons untroubled by critical reasoning, persons blind to the nuances of "idle" theory, are impatient to possess themselves of the perfection, without bothering to take note that the perfection in question is supposed to be based on particular historic conditions. Metaphysical reasoning refuses to accept the dialectical negation of the absolute. It ignores the relative. Having learned that the true, the genuine, the perfect mode of social life has at last been discovered, it insists on having this perfect mode applied to daily existence.

We therefore see that, contrary to its own theoretic claims, this perfect political form has become applicable to all peoples, to all social groups. All that is necessary is that the people concerned want to modify the structure of the State under which it is suffering. Soviets have become the slogan for the proletariat of the most advanced industrial countries, the United States, England, Germany. They are also the slogan for agricultural Hungary, peasant Bulgaria and Russia, where agriculture is just issuing from primitive structures.

The universal efficacy of the soviet régime reaches even farther. Communist publicists seriously speak of soviet revolutions occurring, or about to occur, in Asiatic Turkey, among the Egyptian fellahin, in the pampas of South America. In Corea, the proclamation of a soviet republic is only a matter of time. In India, China and Persia the soviet idea is said to be advancing with the speed of an express train. And who dares to doubt that by now the soviet system has already been adapted to the primitive social conditions of the Bashkirs, Kirghizes, Turkomans and the mountaineers of Daghestan?

No matter what Marxist thought may have to say on the subject, the soviet régime, as such, is not only said to solve the antagonism arising between the proletariat and the bourgeoisie under conditions of highly developed capitalism, but is also presented as the universal State form that cuts through the difficulties and antagonisms arising at any degree of social evolution. In theory, the lucky people bursting into soviets are expected to have passed—at least ideologically—the stage of bourgeois democracy. They are expected to have freed themselves from a number of noxious illusions—parliamentarism, the need for a universal, direct, equal and secret ballot, the need of liberty of the press, etc. Only then can they know the supreme perfection incorporated in the soviet State structure. In practice, however, nations here and there, possessed by the metaphysical negation of the course traced by soviet theory, jump over the prescribed stages. Soviets are the perfect form of the State. They are the magic wand by which all inequalities, all misery, may be suppressed. Having once learned about soviets, who would consent to suffer the yoke of less perfect systems of government? Having once tasted the sweet, who would choose to continue to live on bitterness?

In February 1918, at Brest-Litovsk, Trotsky and Kamenev still defended with great obstinacy the right of peoples to self-determination. They demanded from victorious Germany that this principle be applied, through the instrumentality of the equal and universal ballot, in Poland, Lithuania and Latvia. The historic value of democracy was still recognized at that time. But a year later, at the congress of the Russian Communist Party, the intrepid Bukharine already insisted that the principle of "self-determination of peoples" had to be replaced with the principle of "self-determination of the laboring classes." Lenin succeeded in obtaining the maintenance of the principle of self-determination—for backward peoples—paralleling in this respect certain philosophers who, not wanting to fall out with the Church, would limit the scope of their materialist teachings to animals deprived of the benefits of divine revelation. But it was not for doctrinal reasons that the Communist congress refused to fall in line with Bukharine. Lenin won out with arguments of a diplomatic order. It was said to be unwise to alienate from the Communist International the Hindoos, Persians and other peoples who, though still blind to the revelation, were in a situation of pan-national struggle against the foreign oppressor. Fundamentally, the Communists were in full agreement with Bukharine. Having tasted sweetness, who would offer bitterness to his neighbor?

So that when the Turkish consul at Odessa permitted himself to launch the hoax about the triumph of a soviet revolution in the Ottoman empire, not a single Russian newspaper refused to take the obvious hoax seriously. Not a single publication showed the slightest skepticism concerning the ability of the good Turks to jump over the stages of self-determination, uni-

versal franchise, bourgeois parliamentarism, etc. The mystification was quite successful. Mystifications find a favorable soil
in mysticism. For no less than mystic is the concept of a political
form that, by virtue of its particular character, can surmount all
economic-social and national contradictions.

In the course of the congress of the Independent Social Democratic Party of Germany at Leipzig, good men racked their
brains to discover how to conciliate "all power to the soviets"
with the traditional notions of the Social-Democracy concerning the political forms of the socialist revolutions, especially
with the notion of democracy.

For here is a mystery that escapes the understanding of the
true-believers of Sovietism with the same persistence that
the mystery of the Immaculate Conception has ever escaped
the understanding of the Christian faithful. Sometimes it escaped the understanding of its own creator. . . .

As a result of the extreme class antagonism between the proletariat and the bourgeoisie, the proletariat overthrows the most
complete embodiment of democratic statism. By this act, the
proletariat creates itself a new political mode, which is also
the specific expression of the dictatorship of the proletariat.
Here is the starting point of the "soviet idea."

The political mode thus created is universally applicable. It
fits the needs and consequences of all kinds of social change.
It can clothe the multiform substance of all the revolutionary
acts of the twentieth century. That is the "soviet idea" at the
close of its own evolution.

This dialectical contradiction summarizes the mystery of
"sovietism," which is a mystery beyond the dogmatic comprehension of thinkers, both on the Left and on the Right.

Dictatorship of the Minority

The mechanism of the popular revolutions of the preceding
historic period had the following characteristics.

The role of active factor in the overturn belonged to *minorities* of the social classes in whose interest the revolution devel-

oped. These minorities exploited the confused discontent and the sporadic explosions of anger arising among scattered and socially inconsistent elements within the revolutionary class. They guided the latter in the destruction of the old social forms. In certain cases, the active leader minorities had to use the power of their concentrated energy in order to shatter the inertia of the elements they tried to wield for revolutionary purposes. Therefore, these active leader minorities sometimes made efforts—often successful efforts—to repress the passive resistance of the manipulated elements, when the latter refused to move forward toward the broadening and deepening of the revolution. The dictatorship of an active revolutionary minority, a dictatorship that tended to be terrorist, was the normal coming-to-a-head of the situation in which the old social order had confined the popular mass, now called on by the revolutionaries to forge their own destiny.

There where the active revolutionary minority was not able to organize such a dictatorship, or to maintain it for some time, as was the case in Germany, Austria, France in 1848—we observed the miscarriage of the revolutionary process, a collapse of the revolution.

Engels said that the revolutions of the past historic period were the work of conscious minorities exploiting the spontaneous revolt of unconscious majorities.

It is understood that the word "conscious" should be taken here in a relative sense. It was a question of pursuing political and social aims that were quite definite, though at the same time quite contradictory and utopian. The ideology of the Jacobins of 1793-1794 was thoroughly utopian. It cannot be considered to have been the product of an objective conception of the process of historic evolution. But in relation to the mass of peasants, small producers and workers in whose name they demolished the old régime, the Jacobins represented a conscious vanguard whose destructive work was subordinated to positive problems.

In the last decade of the 19th century, Engels arrived at the

conclusion that the epoch of revolutions effected by conscious
minorities heading unknowing masses had closed for ever.
From then on, he said, revolution would be prepared by long
years of political propaganda, organization, education, and
would be realized directly and consciously by the interested
masses themselves.

To such a degree has this idea become the conception of the
great majority of modern socialists that the slogan: "All power
to the soviets!" was originally launched as an answer to the
need of assuring, during the revolutionary period, the maximum of active and conscious participation and the maximum
of initiative by the masses in the task of social creation.

Read again Lenin's articles and speeches of 1917 and you
will discover that their master thought, "all power to the soviets," amounted then to the following: 1. the direct and active
participation of the masses in the management of production
and public affairs; 2. the obliteration of all gaps between the
directors and the directed, that is, the suppression of any social
hierarchy; 3. the greatest possible unification of the legislative
and executive powers, of the production apparatus and the
administrative apparatus, of the State machinery and the machinery of local administration; 4. the maximum of activity
by the mass and the minimum of liberty for its elected representatives; 5. the total suppression of all bureaucracy.

Parliamentarism was repudiated not only as the arena where
two enemy classes collaborate politically and engage in "pacific" combats, but also as a mechanism of public administration. And this repudiation was motivated, above all, by
the antagonism arising between this mechanism and the unbounded revolutionary activity of the mass, intervening directly in administration and production.

In August 1917, Lenin wrote:

> Having conquered political power, the workers will
> break up the old bureaucratic apparatus; they will shat-
> ter it to its very foundations, until not one stone is left

upon another: and they will replace it with a new one consisting of the same workers and employees, *against* whose transformation into bureaucrats will at once be undertaken, as pointed out in detail by Marx and Engels: 1. not only electiveness, but also instant recall; 2. payment no higher than that of ordinary workers; 3. immediate transition to a state of things when *all* fulfil the functions of control and superintendence, so that *all* become "bureaucrats for a time, and *no one*, therefore can become a bureaucrat." (*The State and Revolution*, page 103, early Russian edition.)

He wrote of the "*substitution of a universal popular militia for the police*," of the "electiveness and recall at any moment of all functionaries and commanding ranks," of "workers' control in its primitive sense, direct participation of the people at the courts, not only in the shape of a jury but also by the suppression of specializing prosecutors and defense counsels and by the vote of all present on the question of guilt." . . .

Reality has cruelly shattered all these illusions. The "soviet State" has not established in any instance electiveness and recall of public officials and the commanding staff. It has not suppressed the professional police. It has not assimilated the courts in direct jurisdiction by the masses. It has not done away with social hierarchy in production. It has not lessened the total subjection of the local community to the power of the State. On the contrary, in proportion to its evolution, the Soviet State shows a tendency in the opposite direction. It shows a tendency toward intensified centralism of the State, a tendency toward the utmost possible strengthening of the principles of hierarchy and compulsion. It shows a tendency toward the development of a more specialized apparatus of repression than before. It shows a tendency toward the greater independence of the usually elective functions and the annihilation of the control of these functions by the elector masses. It shows a tendency toward the total freedom of the executive organisms from the tutelage of the electors. In the crucible of reality, the "power of the soviets" has become the "soviet power," *a power that originally issued from the soviets* but has steadily become independent from the soviets.

We must believe that the Russian ideologists of the soviet system have not renounced entirely their notion of a non-Statal social order, the *aim* of the revolution. But as they see matters now, the road to this non-Statal social order no longer lies in the progressive atrophy of the functions and institutions that have been forged by the bourgeois State, as they said they saw things in 1917. Now it appears that their way to a social order that would be free from the State lies in the hypertrophy—the excessive development—of these functions and in the resurrection, under an altered aspect, of most State institutions typical of the bourgeois era. The shrewd people continue to repudiate democratic parliamentarism. But they no longer repudiate, at the same time, those instruments of State power *to which parliamentarism is a counterweight within bourgeois society:* bureaucracy, police, a permanent army with commanding cadres that are independent of the soldiers, courts that are above control by the community, etc.

In contrast to the bourgeois State, the State of the transitional revolutionary period ought to be an apparatus for the "repression of the minority by the majority." Theoretically, it should be a governmental apparatus resting in the hands of the majority. In reality, the Soviet State continues to be, as the State of the past, a government apparatus resting in the hands of a minority. (Of another minority, of course.)

Little by little, the "power of the soviets" is being replaced with the power of a certain party. Little by little the party becomes the essential State institution, the framework and axis of the entire system of "soviet republics."

The evolution traversed by the idea of the "Soviet State" in Russia ought to help us to understand the psychological basis of this idea in countries where the revolutionary process of today is yet in its initial phase.

The "soviet régime" becomes the means of bringing into power and maintaining in power a revolutionary minority which claims to defend the interests of a majority, though the latter has not recognized these interests as its own, though this majority has not attached itself sufficiently to these interests to defend them with all its energy and determination.

This is demonstrated by the fact that in many countries—it happened also in Russia—the slogan "all power to the soviets" is launched in opposition to the already existing soviets, created during the first manifestations of the revolution. The slogan is directed, in the first place, against the majority of the working class, against the political tendencies which dominated the masses at the beginning of the revolution. The slogan "all power to the soviets" becomes a pseudonym for the dictatorship of a minority. So that when the failure of July 3, 1917, had brought to the surface the obstinate resistance of the soviets to Bolshevik pressure, Lenin tore off the disguise in his pamphlet: *On the Subject of Slogans* and proclaimed that the cry "All Power to the Soviets!" was thenceforward out of date and had to be replaced with the slogan: "All power to the Bolshevik Party!"

But this "materialization" of the symbol, this revelation of its true content, was only a moment in the development of the perfect political form, "finally discovered" and exclusively possessing the "capacity of bringing out the social substance of the proletarian revolution."

The retention of political power by the minority of a class (or classes), by a minority organized as a party and exercising its power in the interests of the class (or classes), is a fact arising from antagonisms typical of the most recent phase of capitalism. It thus offers a difference between the old revolutions and the new. On the other hand, the fact that it is a dictatorship by a minority constitutes a *bond of kinship* between the present revolution and those of the preceding historic period. If that is the basic principle of the governmental mechanism in question, it hardly matters if the exigency of given historic circumstances have made this principle assume the particular form of soviets.

The events of 1792-1794 in France offer an example of a revolution that was realized by means of a minority dictatorship set up as a party: the Jacobin dictatorship. The Jacobin party embraced the most active, the most "leftward," elements of the petty-bourgeoisie, proletariat, and declassed intellectuals. It exercised its dictatorship through a network of multiple institutions: communes, sections, clubs, revolutionary committees. In this network producers' organizations on the style of our workers' soviets were completely absent. Otherwise, there is a striking similarity, and a number of perfect analogies, between the institutions used by the Jacobins and those serving the contemporary dictatorship. The party cells of today differ in no way from the Jacobin clubs. The revolutionary committees in 1794 and 1919 are entirely alike. The committees of poor peasants of today bear comparison with the committees and clubs, composed especially of poor elements, on which the Jacobin dictatorship based itself in the villages. Today, workers' soviets, factory committees, trade union centers, mark the revolution with their stamp and give it its specific character. Here is where the influence of the proletariat in the large industries of today makes itself felt. Nevertheless, we see that such specifically class organisms, such specially proletarian formations, issuing from the milieu of modern industry, are as much reduced to the role of mechanical instruments of a party minority dictatorship as were the auxiliaries of the Jacobin dictatorship in 1792-1794, though the social origins of the latter were entirely different. . . .

Dictatorship over the Proletariat

The revolutionary sectors of the population do not believe themselves able to draw along with them the majority of the country on the road to socialism. Here is the secret of the spread of the "soviet idea" in the confused consciousness of the European proletariat.

Now the majority opposing socialism, or backing parties that oppose socialism, may include numerous worker elements. To the extent that this is true, the principle of "soviet rule" implies not only the repudiation of democracy in the framework of the nation but also the suppression of democracy within the working class. . . .

Charles Naine, the well-known Swiss militant, writes:

> At the beginning of 1918, we were in a panic. There was no time to delay. Soviets of workers, soldiers and peasants had to be formed in Switzerland immediately and a red guard constituted. The knowing minority had to impose its will on the majority, even by brute force. The great mass, the workers, are in economic slavery. They cannot accomplish their own liberation. Their minds are formed by their masters; they are incapable of understanding their true interests. It is left to the knowing minority to free the mass from the tutelage of its present masters. Only after this is done will the mass understand. Scientific socialism is the truth. The minority possessing the knowledge of the truth of scientific socialism has the right to impose it on the mass. Parliament is only an obstruction. It is an instrument of reaction. The bourgeois press poisons the minds of the people. It should be suppressed. Later, that is, after the social order will have been totally transformed by the socialist dictators, liberty and democracy will be reconstituted. Then the citizens will be in the position to form a real democracy; they will then be free from the economic régime which, oppressing them, keeps them at present from manifesting their true will. (Charles Naine: *Dictature du prolétariat ou démocratie*, page 7).

Only the blind and the hypocritical will fail to recognize that Charles Naine has presented here, divested of its usual phraseologic ornamentation, the ideology of Bolshevism. It is in this shape that the latter has been assimilated by the masses in Russia, Germany, Hungary, and wherever Bolshevism has made its appearance.

This phraseological ornamentation does not always succeed in hiding. There is, for example, the important statement by P. Orlovsky [V. Vorovsky, later Soviet representative at Rome, killed in Lausanne, May 1923, *Trans.*], entitled "The Communist International and the World Soviet Republic." The author proposes to deal with the "crux" of the question of the soviet system.

"The soviet system," he writes, "merely *implies* participation of the popular masses in the administration of the State: but it does not *assure* them either mastery or even a predominant influence (in the administration of the State)." . . .

Here is Orlovsky's conclusion:

"Only when the soviet system has put the effective State power in the hands of the Communists, that is to say in the party of the working class, may the workers and other exploited elements obtain access to the exercise of State power as well as the possibility of reconstructing the State on a new basis, conforming to their needs, etc."

In other words, the soviet system is good as long as it is in the hands of the Communists. For "as soon as the bourgeoisie succeeds in possessing itself of the soviets (as was the case in Russia under Kerensky and now—in 1919—in Germany), it utilizes them against the revolutionary workers and peasants, just as the Tsars used the soldiery, sprung from the people, to oppress the people. Therefore, soviets can fulfill a revolutionary role, and free the working masses, only when they are dominated by the Communists. And for the same reason, the growth of soviet organizations in other countries is a revolutionary phenomenon in the proletarian sense—not merely in the petty-bourgeois sense—only when this growth is paralleled by the triumph of communism."

There could be no clearer statement. The *"soviet system" is an instrument which permits State power to slip into the hands of the Communists. The instrument is put aside as soon as it has fulfilled its historic function.* That is never said, of course.

"The Communist Party, that is to say, the party of the working class . . ." The principle is always posed in these words. Not one of the parties—nor even "the most advanced party," nor the "party most representative of the interests of the proletarian class." No, but the "only real worker party.". . .

The soviets fulfilled the role expected of them. The rising tide of bourgeois revolutionary enthusiasm set in motion the worker and peasant masses, washing away their "meanness." Lifted by the wave, the Bolsheviks possessed themselves of the government apparatus. Then the role of the insurrectionary element came to an end. The Moor had accomplished his task. The State that came into being with the aid of the "Power of the Soviets" became the "Soviet Power."

Bertrand Russell

REVOLUTION AND DICTATORSHIP

Editor's Note

"No MATTER what one thinks of Bolshevism, it is undeniable that the Russian Revolution is one of the great events of human history." In 1919, so proclaimed John Reed in his *Ten Days That Shook the World.* Honest, sensitive to human injustice, John Reed—in his account which later came to bear the imprimatur of Lenin—proudly announced that "in the struggle my sympathies were not neutral. . . . Instead of being a destructive force, it seems to me that the Bolsheviki were the only party in Russia with a constructive program and the power to impose it on the country." Hope was the keynote and all eyes were on the future. Given Reed's admirably rebellious nature, his notable journalistic and crusading rather than analytic talent, it is perhaps natural—certainly understandable—that he should have been without qualifications. His book will remain, and deservedly so, a major sourcebook of one view of the Revolution.

But in a reappraisal of what that early period actually signified in the historical sequence of our times, we find Reed's credulous and wide-eyed account superseded by a quieter, lesser-known work which appeared in the following year. In 1920, having visited the Soviet Union, subjected the experience to his observant, affirmative, and yet critical sensibility, Bertrand Russell published his *The Practice and Theory of Bol-*

shevism. Unheralded, it is a work that will greatly repay a contemporary re-reading.

Russell's starting point was not wholly unlike Reed's. To understand Bolshevism, he held, it was not sufficient to view it only in a factual way, although that too obviously was quite necessary. "It is necessary to enter with sympathy or imagination into a new spirit." He agreed with Reed that the occurrence was one of the first magnitude. "The Russian Revolution," he declared, "is one of the great heroic events of the world's history. It is natural to compare it to the French Revolution, but it is in fact something of even more importance." Above all, he wished it well, asserting his belief that socialism is necessary to the world. He recognized the need for the quality of hope and the importance of planning for the future. But where Reed stopped, Russell began. Studying the Bolshevik methodology and relating it to actions he witnessed, he spoke simply: "I do not believe that by this method a stable or desirable form of Socialism can be established." His slim book went on to expound the basis for his judgment, carefully, fraternally, prophetically.

Originally written in 1920, Bertrand Russell's book saw a second edition in London in 1949. This in itself would not be remarkable were it not for the fact that the book was again published in its original state. The only alteration in Mr. Russell's text was the changing of "Communist" to "Socialist" on a number of occasions to take into account changes in usage. His depiction of what was to come, his analysis of events as he witnessed them, these—with remarkably few exceptions—have basically withstood the changes of what has perhaps been the most turbulent period in the history of the world.

Mr. Russell, then, was not a hostile commentator. On the contrary, it was his extreme friendship and good will that impelled him to speak his mind. "The chief thing that the Bolsheviks have done is to create a hope, or at any rate to make strong and widespread a hope which was formerly confined to a few. . . . One might as well describe the Thebaid without

mentioning that the hermits expected eternal bliss as the reward of their sacrifices here on earth. I cannot share the hopes
of the Bolsheviks any more than those of the Egyptian ancho-
rites; I regard both as tragic delusions, destined to bring upon
the world centuries of darkness and futile violence." Again: "I
do not know whether Bolshevism can be prevented from ac-
quiring universal power. But even if it cannot, I am persuaded
that those who stand out against it, not from love of ancient injustice, but in the name of the free spirit of Man, will be the
bearers of the seeds of progress, from which, when the world's
gestation is accomplished, new life will be born." In the selection, "Revolution and Dictatorship," here presented, are
included insights from which the world might well have bene-
fited had it received them with closer attention in 1920.

Bertrand Arthur William Russell, philosopher, mathemati-
cian, teacher, writer, lecturer, was born in England on May 18,
1872. He is the grandson of Lord John Russell, British Foreign
Secretary during the Civil War. His academic career began
with his position of fellow and lecturer at Trinity College, Cam-
bridge University. Since then he has taught in many colleges
and universities, including Harvard, Chicago, California, and
Peking Universities. He has received many awards for scholarship; among them the Sylvester Medal of the Royal Society
in 1934 and the Nicholas Murray Butler Medal in 1915. He has
been a most prolific and varied writer. Perhaps his best-known
works are: *Roads to Freedom; Power; Freedom and Organization; Our Knowledge of the External World; Principia Mathe-
matica* (with A. N. Whitehead); *The Philosophy of Leibniz;
Marriage and Morals;* and *History of Western Philosophy.*

Revolution and Dictatorship by Bertrand Russell

THE Bolsheviks have a very definite programme for achieving Communism—a programme which has been set forth by Lenin repeatedly, and quite recently in the reply of the Third International to the questionnaire submitted by the Independent Labour Party.

Capitalists, we are assured, will stick at nothing in defence of their privileges. It is the nature of man, in so far as he is politically conscious, to fight for the interests of his class so long as classes exist. When the conflict is not pushed to extremes, methods of conciliation and political deception may be preferable to actual physical warfare; but as soon as the proletariat make a really vital attack upon the capitalists, they will be met by guns and bayonets. This being certain and inevitable, it is as well to be prepared for it, and to conduct propaganda accordingly. Those who pretend that pacific methods can lead to the realization of Communism are false friends to the wage-earners; intentionally or unintentionally, they are covert allies of the bourgeoisie.

There must, then, according to Bolshevik theory, be armed conflict sooner or later, if the injustices of the present economic system are ever to be remedied. Not only do they assume armed conflict: they have a fairly definite conception of the way in which it is to be conducted. This conception has been carried out in Russia, and is to be carried out, before very long, in every civilized country. The Communists, who represent the class-conscious wage-earners, wait for some propitious moment when events have caused a mood of revolutionary discontent with the existing Government. They then put themselves at the head of the discontent, carry through a successful revolution, and in so doing acquire the arms, the railways, the State treasure, and all the other resources upon which the power of modern Governments is built. They then confine political power to Communists, however small a minority they may be of the whole nation. They set to work to increase their number by propaganda and the control of education. And meanwhile, they introduce Communism into every department of economic life as quickly as possible.

Ultimately, after a longer or shorter period, according to circumstances, the nation will be converted to Communism, the relics of capitalist institutions will have been obliterated, and it will be possible to restore freedom. But the political conflicts to which we are accustomed will not reappear. All the burning political questions of our time, according to the Communists, are questions of class conflict, and will disappear when the division of classes disappears. Accordingly, the State will no longer be required, since the State is essentially an engine of power designed to give the victory to one side in the class conflict. Ordinary States are designed to give the victory to the capitalists; the proletarian State (Soviet Russia) is designed to give the victory to the wage-earners. As soon as the community contains only wage-earners, the State will cease to have any functions. And so, through a period of dictatorship, we shall finally arrive at a condition very similar to that aimed at by Anarchist Communism.

Three questions arise in regard to this method of reaching Utopia. First, would the ultimate state foreshadowed by the Bolsheviks be desirable in itself? Secondly, would the conflict involved in achieving it by the Bolshevik method be so bitter and prolonged that its evils would outweigh the ultimate good? Thirdly, is this method likely to lead, in the end, to the state which the Bolsheviks desire, or will it fail at some point and arrive at a quite different result? If we are to be Bolsheviks, we must answer all these questions in a sense favourable to their programme.

As regards the first question, I have no hesitation in answering it in a manner favourable to Communism. It is clear that the present inequalities of wealth are unjust. In part they may be defended as affording an incentive to useful industry, but I do not think this defence will carry us very far. However, I have argued this question before in my book on *Roads to Freedom*, and I will not spend time upon it now. On this matter, I concede the Bolshevik case. It is the other two questions that I wish to discuss.

Our second question was: Is the ultimate good aimed at by the Bolsheviks sufficiently great to be worth the price that, according to their own theory, will have to be paid for achieving it?

If anything human were absolutely certain, we might answer this question affirmatively with some confidence. The benefits of Communism, if it were once achieved, might be expected to be lasting; we might legitimately hope that further change would be towards something still better, not towards a revival of ancient evils. But if we admit, as we must do, that the outcome of the Communist revolution is in some degree uncertain, it becomes necessary to count the cost; for a great part of the cost is all but certain.

Since the revolution of October, 1917, the Soviet Government has been at war with almost all the world, and has had at the same time to face civil war at home. This is not to be regarded as accidental, or as a misfortune which could not be foreseen. According to Marxian theory, what has happened was bound to happen. Indeed, Russia has been wonderfully fortunate in not having to face an even more desperate situation. First and foremost, the world was exhausted by the war, and in no mood for military adventures. Next, the Tsarist régime was the worst in Europe, and therefore rallied less support than would be secured by any other capitalist Government. Again, Russia is vast and agricultural, making it capable of resisting both invasion and blockade better than Great Britain or France or Germany. The only other country that could have resisted with equal success is the United States, which is at present very far removed from a proletarian revolution, and likely long to remain the chief bulwark of the capitalist system. It is evident that Great Britain, attempting a similar revolution, would be forced by starvation to yield within a few months, provided America led a policy of blockade. The same is true, though in a less degree, of continental countries. Therefore, unless and until an international Communist revolution becomes possible, we must expect that any other nation following Russia's example will have to pay an even higher price than Russia has had to pay.

Now the price that Russia is having to pay is very great. The almost universal poverty might be thought to be a small evil in comparison with the ultimate gain, but it brings with it other evils of which the magnitude would be acknowledged even by those who have never known poverty and therefore make light of it. Hunger brings an absorption in the question of food, which, to most people, makes life almost purely animal. The general shortage makes people fierce, and reacts upon the political atmosphere. The necessity of inculcating Communism produces a hot-house condition, where every breath of fresh air must be excluded: people are to be taught to think in a certain way, and all free intelligence becomes taboo. The country comes to resemble an immensely magnified Jesuit College. Every kind of liberty is banned as being *"bourgeois"*; but it remains a fact that intelligence languishes where thought is not free.

All this, however, according to the leaders of the Third International, is only a small beginning of the struggle, which must become world-wide before it achieves victory. In their reply to the Independent Labour Party they say:

> It is probable that upon the throwing off of the chains of the capitalist Governments, the revolutionary proletariat of Europe will meet the resistance of Anglo-Saxon capital in the persons of British and American capitalists who will attempt to blockade it. It is then possible that the revolutionary proletariat of Europe will rise in union

> with the peoples of the East and commence a revolu-
> tionary struggle, the scene of which will be the entire
> world, to deal a final blow to British and American capi-
> talism (*The Times*, July 30, 1920).

The war here prophesied, if it ever takes place, will be one
compared to which the late war will come to seem a mere affair
of outposts. Those who realize the destructiveness of the late
war, the devastation and impoverishment, the lowering of the
level of civilization throughout vast areas, the general increase
of hatred and savagery, the letting loose of bestial instincts
which had been curbed during peace—those who realize all
this will hesitate to incur inconceivably greater horrors, even if
they believe firmly that Communism in itself is much to be desired. An economic system cannot be considered apart from
the population which is to carry it out; and the population resulting from such a world-war as Moscow calmly contemplates
would be savage, bloodthirsty and ruthless to an extent that
must make any system a mere engine of oppression and cruelty.

This brings us to our third question: Is the system which
Communists regard as their goal likely to result from the adoption of their methods? This is really the most vital question of
the three.

Advocacy of Communism by those who believe in Bolshevik
methods rests upon the assumption that there is no slavery except economic slavery, and that when all goods are held in
common there must be perfect liberty. I fear this is a delusion.

There must be administration, there must be officials who
control distribution. These men, in a Communist State, are the
repositories of power. So long as they control the army, they are
able, as in Russia at this moment, to wield despotic power even
if they are a small minority. The fact that there is Communism
—to a certain extent—does not mean that there is liberty. If
the Communism were more complete, it would not necessarily
mean more freedom; there would still be certain officials in control of the food supply, and these officials could govern as they

pleased so long as they retained the support of the soldiers. This is not mere theory: it is the patent lesson of the present condition of Russia. The Bolshevik theory is that a small minority are to seize power, and are to hold it until Communism is accepted practically universally, which, they admit, may take a long time. But power is sweet, and few men surrender it voluntarily. It is especially sweet to those who have the habit of it, and the habit becomes most ingrained in those who have governed by bayonets, without popular support. Is it not almost inevitable that men placed as the Bolsheviks are placed in Russia, and as they maintain that the Communists must place themselves wherever the social revolution succeeds, will be loath to relinquish their monopoly of power, and will find reasons for remaining until some new revolution ousts them? Would it not be fatally easy for them, without altering economic structure, to decree large salaries for high Government officials, and so reintroduce the old inequalities of wealth? What motive would they have for not doing so? What motive is possible except idealism, love of mankind, non-economic motives of the sort that Bolsheviks decry? The system created by violence and the forcible rule of a minority must necessarily allow of tyranny and exploitation; and if human nature is what Marxians assert it to be, why should the rulers neglect such opportunities of selfish advantage?

It is sheer nonsense to pretend that the rulers of a great empire such as Soviet Russia, when they have become accustomed to power, retain the proletarian psychology, and feel that their class-interest is the same as that of the ordinary working man. This is not the case in fact in Russia now, however the truth may be concealed by fine phrases. The Government has a class-consciousness and a class-interest quite distinct from those of the genuine proletarian, who is not to be confounded with the paper proletarian of the Marxian schema. In a capitalist state, the Government and the capitalists on the whole hang together, and form one class; in Soviet Russia, the Government has absorbed the capitalist mentality together with the governmental, and the fusion has given increased strength to the upper class. But I see no reason whatever to expect equality or freedom to result from such a system, except reasons derived from a false psychology and a mistaken analysis of the sources of political power.

I am compelled to reject Bolshevism for two reasons: First, because the price mankind must pay to achieve Communism by Bolshevik methods is too terrible; and secondly because, even after paying the price, I do not believe the result would be what the Bolsheviks profess to desire.

Alexander Berkman

THE KRONSTADT REBELLION

Editor's Note

THE entire period of frenzy that was War Communism (1918-21) culminated in what has come to be known as the Kronstadt Rebellion, although the antecedents of the event were intended to be quite pacific. This segment of Russian history, sometimes referred to as "The Third Revolution," is one about which the Soviet leaders would prefer silence. Indicted by the Kronstadt episode are Lenin, Trotsky, Zinoviev and the entire Communist regime.

It is important to know who the sailors and workers of Kronstadt were, what was their past. They were the widely hailed and acclaimed heroes of the November, 1917 Bolshevik Revolution. To the end they were loyal to the idea of the revolutionary state. They died pronouncing this conviction, as expressed in a manifesto: "We will rise or fall under the ruins of Kronstadt, fighting for the bloodstained cause of the laboring people. Long live the power of the Soviets! Long live the world Socialist Revolution!" Here is an early acid test of the character of the Communist dictatorship. Here is no instance of opposition by "counter-revolutionaries," by "foreign interventionists." "bourgeois enemies." The sailor heroes of Kronstadt were precisely those who responded to Lenin's slogans in

1917, who fought so courageously and selflessly—if blindly—for him, who made possible his acquisition of power.

Their tragic story began when they sent an investigating committee to Petrograd to inform them of the situation faced by the workers in that city. These workers had at first demanded bread and fuel, an end to preferential treatment for privileged Communists, increased rations as they had been promised. The answer of Lenin's government was a decree of martial law. Return to your factories or have your rations taken away, was the edict. The situation gradually took on a political coloration. A manifesto in Petrograd read: "First of all the workers and peasants need freedom. They don't want to live by the decrees of the Bolsheviki; they want to control their own destinies." The slogans the Communists used to ride to power were now to haunt them, voiced by those who had supported them and who now demanded that the promises be kept. The strikes continued to spread, despite the government's threats, and they were reinforced by serious peasant revolts.

These facts were what the investigating committee of Kronstadt learned. They discovered that armed bands, soldiers, had been sent to disperse the striking workers. Announcing their solidarity with their comrades, the Petrograd strikers, the sailors of the warships *Petropavlovsk* and *Sevastopol* also reiterated their loyalty to the revolution, to the Soviets, and to the Communist ideal. Despite these well-intentioned petitions, proclamations and declarations of loyalty, Lenin's dictatorship was not deterred. The Communist leaders would tolerate no "opposition" to their dictatorial rule. Exactly what happened at Kronstadt is the subject of Alexander Berkman's important selection. In close touch with the situation, held in high esteem by the "pride of the Revolution," as Trotsky had earlier called the Kronstadt sailors, Berkman played an important role in relating the story of Kronstadt to the world. His essay, published in 1922, a year after the experience he details, has long been unavailable. It is here excerpted at length in the belief that this extremely significant piece of history, an event which brought an end to the period of War Communism and which ushered in the Communist retreat in the form of NEP (New Economic Policy)—about which we shall hear more—is inadequately known at the present time.

Facets of especial interest in this selection, as regards the Communist role, are the already entrenched system of misrepresentation of political fact, the opportunist attempt to tar these simple, revolutionary heroes with the counter-revolutionary brush, the incredible brutality visited on Kronstadt, and the barbaric massacre it entailed. As the story enfolds and made additionally valuable by the moving documents of Kronstadt that Berkman intersperses in his account, the violence of the Soviet repression of the meager revolutionary demands of Kronstadt furnishes an uneasy insight into the entire period of which this was the culminating event.

Alexander Berkman was born in Vilna in November, 1870. In his early teens he joined a revolutionary study group and was soon expelled from school. At 16 he emigrated to the United States. He arrived at a time of unrest, some months after the Haymarket affair, and immediately became a participant in radical activity. He joined the "Pioneers of Liberty" group, and later John Most's anarchist circle. He became a close associate of Emma Goldman and their names are closely connected in the history of the American anarchist movement. The events leading up to his expulsion from the United States are noted briefly in the preface to Emma Goldman's selection in this book. His experiences in the Soviet Union paralleled hers. They had both hailed the coming of the Revolution and had been welcomed in Russia after their arrival; together they grew disillusioned with Bolshevik control of the state after spending two years in Russia, their very last hope disappearing with the occurrence of the Kronstadt massacre. Among Berkman's books are: *The Bolshevik Myth* (1925), the diary of his stay in Russia; *Prison Memoirs of an Anarchist,* his famous account of his fourteen years in an American penitentiary; *What is Communist Anarchism?*; and his pamphlets, "The Russian Tragedy" and "The Russian Revolution and the Communist Party," both published, as was his essay on Kronstadt, in Berlin in 1922. Exiled from the United States, sick, despondent, he committed suicide in France on June 28, 1936.

The Kronstadt Rebellion by Alexander Berkman

I. Labor Disturbances in Petrograd

It was early in 1921. Long years of war, revolution, and civil struggle had bled Russia to exhaustion and brought her people to the brink of despair. But at last civil war was at an end: the numerous fronts were liquidated, and Wrangel—the last hope of Entente intervention and Russian counter-revolution—was defeated and his military activities within Russia terminated. The people now confidently looked forward to the mitigation of the severe Bolshevik régime. It was expected that with the end of civil war the Communists would lighten the burdens, abolish war-time restrictions, introduce some fundamental liberties, and begin the organisation of a more normal life. Though far from being popular, the Bolshevik Government had the support of the workers in its oft announced plan of taking up the economic reconstruction of the country as soon as military operations should cease.

The people were eager to coöperate, to put their initiative and creative efforts to the upbuilding of the ruined land.

Most unfortunately, these expectations were doomed to disappointment. The Communist State showed no intention of loosening the yoke. The same policies continued, with labor militarisation still further enslaving the people, embittering them with added oppression and tyranny, and in consequence paralising every possibility of industrial revival. The last hope of the proletariat was perishing: the conviction grew that the Communist Party was more interested in retaining political power than in saving the Revolution.

The most revolutionary elements of Russia, the workers of Petrograd, were the first to speak out. They charged that, aside from other causes, Bolshevik centralisation, bureaucracy, and autocratic attitude toward the peasants and workers were directly responsible for much of the misery and suffering of the people. Many factories and mills of Petrograd had been closed, and the workers were literally starving. They called meetings to consider the situation. The meetings were suppressed by the Government. The Petrograd proletariat, who had borne the brunt of the revolutionary struggles and whose great sacrifices and heroism alone had saved the city from Yudenitch, resented the action of the Government. Feeling against the methods employed by the Bolsheviki continued to grow. More meetings were called, with the same result. The Communists would make no concessions to the proletariat, while at the same time they were offering to compromise with the capitalists of Europe and America. The workers were indignant—they became aroused. To compel the Government to consider their demands, strikes were called in the Patronny munition works, the Trubotchny and Baltiyski mills, and in the Laferm factory. Instead of talking matters over with the dissatisfied workers, the "Workers' and Peasants' Government" created a war-time *Komitet Oborony* (Committee of Defense) with Zinoviev, the most hated man in Petrograd, as Chairman. The avowed purpose of that Committee was to suppress the strike movement.

It was on February 24 that the strikes were declared. The same day the Bolsheviki sent the *kursanti,* the Communist students of the military academy (training officers for the Army and Navy), to disperse the workers who had gathered on Vassilevsky Ostrov, the labor district of Petrograd. The next day, February 25, the indignant strikers of Vassilevsky Ostrov visited the Admiralty shops and the Galernaya docks, and induced the workers there to join their protest against the autocratic attitude of the Government. The attempted street demonstration of the strikers was dispersed by armed soldiery.

On February 26 the Petrograd Soviet held a session at which the prominent Communist Lashevitch, member of the Committee of Defense and of the Revolutionary Military Soviet of the Republic, denounced the strike movement in sharpest terms. He charged the workers of the Trubotchny factory with inciting dissatisfaction, accused them of being "self-seeking labor skinners (*shkurniki*) and counter-revolutionists," and proposed that the Trubotchny factory be closed. The Executive Committee of the Petrograd Soviet (Zinoviev, Chairman) accepted the suggestion. The Trubotchny strikers were *locked out* and thus automatically deprived of their rations.

These methods of the Bolshevik Government served still further to embitter and antagonise the workers.

Strikers' proclamations now began to appear on the streets of Petrograd. Some of them assumed a distinctly political character, the most significant of them, posted on the walls of the city February 27, reading:

A complete change is necessary in the policies of the Government. First of all, the workers and peasants need freedom. They don't want to live by the decrees of the Bolsheviki: they want to control their own destinies.

Comrades, preserve revolutionary order! Determinedly and in an organised manner demand:

Liberation of all arrested socialists and nonpartisan workingmen;

Abolition of martial law; freedom of speech, press and assembly for all who labor. . . .

Meanwhile the Bolsheviki concentrated in Petrograd large military forces from the provinces and also ordered to the city its most trusted Communist regiments from the front. Petrograd was put under "extraordinary martial law." The strikers were overawed, and the labor unrest crushed with an iron hand.

II. The Kronstadt Movement

The Kronstadt sailors were much disturbed by what was happening in Petrograd. They did not look with friendly eyes upon the Government's drastic treatment of the strikers. They knew what the revolutionary proletariat of the capital had had to bear since the first days of the Revolution, how heroically they had fought against Yudenitch, and how patiently they were suffering privation and misery. . . . They were the staunchest supporters of the Soviet system, but they were opposed to the dictatorship of any political party.

The sympathetic movement with the Petrograd strikers first began among the sailors of the warships *Petropavlovsk* and *Sevastopol*—the ships that in 1917 had been the main support of the Bolsheviki. The movement spread to the whole fleet of Kronstadt, then to the Red Army regiments stationed there. On February 28 the men of *Petropavlovsk* passed a resolution which was also concurred in by the sailors of *Sevastopol*. The resolution demanded, among other things, free reëlections to the Kronstadt Soviet, as the tenure of office of the latter was about to expire. At the same time a committee of sailors was sent to Petrograd to learn the situation there.

On March 1 a public meeting was held on the Yakorny Square in Kronstadt, which was officially called by the crews of the First and Second Squadrons of the Baltic Fleet. 16,000 sailors, Red Army men, and workers attended the gathering. It was presided over by the Chairman of the Executive Committee of the Kronstadt Soviet, the Communist Vassiliev. The President of the Russian Socialist Federated Republic, Kalinin, and the Commissar of the Baltic Fleet, Kuzmin, were present and addressed the audience. It may be mentioned, as indicative of the friendly attitude of the sailors to the Bolshevik Government, that Kalinin was met on his arrival in Kronstadt with military honors, music, and banners.

At this meeting the Sailors' Committee that had been sent to Petrograd on February 28 made its report. It corroborated the worst fears of Kronstadt. The audience was outspoken in its indignation at the methods used by the Communists to crush the modest demands of the Petrograd workers. The resolution which had been passed by *Petropavlovsk* on February 28 was then submitted to the meeting. President Kalinin and Commissar Kuzmin bitterly attacked the resolution and denounced the Petrograd strikers as well as the Kronstadt sailors. But their arguments failed to impress the audience, and the *Petropavlovsk* resolution was passed unanimously. . . .

This Resolution, strenuously opposed—as already mentioned —by Kalinin and Kuzmin, was passed over their protest. After the meeting Kalinin was permitted to return to Petrograd unmolested.

At the same Brigade Meeting it was also decided to send a Committee to Petrograd to explain to the workers and the garrison there the demands of Kronstadt and to request that nonpartisan delegates be sent by the Petrograd proletariat to Kronstadt to learn the actual state of affairs and the demands of the sailors. This Committee, which consisted of thirty members, was arrested by the Bolsheviki in Petrograd. It was the first blow struck by the Communist Government against Kronstadt. The fate of the Committee remained a mystery.

As the term of office of the members of the Kronstadt Soviet was about to expire, the Brigade Meeting also decided to call a Conference of delegates on March 2, to discuss the manner in which the new elections were to be held. The Conference was to consist of representatives of the ships, the garrison, the various Soviet institutions, the labor unions and factories, each organisation to be represented by two delegates.

The Conference of March 2 took place in the House of Education (the former Kronstadt School of Engineering) and was attended by over 300 delegates, among whom were also Communists. . . .

The spirit of the Conference was thoroughly Sovietist: Kronstadt demanded Soviets free from interference by any political party; it wanted nonpartisan Soviets that should truly reflect the needs and express the will of the workers and peasants. The attitude of the delegates was antagonistic to the arbitrary rule of bureaucratic commissars, but friendly to the Communist Party as such. They were staunch adherents of the Soviet *system* and they were earnestly seeking to find, by means friendly and peaceful, a solution of the pressing problems.

Kuzmin, Commissar of the Baltic Fleet, was the first to address the Conference. A man of more energy than judgment, he entirely failed to grasp the great significance of the moment. He was not equal to the situation: he did not know how to reach the hearts and minds of those simple men, the sailors and workers who had sacrificed so much for the Revolution and who were now exhausted to the point of desperation. The delegates had gathered to take counsel with the representatives of the Government. Instead, Kuzmin's speech proved a firebrand thrown into gunpowder. He incensed the Conference by his arrogance and insolence. He denied the labor disorders in Petrograd, declaring that the city was quiet and the workers satisfied. He praised the work of the Commissars, questioned the revolutionary motives of Kronstadt, and warned against danger from Poland. He stooped to unworthy insinuations and thundered threats. "If you want open warfare," Kuzmin concluded, "you shall have it, for the Communists will not give up the reins of government. We will fight to the bitter end."

This tactless and provoking speech of the Commissar of the Baltic Fleet served to insult and outrage the delegates. The address of the Chairman of the Kronstadt Soviet, the Communist Vassiliev, who was the next speaker, made no impression on the audience: the man was colorless and indefinite. As the meeting progressed, the general attitude became more clearly anti-Bolshevik. Still the delegates were hoping to reach some friendly understanding with the representatives of the Government. But presently it became apparent, states the official report,* that "we could not trust comrades Kuzmin and Vassiliev any more, and that it was necessary to detain them temporarily, especially because the Communists were in possession of arms, and we had no access to the telephones. The soldiers stood in fear of the Commissars, as proved by the letter read at the meeting, and the Communists did not permit gatherings of the garrison to take place."

Kuzmin and Vassiliev were therefore removed from the meeting and placed under arrest. It is characteristic of the spirit of the Conference that the motion to detain the other Communists present was voted down by an overwhelming majority. The delegates held that the Communists must be considered on equal footing with the representatives of other organisations and accorded the same rights and treatment. Kronstadt still was determined to find some bond of agreement with the Communist Party and the Bolshevik Government.

The Resolutions of March 1 were read and enthusiastically passed. At that moment the Conference was thrown into great excitement by the declaration of a delegate that the Bolsheviki were about to attack the meeting and that fifteen carloads of soldiers and Communists, armed with rifles and machine guns, had been dispatched for that purpose. "This information," the *Izvestia* report continues, "produced passionate resentment among the delegates. Investigation soon proved the report groundless, but rumors persisted that a regiment of *kursanti*, headed by the notorious Tchekist Dulkiss, was already marching in the direction of the fort Krasnaia Gorka." In view of these new developments, and remembering the threats of Kuz-

---

* *Izvestia* of the Provisional Revolutionary Committee of Kronstadt, No. 9, March 11, 1921.

min and Kalinin, the Conference at once took up the question
of organising the defense of Kronstadt against Bolshevik attack. Time pressing, it was decided to turn the Presidium of the
Conference into a Provisional Revolutionary Committee, which
was charged with the duty of preserving the order and safety
of the city. That Committee was also to make the necessary
preparations for holding the new elections to the Kronstadt
Soviet.

III. The Bolshevik Campaign Against Kronstadt

Petrograd was in a state of high nervous tension. New strikes
had broken out and there were persistent rumors of labor disorders in Moscow, of peasant uprisings in the East and in Siberia. For lack of a reliable public press the people gave
credence to the most exaggerated and even to obviously false
reports. All eyes were on Kronstadt in expectation of momen-
tous developments.

The Bolsheviki lost no time in organising their attack against
Kronstadt. Already on March 2 the Government issued a
prikaz (order) signed by Lenin and Trotsky, which denounced
the Kronstadt movement as a *myatezh,* a mutiny against the
Communist authorities. In that document the sailors were
charged with being "the tools of former Tsarist generals who
together with Socialist-Revolutionist traitors staged a counter-
revolutionary conspiracy against the proletarian Republic."
The Kronstadt movement for free Soviets was characterised
by Lenin and Trotsky as "the work of Entente interventionists
and French spies." "On February 28," the *prikaz* read, "there
were passed by the men of the *Petropavlovsk* resolutions breathing the spirit of the Black Hundreds. Then there appeared on
the scene the group of the former general, Kozlovsky. He and
three of his officers, whose names we have not yet ascertained,
have openly assumed the rôle of rebellion. Thus the meaning of
recent events has become evident. Behind the Socialist-Revo-
lutionists again stands a Tsarist general. In view of all this the
Council of Labor and Defense orders: (1) To declare the

former general Kozlovsky and his aides outlawed; (2) to put the City of Petrograd and the Petrograd Province under martial law; (3) to place supreme power over the whole Petrograd District into the hands of the Petrograd Committee of Defense."

There was indeed a former general, Kozlovsky, in Kronstadt. It was Trotsky who had placed him there as an artillery specialist. He played no rôle whatever in the Kronstadt events, but the Bolsheviki cleverly exploited his name to denounce the sailors as enemies of the Soviet Republic and their movement as counter-revolutionary. The official Bolshevik press now began its campaign of calumny and defamation of Kronstadt as a hotbed of "White conspiracy headed by General Kozlovsky," and Communist agitators were sent among the workers in the mills and factories of Petrograd and Moscow to call upon the proletariat "to rally to the support and defense of the Workers' and Peasants' Government against the counter-revolutionary uprising in Kronstadt." . . .

Moscow . . . continued its campaign of misrepresentation. On March 3 the Bolshevik radio station sent out the following message to the world: . . .

> . . . That the armed uprising of the former general Kozlovsky has been organised by the spies of the Entente, like many similar previous plots, is evident from the bourgeois French newspaper *Matin,* which two weeks prior to the Kozlovsky rebellion published the following telegram from Helsingfors: "As a result of the recent Kronstadt uprising the Bolshevik military authorities have taken steps to isolate Kronstadt and to prevent the sailors and soldiers of Kronstadt from entering Petrograd." . . . It is clear that the Kronstadt uprising was made in Paris and organised by the French secret service. . . .

The Petrograd Committee of Defense, directed by Zinoviev, its Chairman, assumed full control of the City and Province of

Petrograd. The whole Northern District was put under martial law and all meetings prohibited. Extraordinary precautions
were taken to protect the Government institutions and machine
guns were placed in the Astoria, the hotel occupied by Zinoviev
and other high Bolshevik functionaries. The proclamations
posted on the street bulletin boards ordered the immediate
return of all strikers to the factories, prohibited suspension of
work, and warned the people against congregating on the
streets. "In such cases," the order read, "the soldiery will resort
to arms. In case of resistance, shooting on the spot."

The Committee of Defense took up the systematic "cleaning
of the city." Numerous workers, soldiers and sailors, suspected
of sympathising with Kronstadt, were placed under arrest. All
Petrograd sailors and several Army regiments thought to be
"politically untrustworthy" were ordered to distant points,
while the families of Kronstadt sailors living in Petrograd were
taken into custody *as hostages*. The Committee of Defense
notified Kronstadt of its action by a proclamation scattered
over the city from an aeroplane on March 4, which stated: "The
Committee of Defense declares that the arrested are held as
hostages for the Commissar of the Baltic Fleet, N. N. Kuzmin,
the Chairman of the Kronstadt Soviet, T. Vassiliev, and other
Communists. If the least harm be suffered by our detained comrades, the hostages will pay with their lives."

"We do not want bloodshed. Not a single Communist has
been shot by us," was Kronstadt's reply.

IV. *The Aims of Kronstadt*

Kronstadt revived with new life. Revolutionary enthusiasm
rose to the level of the October days when the heroism and
devotion of the sailors played such a decisive rôle. Now, for the
first time since the Communist Party assumed exclusive control
of the Revolution and the fate of Russia, Kronstadt felt itself
free. A new spirit of solidarity and brotherhood brought the
sailors, the soldiers of the garrison, the factory workers, and the
nonpartisan elements together in united effort for their com-

mon cause. Even Communists were infected by the fraternisation of the whole city and joined in the work preparatory to the approaching elections to the Kronstadt Soviet.

Among the first steps taken by the Provisional Revolutionary Committee was the preservation of revolutionary order in Kronstadt and the publication of the Committee's official organ, the daily *Izvestia*. Its first appeal to the people of Kronstadt (issue No. 1, March 3, 1921) was thoroughly characteristic of the attitude and temper of the sailors. "The Revolutionary Committee," it read, "is most concerned that no blood be shed. It has exerted its best efforts to organise revolutionary order in the city, the fortress and the forts. Comrades and citizens, do not suspend work! Workers, remain at your machines; sailors and soldiers, be on your posts. All Soviet employees and institutions should continue their labors. The Provisional Revolutionary Committee calls upon you all, comrades and citizens, to give it your support and aid. Its mission is to organise, in fraternal coöperation with you, the conditions necessary for honest and just elections to the new Soviet."

The pages of the *Izvestia* bear abundant witness to the deep faith of the Revolutionary Committee in the people of Kronstadt and their aspirations toward free Soviets as the true road of liberation from the oppression of Communist bureaucracy. In its daily organ and radio messages the Revolutionary Committee indignantly resented the Bolshevik campaign of calumny and repeatedly appealed to the proletariat of Russia and of the world for understanding, sympathy, and help. The radio of March 6 sounds the keynote of Kronstadt's call:

> Our cause is just: we stand for the power of Soviets, not parties. We stand for freely elected representatives of the laboring masses. The substitute Soviets manipulated by the Communist Party have always been deaf to our needs and demands; the only reply we have ever received was shooting. . . . Comrades! They not only deceive you: they deliberately pervert the truth and

resort to most despicable defamation. . . . In Kronstadt the whole power is exclusively in the hands of the revolutionary sailors, soldiers and workers—not with counter-revolutionists led by some Kozlovsky, as the lying Moscow radio tries to make you believe. . . . Do not delay, comrades! Join us, get in touch with us: demand admission to Kronstadt for your delegates. . . .

The Provisional Revolutionary Committee first had its headquarters on the flagship *Petropavlovsk,* but within a few days it removed to the "People's Home," in the center of Kronstadt, in order to be, as the *Izvestia* states, "in closer touch with the people and make access to the Committee easier than on the ship." Although the Communist press continued its virulent denunciation of Kronstadt as "the counter-revolutionary rebellion of General Kozlovsky," the truth of the matter was that the Revolutionary Committee was exclusively proletarian, consisting for the most part of workers of known revolutionary record. . . .

The Provisional Revolutionary Committee enjoyed the confidence of the whole population of Kronstadt. It won general respect by establishing and firmly adhering to the principle of "equal rights for all, privileges to none." The *pahyok* (food ration) was equalised. The sailors, who under Bolshevik rule always received rations far in excess of those allotted to the workers, themselves voted to accept no more than the average citizen and toiler. Special rations and delicacies were given only to hospitals and children's homes.

The just and generous attitude of the Revolutionary Committee toward the Kronstadt members of the Communist Party —few of whom had been arrested in spite of Bolshevik repressions and the holding of the sailors' families as hostages—won the respect even of the Communists. The pages of the *Izvestia* contain numerous communications from Communist groups and organisations of Kronstadt, condemning the attitude of the Central Government and indorsing the stand and measures

of the Provisional Revolutionary Committee. Many Kronstadt
Communists publicly announced their withdrawal from the
Party as a protest against its despotism and bureaucratic corruption. In various issues of the *Izvestia* there are to be found
hundreds of names of Communists whose conscience made it
impossible for them to "remain in the Party of the executioner
Trotsky," as some of them expressed it. Resignations from the
Communist Party soon became so numerous as to resemble a
general exodus.*. . .

Similarly various other organisations, civil and military, expressed their opposition to the Moscow régime and their entire
agreement with the demands of the Kronstadt sailors. Many
resolutions to that effect were also passed by Red Army regiments stationed in Kronstadt and on duty in the forts. The following is expressive of their general spirit and tendency:

> We, Red Army soldiers of the Fort "Krasnoarmeetz,"
> stand wholly with the Provisional Revolutionary Com-
> mittee, and to the last moment we will defend the Revo-
> lutionary Committee, the workers and the peasants. . . .
> Let no one believe the lies of the Communist proc-
> lamations thrown from aeroplanes. We have no gener-
> als here and no Tsarist officers. Kronstadt has always
> been the city of workers and peasants, and so it will re-
> main. The generals are in the service of the Commu-
> nists . . .
> At this moment, when the fate of the country is in the
> balance, we who have taken the power into our own
> hands and who have entrusted the Revolutionary Com-
> mittee with leadership in the fight—we declare to the
> whole garrison and to the workers that we are prepared
> to die for the liberty of the laboring masses. Freed from
> the three-year old Communist yoke and terror we shall

---

* The Executive Committee of the Communist Party of Russia considered its
Kronstadt Section so "demoralised" that after the defeat of Kronstadt it ordered
a complete re-registration of all Kronstadt Communists.

die rather than recede a single step. Long live Free
Russia of the Working People!

CREW OF THE FORT "KRASNOARMEETZ"
Izvestia, No. 5, March 7, 1921

Kronstadt was inspired by passionate love of a Free Russia
and unbounded faith in true Soviets. It was confident of gaining the support of the whole of Russia, of Petrograd in particular, thus bringing about the final liberation of the country. . . .
It often reproduced in its organ the Moscow proclamations
in order to show to the people of Kronstadt to what depths the
Bolsheviki had sunk. . . .

In simple and frank speech Kronstadt sought to express the
will of the people yearning for freedom and for the opportunity
to shape their own destinies. It felt itself the advance guard, so
to speak, of the proletariat of Russia about to rise in defense of
the great aspirations for which the people had fought and suffered in the October Revolution. . . . It strove for the emancipation of the people from the Communist yoke. That yoke,
no longer bearable, made a new revolution, the *Third Revolution*, necessary. The road to liberty and peace lay in freely
elected Soviets, "the cornerstone of the new revolution." The
pages of the *Izvestia* bear rich testimony to the unspoiled di-
rectness and single-mindedness of the Kronstadt sailors and
workers, and the touching faith they had in their mission as the
initiators of the Third Revolution. These aspirations and hopes
are clearly set forth in No. 6 of the *Izvestia*, March 8, in the
leading editorial entitled "What We Are Fighting For":

> With the October Revolution the working class had
> hoped to achieve its emanicipation. But there resulted
> an even greater enslavement of human personality.
> The power of the police and gendarme monarchy fell
> into the hands of usurpers—the Communists—who, in-

stead of giving the people liberty, have instilled in them only the constant fear of the Tcheka, which by its horrors surpasses even the gendarme régime of Tsarism. . . . Worst and most criminal of all is the spiritual cabal of the Communists: they have laid their hand also on the internal world of the laboring masses, compelling everyone to think according to Communist prescription. . . .

Here is raised the banner of rebellion against the three-year old tyranny and oppression of Communist autocracy, which has put in the shade the three-hundred-year-old despotism of monarchism. Here, in Kronstadt, has been laid the cornerstone of the Third Revolution which is to break the last chains of the worker and open the new, broad road to Socialist creativeness. . . .

Without firing a single shot, without shedding a drop of blood, the first step has been taken. Those who labor need no blood. They will shed it only in self-defense. . . .

That was the program, those the immediate demands, for which the Bolshevik Government began the attack of Kronstadt at 6.45 P.M., March 7, 1921.

V. *Bolshevik Ultimatum to Kronstadt*

Kronstadt was generous. Not a drop of Communist blood did it shed, in spite of all the provocation, the blockade of the city and the repressive measures on the part of the Bolshevik Government. It scorned to imitate the Communist example of vengeance, even going to the extent of warning the Kronstadt population not to be guilty of excesses against members of the Communist Party. The Provisional Revolutionary Committee issued a call to the people of Kronstadt to that effect, even after the Bolshevik Government had ignored the demand of the sailors for the liberation of the hostages taken in Petrograd. . . .

Kronstadt lived in the spirit of its holy crusade. It had abiding faith in the justice of its cause and felt itself the true de-

fender of the Revolution. In this state of mind the sailors did
not believe that the Government would attack them by force of
arms. In the subconsciousness of these simple children of the
soil and sea there perhaps germinated the feeling that *not only
through violence may victory be gained*. The Slavic psychology
seemed to believe that the justice of the cause and the strength
of revolutionary spirit must win. At any rate, Kronstadt refused
to take the offensive. The Revolutionary Committee would not
accept the insistent advice of the military experts to make an
immediate landing in Oranienbaum, a fort of great strategic
value. The Kronstadt sailors and soldiers aimed to establish
free Soviets and were willing to defend their rights against
attack; but they would not be the aggressors.

In Petrograd there were persistent rumors that the Government was preparing military operations against Kronstadt,
but the people did not credit such stories: the thing seemed so
outrageous as to be absurd. As already mentioned, the Committee of Defense (officially known as the Soviet of Labor and
Defense) had declared the capital to be in an "extraordinary
state of siege." No assemblies were permitted, no gathering on
the streets. The Petrograd workers knew little of what was transpiring in Kronstadt, the only information accessible being the
Communist press and the frequent bulletins to the effect that
the "Tsarist General Kozlovsky organised a counter-revolutionary uprising in Kronstadt." Anxiously the people looked
forward to the announced session of the Petrograd Soviet which
was to take action in the Kronstadt matter.

The Petro-Soviet met on March 4, admission being by cards
which, as a rule, only Communists could procure. The writer,
then on friendly terms with the Bolsheviki and particularly
with Zinoviev, was present. As Chairman of the Petograd
Soviet Zinoviev opened the session and in a long speech set
forth the Kronstadt situation. I confess that I came to the
meeting disposed rather in favor of the Zinoviev veiwpoint: I
was on my guard against the vaguest possibility of counter-
revolutionary influence in Kronstadt. But Zinoviev's speech it-

self convinced me that the Communist accusations against the sailors were pure fabrication, without a scintilla of truth. I had heard Zinoviev on several previous occasions. I found him a convincing speaker, once his premises were admitted. But now his whole attitude, his argumentation, his tone and manner— all gave the lie to his words. I could sense his own conscience protesting. The only "evidence" presented against Kronstadt was the famous Resolution of March 1, the demands of which were just and even moderate. Yet it was on the sole basis of that document, supported by the vehement, almost hysterical denunciation of the sailors by Kalinin, that the fatal step was taken. Prepared beforehand and presented by the stentorian-voiced Yevdokimov, the right-hand man of Zinoviev, the resolution against Kronstadt was passed by the delegates wrought up to a high pitch of intolerance and blood thirst—passed amid a tumult of protest from several delegates of Petrograd factories and the spokesmen of the sailors. The resolution declared Kronstadt guilty of a counter-revolutionary uprising against the Soviet power and demanded its immediate surrender.

It was a declaration of war. Even many Communists refused to believe that the resolution would be carried out: it were a monstrous thing to attack by force of arms the "pride and glory of the Russian Revolution," as Trotsky had christened the Kronstadt sailors. In the circle of their friends many sober-minded Communists threatened to resign from the Party should such a bloody deed come to pass.

Trotsky had been expected to address the Petro-Soviet, and his failure to appear was interpreted by some as indicating that the seriousness of the situation was exaggerated. But during the night he arrived in Petrograd and the following morning, March 5, he issued his ultimatum to Kronstadt:

> The Workers' and Peasants' Government has decreed that Kronstadt and the rebellious ships must immediately submit to the authority of the Soviet Republic. Therefore I command all who have raised their hand

against the Socialist fatherland to lay down their arms at once. The obdurate are to be disarmed and turned over to the Soviet authorities. The arrested Commissars and other representatives of the Government are to be liberated at once. Only those surrendering unconditionally may count on the mercy of the Soviet Republic.

Simultaneously I am issuing orders to prepare to quell the mutiny and subdue the mutineers by force of arms. Responsibility for the harm that may be suffered by the peaceful population will fall entirely upon the heads of the counter-revolutionary mutineers.

This warning is final.

TROTSKY
Chairman Revolutionary Military Soviet of the Republic

KAMENEV
Commander-in-Chief

The situation looked ominous. Great military forces continuously flowed into Petrograd and its environs. Trotsky's ultimatum was followed by a *prikaz* which contained the historic threat, "I'll shoot you like pheasants." A group of Anarchists then in Petrograd made a last attempt to induce the Bolsheviki to reconsider their decision of attacking Kronstadt. They felt it their duty to the Revolution to make an effort, even if hopeless, to prevent the imminent massacre of the revolutionary flower of Russia, the Kronstadt sailors and workers. On March 5 they sent a protest to the Committee of Defense, pointing out the peaceful intentions and just demands of Kronstadt, reminding the Communists of the heroic revolutionary history of the sailors, and suggesting a method of settling the dispute in a manner befitting comrades and revolutionists. The document read:

To the Petrograd Soviet of Labor and Defense
Chairman Zinoviev:

To remain silent *now* is impossible, even criminal. Recent events impel us Anarchists to speak out and to declare our attitude in the present situation.

The spirit of ferment and dissatisfaction manifest among the workers and sailors is the result of causes that demand our serious attention. Cold and hunger have produced disaffection, and the absence of any opportunity for discussion and criticism is forcing the workers and sailors to air their grievances in the open. . . .

Concerning the conflict between the Soviet Government and the workers and sailors, we hold that it must be settled not by force of arms but by means of comradely, fraternal revolutionary agreement. Resorting to bloodshed, on the part of the Soviet Government, will not—in the given situation—intimidate or quieten the workers. On the contrary, it will serve only to aggravate matters and will strengthen the hands of the Entente and of internal counter-revolution.

More important still, the use of force by the Workers' and Peasants' Government against workers and sailors will have a reactionary effect upon the international revolutionary movement and will everywhere result in incalculable harm to the Social Revolution.

Comrades Bolsheviki, bethink yourselves before it is too late! Do not play with fire: you are about to make a most serious and decisive step.

We hereby submit to you the following proposition: Let a Commission be selected to consist of five persons, inclusive of two Anarchists. The Commission is to go to Kronstadt to settle the dispute by peaceful means. In the given situation this is the most radical method. It will be of international revolutionary significance.

Petrograd
March 5, 1921

ALEXANDER BERKMAN
EMMA GOLDMAN
PERKUS
PETROVSKY

Zinoviev, informed that a document in connection with the Kronstadt problem was to be submitted to the Soviet of Defense, sent his personal representative for it. Whether the letter was discussed by that body is not known to the writer. At any rate, no action was taken in the matter.

VI. *The First Shot*

Kronstadt, heroic and generous, was dreaming of liberating Russia by the Third Revolution which it felt proud to have initiated. It formulated no definite program. Liberty and universal brotherhood were its slogans. It thought of the Third Revolution as a gradual process of emancipation, the first step in that direction being the free election of independent Soviets, uncontrolled by any political party and expressive of the will and interests of the people. The whole-hearted, unsophisticated sailors were proclaiming to the workers of the world their great ideal, and calling upon the proletariat to join forces in the common fight, confident that their cause would find enthusiastic support and that the workers of Petrograd, first and foremost, would hasten to their aid.

Meanwhile Trotsky had collected his forces. The most trusted divisions from the fronts, *kursanti* regiments, Tcheka detachments, and military units consisting exclusively of Communists were now gathered in the forts of Sestroretsk, Lissy Noss, Krasnaia Gorka, and neighboring fortified places. The greatest Russian military experts were rushed to the scene to form plans for the blockade and attack of Kronstadt, and the notorious Tukhachevski was appointed Commander-in-Chief in the siege of Kronstadt.

On March 7, at 6.45 in the evening, the Communist batteries of Sestroretsk and Lissy Noss fired the first shots against Kronstadt.

It was the anniversary of the Women Workers' Day. Kronstadt, besieged and attacked, did not forget the great holiday. Under fire of numerous batteries, the brave sailors sent a radio greeting to the workingwomen of the world, an act most characteristic of the psychology of the Rebel City. The radio read:

> Today is a universal holiday—Women Workers' Day. We of Kronstadt send, amid the thunder of cannon, our fraternal greetings to the workingwomen of the world. . . . May you soon accomplish your liberation from every form of violence and oppression. . . . Long live the free revolutionary workingwomen! Long live the Social Revolution throughout the world!

No less characteristic was the heart-rending cry of Kronstadt, "Let the Whole World Know," published after the first shot had been fired, in No. 6 of the *Izvestia*, March 8:

> The first shot has been fired. . . . Standing up to his knees in the blood of the workers, Marshal Trotsky was the first to open fire against revolutionary Kronstadt which has risen against the autocracy of the Communists to establish the true power of the Soviets.
>
> Without shedding a drop of blood we, Red Army men, sailors, and workers of Kronstadt have freed ourselves from the yoke of the Communists and have even preserved their lives. By the threat of artillery they want now to subject us again to their tyranny.
>
> Not wishing bloodshed, we asked that nonpartisan delegates of the Petrograd proletariat be sent to us, that they may learn that Kronstadt is fighting for the Power of the Soviets. But the Communists have kept our demand from the workers of Petrograd and now they have opened fire—the usual reply of the pseudo Workers' and Peasants' Government to the demands of the laboring masses.
>
> Let the workers of the whole world know that we, the defenders of Soviet Power, are guarding the conquests of the Social Revolution.

We will win or perish beneath the ruins of Kronstadt, fighting for the just cause of the laboring masses.

The workers of the world will be our judges. The blood of the innocent will fall upon the heads of the Communist fanatics drunk with authority.

Long live the Power of the Soviets!

VII. *The Defeat of Kronstadt*

The artillery bombardment of Kronstadt, which began on the evening of March 7, was followed by the attempt to take the fortress by storm. The attack was made from the north and the south by picked Communist troops clad in white shrouds, the color of which protectively blended with the snow lying thick on the frozen Gulf of Finland. These first terrible attempts to take the fortress by storm, at the reckless sacrifice of life, are mourned by the sailors in touching commiseration for their brothers in arms, duped into believing Kronstadt counter-revolutionary. Under date of March 8 the Kronstadt *Izvestia* wrote:

We did not want to shed the blood of our brothers, and we did not fire a single shot until compelled to do so. We had to defend the just cause of the laboring people and to shoot—to shoot at our own brothers sent to certain death by Communists who have grown fat at the expense of the people. . . .

To your misfortune there broke a terrific snowstorm and black night shrouded everything in darkness. Nevertheless, the Communist executioners, counting no cost, drove you along the ice, threatening you in the rear with their machine guns operated by Communist detachments.

Many of you perished that night on the icy vastness of the Gulf of Finland. And when day broke and the storm quieted down, only pitiful remnants of you, worn and hungry, hardly able to move, came to us clad in your white shrouds.

Early in the morning there were already about a thousand of you and later in the day a countless number. Dearly you have paid with your blood for this adventure, and after your failure Trotsky rushed back to Petrograd to drive new martyrs to slaughter—for cheaply he gets our workers' and peasants' blood! . . .

Kronstadt lived in deep faith that the proletariat of Petrograd would come to its aid. But the workers there were terrorised, and Kronstadt effectively blockaded and isolated, so that in reality no assistance could be expected from anywhere. The Kronstadt garrison consisted of less than 14,000 men, 10,000 of them being sailors. This garrison had to defend a widespread front, many forts and batteries scattered over the vast area of the Gulf. The repeated attacks of the Bolsheviki, whom the Central Government continuously supplied with fresh troops; the lack of provisions in the besieged city; the long sleepless nights spent on guard in the cold—all were sapping the vitality of Kronstadt. Yet the sailors heroically persevered, confident to the last that their great example of liberation would be followed throughout the country and thus bring them relief and aid.

In its "Appeal to Comrades Workers and Peasants" the Provisional Revolutionary Committee says (*Izvestia* No. 9, March 11):

Comrades Workers, Kronstadt is fighting for you, for the hungry, the cold, the naked. . . . Kronstadt has raised the banner of rebellion and it is confident that tens of millions of workers and peasants will respond to its call. It cannot be that the daybreak which has begun in Kronstadt should not become bright sunshine for the whole of Russia. It cannot be that the Kronstadt explosion should fail to arouse the whole of Russia and first of all, Petrograd.

But no help was coming, and with every successive day Kronstadt was growing more exhausted. The Bolsheviki continued massing fresh troops against the besieged fortress and weakening it by constant attacks. Moreover, every advantage was on the side of the Communists, including numbers, supplies, and position. Kronstadt had not been built to sustain an assault from the rear. The rumor spread by the Bolsheviki that the sailors meant to bombard Petrograd was false on the face of it. The famous fortress had been planned with the sole view of serving as a defense of Petrograd against foreign enemies approaching from the sea. Moreover, in case the city should fall into the hands of an external enemy, the coast batteries and forts of Krasnaia Gorka had been calculated for a fight *against* Kronstadt. Foreseeing such a possibility, the builders had purposely failed to strengthen the rear of Kronstadt.

Almost nightly the Bolsheviki continued their attacks. All through March 10 Communist artillery fired incessantly from the southern and northern coasts. On the night of the 12—13 the Communists attacked from the south, again resorting to the white shrouds and sacrificing many hundreds of the *kursanti*. Kronstadt fought back desperately, in spite of many sleepless nights, lack of food and men. It fought most heroically against simultaneous assaults from the north, east and south, while the Kronstadt batteries were capable of defending the fortress only from its western side. The sailors lacked even an ice-cutter to make the approach of the Communist forces impossible.

On March 16 the Bolsheviki made a concentrated attack from three sides at once—from north, south and east. "The plan of attack," later explained Dibenko, formerly Bolshevik naval Commissar and later dictator of defeated Kronstadt, "was worked out in minutest detail according to the directions of Commander-in-Chief Tukhachevsky and the field staff of the Southern Corps. . . . At dark we began the attack upon the forts. The white shrouds and the courage of the *kursanti* made it possible for us to advance in columns."

On the morning of March 17 a number of forts had been taken. Through the weakest spot of Kronstadt—the Petrograd Gates—the Bolsheviki broke into the city, and then there began most brutal slaughter. The Communists spared by the sailors now betrayed them, attacking from the rear. Commissar of the Baltic Fleet Kuzmin and Chairman of the Kronstadt Soviet Vassiliev, liberated by the Communists from jail, now participated in the hand-to-hand street fighting in fratricidal bloodshed. Till late in the night continued the desperate struggle of the Kronstadt sailors and soldiers against overwhelming odds. The city which for fifteen days had not harmed a single Communist, now ran red with the blood of Kronstadt men, women and even children.

Dibenko, appointed Commissar of Kronstadt, was vested with absolute powers to "clean the mutinous city." An orgy of revenge followed, with the Tcheka claiming numerous victims for its nightly wholesale *razstrel* (shooting).

On March 18 the Bolshevik Government and the Communist Party of Russia publicly commemorated the Paris Commune of 1871, drowned in the blood of the French workers by Gallifet and Thiers. At the same time they celebrated the "victory" over Kronstadt.

For several weeks the Petrograd jails were filled with hundreds of Kronstadt prisoners. Every night small groups of them were taken out by order of the Tcheka and disappeared—to be seen among the living no more. . . .

The prisons and concentration camps in the frozen district of Archangel and the dungeons of far Turkestan are slowly doing to death the Kronstadt men who rose against Bolshevik bureaucracy and proclaimed in March, 1921, the slogan of the Revolution of October, 1917: "All Power to the Soviets!" . . .

Kronstadt fell. But it fell victorious in its idealism and moral purity, its generosity and higher humanity. Kronstadt was superb. It justly prided itself on not having shed the blood of its enemies, the Communists within its midst. It had no executions. The untutored, unpolished sailors, rough in manner and speech, were too noble to follow the Bolshevik example of vengeance: they would not shoot even the hated Commissars. Kronstadt personified the generous, all-forgiving spirit of the Slavic soul and the century-old emancipation movement of Russia.

Kronstadt was the *first* popular and entirely independent attempt at liberation from the yoke of State Socialism—an attempt made directly by the people, by the workers, soldiers and sailors themselves. It was the first step toward the Third Revolution which is inevitable and which, let us hope, may bring to long-suffering Russia lasting freedom and peace.

Emma Goldman

TRAVELING SALESMEN OF THE REVOLUTION

Editor's Note

FEW persons have been as abused in America as Emma Goldman. Headstrong as she was, given at times to almost childlike extremism, devotee of idealistic but untenable doctrines, it is still true that few persons have less deserved such treatment. Time has not treated her assailants well.

Born in Russia in 1869, she spent her early adolescence in a factory in St. Petersburg. Unhappy at home, she finally persuaded her father to allow her and her sister, Helena, to leave for the United States. Equipped with twenty-five rubles they traveled in steerage. Three years later, after a stay in Rochester, Emma Goldman arrived in New York City in possession of five dollars and a small handbag. "A new world was before me, strange and terrifying." So it turned out to be! On her very first day in the city she met Alexander Berkman, then a boyish anarchist, who became her lifelong friend and co-worker. After the hanging of the anarchists as the aftermath of the Haymarket bombing in Chicago, she was converted to anarchism, a doctrine she held to her last days. Her career became tumultuous. Working in factories to supply her physical needs, she threw herself into the political and intellectual life of the city. In time she was internationally known as a lecturer and political writer; her notoriety as an agitator—built up by a press which pretended to fear her as "Red Emma"—was great enough to alert the police upon her arrival into a new town. She was arrested countless times, her meetings were broken up, and she did not escape physical abuse. Whenever an act of violence occurred the press seemed ready to relate Emma Goldman to it in some fashion, no matter what were her actual whereabouts.

The fear and trembling that the authorities felt or pretended to feel reached ludicrous heights. After a quiet, routine lecture on "patriotism," on one occasion, a soldier came up to Goldman and held out his hand. Emma grasped it. The audience broke into cheers; they were delighted to see the anarchist leader shaking hands with a soldier. The man thanked her and left. The next morning she discovered that she had unwittingly made news again. The soldier's name was William Buwalda; he was nearly middle-aged and had been decorated by the Army for his service in the Philippines. He had disagreed with Goldman's views but had enjoyed the lecture. After the meeting he had been trailed by plain-clothes men and placed under military arrest. He was to be "court-martialed for attending Emma Goldman's meeting and shaking hands with her." Later, he was indeed court-martialed; he served ten months of his sentence before he was pardoned. This incident is symptomatic of the hysteria that Emma Goldman's name was capable of creating.

When World War I broke out, she opposed it and helped organize the No-Conscription League, to encourage conscientious objectors. For this activity, she and Berkman were arrested for conspiring against the draft. They were convicted and received the maximum penalty of two years in prison and $10,000 fine. When released they were deported to Russia with 247 other dissidents on the old troopship *Buford.* She and Berkman were to spend two years in that country.

Before her deportation, Goldman had spent months lecturing throughout the U. S. in defense of the new Utopia. Few persons have more fervently wished success to the new regime than did Goldman. But the implacable conscience, the inability to lie to herself about injustice, alienated her swiftly from the young but growing dictatorship that she encountered. She proved incapable of turning her attention away from the plight of the people and the lack of freedom. Protesting abuses and terror, she wore out her welcome. She—and Berkman—played an important role in recounting to the Western world the story of the Kronstadt massacre.

After the two anarchists left Russia, they were refused sanctuary by the governments of the world. Finally, they were permitted to take up residence in England. Goldman was quick to recognize the menace of Nazism and lectured widely on this subject in the early Thirties. In 1934, she was permitted to visit the U. S. for ninety days; the short visit over, she reluctantly returned to exile. Berkman suddenly committed suicide and it came as a severe blow for Emma. No longer young, she nevertheless later went to Spain following the outbreak of the Civil War.

In this selection, taken from her *My Further Disillusionment in Russia* (1924), she provides us with an informative glimpse into the atmosphere of two early international Communist congresses, organizations which were later recognizable as a global fifth-column. Apparent already is the basic mechanism of disclaiming what one sees and knows to be true that characterizes the Communist supporter—present also are the Communist "whips" managing the outcome of the meetings in the manner of stage directors, and the chicanery of the leadership cynically playing with the hopes of foreign believers.

Emma Goldman was a prolific writer as well as speaker. She wrote voluminously for her magazine *Mother Earth*, which for the eleven years of its publication managed to keep just one step ahead of its creditors and reached only several thousand readers. Her books include: *Anarchism and Other Essays; The Social Significance of the Modern Drama; Living My Life,* her famed autobiography; and two volumes on her experiences in the Soviet Union. She died in Canada on May 13, 1940.

Traveling Salesmen of the Revolution by Emma Goldman

GREAT preparations were being made by the Communists for the Third Congress of the Third International and the First Congress of the Red Trade Union International. A preliminary committee had been organized in the summer of 1920, while delegates from various countries were in Moscow. How much the Bolsheviki depended upon the First Congress of the Red Trade Union International was apparent from a remark of an old Communist. "We haven't the workers in the Third International," he said; "unless we succeed in welding together the proletariat of the world into the R. T. U. I., the Third International cannot last very long."

The Hôtel de Luxe, renovated the previous year, became the foreign guest house of the Third International and was put in festive attire. The delegates began to arrive in Moscow.

During my stay in Russia I came across three classes of visitors who came to "study the Revolution." The first category consisted of earnest idealists to whom the Bolsheviki were the symbol of the Revolution. Among them were many emigrants from America who had given up everything they possessed to return to the promised land. Most of these became bitterly disappointed after the first few months and sought to get out of Russia. Others, who did not come as Communists, joined the Communist Party for selfish reasons and did in Rome as the Romans do. There were also the Anarchist deportees who came not of their own choice. Most of them strained every effort to leave Russia after they realized the stupendous deception that had been imposed on the world.

In the second class were journalists, newspapermen, and some adventurers. They spent from two weeks to two months in Russia, usually in Petrograd or Moscow, as the guests of the

Government and in charge of Bolshevik guides. Hardly any of them knew the language and they never got further than the surface of things. Yet many of them have presumed to write and lecture authoritatively about the Russian situation. I remember my astonishment when I read in a certain London daily that the teachings of Jesus were "being realized in Russia." A preposterous falsehood of which none but a charlatan could be guilty. Other writers were not much nearer the truth. If they were at all critical of the Bolsheviki they were so at the expense of the whole Russian people, whom they charged with being "crude, primitive savages, too illiterate to grasp the meaning of the Revolution." According to these writers it was the Russian people who imposed upon the Bolsheviki their despotic and cruel methods. It did not occur to those so-called investigators that the Revolution was made by those primitive and illiterate people, and not by the present rulers in the Kremlin. Surely they must have possessed some quality which enabled them to rise to revolutionary heights—a quality which, if properly directed, would have prevented the wreck and ruin of Russia. But that quality has persistently been overlooked by Bolshevik apologists who sacrifice all truth in their determination to find extenuating circumstances for the mess made by the Bolsheviki. A few wrote with understanding of the complex problems and with sympathy for the Russian people. But their voice was ineffectual in the popular craze that Bolshevism had become.

The third category—the majority of the visitors, delegates, and members of various commissions—infested Russia to become the agents of the ruling Party. These people had every opportunity to see things as they were, to get close to the Russian people, and to learn from them the whole terrible truth. But they preferred to side with the Government, to listen to its interpretation of causes and effects. Then they went forth to misrepresent and to lie deliberately in behalf of the Bolsheviki, as the Entente agents had lied and misrepresented the Russian Revolution.

Nor did the sincere Communists realize the disgrace of the situation—not even Angelica Balabanova.* Yet she had good judgment of character and knew how to appraise the people who flocked to Russia. Her experience with Mrs. Clare Sheridan was characteristic. The lady had been smuggled into Russia before Moscow realized that she was the cousin of Winston Churchill. She was obsessed by the desire "to sculp" prominent Communists. She had also begged Angelica to sit for her. "Lenin, Trotsky, and other leaders are going to; aren't you?" she pleaded. Angelica, who hated sensationalism in any form, resented the presence in Russia of these superficial visitors. "I asked her," she afterward related, "if she would have thought of 'sculping' Lenin three years ago when the English Government denounced him as a German spy. Lenin did not make the Revolution. The Russian people made it. I told this Mrs. Sheridan that she would do better to 'sculp' Russian workingmen and women who were the real heroes of the Revolution. I know she did not like what I said. But I don't care. I can't stand people to whom the Russian struggle is mere copy for poor imitations or cheap display."

Now the new delegates were beginning to arrive. They were royally welcomed and fêted. They were taken to show schools, children's homes, colonies, and model factories. It was the traditional Potemkin villages** that were shown the visitors. They were graciously received and "talked to" by Lenin and Trotsky, treated to theatres, concerts, ballets, excursions, and military parades. In short, nothing was left undone to put the delegates into a frame of mind favourable to the great plan that was to be revealed to them at the Red Trade Union and the Third International Congresses. There were also continuous private conferences where the delegates were subjected to a

---

* [She did later, however. Angelica Balabanoff (as her name is usually spelled) is the former secretary of the Communist International. See her *My Life as a Rebel* (1938).—*Ed.*]

** Happy villagers and their model homes, specially prepared and shown to Catherine the Great by her Prime Minister Potemkin to deceive her about the true condition of the peasantry.

regular third degree, Lozovsky—prominent Bolshevik labour leader—and his retinue seeking to ascertain their attitude to the Third International, the dictatorship of the proletariat, and similar subjects. Here and there was a delegate who refused to divulge the instructions of his organization on the ground that he was pledged to report only to the Congress. But such naïve people reckoned without their host. They soon found themselves ostracized and at the Congress they were given no opportunity to make themselves heard effectively.

The majority of the delegates were more pliable. They learned quickly that pledges and responsibilities were considered bourgeois superstitions. To show their ultra-radicalism they quickly divested themselves of them. They became the echoes of Zinoviev, Lozovsky, and other leaders.

The American delegates to the Red Trade Union International were most conspicuous by their lack of personality. They accepted without question every proposition and suggestion of the Chair. The most flagrant intrigues and political machinations and brazen suppression of those who would not be cajoled or bullied into blind adherence found ready support by the American Communist crew and the aides they had brought with them.

The Bolsheviki know how to set the stage to produce an impression. In the staging of the two Congresses held in July, 1921, they outdid themselves. The background for the Congress of the Third International was the Kremlin. In the royal halls where once the all-powerful Romanovs had sat, the awed delegates hung with bated breath upon every word uttered by their pope, Lenin, and the other Grand Seigneurs of the Communist Church. On the eve of the Congress a great meeting was held in the big theatre to which only those whose passports had been approved by the All-Russian Tcheka were admitted. The streets leading to the theatre were turned into a veritable military camp. Tchekists and soldiers on foot and on horseback created the proper atmosphere for the Communist conclave. At the meeting resolutions were passed extending fraternal greetings to "the revolutionists in capitalist prisons." At that very moment every Russian prison was filled with revolutionists but no greetings were sent to them. So all-pervading was Moscow hypnotism that not a single voice was raised to point out the farce of Bolshevik sympathy for political prisoners.

The Red Trade Union Congress was set on a less pretentious scale in the House of the Trade Unions. But no details were overlooked to get the proper effects. "Delegates" from Palestine and Korea—men who had not been out of Russia for years— delegates from the great industrial centres of Bokhara, Turkestan, and Adzerbeydzhan, packed the Congress to swell the Communist vote and help carry every Communist propositon. They were there to teach the workers of Europe and America how to reconstruct their respective countries and to establish Communism after the world revolution.

The plan perfected by Moscow during the year 1920-21, and which was a complete reversal of Communist principles and tactics, was very skilfully and subtly unrolled—by slow degrees—before the credulous delegates. The Red Trade Union International was to embrace all revolutionary and syndicalist organizations of the world, with Moscow as its Mecca and the Third International as its Prophet. All minor revolutionary labour organizations were to be dissolved and Communist units formed instead within the existing conservative trade union bodies. . . .

Here again the American delegates proved themselves worthy of their hire. Most of them had sprung from the Industrial Workers of the World; had indeed arisen to "fame and glory" on the shoulders of that militant American labour body. Some of the delegates had valiantly escaped to safety, unselfishly preferring the Hôtel de Luxe to Leavenworth Penitentiary, leaving their comrades behind in American prisons and their friends to refund the bonds they had heroically forfeited. While Industrial Workers continued to suffer persecution in capitalistic America, the renegade I. W. W.'s living in comfort and safety in Moscow maligned and attacked their former comrades and schemed to destroy their organization. Together with the Bolsheviki they were going to carry out the job begun by the American Vigilantes and the Ku Klux Klan to exterminate the I. W. W. *Les extrêmes se touchent.*

While the Communists were passing eloquent resolutions of protest against the imprisonment of revolutionaries in foreign countries, the Anarchists in the Bolshevik prisons of Russia were being driven to desperation by their long imprisonment without opportunity for a hearing or trial. To force the hand of the Government the Anarchists incarcerated in the Taganka (Moscow) decided on a hunger strike to the death. The French, Spanish, and Italian Anarcho-syndicalists, when informed of the situation, promised to raise the question at an early session of the Labour Congress. Some, however, suggested that the Government be first approached on the matter. Thereupon a Delegate Committee was chosen, including the well-known English labour leader, Tom Mann, to call upon the Little Father in the Kremlin. The Committee visited Lenin. The latter refused to have the Anarchists released on the ground that "they were too dangerous," but the final result of the interview was a promise that they would be permitted to leave Russia; should they, however, return without permission, they would be shot. The next day Lenin's promise was substantiated by a letter of the Central Committee of the Communist Party, signed by Trotsky, reiterating what Lenin had said. Naturally the threat of shooting was omitted in the official letter.

The hunger strikers in the Taganka accepted the conditions of deportation. They had for years fought and bled for the Revolution and now they were compelled to become Ahasueruses in foreign lands or suffer slow mental and physical death in Bolshevik dungeons. The Moscow Anarchist groups chose Alexander Berkman and A. Shapiro as their representatives on the Delegates' Committee to arrange with the Government the conditions of the release and deportation of the imprisoned Anarchists.

In view of this settlement of the matter the intention of a

public protest at the Congress was abandoned by the delegates. Great was their amazement when, just before the close
of the Congress, Bukharin—in the name of the Central Committee of the Communist Party—launched into a scurrilous
attack on the Anarchists. Some of the foreign delegates, out-
raged by the dishonourable proceeding, demanded an opportunity to reply. That demand was finally granted to a representative of the French delegation after Chairman Lozovsky
had exhausted every demagogic trick in a vain attempt to
silence the dissenters.

At no time during the protracted negotiations on behalf of
the imprisoned Anarchists and the last disgraceful proceedings at the Red Trade Union Congress did the American Communist delegates make a protest. Loudly they had shouted for
political amnesty in America, but not a word had they to say
in favour of the liberation of the politicals in Russia. One of the
group, approached on behalf of the hunger strikers, exclaimed:
"What are a few lives or even a few hundred of them as against
the Revolution!" To such Communist minds the Revolution had
no bearing on justice and humanity.

In the face of abject want, with men, women, and children
hungrily watching the white bread baked for the Luxe Hotel
in its adjoining bakery, one of the American fraternal delegates
wrote to a publication at home that "the workers in Russia control the industries and are directing the affairs of the country;
they get everything free and need no money." This noble delegate lived in the palatial home of the former Sugar King of Russia and enjoyed also the hospitality of the Luxe. He indeed
needed no money. But he knew that the workers lacked even
the basic necessities and that without money they were as
helpless in Russia as in any other country, the week's *payok*
not being sufficient for two days' existence. Another delegate
published glowing accounts dwelling on the absence of prosti-
tution and crime in Moscow. At the same time the Tcheka was
daily executing hold-up-men, and on the Tverskaya and the
Pushkin Boulevard, near the Luxe Hotel, street women mobbed

the delegates with their attentions. Their best customers were the very delegates who waxed so enthusiastic about the wonders of the Bolshevik régime.

The Bolsheviki realized the value of such champions and appreciated their services. They sent them forth into the world generously equipped in every sense, to perpetuate the monstrous delusion that the Bolsheviki and the Revolution are identical and that the workers have come into their own "under the proletarian dictatorship." Woe to those who dare to tear the mask from the lying face. In Russia they are put against the wall, exiled to slow death in famine districts, or banished from the country. In Europe and America such heretics are dragged through the mire and morally lynched. Everywhere the unscrupulous tools of the great disintegrator, the Third International, spread distrust and hatred in labour and radical ranks. Formerly ideals and integrity were the impulse to revolutionary activity. Social movements were founded upon the inner needs of each country. They were maintained and supported by the interest and zeal of the workers themselves. Now all this is condemned as worthless. Instead the golden rain of Moscow is depended on to produce a rich crop of Communist organizations and publications. Even uprisings may be organized to deceive and mislead the people as to the quality and strength of the Communist Party. In reality, everything is built on a foundation that crumbles to pieces the moment Moscow withdraws its financial support. . . .

Victor Serge

VIGNETTES OF NEP

"Three years of practical experience destroyed the theories that Lenin passionately believed and disseminated during seventeen years of refugee residence in western Europe." Workers Before and After Lenin *by Manya Gordon.*

"The New Economic Policy . . . means a transition to the restoration of capitalism in no small degree."—Lenin in 1921.

Editor's Note

THE New Economic Policy (NEP) was instituted in 1921. Lenin's "strategic retreat" from the "militant" policies of War Communism made for an almost immediate change in the economic life of the Soviet Union. Re-establishing a limited private market, as it did, inviting foreign capital, legalizing non-state businesses, taxing peasants instead of requisitioning crops—these measures resulted in food again appearing in the shops, Soviet citizens being able to dress better. Living standards rose perceptibly. A new class of traders, the Nepmen, came into existence. One facet of Soviet life, however, did not change: repression continued, the dictatorship permitted no political freedom to become admixed with "economic freedom," however restricted was the latter. With the end of NEP, half a dozen years later, there was again to be a massive onslaught on the part of the Soviet state, including another war on the peasants, and the reins of power were to be held firm in the interim. (The period of NEP was also to witness the death of Lenin in 1924, and the emergence of Stalin as full victor in his battle with Trotsky; in 1927 the latter would

124

be formally expelled from the Communist Party, and in 1928 would already be in exile at Alma-Ata.) In 1921, however, the Communist state—to repair its wounds from the three years of War Communism, from famine, from the widespread discontent that had brought the regime to the brink of collapse, from falling production scales, from shoddy output—turned its back for the moment, a long moment, on Communism. Repudiating by its new policy that which it had taught and implemented as "necessary," and at such a horrible human and economic cost, the Russian state now prospered, comparatively and temporarily, for the first time since the Bolshevik seizure of power. By instituting the very policies they had fought against!

In this selection Victor Serge presents a vivid insight into the psychological atmosphere of the years of the New Economic Policy. At first one is aware of the general relaxation accompanying the less burdensome non-Communist economic innovations, then the insistent line of frustration, futility, and desperation evidencing itself as political repression increases. Since Serge deals here with the beginning and culminating periods of NEP, this contrast is especially clear. We are introduced to the Party idealists who had been taught to sanction even murder in the name of the new and higher "ethic" that made such conduct not reprehensible but noble. These were the men who had undergone privations of the most extreme sort for the new world in birth. Now, with the start of NEP, they witness the re-introduction of that which they had fought against, which they had been told was despicable, sufficiently so as to merit the suspension of all morality in its erasure. Unlike the citizenry which welcomes the "retreat," the Party idealists are sunk in gloom. Serge deals also with the personalities of the leaders at the helm, as he appraised them, most of whom were to fall victims to Stalin's executioners in the 1930s. In this survey too are the new victims of NEP, those whose only offense was often dissenting opinions, others who "thought" of striking a blow at the repressive state they found hateful, still others who were guilty of no crimes at all—wise men, some less wise, some sentimental, death was often the sentence of all. Perhaps symbolizing the period best, the "revolution at dead end," are the heartbroken suicides. The tracts of the Revolution had built an icon to economics and now a strange axiom for this context was again manifesting itself, bread alone—and living standards were still far from adequate—was not enough. Freedom was no closer, each passing year made it more distant. Serge's closeness to the events and moods he depicts, his long service and devotion to the stated ideals of Communism and the Soviet state, allow him in this retrospective panorama to penetrate the political facades and take us to the heart of the matter, to show us what the years of NEP, and the continued dictatorship, meant to the people.

In terms of experience and opportunity for observation, few persons have been better equipped than Victor Serge, former highly-placed and important member of the Communist International, to write on Soviet history and politics. He was born Victor Lvovich Kibalchich in Brussels in 1890; his parents were revolutionary exiles. His childhood was spent in Belgium and England and as a young man he worked in various trades, as a photographer and draftsman as well as journalist and translator. In 1913 he found himself implicated in an assassination case directed against a number of anarchists. Innocent, he nevertheless used the occasion to defend anarchist principles, which he held, and was rewarded with several years in a penitentiary. He participated in the revolutionary attempt of the Catalonians in Spain in 1917, after having gone to that country to assume an active role with the syndicalists and anarchists. Two years later he was exchanged as a Bolshevik hostage for a French officer who had been arrested in Russia, after having been arrested earlier by the Clemenceau government during a trip through France to Russia. Arriving in Petrograd he soon joined the Communist Party. His service to the Soviet state included being sent on dangerous, undercover missions abroad; for many years he also held the post of managing editor of the official world publication, *Communist International*.

A new phase in his political history appeared when the Trotskyist opposition was organized; he became an active spokesman for this view. Again, he won only prison, this time from the Soviet state he had served so faithfully. He received this sentence after he, and thousands of other Trotskyists, were expelled from the Party in 1928. In 1933 he was again sentenced and deported to Siberia. He was finally released in 1936 after international protests had been made in his behalf. Serge's Soviet citizenship was withdrawn and he was banished from the USSR. On November 18, 1947, after several unsuccessful attempts to be admitted into the United States, he died in Mexico City of a heart attack.

He was the author of many books and articles, including the well-known *Russia Twenty Years After* and *Year One of the Russian Revolution*. In addition to his political writings he published several novels in French and English, the last being *The Long Dusk*. This selection is a portion of excerpts from his as yet unpublished memoirs which appeared in *Politics* in 1944-46.

#

Vignettes of NEP by Victor Serge

In the spring of 1921, Lenin wrote a long article defining the NEP: no more requisitions, no more taxes in kind from the peasants; freedom to buy and sell; removal of the restrictions on production by craftsmen; concessions on attractive terms to foreign capital; freedom of enterprise—within limits, to be sure, but limits imposed by the Soviet citizenry themselves. What it added up to was a partial restoration of capitalism, and Lenin admitted it in so many words. At the same time he denied the country any political freedom whatever: "The Mensheviks will remain locked up!" And he proclaimed a party purge, directed against those revolutionaries who had come from other parties—*i.e.*, who had not been saturated with the Bolshevik way of thinking. Within the party, this meant a dictatorship of the old Bolsheviks, plus disciplinary measures aimed not at the opportunists but at the critics.

Some time afterwards, during the Third Congress of the International, I went to hear Bukharin lecture before the foreign delegates. His case for the NEP ran in terms of "the impossibility of finishing off the rural *petite bourgeoisie* (the peasants, with their attachment to small property-holdings) in a single blood-letting—an impossibility which is itself the result of the isolation of the Russian revolution." If a German revolution, backed up by Germany's industrial capacity, had come to our assistance, we would have pressed forward along the path of all-out communism, even if it had called for bloodshed. I do not have Bukharin's text before me, but I printed it once, and I am sure this is an accurate summary. It surprised me all the more because I had run into Bukharin several times at Zinoviev's, and genuinely admired him.

Lenin, Trotsky, Karl Radek, and Bukharin had, beyond question, come to be the brains of the revolution. They spoke the same Marxist language, and had the same background of experience with European and American socialism. Moreover, they understood each other so well, with so little need to depend upon the spoken word, that they actually seemed to think *collectively*. (The Party in fact drew its strength from its collective thinking.) Compared to them, such a man as Lunacharsky, People's Commissar of Public Education (a playwright, a poet, an able though pretentious public speaker, he had translated Hoelderlin into Russian, and set himself up as a protector of futurist painters) seemed to be a mere dilettante. Beside

them, Zinoviev was just a rabble-rouser, a popularizer of ideas
furnished by Lenin. Chicherin, specializing in questions of foreign policy, kept to his archives. The wily Kalinin, chosen for
his job because of his good peasant head and his intuitive
knowledge of popular feeling and opinion, was a representative
figurehead. There were other big names in the party, men of
proven worth; but they were secondary figures, who gave full
time to practical tasks: Krassin, Pyatakov, Sokolnikov, Smilga,
Rakovsky, Preobajensky, Joffe, Ordjonikidze, Dzerjinsky.

Nicholas Ivanovitch Bukharin, now 33 years old, had been
a militant for fifteen years. He had lived through a period of
exile in Onega, had been with Lenin in Crakow, and had done
party work in Vienna, Switzerland, and New York. A tireless
researcher in economics, he had worked out, even before Lenin,
a doctrine of the complete overthrow of the capitalist State.
His mind was both effervescent and rigorously disciplined; always alert, always active. The high forehead, the thin hair, the
slightly turned-up nose, the chestnut-brown mustache and
chin-beard—all made him look the picture of the average Russian. His careless clothing only completed this picture. He
dressed in the most devil-may-care fashion imaginable—as if
he had never found time to get a suit that fitted him. His normal expression was jovial, and even when he was silent, the
look in his eye, sharpened by a humorous sparkle, was that of
a man about to venture a witticism. He devoured books in several languages, and spoke lightly about the most serious subjects. You knew, a moment after you met him, that what he
most enjoyed was turning ideas over in his head. Young people
always crowded about him, and hung smiling on every incisive
word he spoke. He had a great contempt for the trade union
bonzes and the parliamentary politicians of the Western countries, and never missed a chance to ridicule them.

Because he spoke all other languages with an incredibly bad
accent, we used to say that Karl Radek (35 years old at the
time) expressed himself in his own idiom no matter what lan-

guage he was using. A Galician Jew, he had grown up with the
socialist movements in Galicia, Poland, Germany and Russia
—all at the same time. He was a brilliant writer, with an equal
flair for synthesis and sarcasm; and an uncompromising realist.
Thin, rather small, nervous, he was always ready with an anec-
dote—as often as not with one with a sharp point to it. Like
an old-time pirate, he let his beard grow in a fringe around his
clean-shaven face. His features were irregular, and because he
was extremely near-sighted he always wore thick tortoise-shell
glasses. His walk, his quick gestures, his pout, his way of screw-
ing up his face, every muscle of which moved as he talked along
without ever stopping, all had something monkey-like about
them which it was amusing to watch.

In 1918, when Lenin was considering a mixed economy,
these two men, Radek and Bukharin, had been the first to speak
up in favor of the nationalization of large industries. That same
year, in the course of the negotiations at Brest-Litovsk, they
had accused Lenin, some 15 years their senior, of opportunism,
and had romantically demanded all-out resistance by the Soviet Republic against the German Empire. In 1919 Radek had
put his daring and good sense into an attempt to guide the
Spartacist movement in Germany, and by pure luck had survived the assassination of his friends Rosa Luxemburg, Karl
Liebknecht, and Leo Tychko (Jogiches). I had myself watched
him use his satirical dialectic on the German moderates, and
make life miserable for them. I can see him now, hitching up
his trousers (they were always too big for him) as he took his
stance beside the dispatch box, and demonstrating, after an
ear-splitting *"Parteigenossen!,"* that the days of the old regime
in Europe were numbered. Though more of an improviser than
a theoretician, he was also a scholar, and read all the learned
journals he could lay his hands on. He was now being called a
Rightist, because he had no use for the German Communist
Party, and because he believed that, for the time being any-
how, there was no likelihood of revolutionary uprising in Central Europe.

The Third Congress of the Communist International met in Moscow. Save for a certain letdown in intensity, its mood was much the same as that of the preceding Congress, though the attendance was larger. With the NEP, food had become less scarce, and the atmosphere by now was heavy with the smell of appeasement. The delegates from abroad asked no questions about the tragedy at Kronstadt, and all but a handful deliberately closed their minds to information about it. They condemned the Workers' Opposition without even giving it a hearing. And they considered the NEP—I quote one of the French delegates—an "inspired turn to the Right that had saved the revolution." But it doesn't take much inspiration to yield to a famine, or to back out of a hopeless situation. The truth is, rather, that the spectacular character of the Russian Revolution, even at this time, meant abdicating the right to do your own thinking. Lenin defended the NEP—in a speech delivered at the Kremlin, among the tall gilded columns of the throne room of the Imperial Palace. As he spoke, he stood under a canopy of crimson velvet, embroidered with the emblem of the Soviets. When he came to international strategy, he argued in favor of a breathing spell, and an attempt to win over the masses. He was easy, warm, friendly; and he expressed himself as simply as he knew how to—as if determined to get across with every gesture the fact that the head of the Soviet government and of the Russian Communist Party was still just another comrade—the most eminent one, it is true, because of his recognized intellectual and moral leadership, but no more than that, and one who would never become just another statesman or just another dictator. He had obviously determined to carry the International with him by persuasion. Now and then, he would leave the speakers' stand and take a seat on the steps, near the stenographers. With his note-pad on his knee he would break in with an occasional wisecrack that made everybody laugh, and a mischievous smile would light up his face. Or he would buttonhole one or another of the least known and least conspicuous foreign delegates, draw him into a corner, and, man to man, press home the points he'd been making: The party must turn to the masses! Yes, to the masses! The party must not become sectarian! The NEP was not nearly so dangerous as it might look from the outside, because the party had the situation completely in hand. The capitalist concessionaires from abroad would have a hard row to hoe! As for the neo-capitalists inside the country—well, the thing to do was fatten them up for a while, like chickens, and then, when they began to cause trouble, gently wring their necks, which it would be easy enough to do.

On several occasions I happened to see him on his way home after one of the sessions—dressed in the familiar cap and jacket, alone, marching along with quick step with the Kremlin cathedrals towering up above him on either side. And once I was present when, genial as always, his face shining with health and good spirits, he took Bela Kun apart in a mercilessly abusive speech. It was at a meeting of the Executive Committee of the International, held during this same Congress in the ballroom of a hotel, the Continental, I think; that speech of Lenin's was a real turning point in the history of Communist policy.

Trotsky attended many of the Congress' sessions. Nobody ever carried the burden of a great destiny more gracefully. Still only 41 years old, there was little—of power, popularity, fame—left for him to win: tribune of Petrograd in two revolutions; creator of the Red Army, which he literally, as Lenin put it to Gorki, "pulled out of his hat." Victor in such decisive battles as Sviajsk, Kazan, Poulkovo; Organizer of Victory ("Our Carnot," Radek called him). In oratorical gifts, in organizational capacity (first the army, then the railroads), in ideological brilliance, he overshadowed Lenin, who was his superior in only one respect (but a most important one): before the revolution he had been the undisputed leader of the tiny Bolshevik Party, which supplied the cadres of the new state organization, and whose sectarian spirit distrusted the rich and subtle mentality of the chairman of the supreme War Council.

At one time during the Congress little groups here and there were talking of Trotsky for the chairmanship of the International. But Lenin preferred to keep the "world party" in the hands of his own mouthpiece. [Zinoviev.—*Ed.*]

Trotsky's own attention was given to Soviet economy. He came to the session dressed in a white uniform of special design, without insignia. The headgear, white also, was a broad, flat garrison cap. The effect, what with his huge chest, his jet-black hair and beard, the sparkle of his eye-glasses, was imposing. He lacked Lenin's easy way with people; there was a touch of the authoritarian in his bearing. That, at least, is how he looked to my friends and me, who though Communists still had our critical faculties about us. We admired him greatly, but were not fond of him. His severity, his insistence on punctuality both in the office and on the battlefield, his invariable correctness (at a time when nobody else was paying much attention to formalities), all lent themselves to malicious gossip. I was indifferent to that, but the solutions he proposed for the problems then under discussion struck me as downright dictatorial. Had he not favored absorption of the trade unions by the state —while Lenin, rightly, had wished to leave the unions a certain degree of independence? We did not grasp the fact that trade-union pressure would perhaps have imposed a wholesome proletarian orientation upon the State itself. Had he not created the labor battalions? Had he not proposed militarization as a remedy for the unbelievably disorganized condition of industry? We didn't know that, still earlier, in the Central Committee, he had tried unsuccessfully to put an end to requisitioning. The labor battalions had been an acceptable expedient during the demobilization period. Had he not signed a manifesto, a shamefully threatening one, against Kronstadt? The truth was that he had been in the thick of things, of everything, acting with a vigor which was both sure of itself and willing to seek solutions first in one direction and then in another.

During one of the sessions he left the speakers' stand, came over to where our French group was sitting, and gave us his own interpretation of the speech he had just made. His French, though ungrammatical, was fluent and expressive. When he was heckled about the terror, about violence, about party discipline, he responded sharply. Our little group—Paul Vaillant-Couturier, Andre Morizet, Andre Julien, Fernand Loriot, Jacques and Clara Mesnil, and Boris Souvarine, among others —seemed to irritate him. Trotsky was courteous, cordial even, but implacable in his argumentation. On another occasion he tore into the Spanish delegate, Arlandis, who resented the persecution of the anarchists. Trotsky, seizing him by his coat collar, almost shouted: "I'd like to see the same thing happen to you, you petit-bourgeois."

The NEP, though it had been in effect only a few months, was giving marvelous results. You could tell the difference from week to week: food was easier to get; there was less speculation; the restaurants were reopening their doors. More incredible still, they were selling pastries, edible pastries, mind you, at a ruble apiece! The general public was beginning to breathe more easily, and there was a good deal of loose talk about the return to capitalism . . . and prosperity. The confusion among the rank and file of the party, on the other hand, was appalling. What did we fight for, spill so much blood, accept so many sacrifices? Those who had fought in the civil war asked such questions bitterly. Most of them lacked all the necessities: clothes, decent lodgings, money; and now everything was turning back into exchange-value. You had the feeling that money, dethroned, had been restored to its kingdom.

Myself, I was more hopeful. I saw some good in the turn things had taken, although the reactionary aspect of the change—the arbitrary snuffing out of every trace of democracy —disturbed and hurt me. Would any other ending to the drama of War Communism have been possible? It was a problem of merely theoretical interest, but one well worth thinking about. I developed some ideas about it, and set them forth, on the occasion I best remember, to two Spanish socialists I had a talk with at the Hotel Lux. (Fernando de los Rios was one of them.) They ran as follows:

Because of its intolerance, and because it has arrogated to itself an absolute monopoly of power and initiative in all fields, the Bolshevik regime reached a dead end. It has spread a sort of general paralysis over the country, and had put the revolution in a desperate position. The big concessions to the peasants had been unavoidable; but small-shop production, middle-sized stores, and even some industries could have been revived by merely appealing to the initiative of groups of producers and consumers. By granting freedom of action to the State-strangled cooperatives, by calling economic associations into existence, large-scale recovery could have been achieved almost overnight. The country was out of shoes and out of leather; but the rural districts had leather, and shoemakers' cooperatives, if they had been let alone, would have got hold of it and would have gone into action at once. They would have had to sell at relatively high prices, but at one and the same time the State could have assisted them in their operations and exercised a downward pressure on their prices. These, in any case, would have been below those charged on the black market. I saw, in Petrograd, what was happening to the book trade. The stocks of the bookstores, taken over by the State, were rotting away in basements. In the spring, the basements often filled up with water. So we were downright grateful to the thieves who salvaged items and—illegally, of course—put them back into circulation. If the books had been turned over to associations of booklovers, the book trade could have been saved in no time. In a word, I favored a "communism of associations" —in contrast to the existing State communism. The clashes of interest between such associations, the disorder natural to beginnings, would have caused less trouble than we were having with our highly bureaucratic centralization, with its red-tape and its muddling. I thought of the scheme not as something to be handed down by the State from on high, but rather as resulting from the harmonizing, by congresses and meetings of specialists, of initiatives working up from below. However, since the Bolshevik mind had already conjured up other solutions, it was all a venture in pure theory. . . .

After Kronstadt there was a new reign of terror in Petrograd. The Cheka had just "liquidated" the Tagantsev conspiracy by executing some thirty persons. I had known Professor Tagantsev a little: a skinny little old man with white whiskers, a jurist, and a university teacher with a long record of service there in the former capital city. Along with Tagantsev they shot a lawyer by the name of Bak, to whom I had now and then sent translation jobs. With me, Bak had never made any secret of his counter-revolutionary opinions. The gifted poet Nicolas Stepanovitch Goumilev, my comrade (and sometimes my adversary) from days in Paris, was shot at the same time as Tagantsev and Bak. I dropped in at the Moyka Art House, where he shared a room with his very young wife—a tall girl with a slender neck and the eyes of a frightened gazelle. It was a tremendous room, with walls decorated with swans and lotus —the former bathroom of a merchant with a taste for swans-and-lotus poetry. "You haven't heard?" Goumilev's young wife said to me in a low voice. "They took him away day before yesterday." The comrades at the Soviet Executive tried to quiet my fears, but at the same time made me feel uneasy: Goumilev was being well treated at the Cheka. For a while every night he recited his poems—poems overflowing with vigor and high purpose—for the Chekists. But he confessed that he had drafted certain political documents for the counter-revolutionary group. That seemed likely enough. Goumilev had never concealed his opinions. During the Kronstadt rebellion the university crowd had evidently believed the regime was about to collapse, and had planned to take a hand in liquidating it. The "conspiracy" had gone no further than that. The Cheka prepared to shoot everybody. "We mustn't go soft now." One comrade journeyed all the way to Moscow to ask Dzerjinsky a question: "Wasn't it a little too much to shoot one of the two or three great poets of Russia?" "Can we make an exception of

the poet," Dzerjinsky replied, "and still shoot the others?" The
spot chosen for the execution was at the edge of a forest; and
Goumilev, with his cap pulled down over his eyes and a cigarette drooping from his lips, fell at dawn—with the same peace
of mind he had expressed in one of the poems he brought back
with him from Ethiopia: "I stood fearless in the sight of the
Lord God." That, at least, is how it was told to me. . . . I re-
read, with mingled admiration and horror, his *The Worker*, in
which he described a gentle, grey-eyed man who, before going
to bed, shaped "the bullet which will bring me death." The
faces of Nicolas and Olga Goumilev were going to haunt me
for years.

I know, of course, that in the great revolutions of the past,
terror could not have been dispensed with; that revolutions
aren't made according to the wishes of men of good will, but
rather follow their own laws, moving with the destructive fury
of the hurricane; that our duty in a revolution is to forestall unnecessary defeat by fighting with whatever weapons history
places in our hands. But I have come to see, also, that the con-
tinuance of the terror beyond the end of the Civil War, into the
period of economic freedom, was a big mistake—and a demor-
alizing one. I believed then, and I still believe, that if at the
beginning of that period the new regime had proclaimed its
socialist respect for human life and for individual rights, no
matter whose, its strength would have increased a hundred-
fold. Convinced as I am of the probity and intelligence of the
regime's leaders, I am still asking myself why it did not do that.
What psychoses—of fear and of authority—tied its hands?

The Revolution at Dead-End

It is raining, the docks are black. Two rows of street lights
hang at long intervals in the night; between them are the black
waters of the Neva. On either side, the dark city. Inhospitable.
It has not yet emerged from its wretchedness. Four days before, I had seen a great glow over the night sky above Berlin,
which had just gone through an inflation more fabulous than

our own. We had never spent more than a million on a lemon; in Berlin a postage stamp had cost trillions.

Why does this despondency persist on our Russian soil? Leaving the customs house, we are met by a skeleton outfit splashing through the mud puddles—ghost-like horse and rattling carriage, as though we were living in Gogol's time, entering some forlorn city. . . . It has always been like this. Returning to Russian soil is always poignant. "Russian soil," the poet Tyuchev writes, "Christ in bondage has covered every inch of you." And the Marxist explains it: "The production of commodities was never sufficient, the means of communication were always lacking. . . ." The poor (and there are some Christs among them), slaves to want, have always been forced to set out barefoot, with knapsacks on their backs, wandering from one steppe to another, never stopping in their flight, always seeking. . . .

I find myself in a peaceful but depressing atmosphere. Lutovinov has committed suicide. The organizer of the metal-workers had been wandering about at night with Radek in Berlin. The cocktails of the Kurfuerstendamm burned his throat. "What messes the bourgeoisie invents to intoxicate itself with!—What am I going to do when I get home? I've told the Central Committee over and over again that we must re-examine the salary problem. Our metal-workers are going hungry. So the Sanitary Commission of the party sent me abroad for my health. . . ."

Glazman has committed suicide. Few people are aware of this incident, which took place in the entourage of Trotsky, president of the Supreme War Council. It is spoken of only in whispers. And Glazman is not the only one.

Expelled from the party for having opposed the "New Line," some young men have gotten hold of revolvers—to turn against themselves. Young women, as everybody knows, prefer veronal. What good is life if the party refuses us the right to serve? This new-born world is calling us, we belong to it alone—and in its name somebody spits in our faces. "You are unworthy . . ." Are we unworthy because we represent the throbbing body and unworthy thought of the revolution? It is better to die. The curve of suicides is rising. An extraordinary session of the Central Control Commission is called.

Eugenie Bogdanovna Bosh has committed suicide. Nothing has been printed abroad about the death of one of the greatest Bolshevik figures. Since the Civil War, she had headed with Piatakov the first Soviet government in the Ukraine; dealt severely with the difficulties in Astrakhan, and the counter-revolutionary peasants in Perm; she had commanded armies—and she had always slept with a revolver under her pillow. The party discussion in 1923, the juggling with workers' democracy by the Central Committee with its ambiguous resolutions, the purging of the universities, the dictatorship of the secretaries—all this saddened her, while sickness hollowed out her strong square fighter's face with its deep eyes. When Lenin died, she made her decision. What could be done, with the party misled and divided? With Ilyich gone, what was there to wait for, when she could do nothing herself? Lying in bed, she shot herself in the temple. The committees deliberated on the question of funeral rites. The formalists argued that suicide, even when justified by an incurable disease, remained an undisciplined act. Besides, in this case the act of suicide bore witness to a spirit of opposition. No national funeral, only a local one. No urn in the Kremlin wall; a place according to her official rank with the Communists in the Novo-Devichy Cemetery. . . . Forty lines of obituary in *Pravda*. Preobrazhensky declared that this was nothing but underhanded censorship. When she had been resisting the Germans, the Ukrainian nationalists, the Whites, the rural Vendée, what humorist would have inquired into her official rank in the party hierarchy? The very idea did not exist then. Preobrazhensky was requested to hold his tongue. The fleshly spectre of Lenin, stripped of all substance and of all spirit, lies in his Mausoleum, while the hierarchy, living and devouring like unnatural beasts, has only just begun to show us. . . .

Serge Yessenin, our matchless poet, has committed suicide.
The telephone rang: "Come quickly, Yessenin has killed himself. . . ." I rushed out into the snow, went up to a room in the
Hotel International. I could hardly recognize him; he no longer
looked the same. The evening before, he had been drinking
quite naturally and then had said goodby to his friends. "I
want to be alone. . . ." Waking up sadly that morning, he felt
the desire to write something. He had neither pencil nor foun-
tain-pen in his room; there was no ink in the hotel ink-stand,
but he found a razor-blade with which he slashed his wrist.
And with a rusty pen wet with his own blood, Yessenin wrote
his last lines:

> Au revoir, my friend, au revoir . . .
> . . . There is nothing new about dying in this life,
>   but there is surely nothing new about living.

He asked that no one be permitted to enter. They found him
hanging, a suitcase strap around his neck, his forehead bruised
by falling in death against a steam-pipe. Washed, his hair
combed, the hair more brown than gold, he lay on his deathbed; his face had stiffened, he wore an expression of cold and
distant severity. "One would think him a young soldier who
died alone," I thought, "after having been bitterly defeated."
Thirty years old, at the height of his fame, married eight times.
. . . He was our greatest lyric poet, the poet of the Russian
campaigns, of the Moscow cafes, of Bohemian singing during
the revolution. He has sung the victory of the steel horse over
the russet colt in the "fields without light." His verses are filled
with dazzling images, yet they are as simple as village talk. He
considered his own plunge into the abyss: "Where has your
rashness led me, oh my head?" "I have been dishonorable, I
have been wicked—but only to burn more brilliantly. . . ."
He had tried to put himself in tune with the times—and with
our regimented literature:

*I am a stranger in my own country . . . My poetry
is no longer needed, and I myself am in the way . . .
Blossom, oh youth, with your sound bodies . . . Your
life is different, your songs are different . . . I am not
a new man, I have one foot in the past—and yet, although I stagger, although I limp, I would join the co-
horts of steel once again. . . .*

> *That's it, the unbending harshness,*
> *The whole tale of men's sufferings!*
> *The sickle cuts the heavy ears of grain*
> *As one cuts the throat of a swan.*

Vladimir Mayakovsky, second in popularity only to Yessenin,
addressed a reproachful goodby to him:

> *Now you have passed away, as we say, to the other*
> *world. . . .*
> *The void. . . . You whirl round and round, jostling*
> *the stars. . . .*

Mayakovsky, athletic, clothed in a kind of jeering violence,
hammered out his goodby before an audience for whom this
death had become symbolic:

> *This globe is not too well equipped for happiness.*
> *We must try to seize happiness at some future time!*

And Mayakovsky is soon to kill himself, with a bullet in his
heart; but that is another story. Through the snowy night, we
carry the body of Serge Yessenin. This is no time for dreams or
lyrics. Farewell, poet!

Lenka Panteleyev, a Kronstadt sailor in 1917, one of those
who battered down the gates of the Winter Palace with the
butt of his gun, has just ended his career in Leningrad. A legend grew up about him in the swamps where legends grow,

for we have swamps again. When money came back into use, Lenka felt his end near at hand. He was not a man of ideas, he was an equalitarian. He turned bandit to plunder the first jewelry shops opened by the first neocapitalists of the Nep. A day or two before, the militiamen who told me this tale, and who admired Lenka, had surrounded him in his hide-out (he had been betrayed, of course). There were women and drink. He came in, threw down his leather jacket, tossed off a glass of vodka, took up his guitar. What should he sing? "Roll under the axe, head of Stenka Razin. . . ." They struck him down while he was still singing. This dangerous guitar was silenced. The militiamen, who got forty rubles a month, wore on their caps the red star which the Panteleyevs had put there.

The sordid taint of money could again be seen on everything. The ostentatious shop-windows of the grocery stores were filled with fruits from the Crimea and wines from Georgia, but a postman earned fifty rubles a month. There were 150,000 unemployed in Leningrad alone; the allowance they received ranged from twenty to twenty-seven rubles a month. Agricultural day-workers and servants received fifteen rubles (with meals, it is true). Party functionaries got as much as 180 to 225 rubles a month, like skilled workers. There were many beggars, and abandoned children; many prostitutes. We had three casinos in the city, where baccarat, roulette, and chemin-de-fer were played; low dives, the scenes of many crimes. The hotels which were run for foreigners and high functionaries had bars in which there were tables covered with soiled white linen, dusty palms, and assiduous waiters who knew secrets unknown to the revolution. What will you have? Some dope? Thirty girls, painted and bejeweled, lounge about the Europa bar, with men in fur coats and caps drinking from brimming glasses, of whom one-third are thieves, another third swindlers, and the last third melancholy workers and comrades who, by three o'clock in the morning have begun to quarrel with each other, and sometimes draw their knives. Then someone cries out with a strange pride (I heard it only the other night), "I

have been a party member since 1917!" The year when the
world shook. On snowy nights, sleighs drawn by proud thor-
oughbreds and driven by coachmen as bearded as those of the
night-owls of czarist days draw up there before dawn. And a
director of a nationalized factory, a wholesaler of textiles from
the Lenin factory, an assassin sought after by the informers
who drink with him—all these take with them, squeezed tightly
together on the narrow seats, daughters of Ryazan and of the
Volga, daughters of famine and revolution, who have only their
youth to sell and are too thirsty for life to be among those on
the suicide list which I check over in my editorial office. Leningrad lived at the price of ten to fifteen suicides a week, chiefly
young people under thirty.

One could take the elevator and find on the roof of the Hotel
Europa another bar, just like those in Paris or Berlin, brightly
lit, with dancing and jazz, and even more dismal than the one
on the street-level. I was there with another writer at the beginning of a party, while the hall was still deserted, when Mayakovsky strode in with his athletic gait. He leaned on his elbow
near us. "Are things all right? Yes, I suppose they're all right!
Merde!—Do you think I'm a hypocrite? No. But some day I'll
blow my brains out. Everybody's a swine!" This was several
years before his suicide. He was earning a great deal of money
writing official poetry for the press, still very powerful poetry
at times.

We wanted to remain a party of poor people, but money
very gradually became most important. Money rots everything
—and yet it also makes life spring forth everywhere. In less
than five years, freedom of trade has accomplished miracles.
There is no more starvation; an extraordinary zest for life
rises up about us, carrying us along, but the worst of it is we
feel we are rapidly being swept down hill. Our country is a
great convalescent body, but on this body whose flesh is our
flesh we see the blotches spreading.

When I was president of a cooperative apartment-house, I
supported some girl student in a long-drawn-out struggle to ac-

quire a maid's room in this "bourgeoisified" house. The house accounts submitted to me by an engineer had been falsified, but I had to sign them anyway. One of our fellow-tenants was becoming rich quite openly by reselling at high prices goods which a socialist factory sold him cheap because of his small salary. The explanation: the demand for manufactured articles exceeded the supply by about 400 million rubles. The workers escaped their miserable quarters by going to the cabarets. Housewives in the Red Putilov Works section begged the party committees to find a way to turn over to them a part of the salaries of their drunkard husbands. . . . On pay-days, some proletarians lay dead-drunk on the sidewalks, and others reviled you as you passed. I was despised as a bespectacled intellectual. A children's aid committee owned and ran the Vladimirsky Club, a vicious gambling-den. It was there that I saw a woman struck in the face and thrown down the stairs half dressed. The manager came over to me, and said calmly, "What makes you so indignant? She is only a street-walker. You ought to have my job!" This manager was a Communist; we were in the same party.

Trade produces a certain liveliness, but it is the most polluted kind of trade imaginable. Retail trade, the distribution of manufactured articles, has passed into the hands of private enterprise which has defeated both the cooperatives and the state-controlled trade. Where does this capital come from, which did not exist five years ago? From robbery, fraudulent speculation, and the most ingenious "combinations." Some cheap peddlers start a false cooperative; they bribe functionaries to give them credit, raw material, and orders. They had nothing yesterday, but now the Socialist state has supplied them with everything (under certain burdensome conditions), because contracts, agreements, and the granting of orders are all perverted by corruption. Once started, they go on trying everywhere to make themselves the middle-men between socialized industry and consumer. They double prices. Soviet trade, due to our industrial weakness, has now become the field of activity for a flock of vultures, in whom one can see the makings of the toughest and shrewdest capitalists of tomorrow. In this respect, the Nep is unquestionably a defeat. The prosecutors, from Krylenko down, spend their time vainly bringing speculators to trial. A shabby little fellow, with a ruddy face, very talkative, called Plyatsky, is in Leningrad in the middle of all this corruption and speculation. This businessman out of Balzac is behind a long string of enterprises, has bribed functionaries in all the bureaus; and he is not shot, because he is really needed, he keeps the wheels turning. The Nep has become a racket. This is also true in the rural districts, although it is somewhat different there. One year's sheep-breeding in the south has produced Soviet millionaires of a strange kind, former Red Partisans, whose daughters live in the most beautiful hotels in the Crimea and whose sons gamble for large stakes at the casinos.

In another field, the huge fees paid to authors encourage the slow growth of an official literature. The hack playwrights Shchegolev (the historian) and Alexei Tolstoy have amassed hundreds of thousands of rubles for some silly plays about Rasputin and the Empress; and the goal of many of our young writers is to imitate them. All they have to do is to write to the public's taste and at the same time follow the directives of the cultural section of the Central Committee. Not that this is so easy. It is becoming obvious that we are going to have a conformist and corrupt literature in spite of the remarkable resistance of the majority of young Soviet writers. . . . Although we are starting life anew, we can see everywhere things which have escaped us, which threaten us, which will be our ruin.

Konstantinov solved the equation. We knew each other without ever having met. I detested him, but I was beginning to understand him. Someone said to me, "He is scholarly and collects autographs. He has manuscripts of Tolstoy, Andreyev, Chekhov, Rozanov. . . . He is a materialist, but he has begun to visit mystics. Perhaps a little cracked, but intelligent. A former Chekist. He says he likes you very much. . . ." In a house located on the right bank, I met some people standing about under a chandelier. One old man told us about Rozanov, in whom there was something of Nietzsche, Tolstoy, and Freud, all sublimated in a sensual Christianity rebelling against itself. A kind of saint, although a prey to *idées fixes,* he had thoroughly studied the moral and the sexual problems. A bit of a scoundrel through thinking himself one—not that he wanted to be one, but he told himself that basically everyone is, in spite of everything. Author of "Fallen Leaves," a book of meditations on life, death, hypocrisy, unclean flesh, and the Savior; a book written on sheets of toilet paper in the w. c. . . . He died about the same time as Lenin, and left a deep impression on the Russian intelligentsia. They spoke of him as though he had just left the apartment. There were some young women there, and a tall lean man with a small, blond mustache and a colorless, expressionless face, whom I immediately recognized as Ott, the director of the administrative services of the Cheka in 1919-20. An Esthonian or Lett, and characterized by a bloodless immobility, he was the one who handled all the scribbling during the period of the executions. Konstantinov, bald-headed, with a bony nose, eyeglasses; I did not remember him, although he treated me as an old acquaintance. Late in the evening he told me privately, "You know me all the same. I was the examining magistrate in the Bayrach affair. . . ."

I remembered him. In 1920, along with a French Communist, I had waged a long struggle against him to save some men who were surely innocent but whom he seemed to want shot at any cost. I shall not go into this unimportant matter. There had been the incident of the bloody shirt which had been brought to me from prison, the incident of the young woman with the face of an odalisque for whom the sadistic judge had set fantastic traps and to whom he had made certain insulting proposals; there had been many incidents, and we had finally saved the accused by going to the very top man in the Cheka, Xenofontov, I believe. At the Cheka in Petrograd, the comrades had spoken to me about the examining magistrate in equivocal terms. A hard man, incorruptible (he only pretended to be willing to sell his mercy), a sadist perhaps, "but you understand—it is psychology!" I avoided meeting him again, believing he was a dangerous person, a professional maniac. Seven years later, he offered me tea as if we were friends.

"Your protégés went to Constantinople, where they have doubtless become big speculators. You were very wrong to take so much trouble to keep me from liquidating them. I knew that strictly speaking they were innocent, but we had many other things against them. Well, it doesn't matter now. In other circumstances, even greater people than you could not prevent me from carrying out my revolutionary duty. . . . It was I who . . ."

In January, 1920, when Lenin and Dzerzhinsky were proclaiming the abolishment of the death penalty, Konstantinov was one of those Chekists who ordered a night execution at the very moment that the decree was being printed. Several hundred suspects were massacred.

"Ah, it was you who . . ." And now?

He was on the periphery of the party now, not completely excluded, but pensioned, tolerated. From time to time he would take the train to Moscow and go to the Central Committee, where an important secretary would receive him. Konstantinov would carry his secret dossier, bulging with choice bits of information, and supplemented by his memory, whose accusations were irrefutable. He would show proofs, make accusations, name high personages, yet, never dared to tell everything. He would have been killed. Now he proposed to tell me nearly all. Whence this confidence in me? "You are an oppositionist? You are missing the whole point of the matter. You don't even suspect anything. . . ." He began by making some allusions, and we spoke of what was happening. Of what Lenin had foreseen when he said, "You think you are running the machine but it is running you, and suddenly there are other hands at the wheel."

Figures on unemployment, wage-scales; seizure of the home

market by private businessmen resulting from plunder of the
state; privation in the villages and the creation of a peasant
bourgeoisie; weakness of the Comintern and the Rapallo policies; wretchedness in the cities and the arrogance of the newly
rich—do these results seem natural to you? "And have we done
all that we have done, just for this?"

He put his cards on the table and told me his secret. The
secret that we have all been betrayed. There was treachery in
the Central Committee while Lenin was still alive. He knew
names, he had proofs. He could not tell me all, it was too serious
a matter; they knew that he knew. If anyone should suspect
that I learned it from him I should be lost. It is tremendous and
appalling. To combat this plot, one must have a profound perception, an inquisitorial genius, and absolute discretion. At the
risk of his life, he had submitted to the Central Committee his
analysis of the great crime which he had studied for years. He
whispered the names of foreigners, of the most powerful capitalists, and of many others to which he attached some occult
significance. He mentioned a city in America. I followed his
argument with the blank uneasiness which one might feel in the
presence of a logical lunatic. And I saw that he had the inspired
look of a madman. But in what he said there was the germ of a
basic idea, and it was not the idea of a madman: "We did not
fight the revolution for this."

We left each other bound by a feeling of mutual confidence.
It was a white night. The street cars had stopped running, and
Ott and I walked away together. Crossing a bridge which stood
between the dull sky and the mist-colored water, I realized that
my companion had not changed in six years. He still wore the
long cavalry coat without insignia; he had the same phlegmatic
air and the same half-smile under his pale little mustache as if
he were leaving the Cheka building on a white night in 1920.
He was in entire agreement with Konstantinov. The argument
was sound, wasn't it? We hold the threads of this plot against
the first socialist republic, this monstrous plot with world-wide
ramifications. . . . But everything can be saved, if only . . .

There are still some men in the Central Committee. But who are they?

The quiet city at two o'clock in the morning opened its long empty vistas. It seemed indifferent; a cold design in stone, full of memories. We had passed the blue cupola of the Mosque. On the little hill on the right, the five heroes of the Decembrist plot were hanged in 1825. On the left, in that little palace which once belonged to one of Nicholas II's favorites, the Bolshevik plot was organized in 1917. The gilded spire of the Peter-Paul fortress appeared above the casemates and the river; a prisoner there, Nechayev dreamed his grandiose plot to overthrow the empire. The conspirators of the "People's Will" group died there—died of starvation, in 1881-83. (Many of their younger disciples survived, the link between the older group and our own.) We approached the tombs on the Field of Mars, enclosed by ramparts of red granite. Our tombs. Opposite, in St. Michael's Palace, Paul I had been assassinated by his own officers. "Just one conspiracy after another," said Ott, smiling. "But that was all child's play. Today . . ." I had a notion to reply (but it would have been useless with these victims of an obsession): "Nowadays it is not nearly so easy. It is another thing altogether. And the conspiracies which you are inventing, my poor Ott, are quite superfluous. . . ."

I sketch these portraits and recall these chance remarks of the year 1926 because they show that even then there were vague beginnings of an atmosphere of psychosis. The whole USSR, for many tragic years, was to suffer from this psychosis more and more intensely; it is a psychological phenomenon unique in history. (Konstantinov was deported to Central Siberia in the early thirties, and disappeared.)

Then the dramatic story of Chubarev Lane disturbed the calm of the workers' city of Leningrad by revealing the conditions under which some of our young people lived. About fifteen young workers of the San-Galli factory had raped a poor girl of their own age in an empty lot close to the October Station. This was the Ligovka section, a squalid slum of filthy

tenements. The Control Commission of the party, over-
loaded with nasty little matters of morality, were confronted
with a kind of epidemic of collective rapes. Doubtless, sexuality,
long repressed by revolutionary asceticism and then by poverty
and famine, was beginning to recover its insistence in a society
suddenly deprived of spirituality. Two affairs of the same kind
became the subject of an inquiry. They took place at the House
of Students in Zhelyabova Street, the former Hotel Medved, a
few doors from where I was living. During the same evening,
two parties in different rooms had ended by a young girl being
left to the mercies of several drunken young males. . . . I
visited this house with a Sanitary Commission. The rooms,
nearly bare of furniture, were horribly poverty-stricken. Clothes
hung from the window latches. Some pots and little tin wash-
basins stood on the floor, and books were flung in the corners
along with shabby, down-at-heel shoes. On the iron beds,
generally without mattresses, boards had been placed, and a
quilt placed on these to be used as a mattress. Wherever there
were sheets, they were gray with dirt. In a large room where
there was nothing but a quilt on the plain boards we found
three young people asleep, two boys with a girl between them.
Promiscuity was growing under these conditions of miserable
squalor. Books like those of Alexandra Kollontay were promul-
gating an absurdly simple theory of free love; a childish materialism was reducing the "sexual need" to its fundamental of
carnal desire. "We have intercourse for the same reason that
we drink a glass of water, to slake our thirst." The more advanced young people, in the universities, followed Enschmen's
theory, disputed by Bukharin, on the disappearance of morals
in the future communist society. . . .

A trial for propaganda purposes of the fifteen culprits of
Chubarev Lane took place under the portrait of Lenin in the
Workers' Club. Rafail, editor of the Leningrad *Pravda,* presided, a bald, crafty-looking functionary. He did not seem to
understand at any time what depths of human wickedness and
poverty-induced decay he was being compelled to plumb in

the name of workers' justice. A room filled with men and women workers followed the testimony in an atmosphere of weary endurance. The fifteen accused looked like guttersnipes, and combined the more brutal elements of both the proletarian and peasant types. They confessed freely, and also informed on the others, gladly giving details, understanding nothing when anything but facts were mentioned, and finding that enough fuss was made over things as they were already without inventing stories. What is more natural than sex in the desert wastes? And if she prefers to sleep with four or five or six? She would become just as pregnant and diseased if she had slept with only one. And if she refuses, perhaps it is because she has "prejudices." I still remember some bits of testimony. The lack of self-consciousness of the culprits seemed so primitive that Rafail, accustomed to committees, was continually disconcerted by it. He had just made some senseless remarks about the new culture and good Soviet morals. A small blonde lad with a short, flat nose answered him:

"I don't know what they are."

Rafail went on, "I suppose you'd prefer the bourgeois morals of the foreigners?"

It was absurdly stupid. The boy replied, "I don't know anything about them. I've never been abroad."

"You might know about them by reading foreign newspapers."

The accused answered, "I've never even seen the Soviet papers. I get my culture from the streets."

Five of the accused were condemned to death. In order to be able to execute them, the authorities had to twist the law, and they were accused of being bandits. On the evening of the verdict, I saw a purple glow in the sky over the city. I walked towards this light, and saw that the whole San-Galli works were in flames. The condemned were executed the following day. Rumor had it that the workers who had started the fire were secretly executed, but this was impossible to verify.

I decided to get to know our social inferno, which flared up so brightly at night. I went down into the Soviet night shelters. I was there when some girls were shipped out by administrative decree to the concentration camps of the far north. I can safely say that Dostoyevsky saw very little, or at least, nothing has been improved in certain dark recesses of the world since Dostoyevsky's day. *Fréres clochards de Paris,* how difficult is social transformation!

Boris Souvarine

THE CULT OF LENIN

Editor's Note

[V. I. LENIN, born Vladimir Ilych
Ulianov, was that most rare of creatures, a dictator without
obsessive needs for personal aggrandizement, a dictator not
lacking in humility. It was his to achieve what is possible for
so few: a seminal role in the alteration of the course of the
world. The Bolshevik Revolution was the ten days that shook
the world, and Lenin was the prime shaker. The intensified
reverberations that the years have brought, the total subjugation of the Russian people, a dictatorial state grown into a totalitarian society—these are to a considerable extent the hom-
age of time to him, an ominous tribute that he would perhaps
not fully enjoy. There are the words of the late Krupskaya, his
devoted wife, to the effect that if Ilych were alive he would
be in prison. The revolution for "liberation" which resulted in
another imprisonment of the Russian people, albeit of a more
complete kind, would probably have jailed him too. In one
respect, there is no need to guess what would have happened.
In regard to Lenin's closest associates the record tells us what
did happen. Joseph Stalin has removed them from the ranks
of the living with a ferocity that would have delighted a long
succession of absolutistic Russian rulers. At that, it is doubtful
if Lenin would merely have been put in prison.

In his last advice to the party, Lenin called for Stalin to be
replaced as General Secretary. He castigated him for lacking

153

in loyalty, among other deficiencies in character. "Comrade
Stalin," he wrote, "having become General Secretary, has
concentrated an enormous power in his hands; and I am not
sure that he always knows how to use that power with sufficient
caution." There followed: "I propose to the comrades to find a
way to remove Stalin from that position . . ." (Stalin himself
later publicly conceded the authenticity of this document; see
"Lenin's 'Testament' and a Note of Background" in this book.)
At another time he had warned presciently regarding Stalin:
"This cook will concoct nothing but peppery dishes." But Lenin
was soon to die, impotent in the clutch of a dreadful illness.
The "peppery dishes" of the new cook exceeded all expectations.

Whether the prospect disheartened Lenin or not, history has
established Joseph Stalin not only as his successor but as his
rightful "heir," a son personally not worthy of his father, but
politically his natural son. There is much unnecessary confusion
on this point. Leon Trotsky and the followers he enlisted
have accused Stalin of a "betrayal" of Leninism, of the Communist revolution. With the specific crimes, atrocities and
outrages which they properly credit to Stalin, one can only
agree. Their "betrayal" explanation, a quite separate question,
is dramatic, simplistic, and it has caught the fancy of many
who are otherwise not attracted by the Trotskyist view, and
who fail to grasp the actual significance of this explanation, and
the reason for it—in short, who fail to appreciate the manner
in which, under the guise of attacking Stalinist dictatorship,
it involves them in a defense of Leninist dictatorship. Actually
Stalin has continued to develop, not subvert, the Leninist potential. Again, if the prospect which was apparently quite
clear to Lenin in his last days distressed him, it was a tribute
to his underlying humanity; but he was evaluating in reality
his own achievements, the fruit of his own program for which
he had sacrificed the blood of so many. The seed of the new
despotism was planted and watered under the aegis of Lenin,

not Stalin who, while by no means absent, had yet to emerge
fully from the wings.

The leader of a small band lashed by a selfless righteousness
given in previous times to sects of religious fanatics, Lenin invoked determinedly "history" as his mandate as others have
misused and gluttonized on the diet of "God." In the name of
morality, of a "higher" kind, he disregarded completely once
in power those democratic processes for which generations of
Russians had fought and died, apparently mistakenly. The new
redemptionist age was to be imposed by force on the Russian
people. All that has remained is the apparatus of dictatorial
imposition.

If not overly impressed with the personal rewards of unrestricted power, he was driven by the need for power itself, and
he was not scrupulous as to how he achieved or retained it. On
the eve of his *coup* in 1917, he warned the leaders of his inner
circle that "history will not forgive" them if they did not seize
power that very evening. Shortly before (and after) the *coup*
when Zinoviev and Kamenev, two of his closest Bolshevik associates, dissented, his response to them was characteristic.
He branded them as "strike-breakers" and worse. "No self-
respecting party," Lenin heatedly told the inner circle, "can
tolerate strike-breakers in its midst. That is obvious." To a dictatorial mentality it was; it is less obvious to those who find the
democratic system not despicable.

His contempt for those who believed in democratic parliaments was considerable, for firm advocates of democratic parliamentarism even greater. As Zinoviev and Kamenev had, with
one nasty flourish of his tongue, become "strike-breakers," democratic opponents became "opportunists," "White Guards,"
"counter-revolutionaries."

A sample statement of his credo:

> "The opportunists, including the Kautskians [Karl
> Kautsky], are 'teaching' the people a mockery of the
> teachings of Marx: the proletariat, forsooth, must first

gain a majority with the help of universal suffrage; then, having gained this majority, it must take over the power of the state; and, finally, on the basis of this 'consistent' (or 'pure' as it is called now) democracy, it must proceed to organize socialism. We, on the other hand, declare, on the basis of the teachings of Marx and the experience of the Russian revolution, that the proletariat must first overthrow the bourgeoisie and conquer the power of the state, and then use the power of the state, *i.e.*, the dictatorship of the proletariat, as an instrument of its class in order to gain the sympathy of the majority of the toilers." (Vol. 6, page 473.)*

Lenin was saying again, among other things, what he had stated to his conspiratorial collaborators on the eve of the *coup:* "*The seizure of power is a matter of insurrection; its political purpose will be clear after the seizure.*" Its "purpose" had made itself clear rapidly.

In unacademic terms, this kind of doctrine is familiar as a demand for a political blank check. The taking of power was a technical problem, done in the name of the masses. Rule would also be a technical problem, done also in the name of the masses. The technicians, responsible only to themselves, unrequestedly assumed the obligation of dictatorially imposing their program—which, indeed, was to be made clear *after the coup*—in the name of the masses.

"Dictatorship is power," Lenin instructed the "opportunist" Karl Kautsky, in his famed polemic against the democratic socialist leader, "based directly on force, and unrestricted by any laws. The revolutionary dic-

* The sources for Lenin's statements cited in this preface are volumes 6, 7, 8 and 9 of his *Selected Works;* in order: *From the Bourgeois to the Proletarian Revolution; After the Seizure of Power; The Period of War Communism;* and *New Economic Policy.* This edition, printed in Moscow, is not only an authorized version but is the official English translation as well, as issued by the Marx-Engels-Lenin Institute.

tatorship of the proletariat is power won and maintained
by the violence of the proletariat against the bourgeoisie, power that is unrestricted by any laws." (Vol. 7,
page 123.)

It is understandable that in the name of righteousness Lenin
should have recognized no differences among his opponents, as
Stalin does not among his. His simple technique was that of
reduction and amalgam; reduce everything you despise to a
slogan or epithet ("bourgeois," "White Guard") and then drape
it as a shroud about the shoulders of your opponents *en masse.*

> "You are the violators of freedom, equality and de-
> mocracy—they shout at us on all hands, pointing to the
> inequality of the worker and peasant under our constitu-
> tion, to the dispersal of the Constituent Assembly, to
> the forcible confiscation of surplus grain, and so forth.
> . . . But we shall never recognize equality with the
> peasant profiteer, just as we do not recognize 'equality'
> between the exploiter and the exploited, between the
> full and the hungry, and the 'freedom' of the former to
> rob the latter. And those educated people who refuse to
> recognize this difference we shall treat as White Guards,
> even though they may call themselves democrats, So-
> cialists, internationalists, Kautskys, Chernovs and Mar-
> tovs." (Vol. 8, page 10.)

He was exerting his divine right to characterize his opponents, not as they were, but in terms he found acceptable,
simple terms: either for or against us. It was difficult to explain
to the country why a "socialist" revolution would soon fully suppress the followers of such distinguished and universally-
respected socialists; it was easier to create a slogan, an endless
incantation of war against the "bourgeoisie," and to pin the
label to all who opposed him. Thus, Julius Martov, his old and
dear friend, a lifelong foe of tyranny, Martov was now—to

Lenin—a "White Guard." Karl Kautsky, the internationally admired socialist theoretician, the man whom Lenin once said understood Russia better than all the European socialists, the man
Lenin had once revered above all others with the exception
of Karl Marx and Engels, Karl Kautsky was now a "White
Guard." Victor Chernov, the elected chairman of the Constituent Assembly, which had been for the one day of its existence
the united voice of anti-tsarist Russia, Chernov who had been
the co-founder of the Socialist Revolutionaries, the great party
of agrarian socialism, was now a "White Guard." One must
know the records of these men, and those of so many others,
must appreciate what they stood for, their undisputed integrity, their lifelong visions and fight for a democratic Russia, to
grasp at all the full villainy of Lenin's characterization. And
after having transformed these men, as if by decree, into
"White Guards," and having a resolute policy against "White
Guards," he promptly fulfilled his noble and dedicatory task
by suppressing every non-Communist voice in the Russia he
was "liberating."

Thus he could openly state: "The place for Mensheviks and
Socialist Revolutionaries, [whether] open or disguised as non-
party, is in prison. . ." (Vol. 9, page 198.) This sounds, as yet,
as only a dire threat for the dire future, but it was already a sad
actuality. In the same article, Lenin makes this only too clear,
in a statement written as if to resolve all doubt: "We will keep
the Mensheviks and Socialist Revolutionaries, whether open
or disguised as non-party, in prison." (*Ibid.*, page 199.)

His either-or formulations led him to postulate a view
on parliamentary democracy ("bourgeois" democracy) which
aroused the enmity of the democratic world when voiced in a
variant form by more recent dictators.

> "Only two forces, in fact, exist: the dictatorship of the
> bourgeoisie and the dictatorship of the proletariat. Who-
> ever has not learnt this from Marx, whoever has not

learnt this from the works of all the great socialists, has never been a socialist, has never understood socialism, and has only called himself a socialist." (Vol. 8, page 170.)

". . . a democratic republic is a bourgeois-democratic republic, which has already become antiquated from the point of view of the problems which imperialism has placed on the agenda of history. They show that there is no *other* alternative: *either* the Soviet government triumphs in every advanced country in the world, *or* the most reactionary imperialism triumphs . . . One or the other. There is no middle course." (Vol. 8, pages 148-9.)

"General talk about freedom, equality and democracy is in fact but a stereotyped repetition of conceptions which are only a cast from the relations of commodity production. To attempt to solve the concrete problems of the dictatorship of the proletariat by means of such general talk is to accept the theories and principles of the bourgeoisie all along the line." (Vol. 8, page 12.)

Evident also in Leninism, and made hugely more articulate in Stalinism, is his formulation of a political double standard: one code for Communists and another for all others. If one were to attempt to unearth in Lenin's writings and pronouncements objective criteria for judging the rightness and wrongness of specific kinds of action the task would soon be found to be impossible. By this is meant that specific actions (suppressions of parliaments, banning of parties, and so on) when perpetrated by non-Communist governments are wrong—but when perpetrated by the Communist state are correct, moral. The only principle for "rightness" in this body of floating ethics is ostensibly and actually whether or not the Communists are the instruments of the action. The Provisional Government, for example, was cynically accused by the Bolsheviks of delaying the calling of the Constituent Assembly which all democratic

Russia awaited eagerly; when the elections, scheduled by the Provisional Government and held under the Communist Government—Lenin having quite wisely insisted on his *coup* preceding the elections—gave the Communists only one quarter of the votes, the latter immediately bayoneted it out of existence. The Provisional Government, nevertheless, and remarkably, continues to be a target for abuse on this matter in Communist quarters; Lenin's suppression, although not much discussed, is praised when such discussion is unavoidable!

Many readers in 1949 were rightly impressed by the late George Orwell's *Nineteen Eighty-Four;* the examination of the concept of "double think" so aptly described the substance of Communist propaganda and philosophy. But Stalin is the chief user not the inventor. Here is an archetype of Lenin's "double think" principle:

> "If war is waged by the exploiting class with the object of strengthening its class rule, such a war is a criminal war, and 'defencism' in *such* a war is a base betrayal of socialism. If war is waged by the proletariat after it has conquered the bourgeoisie in its own country, and is waged with the object of strengthening and extending socialism, such a war is legitimate and 'holy.' "
> (Vol. 7, page 357.)

Before Russia was induced by the Nazi attack to unwillingly enter into World War II, that war, said the Communists, was "imperialistic." After the Russian entry, it was holy. American Marshall Plan aid for Europe is "imperialistic," but Russia's gobbling up of many European countries is "holy." More than "double think," however, is involved; the principle is at the heart of Communism's global view. So-called security, in the cynical avowal, comes only with world domination; so long as any periphery of the expanding Communist world touches a non-Communist state, Communism's "security" is threatened.

It calls for no elaborate explanation to indicate the point at which Communist "security" is finally achieved.

> "We are living," said Lenin, "not merely in a state, but in a *system of states,* and the existence of the Soviet Republic side by side with imperialist states for a long time is unthinkable. One or the other must triumph in the end. And before that end supervenes, a series of frightful collisions between the Soviet Republic and the bourgeois states will be inevitable." (Vol. 8, page 33.)

> Again: "As soon as we are strong enough to defeat capitalism as a whole we shall immediately take it by the scruff of the neck." (Vol. 8, page 282.)

> And again: "As long as we have not conquered the whole world, as long as, from the economic and military standpoint, we are weaker than the capitalist world, we must adhere to the rule that we must know how to take advantage of the antagonisms and contradictions existing among the imperialists." (Vol. 8, pages 279-80.)

> And again: "As long as capitalism and socialism exist, we cannot live in peace: in the end, one or the other will triumph—a funeral dirge will be sung either over the Soviet Republic or over world capitalism." (Vol. 8, page 297.)

As the Stalinist state each day brings these Communist aims closer to total realization, speculation absurdly persists on whether Stalin—whose basic writings consist almost solely of quotations and paraphrases from Lenin—adheres to this Communist philosophy. *Which of these central tenets, it may be asked, has Stalin "betrayed?"*

Lenin cleared the woods of democracy and made it possible for Stalin to plant his own totalitarian trees. It is an unpleasant conclusion, for it is more encouraging to speak of a white ideal being splattered by black betrayal—and so we have the

spectacle of a number of avid foes of Stalinist-Communism nos-
talgically remembering Leninist-Communism. The growth
in extent and odiousness between Leninist-Communism and
Stalinist-Communism represents rather clearly the cumulative
dividends of absolute power; an over-quoted, but insufficiently
understood, dictum of Lord Acton's is much to the point.

There indeed *was* a betrayal, a betrayal of the idealistic
hopes of a large segment of the world that came with the fall of
tsarism, a betrayal of the aspirations of the Russian people for
freedom, a heroic struggle that was repaid with a new saddle
of dictatorship as soon as the old was lifted, a new despotism
the scope and quality of which is at present unrivaled, and
which has been matched in all history only by the infamy of
Nazi Germany. But who is responsible for *that* betrayal? A
man can ask no more than to be judged by the fruits of his endeavor. At the time of Lenin's death, the Communist state held
the Russian people in an iron grip of repression—this was Lenin's state, and already, in effect, Stalin's state. In 1921 Lenin
was compelled to "strategically" turn his back on Communism
—he had no recourse—and institute the NEP, a significant
embracing of capitalist restoration; he needed to do this to prevent the regime from falling, to quell dissent, to allow the barest
necessities of life to be obtained. Three years of Leninist Communism had reduced Russia to a shambles. But, for all the economic innovations, the political dictatorship continued, repression was intensified.

It may seem strange to some that a man's fanatic dedication
to "ultimate" ideals can be conceded, and that he can yet be
held responsible for the most inhuman devastation of the human spirit and condition. It remains a fact, and by no means a
mysterious one. It is a sad truth, but nevertheless a truth: "benevolent" tyranny fails to produce results much different from
those of "unbenevolent" tyranny.

A "dictator without vanity" dies, as Lenin did in January,
1924, and his power is won by a dictator much given to vanity,

to the encouragement of near idolatry, the "Leader," the man
after whom cities are named at his request or certainly with his
permission, poetry written, paintings painted. The slogans of
the devoted, and selfless, fanatics of yesterday, the cause of the
initial "benevolent" dictatorship, remain—but even the camouflage of benevolence wears thin. Not only has the new leader
absolute power, he has (miracle of miracles!) a legion of followers throughout the world, blind to three decades of history,
who continue to affirm their devotion to the slogans, and, after
denouncing dictatorship, get in line behind the dictator. The
original fanatic desire for a world revolution, to "free the wage
slaves," is gone—the citizens of the liberated country have
themselves been permanently enslaved. But the tactical
weapon of "world revolution" remains—support throughout
the world for the dictatorial regime that steps steadily toward
world *conquest*. The "dictator without vanity" dead, there
springs up a "cult" about him, each faction fighting for his
mantle. The triumphant new dictator deifies his predecessor;
in truth, he owes much to him. The old dictator is literally mum-
mified and put on display—an ironic reminder, perhaps, of
the dead ideal which continues to be paraded as a living reality.

But if here we have been concerned with the methods of
Leninism, elsewhere in this book our interest has been with
the record that these methods achieved. In this summary selection, Boris Souvarine presents us with an incisive political
portrait of the dead dictator, his personal contradictions, his
varying ideas before and after his seizure of power, the tragedy
he wrought, the political capital that is made of him after his
death. What remains of Lenin's work? That is one of the focal
questions to which this essay turns, and performs a remarkable achievement of summary, synthesis and analysis. It is not
surprising that it should be Boris Souvarine who should succeed in placing this difficult subject in such an enlightening
perspective. His credentials are those born of intimacy with the
international Communist movement, and of a distinguished,

independent scholarly aptitude. He was one of the founders of the French Communist Party, and studied Soviet Russia, Lenin and the international movement closely, and at first hand, as a member of the Executive Committee of the Communist International. He is widely known as the author of *Stalin,* an indispensable biography of the dictator, which is an extraordinarily informative book on the results of the Russian Revolution as well. At present he is a member of the staff of the Institut Internationale d'Histoire Sociale in Paris. This selection appeared in the Summer, 1939, issue of *The Modern Quarterly.*

#

The Cult of Lenin by Boris Souvarine

ON JANUARY 21, 1924, the Moscow militia ordered all building superintendents, caretakers and *concierges* to decorate their buildings with red flags trimmed with black mourning bands. Thus the population learned that somebody important had died. But who? People were indifferent. There had been too much suffering during civil war, misery and dictatorship were still too burdensome to permit the leisure necessary to an interest in such matters. On the next day a government communique was issued: "Yesterday, January 21, at 6:50 p. m., at Gorki near Moscow, Vladimir Ilych Ulianov (Lenin) died suddenly. The proximity of a fatal end had not been indicated in any way." And so on. Thus insensibly did the Russian revolution enter a new phase.

The report of an autopsy signed by eleven doctors and professors of medicine diagnosed a cerebral hemorrhage due to arterio-sclerosis. The anatomical-pathological analysis described a sclerotic state so far advanced that it is hardly comprehensible how the patient could still have lived, much less thought. The People's Commissar for Public Health ended an article with these words: "Thus the autopsy on the body of Vladimir Ilych established an *Abnützungssclerose* (sclerosis due to attrition) as the principal cause of the illness and death. It revealed that superhuman intellectual labor, constant emotions and continuous anxiety, brought our chief to an untimely end." Under the chairmanship of Dzerzhinsky an organizing committee got to work to arrange the funeral ceremonies.

The preparations took six days. A temporary mausoleum was hastily constructed on the Red Square in front of the Kremlin. The embalmed corpse was on view at the House of Trade Unions, the old Nobles Club, where the crowd could file by in a properly organized procession. The closest companions of the deceased lost no time in starting to exploit the cadaver politically. One hour after the death Zinoviev, in an article entitled "Six Days Russia Will Not Forget," described what happened: "We are going to the dead Ilych: Bukharin, Tomsky, Kalinin, Stalin, Kamenev and I. Rykov is sick in bed." Around the cold corpse of their master, the disciples were already mounting a jealous guard, watching in order to prevent any one or several among them from appropriating his memory, such an invaluable historical capital.

On Sunday, January 27, the burial day, the first guard of honor took up its post around the coffin: it was composed of Zinoviev, Stalin, Kalinin and Kamenev. Every ten minutes there was a change of guard: first Bukharin, Rykov, Molotov and Tomsky; then Dzerzhinsky, Chicherin, Petrovsky and Sokolnikov; then Kiubyshev, Ordzhonikidze, Pyatakov, and Yenukidze. And so on. In cold weather memorable even for Moscow, Lenin's endless funeral cortége set out. Exactly at four o'clock throughout the immense territory of all the Russias, work was suspended, and for three minutes factories, shops, mills, railroads, locomotives, ships in the ports, sounded their whistles or sirens. Artillery salutes and salvos resounded in all the garrisons, as well as from the naval and coast defense batteries. At the same instant on the mausoleum Stalin, Zinoviev,

Molotov, Bukharin, Rudzutak, Tomsky and Dzerzhinsky lifted the coffin to descend to the crypt. . . .

"Lenin is dead, long live Leninism!" proclaimed with one voice the accredited Leninists, in a consolatory formula.

I

Fifteen years have passed. With two or three exceptions, all those men who then pressed about the tomb have perished, by an infamous or tragic mysterious death, by the will of Lenin's successor, or rather of him who knew how to make off with the heritage. Fifteen years have passed. What remains of Lenin, what remains of Leninism?

Joining the revolutionary movement in 1888 at the age of 18, the future Lenin (he was born Ulianov) did not claim and never was to claim to have made any doctrinal innovations. Down to his death, he made it a sort of point of honor to be nothing but a disciple of Karl Marx. Whether he succeeded in doing that is another matter, a matter of debate hinging on a certain casuistry. He boasted the most classical Marxism and aspired to fight for political democracy as the preliminary and necessary condition for the conquest of that economic democracy which, some fine day, was to be the socialism of his dreams. His professions of democratic faith are incessant, repeated, multiplied, down to the October revolution.

But in 1902 his first writing over the name of Lenin sounded an unprecedented note for Marxists of the day. Under the title *What Is to be Done?* we have a veritable technical handbook of civil war which links the author to Blanqui and the pioneers of Russian "populism," terroristic and conspiratorial. In the service of a fixed doctrine which will become more and more rigid and dogmatic, Lenin extols the development of professional revolutionaries, of a disciplined military organization, capable of maneuvering with its leaders, its staff, its specialists.

Beginning in 1903, at the Russian Social-Democratic Congress held in London, where two tendencies, the "hards" and the "softs," still vague as to ideas but distinct as to temperament, shaped themselves, he took command of the "hards," the future Bolsheviks,* demonstrating at thirty-three his irresistible call to leadership and standing his ground even in the face of a possible split. He affirmed the necessity of organizing "a secret circle of leaders" in order to set into motion "the largest possible mass." He was already taxed with dictatorship, accused of wanting to initiate a veritable state of siege within the party. He was regarded as a Robespierre. Nothing daunted, he even found the comparison flattering.

In the ensuing controversies, all the theoreticians of Marxism, in Russia and in Germany, took sides against him. He persisted, defended himself, attacked. To those who spoke indignantly of Jacobinism, even of Bonapartism, he replied by denouncing their "opportunistic or anarchistic corruption," and declared himself the Jacobin of the proletariat as opposed to the orthodox Marxist Gironde. Two of his friends of yesterday, Trotsky and Plekhanov, forecast precisely that, put into practice, his theories would end in personal omnipotence. Several pamphlets and numerous articles were interchanged without result. "Maximilian Lenin," as Trotsky dubbed him, tired of sterile arguments, dreamt of setting out for America. But meanwhile the Russo-Japanese war broke out in 1904, and, in January of the following year, "Bloody Sunday" ** in St. Petersburg set the first Russian revolution under way.

II

The professional revolutionaries dear to Lenin amounted to nothing, particularly in the spontaneous creation of the first soviets. In a general way, nobody foresaw anything. Lenin first distrusted the soviets, for his followers saw therein a reactionary competitor. But he grasped his mistake quickly

* [The "softs," opposed to a dictatorial party, were to become the Mensheviks—*Ed.*]

** [January 22, 1905 when Father Gapon led thousands of workers to the Winter Palace to make a personal plea to the "true Czar with a valiant heart" about working conditions; they were fired upon—*Ed.*]

enough and pressed the party to take advantage of these new organs of revolution, and he followed their movement. As for doctrine, he did not abate an inch: the revolution must support the bourgeoisie, develop capitalism, "found a democratic republic as the final form of bourgeois domination." The conceptions of Trotsky as to the permanent Russian and international revolution, and the coming establishment of a socialist power were, to Lenin, "absurd semi-anarchistic conceptions."

After the abortive revolution of 1905, during which he kept in the shadows, Lenin expected a new explosion, this time a decisive one. He was wrong. Having called for the boycott of the elections to the Duma, he recognized his mistake, adopted an opposite tactic, fought his own supporters who clung to an intransigent position, resigned himself to re-establishing the unity of the Party. He had condemned the terroristic activity of the Social-Revolutionaries; he now endorsed it for himself, justified violent expropriations, assassinations, reprisals, and was free subsequently to disavow "combativeness degenerated to adventurism." His socialist adversaries reminded him of morality, of which he contrived elastic and contradictory definitions. Trotsky denounced his "sectarian spirit," his "ideological fetishism," Martov condemned the Bolsheviks as a "new Jesuit order." In 1914 the great war swept away the old quarrels and posed new problems.

Lenin first refused to believe in the "treason" of the German Social-Democracy. Could he have been so wrong? He had to bow to the evidence. Thereupon he furiously attacked the mother-section and the sister-sections of the Second International, and called for the founding of a third. He worked out the theory of "revolutionary defeatism." At the beginning of 1917 he was doubtful of ever seeing the hoped-for revolution, but in February-March of the same year czarism finally collapsed. Contrary to his expectation, revolution preceded defeat.

Taken unawares, he began to repeat his old and quite modest democratic program. But soon he changed his mind and put

socialist demands to the fore. For the events in Russia led him
to forecast a socialist revolution in all Europe. In April he called
for "all power to the Soviets" in order to accomplish the nationalization of the land, the right of nationalities to separate from
Russia, the merger of banks, workers' control of production,
the abolition of the police and of the permanent army of officials. His Marxist critics considered him an anarchist, a new
Bakunin. In July he withdrew his slogan of power for the Soviets, and proposed the dictatorship of the proletariat exercised
by his Party, a change which was motivated by the imminence
of the general European revolution. Now he subscribed to
Trotsky's thesis, which he had formerly subjected to ridicule.
Then he changed his mind again, and reaffirmed the formula
of Soviets of a "higher and democratic type," and guaranteed
that a Soviet power would assure the peaceful development of
the revolution, the peaceful competition of parties within the
republic. At the same time, he insisted on the earliest possible
calling of the Constituent Assembly.

III

As soon as the Bolsheviks got a majority in the Petrograd and
Moscow Soviets, Lenin felt that they could and must take
power. With the first symptoms of trouble in Germany, he was
certain of the proximity of a "world proletarian revolution." In
September he demanded action. In October he had no patience
with slowness, he was irritated by hesitation, he stamped his
foot with rage: "It is a crime to wait." He believed that "Kerensky & Co." were going to surrender Petrograd to Germany.
He was mistaken. He was afraid of a separate peace between
England and the central powers. He was mistaken again. He
saw the international socialist revolution coming. Another mistake. But with an argument based on three mistakes, he put
over, on October 23, the decision to make an insurrection
within a short time. He tormented his lieutenants, precipitated
the denouement: "Any delay is tantamount to death; everything hangs on a hair. . . ." On November 7, under Trotsky's

leadership, the Bolshevik revolution conquered without danger and triumphed without glory; in the capital at least nothing and nobody set up any obstacle to it. Lenin later said: "It was easy to begin a revolution in such a country. It was easier than to lift a feather."

Now began the difficulties. The new regime had to resolve immediately several vital questions: the agrarian problem, the right of nationalities, war and peace. It had to live up to democratic promises: abolition of the death penalty, convocation of the Constituent Assembly, civil liberties, workers' control of production, socialization by stages. How would Lenin carry out his program?

He had changed his mind several times about the agrarian question. At the time of the first revolution, he called for the confiscation of the great estates for the benefit of the small peasants. Later he supported nationalization of the land, that is to say, general expropriation. Finally, when in power, he decreed the transfer of large estates to the local Soviets or agricultural committees. He thus established, in order not to mince matters and to neutralize the peasantry, a new individualistic property instead of taking the road of socialism. Thus he prepared insoluble contradictions for the future. Having promised the land to the peasants, he deprived them of their harvests to feed the cities. Everything turned out as badly as possible: famines, civil war in the countryside, militarization of agriculture, constant exactions and killings.

He also changed his mind several times about the question of nationalities. He successively defended the right of nations to dispose of their own fate, democratic centralism against federalism ("for the Jacobins, against the Girondins"); he agreed to separatism only as an exception or a transition toward the one and indivisible republic; he regarded separation as a right and federation as a duty; he proclaimed that the interest of socialism is superior to the right of self-determination of the nations; finally, once in power, he smashed separatism by violence and imposed the Soviet order on all the nationalities of old Russia by means of the Red Army. Subsequently, he promoted the culture of regional nationalities and aroused centrifugal forces which had to be incessantly repressed at the cost of many victims, and with which his successors would some day have to reckon.

He had undertaken either to obtain a "democratic peace" or to wage a "revolutionary war" against Germany; he had to submit at Brest-Litovsk to a peace which he characterized as "shameful." He had declared against any separate peace; he was forced to sign one. He had counted on the support of a European, indeed of a "world" socialist revolution; he came to answer the naive who persisted in their illusions: "Can a serious revolutionary believe in fables?"

He had protested against the re-establishment of the death sentence in the army; he extended its application to the civil population. He demanded at the top of his lungs the immediate calling of the Constituent Assembly; it was he who dissolved it. He would not hear of the transfer of the capital from Petrograd to Moscow; later he ordered the shift himself. He forecast the peaceful competition of parties; he instituted a monopoly. Workers' control of production? A complete failure. The labor armies? A disastrous setback. Instead of the merger of banks, the state took them over and confiscated all their property. Instead of socialization by stages, socialization was promoted by forced marches.

He had promised "complete freedom of the press"; he extinguished both freedom and the press. All the democratic gains disappeared in succession, even freedom of conscience: religious persecutions were added to political. He had accepted the terror in principle as an expedient of civil war, temporary, provisional, to solidify the so-called "democratic dictatorship"; he perpetuated its employment and made a virtue of necessity, a permanent regime out of an exceptional one. Instead of the dictatorship of the proletariat, a Party dictatorship was established, then, as he himself put it, a new "oligarchy" arose. During the civil war the Party transformed itself into an institution of military type and organized the State in its own image. The Soviets and the trade unions served as instruments of power. The state of siege became the normal state of what was called Soviet society, and an omnipresent police installed itself, proliferating and swarming until it dominated everything.

IV

Lenin, parroting all his doctrinal teachers, declaimed that it was impossible to establish socialism in a single country, especially such a backward one as Russia. But thereafter he acted as though he thought exactly the opposite. Driven into a blind alley, he neatly executed a turnabout which he called NEP (new economic policy) and he christened his previous aberration "military communism." He always knew that his pretended socialism was in truth, nothing but state capitalism. Due to the contradiction between theory and practice, or to the arterio-sclerosis which paralyzed his cerebral faculties, he no longer had clear-sightedness nor the opportune courage to draw political deductions from his economic considerations. The more he resigned himself to concessions of an economic order, the more he reinforced the political dictatorship, expressly threatening his old socialist comrades with death. Thus he provided Stalin with the formula, "not to shrink from barbarous means of fighting barbarism," in whose name innumerable human lives have been sacrificed. On the ruins of the old ruling classes a new social stratum formed itself, that of the bureaucracy, profiteering, harsh, avid, a political, technical, police and military bureaucracy which dug itself into a new mode of man's exploitation of man. When Lenin perceived the evil, it was too late; arterio-sclerosis rapidly overcame him. On his death, all the conditions were present for the future construction of a sort of fascist totalitarian state.

The *Complete Works* of Lenin contain all his writings and speeches in thirty compact, large volumes, augmented by a series of volumes called the *Collected Works*. The latter preserve all Lenin's literary remains which have been found, his rough drafts, note-books, sketches, outlines for reports or articles, minor papers, correspondence. We are spared nothing except what might harm Stalin. A special Institute works on this publication, with an army of archivists, copyists, translators, annotators, editors. Everything is transcribed, photographed, engraved, reproduced, printed. They are something to see, those pages covered with citations, references, quotation marks, parentheses, brackets, interrogation and exclamation points, underlinings and insertions, blue-pencilings, notations and erasures! These sixty-odd volumes constitute the printed sum of Leninism. In addition, there are what may properly be called the works: books, pamphlets, studies, articles classified thematically, are published separately in all possible formats and all sorts of bindings. The total run is fantastic, reaching a figure of dozens of millions. *Komsomolskaya Pravda* reports 115,066,575 copies of various works by Lenin published since the October revolution, of which more than 108,000,000 were issued since Lenin's death. There are translations into 80 languages. And on top of all this is an enormous and comical hagiographic literature, plus an incommensurable literature of popularization.

But none of this would have existed had Lenin not seized power in 1917. Assuming another course of events, an accidental factor, and perhaps nobody would have published *The State and Revolution* or, in any case, republished *The Development of Capitalism in Russia* or *Materialism and Empirio Criticism*. As far as their intrinsic value goes, Lenin's writings would have found but few readers. It is not the thinker, writer, orator or theoretician who makes an impression by his *Complete Works,* but rather the bold victor of October. Several of these writings or reports have retained their high documentary or analytical quality, but no more nor less so than dozens of works published and forgotten by his contemporaries. The majority are conscientious compilations which have become anachronistic. As for the articles, full of repetitions and contradictions, they add nothing to his glory, despite their biographical interest.

In truth, Lenin was above all else a great civil war captain, organizer, trainer, tactician and strategist. At the decisive moment, he saw power go begging, he was able to grasp it—because he was permitted to do so. Before that, he had had the merit of preparing himself; subsequently he had the talent to hang on. But, as the price of power, he was obliged bit by bit to renounce his principles, abandon his program, compromise his work forever. A statesman of incontestable breadth of vision, he showed himself capable of temporizing, maneuvering, adapting, repressing, conceding, now taking the offensive, now beating an opportune retreat. And he dominated chaos (toward whose creation, moreover, he contributed not a little), restored order, a hierarchy, a social discipline, an economic life. But he did not found a normal or stable order, rational and durable institutions—whether one takes as criteria his own ideas or the results of his experiment. He left nothing viable. Fifteen years after his death no great deal remains of his theoretical abstractions or of his practical constructs, and his memory has been tarnished by epigones.

Of the man, there remains the memory and the example of sincere convictions, of absolute disinterestedness, of an inflexible will aspiring toward a single goal: the socialist ideal. He was obviously not the original thinker, still less the profound philosopher which ignoramuses misled by cynics would like to see in him. His "scientific" pretensions provoke a smile, but his transcendental intentions permit of no contempt. He still inpires respect by the broadness of his culture, the probity of his studies, the intensity of his labor. As for his natural intelligence, simultaneously lively and simplistic, it could seduce by its peasant shrewdness or repel by its over-schematicness. "Lenin is a genius of an imbecile," Radek once said to the present writer. The same idea is embodied in a moujik's maxim applied to Lenin by his socialist critic Victor Chernov: "As for being intelligent, he is that, of course, but his intelligence is stupid."

Finally, one can discover in Lenin nothing of affectation, of meanness, of vulgarity. His human worth would be plain if only by the way in which he publicly recognized his mistakes. But he was unable to admit the chief one, because that would have meant disavowing himself and renouncing Bolshevism.

V

Of his work nothing worthwhile remains, taking into account what his heirs did with the inheritance and contrasting theory with practice, fine promises with disillusioning actions. Where is the State without police, without army, without officialdom? Where are the trade unions and the Soviets? The Party itself has disappeared unhonored and unsung and the Communist International did not outlive its founder. True, a sort of political and police agency of the Russo-Bolshevik state has persisted under the name of the Comintern, but it is alien to its initial inspiration. What has become of the liberties, the democracy, the rights of nations, the rights of man? The thousands of decrees which Lenin signed are gone with the wind. The millions of volumes which Lenin would not have published—nobody takes them seriously. Lenin is dead and embalmed, Leninism dead and buried, the Leninists dead and dishonored by mutual assassination. A new czarism is installing itself for a long stay, one infinitely worse than the former, which was not totalitarian. If Lenin could, from his Asiatic mausoleum, contemplate the picture which is Russia and which he did not foresee, most assuredly he would not be proud.

Max Eastman

THE CHARACTER AND FATE OF LEON TROTSKY

Editor's Note

THE stature of Leon Trotsky is generally conceded even by his opponents, excluding, of course, the Stalinists. He was a brilliant writer, revolutionary leader, historian, military mind. Yet there have been questions about his sagacity as politician—a subject of historical and political interest—that have not been satisfactorily answered, certainly not by Trotsky. There is, for example, his political conduct after the death of Lenin, during the period which Stalin used so cynically to cement his way to complete power. When Lenin died in 1924, Trotsky was on his way to Sukhum in the Caucasus. At this tense time, when power had been fought for outside Lenin's sickroom, Trotsky was making this journey to try to rid himself of what he described shortly before his assassination in Mexico as a "dogged, mysterious infection, the nature of which still remains a mystery to my physicians." This was to be, politically, an extremely expensive, probably psychosomatic, illness. He received news of Lenin's death en route and sent a wire asking when the funeral would take place. Moscow's reply was that the day was Saturday and that he would not be able to return in time. *The telegram was from Stalin*, who solicitously added: "The Politburo thinks that because of the state of your health you must proceed to Sukhum." The telegram alone, it would seem, should have made Trotsky suspicious. In view of the political setting and Stalin's role, the latter being at this time already only too clear, one would think that Trotsky would have sped back to Moscow if only to be there immediately *after* Lenin's funeral. Later, Trotsky learned that the date had been changed to Sunday; he could have returned in time. He had been outmaneuvered by Stalin. When he did return, moreover, he chose to maintain an inexplicable silence, thus allowing Stalin to keep busy in his quest for power. In addition, when Trotsky finally spoke he sounded conciliatory. This at a time when his name was linked throughout the Soviet Union with that of Lenin.

This inadequately explained episode opens up the entire question of Trotsky as politician. Max Eastman has known Trotsky closely; he was translator of Trotsky's monumental *History of the Russian Revolution,* author of a biography of the revolutionary leader, and friend. He never, however, was a Trotskyite, contrary to a popular notion. Although this portrait was written in 1942, as part of Eastman's *Heroes I Have Known,* it develops views he held regarding this side of Trotsky's personality as early as 1924, when he knew and observed Trotsky in Russia. An early statement of this partial appraisal was made in Eastman's *Since Lenin Died,* published in 1925, and especially in the chapter, "Trotsky's Bad Tactics." That book, by the way, was one of the first revelatory American accounts of Stalin's ruthless rise to power.

Mr. Eastman in his evaluation of Trotsky as politician does not, of course, pretend that the entire explanation for that crucial period—as regards the struggle for power—is to be found in his assessment. A stage had been reached in the USSR, and in the "degenerated" Communist Party, which might have dictated—given all the circumstances—Stalin's taking of power. But that did not remove Trotsky from his responsibility as politician from waging a far more ferocious fight than he did. Our interest here, however, is not one of partisanship. An attitude toward Trotsky has been indicated elsewhere in this book, in John Dewey's statement on the revolutionary leader which is cited in the preface to Trotsky's own selection. We *are* interested in a suggestive view, Mr. Eastman's, of a possibly understressed aspect of one of the fathers of the Bolshevik revolution, and in the light it may throw on an important historical period.

Max Forrester Eastman was born in Canandaigua, New York, on January 4, 1883. Both his parents, and his grandfather, were ministers. He was educated at Williams College and Columbia University, and as a young man taught philosophy at the latter institution. During this period he wrote his widely read *Enjoyment of Poetry*. In 1910, developing politically at the same time, he organized the first Men's League for Woman Suffrage in the United States, and after that became interested and active in radical politics. He helped found *The Masses* and served it as its first editor, from 1913-17. During World War I this magazine was suppressed by the government for opposing the war. Eastman, and his sister, next started *The Liberator*, and he remained with that magazine until 1922. The Soviet Union was then in its formative years and Eastman went to study the country and observe the situation at first hand. He remained in that country for two years, marrying Eliena Krylenko there (whom he brought back to the U. S. with him), and later, after continuing his study of Marxism and Soviet politics, wrote several works on both subjects. Mr. Eastman's well-known books are: *Enjoyment of Laughter; Stalin's Russia and the Crisis in Socialism; Artists in Uniform; The Literary Mind; Marxism, Is It Science?* He has also written, among others, four books of poetry, a novel, and is the compiler and narrator of *From Czar to Lenin* (1937), a motion-picture history of the Russian Revolution. Most recently he has published *Enjoyment of Living*, volume one of his autobiography.

The Character and Fate of Leon Trotsky by Max Eastman

TROTSKY stood up gloriously against the blows of fate during his last years—demotion, rejection, exile, systematized slanderous misrepresentation, betrayal by those who had understood him, repeated attempts upon his life by those who had not, the certainty of ultimate assassination. His associates, his secretaries, his relatives, his own children, were hounded to death by a sneering and sadistic enemy. He suffered privately beyond description, but he never relaxed his monumental self-discipline. He never lost his grip for one visible second, never permitted any blow to blunt the edge of his wit, his logic or his literary style. Under afflictions that would have sent almost any creative artist to a hospital for neurotics and thence to the grave, Trotsky steadily developed and improved his art. His unfinished life of Lenin, which I had partially translated, would have been his masterpiece. He gave us, in a time when our race is woefully in need of such restoratives, the vision of a man.

Of that there is no more doubt than of his great place in history. His name will live, with that of Spartacus and the Gracchi, Robespierre and Marat, as a supreme revolutionist, an audacious captain of the masses in revolt. Beyond these clearly shining facts, however, the doubts about Trotsky, the problems of his character, are many and complex. Few great men lend themselves to false portraiture and extreme overcorrections of it as he does. His inward nature, like Robespierre's, will remain a subject of hot argument while history lasts. Moreover, those in a position best to give testimony, his colleagues in great action, are all dead or destroyed. Stalin has not left one to tell the story. I have been less close to him than many knowing of our literary collaboration think; but I have received a definite impression of his character which is surely worth setting forth.

As a young man of twenty-six Trotsky presided over the revolution of 1905, the first assault of the Russian masses on the Tsar's government. Twelve years later he organized and led the victorious October revolution of 1917, a model for all insurrections and one of the turning points in history. In the next years he created a revolutionary army out of hungry and bedraggled hordes, and fought off on seven fronts the invading forces of Europe. He played, next to Lenin, the major role in founding the Soviet state. And when it was done, he wrote a three-volume history of these events that holds a permanent place in the world's literature. With all this behind him, he died in a strange loneliness, hunted out of every country, starved of friendship, imprisoned without being protected, robbed almost of the company of the earth.

The causes of this sad story are of course as complex as the forces he attempted to manipulate. But large among them, in my view, looms a singular defect or weakness in his own motivation. When I went to Russia in 1922 he was more popular among the masses than Lenin was. He was a military victor and a national hero. His oratorical ability, which surpassed that of all his rivals put together, seemed to guarantee this popularity. His prestige and personal power, had he known how, or wished, to use them, were invincible. And to certify this, Lenin, when he fell sick, offered to make him vice-president of the Council of People's Commissars—offered, that is, to designate Trotsky before the world as his successor, an act which would have made the rise of Stalin, whom they both despised, well-nigh impossible.

Trotsky declined the offer. He stood meekly aside while Stalin organized a political machine capable of displacing him at Lenin's death. When the expected death occurred he was en route to the Caucasus, and to the amazement of all did not come back to make the funeral oration. He let Stalin push him off with a lying telegram about the date—and complained about it long after:

"I immediately telegraphed the Kremlin: 'I deem it necessary to return to Moscow. When is the funeral?' The reply came in about an hour: 'The funeral will take place on Saturday. You will not be able to return in time . . . Stalin.' Why this hurry? Why precisely Saturday? But I did not feel that I should request postponement for my sake alone. Only in Sukhum did I learn that it had been changed to Sunday."

There had been no change. Lenin's body lay in state four days. Trotsky could have returned from twice as far. He did not want to be there. He did not want to fight for power. He sidestepped the power at every vital turn, rationalizing his conduct by appeals to etiquette or ethical punctilio. The future of the revolution was at stake, but its leader "did not feel that he should request postponement for his sake alone"!

Having evaded the power at these two crises, Trotsky adopted, while Stalin laid the groundwork for his counterrevolutionary tyranny, a "policy of silence," disheartening to his followers, bewildering to the Russian masses, astounding to the whole world. In 1925, when I crashed that silence with my book *Since Lenin Died*, exposing Stalin's conspiracy to seize the power, and quoting Lenin's deathbed warning to the party against Stalin and endorsement of Trotsky as "the ablest man in the Executive Committee," he disavowed my book. He disavowed it, although he himself had given me the key facts, and done so with the express understanding that I would publish them. He denied over his signature that there was any such thing as this document, called "Lenin's Testament," which I had quoted directly from his lips. To be sure, he disavowed his disavowal long after, exonerating me and endorsing me beyond my merits, but by that time Stalin was secure. Trotsky will go down to posterity as a great man, one of the few great men who ever wrote history as brilliantly as he made it. But he will go down as a great man who let himself be jockeyed out of his hold on history by a "mediocrity," as he himself so often called his enemy.

Of all mistaken judgments of him, the most fantastic is that he was, in his last years, eaten up with a yearning to "come back." His basic policy, since Stalin established his dictatorship, has been to advocate the overthrow of Stalin, but at the same time the defense of the Soviet Union. The workers of the world, he has insisted, while rejecting Stalin's tyranny, must defend the Russian state, if necessary with arms in their hands. After the Stalin-Hitler pact and the invasion of Finland this was almost quixotic, but Trotsky stuck to it. That made it seem plausible that he wanted to return to power—but only to those who did not realize that he had dropped the power when he had it, dodged it when it was thrust at him.

Trotsky advocated the defense of the Soviet Union, and insisted on calling Stalin's one-man rule a "workers' state," because he was an orthodox Marxian, and according to Marx only the workers can expropriate the private capitalists. If it was Stalin's bureaucracy and not the Russian proletariat that nationalized the Russian land and industries, then Trotsky's whole philosophy of life, his inward flame of faith, was wrong. That is why he stuck out loyally for the defense of Stalin's Russia as a workers' state even when it cost him the last appearances of good sense. And Stalin, of course, foiled him once more in the very hour of death—placing in the assassin's pocket a prepared statement that he had killed Trotsky because Trotsky had urged him to "sabotage the Soviet Union." Everyone has read that statement. Few will ever read the torrent of Trotsky's sixteen years of impassioned argument to the contrary.

Trotsky was not eaten up with any yearning at all. It was natural to him to be in opposition, to be fighting with a sense of righteous indignation those who ruled. That is what, in his deep self, he wanted. He would rather be right than President —yes, and more: he would rather be right and *not* President. That was his weakness. Some say that he dreaded to become a Bonaparte, and I think that that thought did dwell in his mind. But deeper and nearer the heart of this overconfident brandisher of programs was an instinctive distaste for the power to put them through.

Others, who realize that Trotsky dodged the power, imagine that he did so because his pride was hurt—he wanted power handed to him on a golden platter. In France a book was published on this subject, *La Vie orgueilleuse de Trotsky*. It is pure nonsense. Trotsky did like admiration, and liked it fairly thick. Worse than that, he did not know he liked it. He thought he was very "impersonal," "objective," as Marxists are supposed to be. In his *History of the Russian Revolution* he always speaks of himself in the third person. "The then head of the Red Army did thus and so," he says. Once he alludes to himself in the same passage as "the author of these lines" and "the then head of the Red Army," not realizing that two impersonals make an especially obtrusive personal. Genuine modesty would say simply: "I did thus and so." But Trotsky did not know that. He did not know himself. That made it possible to influence him sometimes by mixing flattery with only a fair argument. But not often—not on questions of principle. His vanity was superficial.

His consecration to the cause of socialism was deep. It was absolute. I talked about Trotsky's famous pride one day with his first sweetheart, one who loved him and conspired with him when he was eighteen, married him, and bore him two children in Siberian exile.

"Arrogance," she said, "would be a better word than pride. Leon Davidovich is self-assertive and explosive, a little difficult that way sometimes in personal life, but he is the most consecrated person I ever met. Nothing, absolutely nothing—not even a disgraceful death—would swerve him from the path of his objective duty to the revolution." I quote her because she was an exceptionally wise, warm, and judicious person, herself a devoted Communist. But I could quote to the same effect anybody who ever really knew Trotsky.

I think the main reason Trotsky sidestepped the power is a good one—namely, that he could not wield it. He could not handle men. He did not live among men. He lived among ideas. As a politician in the narrow sense, the Jim Farley sense, Trotsky was a total loss. He had no genial tastes or habits. He did not "smoke, drink, chew, swear, dance, nor play cards." He could not bring an improper word to his lips. He tried once to tell me the obscene remark made by Stalin when he first read Lenin's "Testament." It had to be conveyed in a paragraph of fastidious circumlocutions.* He hated the smell of tobacco, hated a speck of ashes on his desk. He could not put his feet up on a chair; he lacked the art. He dressed like a dude—not in bad taste, but too immaculately. And although he could laugh heartily, he had also, when embarrassed, a nervous clicking giggle in his throat, a sort of ghost laugh that made you feel he was not present in reality at all.

I once attended an anniversary smoker in the Kremlin where all the old Bolsheviks used to assemble, as the Dutch Treat Club does, to put on some fool acts and exchange a little jovial gossip jazzed up with alcohol. Somebody played *The Volga Boat Song* on all the various parts of a kitchen stove. Trotsky wandered among those old revolutionists, of whom he was then still the chief, like a lost angel, faultlessly clad as always, with a brand-new shiny manuscript case under his arm, a benign sort of Y.M.C.A. secretary's smile put on for the festivities, but not an offhand word to say to anybody. It seems a funny epithet to use about a commander in chief, but he reminded me of Little Lord Fauntleroy.

I remembered, of course, that these were for the most part veterans of a party to which he had come over only in the hour of action, a party which, even when he led them, insisted upon regarding him as an outsider. But why, when his loyalty had been so tested, and his service to the party greater than that of anyone but Lenin—why did they hold him off? Why could Trotsky never win his way in, with no matter what achievements, to the heart of the Bolshevik party? I felt that what I

---

* "On receiving and reading Lenin's Testament, Stalin said: 'The —— —— —— —— dirtied himself and dirtied us!' He did not use the word *dirtied*, but another far more 'naturalistic' word which you can find in Dal's dictionary. The dashes represent genuine-Russian abuse. The whole incident was reported to me by a person present when it happened."

saw was the reason for this strange fact, not merely its result.

To correct the impression, you have to remember that all those men knew Trotsky for the bravest of the brave. He had defied two governments, daring them to arrest him while he organized their overthrow. He had refused to go underground, as Lenin did, in the dangerous July days when tsarist generals undertook to liquidate the Bolsheviks. As head of the Red Army he had been criticized for the recklessness with which he exposed himself to rifle fire. He was not the kind of general who dies in bed. They knew, also, that at the drop of the hat he could mount the platform and raise them out of their chairs with a revolutionary speech. They respected him, but he was not one of them.

That would not have mattered fatally if he had had the gift of personal friendship. He lacked that also. Aside from his quiet, thoughtful wife, toward whom his attitude was a model of sustained gallantry and inexhaustible consideration, he had, in my opinion, no real friends. He had followers and subalterns who adored him as a god, and to whom his coldness and unreasonable impatience and irascibility were a part of the picture. And he had admiring acquaintances charmed by his brilliant conversation and those "beautiful manners" for which he was famous at the age of five. But in a close and equal relation he managed to get almost everybody "sore." One after another, strong men would be drawn to him by his deeds and brilliant conscientious thinking. One after another they would drop away.

Lacking both sympathetic imagination and self-knowledge, he seemed spiritually, in an intimate relation, almost deaf and dumb. He would talk with you all night long, very candidly and about everything under the sun, but when you went home at dawn you would feel that you had not been with him. You had received no personal glance out of those cold light-blue eyes. You had heard no laughter but of mockery. You had been exchanging ideas with a brilliant intellect, one that had heard about friendship and had it explained to him, and with consummate skill and intelligence was putting on the act. That, at least, was my experience.

People who disliked Trotsky were always calling him an actor. He was not an actor when motivated by ideas. His passion for ideas was instinctive, deep, disciplined. His loyalty to ideas was absolute. It was his whole natural self. He had no other loyalty (once more making exception of his wife—or rather, I assume, his family), and therefore in personal relations he *was* in some degree an actor. The part he played was that which a high idea of personal relations demanded of him, but since the whole feeling was not there he fell often and too easily out of the part.

He would make promises and forget them, make contracts and try to squirm out of them, conveniently failing to remember the aspect that was important to the party of the second part. When he arrived in Prinkipo and was in a way to be mulcted by American publishers and their agents, I took on the job of his literary agent as well as personal representative in this country. Much of my spare time was spent trying to get contracts amended or backed out of, contracts that he had signed without quite clearly noticing what he was giving as well as getting. It seemed to me that his idea of how a revolutionist should act would dictate a proud recklessness in signing a contract, and then the authentic impulses and real necessities of his being would demand a cancellation. At any rate, I remember that two years of work trying to help Trotsky do business as a frantic period. I would as soon have tried to straighten out the affairs of General Grant.

That "ability to deal with people," for which old John D. Rockefeller used to say he would pay more than for any other commodity, consists essentially in treating people as ends and not means. It consists in remembering that they are ends even when you are using them as means. Try as he would, Trotsky could not remember that for long. Sooner or later he would repel every associate not willing to take the position of an instrument in his hands. Of his genius for losing friends and alienating people there is a wealth of private anecdotes, and mine is too long to tell. But here is a little piece of it:

One of our amusements while I stayed with him in Prinkipo in 1932 was for him to dictate letters to me in his then horrendous English, and let me fix them up. It was entertaining, for although he had no grammar, he had a prodigious vocabulary. One day he showed me a letter from some woman in Indiana asking him please to look up her relatives in Russia. He asked me if I knew her name, and when I said, "No, it's just some half-wit," he agreed. I crumpled the letter and started to throw it in the wastebasket. He stopped me with a cry as though I were stepping on a baby's face.

"Is *that* the way you treat your correspondence! What kind of a man are you? That letter has to be filed by my secretaries!"

I straightened out the letter and passed it over to him, laughing.

"Did you keep letter files," I asked, "in the days when you were a penniless agitator in Paris and Vienna? I'm not an army commander. I'm a poor writer."

He relaxed then, and smiled: "Well, I like to keep things in order so far as I can."

The incident in itself was not in the least unpleasant. But in a day or two another question arose between us. I was leaving for a trip through the Near East, and he had just finished a long article that I was supposed to translate. I said I would do it on the train and send the translation from Jerusalem to a literary agent in New York.

He said that he would rather let the literary agent find a translator. I pointed out the scarcity of good Russian translators, and the unlikelihood that a commercial agent could find one or recognize one when found.

"Well, I don't want my articles carted around over Europe and Asia!" he said.

I answered: "Your literary agent is just as likely as not to send it to Canada or San Francisco to be translated."

Again he flared up as though ignited by a fuse.

"I don't want my articles translated by people who crumple up letters and throw them in the wastebasket!"

It was an angry shout. In view of what I had been doing for him, it was, moreover, unreasonable to the *n*th degree. To anybody but Trotsky, and perhaps Shakespeare, I would have said: "To hell with your articles!" and walked out. As it was, I recalled by good luck the criticism Lenin made of him in his "Testament." I recalled it very exactly and rolled it off in perfect Russian:

"Lyef Davidovich," I said, "I can only answer you in the words of Lenin: 'Comrade Trotsky is inclined to be carried away by the administrative aspect of things.'"

I must say that he laughed at my thrust with great good nature, and dropped into his chair and relaxed. Inside of two minutes he was proposing that we collaborate on a drama about the American Civil War.

"You have poetic imagination," he said, "and I know what civil war is as a fact."

It was a poor time to suggest collaboration—mighty poor. It shows what I mean by saying that Trotsky did not know himself or others. In relations with concrete people, he was often no less than obtuse. He had a blind spot. His life was in his head. A poorer politician never lived.

This fact has somehow to be reconciled with the existence in Trotsky's historic writings of certain abstract or retrospective understandings, both of the masses and of individual men, that are sympathetic and subtle. It is perhaps largely a matter of interested attention. When contemplating people in idea the man's full powers came into play, and he might describe their moods and characters with penetration. His *conception* was better than his *perception* of what men are and how they feel. For that reason, while both his tact and his tactics were usually bad, his large-scale strategy, political as well as military, was often superbly good.

To illustrate this, it should suffice, while Hitler's armies occupy the richest parts of Russia, to read Trotsky's advice given

to Stalin's government as far back as 1931. A year before Hitler
seized power, he wrote:

> In my opinion this is how the Soviet Government
> ought to act in case of a fascist coup in Germany. Upon
> receiving the telegraphic communication of this event I
> would, in their place, sign an order for the mobilization
> of the army reserves. When you have a mortal enemy
> before you, and when war flows with necessity from
> the logic of the objective situation, it would be unpar-
> donable lightmindedness to give that enemy time to
> establish and fortify himself, conclude the necessary
> alliances, receive the necessary help, work out a plan of
> concentric military actions and thus grow up to the di-
> mensions of a colossal danger. (*Liberty,* July 16, 1932.)

A year later Trotsky sounded the alarm again:

> Have the Stalinists perhaps assimilated the pacifist
> wisdom of the "purely defensive" war being the only
> permissible one? "Let Hitler attack us first, then we will
> defend ourselves." . . . He who leaves to the enemy a
> complete liberty of initiative is a traitor, even if the mo-
> tives for his treason are not to render service to imperi-
> alism, but consists of petty bourgeois weakness and
> political blindness. (*The Militant,* April 8, 1933.)

After Stalin concluded his pact with Hitler and boasted that
it gave security to the Soviet Union, Trotsky warned:

> In spite of the Kremlin's territorial seizures, the in-
> ternational position of the USSR is worsened in the
> extreme. The Polish buffer has disappeared. The Ruma-
> nian buffer will disappear tomorrow. Mighty Germany,
> master of Europe, has acquired a common frontier with
> the USSR. Scandinavia is occupied by this same Ger-

many. Her victories in the west are only preparation for a gigantic move toward the east. ("The Kremlin's Role in the War," June 17, 1940.)

Russia could ill afford to have a pickaxe sunk in a brain like that.

Lenin combined intellect and idealism with a mastery of the craft of politics. Trotsky inherited the intellect and idealism, Stalin the craft—a fatal split. Every move that Trotsky made when Stalin opened his attack on him was inept. At first, as I have said, he did not move at all. He stayed in bed while Stalin falsified his writings and misrepresented him without limit in the party press. Supposedly, he had one of his mysterious fevers, but he would not have had a fever if the fight had been of mass against class. Trotsky could have gone into the factories and barracks with a few forthright speeches and raised every fighting revolutionist in Moscow and Leningrad against the Stalin clique. But that would have meant war. Lenin would have waged that little war without a moment's hesitation, because Lenin sensed things in their practical terms. Trotsky was theoretical, and there was no place in his theories for any war but that between the workers and the *bourgeoisie*.

Moreover, he was squeamish; he was disgusted when he should have been enraged. His wife told me at the time, with tears flowing from her eyes, that he never read a word of the attacks that were made on him. "He couldn't stomach all that filth."

During that winter of 1924 while Trotsky gave him a free hand, Stalin changed the entire membership of the party and changed the essential policy of the press. By June, when the party held its convention, he had the delegates in the palm of his hand. Trotsky emerged then from his mysterious silence like Achilles from his tent, but not to fight for his and Lenin's trampled policies—only to make what he considered a diplomatic speech.

"The party can never make a mistake," he said.

Incredible as it may seem, that is what he said. That was his idea of being a crafty politician. He also declared his readiness to go into the trenches and fight with the humblest soldier in defense of the revolution. Somebody yelled:

"That isn't what we expected from you, Comrade Trotsky. We expected leadership!"

It was certainly the most ill-judged speech I ever listened to. I had just been talking to him about his real opinions. In fact, it was in a little nook behind the platform at that convention that he told me about Lenin's "Testament," his last letter to the party, which Stalin had withheld from them and locked up in the safe. He quoted the main phrases of it for me to use. I was leaving Russia the next day, and we said good-by.

"What are you going to do when you get home?" he asked.

"I'm not going to do anything except write books."

He smiled a deprecating smile and I added: "I believe in the class struggle, but I love peace."

"You love peace? You ought to be arrested," he said.

I agreed; and that was, it seemed, our farewell word. But right after that he got up and made this insincere, inept, inadequate—to my mind blunderingly stupid—speech. I could not refrain from going up and drawing him into our nook again and telling him what I thought he ought to do.

"In God's name," I said, or words to that effect, "why don't you peel off your coat and roll up your sleeves and sail in and clean them up? Read the 'Testament' yourself. Don't *let* Stalin lock it up. Expose the whole conspiracy. Expose it and attack it head on. It isn't your fight, it's the fight for the revolution. If you don't make it now, you'll never make it. It's your last chance."

He looked at me in some surprise. I had been on the whole a respectful biographer. He even weighed my advice seriously for a moment. Then he assumed a quizzical expression.

"I thought you said you loved peace," he said.

I knew then, as certain wise old Bolsheviks had told me, that although Trotsky's policies were right, he never could take

Lenin's place. It was always the policies, not Trotsky's leadership, that they were fighting for. That made the fighting weak.

Trotsky must have been at least dimly aware of this himself. No man could be so lonely and not know it, or at least feel it, and not have it influence his acts. I asked him once why he declined the offer of Lenin to make him acting head of the government.

"Stalin and Zinoviev and Kamenev had already ganged up on me," he said. "What could I do with a majority of the Politburo working against me?"

What could he do? Kamenev was his brother-in-law. He could ask him into the War Department for a glass of tea, to talk it over man to man. He could ask one or two others in— Bukharin, especially, who adored him. He could *use* his charm and his overpowering prestige. He could play the heart as well as the head. That was really all he had to do. But that was beyond his powers.

Trotsky sidestepped the heritage of Lenin because he was inadequate to it. Although incapable of saying so even to himself, he *felt* inadequate to it. He could command minds; he could command armies; he could sway masses from the safe distance of the platform. In the time of revolutionary storm, when all men were lifted by high hopes or billowing desperations into the realm of ideas, and their motives actually became on a large scale impersonal, Trotsky, with his trim presence, audacious will, and ironical white logic, was all that a great historic character could be. He was the very concept of a hero. But in calmer times he could not bring two strong men to his side as friends and hold them there.

That, I think, is the secret of the sad arc traced by his life story, his rise to supreme heights under another leader and in an epoch of war and insurrection, his incredibly swift decline when skill in politics and his own leadership were called for.

LENIN'S 'TESTAMENT' AND A NOTE OF BACKGROUND*

In several places in this book the reader will find references to a document of Lenin's which has come to be known as his "Testament." The description is appropriate, for the message in question was Lenin's last advice to the Communist Party. It is not here presented, however, in a sense of partisanship between Stalin and Trotsky. Contrary to some popular opinion, Lenin did not explicitly state a preference as to his political heir. The importance of the testament lies, to my mind, in the clear statement of Lenin's latter-day appraisal of Stalin, the light that this altered attitude sheds on the young dictatorial state and on the man who was soon to head it completely, and Lenin's seeming recognition one year before his death, along with other indications, of the morass into which his dedication to dictatorial means of salvation had thrown the Communist state.

First it is important for this short and significant document to be read. It follows in full:

* * *

By the stability of the Central Committee, of which I spoke before, I mean measures to prevent a split, so far as such measures can be taken. For, of course, the White Guard in *Russkaya Mysl* (I think it was S. E. Oldenburg) was right when, in the first place, in his play against Soviet Russia he banked on the hope of a split in our party, and when, in the second place, he banked for that split on serious disagreements in our party.

* By the editor.

Our party rests upon two classes, and for that reason its instability is possible, and if there cannot exist an agreement between those classes its fall is inevitable. In such an event it would be useless to take any measures in general to discuss the stability of our Central Committee. In such an event no measures would prove capable of preventing a split. But I trust that is too remote a future and too improbable an event to talk about.

I have in mind stability as a guarantee against a split in the near future, and I intend to examine here a series of considerations of a purely personal character.

I think that the fundamental factor in the matter of stability —from this point of view—is such members of the Central Committee as Stalin and Trotsky. The relation between them constitutes, in my opinion, a big half of the danger of that split, which might be avoided, and the avoidance of which might be promoted, in my opinion, by raising the number of members of the Central Committee to fifty or one hundred.

Comrade Stalin, having become General Secretary, has concentrated an enormous power in his hands; and I am not sure that he always knows how to use that power with sufficient caution. On the other hand, Comrade Trotsky, as was proved by his struggle against the Central Committee in connection with the question of the People's Commissariat of Ways and Communications, is distinguished not only by his exceptional ability—personally, he is, to be sure, the most able man in the present Central Committee—but also by his too far-reaching self-confidence and a disposition to be far too much attracted by the purely administrative side of affairs.

These two qualities of the two most able leaders of the present Central Committee might quite innocently, lead to a split, and if our party does not take measures to prevent it, a split might arise unexpectedly.

I will not further characterize the other members of the Central Committee as to their personal qualities. I will only remind you that the October episode of Zinoviev and Kamenev was not, of course, accidental, but that it ought as little to be used against them personally as the non-Bolshevism of Trotsky.

Of the younger members of the Central Committee, I want

to say a few words about Bukharin and Pyatakov. They are, in my opinion, the most able forces (among the youngest) and in regard to them it is necessary to bear in mind the following: Bukharin is not only the most valuable and biggest theoretician of the party, but also may legitimately be considered the favorite of the whole party; but his theoretical views can only with the very greatest doubt be regarded as fully Marxian, for there is something scholastic in him (he has never learned, and I think never has fully understood, the dialectic).

And then Pyatakov—a man undoubtedly distinguished in will and ability, but too much given over to administration and the administrative side of things to be relied on in a serious political question.

Of course, both these remarks are made by me merely with a view of the present time, or supposing that these two able and loyal workers may not find an occasion to supplement their one-sidedness.

December 25, 1922

Postscript: Stalin is too rude, and this fault, entirely supportable in relations among us Communists, becomes insupportable in the office of General Secretary. Therefore I propose to the comrades to find a way to remove Stalin from that position and appoint another man who in all respects differs from Stalin only in superiority—namely, more patient, more loyal, more polite, and more attentive to comrades, less capricious, etc. This circumstance may seem an insignificant trifle, but I think that from the point of view of preventing a split and from the point of view of the relation between Stalin and Trotsky which I discussed above, it is not a trifle, or it is such a trifle as may acquire a decisive significance.

Lenin

January 4, 1923

❂   ❂   ❂

The authenticity of the testament has long been established beyond question; as we shall see, its call for the removal of Stalin has been confirmed by the best possible source in this case, Joseph Stalin. The object of an attempt at suppression by

Stalin, then its very existence denied by Stalinist adherents, the document was first revealed to the non-Communist world in the *New York Times* of October 18, 1926, to which it had been sent by Max Eastman.* In 1927 the argument about its existence came to an end. Stalin himself verified its existence and contents; too many party leaders knew of the document, a new tack had to be tried. Primly, Stalin denied that there had ever been an attempt by him to suppress Lenin's last advice.

> "It is said," wrote Stalin in the *International Press Correspondence* of November 17, 1927, a Comintern publication, "that in the 'Testament' in question, Lenin suggested to the Party Congress that it should deliberate on the question of replacing Stalin and appointing another comrade in his place as General Secretary of the Party. This is perfectly true."

He also said, lamely:

> "The Opposition raised a cry—you heard it, all of you —that the Central Committee of the Party was 'keeping Lenin's "Testament" concealed.' . . . It has been proved over and over again that nobody has concealed or is concealing anything, that Lenin's 'Testament' was read to that Party Congress. That the Party Congress resolved unanimously not to publish the 'Testament,' among other reasons because Lenin himself did not wish or demand its publication. . . ."

After his disavowal of any attempt to suppress the document, Stalin made the already quoted admission that Lenin had called for his removal from his post. "This is perfectly true," said Stalin.

We shall bypass Stalin's insistence that he had not attempted to suppress the document; the fact that twenty-three years

* Later included as a supplement to *The Real Situation in Russia* (1928) by Leon Trotsky, published by Harcourt, Brace and Co.

after his verification of its existence, and twenty-seven years after its dictation by Lenin, it is still not publicly available in the Soviet Union and its existence is again denied by all Communist parties the world over is sufficient to indicate the quality of veracity in Stalin's statement. But, except for an additional insight into Stalin's character, his democratic pose is of little importance. What is important is his authentication of Lenin's last message to the party, and of still greater importance, of course, is the document itself.

The political will was written one year before Lenin's death and dictated to his secretary. Since Lenin's active political life ceased in March, 1923, and his death followed in January of the following year, the document stands as his last judgment of the leaders of the party and his suggestions for the future. The first official reading of the testament occurred before the Council of Elders, or provincial leaders, at the Thirteenth Congress of the Party of May 22, 1924. At first, knowledge of the testament was held by two persons, Lenin's wife, Krupskaya, and the stenographer who had taken it down, N. Volodicheva. Krupskaya kept the message private until all hope for Lenin's recovery had vanished. After his death she delivered it to the Secretariat of the central committee so that Lenin's wish that it be brought before the party could be followed.

The party machine at that time was under the control of three men nominally, Zinoviev, Kamenev and Stalin; in fact under the control of Stalin. From that point onwards Stalin's ascent in terms of power was to be one of uninterrupted success. The decision to keep the document from the attention of the party was made under his aegis, and over Krupskaya's protests.

In 1925 Max Eastman in *Since Lenin Died* described what happened:

> "At the next convention (May, 1924) the machine organized by Stalin and Zinoviev was already strong enough to defy the last will and testament of Lenin. The

central committee of the party, by a vote of about thirty
against ten—and against the demand of Lenin's wife—
decided not to read his last letter to the party. Thus one
of the most solemn and carefully weighed utterances
that ever came from Lenin's pen was suppressed—in the
interests of 'Leninism' by that triumvirate of 'Old Bolsheviks,'—Stalin, Zinoviev and Kamenev, who govern
the Russian Communist Party." He added these details:
"They decided that it might be read and explained privately to the delegates—kept within the bureaucracy,
that is to say—but not put before the party for discussion, as Lenin directed."

Trotsky learned of the testament when it came before the
Council of Elders. After Max Eastman printed the codicil, Trotsky, in order to conciliate his opponents, shamefully tried to
cast doubt on Eastman's publication. He did this, however, in
a manner which indicated that the testament existed.* He has
since told what methods were taken to limit the audience for
the testament:

> "The *troika* introduced through one of its henchmen,"
> he wrote in his pamphlet "The Suppressed Testament of
> Lenin" (1935), "a resolution previously agreed upon
> with the provincial leaders: the document should be
> read to each delegation separately in executive session;
> no one should dare to make notes; at the plenary session
> the testament must not be referred to. With the gentle
> insistence characteristic of her, Krupskaya argued that
> this was a direct violation of the will of Lenin, to whom
> you could not deny the right to bring his last advice
> to the attention of the party. But the members of the
> Council of Elders, bound by factional discipline, re-
> mained obdurate; the resolution of the *troika* was
> adopted by an overwhelming majority."

* Cf. *Stalin and German Communism* by Ruth Fischer (1948), page 241, a
book considerably wider than its title.

One of Lenin's hopes was that his message might alleviate the conflict for power in the party; it served to intensify it. Karl Radek, then a member of the central committee, sat besides Trotsky during the reading. He told Trotsky: "Now, they won't dare go against you." Trotsky states that he replied, and it was a most informed answer: "On the contrary, they will have to go to the limit and moreover as quickly as possible." But, actually, Stalin was already in full command of the situation. As Trotsky sadly concedes: "The machine was already in complete control."

Trotsky calls a still later letter, dictated by Lenin on March 5, 1923, Lenin's very last surviving document; in it Lenin severed "all personal and comradely relations with Stalin."

In 1926, a year after his break with Stalin, Zinoviev said: "At the beginning of the year 1923, Vladimir Ilyich, in a personal letter to Comrade Stalin, broke off all comradely relations with him."

In 1927 Stalin printed his article in *International Press Correspondence,* stating that it was "perfectly true" that Lenin had called for his removal; in 1929 he quoted the testament in his fight against Bukharin. In 1950 the Communist parties of the world again deny the existence of the testament.

Some who are desirous of dissociating Lenin from Stalin seem content to let the matter rest with the above facts. The conclusion then seems clear: Stalin, the usurper, was recognized for what he was by Lenin who attempted to bring about his downfall but was prevented from doing so by his illness. This presents the matter too simply. If these were all the relevant facts, it would nevertheless stand only as a partial "clearance" of Lenin; politically, he would still have paved the way for Stalin, or another of like character, by his fanatic insistence on dictatorial rule. A closer background examination, however, brings one to quite a different conclusion.

No man was more devoted to the historical separation of Leninism and Stalinism than was Leon Trotsky. The first he

revered and the second he detested. And yet in his biography
of Stalin, he makes the following interesting, and significant,
disclosures.

> "I soon noticed that Lenin was 'advancing' Stalin,
> valuing in him his firmness, grit, stubbornness, and to a
> certain degree his slyness, as attributes necessary in the
> struggle."

And again:

> "I remember during the Civil War asking a member
> of the Central Committee, Serebryakov, who at that
> time was working with Stalin in the Revolutionary
> Council of War of the Southern Front, whether he could
> not manage without Stalin for the sake of economizing
> forces? Serebryakov replied: 'No, I cannot exert pres-
> sure like Stalin. It is not my speciality.'" Comments
> Trotsky: "The ability to 'exert pressure' was what Lenin
> prized so highly in Stalin."

Trotsky's dilemma is clear: how, in the face of the above, and
other like data, to break the link between Lenin and Stalin? He
stresses emphatically that Lenin found Stalin devoid of finer
qualities. "He did not expect of him any independent ideas,
political initiative or creative imagination." But that is to miss
the entire point! The major significance of Lenin's admiration
for Stalin's ability to "exert pressure" (here Trotsky is being
much too vague in the description of Stalin's methods, and
for obvious reasons) is that, whether Lenin personally felt inclined towards Stalin or not, his regime called for the services
of men of Stalin's brutal makeup to do the regime's brutal work.
Boris Souvarine in his *Stalin* makes the point cogently:

"There is no ground for Trotsky's hypothesis that
Lenin, who had only just met Stalin from time to time
before he returned to Russia, formed an unfavorable
opinion of him after seeing him actually at work. That
appears to be an anachronism. Lenin respected Stalin
not for his brain but for his fist. It was several years before he changed his opinion of the 'wonderful Geor-
gian.'"

Both Trotsky and Stalin were tutored in the service of Lenin;
neither believed in democracy for non-Communists, for the
mass of the country. Democracy, in the code of the Bolsheviks,
was at best democracy for the party. Stalin continued his notable activities which Lenin had valued so highly and in time
extended the repressive means that he, and the more important
Communist leaders, had utilized against all "enemies" of the
Bolsheviks. But this time many of the Bolsheviks were suddenly
stricken with morality, for *they* were falling as Stalin's next victims, a natural enough—if horrible—development, one they
might have anticipated from their study of previous tyrannies.
It is therefore of importance to note Lenin's latter-day concern,
such as it was, with the direction of his State; it helps to characterize with the aid of a most authoritative source the nature
of young Soviet Russia circa 1923. But the greater lesson was,
so far as we know, not to make itself clear to Lenin during
his lifetime; for that knowledge would have meant repudiating
himself and what he had taught and implemented. For the lesson was not that half a dozen years after the Communist coup
d'état the same Communist revolution had degenerated. The
moral was the same as it had been at the start, as seen by
democratic opponents whom Lenin had ruthlessly labelled
"counter-revolutionary" and had so ruthlessly suppressed: that
dictatorship and terror, however bolstered by idealistic slogans, is productive only of greater dictatorship and terror, and,

soon enough, of internal dictatorship and terror of the most complete kind among the clique of dictators themselves. That, for those who needed to learn it, and there were and are many, is the most obvious overall lesson of the Communist Revolution.

Joseph Stalin

W H A T   I   B E L I E V E

"We Communists are people of a special mould. We are made of special material. We are those who comprise the army of the great proletarian strategist, the army of Lenin. There is nothing higher than the honor of belonging to this army." Joseph Stalin.

Editor's Note

IN THE preface to Boris Souvarine's selection we had occasion to comment on those who formulate the "betrayal of Leninism" indictment against Stalin, in preference to the actual charge of betrayal of the Russian people which Stalin shares with Lenin. In choosing thus to obscure the Leninist roots of Stalinism, these persons have performed the additional disservice of drawing attention away from Stalin's writings, especially on the subject of Lenin and Leninism. It is the partial purpose of this selection to make redress for that situation. Stalin, wrote Trotsky, with what must have been self-satisfaction, "is neither a thinker, a writer nor an orator." Trotsky, on the other hand, possessed all these many talents. There is no need to labor the point; political acuteness need hardly be synonymous with intellectual stature. The image of Stalin as a non-entity (or "mediocrity," to use Trotsky's word) is consoling. But absurd underestimation of our adversary is also masochistic.*

Stalin's very defects make his rather dull writings all the

---

* Cf. James Burnham's "Lenin's Heir," *Partisan Review,* Winter 1945.

more valuable to us. They possess a blunt quality which is not capable of misconstruction. More, his very lack of theoretical ingenuity (the leaning on Lenin, which his literary critics so deplore) reveal to us plainly, even nakedly, the sources of his inspiration, the credo that he has followed and expanded in practice.

There are differences, to be sure, between the master and the faithful pupil turned master. Lenin, as often said, was relatively free of "vanity." He permitted himself the full exercise of his dictatorial powers, but he did not attempt to draw personal rewards from his actions. His concentration on suppression, compulsion, dictatorship, hatred for democratic forms, amounted in practice to monomania, whatever the belated theoretical justifications, and it is of little consolation to grant, in the interests of "fairness," that he was honestly convinced that ultimate good would come from such policies. There is no reason for doubting his "sincerity," the selflessness of his devotion to his cause. The point is that one does not reasonably implement private prophetic hopes at the cost of other people's lives. Lenin lived moderately, however, denying himself great luxury. He shunned titles (although he retained power, and despotic power), physical works in his honor, and ostentatious tribute. Stalin, his successor, suffers from no such asceticism. As is apparent to anyone who observes the products of Soviet cultural life, the entire creative output of those who must grovel before the dictatorship, the glorification of Stalin is a prime task, a full time task. His picture—as did Hitler's in Germany—seemingly covers all the walls of the Soviet Union. Poets, musicians, artists, craftsmen seek redemption and advancement by dedicating and building works about Stalin. No artist, however famed, is absolved from this highest of tasks. Dmitri Shostakovich, for example, produced a new oratorio in December, 1949, after a crackdown on composers and others by the cultural bosses. The success of the new work lay in its theme: a glorification of

Stalin's reforestation plan. A specimen verse (by Evgeny Dol-matovsky, poet):

> We are ordinary Soviet people,
> Communism is our glory and honor.
> If Stalin said it will be,
> We will answer, Leader, it is!

This abject, and dictated, glorification of the dictator has produced a disheartening body of literature which is unrivaled in the entire world, if not in all history. In *Russia Twenty Years After*, Victor Serge has collected some prize examples, including what surely must be the ultimate encomium: the seeming attribution to Stalin of the creation of the world. It is by a Uzbek poet, and did not appear in *College Humor* in jest but in *Pravda* on August 28, 1936, in utter seriousness:

> O great Stalin, O leader of the peoples,
> Thou who broughtest man to birth,
> Thou who fructifiest the earth,
> Thou who restoreth the centuries,
> Thou who makest bloom the spring,
> Thou who makest vibrate the musical cords
>
> .   .   .   .
>
> Thou, splendor of my spring, O Thou
> Sun reflected by millions of hearts*

After reproducing examples of other such artistic accomplishments, Serge comments:

* "Your congratulations and greetings I credit to the great party of the working class that created me and raised me in its own image," said Stalin, on the occasion of his fiftieth birthday. (Quoted by Harrison Salisbury in his Moscow dispatch of December 3, 1949, to the *New York Times,* as preparations were in full swing for the celebration of the seventieth birthday of the Soviet Being "who broughtest man to birth.")

"The reader will excuse these tedious quotations if he only remembers that a people of 170,000,000 has had no other spiritual nourishment for many years; that this people finds these texts again and again, every day, in every periodical; that they are shown in large letters in the cinemas, the theatres, the hospitals, the prisons, the stores, the clubs, the schools, the barracks, the streets. It would be wrong to conclude, as do certain travelers who are, in reality, not very conscientious, that this shows a widespread mysticism among the masses. Messages of this sort are written by the local secretaries of the party on the precise instructions of the propaganda section of the Central Committee. They are manufactured, the audience raises its hand (woe to him who would shrug his shoulders!), and everybody goes home, happy at not having to think about it any more."

A pregnant clue to the personal disparity between Lenin and Stalin is to be found in the latter's remarkable reminiscence of his first meeting with Lenin:

"I first met Lenin in December 1905 at the Bolshevik conference in Tammerfors (Finland). I was hoping to see the mountain eagle of our Party, the great man, great not only politically, but if you will, physically, because in my imagination I pictured Lenin as a giant, stately and imposing. What, then, was my disappointment to see a most ordinary-looking man, below average height, in no way, literally in no way, distinguished from ordinary mortals. It is accepted as the usual thing for a 'great man' to come late to meetings so that the assembly may await his appearance with bated breath; and then, just before the great man enters, the warning whisper goes up: 'Hush! . . . Silence! . . . He's coming.' This rite did not seem to me superfluous, because it creates an impression, inspires respect. What, then, was my disappointment to learn that Lenin had arrived at the conference before the delegates, had settled himself somewhere in a corner, and was unassumingly carrying on a conversation, a most ordinary conversation with the most ordinary delegates at the conference. I will not conceal from you that at that time this seemed to me to be rather a violation of certain essential rules." (*Stalin on Lenin*, Moscow: 1946.)

It would be impossible in the short space of a single selection to represent in any comprehensive way the huge shadow that the career of Stalin has thrown on the earth. An entire library, and a vast one, exists and it is to be hoped that the reader will start with Boris Souvarine's biography of the dictator. In a tragic sense, the enormous toll of lives and liberty indicated in this book forms the substance of a kind of political biography of Stalin—for after the death of Lenin, until the present, his personal presence has been manifest in all important decisions taken by the Soviet state; he is inextricably involved, of course, in what the Soviet Union is today. It is therefore most pertinent to our task to have Stalin speak for himself.

What shall we have him speak about? To all of the similarities between Soviet Communism and Nazism must be added the characteristic advance notice of intentions, announcements which in both instances have been tragically neglected by the democratic West. In the case of Soviet Communism the pronouncements are of even greater value than were the improvisations of Hitler, for Leninism-Stalinism, whatever else they may represent, are not megalomaniac ravings. They are a body of assumptions, deductions and conclusions of a closed system of thought, of the "principles" and aspirations which have formed the underlying basis for three decades of Soviet practice. We do ourselves no service when we derogate the efficacy of the doctrines of our adversaries. If we cannot hope to find humanistic enlightenment, as we cannot, in the writings of the leaders of the Soviet state, we nevertheless would do well to familiarize ourselves with their teachings. It is in a sense ludicrous that today, when much of the blueprint has already been fulfilled, it is still necessary to need to direct anyone's attention to the ideological blueprint itself.

Save for calculated vagaries of conciliatory and temporary turns of the party line, Stalin has repeated his basic conclusions again and again—and chameleon-like Soviet policy itself has been the means by which these unvarying principles have been implemented. Appeasement of Stalin's regime—a fearful trust based on the hope that he does not believe what he has so plainly stated—has merely allowed him to transform doctrine into actuality. It is pathetic to believe that empirical knowledge of continuing expansionist success—based in significant part on the fanatic tenacity with which those tenets are held—should deter him when his regime is quite possibly on the threshold of total triumph.

Communism has existed psychologically and politically on two levels, covert and manifest, and Stalin's writings demonstrate these mechanisms consummately. They convey the orthodoxies of the system to Communist readers throughout the world rather plainly; simultaneously, they are embedded with disavowals of what is clearly said. A technique that repudiates what is said at the time that these things are said may seem to result in nothing being said. The Stalinists, at times, are content for this to be thought: but it does not explain why such writings should be so strenuously composed and so widely distributed. After describing, for example, the dictatorial processes of administration and control by means of which all units of life in the USSR are dominated by the Communist Party, Stalin is not above affirming, rhetorically, that the opposite is true. Thus, the Communist adherent is brought close to the facts, and is yet able to bring forth democratic sounding *slogans* when the non-Communist finds his way to Stalin's texts and is somewhat alarmed. Another example: in the present selection Stalin informs us helpfully, "In the Soviet Union only one party can exist, the Communist Party." Nevertheless, he concludes that the Soviet Constitution is the most democratic in the world. Put that bluntly, it calls for no great perception to understand the fraud that is being practiced, words standing for things, ashes called ice cream because the latter, in a certain context, produces a more joyful response.

"When *I* use a word," Humpty Dumpty said, in rather a scornful tone, "it means just what I choose it to mean—neither more nor less."

"The question is," said Alice, "whether you *can* make words mean so many different things."

"The question is," said Humpty Dumpty, "which is to be master—that's all."

The method is not diabolically clever as some anti-Communists who have pridefully learned to follow it maintain. It is quite simple, crude in fact, and it is to be doubted whether it would be as efficient if it were more involved, but it is efficient. Examine the arguments that are raised when Stalin's writings are cited at all—that is, when he is quoted by an anti-Communist writer. The most familiar complaint is that he is being quoted out of context. But any method short of verbatim reproduction of the many hundreds of pages of the speeches, reports, interviews, correspondence, which compose his writings is quotation out of context. Nevertheless the charge is met frequently with approving recognition. After all, we do live in a world in which many things are quoted misleadingly. That the Communists themselves quote Stalin (and Lenin) in precisely the same manner—often the same sentences—when the party line decrees, is helpfully forgotten. So we go on to the next point. We write that Stalin at such and such a time said that there can be only one party in the Soviet Union; we therefore accept this as an admission that the Soviet Union is not a democracy. The rebuttal is that we are misquoting again. "In the very next sentence"—the argument may run, it always sounds devastating —"Stalin says that the Soviet Union is the most democratic nation in the world. Why did you not quote that?" The answer quite simply is that an independent fact, one which corresponds to real circumstances, is not eradicated by a rhetorical flourish. Stalin's protestation may be quoted; it is not without interest as an expression of typical Soviet cynicism. But it has literally nothing to do with his admission. If the Communist desires to interpret democracy as a system without rival parties, without freedom of expression, without free newspapers, and so on, he has a right to do so. But a legitimate argument on his part then must sound like this: the Soviet Union is the most democratic in the world, meaning democracy to be that system which has least opportunity for free expression, rival viewpoints, etc. But the Communists do not argue in this manner, of course, and it is hardly an oversight.

Stalin's international views were most clearly expressed in the period when they were farthest from realization. They have been reiterated since many times with varying degrees of candor. His action which has stemmed from these "principles" has been depressingly clear.

As our former Ambassador to the Soviet Union, Walter Bedell Smith has said in *My Three Years in Moscow* (1950):

> "When comparisons are made between what Stalin has said to foreigners and what he has said to his own people in the basic literature of the Communist Party, in which their program is clearly spelled out, it is impossible to avoid the conclusion that the Generalissimo is capable of contradicting himself and even, on occasion, of deliberately deceiving his auditor."

We shall therefore do the Soviet dictator the disservice of focusing on one of his writings which is least known. This should, perhaps, be amended; least known, that is, to the publics of the Western nations. To Stalinists throughout the world it is mandatory reading. His *Foundations of Leninism* was originally delivered as a series of lectures at Sverdlov University, Moscow, in April, 1924. We shall therefore be reminded by some, oblivious to all of Soviet history, that many years have passed since then. But that shall not explain to us why *Foundations of Leninism* is sold in every Communist bookstore, is a "bible" in every Communist study course, *today!* Nor shall it explain why it has been printed in edition after edition, translated into almost every language of the world, sold in the millions of copies since its appearance, why it has never been allowed to go out of print, nor why it is always available in inexpensive, attractive formats. (*Mein Kampf* incidentally was first published in 1925; needless to say it did not become "obsolete" until the day of Hitler's defeat.) No, we may charge Stalin with many crimes but we cannot with justice say that he has wholly concealed his plans from us.

Our intention here can be no more than to provide the reader with a taste of Stalin's reasoning, argumentation, statement of aims and general manner of approach to problems. The extended extracts from *Foundations of Leninism* which follow are briefly supplemented by various shorter statements made at different times. It is to be hoped that this selection will induce the reader to a fuller examination of Stalin's works—there is no substitute for this quite dreary task. The editions we have drawn on for the purposes of reproduction in this selection, except as otherwise noted at the point of insertion, are two collections of Stalin's writings in the official Soviet English translations. They are: *Leninism* I and II (Moscow, 1933-34) and *Problems of Leninism* (Moscow, 1945), the latter title being the name of an important short work by Stalin as well as the title for the combined selected works. *Foundations of Leninism* is easily available in the United States as Volume 18 of the "Little Lenin Library," printed and distributed by International Publishers. *Problems of Leninism*, a companion work, is Volume 19 of the same low-priced series.

What I Believe by Joseph Stalin

From *Foundations of Leninism*

WHAT is Leninism: Some say that Leninism is the application of Marxism to the peculiar conditions of the situation in Russia. This definition contains a particle of truth, but not the whole truth by any means. Lenin, indeed, applied Marxism to Russian conditions, and applied it in a masterly way. But if Leninism were only the application of Marxism to the peculiar situation in Russia it would be a purely national and only a national, a purely Russian and only a Russian phenomenon. We know, however, that Leninism is not merely a Russian, but an international phenomenon rooted in the whole of international development. . . .

What, then, in the last analysis, is Leninism?

Leninism is Marxism of the era of imperialism and of the proletarian revolution. To be more exact, Leninism is the theory and tactics of the proletarian revolution in general, the theory and tactics of the dictatorship of the proletariat in particular. Marx and Engels pursued their activities in the pre-revolutionary period (we have the proletarian revolution in mind), when developed imperialism did not yet exist, in the period of the proletarians' preparation for a revolution, in the period when the proletarian revolution was not yet an immediate, practical inevitability. Lenin, however, the disciple of Marx and Engels, pursued his activities in the period of developed imperialism, in the period of the unfolding proletarian revolution, when the proletarian revolution had already triumphed in one country, had smashed bourgeois democracy and had ushered in the era of proletarian democracy, the era of the Soviets.

THE PROLETARIAN REVOLUTION:* Formerly it was the accepted thing to speak of the existence or absence of objective conditions for the proletarian revolution in individual countries, or, to be more precise, in one or another developed country. Now this point of view is no longer adequate. Now we must speak of the existence of objective conditions for the revolution in the entire system of world imperialist economy as an integral unit; the existence within this system of some countries that are not sufficiently developed industrially cannot serve as an insurmountable obstacle to the revolution, *if* the system as a whole, or, more correctly, *because* the system as a whole is already ripe for revolution.

Formerly it was the accepted thing to speak of the proletarian revolution in one or another developed country as of something separate and self-sufficient, facing a separate national front of capital as its opposite. Now, this point of view is no longer adequate. Now we must speak of the world proletarian revolution; for the separate national fronts of capital have become links in a single chain called the world front of imperialism, which must be opposed by a common front of the revolutionary movement in all countries.

PROSPECTS FOR THE REVOLUTION: Where will the revolution begin? Where, in what country, can the front of capital be pierced first? Where industry is more developed, where the proletariat constitutes the majority, where there is more culture, where there is more democracy—that was the reply usually given formerly.

No, objects the Leninist theory of revolution; *not necessarily where industry is more developed,* and so forth. The front of capital will be pierced where the chain of imperialism is weakest, for the proletarian revolution is the result of the breaking of the chain of the world imperialist front at its weakest link; and it may turn out that the country which has started the revolution, which has made a breach in the front of capital,

* [Subtitles added.—*Ed.*]

is less developed in a capitalist sense than other, more developed, countries, which have, however, remained within the framework of capitalism. . . .

Where will the chain break in the near future? Again, where it is weakest. It is not precluded that the chain may break, say, in India. . . .

It is also quite possible that the chain will break in Germany. . . .

THE COMPLETE VICTORY OF SOCIALISM: But the overthrow of the power of the bourgeoisie and establishment of the power of the proletariat in one country does not yet mean that the complete victory of Socialism has been ensured. After consolidating its power and taking the peasantry in tow, the proletariat of the victorious country can and must build up a Socialist society. But does this mean that it will thereby achieve the complete and final victory of Socialism, *i.e.*, does it mean that with the forces of only one country it can finally consolidate socialism and fully guarantee that country against intervention and, consequently, also against restoration? No, it does not. For this the victory of the revolution in at least several countries is needed. Therefore the development and support of revolution in other countries is an essential task of the victorious revolution. Therefore, the revolution in the victorious country must regard itself not as a self-sufficient entity but as an aid, as a means of hastening the victory of the proletariat in other countries.

Lenin expressed this thought in a nutshell when he said that the task of the victorious revolution is to do "the utmost possible in one country *for* the development, support and awakening of the revolution *in all countries*." (Lenin, *Selected Works*, Vol. VII, p. 182.)

THE DICTATORSHIP OF THE PROLETARIAT: The question of the proletarian dictatorship is above all a question of the main content of the proletarian revolution. The proletarian revolution, its movement, its scope and its achievements acquire flesh and blood only through the dictatorship of the proletariat. The dictatorship of the proletariat is the instrument of the proletarian revolution, its organ, its most important mainstay, brought into being for the purpose of, firstly, crushing the resistance of the overthrown exploiters and consolidating the achievements of the proletarian revolution, and, secondly, carrying the proletarian revolution to its completion, carrying the revolution to the complete victory of Socialism. The revolution can vanquish the bourgeoisie, can overthrow its power, without the dictatorship of the proletariat. But the revolution will be unable to crush the resistance of the bourgeoisie, to maintain its victory, and to push forward to the final victory of Socialism unless, at a certain stage in its development, it creates a special organ in the form of the dictatorship of the proletariat as its principal mainstay. . . .

The dictatorship of the proletariat arises not on the basis of the bourgeois order, but in the process of the breaking up of this order after the overthrow of the bourgeoisie, in the process of the expropriation of the landlords and capitalists, in the process of the socialization of the principal instruments and means of production, in the process of violent proletarian revolution. The dictatorship of the proletariat is a revolutionary power based on the use of force against the bourgeoisie.

The state is a machine in the hands of the ruling class for suppressing the resistance of its class enemies. *In this respect* the dictatorship of the proletariat does not differ essentially from the dictatorship of any other class, for the proletarian state is a machine for the suppression of the bourgeoisie. But there is one *substantial* difference. This difference consists in the fact that all hitherto existing class states have been dictatorships of an exploiting minority over the exploited majority, whereas the dictatorship of the proletariat is the dictatorship of the exploited majority over the exploiting minority.

ON DEMOCRACY: The theory of "pure" democracy is the theory of the upper stratum of the working class, which has been broken in and is being fed by the imperialist robbers. It was brought into being for the purpose of concealing the ulcers of capitalism, of touching up imperialism and lending it moral strength in the struggle against the exploited masses. Under capitalism there are no real "liberties" for the exploited, nor can there be, if for no other reason than that the premises, printing plants, paper supplies, etc., indispensable for the actual enjoyment of "liberties" are the privilege of the exploiters. Under capitalism the exploited masses do not, nor can they, really participate in the administration of the country, if for no other reason than that, even under the most democratic regime, governments, under the conditions of capitalism, are not set up by the people but by the Rothschilds and Stinneses, the Rockefellers and Morgans. Democracy under capitalism is *capitalist* democracy, the democracy of the exploiting minority, based on the restriction of the rights of the exploited majority and directed against this majority.

THE FALLACY OF PEACEFUL DEVELOPMENT: The dictatorship of the proletariat cannot arise as the result of the peaceful development of bourgeois society and of bourgeois democracy; it can arise only as the result of the smashing of the bourgeois state machine, the bourgeois army, the bourgeois bureaucratic machine, the bourgeois police.

In a preface to *The Communist Manifesto* Marx and Engels wrote:

> "The working class cannot simply lay hold of the ready-made state machine and wield it for its own purposes."

In a letter to Kugelmann (1871) Marx wrote that the task of the proletarian revolution is "no longer as before, to transfer the bureaucratic military machine from one hand to another, but to *smash* it, and that is a preliminary condition for every real people's revolution on the Continent."

Marx's qualifying phrase about the Continent gave the opportunists and Mensheviks of all countries a pretext for proclaiming that Marx had thus conceded the possibility of the peaceful evolution of bourgeois democracy into a proletarian democracy, at least in certain countries outside the European continent (England, America). Marx did in fact concede that possibility, and he had good grounds for conceding it in regard to England and America in the seventies of the last century, when monopoly capitalism and imperialism did not yet exist, and when these countries, owing to the special conditions of their development, had as yet no developed militarism and bureaucracy. That was the situation before the appearance of developed imperialism. But later, after a lapse of thirty or forty years, when the situation in these countries had radically changed, when imperialism had developed and had embraced all capitalist countries without exception, when militarism and bureaucracy had appeared in England and America also, *when the special conditions for peaceful development in England and the United States had disappeared* [My italics—Ed.]—then the qualification in regard to these countries necessarily could no longer hold good.

"Today," said Lenin, "in 1917, in the epoch of the first great imperialist war, this qualification made by Marx is no longer valid. Both England and America, the greatest and the last representatives—in the whole world—of Anglo-Saxon 'liberty,' in the sense that militarism and bureaucracy were absent, have today plunged headlong into the all-European, filthy, bloody morass of bureaucratic-military institutions to which everything is subordinated and which trample everything under-foot. Today, in England and in America, too, the preliminary condition for 'every real people's revolution' is the *smashing*, the *destruction* of the 'ready-made state machine' (brought in those countries, between 1914 and 1917, to general 'European' imperialist perfection)." (Lenin, *Selected Works*, Vol. VII, p. 37.)

In other words, the law of violent proletarian revolution, the law of the smashing of the bourgeois state machine as a preliminary condition for such a revolution, is an inevitable law of the revolutionary movement in the imperialist countries of the world.

REFORM AND REVOLUTION: What is the difference between revolutionary tactics and reformist tactics?

Some think that Leninism is opposed to reforms, opposed to compromises and to agreements in general. This is absolutely wrong. Bolsheviks know as well as anybody else that in a certain sense "every little helps," that under certain conditions reforms in general, and compromises and agreements in particular, are necessary and useful.

"To carry on a war for the overthrow of the international bourgeoisie," says Lenin, "a war which is a hundred times more difficult, protracted and complicated than the most stubborn of ordinary wars between states, and to refuse beforehand to manoeuvre, to utilize the conflict of interests (even though temporary) among one's enemies, to refuse to temporize and compromise with possible (even though temporary, unstable, vacillating and conditional) allies—is not this ridiculous in the extreme? Is it not as though, when making a difficult ascent of an unexplored and heretofore inaccessible mountain we were to refuse beforehand ever to move in zigzags, ever to retrace our steps, ever to abandon the course once selected and to try others?" (Lenin, *Selected Works,* Vol. X, p. 111.)

Obviously, therefore, it is not a matter of reforms or of compromises and agreements, but of the use people make of reforms and compromises.

To a reformist, reforms are everything, while revolutionary work is something incidental, something just to talk about, mere eyewash. That is why, with reformist tactics under the bourgeois regime, reforms are inevitably transformed into an instrument for strengthening that regime, an instrument for disintegrating the revolution.

To a revolutionary, on the contrary, the main thing is revolutionary work and not reforms; to him reforms are the by-products of the revolution. That is why, with revolutionary tactics under the bourgeois regime, reforms are naturally transformed into instruments for disintegrating this regime, into instruments for strengthening the revolution, into a base for the further development of the revolutionary movement.

The revolutionary will accept a reform in order to use it as an aid in combining legal work with illegal work, to intensify, under its cover, the illegal work for the revolutionary preparation of the masses for the overthrow of the bourgeoisie.

THE COMMUNIST PARTY: . . . The Party must be armed with revolutionary theory, with a knowledge of the laws of the movement, with a knowledge of the laws of revolution. Without this it will be incapable of directing the struggle of the proletariat, of leading the proletariat. The Party cannot be a real party *if it limits itself to registering what the masses of the working class feel and think* [My italics—Ed.], if it drags at the tail of the spontaneous movement, if it is unable to overcome the inertness and the political indifference of the spontaneous movement, if it is unable to rise above the momentary interests of the proletariat, if it is unable to elevate the masses to the level of the class interests of the proletariat. The Party must stand at the head of the working class; it must see farther than the working class; it must lead the proletariat, and not follow in the tail of the spontaneous movement. . . .

I have spoken of the difficulties of the struggle of the working class, of the complicated conditions of the struggle, of strategy and tactics, of reserves and manoeuvring, of attack and retreat. These conditions are no less complicated, if not more so, than the conditions of war. Who can find his bearings in these conditions, who can give correct guidance to the proletarian millions? No army at war can dispense with an experienced General Staff if it does not want to court certain defeat. Is it not clear that the proletariat can still less dispense with such a General Staff if it does not want to give itself up to be devoured by its mortal enemies? But where is this General Staff? Only the revolutionary party of the proletariat can serve as this General Staff. The working class without a revolutionary party is an army without a General Staff. The Party is the General Staff of the proletariat. . . .

The Party is the highest form of organization of the proletariat . . . it is at the same time an *instrument* in the hands of the proletariat *for* achieving the dictatorship where that has not yet been achieved and *for* consolidating and expanding the dictatorship where it has already been achieved. . . . But the proletariat needs the Party not only to achieve the dictatorship; it needs it still more to maintain the dictatorship, to consolidate it and expand it in order to achieve the complete victory of Socialism. . . .

The proletariat needs the Party for the purpose of achieving and maintaining the dictatorship. The Party is an instrument of the dictatorship of the proletariat.

IRON DISCIPLINE AND FACTIONALISM: Iron discipline does not preclude but presupposes conscious and voluntary submission, for only conscious discipline can be truly iron discipline. But after a contest of opinion has been closed, after criticism has been exhausted and a decision has been arrived at, unity of will and unity of action of all Party members are the necessary conditions without which neither Party unity nor iron discipline in the Party is conceivable.

> "In the present epoch of acute civil war," says Lenin, "a Communist Party will be able to perform its duty only if it is organized in the most centralized manner, only if iron discipline bordering on military discipline prevails in it, and if its Party centre is a powerful and authoritative organ, wielding wide powers and enjoying the universal confidence of the members of the Party." (Lenin, *Selected Works*, Vol. X, p. 204.)

This is the position in regard to discipline in the Party in the period of struggle preceding the achievement of the dictatorship.

The same, but to an even greater degree, must be said about discipline in the Party after the dictatorship has been achieved. [My italics—Ed.]

> "Whoever," says Lenin, "weakens ever so little the iron discipline of the Party of the proletariat (especially during the time of its dictatorship) actually aids the bourgeoisie against the proletariat." (Lenin, *Selected Works*, Vol. X, p. 84.)

But from this it follows that the existence of factions is incompatible with the Party's unity or with its iron discipline. It need hardly be proved that the existence of factions leads to the existence of a number of centres, and the existence of a number of centres connotes the absence of one common centre in the Party, the breaking up of the unity of will, the weakening and disintegration of discipline, the weakening and disintegration of the dictatorship. Of course, the parties of the Second International, which are fighting against the dictatorship of the proletariat and have no desire to lead the proletarians to power, can afford such liberalism as freedom of factions, for they have no need at all for iron discipline. But the parties of the Communist International, which base their activities on the task of achieving and consolidating the dictatorship of the proletariat, cannot afford to be "liberal" or to permit freedom of factions. The Party represents unity of will, which precludes all factionalism and division of authority in the Party.

Hence Lenin's warning about the "danger of factionalism from the point of view of Party unity and of effecting the unity of will of the vanguard of the proletariat as the fundamental condition for the success of the dictatorship of the proletariat," which is embodied in the special resolution of the Tenth Congress of our Party "On Party Unity."

Hence Lenin's demand for the "complete elimination of all factionalism" and the "immediate dissolution of all groups, without exception, that had been formed on the basis of various platforms," on pain of "unconditional and immediate expulsion from the Party." (*Ibid.*)

*   *   *

From *The Road to October*
December 17, 1924

THE WORLD REVOLUTION: Most probably, the world revolution will develop along the line of a number of new countries breaking away from the system of the imperialist countries as a result of revolution, while the proletarians of these countries will be supported by the proletariat of the imperialist states. We see that the first country to break away, the first victorious country, is already being supported by the workers and the labouring masses in general of other countries. Without this support it could not hold out. Undoubtedly, this support will increase and grow. But there can also be no doubt that the very development of the world revolution, the very process of the breaking away from imperialism of a number of new countries will be more rapid and more thorough, the more thoroughly Socialism fortifies itself in the first victorious country, the faster this country is transformed into a base for the further unfolding of the world revolution, into a lever for the further disintegration of imperialism.

While it is true that the *final* victory of Socialism in the first country to emancipate itself is impossible without the combined efforts of the proletarians of several countries, it is equally true that the development of the world revolution will be the more rapid and thorough, the more effective the assistance rendered by the first Socialist country to the workers and labouring masses of all other countries.

In what should this assistance be expressed?

It should be expressed, first, in the victorious country achieving the "utmost possible in one country *for* the development, support and awakening of the revolution *in all countries.* (Lenin, *Selected Works,* Vol. VII, p. 182.)

Second, it should be expressed in that the "victorious proletariat" of one country, "having expropriated the capitalists and organized its own Socialist production, would stand up *against* the rest of the world, the capitalist world, attracting to its cause the oppressed classes of other countries, raising revolts in those countries against the capitalists, and in the event of necessity coming out even with armed force against the exploiting classes and their states." (Lenin, *Selected Works,* Vol. V, p. 141.)

The characteristic feature of the assistance given by the victorious country is not only that it hastens the victory of the proletarians of other countries, but also that, by facilitating this victory, it ensures the *final* victory of Socialism in the first victorious country.

Most probably, in the course of development of the world revolution, side by side with the centres of imperialism in individual capitalist countries and the system of these countries throughout the world, centres of Socialism will be created in individual Soviet countries and a system of these centres throughout the world, and the struggle between these two systems will fill the history of the development of the world revolution.

"For," says Lenin, "the free union of nations in Socialism is impossible without a more or less prolonged and
stubborn struggle by the Socialist republics against the
backward states." (*Ibid.*)

The world significance of the October Revolution lies not
only in that it constitutes a great start made by one country in
causing a breach in the system of imperialism and that it is the
first centre of Socialism in the ocean of imperialist countries,
but also in that it constitutes the first stage of the world revolution and a mighty base for its further development.

Therefore, not only those are wrong who forget the international character of the October Revolution and declare the victory of Socialism in one country to be purely national, and only
a national, phenomenon, but also those, who, although they
bear in mind the international character of the October Revolution, are inclined to regard this revolution as something passive, merely destined to accept help from without. Actually, not
only does the October Revolution need support from the revolution in other countries, but the revolution in those countries
needs the support of the October Revolution in order to accelerate and advance the cause of overthrowing world imperialism.

*   *   *

From *Report to the Fourteenth Conference of the Russian Communist Party, May 9, 1925*

WHO WILL DEFEAT WHOM? After the October victory,
we entered on the third strategic period, the third stage of the
revolution, the objective of which is the overthrow of the bourgeoisie throughout the world. It is difficult to foresee how long
this period will last. At any rate, it is certain to be protracted,
just as it is certain to have its ebbs and flows. At the present
time, the international revolutionary movement has entered a
period of the ebb of the revolution; and, for a number of rea-

sons which I shall discuss later, this ebb will give way to a new flow of the tide, which may end in the victory of the proletariat, but, on the other hand, may not end in victory and may be succeeded by another ebb, which in its turn will be followed by another revolutionary flow. The liquidators of our period say that the present lull marks the end of the world revolution. They are mistaken now, just as they were mistaken before, during the first and the second stages of the revolution, when they regarded every ebb in the revolutionary movement as the utter defeat of the revolution.

Such are the oscillations within each stage of the revolution, within each strategic period.

What do these oscillations signify? Do they signify that Lenin's thesis concerning the new epoch of world revolution has lost, or may lose, its significance? No, of course not! These oscillations merely show that the revolution does not usually develop along a straight, continuously ascending line, not as a continuously swelling upsurge, but that it develops in zigzags, in advances and retreats, in the ebb and flow of tides, which in the course of development harden the forces of the revolution and prepare for its final victory.

Such is the historical meaning of the period of the ebb-tide of the revolution that has set in, such is the historical meaning of the present lull.

But this ebb is only one aspect of the matter; the other aspect is that, side by side with the ebb of the revolutionary tide of Europe, we have the rapid growth of the economic development of the Soviet Union and the growth of its political might. In other words, we have not only the stabilisation of capitalism, we have at the same time the stabilisation of the Soviet system. Thus we have two stabilisations: the temporary stabilisation of capitalism and the stabilisation of the Soviet system. The setting in of a certain temporary equilibrium between these two stabilisations—such is the characteristic feature of the present international situation.

But what is stabilisation? Is it not stagnation? And if stabilisation is stagnation can we apply the term to the Soviet system? No; stabilisation is not stagnation. Stabilisation is the consolidation of a given position and its further development. World capitalism has not only consolidated itself in its present position; it is advancing and developing, widening its sphere of influence and multiplying its wealth. It is not true that capitalism is incapable of further development, that the theory of the decay of capitalism (advanced by Lenin in his book *Imperialism*) excludes the development of capitalism. In his book *Imperialism*, Lenin fully proved that the growth of capitalism does not cancel, but presupposes and prepares for, the progressive decay of capitalism. Thus we have two stabilisations. At the one pole we find capitalism stabilising itself, consolidating the position it has reached and continuing its development. At the other pole we find the Soviet system stabilising itself, consolidating the positions it has won and marching forward on the road to victory.

Who will defeat whom?—That is the essence of the question.

*   *   *

From *Interview with the First American Labor Delegation, September 9, 1927*

ON RELIGION: The Party cannot be neutral towards religion, and it does conduct anti-religious propaganda against all and every religious prejudice because it stands for science, while religious prejudices run counter to science. . . . Have we suppressed the reactionary clergy? Yes, we have. The unfortunate thing is that it has not been completely liquidated. Anti-religious propaganda is a means by which the complete liquidation of the reactionary clergy must be brought about. Cases occur when certain members of the Party hamper the complete development of anti-religious propaganda. If such members are expelled it is a good thing because there is no room for such 'Communists' in the ranks of the Party.

From *Interview with Foreign Workers' Delegations,* November 5, 1927

THE SECRET POLICE: The G.P.U. or Cheka is a punitive organ of the Soviet government. It is more or less similar to the Committee of Public Safety which existed during the great French Revolution. It punishes primarily spies, plotters, terrorists, bandits, speculators and forgers. It is something in the nature of a military political tribune set up for the purpose of protecting the interests of the revolution from attacks on the part of the counter-revolutionary bourgeoisie and their agents. . . . It must be admitted that the G.P.U. aimed at the enemies of the revolution without missing. By the way, this quality of the G.P.U. still holds good. It has been, ever since, the terror of the bourgeoisie, the indefatigable guard of the revolution, the unsheathed sword of the proletariat. . . .

I understand the hatred and distrust of the bourgeoisie for the G.P.U. I understand the various bourgeois tourists who, on coming to the U.S.S.R. inquire before anything else as to whether the G.P.U. still exists and whether the time has not yet come for its liquidation. This is comprehensible and not out of the ordinary. But I cannot understand some workers' delegates who, on coming to the U.S.S.R., ask with alarm as to whether many counter-revolutionaries have been punished by the G.P.U. and whether terrorists and plotters against the proletarian government will still be punished by it and is it not time yet for its dissolution. Why do some workers' delegates show such concern for the enemies of the proletarian revolution? How can it be explained? How can it be justified?

They advocate a maximum of leniency, they advise the dissolution of the G.P.U. . . . But can anyone guarantee that the capitalists of all countries will abandon the idea of organising and financing counter-revolutionary plotters, terrorists, incendiaries, and bomb-throwers after the liquidation of the G.P.U.? . . .

I do not mean to say by this that the internal situation of the country is such as makes it necessary to have punitive organs of the revolution. From the point of view of the internal situation, the revolution is so firm and unshakable that we could do without the G.P.U. But the trouble is that the enemies at home are not isolated individuals. They are connected in a thousand ways with the capitalists of all countries who support them by every means and in every way. We are a country surrounded by capitalist states. The internal enemies of our revolution are the agents of the capitalists of all countries. The capitalist states are the background and basis for the internal enemies of our revolution. In fighting against the enemies at home we fight the counter-revolutionary elements of all countries. Judge for yourself whether under such conditions we can do without punitive organs as the G.P.U. . . .

The G.P.U. is necessary for the revolution and it will continue to live and strike terror into the hearts of the enemies of the proletariat.

*   *   *

From *Report to the Eighth Congress of Soviets*
November 25, 1936

THE SOVIET CONSTITUTION AND ITS CRITICS: I must admit that the draft of the new Constitution does preserve the regime of the dictatorship of the working class, just as it also preserves unchanged the present leading position of the Communist Party of the U.S.S.R. If the esteemed critics regard this as a flaw in the Draft Constitution, that is only to be regretted. We Bolsheviks regard it as a merit of the Draft Constitution.

As to freedom for various political parties, we adhere to somewhat different views. A party is a part of a class, its most advanced part. Several parties, and, consequently, freedom for parties, can exist only in a society in which there are antagonistic classes whose interests are mutually hostile and irreconcilable —in which there are, say, capitalists and workers, landlords and peasants, kulaks and poor peasants, etc. But in the U.S.S.R. there are no longer such classes as the capitalists, the landlords, the kulaks, etc. In the U.S.S.R. there are only two classes, workers and peasants, whose interests—far from being mutually hostile—are, on the contrary, friendly. Hence there is no ground in the U.S.S.R. for the existence of several parties, and, consequently, for freedom for these parties. In the U.S.S.R. there is ground only for one party, the Communist Party. In the U.S.S.R. only one party can exist, the Communist Party, which courageously defends the interests of the workers and peasants to the very end. . . .

They talk of democracy. But what is democracy? Democracy in capitalist countries, where there are antagonistic classes, is, in the last analysis, democracy for the strong, democracy for the propertied minority. In the U.S.S.R., on the contrary, democracy is democracy for the working people, *i.e.*, democracy for all. But from this it follows that the principles of democratism are violated, not by the draft of the new Constitution of the U.S.S.R., but by the bourgeois constitutions. That is why I think that the Constitution of the U.S.S.R. is the only thoroughly democratic Constitution in the world.

* * *

From *Report to the Eighteenth Party Congress* March 10, 1939

THE SOVIET STATE: It is sometimes asked: "We have abolished the exploiting classes; there are no longer any hostile classes in the country; there is nobody to suppress; hence there is no more need for the state; it must die away.—Why then do we not help our Socialist state to die away? Why do we not strive to put an end to it? Is it not time to throw out all this rubbish of a state?"

Or further: "The exploiting classes have already been abolished in our country: Socialism has been built in the main; we are advancing towards Communism. Now, the Marxist doctrine

of the state says that there is to be no state under Communism.
—Why then do we not help our Socialist state to die away? Is
it not time we relegated the state to the museum of antiqui-
ties?"

These questions show that those who ask them have conscientiously memorized certain propositions contained in the
doctrine of Marx and Engels about the state. But they also show
that these comrades have failed to understand the essential
meaning of this doctrine; that they have failed to realize in what
historical conditions the various propositions of this doctrine
were elaborated; and, what is more, that they do not understand
present-day international conditions, have overlooked the capitalist encirclement and the dangers it entails for the Socialist
country. These questions do not only betray an underestimation
of the capitalist encirclement, but also an underestimation of
the role and significance of the bourgeois states and their organs, which send spies, assassins and wreckers into our country
and are waiting for a favourable opportunity to attack it by
armed force. They likewise betray an underestimation of the
role and significance of our Socialist state and of its military,
punitive and intelligence organs, which are essential for the defence of the Socialist land from foreign attack. It must be confessed that the comrades mentioned are not the only ones to sin
in this underestimation. All the Bolsheviks, all of us without
exception, sin to a certain extent in this respect. Is it not surprising that we learned about the espionage and conspiratorial
activities of the Trotskyite and Bukharinite leaders only quite
recently, in 1937 and 1938, although, as the evidence shows,
these gentry were in the service of foreign espionage organizations and carried on conspiratorial activities from the very first
days of the October Revolution? * How could we have failed to

---

* [The "evidence" to which Stalin refers is that of the infamous Moscow
Trials. In 1918 Stalin spoke differently: "All the work of practical organization of the insurrection," he wrote, "was conducted under the direct leadership of the President of the Petrograd Soviet, Comrade Trotsky." Trotsky's
eminent role in the Communist Revolution is indisputable. As the chief technician of the *coup* Trotsky's role even exceeded that of Lenin in the actual

notice so grave a matter? How are we to explain this blunder? The usual answer to this question is that we could not possibly have assumed that these people could have fallen so low. But that is no explanation, still less is it a justification: for the blunder was a blunder. How is this blunder to be explained? It is to be explained by an underestimation of the strength and consequences of the mechanism of the bourgeois states surrounding us and of their espionage organs, which endeavour to take advantage of people's weaknesses, their vanity, their slackness of will, to enmesh them in their espionage nets and use them to surround the organs of the Soviet state.

* * *

From *Speech of February 9, 1946**

THE REAL CAUSE OF WORLD WAR II: It would be wrong to think that the Second World War was a casual occurrence or the results of mistakes of any particular statesmen, though mistakes were undoubtedly made. Actually, the war was the inevitable result of the development of the world economic and political forces on the basis of modern monopoly capitalism. Marxists have declared more than once that the capitalist system of world economy harbors elements of general crises and armed conflicts and that, hence, the development of world capitalism in our time proceeds not in the form of smooth and even progress but through crises and military catastrophes.

The fact is, that the unevenness of development of the capitalist countries leads in time to violent disturbance of equilibrium in the world system of capitalism, that group of capitalist

taking of power. What Stalin is therefore saying above is that the Bolshevik Revolution was made by men "in the service of foreign espionage organizations." These same men, of course, founded the Communist state. But responsive as we are to revealing disclosures about Soviet history, we are also, alas, concerned with *accurate* information and so we must refuse this proffered anti-Communist aid of Stalin's.—*Ed.*]

* [Text of this important address will be found in *The Strategy and Tactics of World Communism* (1948), a several hundred page report of the Foreign Affairs Committee of the U. S. House of Representatives containing much source material.—*Ed.*]

countries which considers itself worse provided than others with raw materials and markets usually making attempts to alter the situation and repartion the "spheres of influence" in its favor by armed force. The result is a splitting of the capitalist world into two hostile camps and war between them.

Perhaps military catastrophes might be avoided if it were possible for raw materials and markets to be periodically redistributed among the various countries in accordance with their economic importance, by agreement and peaceable settlement. But that is impossible to do under present capitalist conditions of the development of world economy.

Thus the First World War was the result of the first crisis of the capitalist system of world economy, and the Second World War was the result of a second crisis.

*   *   *

From *Speech at Moscow Soviet Meeting on 32nd Anniversary of the Bolshevik Revolution** by *G. M. Malenkov*

Comrades, today the peoples of the Soviet Union and our friends abroad are celebrating the 32nd Anniversary of the Great October Socialist Revolution.

The Soviet people look upon the results of their struggle and work with feelings of legitimate pride. The times in which you and I are living, comrades, will go down in the history of our country as the Great Stalin Epoch. . . .

It is precisely the successes of the camp of peace that drive

* [These extracts from the address of G. M. Malenkov are included not only because of the clarity with which the current Soviet line is stated, and because of Malenkov's position as Secretary of the Central Committee of the Communist Party of the Soviet Union, but also because it is an introduction to the man who may replace Stalin upon his death or retirement as the head of the Soviet state. Widespread conjecture by close observers of the USSR views Malenkov as the prime contender for this position. The text is excerpted from "On the Sure Road to New Victories" (1949), Malenkov's speech in pamphlet form, published by the *Soviet News* (London).—*Ed.*]

the warmongers to increasing frenzy. The programme of the main enemies of peace becomes more nakedly revealed every day.

This programme envisages the creation by means of violence and new wars of an American world empire, which in scale is to surpass any of the world empires built by conquerors in the past. The idea is nothing more nor less than to turn the whole world into a colony of the American imperialists, to reduce the sovereign peoples to the status of slaves.

In what way do these insensate designs of "Americanising" all countries and continents differ from the maniacal plan of Hitler and Goering for the "Germanisation" first of Europe and then of the whole world? In what way do these designs differ from the no less maniacal plans of Tanaka and Tojo for the subjugation of all Asia and the Pacific to the Japanese imperialists? Actually only in the fact that the aggressive programme of the instigators of a new war surpasses the plans of their German and Japanese predecessors taken together.

Does not the policy of preparing war lie at the foundation of the notorious "Marshall Plan"? We know that the annual allocations for so-called "aid" to the West European countries under the "Marshall Plan" amount to round about 4,000 million dollars. Yet at the same time we find that the main Marshallised countries, under the pressure of the United States, are spending over 6,000 million dollars annually on the armaments race, on a riot of militarism. . . .

Parallel with the development and progress of the Soviet Union, the forces of democracy and socialism are growing in numbers and strength all over the world.

In 1949, the people's democracies of Central and South-East Europe—Czechoslovakia, Poland, Bulgaria, Hungary, Rumania and Albania—advanced along the road of socialist construction. . . .

The imperialists express their "disapproval" of the State regimes in the people's democracies. This is not surprising. It would be unnatural to expect any other attitude on their part towards countries where the people are in power and whose national sovereignty is not to be bought and sold.

It would, so to speak, not be half so bad if the imperialists merely confined themselves to verbal disapproval. But they do not stop at this. They go to the length of unceremoniously interfering in the domestic affairs of the people's democratic Republics. They engage in criminal subversive activity against these countries, principally using for this purpose the Yugoslav gang of fascist spies and saboteurs.

The trial in Budapest of the espionage centre of Rajk and his accomplices revealed that the warmongers and their Yugoslav lackeys stop at nothing. They are trying to halt the historic advance of the people's democratic Republics, and to pave the way to imperialist armed intervention against them with the object of turning them into their colonies.

But at the same time the Budapest trial demonstrated that the subversive schemes of the imperialists against the people's democracies are sustaining defeat after defeat. The Tito-Rankovic clique of fascist nationalists were completely exposed as espionage agents of imperialism, utilised by the imperialists for hostile action against the Soviet Union and the people's democracies.

This exposure was a severe blow to the imperialists' machinations. Now neither the masters themselves nor their Yugoslav henchmen can succeed in masking themselves, for the masks have been torn away. The perfidious schemes have been laid bare, the criminals have been caught red-handed. . . .

One exceptional success of the camp of peace and democracy was the establishment of a peace-loving German Democratic Republic. This is a fact of first-rate international importance. . . .

Undoubtedly, given the peace-loving policy of the German Democratic Republic, side by side with the peace-loving policy of the Soviet Union, which enjoys the sympathy and support of the European peoples, the cause of peace in Europe can be considered to be guaranteed. . . .

Of historic significance for the consolidation of the cause of peace is the victory of the Chinese people, who have emancipated themselves from the age-long tyranny of feudal reaction and the yoke of foreign imperialism.

Lenin said in 1923 that the issue of the world struggle between capitalism and Communism depended in the final analysis on the fact that Russia, India and China constituted the overwhelming majority of the population of the world, and that this majority was being drawn with extraordinary rapidity into the struggle for its emancipation. With the victory of the Chinese people, the people's democracies of Europe and Asia together with the Soviet Socialist Power embrace a population of approximately 800 million. . . .

As far back as 1925 Comrade Stalin said: "The forces of the revolutionary movement in China are incalculable. They have not yet made themselves properly felt. But they will make themselves felt in the future. The rulers of the East and West who do not see these forces and do not reckon with them in due measure will suffer from this . . ."

Comrade Stalin's prediction has been fully confirmed by history. The Chinese Communist Party, steeled in the fire of the national liberation struggle and armed with the all-conquering teachings of Marxism-Leninism, has proved equal to its historic mission. Guided by its tried and tested leader, Mao Tse-tung, it organised and united the workers, peasants, intellectuals, all the patriotic forces of the nation. It built a powerful People's Liberation Army, which smashed the Kuomintang hordes armed with American weapons and virtually directed by American staffs. . . .

And so we may confidently say that the forces of democracy and socialism are growing while the forces of capitalism and the warmongers are waning. . . .

Incidentally, one of the features of the present American crisis is that it is developing at a time when the American monopolists have subordinated practically the whole economy of the capitalist world to their service. With the help of the so-called "Marshall Plan" they artificially dispose of commodities which cannot find a sale at home, and through the programme of arming foreign states they artificially keep a number of branches of industry loaded with orders. . . .

Guided by the genius of Comrade Stalin, our teacher and leader, we face the morrow with confidence. We firmly know that the world-wide triumph of socialism and democracy is inevitable.

II. The Second Decade

FROM DICTATORSHIP TO TOTALITARIAN SOCIETY

(1928-1939)

Part Two

I N T R O D U C T I O N

THE first Soviet decade proved crucial. The dictatorship installed in that period grew under the impact of each succeeding crisis. The restraining influence that might have been exerted by independent forces was absent—after Kronstadt, popular rebellion was no longer possible. The Soviet totalitarian state as we know it was coming into existence; the second terrible decade was the crucible in which it was formed. Four major "events" of decisive importance vividly illustrate the development: forced industrialization; collectivization; the physical liquidation of the Communist opposition in the long St. Bartholomew's Eve of purges and trials, representing as it did the final triumph of Stalin as the most unlimited sovereign in all of Russia's absolutistic history; and the symbolic, and actual, culmination of these climactic years in the Nazi-Soviet Pact.

In 1922, in a moment of good-humored desperation, Lenin criticized Communist inefficiency by saying: "This is not new, not economic, and not a policy, but sheer mockery." The imposition of Communist policy by assault during the period of War Communism (1918-21) had proven bankrupt in action. Rising internal dissent, peasant rebellions, demonstrations by workers and strikes, finally Kronstadt, had compelled Lenin to make a "strategic retreat." It is known that he did not view the NEP as short-term policy; he was preparing himself, however unwillingly, to live with it for a considerable time to come. His sense of reality convinced him that he could not do otherwise. When he died in 1924 the "burlesque on capitalism" * had not yet come to an end; it petered out, however, about four years later. The Stalinist system was now readying itself for the second great assault.

The end of NEP was extraordinarily instructive regarding the possibilities of "doing business with the Communists," to use the term in its broadest sense. Russians who performed private trading and other activities that the regime had assured them were permissible were later jailed, imprisoned, and exiled for no other crime than having done what they were told they could do with impunity, and sometimes encouraged to do.

Here is a tail end of NEP report:

> "A great many of the Siberian prisoners in Russia today consists of those 'NEP people' who were supported by the Government as long as it needed them for the reorganization of their ruined industry and trade, but were banished to Siberia as soon as their services could be dispensed with. The authorities contrived to combine business with pleasure by deporting to Siberia not only the guilty NEP people who had 'speculated professionally' or 'lived on games of chance,' but also their whole families, in this way setting free many houses in Moscow. The shortage of houses in Moscow is very great." **

Economically, NEP had allowed the state to put a little "financial fat" under its governmental belt, but conditions were still depressing.*** To the extent that private trading activi-

---

* The term is Eugene Lyons'. See his *Assignment in Utopia*.
** *The Mind and Face of Bolshevism* (1927) by Rene Fulop-Miller.
*** "National production," sums up *Communism in Action*, the factual report of the research specialists of the U. S. Library of Congress, "was still below pre-revolutionary times in a country whose national production had never been

ties, and other such non-Communist features, brought about an improvement in conditions, the gloom of the Communists deepened. "The rising tide of capitalism was visible everywhere," Leon Trotsky has forlornly written.

The fateful year of change was 1928. The period it ushered in Stalin has called the "great change." So it was. Let us trace its antecedents.

The Left Opposition Communists had several years earlier proposed an accelerated industrialization campaign and a more intense development of agricultural collectives, the peasantry having virtually ignored the latter when joining was voluntary. Stalin mocked at this proposal, stating quite accurately that the condition of Soviet Russia would not permit, either in resources or living standards, such convulsive measures. To independent observers it was clear that these moves, which would need to be financed by what could be expropriated from the lean "reserves" of the peasants and workers, would create living conditions that would make tsarism in retrospect seem fraught with everyday abundance for the common man. Stalin ridiculed the opposition as "super industrialists" and economic romantics.

It should be made clear that considerations of democracy for the country as a whole entered into the thinking of neither Communist faction. Both maintained their beliefs in Leninism and the principle of the "dictatorship of the proletariat," which, from the start, had meant dictatorship over the proletariat and the country as a whole. But it is important to understand the antecedents of the Five Year Plan, for Stalin's zigzags at that time help reveal the haphazard and irresponsible basis on which the supposedly carefully considered Five Year Plan, which was indeed to convulse Russia, was built.

In the internal struggle for power, Stalin at this point feigned

outstanding. . . . Despite the confiscation of all productive property, the socialization of all industry, and the steep increase in the total number of industrialized workers in Soviet Russia, neither total industrial production nor the plane of living of the workers was greater a decade after the Revolution than they had been in Czarist times."

the role of a conservative. He posed as the great supporter of the peasantry. "Enrich yourselves," was the famous slogan as voiced by Bukharin, then chief theoretician for the ruling clique, to the peasantry. In 1925 Stalin went so far as to favor, or pretend favoring, steps for the denationalization of the land. In a set-up question he was asked by a Soviet journalist whether it might "not be expedient in the interest of agriculture to deed over to each peasant for ten years the parcel of land tilled by him?" "Yes," Stalin answered, in a celebrated reply, "and even for forty years."

Forced industrialization and forced collectivization (confiscation of private peasant holdings in actuality) clearly indicated civil war with the peasantry and extreme suffering for the working class in the cities, plus other dire results which were incalculable. Stalin had stressed this himself, it must be remembered, and said so enthusiastically; it was his position of opposition to the "super industrialists." In 1925 he said: "Since, however, there is great lack of capital in this country, we have good reason to expect that in the future the growth of our industry will not proceed so rapidly as it has in the past." Also: "We might devote double the present sum to the development of industry, so that, owing to the lack of sufficiency of free capital, we should not be able to keep step with that development, and there would certainly be a fiasco."

This made good sense. To repeat, the country was in no way fitted for an extreme program of industrialization. Living standards were abysmal; whatever capital for building was raised could be taken only from the already discontented and quite poor Russian people. A large source of funds for pre-revolutionary construction had come from foreign loans and investments; these were no longer forthcoming. The peasant's basis of security, even under a dictatorship, was his land—it was the basis for his remote, limited freedom as well. Regimented life in a collective was the counterpart of the regimented life of an industrial worker for the state. The peasant would not willingly give up what he had, his cow or chickens and mostly very small land holdings. At the start, during their rise to power, land for the peasants was one of the most popular slogans of the Bolsheviks. Collectivization meant the confiscation of all of these.

Stalin made another prescient statement which is worthy of remembrance:

> "We might greatly increase exports, without paying heed to any other of the main constituents of our economic life. We might do this regardless of the condition of the home market. The consequences of such a policy would inevitably be to produce great complications in the towns, owing to an enormous increase in the price of agricultural produce, this meaning a decline in real wages and a sort of *artificially organized famine* with all its disastrous consequences." *

What gives enormous significance to these seemingly esoteric facts—Stalin's predictions of fiasco, the possibility of "artificially organized famine," "disastrous consequences"—is that soon after, with the fall of the opposition, *Stalin was to reverse himself completely!* Having used the time lag to decimate his opponents, he now proceeded to steal their program, and to expand it unrecognizably. As his biographer Boris Souvarine puts it: "Freed from the 'super industrialists,' Stalin hastened on with super-industrialization." And he brought into being all the disaster that he himself had predicted—when fighting the opposition—and more!

Anton Ciliga, the former Yugoslavian Communist, has described in a discussion of his own political development an attitude of the time among Communists. When Stalin reversed

* Address before Fourteenth Party Congress, May, 1925; text in his *Leninism,* London, published by British Communist Party, 1928.

his position and became a super industrialist himself, "I first
imagined that this signified a proletarian and revolutionary rebirth of the Communist Party. I began to reproach myself for
my doubts about the future of the revolution in Russia." But
the new development—ruthless industrialization and forced
collectivization—still did not fit the state into either of the
seemingly two Marxist categories. The state turned its back
on capitalism, abandoning the NEP, but socialism was now
still farther away. "In the autumn of 1929," Ciliga writes in
The Russian Enigma, "this hope in Stalin and his group had
long since vanished." There was less democracy than before,
"the workers still had as few rights as ever, and society had in
no way evolved towards socialism." The Marxist mind was in
a quandary. "One had therefore to conclude that the trend was
towards the restoration of private capital. . . . From it followed that the 'Left' attitude of Stalin reflected only the 'Centre' waverings between socialism and capitalism and that Stalin,
notwithstanding all his zigzaggings to the Left, was to lean
more and more toward the kulaks and private capitalism. That
is how theory would have it. Reality was quite different."

Reality was, indeed, quite different; there was a third road
and Soviet Russia was well along on it. Centralization without
democracy was not socialism, at least not the enhanced democratic state that idealists had conceived and for which they had
sacrificed so much; also, it was certainly not capitalism of any
recognizable variety. A new system was being born, for which
there was no basis for recognition in Marxist theory: the modern totalitarian state—what Rudolf Hilferding in this book
calls "totalitarian state economy," and what others have attempted to identify as "state capitalism." The Five Year Plan,
the highly touted Five Year Plan, was the womb in which this
new and monstrous state development was being born.

The real results of the Plan were soon apparent. The worker
became an economic as well as political prisoner of the state.
He needed passports—as decreed in December, 1932—to
travel from place to place in Russia. This strange document

was followed by an employment dossier. The slightest offense
to the state—by no means necessarily political—resulted in
his severance from his livelihood. His working conditions, as
was necessary to the needs of the "Plan," were depressed to the
direct extent that industrialization was stepped up, a simple
fact which yet managed to escape the attention of those
observers abroad who automatically equated heightened industrialization with increased living standards. In addition,
machinery had to be bought abroad in great quantities and
the exports in payment were the produce and commodities that
the people so badly needed. There was still another factor
in the unprecedented degradation of the Russian worker: industrialization concentrated feverishly on heavy industry, not
on consumer goods, a concentration that has continued to the
present day, producing much armament and giant edifices,
many guns and little butter. Succeeding Plans have thus—in
conjunction with the tremendous costs of sustaining the governmental and police bureaucracy, a "detail" that is sometimes
overlooked—continued unmysteriously to depress living standards.

The Plan called for ever increasing numbers of workers, and
many of these were recruited in an interesting manner:

> "All reserves of manpower seemed to have been
> absorbed during the first two years of the Five Year
> Plan. Unemployment disappeared, and the labor short-
> age became a serious problem. . . . By keeping wages
> low the government and the trade unions were able to
> achieve another success, namely, to force wives and
> daughters of workers into jobs. The lower the income
> of the principal wage earner of a family, the more nec-
> essary it becomes for other members of the family to
> seek employment. Female and child labor increased
> rapidly after 1928." (Dallin and Nicolaevsky, *Forced
> Labor in Soviet Russia*.)

The peasant faced more than extreme privation: he came to know the "artificially organized famine" that Stalin himself had so wisely predicted, then produced, an avoidable famine which, in extent and numbers of deaths, remains one of the most horrible events of many horrible events in the modern world.

For both peasant and worker, for all Russians, the Five Year Plan brought another development: the creation of a slave labor force which has continued to grow until it is measured in millions. This too managed to evade the attention of those who were shouting hosannas about the Plan, and continuing Plans. Vast territories were settled and worked by prison labor which was now used "profitably" in the most shocking conceivable way: as cheap, expendable labor, labor which could be replaced at will, and which could be drawn, as needs arose, from a gigantic body—the entire Russian people.

Combined, these were the methods—so fervently recommended by some to the American people—by which the Soviet Union "solved" the problem of unemployment. These were the methods by which the dictatorial state was brought to totalitarian maturity.

In the early 1930s Karl Kautsky reemphasized the human aspect that is the only criterion for decently judging governmental accomplishment. He merits a lengthy hearing, for his comments cut incisively through the inhuman paeans of those who echoed—and echo—the Soviet line so vociferously, and ignorantly:

> "The construction program carried out under Stalin's reign," wrote Kautsky in 1933, "is by no means unprecedented. Other rulers before Stalin who commanded the services of large masses of docile, helpless labor whom they sacrificed mercilessly to their plans were able, even in primitive times, to build huge edifices which roused astonishment, edifices the construction of which was brought about by tremendous sacrifices and expenditures of human lives, and which did not,

however, move the 'leader' in the least. The builders of
the pyramids have been cited in this connection. The
Roman Caesars and the Rajahs of India astonished the
world with similar remarkable performances by using
the labor of millions of cheap slaves over whom they
held sway. Nor did they confine themselves to luxury
construction. The Roman Caesars built not only great
amphitheaters and bath houses but also very fine roads
connecting all parts of the great empire, water systems,
etc. Many persons who admire these accomplishments
fail to realize that because they rested on slave labor
they led ultimately to the destruction of the state.

"The Pharaohs of Egypt and the despots of Babylonia
and India built not only great palaces, temples, mauso-
leums but also huge works, dams, reservoirs, and canals
without which agriculture could not endure. Marx characterized these works as part of the material foundations
of the despotism of those regions. He did not regard
them as the material basis of a socialist society.

"The fact that the present rulers of the Kremlin follow
these examples of Asiatic despots does not signify a fundamental change in the face of the world. Neither the
brutality of the rulers nor the enslavement of the ruled
is altered by these achievements. It is not technical and
economic innovations but the human aspects of a society that matters. Many see only the construction of
plants and collectives, but fail to perceive the rise of a
new aristocracy which controls these new means of production and exploits them for its own purposes. . . .

"The fruit of the Bolshevist regime has been the
establishment of a new class rule. The Bolsheviks, to be
sure, have destroyed the old classes, but new classes,
new elements of aristocracy have arisen under their
regime. They have arisen of necessity from the conditions of Bolshevist dictatorship, although they may be
invisible at first glance because they had not been fore-

seen in Bolshevist ideology and phraseology. But they are there, nevertheless. They are striking ever deeper root and are becoming in ever increasing measure the determining factor in the actions and aspirations of Bolshevism. Its ultimate Communist objective is becoming more and more a matter of decoration, a mere memory of allurement for socialist idealists whom the dictator seeks to utilize for his own purposes. . . . State slavery does not become Socialism merely because the slave drivers call themselves Communists. The methods of dictatorship in general and of the Five Year Plan in particular do not constitute the road to Socialism, but rather the road away from it." (Excerpt from "Is Soviet Russia a Socialist State," in *Social Democracy Versus Communism*, a collection of Kautsky's essays during 1932-37, New York: Rand School Press, 1946.)

* * *

This is the meaning of Stalin's achievement (a new class society, loss of every democratic liberty, a new slave force) even when we credit fully *every* Soviet industrialization claim.

The Communists failed, however, to utilize the argument of industrial advance as a basis for exulting in Japan's "superiority," despite the incredible industrial development of that country in the twentieth century. On the contrary, Fascist Italy's boast that it had "made the trains run on time" was recognized precisely for what it was—mockery of the concept of human justice under the guise of mechanical advance. These are aspects obscured by the absurd Soviet ideological promissory note to "surpass and overtake" American production.

Let us examine one of the most publicized Soviet innovations: the "new and higher standard" of the Stakhanov movement. "The Stakhanov movement," said Stalin himself, in an address to the First Conference of Stakhanovites of Industry and Transport in 1935, "as an expression of new and higher standards of output, is a model of that high productivity of

labor which socialism alone can give and which capitalism
cannot give."

Here are the facts. In 1935 Alexei Stakhanov, a coal miner,
cut fourteen times as much coal as the norm. He later explained
his remarkable achievement by reporting that he had observed
that the other hewers used their drills only during part of the
shift; they did this to clear away what they had cut. He thus
concluded, and rightly, that a "team would produce better
results if one man cut the coal and the others performed the
subsidiary work." Arthur Koestler has commented appropri-
ately on this "new" phenomenon: "A division of labor was
achieved which for decades has been a matter of course in the
rationalized mining industry of the West."

But more than a pathetic boast was involved:

> "Piece work wages were reintroduced: they were the
> object of hate under the capitalist regime, yet excellent
> under the emblem of the hammer and sickle. . . . They
> sought for and found 'things which had long existed and
> were well known' elsewhere—under the names of Tay-
> lorism and the sweating system—but only too well
> known already in the USSR as 'socialist emulation' and
> 'shock labor.' . . . A quantitative increase of produc-
> tion was only achieved to the detriment of the quality of
> the products, at the cost of a disastrous increase in waste,
> in a heavy wear and tear of machinery, and of a pre-
> mature exhaustion of man-power. If by this means some
> thousands of future foremen and managers have sprung
> from the ranks to become to some degree privileged, the
> selection could have been accomplished more soundly
> and beneficially and with less ostentation. The numer-
> ous assassinations of stakhanovists by their companions
> in bondage, the antagonisms in the factories and work-
> shops . . . testified to a state of mind among the work-
> ers quite other than the enthusiasm prescribed by 'our
> beloved hero,' Stalin. In short, stakhanovism served only

to introduce into the so-called 'socialist fatherland,' in
an aggravated form, methods in use in capitalist countries where the communists ceaselessly demand their
abolition. To attain such an end it was more than useless
to cause the shedding of so much blood and the flowing
of so many tears." (Souvarine's *Stalin*.)

The Soviet actuality, as compared with the grandeur of Soviet claims, has been little different in quality in other connections. The substance was ruthless assault, frequently subverting
the potentialities inherent in the industrial techniques that
were derivatively borrowed and equipment bought from other
nations. Machinery bought abroad, paid for with all that could
be squeezed from the Russian workers and peasantry (the
only sizable source for funds before the post-World War II
looting of European countries), was frequently ruined in use,
a fact, as we shall see, not denied by the Soviet leaders. It is
true, however, that the state preferred "sabotage" explanations to the much simpler and human truth that there was a
grave shortage of skilled technicians, and that terrorized, un-
derfed, and overworked men and women were not efficient
workers. Other errors and failures of the regime were pinned
to the backs of "class enemy" scapegoats, and thus the double
purpose of face-saving and recruitment of more forced labor
were simultaneously served. In the Moscow Trials—the pe-
nultimate triumph—Stalin attributed his own failures to the
Communist opposition. By means of a surrealist amalgam of
connections, the Nazis, the Mikado, foreign capitalist agents,
and others, the opposition was charged with sabotaging the
Five Year Plan. As in the period of War Communism all dictatorial steps were later explained away as "necessary," a
phrase that covers whatever is done. The foreign fellow travelers, for their part, would sometimes concede "excesses"—but
always in the past tense—and explain them away as history,
conveniently forgetting, as has often been said, that all injustice
ultimately becomes "history," and in this case a history still

being made. But underneath the vituperation of the dictatorship, there were on occasion more reliable clues to Soviet failures, but they needed to be sought avidly—an undertaking
that proved too arduous for many. We have these disquieting
words of Stalin, for example, spoken in 1931 before the First
All-Union Conference of Managers of Soviet Industry:

> "What does directing production mean? There are
> people among us who do not always treat the question
> of factory management in a Bolshevik way. There are
> many people among us who think that to direct means
> to sign papers. . . . It must be admitted to our shame
> that even among us Bolsheviks there are not a few who
> direct by signing papers. But as for going into the details
> of the business, learning technique, becoming master of
> the business—why, by no manner of means." (*Problems
> of Leninism,* Moscow, 1945, page 354.)

This is reasonable, but how much consolation could it provide
to the "wreckers"—arrested in great numbers both before and
after the statement (and still being arrested)—who felt the
wrath of the dictatorship for their guiltless actions?

> "Of course, the underlying cause of wrecking activities
> is the class struggle. . . . This alone, however, is not an
> adequate explanation for the luxuriant growth of wreck-
> ing activities. How is it that sabotage has assumed such
> wide dimensions? Who is to blame for this? We are to
> blame. Had we handled the business of industrial man-
> agement differently, had we started much earlier to
> learn the technique of the business, to master technique
> . . . the wreckers could not have done so much dam-
> age. . . . You can write as many resolutions as you
> please, take as many vows as you please, but, unless you
> master the technique, economics and finance of the mill,
> factory or mine, nothing will come of it."

But what were these strands of explanation as compared with the torrent of almost mystical claims that poured from the pens of Soviet partisans, accepting each resolution as an achievement, every slogan as an actuality, and bolstering the dictatorship by enthusiastically indicting "wreckers," "foreign capitalist agents," "opposition elements," for every dictatorial fiasco.

> "Of course," said Stalin, in a 1935 address to the graduates of the Red Army Academies, "it never even occurred to us to turn from the Leninist road. Moreover, once we stood firmly on this road, we pushed forward still more vigorously, brushing every obstacle from our path. True, in pursuing this course we were obliged to handle some of these comrades [in the opposition] roughly. But that cannot be helped. I must confess that I too had a hand in this."

He neglected to add that millions of Russians were among the "obstacles" in his path. They remain in his path. And more than one disillusioned ex-Communist was remembering Balzac's pungent reflection: "Popular revolutions have no more implacable enemies than the men they raised to power."

*   *   *

In 1925, Stalin furnished a vivid preview of the massacre of the best known Communists that was to come. Characteristically, his statement was in the form of a charge against his Communist critics. "The methods of lopping off," he said, "the method of bloodletting . . . is dangerous, and infectious. Today you lop off one limb; tomorrow, another, the day after tomorrow, a third—and what is left of the Party?" In the grim period of purges and trials that lay ahead Stalin was to complete the process that he had so expertly described.

He permitted the opposition to linger, first using one against the other, then a third against the second: expulsions, harassment, finally the bloody purges and trials. Throughout the

world men and women of good will, of all political shadings,
declared themselves in continuing disagreement with the Communist opposition—which disagreed with Stalin over methods
not goals—but attempted in the courts of international opinion
to combat this newest, startling injustice of Soviet Russia. The
trials and purges—hundreds of thousands falling without a
trial of any sort—this new turn stripped completely (for all
who would see) the Communist myth from the ghastly actualities it shrouded. The dictatorial wheel had come full turn:
the Communist founding fathers themselves were falling victim
to the Frankenstein's monster they had created.

One ex-Communist, from his own experience, has furnished
us an extremely vivid insight into the duplicity of the Stalinist
state at the beginning of the decade that was to later witness
the trials and purges:

> "What is especially striking is that in the period of
> 1929-30 neither the GPU nor any other party organ
> insisted on a change of viewpoint. All they asked for was
> a *declaration.* Privately, they even conceded that the
> opposition could be right 'in certain things.' But they,
> nevertheless, insisted most intransigently that the of-
> ficial declaration should contain the very opposite: that
> the official party machine was 100 percent right and the
> opposition 100 percent wrong. This was asked for 'in
> order to safeguard and strengthen the authority of the
> party.' This fact is very important for understanding
> the mechanism of political and social life in the USSR.
> The Russian Communists are absolutely impregnated,
> or, to speak more exactly, infected with the theory of
> the 'two truths,' one the 'true-truth' meant for the initi-
> ate, for the restricted circle of the country's directors,
> and the other the 'lie-truth,' better suited for the great
> mass of the people." (Anton Ciliga, *International Re-
> view,* February, 1937.)

Later, declarations of loyalty from those whom the regime saw fit to view as "opposition" were unacceptable, no matter how fervently composed. Nor could the accused count on his safety even if he genuinely believed in Stalinism, for there arose the remarkable doctrine of "unconscious deviations." The believer in Stalinism, he who stated he believed, who *believed* he believed, might still have lurking in his recesses "deviations" that were apparent only to the X-ray vision of the secret police.

The second decade ended fittingly in the Nazi-Soviet Pact, a non-aggression and mutual assistance pact, which Stalin adhered to more strenuously than to any other agreement into which he has ever entered the Soviet Union, an agreement that ended only when the Nazis chose to end it.

There are two historic mementos, and a world war, among other by-products, that commemorate this most distinguished of acts of a totalitarian state in its full maturity.

A telegram from Von Ribbentrop, representing Nazi Germany, to Stalin on his sixtieth birthday, in the unforgettable year of 1939: "REMEMBERING THOSE HISTORIC HOURS IN THE KREMLIN WHICH LAID THE FOUNDATION FOR THE DECISIVE TURN IN THE RELATIONSHIP BETWEEN OUR TWO GREAT PEOPLES AND THUS CREATED THE BASIS FOR A LONG AND LASTING FRIENDSHIP, I BEG YOU TO ACCEPT ON YOUR SIXTIETH BIRTHDAY MY WARMEST CONGRATULATIONS."

Stalin's telegram to Von Ribbentrop: "THE FRIENDSHIP OF THE PEOPLES OF GERMANY AND OF THE SOVIET UNION, CEMENTED BY BLOOD, WILL LONG REMAIN FIRM."

Vladimir V. Tchernavin

SLAVE LABOR AND BIG BUSINESS

"Do not ask for incriminating evidence to prove that the prisoner opposed the Soviet Government either by arms or word. Your first duty is to ask him what class he belongs to, what were his origin, education and occupation. These questions should decide the fate of the prisoner. This is the meaning and essence of Red Terror. . . ." Orders of Latsis, a leader of the Cheka, the Soviet political police (Pravda, December 25, 1918, p. 1).

Editor's Note

THE Russian intellectuals met a curious as well as frightful fate after the Russian Revolution. During the period of Red Terror—aptly named by the Communists themselves—"origins," not views, let alone actions, often determined one's fate. Latsis' instructions, quoted above, symbolizes this especially brutal period. The treatment of the intellectuals was paradoxical because it had been this element in the Russian population that had long helped to keep alive the flames of rebellion in the days of Tsarism. As William Henry Chamberlin, the veteran Moscow correspondent of the *Christian Science Monitor*, wrote in 1931 in his *Soviet Russia:*

> To be uprooted and displaced by a social upheaval to which one is indifferent or hostile (the fate of the old Russian aristocracy and bourgeoisie) is, of course, painful and disconcerting to the persons affected. But to be swept aside by a revolutionary storm which one regarded, in anticipation, with sympathy, or even helped

255

to raise (the fate of the Russian radical and liberal intelligentsia)—here is surely material both for tragedy
and irony. Madame Rolland, guillotined by her revolutionary associates of yesterday and dying with her last
bitter apostrophe to liberty on her lips, is a figure of
more historical dramatic pathos than Marie Antoi-
nette . . .

The non-Communist intellectual had to be watched, then
harassed by the Bolsheviks because his talents for questioning,
for objecting to injustice, that had served the revolutionary
cause so well, directly and indirectly, were now no longer assets
when a new and "higher" autocracy asserted itself.

In September, 1930, *Pravda* ominously announced the "discovery of a counter-revolutionary organization to wreck the
workers' food supplies." There followed a harrowing list of
"wreckers," and their "confessions." Forty-eight eminent specialists, renowned scientists—all were wreckers, all confessed.
No evidence was forthcoming. Mass arrests followed. The procedure was later to become better known. Origins of the accused were stressed: A. V. Ryazantsev, "professor, gentleman
by birth, member of the board of directors of the Central Cold
Storage Trust . . ."; M. Z. Karpenko, "gentleman by birth,
head engineer of. . . ." Their only ostensible crime was in being intellectuals and scientists. "To be shot" was the verdict,
and then the laconic denouement, "The sentence has been
carried out." Signed: Menzhinsky, head of the GPU.

Tatiana Tchernavin, wife of the author of this selection, has
described the effect produced on the intellectuals.

No more than a week had passed after the execution
of the "forty-eight," but one might have thought that the
intellectuals had been stricken by plague: thousands
were in prison, and those that were still free were a
pitiful sight. No one argued any more or talked of justice
or felt secure in the sense of his own rectitude. Prison,
death or exile were the fate of all; it would have been

shameful to expect mercy, when one's friends lay buried
in a nameless grave, and their widows and children
suffered in far-off exile. (*Escape from the Soviets*, 1934.)

Her husband, Vladimir Tchernavin, of humble but non-
proletarian origins, was soon arrested as a "wrecker." He was
a Russian scientist who in his youth had joined the explorer
V. V. Sapojnikoff as a collector-zoologist. Later he carried on
independently and conducted scientific expeditions to Mon-
golia and elsewhere. He continued his academic studies and
became a specialist in ichthyology. After the Revolution he
taught in several Russian institutions. In 1925 he was advanced to the position of Director of Production and Research
Work of the North State Fishing Trust, the state-owned industry organized to deal with the fishing business of the region
on the Arctic Ocean. Just prior to his arrest he was Professor
of Ichthyology at the Agronomic Institute of Leningrad. After
his arrest he was sent to the Northern Camps. Here, because
of his background, he was given the task of organizing the exploitation of forced labor in the fishing industry. This was not
only to lead to an opportunity for escape to Finland, with his
wife and son, but to a book which is one of the most valuable
on the early period of mass forced labor. The concentration
camps in the Soviet Union were undergoing a thorough change
and Professor Tchernavin was in a strategic position to study its
manifestations. Originally the camps were designed as punitive
sites for political and other prisoners. Now, the Soviet state had
come to recognize the economic value of expendable labor:
labor that did not have to be paid for, that cost nothing to obtain, and that could be replaced by more arrests. This tendency
blossomed during the inauguration of the Five Year Plans
when slave labor became an integral part of these campaigns,
and gradually of the entire Soviet economy. Professor Tchernavin's *I Speak for the Silent* (1935) is a mine of human-
interest material, of how forced laborers live and die, of the
system that embraces them. For this book, however, we have

selected an extremely valuable chapter on the early economic uses to which forced labor was put, the kind of slave economy that was steadily coming into existence and which is now inextricably a part of the entire Soviet structure.

Valuable data on the role of forced labor in the successive Five Year Plans will be found in *Forced Labor in Soviet Russia* (1947), by David J. Dallin and Boris I. Nicolaevsky, the most extensive and authoritative presentation and analysis of the overall subject to date. The text of the Corrective Labor Codex of the Russian Soviet Federated Socialist Republic, an intriguing and revolting document, will be found in *Slave Labor in Russia* (1949), the report of the American Federation of Labor to the United Nations, a book containing many informative and tragic eyewitness accounts by former inmates of Soviet concentration camps.

#

Slave Labor and Big Business by Vladimir V. Tchernavin

F ROM my own investigations of the Fisheries Section and, as time went on, from conversations with prisoners in other sections and in the central administration of the camp, its complicated structure and its operations as a productive commercial enterprise were becoming clear to me. Let me describe them.

In 1931 the Solovetzki camp reached the height of its development. It contained fourteen sections. The river Swir and Lake Ladoga formed its southern boundary; its northern limit was the Arctic Ocean. The enterprises of this so-called camp extended approximately 1500 kilometers along the Murmansk railroad, taking in also the whole of Karelia. It was still growing and tending to expand beyond these limits. To the east this was checked by another enormous enterprise owned by the

GPU—the Northern Camps of Special Designation—and to the west by the closeness of the Finnish frontier. Therefore the camp was reaching out to the islands of the Arctic Ocean, Kolgoueff and Vaigash, and to the southern shore of the Kola Peninsula (Kandalaksha and Terek shores of the White Sea). The number of prisoners was increasing daily. Enormous projects were being carried out and plans for even wider activities were under way.

Operating independently on the territory of the so-called autonomous Republic of Karelia the Solovetzki camp established there, on a large scale, its own commercial enterprises, duplicating all the enterprises of that state. The camp had its own fisheries and lumber camps, its own brick-yards, road construction, agricultural and cattle farms—all of which were completely stifling Karelian industry. Besides these activities of a permanent nature the camp also undertook work of temporary character on a still larger scale. Some of this work had a definitely strategic purpose; for example, the construction of the White Sea-Baltic Canal (actually the joining of the Onega Bay of the White Sea with Lake Onega), the building of highways to the Finnish frontier, the reclaiming and levelling of large expanses of swamps and woods for military airports, the erection in the most important strategic points (Kem, Kandalaksha, Loukhi and others) of whole towns for quartering troops, with barracks to accommodate thousands of men, hospitals, warehouses, bathhouses, bakeries and so on. Besides this, in 1930-31 the camp also engaged in activities of an economic nature: the clearing of marsh land to be used for camp farms, preliminary work for the construction of a Soroka-Kotlas railroad which was to join the Siberian trunk line with the Murmansk railroad (this work was abandoned in 1931), the preparation of firewood for Moscow and Leningrad, and other activities.

In 1932 the GPU evidently decided that the Solovetzki camp had grown too big and it was, therefore, reorganized. After many changes, two new independent camps—the White

Sea-Baltic camp (for the construction of the canal) and the Swir camp (for preparation of firewood for Moscow and Leningrad)—were finally formed and were no longer a part of Solovetzki.

Each camp had many sections. Every section was a complete commercial entity, similar to those which in the U.S.S.R. are called "trusts," designed to make profits by productive commercial operations. Each section had its own budget, its invested and working capitals. The administration of the section, as in all Soviet "trusts," included the following departments: planning, production, technical, commercial, bookkeeping and executive. The higher officers were usually three in number: the section chief and his two assistants. The section was composed of production and commercial units the nature of which depended on the section's activity: factories, trades, agricultural farms, lumber camps and so on. Each section worked in a definite production field and had its own distinct territory. The marketing of its product was effected either independently in the Soviet market or through intermediaries. Goods produced by sections using forced labor and sold in the home market were often stamped with their trademark. As I have said, the trademark of the Solovetzki camp was an elephant. Dealings with foreign markets were, of course, handled through the *Gostorg* (State Trade Commissariat) and sometimes even through a second intermediary, in order better to conceal the origin of the goods. The Section of Fisheries, the *Ribprom,* in which I worked, had a canning factory, a fish-smoking factory, a shop for construction and repair of ships, a net factory and over twenty fisheries scattered along the shores of Onega and Kandalaksha bays of the White Sea, on the Solovetzki Islands and on the Murman coast of the Arctic Ocean.

The sections were unified by and subordinated to the administration of the camp which regulated, combined and controlled their activity. The result was a very unwieldy and complicated bureaucratic body entirely unnecessary from the point of view of production efficiency. Furthermore, in Moscow there was a central organization independent of the camp administrations, for the combining, regulating and controlling of the activities of camp sections, composed of specialists in various fields of industry. Each specialist was in charge of one branch of industrial activity in *all* the camps. Thus, for instance, a certain Bikson was managing the fishing industry at the Moscow GPU. He was a former fish merchant, had been deported to the Solovetzki camp and finally had entered the service of the GPU.

In this way the section had two masters: the administration of the camp and the council of specialists in Moscow. Both took every opportunity to meddle in the economic life of the section, although all the responsibility for the work remained with the section itself. Such a system of dual subordination is characteristic of all Soviet enterprises and those of the GPU were no exception.

Like all other Soviet enterprises the camp sections formulated yearly and five-year plans, which were combined, along one line, into the general plan of the particular camp, and along another line, into the general plan for the given branch of industry by the GPU. There is no doubt that these plans were finally included in the *Piatiletka.* The industrial enterprises of the GPU, based on slave labor of prisoners, are growing from year to year and becoming a factor of decisive importance in the general economic activity of the U.S.S.R.

The concentration camps, therefore, are actually enormous enterprises operating in the same field with similar "free" Soviet State institutions. The management of the former is concentrated in the GPU, of the latter, in various commissariats. In many cases the scale of the work carried on by the GPU is larger than that of the corresponding Soviet institutions; it is quite probable, for instance, that the GPU lumber operations exceed those of free lumber "trusts." Communication construction has almost entirely passed into the hands of the GPU, and entire camps with hundreds of thousands of slaves are engaged in these works—the White Sea-Baltic Canal, the Moscow-

Volga Rivers Canal, the Sizran and Koungour railroads and the gigantic Bamlag, Baikal-Amour railroad development. It would seem that the planned economy, proclaimed by the Soviets, would have precluded the existence on such a grand scale, of an industrial organization paralleling the state industry, but the point is that *the GPU in the U.S.S.R. is not simply a state institution, it is actually a state within a state.* The GPU has its own troops, its own navy, millions of its own subjects (the prisoners in camps), its own territory where Soviet authority and laws do not function. The GPU issues its own currency, forbids its subjects to use Soviet currency and does not accept it in its stores. The GPU proclaims its own laws for its subjects, has its own jurisdiction and prisons. It is not surprising, therefore, that it maintains its own industry, parallel to Soviet industry.

There can be no exact comparison between GPU and State enterprises because the former have peculiar features differentiating them from all other business ventures, whether Soviet or not. They deserve the attention of economists.

As I continued my studies of the Fisheries Section I was struck by several of these unique features which it revealed. The invested capital was negligible, the cost of production unusually low, and the profits enormous. With a catch of 700 tons, and the purchase of a similar quantity from fishermen—a total of 1400 tons—the *Ribprom* had earned in 1930 a net profit of one million roubles. Compare this with the record of the North State Fishing Trust which in 1928, with a catch of 48,000 tons, earned a profit of less than one million roubles.

All the production buildings of this enterprise—considered as part of the invested capital—were nothing but barracks of a temporary type. The largest establishments—the canning, fish-smoking and net factories—were housed in large barns on the verge of collapse. The equipment was primitive; at the canning factory, for instance, there was neither running water nor fresh water; sea water was used. At most of the fisheries the salting was carried on in the open as no buildings were available.

There was no refrigeration of any kind—not even ice-cellars. Mechanization of work was entirely absent—everything was done by hand.

In consequence, depreciation of invested capital plays almost no part in the computation of costs. In this respect all enterprises of camps, even those engaged in such complicated works as the construction of the White Sea-Baltic Canal, present an extraordinary similarity. All work is carried on by hand, not a single building of real capital type is erected, all service buildings are constructed as cheaply as possible. This is a feature unknown in Soviet enterprises, where enormous sums are being spent for capital construction and mechanization, often without any rhyme or reason except that of "overtaking and outstripping."

Why this difference? First, the camp enterprises are not intended for "show," and second—this is the chief reason—the camps have *slave labor*. This personnel is actually the invested capital of the GPU enterprises; it takes the place of expensive equipment and machinery. Machines require buildings, care, and fuel of a certain quality and in fixed quantity. Not so with these prisoner-slaves. They need no care, they can exist in unheated barracks which they build themselves. Their fuel ration —food—can be regulated according to circumstances: one kilogram of bread can be reduced to 400 grams, sugar can be omitted entirely; they work equally well on rotten salted horse or camel meat. Finally the slave is a universal machine; today he digs a canal, tomorrow he fells trees, and the next day he catches fish. The only requisite is an efficient organization for compelling him to work—that is the "specialty" of the GPU.

But that is not all. This invested capital costs nothing to obtain as slaves did in capitalistic countries when slavery existed; the supply is limitless and there is neither interest to pay on funded debts nor any depreciation reserve to be set up when the balance sheet is made out.

And then there is the matter of wages, salaries, social insurance, union dues, and so on, all of which may be grouped as "labor costs," of vital importance to Soviet business. The GPU does not have to worry about these. Among the thousands of workmen in a camp section not more than a few free hired employees get salaries; the remainder work without pay. It is true that the GPU pays out premiums to those prisoners who work irreproachably, but this represents not more than 3 or 4 per cent of what the GPU would have to pay a free worker. And even this miserly pay is not in Soviet money, but in GPU scrip. The prisoner can buy for it (only in GPU stores) an insignificant quantity of food which is the waste that otherwise could not be sold. Here again the GPU makes money.

Thus, labor costs cannot be said to influence seriously the cost of production in the GPU. The absence of these two items of expense—depreciation and wages—gives the GPU a saving of not less than 35 per cent in such a venture as the fisheries, and a considerably greater saving in works like the construction of the White Sea Canal.

Moreover, the GPU trademark guarantees an assured home market for its goods—a Soviet purchaser never refuses goods offered him by this "firm," which are sold in open violation of trade regulations of the Soviet Government. A mark-up of 100 to 150 per cent over cost is the usual GPU figure according to its own "plans," and this mark-up is practically synonymous with "profit"—whereas the Soviet State enterprises are not allowed a profit of more than 8 per cent. Actually the GPU is not content with the limit approved in their plans and often sells its goods with a mark-up of 200-300 per cent and sometimes even more.

Here is an example. The Section of Fisheries dealt in fish which it caught or bought from free fishermen, who sold their catch both to the GPU and to other State enterprises (Corporations and Trusts) at fixed prices established by the local executive committee.* The Section of Fisheries bought frozen

* The sale of fish to private individuals, or at a price higher than the one established, is strictly prohibited and is done only secretly and in very small quantities.

herring from the fishermen at the fixed price of 10 kopeks the kilogram, delivered to the warehouse of the Section, where it would be resold, on the spot, to another GPU organization— called "Dynamo"—for 1 rouble (100 kopeks) the kilogram. The new purchaser would cart it to the State Kem Inn, two blocks away, and sell it there for 3 roubles (300 kopeks) the kilogram. That ended the transaction for the GPU. I might add that the State innkeeper, who had nothing to fear from the authorities, would salt it slightly and retail it in his restaurant at one rouble a fish. The White Sea herring is small—there are fifty to sixty in a kilogram—so that the consumer was buying them at the rate of fifty to sixty roubles the kilogram, which was 500 to 600 times the fixed price of 10 kopeks established by Soviet authorities.

I have already pointed out that the GPU was getting rid of its defective merchandise with the greatest ease. Such merchandise is the bane of all Soviet enterprises. Worthless raw materials, inexperienced labor, complicated machinery which nobody can properly handle, extreme haste, uneducated Communist-managers at the head of enterprises, all these factors bring the amount of defective goods to a colossal percentage which wrecks all plans and estimates. In this respect the GPU "businesses" are in a favored position compared with their Soviet competitors. Rarely would a purchaser dare to claim that the GPU had sent him defective goods; he would simply pass them on to the indulgent Soviet consumer. And if the goods are so defective that even the GPU cannot dispose of them in the open market, they are sold, in GPU stores, to prisoners at prices often higher than those of regular GPU goods in the open market. They are also handed out as a premium for "shock" work. The hungry prisoner is happy to get even this.

Widely developed graft is another distinctive feature of all GPU enterprises. Bribes are taken on every occasion and without any reason by everybody from the highest Moscow GPU officials down to the last hired man of the guard. Graft in the inner life of the GPU and their camps has grown such deep roots that it has come to be regarded as a natural condition and the free hired GPU officials openly give and accept bribes unashamed. Money in the U.S.S.R. has little, or rather only a conventional value. Monetary bribes, as such, figure only in fantastic GPU "cases" in which foreign capitalists are supposedly buying Soviet specialists with "Soviet currency." Actually it is doubtful if anyone in the U.S.S.R. could be tempted by Soviet money. Be that as it may, the GPU accepts bribes only in kind, the quality and quantity depending upon the particular case and the rank and position of the person receiving the bribe.

The Section of Fisheries used its own products—fish—as bribes. The Moscow GPU Comrade Boki (member of the OGPU council, in charge of camps) and his equals were given salmon designated for export to England, and a special kind of Solovetzki herring marked by four zeros. In fact, "four zeros" herring was never placed on the market but was reserved for bribes. The export salmon and the "four zeros" herring were also given to the chief of the camp and to the chiefs of the investigation department. Officials of lesser importance received salmon of inferior quality, a box or two of ordinary smoked White Sea herring; the lower officials a few cans of preserved fish. In some cases these bribes were masked by the sending of a bill for a ridiculously small amount.

Whenever a "plan" or a report was to be submitted to the camp administration or to Moscow, the necessary preparations proceeded along two contrasting lines: in the offices, the prisoner-specialists worked day and night compiling memoranda; in the storeroom, other prisoners packed fish in barrels, boxes and baskets—this was the more important work. The Chief of Section, Simankoff, often with both of his assistants, personally supervised the packing, inspected the "presents" which were being sent to those "higher up," and themselves carefully marked the destination of each package. God forbid that an assistant should get a larger "present" than a chief. And the practice was the same when higher authorities came on an of-

SLAVE LABOR—*Vladimir V. Tchernavin* 267

ficial visit. The main concern was to arrange a good reception
and to prepare a pleasing package as a gift. The Section of
Fisheries was no exception in this respect. All sections sent
"presents" to the chiefs. The Agricultural Section sent hams,
butter, and the best vegetables; to local authorities it sent
cream and to the ladies, flowers. The shoe and clothing factories, among whose prisoner-workmen were the best tailors and
cobblers of Leningrad and Moscow, dressed and shod their
chiefs and their families, while the Handicraft Section made
elaborately carved boxes for their superiors.

Such a system of universal graft no doubt adds color to the
life of GPU officials.

Eugene Lyons

THE PRESS CORPS CONCEALS A FAMINE

"I spent the winter of 1932-33 mainly in Kharkov, then capital of the Ukraine. It was the catastrophic winter after the first wave of collectivization of the land. . . . Travelling through the countryside was like running the gant-let: the stations were lined with begging peasants with swollen hands and feet, the women holding up to the carriage windows horrible infants with enormous wobbling heads, sticklike limbs, swollen, pointed bellies. . . . Under my hotel room window in Kharkov funeral processions marched past all day." The Yogi and the Commissar *by Arthur Koestler.*

Editor's Note

SOON after the Bolshevik seiz-ure of power, the first Soviet war against the peasants began. Heavy requisitions, and other confiscatory measures, caused the Russian peasantry to fight back by reducing acreage. When atop Soviet economic policy came drought the grotesque famine of the period of War Communism was the result. But in spite of this vast suffering, the Soviet state lost round one. The widespread discontent, the peasant uprisings, and finally the Kronstadt rebellion forced from the regime the concessions of the New Economic Policy, with its semi-capitalist innova-tions. In 1928, after the breathing spell of NEP, Stalin, who had emerged as the prime holder of power, completed prepara-tions for round two in the internal Soviet agricultural war, a war more costly in lives than many a major military war. The continued distaste for Soviet collectives was irrefutably dem-onstrated by the fact that during the period of NEP, when join-ing collectives was voluntary, less than two per cent of the peasantry chose to do so. It was therefore apparent that the most drastic measures would need to be undertaken in the new drive for collectivization. Stalin, as events soon showed, was quite prepared.

The result was summed up by Anton Ciliga, the former Yugoslavian Communist, in his *The Russian Enigma* (London, 1940): "From 1928 to 1933 bureaucrats and peasants waged one of the most grandiose class-conflicts human history has known." Stalin resorted to an ultimate strategy that was to bring him victory: *organized famine.*

"There is no actual starvation or deaths from starvation but there is widespread mortality from diseases due to malnutrition." Using this incredible sentence—soberly printed in one of the world's most reputable newspapers—as a key, Eugene Lyons in this selection brings us close to one of the world's best hidden atrocities, the Russian famine of 1932-33. This event has instructive value both as brutal "incident" and as symbol. As the author accurately notes: "Years after the event—when no Russian Communist in his senses any longer concealed the magnitude of the famine—the question whether there had been a famine at all was still being disputed in the outside world." That was written in 1937; in some quarters the "controversy" has not ended yet.

William Henry Chamberlin, an eyewitness in the famine areas, from whom we shall hear again on the subject in a next selection, has stated in *Russia's Iron Age:* "Of the historic responsibility of the Soviet Government for the famine of 1932-33 there can be no reasonable doubt. In contrast to its policy in 1921-1922, it stifled any appeal for foreign aid by denying the very fact of the famine and by refusing to foreign journalists the right to travel in the famine regions until it was all over. Famine was quite deliberately employed as an instrument of national policy, as the last means of breaking the resistance of the peasantry to the new system where they are divorced from personal ownership of the land and obliged to work on the conditions which the state may dictate to them and deliver up whatever the state may demand from them."

Forcible collectivization against the will of the peasants, millions dead of starvation, famine as a political weapon, failure to halt exports to feed the dying, prohibition of possible relief measures, indeed, cynical official denial that a famine existed, thorough exercise of censorship to keep the news from the world—this is the essence of the Soviet agricultural victory about which so many "liberals" have written so entrancingly!

Eugene Lyons was born in Uzlian, Russia on July 1, 1898. His youth was spent in the slums of New York. Idealistic, rebellious, he was soon to cultivate an interest in political activity and theory. He took courses in Marx and Spencer and distributed leaflets for socialist candidates as a member of the Young People's Socialist League. He has attended both New York's City College and Columbia University. He served as private in the U. S. Army in World War I and after his demobilization pursued a journalistic career, working for the *Erie* (Pa.) *Dispatch, Financial America,* and other publications. In the autumn of 1920, when Italian workers seized plants in Milan and ran up the flag of revolution, the young writer traveled in steerage to Naples as correspondent for two impecunious leftwing outfits, *Federated Press* and the *Liberator.* When he returned he joined the defense camp of Sacco and Vanzetti. After the execution of the two defendants, the indignant and heartbroken writer shut himself in a room for more than two weeks and wrote at top speed his first book, *The Life and Death of Sacco and Vanzetti.* After being translated into several languages, the book was some years later to be paid the supreme Nazi compliment of burning. In the next five years Lyons edited *Soviet Russia Pictorial,* and worked as Assistant Director of *Tass,* the official Soviet news agency. He did not, however, join the Communist Party. In 1927 he was appointed United Press Russian correspondent, a post he held until 1934, and he, his wife, and their five-year-old daughter, sailed for "the land of our dreams." What he learned there is a better-known part of his story. For his own detailed account, readers are referred to his *Assignment in Utopia* (1937), from which this selection was taken.

Mr. Lyons is also the author of *Moscow Carrousel; Stalin: Czar of All the Russias; The Red Decade;* and a biography of Herbert Hoover. He edited *We Cover the World,* and *Six Soviet Plays.* He has written many articles and has been the editor of *The American Mercury.* At present he is a Roving Editor of the *Reader's Digest.*

#

The Press Corps Conceals a Famine by Eugene Lyons

"THERE is no actual starvation or deaths from starvation but there is widespread mortality from diseases due to malnutrition."

This amazing sophistry, culled from a New York *Times* Moscow dispatch on March 30, 1933, has become among foreign reporters the classic example of journalistic understatement. It characterizes sufficiently the whole shabby episode of our failure to report honestly the gruesome Russian famine of 1932-33.

The circumstance that the government barred us from the afflicted regions may serve as our formal excuse. But a deaf-and-dumb reporter hermetically sealed in a hotel room could not have escaped knowledge of the essential facts. Reporting, as we did daily, industrial victories in the Baikal region or Tajikistan without personal investigation, we had small warrant for withholding and minimizing and diluting the famine story because we were prohibited to make personal investigation. Whatever doubts as to the magnitude of the disaster may have lingered in our minds, the prohibition itself should have set at rest.

The episode, indeed, reflects little glory on world journalism as a whole. Not a single American newspaper or press agency protested publicly against the astonishing and almost unprecedented confinement of its correspondent in the Soviet capital or troubled to probe for the causes of this extraordinary measure.

The New York *Times,* as the foremost American newspaper, is automatically selected for investigation in any test of American reporting. But it was certainly not alone in concealing the famine. The precious sentence quoted above was prefaced with its correspondent's celebrated cliche: "To put it brutally—you can't make an omelette without breaking eggs." A later dispatch enlarged upon the masterpiece of understatement and indicated how the eggs were being broken. Asserting that "in some districts and among the large floating population of unskilled labor" there "have been deaths and actual starvation," he catalogued the maladies of malnutrition as "typhus, dysentery, dropsy, and various infantile diseases." The maladies, in short, that always rage in time of famine.

Not until August 23 did the *Times* out of Moscow admit the famine. "It is conservative to suppose," it said, that in certain provinces with a total population of over 40,000,000 mortality has "at least trebled." On this basis, there were two million deaths more than usual. In addition, deaths were also "considerably increased for the Soviet Union as a whole." This dispatch came one day behind an uncensored cable to the New York *Herald Tribune* by Ralph Barnes, in which he placed the deaths in his ultra-conservative fashion at no less than one million. The Barnes story was front-paged and the *Times* could no longer ignore the subject. Its own admission followed, raising Barnes' ante. By a singular twist of logic, the *Times* story introduced the admission of famine with this remarkable statement:

> Any report of a famine in Russia is today an exaggeration or malignant propaganda. The food shortage which has affected almost the whole population in the last year and particularly in the grain-producing prov-

inces—the Ukraine, North Caucasus, the lower Volga region—has, however, caused heavy loss of life.

The dividing line between "heavy loss of life" through food shortage and "famine" is rather tenuous. Such verbal finessing made little difference to the millions of dead and dying, to the refugees who knocked at our doors begging bread, to the lines of ragged peasants stretching from Torgsin doors in the famine area waiting to exchange their wedding rings and silver trinkets for bread.

These philological sophistries, to which we were all driven, served Moscow's purpose of smearing the facts out of recognition and beclouding a situation which, had we reported it simply and clearly, might have worked up enough public opinion abroad to force remedial measures. And every correspondent, each in his own measure, was guilty of collaborating in this monstrous hoax on the world. Maurice Hindus, though among the most industrious apologists for Stalin, was kept waiting nearly a month for a visa during the famine and finally was admitted on condition that he should not go outside of Moscow. During his 1933 visit, therefore, he did not go to his native village as in the past. In his books, articles and lectures, curiously, he does not allude to that enforced omission and its causes.

The very next day after the *Times*' half-hearted admission from Moscow, its representative in Berlin, Frederick T. Birchall, talked to a group of foreigners just returned from the famine territory, among them a reputable American. "The revelations of what they have seen in the last few weeks," Birchall cabled, "indicate that the recent estimate of four million deaths due indirectly to malnutrition in agricultural Russia in recent months may be rather an understatement than an exaggeration." The word "malnutrition" had, by dint of repetition, taken hold even outside Russia—a clean triumph for planned censorship.

All of us had talked with people just returned from the famine regions. Jack Calder, as honest a man as ever drew a Soviet paycheck, returned from a long tour of Kazakstan with stories to curdle one's blood. Perched on a high stool at the Metropole valuta bar, we listened to his graphic description of Kazakstan roads lined with stiff corpses like so many logs. Most of us saw the pictures taken by German consular officials in the Ukraine showing scenes of horror reminiscent of the Volga famine of 1921. Few of us were so completely isolated that we did not meet Russians whose work took them to the devastated areas, or Muscovites with relatives in those areas. Around every railroad station in the capital hundreds of bedraggled refugees were encamped, had we needed further corroboration; they gathered faster than the police could clear them away.

The truth is that we did not seek corroboration for the simple reason that we entertained no doubts on the subject. There are facts too large to require eyewitness confirmation—facts so pervasive and generally accepted that confirmation would be futile pedantry. There was no more need for investigation to establish the mere existence of the Russian famine than investigation to establish the existence of the American depression. Inside Russia the matter was not disputed. The famine was accepted as a matter of course in our casual conversation at the hotels and in our homes. In the foreign colony estimates of famine deaths ranged from one million up; among Russians from three millions up. Russians, especially communists, were inclined to cite higher figures through a sort of perverse pride in bigness; if it called for Bolshevik firmness to let a million die, it obviously called for three times as much firmness to kill off three million. . . .

The first reliable report of the Russian famine was given to the world by an English journalist, a certain Gareth Jones, at one time secretary to Lloyd George. Jones had a conscientious streak in his make-up which took him on a secret journey into the Ukraine and a brief walking tour through its countryside. That same streak was to take him a few years later into the interior of China during political disturbances, and was to cost him his life at the hands of Chinese military bandits. An earnest and meticulous little man, Gareth Jones was the sort who carries a note-book and unashamedly records your words as you talk. Patiently he went from one correspondent to the next, asking questions and writing down the answers.

On emerging from Russia, Jones made a statement which, startling though it sounded, was little more than a summary of what the correspondents and foreign diplomats had told him. To protect us, and perhaps with some idea of heightening the authenticity of his reports, he emphasized his Ukrainian foray rather than our conversation as the chief source of his information.

In any case, we all received urgent queries from our home offices on the subject. But the inquiries coincided with preparations under way for the trial of the British engineers. The need to remain on friendly terms with the censors at least for the duration of the trial was for all of us a compelling professional necessity.

Throwing down Jones was as unpleasant a chore as fell to any of us in years of juggling facts to please dictatorial regimes —but throw him down we did, unanimously and in almost identical formulas of equivocation. Poor Gareth Jones must have been the most surprised human being alive when the facts he so painstakingly garnered from our mouths were snowed under by our denials.

The scene in which the American press corps combined to repudiate Jones is fresh in my mind. It was in the evening and Comrade Umansky, the soul of graciousness, consented to meet us in the hotel room of a correspondent. He knew that he had a strategic advantage over us because of the Metro-Vickers story.* He could afford to be gracious. Forced by competitive journalism to jockey for the inside track with officials, it would have been professional suicide to make an issue of the famine at this particular time. There was much bargaining in a spirit

* [The trial of a number of British specialists, and a greater number of Russians, in 1933—*Ed.*]

of gentlemanly give-and-take, under the effulgence of Umansky's gilded smile, before a formula of denial was worked out.

We admitted enough to soothe our consciences, but in round-
about phrases that damned Jones as a liar. The filthy business
having been disposed of, someone ordered vodka and *zakuski,*
Umansky joined the celebration, and the party did not break
up until the early morning hours. The head censor was in a mel-
lower mood than I had ever seen him before or since. He had
done a big bit for Bolshevik firmness that night.

We were summoned to the Press Department one by one
and instructed not to venture out of Moscow without submit-
ting a detailed itinerary and having it officially sanctioned. In
effect, therefore, we were summarily deprived of the right of
unhampered travel in the country to which we were accredited.

"This is nothing new," Umansky grimaced uncomfortably.
"Such a rule has been in existence since the beginning of the
revolution. Now we have decided to enforce it."

New or old, such a rule had not been invoked since the civil
war days. It was forgotten again when the famine was ended.
Its undisguised purpose was to keep us out of the stricken regions. The same department which daily issued denials of the
famine now acted to prevent us from seeing that famine with
our own eyes. Our brief cables about this desperate measure of
concealment were published, if at all, in some obscure corner
of the paper. The world press accepted with complete equa-
nimity the virtual expulsion of all its representatives from all of
Russia except Moscow. It agreed without protest to a partnership in the macabre hoax.

Other steps were taken to prevent prying. Until then, foreigners arriving at the frontier received their passports as soon
as the train got under way. Now the passports were retained
by the authorities until just before the train pulled into Moscow
—thus guaranteeing that no foreigner would drop off en route
for unchaperoned research.

When M. Herriot, the liberal French statesman, arrived in

Russia at Odessa, the one French correspondent in the country, M. Lusiani, demanded the right to meet him. The Press Department finally gave its permission—on Lusiani's solemn undertaking to remain with the official party and not to stray into the countryside. M. Herriot, conducted along the prescribed road between Odessa and Moscow, completely surrounded by high functionaries, was able to say honestly when he returned to Paris that he had not personally seen any famine. Neither had Lusiani.

2

I was not the first Moscow observer to remark that God seems to be on the side of the atheists. What the Kremlin would have prayed for, had it believed in prayer, was perfect weather, and that is what it received that spring and summer: perfect weather and bumper crops. The fields had been planted under the aegis of the newly established *Politotdyels* (Political Departments) with unlimited authority over the peasants. Food rations barely sufficient to sustain life had been distributed only to those actually at work in the fields. Red Army detachments in many places had been employed to guard seed and to prevent hungry peasants from devouring the green shoots of the new harvest. In the midst of the famine, the planting proceeded, and the crops came up strong and plenteous. The dead were buried—for the living there would be bread enough and to spare in the following winter.

Belatedly the world had awakened to the famine situation. We were able to write honestly that "to speak of famine *now* is ridiculous." We did not always bother to add that we had failed to speak of it or at best mumbled incomprehensibly *then,* when it was not ridiculous. Cardinal Innitzer, Archbishop of Vienna, made the first of his sensational statements about Soviet agrarian conditions on August 20, when those conditions were already being mitigated. Certain anti-Soviet newspapers in England and America began to write about the famine at about the time it was ended, and continued to write about it long after it had become history: their facts were on the whole correct, but their tenses were badly mixed. The most rigorous censorship in all of Soviet Russia's history had been successful —it had concealed the catastrophe until it was ended, thereby bringing confusion, doubt, contradiction into the whole subject. Years after the event—when no Russian communist in his senses any longer concealed the magnitude of the famine—the question whether there had been a famine at all was still being disputed in the outside world!

In the autumn, the Soviet press was exultant. Lazar Kaganovich was given most of the credit for the successful harvest. It was his mind that invented the Political Departments to lead collectivized agriculture, his iron hand that applied Bolshevik mercilessness. Now that a healing flood of grain was inundating the famished land, the secrecy gradually gave way. Increasingly with every passing month Russian officials ceased to deny the obvious. Soviet journalists who had been in the afflicted areas now told me personally such details of the tragedy as not even the eager imaginations of Riga and Warsaw journalists had been able to project. They were able to speak in the past tense, so that their accents were proud boasts rather than admissions.

The Kremlin, in short, had "gotten away with it." At a cost in millions of lives, through the instrumentalities of hunger and terror, socialized agriculture had been made to yield an excellent harvest. Certain observers now insisted in print that the efficacy of collectivization had been demonstrated; nothing, of course, had been demonstrated except the efficacy of concentrated force used against a population demoralized by protracted hunger.

There were few peasant homes in the worst of the famine districts which had not paid a toll in life for this harvest. In hundreds of villages half the population was gone: some had been killed by the "diseases of malnutrition" and others had fled to seek food. In September and October, Chamberlin, Duranty, and others who visited southern Russia still found half-deserted villages. It would be years before the memory of this fearful time would lose its poignancy in the Ukraine and North Caucasus, in Kazakstan and Lower Volga. And there were those who believed, as I did, that the memory was indelible and would rise to plague those who had decided in cold blood to let the villages starve. But in the cities, at least, a new optimism was born.

The attitude of the professional friends of the U.S.S.R. on the famine went through a curious cycle. First, while the disaster was under way, they made furious denials. Since then, they have tended to admit the facts but to explain them away as unavoidable, and as a just and proper punishment meted out to a "rebellious" peasantry. "Why harp on something that is by now history?" sums up their reproachful objection to a reminder of the period. But all great social crimes, given time, become history. By that fantastic logic, time has wiped out the guilt of those who perpetrated the Inquisition and the St. Bartholomew's Night massacres, the World War and the fascist destruction of Vienna's socialist housing, the Reichstag fire and the fascist attack on democratic government in Spain. The Kremlin had foreseen the famine and permitted it to run its course of death and horror for political reasons. The philosophy which made such a decision possible, the mad arrogance of rulers condemning millions to death, are not justified by the fact that the dead are buried and the survivors being fed.

How many millions actually died will never be known accurately. It is not generally understood abroad that the Soviet government *stopped the publication of vital statistics for the period in question,* although such statistics were published as a matter of routine in previous years; otherwise it would be a simple matter to compare the death-rate for the winter and spring of 1932-33 with the normal death-rate.

Estimates made by foreigners and Russians range from three to seven millions. Chamberlin, after his journey through the devastated districts, described in detail in his *Russia's Iron Age,* placed the cost in life at four million. Duranty, after a similar journey, withdrew his previous estimate that the death-rate had increased threefold as far as the North Caucasus was concerned but stated that "he is inclined to believe that the estimate he made for the Ukraine was too low." A more than trebled death-rate in the Ukraine would bring the famine deaths in that one area alone to a million and a half. Maurice Hindus, after years of vagueness on the subject, finally settled on "at least three million" as his estimate.

Southern Russia, after many months of total news blockade, was opened to foreign correspondents in easy stages. The first to be given permission to travel in the forbidden zones were the technically "friendly" reporters, whose dispatches might be counted upon to take the sting out of anything subsequent travelers might report. Duranty, for instance, was given a two weeks' advantage over most of us. On the day he returned, it happened, Billy* and I were dining with Anne O'Hare McCormick, roving correspondent for the New York *Times,* and her husband. Duranty joined us. He gave us his fresh impressions in brutally frank terms and they added up to a picture of ghastly horror. His estimate of the dead from famine was the most startling I had as yet heard from anyone.

"But, Walter, you don't mean that literally?" Mrs. McCormick exclaimed.

"Hell I don't. . . . I'm being conservative," he replied, and as if by way of consolation he added his famous truism: "But they're only Russians. . . ."

Once more the same evening we heard Duranty make the same estimate, in answer to a question by Laurence Stallings, at the railroad station, just as the train was pulling out for the Polish frontier. When the issues of the *Times* carrying Duranty's own articles reached me I found that they failed to mention the large figures he had given freely and repeatedly to all of us.

---

* [The author's wife—*Ed.*]

OUT OF THE DEEP: LETTERS
FROM SOVIET TIMBER CAMPS

THE following few excerpts are from a collection of letters from Soviet timber camps, written by different persons at forced labor in various places, that appeared in a disturbing volume published in England in 1933. The names of the writers, the methods by which the letters were mailed, and other details had to be withheld for the usual reasons, but their authenticity is beyond question. *Out of the Deep,* the name given to the collection, carries a preface by the late Sir Bernard Pares, known not only for his knowledge of Soviet affairs but for his friendship for the Soviet Union. In it, he states: "I have seen the originals of the letters here printed, with their postmarks. I can have no doubt of their authenticity, for numbers of other materials obtained from trustworthy sources have confirmed, not only the general tenor of these statements, but often the actual details. . . ."

In an introduction Hugh Walpole provides other background information. "The letters in this book are the result of the Collectivist agricultural policy of the Russian Government." The tragic letters, of which only a taste is provided here, are said to be those of *kulaks,* that most elastic of Soviet concepts. This class, the "well-to-do peasants," has been the object of extraordinary efforts on the part of the Soviet regime. *Kulaks* were to be "liquidated as a class." Excluded from the agricultural collectives, their holdings were confiscated, and they were removed ("deported") to sparsely settled and little-worked Soviet territory. Against them was instituted one of the most merciless campaigns in all history. Entire families were arrested and sent to forced labor, where many died; other families were broken up and shipped separately; a huge number was physically "liquidated."

The causes of this upheaval were more than "ideological." The "kulaks" were excellent scapegoats; to them could be attributed many of the failures of the regime. In addition, as Mr. Walpole explained: "The needs of a rapidly developing industry, which did not readily attract voluntary labor, soon showed that wholesale deportation rather than sentencing was needed. Besides, if dispossessed, their lands, cattle and machinery would be valuable assets to the kolkhozy. There followed then a sweeping and merciless policy."

Just how wealthy was a kulak? In an important sense the question is irrelevant, for in no other country in the world, except Nazi Germany where the Jews were the scapegoats, has there been a campaign for the wholesale "liquidation of a class," with human life held in equal contempt. But the brutality involved grows more grotesque if we seek an answer to the question. "The 'wealth' which brought on these disabilities," Mr. Walpole noted, and the full literature on the subject bears him out, "might not be more than a couple of cows and horses, or part ownership of a tea house or village inn, or even the possession of a sewing machine." In his A History of Russia (1944), Professor Vernadsky, in another context, comments informatively: "It is interesting to know what the Soviet leaders meant by the various classes of peasants. According to the data presented to the Fifteenth Party Conference [1926], the poorer peasants were those with an annual per capita income of $39; the middle group had an annual income of $46; and the richer peasants, $88."

As one reads these letters, dated 1931 and 1932, it is impossible not to think of other letters, almost unbelievable, but all too true, that were smuggled out of Nazi Germany. It is still more disheartening to reflect that the charge against the Russians is not even that of aping the Nazis. Hitler and his minions had yet to come to power! And still, this was no new development for Communist Russia, however new was the specific policy from which it stemmed. For an earlier distressing black book of letters from prisons, documents, excerpts from Soviet laws see *Letters from Soviet Prisons* (New York, 1925), assembled by the International Committee for Political Prisoners, and prefaced by statements by many internationally known persons. See also G. P. Maximoff's insufficiently known *The Guillotine at Work: Twenty Years of Terror in Russia* (1940), published by the Alexander Berkman Fund, a comprehensive book of data and documents.

January 31, 1931

. . . WE LIVED in "C," but were sent away nearly a year ago. First we were five months in the Urals, and from there we were sent to the "O" district, where we had to work at stonebreaking.

Dear brothers and sisters, if it be possible we pray you to send us something to eat, even if it is only a little dripping. My family numbers eight souls, of whom only four are able to work, and here those who do not work receive nothing, so that our lack of food is very great. We are in exile and have no rights. Therefore we turn to you, our brothers, for help. At home they took everything away from us, so that we live here without anything . . .

Forgive me, I do not even know where to address this letter, but yet I will try to send it to "Q." Perhaps there will be some kind brothers who will take pity on me and my poor family. . . . We are in a barrack, 366 people.

————.

* * *

February 1, 1931

Dear ————

I received your letters some time ago and the parcel yesterday. The latter had already been here three weeks; but as long as we have not completed the task imposed on us parcels are not handed out. As a sick woman mine was given to me. I send you my very warmest thanks from here, and hope God will repay you. Our Saviour says: 'Whatever thou hast done for my most humble brothers, that hast thou done unto me.' And the humblest and most despised of mankind in this world are we. It is impossible to describe the need, grief, pain and humiliation which we are suffering here. Everyone is forced to work, from the ages of 12 to 70 and over, in fact anyone who is still able to stand on his feet; some of them are even taken from their sick-beds. They wanted to take one man by force and refused to believe he was ill, and the same evening he died, leaving a sick wife with three children. He suffered famine for a long time and could get no support anywhere. Then a parcel came for him, but it was not given to him because he had not carried out the task imposed upon him. Three days after his death the family received the parcel.

The work is very hard and unfamiliar. Felling gigantic trees, sawing them in lengths of 1½ metres, and then splitting them and piling them up; for that they get 40 kop. for one cubic; the norm for children is one cubic, for workers of little strength 2, for workers of full strength 3.75, and 40 kop. is paid for one cubic! Those who earn 1.60 kop. get 800 grammes of bread; the smaller the task the smaller the quantity of bread. On an average the full worker does 2 cubics.

Those who do not complete the imposed task get no day

of rest; for instance, my son, and indeed all men and young women work fifteen miles away from us, and have not had a day of rest since January 6th, working not less than sixteen hours per day or more. It has happened that they were only allowed to sleep one hour a night, and quite often only three hours a night. This has been slightly modified now because so many get frozen limbs. Then there is no pause for food between work; they take a small piece of bread—many have none—with them to eat, which freezes to stone immediately; and in the evenings or at night when they return home, whoever wants tea or something warm to eat has to prepare it first. The arrangements for cooking are very bad, there is one stove for about 120 people, so that many go to bed without anything warm to eat at all. Plenty of vermin exists, for since the 6th nobody has changed and no one may go home until they have finished their task.

Here where we are it is no better, they have taken everybody who remained, chiefly women, even those who have babies of two months old (their mothers, however, are allowed to go home at noon to feed them), and for the rest of the day they are left to a pack of children of which the eldest is ten years old. They took women of 65 and men of over 70. The worst, though, is that they are all starving (many are already swollen), and freezing, for clothing is not supplied. It would be impossible to get felt shoes, even the necessary bast shoes are not available. Many simply work on rags and that is why there are such a number with frozen feet. I got news some days ago that my son and daughter-in-law have frozen feet.

I could not console myself for the loss of my husband, but I will mourn for him no longer, he is freed from all this. I myself am not working because I have been in hospital. I am still writing this letter in bed, but I am not sure for a moment whether they are not going to drag me out of it, for they have been pressing me enough already. Doctors certificates are of no avail, they are simply torn up. My room mate (there are three families in one room) has a boy aged four. She has been working from

January 20th without a break. She has, however, to wash, bake, cook, and look after me as well: she generally sits in the cold as she has no time to get wood. No one looks after the children.

Often one becomes desperate and asks: "Lord, why dost thou try us so sorely, and how have we merited this?* Were we not true and faithful subjects? Did we not live according to the saying 'Bow to the Powers who rule over thee,' even when they seem strange? We subjected ourselves willingly and patiently to everything." It would all be much easier if we felt guilty, but we may say with a good conscience that we are suffering innocently. . . .

*   *   *

March 23, 1931

———,

Accept my heartfelt thanks for all the love and friendliness you have shown my old mother and myself. It is a great help to us, and may the good Lord bless you twofold.

So many things happened about the time the parcels arrived. Dear lady, you have no idea how we live here, and even if I told you the whole truth now, you would still say this cannot be possible. How could you understand a state of affairs in which a mass of people who have worked for nearly a year conscientiously and with all their strength, are at the end of that time treated more cruelly than the vilest animals?

Terrible and appalling things happen here, yet we say nothing. Mothers and fathers stand weeping to see their children so maltreated and driven to work. It is enough to break one's heart, and there is no help anywhere. How we long to live as free citizens! We are all sighing and groaning under the yoke of "free-

---

* [Stalin's words may be read as an answer: "To attack the kulaks means to smash the kulaks, to liquidate them as a class. Without these aims, attack is a declamation, mere scratching, empty noise, anything but a real Bolshevist attack. To attack the kulaks means to make proper preparations and then deliver the blow, a blow from which they could not recover. That is what we Bolsheviks call a real attack." (*Speech by Stalin at the conference of Marxist Agrarians, December 27, 1929.*) Admitting some "excesses," Stalin quoted a proverb in defense: "Weep not for the hair when the head is off."—*Ed.*]

dom." Things in this country are far worse than they were a hundred years ago.

How can one live on half a pound of bread a day, and then walk 10 to 30 kilometres to work? It is terrible. Whatever poor people come to these slave colonies are worked to death. If one could only find someone who had eyes to see how they are trying to carry Socialism into practice!

I shall add a few names of people at the address to which you sent our gifts. They are people to be pitied just as much as ourselves. I thank you again for the flour, groats, rice and bacon. These are things we have not seen for a whole year.

————.

❋   ❋   ❋

DEAREST FRIENDS:

Because there is no one we can turn to in our terrible need and shortage of food, we feed for the most part on different kinds of grasses, just like beasts; death has come to many through eating too much of these grasses. I therefore turn to you and beseech you to send food very soon. May the good Lord repay you for the good you may do to us exiles.

I send you my grateful thanks in advance.

With greetings,

————.

❋   ❋   ❋

August 19, 1932

That dark cloud of terror, starvation, is gathering closer about our heads from day to day. Masses of people are dying. The instinct to live forces us to beg for what you sent us last year of your own free will, or at any rate without our knowing anything about it. Please help us if you can; in our terrible plight of starvation every help is a double help.

Please forgive this letter . . .

From,

————.

William Henry Chamberlin

DEATH IN THE VILLAGES

"Because the famine coincided with the triumphant finish of the first Piatiletka [Five-Year Plan] in four years, the press was hysterical with boasts of 'our achievements.' Yet the deafening propaganda could not quite drown out the groans of the dying. To some of us the shouting about the new 'happy life' seemed ghoulish, more terrifying even than the famine itself." I Chose Freedom, by Victor Kravchenko.

Editor's Note

THESE two brief entries from William Henry Chamberlin's Russian diary are to be read as a continuation to Mr. Lyons's selection. In "The Press Corps Conceals a Famine," we were told why and how the news of the famine was kept from the outside world. Now, we are given a glimpse into the reality in the villages that was being so carefully hidden. Mr. Chamberlin—until then a friendly but not uncritical interpreter of Soviet affairs—visited three widely separated districts, Kropotkin, in the North Caucasus, and Poltava and Byelaya Tserkov, in the Ukraine. What he saw has been reported in horrifying and edifying detail in the chapter, "The Ordeal of the Peasantry," in his *Russia's Iron Age* (1934). Here, from the same book, are two diary notes on his trip to the village of Cherkass which furnish us in microcosm with a picture of the overall famine, with its death toll of millions.

"The Soviet Government," concluded Mr. Chamberlin, "could easily have averted the famine from its own resources if it had desired to do so. A complete cessation of the exports of foodstuffs in 1932 or the diversion of a small amount of foreign currency to the purchase of grain and provisions would have achieved this end."

William Henry Chamberlin was born in Brooklyn, on February 17, 1897. He graduated from Haverford College in the year of the Russian Revolution. In the next six years he was assistant managing editor of the Philadelphia *Press,* and assistant book editor of the New York *Tribune.* In 1922 he was appointed to the position in which he was to become internationally known as a commentator on the Soviet Union, Moscow correspondent of the *Christian Science Monitor.* He remained in this post for thirteen years. His political evolution in the USSR paralleled that of many other observers. When he first arrived he was enthusiastically pro-Soviet. He believed that the Bolshevik model was "the panacea for war and for all social injustice." This idealistic faith was steadily diminished by the impact of many successive events, and by the increasingly dictatorial bent of the regime. Nevertheless he maintained his hope and charitable expectations for a number of years. The final turning point was his trip through the famine regions. In 1939-40 he served as chief Far Eastern correspondent for the *Monitor.* In recent years he has been a lecturer at Yale, Harvard, and other universities, contributor to many publications, an editor of *The New Leader,* and has continued to write expert books on world affairs. Among his many books are: *Soviet Russia; The Soviet Planned Order; The Russian Revolution* (two volumes); *Japan Over Asia; Confessions of an Individualist; The World's Iron Age; The Russian Enigma; America, Partner in World Rule;* and *The European Cockpit.*

Death in the Villages by W. H. Chamberlin

October 1933.—We have just returned from one of the most interesting and certainly from the saddest of our many trips in the Russian villages. For as soon as the long-withheld and reluctantly granted permission to travel outside of Moscow was received we went to the North Caucasus and to Ukraina, to find out how much truth there was in the rumors of wholesale starvation among the peasants there during the past winter and spring. What we found was little short of the worst we had heard, and certainly explains the extraordinary action of the Soviet authorities in forbidding, over a period of several months, all travel in the famine regions by foreign correspondents. Everywhere a death rate that ranged remarkably close around the average figure of 10 per cent, according to the testimony of responsible local officials. Stories of whole families that had died off, leaving one or two survivors. Stories of cannibalism. A dreary, poverty-stricken, miserable population, shaking with malaria, in the once-fertile Kuban Valley, now overgrown with a thick crop of weeds.

Quite by chance the last village we visited was at once the most terrible and the most dramatic. It is called Cherkass, and it lies about seven or eight miles to the south of Byelaya Tserkov, a Ukrainian town southwest of Kiev. Here the "normal" mortality of 10 per cent had been far exceeded. On the road to the village, former ikons with the face of Christ had been removed; but the crown of thorns had been allowed to remain— an appropriate symbol for what the village had experienced. Coming into the village, we found one deserted house after another, with window-panes fallen in, crops growing mixed with weeds in gardens with no one to harvest them. A boy in the dusty village street called the death roll among the families he knew with the stolid impassivity that one sometimes found among the peasants in the face of the catastrophe of the preceding winter and spring.

"There was Anton Samchenko, who died with his wife and sister; three children were left. With Nikita Samchenko's family, the father and Mikola and two other children died; five children were left. Then Grigory Samchenko died with his son Petro; a wife and daughter are left. And Gerasim Samchenko died with four of his children; only the wife is still living. And Sidnor Odnorog died with his wife and two daughters; one girl is left. Gura Odnorog died with his wife and three children; one girl is still alive."

The secretary of the local Soviet, a young man named Fischenko, put the tragedy of the village in concrete figures. During the previous winter and spring, 634 out of the 2072 inhabitants of the village had died. During the past year there had been one marriage in the village. Six children had been born; of these, one had survived.

"It's better not to bear children than to have them die of hunger," said a woman in the office of the Soviet.

"No," argued a boy; "if no children are born, who can till the land?"

I think the individual tragedy which stood out most strongly in Cherkass was that of a woman with whom we talked who had lost her three children. "They were such good children, such *uchenie* (learned) children," she said, weeping bitterly. To me the right of these unknown children, and the uncounted others of whom they were only the symbol, to live is higher than the right of the dictators in the Kremlin to launch a programme of overstrained and overhastened militarist and industrial expansion, to force on the peasants a system so hateful that it could only be finally clamped down with the use of the last and most terrible weapon—organized famine.

December 1933.—Kalinin made a curious reference to the famine in addressing the All-Union Soviet Executive Committee.

He said: "Political impostors ask contributions for the 'starving' of Ukraina. Only degraded disintegrating classes can produce such cynical elements."

So, according to the Soviet President, the famine in Ukraina is nothing but the malicious invention of "degraded disintegrating classes." And not one Ukrainian delegate in the Soviet Executive Committee had a word of contradiction. I wonder whether Kalinin's speech will reach Cherkass, and what effect it will produce there.

André Gide

RETURN FROM THE USSR

Editor's Note

"WHO shall say what the So-
viet Union has been to us?" once asked André Gide, France's
most distinguished contemporary man of letters, in speaking
of an attitude that he previously held regarding the USSR.
"More than a chosen land—an example, a guide. What we have
dreamed of, what we hardly dared to hope, but towards which
we were straining all our will and all our strength, was coming
into being over there. A land existed where Utopia was in process of becoming reality." Four days after his arrival in Moscow
on June 20, 1936, he gave—on the occasion of Maxim Gorky's
funeral—a public address in Red Square. "The fate of culture," he said, "is bound up in our minds with the destiny of
the Soviet Union. We will defend it."

What is necessary to disillusion such a friend? The record
of Gide's comradeship—even adoration—for the Soviet Union,
in the years before his first-hand observation of that country,
is not often presented by Soviet admirers. It was precisely because of this earlier benediction by the great man of international culture—in addition to his perceptive account—that his
report on his journey was instrumental in arousing world-wide
discussion. This becomes even more impressive when the
reader, in turning the pages of M. Gide's book, rapidly un-
derstands that every effort has been made on the side of
understatement. In the long career of this renowned writer,

rabble-rousing is one trait with which he has demonstrated no familiarity. In this context, his honest, modestly presented findings have successfully challenged rebuttal despite an almost unprecedented campaign of abuse, both personal and political, directed against him.

It is significant to note that in the preface to his *Return from the USSR* (1937),* from which we present Chapters 3 and 5, he chose to take as his text the Homeric hymn to Demeter, which characterized his stand at the time perfectly. That work relates how the great goddess, while searching for her daughter, came upon the court of Keleos. She was disguised as a humble wet nurse, and as such went unrecognized. Queen Metaneira put in her care the latest-born child, the infant Demophoon. Every evening, Demeter—moved by an ardent desire to bring the infant to a state of godhood—placed the child secretly on a glowing bed of embers. The great cruelty involved was intended as great love. "I imagine," wrote Gide, "the mighty Demeter bending maternally over the radiant nursling as over the future race of mankind. He endures the fiery charcoal; he gathers strength from the ordeal. Something superhuman is fostered in him, something robust, something beyond all hope glorious. Ah, had Demeter only been able to carry through her bold attempt, to bring her daring venture to a successful issue! But Metaneira becoming anxious, says the legend, burst suddenly into the room where the experiment was being carried on and, guided by her mistaken fears, thrust aside the goddess at her work of forging the superman, pushed away the embers, and, in order to save the child, lost the god."

A most efficacious Soviet method for impressing prominent visitors has been to show them "Potemkin Villages," or unrepresentative model exhibits: special schools, social welfare centers, rest homes for workers. The admiring tourist can then write home truthfully that he has not seen any forced labor centers and similar facets of Soviet life; he most certainly has

* See also his *Afterthoughts*, published in the following year.

not. This cynical approach, which the Communists did not hesitate to use—along with other like techniques—on André Gide, worked badly. It is a testimonial to the sagacity of Gide that he should have so clearly grasped the essentials of the Soviet system, even, or especially, in the presence of these untypical "show" conditions. He is generous in his praise. He admires rest homes that surround a town; nevertheless, he looks about him. "But it is painful to see next door to all this that the workmen who are employed in the construction of the new theatre should be so badly paid and herded in such sordid barracks. . . ." He does not fail to observe the contempt in which servants ("inferiors") are held.

There is still a larger lesson, a key to the psychology of the Communist ruling caste; the point has been made well by "Ypsilon," two ex-Communists, in their interesting book, *Pattern For World Revolution* (1947):

> The Russians, masters at organizing humanistic congresses abroad, committed fatal blunders in their treatment of foreigners at home. They completely misjudged André Gide, believing that an exhibition of luxury and comfort equalling and surpassing that to which he was accustomed in France would dissolve the last doubts that might linger in the mind of the humanist from the West. They provided the finest limousines, special de luxe trains with private cars, elaborate banquets, everything that had caused André Gide to doubt and despise the civilization of the West. This was not a foolish blunder committed accidentally by his Russian guides. It was a spontaneous if unconscious expression of their own order of values by the new Russian elite whom Gide had taken for pioneers of humanism. They were offering him on his journey of discovery the very things they themselves longed for. They were measuring him by their own standards.

André Gide was born in Paris on November 21, 1869. His initial work, *Les Cahiers d'André Walter,* appeared in 1891. By 1925 he had already published thirty additional books which spread his fame as an artist far past the borders of his native land. Few careers have been as unceasingly fruitful. As he neared his sixtieth year, for example, he published in noteworthy succession: *Si le grain ne meurt,* an autobiography; *Numquid et tu?,* a book of prayers; and the Counterfeiters, which is probably his best-known work. In recent years his journals have been put before the American public. In 1947 he received the Nobel Prize for literature. At present M. Gide continues to live and write in Paris.

Return from the USSR by André Gide

In the U.S.S.R. everybody knows beforehand, once and for all, that on any and every subject there can be only one opinion. And in fact everybody's mind has been so moulded and this conformism become to such a degree easy, natural, and imperceptible, that I do not think any hypocrisy enters into it. Are these really the people who made the revolution? No; they are the people who profit by it. Every morning the *Pravda* teaches them just what they should know and think and believe. And he who strays from the path had better look out! So that every time you talk to one Russian you feel as if you were talking to them all. Not exactly that everyone obeys a word of command; but everything is so arranged that nobody can differ from anybody else. Remember that this moulding of the spirit begins in earliest infancy. . . . This explains their extraordinary attitude of acceptance which sometimes amazes you if you are a foreigner, and a certain capacity for happiness which amazes you even more.

You are sorry for those people who stand in a queue for hours; but they think waiting perfectly natural. Their bread and vegetables and fruit seem to you bad; but there is nothing else. You find the stuffs and the articles which you are shown frightful; but there is no choice. If every point of comparison is removed, save with a past that no one regrets, you are delighted with what is offered you. What is important here is to persuade people that they are as well off as they can be until a better time comes; to persuade them that elsewhere people are *worse* off. The only way of achieving this is carefully to prevent any communication with the outside world (the world beyond the frontier, I mean). Thanks to this the Russian workman who has a standard of living equal or even noticeably inferior to that of a French workman thinks himself well off, *is* better off, much better off, than a workman in France. Their happiness is made up of hope, confidence, and ignorance.

It is extremely difficult for me to introduce any order into these reflections, owing to the interweaving and overlapping of the problems. I am not a technician and what interests me in economic questions is their psychological repercussion. I perfectly understand the psychological reasons which render it necessary to operate in close isolation, to prevent any leakage at the frontiers; in present-day conditions and so long as things have not improved, it is essential to the inhabitants of the U.S.S.R. that this happiness should be protected from outside influences.

We admire in the U.S.S.R. the extraordinary *élan* towards education and towards culture; but the only objects of this education are those which induce the mind to find satisfaction in its present circumstances and exclaim: "*Oh! U.S.S.R. . . . Ave! Spes unica!*" And culture is entirely directed along a single track. There is nothing disinterested in it; it merely accumu-

lates, and (in spite of Marxism) almost entirely lacks the critical faculty. Of course I know that what is called "self-criticism"
is highly thought of. When at a distance, I admired this and I
still think it might have produced the most wonderful results,
if only it had been seriously and sincerely applied. But I was
soon obliged to realize that apart from denunciations and complaints ("The canteen soup is badly cooked" or "The club read-
ing-room badly swept"), criticism merely consists in asking
oneself if this, that, or the other is "in the right line." The line
itself is never discussed. What is discussed is whether such and
such a work, or gesture, or theory conforms to this sacrosanct
line. And woe to him who seeks to cross it! As much criticism
as you like—up to a point. Beyond that point criticism is not
allowed. There are examples of this kind of thing in history.

And nothing is a greater danger to culture than such a frame
of mind. I will go more fully into this later on.

The Soviet citizen is in an extraordinary state of ignorance
concerning foreign countries.* More than this—he has been
persuaded that everything abroad and in every department is
far less prosperous than in the U.S.S.R. This illusion is cleverly
fostered, for it is important that everyone, even those who are
ill satisfied, should be thankful for the régime which preserves
them from worse ills.

Hence a kind of *superiority complex,* of which I will give a
few examples:

Every student is obliged to learn a foreign language. French
has been completely abandoned. It is English and especially
German that they are supposed to know. I expressed my surprise that they should speak them so badly; in our countries a
fifth-form schoolboy knows more.

One of the students we questioned gave us the following explanation (in Russian and Jef Last translated it for us):

"A few years ago Germany and the United States still had
something to teach us on a few points. But now we have noth-

---

* Or at least he is only informed as to things which will encourage him in
his own frame of mind.

ing more to learn from foreigners. So why should we speak their language?" *

As a matter of fact, though they do take some interest in what is happening in foreign parts, they are far more concerned about what the foreigner thinks of them. What really interests them is to know whether we admire them enough. What they are afraid of is that we should be ill informed as to their merits. What they want from us is not information but praise.

Some charming little girls who gathered round me in a children's playground (which I must say was entirely praiseworthy, like everything else that is done here for the young) harried me with questions. What they wanted to know was not whether we have children's playgrounds in France, but whether we know in France that they have such fine children's playgrounds in the U.S.S.R.

The questions you are asked are often so staggering that I hesitate to report them. It will be thought that I have invented them. They smile sceptically when I say that Paris too has got a subway. Have we even got street-cars? Buses? . . . One of them asks (and these were not children, but educated workmen) whether we had schools too in France. Another, slightly better informed, shrugged his shoulders; "Oh yes, the French have got schools; but the children are beaten in them." He has this information on the best authority. Of course all workers in our country are wretched; that goes without saying, for we have not yet "made the revolution." For them, outside the U.S.S.R. the reign of night begins. Apart from a few shameless capitalists, everybody else is groping in the dark.

Some educated and most "refined" young girls (at Artek camp, where only exceptional characters are admitted) were highly surprised when I mentioned Russian films and told them that *Chapaiev* and *We are from Kronstadt* had had a great success in Paris. Had they not been assured that all Rus-

* Confronted by our undisguised amazement, the student, it is true, added: "I understand—we all understand today—that such an argument is absurd. A foreign language, when it no longer serves for learning, may still serve for teaching."

sian films were banned in France? And, as those who told them so are their masters, I could see perfectly well that it was my word they doubted. The French are so fond of pulling one's leg!

In a circle of naval officers on board a battleship which had just been presented to our admiration ("This one is entirely made in the U.S.S.R."), when I went so far as to say that I was afraid that people in the Soviet Union were less well informed about what is being done in France than the people in France about what is being done in the Soviet Union, a distinctly disapproving murmur arose: "The *Pravda* gives us sufficient information about everything." And suddenly somebody in a lyrical outburst, stepping out from the group exclaimed: "In order to describe all the new and splendid and great things that are being done in the Soviet Union, there would not be paper enough in the whole world."

In that same model camp of Artek, a paradise for model children and infant prodigies, all hung round with medals and diplomas—and that is just what makes me vastly prefer some other camps for pioneers, which are more modest and less aristocratic—a child of thirteen, who I understood came from Germany, but who had already been moulded by the Union, guided me through the park, showing off its beauties. He began to recite:

> Just look! There was nothing here till quite recently . . . and then suddenly—this staircase appeared. And it's like that everywhere in the Soviet Union. Yesterday nothing; tomorrow everything. Look at those workmen over there, how hard they're working! And everywhere in the Soviet Union there are schools and camps like these. Of course they're not quite so wonderful as this one, because this camp of Artek has not got its equal in the world. Stalin takes a special interest in it. All the children who come here are remarkable.

Later on you'll hear a child of thirteen who is going

to be the best violinist in the world. His talent has already been so highly thought of that they have made him a present of a historic violin, a violin that was made by a very famous violin-maker who lived a long while ago.*

And here—look at this wall! Could you possibly tell that it had been built in ten days?

The child's enthusiasm seemed so sincere that I took good care not to point out that this retaining wall which had been too hastily constructed was already fissured. He only consented to see, was only able to see, what satisfied his pride, and he added in a transport:

"Even the children are astonished!" **

These children's sayings (sayings which had been prompted, and perhaps taught) appeared to me so revealing that I wrote them down that very evening and relate them here verbatim.

And yet I do not want it to be thought that I have no other memories of Artek. It is quite true that this children's camp is wonderful. It is built on overhanging terraces that go right down to the sea, and this splendid site is used to the best advantage with great ingenuity. Everything that one can imagine for the well-being of children, for their hygiene, for their physical training, for their amusement, for their pleasure, has been

---

* Shortly afterwards I heard this little prodigy play some Paganini and then a pot-pourri of Gounod on his Stradivarius, and I must admit that he was amazing.

** Eugène Dabit, when in the course of conversation I mentioned this superiority complex, to which his own extreme modesty made him particularly sensitive, handed me the second volume of *Dead Souls* which he was re-reading. At the beginning there is a letter from Gogol in which Dabit pointed out the following passage: "There are many among us, and particularly among our young people, who exalt the Russian virtues far too highly; instead of developing these virtues in themselves, all they think of is showing them off and saying to Europe: 'Look, foreigners, how much better we are than you!' This swaggering is terribly pernicious. While it irritates other people, it also damages the person who indulges in it. Boasting degrades the finest action in the world. As for me, I prefer a momentary dejection to self-complacency."

This Russian "swaggering" that Gogol deplores is fostered and emboldened by the present system of education.

assembled and arranged along the terraces and slopes. All the children were glowing with health and happiness. They seemed very much disappointed when we told them that we couldn't stay till the evening; they had prepared the traditional camp-fire, and decorated the trees in the lower garden with streamers in our honour. I asked that all the rejoicings, the songs and dances which were to have taken place in the evening, should be held instead before five o'clock. We had a long way to go and I insisted on getting back to Sebastopol before night. It was just as well that I did so, for it was that very evening that Eugène Dabit, who had accompanied me on my visit, fell ill. However, nothing as yet foreshadowed this and he was able to enjoy to the full the performance that the children gave us, and particularly a dance by the exquisite little Tajikistan girl called, I think, Tamar—the very same little girl that is portrayed being embraced by Stalin in those enormous posters that cover the walls of Moscow. Nothing can express the charm of the dance or the grace of the child. "One of the most exquisite memories of the Soviet Union," as Dabit said to me; and I thought so too. It was his last day of happiness.

The hotel at Sochi is very pleasant; its gardens are extremely fine and its beach highly agreeable; but the bathers there at once want to make us admit that we have nothing comparable to it in France. A sense of decency restrains us from saying that there are better places in France—much better places.

No, what we admire at Sochi is the fact that this semi-luxury, this comfort, should be placed at the disposal of the people—if, that is, those who come to stay here are not once more a privileged set. In general, the favoured ones are the most deserving, but they are favoured on condition they conform—"keep to the line"; and these are the only people who enjoy advantages.

What we admire at Sochi is the great quantity of sanatoriums and rest-houses, all wonderfully well equipped, that surround the town. And how excellent that they should all be built for the workers! But it is painful to see next door to all this that the workmen who are employed in the construction of the new theatre should be so badly paid and herded in such sordid barracks. . . .

If I speak in praise of the hotel at Sochi, what words shall I find for the one at Sinop, near Sukhum, which was vastly superior and could bear comparison with the best, the finest, the most comfortable hotels in foreign seaside resorts. Its magnificent garden dates from the *ancien régime,* but the hotel building itself is of recent construction, and has been very ingeniously fitted up. Both the outside and the inside are delightful to look at and every room has a private bathroom and private terrace. The furnishing is in perfect taste, the cooking excellent, among the best we had tasted in the U.S.S.R. Sinop hotel seems to be one of the places in the world where man is nearest to being happy.

A sovkhoz* has been set up in the neighbourhood in order to cater for the hotel. There I admired the model stables, the model cattle-sheds, the model pigsties, and especially a gigantic hen-house—the last word in hen-houses. Every hen has a numbered ring on its leg, the number of eggs it lays is carefully noted, each one has its own little box where it is shut up in order to lay its eggs and only let out when it has laid them. (What I can't understand is why, with all this care, the eggs we get at the hotel are no better.) I may add that you are only allowed to enter the premises after you have stepped on a carpet impregnated with a sterilizing substance to disinfect your shoes. The cattle of course walk round it—never mind!

If you cross the stream which bounds the sovkhoz, you come upon a row of hovels. There four people share a room measuring eight feet by six, which they rent for two roubles per head per month. The luxury of a meal at the sovkhoz restaurant, which costs two roubles, is beyond the means of those whose monthly salary is only seventy-five roubles. They have to content themselves with bread supplemented by dried fish.

* State farm.

I do not protest against the inequality of salaries; I grant that it was necessary. But there are means of remedying differences of condition; now I fear that these differences, instead of getting less, are actually on the increase. I fear that a new sort of workers' bourgeoisie may soon come into being. Satisfied (and for that very reason conservative, of course!), it will come to resemble all too closely our own petty bourgeoisie.

I see everywhere the preliminary symptoms of this.* And as we cannot doubt, alas, that bourgeois instincts, degraded, greedy, self-centred, slumber in many people's hearts notwithstanding any revolution (for many can hardly be reformed entirely from the outside), it disquiets me very much to observe, in the U.S.S.R. today, that these bourgeois instincts are indirectly flattered and encouraged by recent decisions that have been alarmingly approved of over here. With the restoration of the family (in its function of "social cell"), of inheritance, and of legacies, the love of lucre, of private ownership, is beginning to dominate the need for comradeship, for free sharing, and for life in common. Not for everybody, of course; but for many. And we see the reappearance, not of classes no doubt, but of social strata, of a kind of aristocracy; I am not referring here to the aristocracy of merit and of personal worth, but only to the aristocracy of respectability, of conformism, which in the next generation will become that of money.

* The recent law against abortion has horrified all whose salaries are insufficient to enable them to found a family and to bring up children. It has also horrified others, but for different reasons. Had it not been promised that a sort of referendum, a popular consultation, should be held on the subject of this law, to decide whether or not it should be enacted and applied? A huge majority declared itself (more or less openly, it is true) against this law. But public opinion was not taken into consideration, and to the almost general stupefaction, the law was passed in spite of all. The newspapers, of course, had chiefly published approvals. In the private conversations I was able to have with a good many workmen on this subject, I heard nothing but timid recriminations and resigned complaints.

Can this law be to a certain degree justified? At any rate, it was occasioned by some deplorable abuses. But from a Marxist point of view, what can one think of that other, older law against homosexuals? This law, which assimilates them to counter-revolutionaries (for non-conformism is hunted down even in sexual matters), condemns them to a sentence of five years' deportation, which can be renewed if they are not reformed by exile.

Are my fears exaggerated? I hope so. As far as that goes, the Soviet Union has already shown us that it was capable of abrupt reversals. But I do fear that in order to cut short these bourgeois tendencies that are now being approved and fostered by the rulers, a revulsion will soon appear necessary which will run the risk of becoming as brutal as that which put an end to the N.E.P.

How can one not be shocked by the contempt, or at any rate the indifference, which those who are and feel themselves "on the right side" show to "inferiors," to servants,* to unskilled workmen, to "dailies," male and female workers by the day, and I was about to say to "the poor." There are no more classes in the U.S.S.R.—granted. But there are poor. There are too many of them—far too many. I had hoped not to see any—or, to speak more accurately, it was in order *not* to see any that I had come to the U.S.S.R.

Add to this that philanthropy, or even plain charity, is no longer the correct thing. ** The State takes charge of all that. It takes charge of everything and there is no longer any need— granted—for private help. This leads to a kind of harshness in mutual relations, in spite of all comradeship. Of course I am not referring to relations between equals; but as regards those "inferiors" to whom I have alluded, the "superiority complex" is allowed full play.

This petty bourgeois spirit, which I greatly fear is in process of developing, is in my eyes profoundly and fundamentally counter-revolutionary.

But what is known as "counter-revolutionary" in the U.S.S.R. of today is not that at all. In fact it is practically the opposite.

* As a counterpart to this, how servile, how obsequious the servants are! Not the hotel servants, who are usually full of self-respect, although extremely cordial, but those who come into contact with the leaders and the "responsible administrators."

** But I hasten to add the following: in the public gardens of Sebastopol I saw a crippled child, who could only walk with crutches, pass in front of the benches where people were taking the air. I observed him for a long time while he went round with a hat. Out of twenty people to whom he applied, eighteen gave him something, but they would no doubt not have allowed themselves to be touched had he not been a cripple.

The spirit which is today held to be counter-revolutionary
is that same revolutionary spirit, that ferment which first
broke through the half-rotten dam of the old Tzarist world. One
would like to be able to think that an overflowing love of mankind, or at least an imperious need for justice, filled every heart.
But when the revolution was once accomplished, triumphant,
stabilized, there was no more question of such things, and the
feelings which had animated the first revolutionaries began to
get in the way like cumbersome objects that have ceased to be
useful. I compare these feelings to the props which help to
build an arch but which are removed when the keystone is in
place. Now that the revolution has triumphed, now that it is
stabilized and moderated, now that it is beginning to come to
terms, and, some will say, to grow prudent, those that the revolutionary ferment still animates and who consider all these successive concessions to be compromises become troublesome, are
reprobated and suppressed. Then would it not be better, instead of playing on words, simply to acknowledge that the revolutionary spirit (or even simply the critical spirit) is no longer
the correct thing, that it is not wanted any more? What is
wanted now is compliance, conformism. What is desired and
demanded is approval of all that is done in the U.S.S.R.; and
an attempt is being made to obtain an approval that is not mere
resignation, but a sincere, an enthusiastic approval. What is
most astounding is that this attempt is successful. On the other
hand the smallest protest, the least criticism, is liable to the
severest penalties, and in fact is immediately stifled. And I
doubt whether in any other country in the world, even Hitler's
Germany, thought be less free, more bowed down, more fearful (terrorized), more vassalized.

II

Before going to the Soviet Union, I wrote the following passage:

> I believe that a writer's value is intimately linked to
> the force of the revolutionary spirit that animates him

—or to be more exact (for I am not so mad as to believe that only left-wing writers have artistic value), to the force of his spirit of opposition. This spirit exists as much in Bossuet and Chateaubriand, or at the present time in Claudel, as in Molière, Voltaire, Victor Hugo, and so many others. In our form of society, a great writer, a great artist, is essentially non-conformist. He makes head against the current. This was true of Dante, of Cervantes, of Ibsen, of Gogol. It is not true apparently of Shakespere and his contemporaries, of whom John Addington Symonds says so well: "What made the playwrights of that epoch so great . . . was that they [the authors] lived and wrote in fullest sympathy with the whole people." * It was no doubt not true of Sophocles and certainly not of Homer, who was the voice, we feel, of Greece itself. It would perhaps cease to be true the day that . . . But this is the very reason that we turn our eyes with such anxious interrogation to the Soviet Union. Will the triumph of the revolution allow its artists to be borne by the current? For the question arises: what will happen if the transformation of the social State deprives the artist of all motive for opposition? What will the artist do if there is no reason for him to go *against* the current, if all he need do is to let himself be carried by it? No doubt as long as the struggle lasts and victory is not perfectly assured, he can depict the struggle, and by himself fighting, contribute to the triumph. But afterwards . . . ?

This is what I asked myself before visiting the U.S.S.R.

"You see," explained X, "it wasn't at all what the public asked for; not at all the kind of thing we want nowadays. Before this he had written a very remarkable ballet which had been greatly admired." (*He* was Shostakovich, whom I had heard praised in terms usually reserved for geniuses.) "But what is

* General Introduction to the Mermaid Series.

the public to do with an opera that leaves them with no tunes to hum when they come out?" (Heavens! Is this the stage they're at? I thought to myself. And yet X is himself an artist and highly cultivated, and I had never before heard him say anything that was not intelligent.)

"What we want nowadays are works everyone can understand, and understand immediately. If Shostakovich doesn't feel that himself, he will soon be made to by losing all his listeners."

I protested that often the finest works, and even those that eventually become the most popular, were at first appreciated by only a very small number of people. "Why, Beethoven himself," I said, and handed him a volume I happened to have on me at that very moment. "Here! Read what he says."

"*In Berlin gab ich auch*" (Beethoven is speaking), "*vor mehreren Jahren ein Konzert, ich griff mich an und glaubte, was Recht's zu leisten und hoffte auf tüchtigen Beifall; aber siehe da, als ich meine höchste Begeisterung ausgesprochen hatte, kein geringstes Zeichen des Beifalls ertönte.*" *

X granted that in the U.S.S.R. a Beethoven would have found it very difficult to recover from such a failure. "You see," he went on, "an artist in our country must first of all keep in line. Otherwise even the finest gifts will be considered *formalism*. Yes, that's our word for designating whatever we don't wish to see or hear. We want to create a new art worthy of the great people we are. Art today should be popular or nothing."

"You will drive all your artists to conformism," I answered. "And the best, those who refuse to degrade their art, or will not allow it to be subservient, will be reduced to silence. The culture you claim to serve, to illustrate, to defend, will put you to shame."

Then he declared I was arguing like a bourgeois. That, for

---

* "Several years ago I too gave a concert in Berlin. I exerted myself to the utmost and thought I had really accomplished something excellent; I hoped therefore for vigorous applause; but just imagine, after I had given utterance to my highest inspiration, not the smallest sign of approbation was heard." (Goethe's *Briefe mit lebensgeschichtlichen Verbindungen.* Vol. II, p. 287.)

his part, he was convinced that Marxism, which had already produced such great things in other domains, would also produce works of art. He added that what prevented such works from arising was the importance that was still attached to a bygone past.

His voice became louder and louder, and he seemed to be giving a lecture or reciting a lesson. This conversation took place in the hall of the hotel at Sochi. I left him without saying anything more. But a few moments later he came to my room and, in a low voice this time, "Of course," he said, "you are perfectly right . . . but there were people listening to us just now . . . and I have an exhibition opening very soon."

X is a painter.

When we first arrived in the U.S.S.R., public opinion had barely recovered from the great quarrel of Formalism. I tried to understand what this word meant and this is what I made out:

The accusation of formalism was levelled at any artist who was capable of attaching less importance to *content* than to *form*. Let me add at once that no *content* is considered worthy of interest (or, to be more accurate, is tolerated) unless it is inclined in a certain direction. The work of art is considered formalist if it is not inclined at all and therefore has no direction (I use the word in both meanings). I confess I cannot write these words of *form* and *content* without a smile. But it would be more proper to weep that this absurd distinction should be a determining consideration in criticism. That it may have been useful politically is possible; but then stop talking of culture. Culture is in danger when criticism is not free.

In the U.S.S.R., however fine a work may be, if it is not in line it scandalizes. Beauty is considered a bourgeois value. However great a genius an artist may be, if he does not work in line, attention will turn away—will *be* turned away—from him. What is demanded of the artist, of the writer, is that he shall conform; and all the rest will be added to him.

At Tiflis I saw an exhibition of modern art which it would perhaps be charitable not to speak of. But after all, these artists had attained their object, which is to edify, to convince, to convert (episodes of Stalin's life being used as the themes of these illustrations). Oh! it's very certain that none of these people were "formalists." Unfortunately they were not painters either. They made me think of Apollo, who, when he was set to serve Admetus, had to extinguish all his rays and from that moment did nothing of any value, or at any rate nothing of any good to us. But as the U.S.S.R. was no better at the plastic arts before the revolution than after it, let us keep to literature.

"In the days of my youth," said X, "we were recommended certain books and advised against others; and naturally it was to the latter that we were drawn. The great difference today is that the young people read only what they are recommended to read and have no desire to read anything else."

Thus Dostoievski, for instance, finds today very few readers, without our being able to say exactly whether young people are turning away (or being turned away) from him—to such an extent are their minds moulded.

If the mind is obliged to obey a word of command, it can at any rate feel that it is not free. But if it has been so manipulated beforehand that it obeys without even waiting for the word of command, it loses even the consciousness of its enslavement. I believe many young Soviet citizens would be greatly astonished if they were told that they had no liberty of thought, and would vehemently deny it.

And as it always happens that we recognize the value of certain advantages only after we have lost them, there is nothing like a stay in the U.S.S.R. (or of course in Germany) to help us appreciate the inappreciable liberty of thought we still enjoy in France—and sometimes abuse.

At Leningrad I was asked to prepare a little speech to be addressed to a meeting of writers and students. I had only been a week in the country and was trying to tune in to the correct key. I therefore submitted my text to X and Y. I was at once

given to understand that my text was far from being in the
right key or the right tone, and that what I was intending to
say would be most unsuitable. Oh! it didn't take me long to
realize this by myself. As for the speech, it was never delivered.
Here it is:

> I have often been asked my opinion of present-day
> Soviet literature. I should like to explain why I have
> always refused to give it. I shall be able at the same time
> to repeat with greater precision one of the passages of
> the speech I made in the Red Square on the solemn oc-
> casion of Gorki's funeral. I was speaking of the "new
> problems" which had been raised by the very triumph
> of the Soviet Republics, problems, I said, which it would
> not be the least of the U.S.S.R.'s glories to have intro-
> duced into history and to have presented to our medita-
> tions. As the future of culture seems to me to be closely
> bound up with their solution, it will perhaps not be
> amiss if I return to the subject with greater particu-
> larity. . . .

*   *   *

> The great majority, even when composed of the best
> individuals, never bestows its approbation on what is
> new, potential, unconcerted, and disconcerting in a
> work; but only on what it can *recognize*—that is to say,
> the commonplace. Just as once there were bourgeois
> commonplaces, so now there are revolutionary common-
> places; it is important to know it. It is important to real-
> ize that the essential value of a work of art, the quality
> that will ensure its survival, never lies in a conformist
> adherence to a doctrine, be that doctrine the soundest
> and the surest possible; but rather in formulating ques-
> tions that forestall the future's, and answers to questions
> that have not yet been formulated. I am very much
> afraid that many works, imbued with the purest spirit
> of Marxism, and on that account so successful today,

will soon emit to the noses of tomorrow the insufferable odour of the clinic; and I believe that the works that will live most victoriously will be those that have freed themselves successfully from such preoccupations.

When the revolution is triumphant, installed, and established, art runs a terrible danger, a danger almost as great as under the worst fascist oppression—the danger of orthodoxy. Art that submits to orthodoxy, to even the soundest doctrines, is lost—wrecked upon the shoals of conformism. What the triumphant revolution can and should offer the artist is above all else liberty. Without liberty art loses its meaning and its value.

Walt Whitman, on the death of President Lincoln, wrote one of his most beautiful poems. But if this poem had been imposed, if Whitman had been forced to write it by order and in conformity with an accepted canon, his threnody would have lost all its virtue and its beauty; or rather, Whitman could not have written it.

And as, quite naturally, the assent of the greatest number, with its accompanying applause, success, and favours, goes to the qualities the public is best able to recognize—that is say, to conformism—I wonder with some anxiety whether perhaps in this great Soviet Union there may not be vegetating obscurely, unknown to the crowd, some Baudelaire, some Keats, or some Rimbaud, who by very reason of his worth cannot make himself heard. * And yet he, of all others, is the one who is of

---

* But, they will say, what concern have we today with a possible Keats, Baudelaire, Rimbaud, or even Stendhal? The only value they have in our eyes now is the degree in which they reflect the moribund and corrupt society of which they were the melancholy products. If the new society of today is unable to produce them, so much the worse for them, but so much the better for us, who have nothing more to learn from them or their like. The writer who can be of service to us today is the man who is perfectly at his ease in this new form of society and whose spirit is intensified by what would have hampered the others. In other words, the man who approves, enjoys, and applauds.

Exactly. And I think that the writings of those applauders are of very slight value or service, and that if the people wish to develop their culture, they had far better not listen to them. Nothing is so useful for developing culture as to be forced to think.

importance, for those who are at first disdained, like
Rimbaud, Keats, Baudelaire, and even Stendhal, are
those who tomorrow will be the greatest.

As for what might be called "mirror" literature—that is to say, books that
confine themselves to being a mere reflection (of a society, event, or period)—I
have already said what I think of them.

Self-contemplation (and admiration) may be the first interest of a society
that is still very young; but it would be extremely regrettable if this first interest were also the sole and the last.

Leon Trotsky

WHY STALIN TRIUMPHED

"Of Christ's twelve apostles, Judas alone proved to be a traitor. But if he had acquired power, he would have represented the other eleven apostles as traitors, and also all the lesser apostles, whom Luke numbers as seventy." Stalin by *Leon Trotsky.*

Editor's Note

THE key to Leon Trotsky's view of the meaning of Stalinism may be found in the title of his most suggestive book on the subject, *The Revolution Betrayed.* Stalin, in his view, is not the rightful inheritor of Lenin's mantle but the usurper of power, the prime representative of a tendency of reaction, of counter-revolution, of Thermidor, in the parallel he draws with the French Revolution, that carried the Soviet state far from its original aims. In short, Stalin is the personification and the captain of the new ruling caste that betrayed the Bolshevik Revolution. Trotsky was not a Carlylean and his case is rarely personally aimed at Stalin alone. "Stalin took possession of power," he maintained in his biography of the dictator, "not with the aid of personal qualities, but with the aid of an impersonal machine. And it was not he that created the machine, but the machine that created him. . . . Stalin headed the machine from the moment he cut off the umbilical cord that bound it to the idea and it became a thing unto itself." The revolutionary fervor of the masses had spent itself. Stalin used the weariness to ride to power. The revolutionary ideas of Lenin and Trotsky were in retreat. The pale medioc-

WHY STALIN TRIUMPHED–*Leon Trotsky* 315

rity, Stalin, who took power "before the masses had learned to distinguish his figure from others during the triumphal procession across Red Square" saddled his bureaucracy on the state. In brief, that is the explanation of Leon Trotsky.

It is an appealing explanation but ultimately unsatisfactory. As much as any man Trotsky has demonstrated brilliantly the brutality and inhumanity of the regime, the absence of any freedom, the rewriting of history, the eradication of opposition. What he has not done, and what makes his explanation unsatisfactory, is to understand that Stalinism is the logical culmination of Leninism, of Bolshevism. That Stalinism is the betrayer of every elemental decency is written indelibly in the history of our time. That it is also the continuation and expansion of Leninism—denial of democracy, willful use of repressive means against opponents, use of terror, compulsion, imprisonment, to establish policies contrary to popular will, all of which were Leninism—is also evident. One does not betray what one apes and enlarges. If Trotsky has a quarrel it is not only with Stalinism but also with Leninism, a fact he unfortunately resisted until the day of his death.

His "explanation" led him into erroneous, and expensive, miscalculations. Since Stalin rode to power, in his view, because revolutionary feeling had died ("In the last analysis, Soviet Bonapartism owes its birth to the belatedness of the world revolution"), he waited patiently for a possible change in Russia that was to coincide with the new revolutionary risings in Western Europe. Neither came. Trotsky expected World War II to bring about such risings; he was again mistaken. What did happen instead was the forcible imposition of Soviet might on a vast stretch of European territory, the reduction of independent thought in the conquered countries to servility to Russia, the imprisonment and "liquidation" of all dissident elements; in short, the spread of Russian "accomplishments" to Western Europe, a continuation of Russian oppression where a war had just been fought ostensibly to put an end to Nazi oppression.

His erroneous notions of the meaning of Stalinism forced him into a weird position. He espoused the Soviet Union as basically progressive (a "Workers' State") in contradiction to everything he had revealed about the dictatorship. This delusion had its roots in the dogmatic belief that a nationalized economy is progressive *per se* as compared to capitalist economy. From this position it was just one short step to a call for the "defense" of the Soviet state—and, in practice, no matter what imperialistic activity *it* engaged in. This was most clearly demonstrated at the time of the Soviet rape of Poland and the invasion of Finland (the latter, by the way, already almost forgotten history). Trotsky's "anti-Stalinism" at those times reduced itself to a request that Polish and Finnish workers help Stalin enslave them by supporting the Red Army.* While indicting Stalin, he continued thus to declare his loyalty to whatever Stalin's Russia did! It is in more than a spirit of irony that some have referred to Trotsky as Stalin's "loyal opposition." The persistence with which Trotsky adhered to this absurd view is as remarkable as it is disheartening to think of what can befall the human intelligence. In 1928, when he was already in exile at Alma-Ata, he wrote: "The estimation of the present epoch and its inner tendencies and especially the evaluation of the experiences of the last five years prove to us that *the Opposition needs no soil other than that of the Communist International. No one will succeed in tearing us away from it. Our ideas will become its ideas and they will find their expression in the program of the Comintern.*" (*The Strategy of the World Revolution,* 1930; Trotsky's italics.) In his most mature expression of his position, in *The Revolution Betrayed* (1937), he asserted: "Our brief analysis is sufficient to show how absurd are the attempts to identify capitalist state-ism with the Soviet

---

* As Sidney Hook has put it: "As far as Russia's foreign policy is concerned, Trotsky, even when he criticizes Stalin's blunders, calls for unconditional defense of the U.S.S.R. and active aid to the Red Army even when it is depriving workers in other countries of their lives and liberties. Thus, he has called upon the workers of Poland and Finland to help the Red Army and the G.P.U. in their brutal invasions." (*Reason, Social Myths and Democracy,* page 179.)

system. The former is reactionary, the latter *progressive.*" (My italics.) In a written interview with the *St. Louis Post-Dispatch* on February 14, 1940, he again reiterated his stand: first he was with the Soviet Union against all "enemies," then against Stalin's oligarchy. That was the order. "From what I said above, you will see clearly where I stand in relation to this grouping of forces: on the side of the USSR entirely and unconditionally; before all—against imperialisms of all labels; after that— against the Kremlin oligarchy. . . ." A few months later he was to die, with a pickaxe in his brain, at the hands of the side which he pledged to support "entirely and unconditionally."

This suicidal position, for all Trotsky's brilliance in indicting the Stalin regime, has little to recommend it. Even in the ranks of his staunchest supporters there have been many who were no longer capable of putting up with the brutal nonsense of supporting a regime—in whatever way—that they themselves characterize as murderous merely because of the shibboleth of nationalized property, an economic base in the USSR, in the complete absence of any democracy, that serves as one of the major means of entrenchment for the Soviet masters and regimentation for the Soviet workers. It is impossible not to find Trotsky's position more than a bit unreal, a daydream, or nightmare, created not by independent appraisal of objective facts but conjured into existence by ideological hypnosis. But this dissent, fully necessary as it is, should not be used to blur the unrivaled record of the Soviet regime in rewriting history, in conducting a bloody, permanent purge not only against the Russian people but against those who brought the Communists to power. One does not have to agree with a man to recognize the character of the state that murders him, and countless others, for holding opposing views. Trotsky's detailed, documented, and informed exposure of the record—if not the antecedents and meaning—of the Stalinist dictatorship stands quite independent, whatever he may have thought, of his own explanatory and programmatic views. As factual exposes, they are of extreme importance.

Were there no more than the above—Trotsky's "defense" of
the Soviet Union—the charges raised against him at the Moscow Trials (of conspiracy with the Nazis against the USSR,
ad nauseum) would be revealed for the hoax they are, but that
is by no means the only indication of their falsity. In 1937, for
example, an independent commission under the chairmanship
of John Dewey, foremost American philosopher, an anti-Trot-
skyite, held hearings in Mexico to determine the guilt or non-
guilt of Leon Trotsky in regard to Stalin's charges at the trials.
Professor Dewey has summed up the commission's findings:
"As a result of its prolonged, thorough, and impartial investigation—for none of its ten members is a Trotskyite or affiliated
in any way with his theories and activities—it found Trotsky
and his son innocent of the charges brought against them." For
nine months the commission held hearings in Mexico, New
York and Paris. Among other things, the commission found that
the Russian prosecutor (Vishinsky of UN fame) had made no
effort to follow the rules of procedure for Russian law, laid
down by the prosecutor himself in a book he had edited. It was
further found that alleged diabolical interviews with Trotsky,
supposed to have taken place in Copenhagen, Paris and Oslo,
never took place, this being established by a mass of notarized
depositions—many by opponents of Trotsky—which placed
Trotsky elsewhere, and other like findings. Two published volumes of this commission—*Not Guilty* and *The Case of Leon
Trotsky*—containing evidence and hearings, are available, and
make for extremely interesting reading. The verdict of the
commission was that the trials were frame-ups.

Dewey has voiced a personal conclusion which should be of
interest. It helps place Leon Trotsky and suggests an attitude
toward his position for American liberals:

> I have always disagreed with the ideas and theories
> of Leon Trotsky and I disagree with him now, if pos-
> sible, more than ever. It is undoubtedly true that Trot-
> sky has adhered more closely to the pure Marxian line

than has the Stalinist regime. . . . If Trotsky had remained in power, he might have attempted to retain more democracy within the party itself. But he has never faced the question whether democracy within the party can be maintained when there is complete suppression of democracy outside the party. The line of democracy is an exacting master. The limitation of it to a small group involves such a contradiction that in the end democracy even within the party is bound to be destroyed. Aside from this point, the essential evils of violent revolution and of dictatorship by a class remain in full force in Trotsky's Marxian philosophy. . . . (Interview with John Dewey by Agnes E. Meyer, *Washington Post,* December 19, 1937.)

It is impossible in this space to provide an expanded sketch of the dramatic life of the revolutionary leader and its tragic end. Such a biography would start with his birth as Lev Davidovich Bronstein in Elizavethgrad, Russia, in 1879, six weeks before the birth of Stalin, his education at the University of Odessa, his organizing of Russian workers while in his teens, his exile to Siberia at the age of nineteen, his early intimacy with Lenin in London in the early 1900s, his role in the Petersburg Soviet in 1905, then again exile and escape, imprisonment during World War I, expulsion from France, arrest in Spain, deportation, residence in the U. S., return to Russia after the March Revolution where he soon joined the Bolsheviks; the rest is part of contemporary history, an eminence in Russia second only to Lenin, defeat by Stalin, exile, banishment, a search for sanctuary, attacks on his life, finally death at the hands of the assassin, Jacson, on August 20, 1940, in Mexico.

Trotsky was an immensely gifted writer and his publications are many: his three-volume *History of the Russian Revolution; Lenin; Lessons of October; My Life; Literature and Revolution; Problems of the Chinese Revolution;* the *Stalin School of Falsification;* and other books, pamphlets, and articles. This selection is from *The Revolution Betrayed.*

Why Stalin Triumphed by Leon Trotsky

THE historian of the Soviet Union cannot fail to conclude that the policy of the ruling bureaucracy upon great questions has been a series of contradictory zigzags. The attempt to explain or justify them by "changing circumstances" obviously won't hold water. To guide means at least in some degree to exercise foresight. The Stalin faction have not in the slightest degree foreseen the inevitable results of the development; they have been caught napping every time. They have reacted with mere administrative reflexes. The theory of each successive turn has been created after the fact, and with small regard for what they were teaching yesterday. On the basis of the same irrefutable facts and documents, the historian will be compelled to conclude that the so-called "Left Opposition" offered an immeasurably more correct analysis of the processes taking place in the country, and far more truly foresaw their further development.

This assertion is contradicted at first glance by the simple fact that the faction which could not see ahead was steadily victorious, while the more penetrating group suffered defeat after defeat. That kind of objection, which comes automatically to mind, is convincing, however, only for those who think rationalistically, and see in politics a logical argument or a chess match. A political struggle is in its essence a struggle of interests and forces, not of arguments. The quality of the leadership is, of course, far from a matter of indifference for the outcome of the conflict, but it is not the only factor, and in the last analysis is not decisive. Each of the struggling camps moreover demands leaders in its own image.

The February revolution raised Kerensky and Tseretelli to power, not because they were "cleverer" or "more astute" than the ruling tzarist clique, but because they represented, at least temporarily, the revolutionary masses of the people in their revolt against the old regime. Kerensky was able to drive Lenin underground and imprison other Bolshevik leaders,* not because he excelled them in personal qualifications, but because the majority of the workers and soldiers in those days were still following the patriotic petty bourgeoisie. The personal "superiority" of Kerensky, if it is suitable to employ such a word in this connection, consisted in the fact that he did not see farther than the overwhelming majority. The Bolsheviks in their turn conquered the petty bourgeois democrats, not through the personal superiority of their leaders, but through a new correlation of social forces. The proletariat had succeeded at last in leading the discontented peasantry against the bourgeoisie.

The consecutive stages of the great French Revolution, during its rise and fall alike, demonstrate no less convincingly that the strength of the "leaders" and "heroes" that replaced each other consisted primarily in their correspondence to the character of those classes and strata which supported them. Only this correspondence, and not any irrelevant superiorities whatever, permitted each of them to place the impress of his personality upon a certain historic period. In the successive

* [After an abortive Bolshevik-led armed uprising in July, 1917. "The failure of the first Bolshevik uprising," writes Professor Vernadsky in his *A History of Russia* (1940), "might have been a turning point in the history of the Russian Revolution. It was the right moment to enforce the authority of the Government in Petrograd. But this opportunity was not seized by the Government. Some Bolshevik leaders, including Trotsky, were arrested; Lenin fled to Finland; but the Bolsheviks were not outlawed in the Soviet." In September a second blow was directed against the Provisional Government in the form of a revolt led by General Kornilov which collapsed when all the socialist organizations—including the Bolsheviks—came to Kerensky's support. Following this the arrested Bolsheviks were released and they set about preparing for the third, and final, blow which came in November when Lenin made his successful *coup*. The circumstances enjoyed by the Bolsheviks are more than suggested by Lenin's "A Letter to the Comrades," written on October 29-30, 1917. (*Selected Works*, volume 6.) In it, Lenin speaks of "we, with our dozens of newspapers, freedom of assembly." He tells his followers that, as revolutionists, they are "the best situated in the world." He noted these things, of course, not in praise of the Provisional Government against which he was conspiring—but to stress how advantageous the situation was for the insurrection that he made soon after.—*Ed.*]

supremacy of Mirabeau, Brissot, Robespierre, Barras and Bonaparte, there is an obedience to objective law incomparably
more effective than the special traits of the historic protagonists
themselves.

It is sufficiently well known that every revolution up to this
time has been followed by a reaction, or even a counter-revolution. This, to be sure, has never thrown the nation all the way
back to its starting point, but it has always taken from the people the lion's share of their conquests. The victims of the first
reactionary wave have been, as a general rule, those pioneers,
initiators, and instigators who stood at the head of the masses
in the period of the revolutionary offensive. In their stead
people of the second line, in league with the former enemies of
the revolution, have been advanced to the front. Beneath this
dramatic duel of "coryphées" on the open political scene, shifts
have taken place in the relations between classes, and, no less
important, profound changes in the psychology of the recently
revolutionary masses.

Answering the bewildered questions of many comrades as to
what has become of the activity of the Bolshevik party and the
working class—where is its revolutionary initiative, its spirit of
self-sacrifice and plebeian pride—why, in place of all this, has
appeared so much vileness, cowardice, pusillanimity and careerism—Rakovsky referred to the life story of the French revolution of the eighteenth century, and offered the example of
Babeuf, who on emerging from the Abbaye prison likewise
wondered what had become of the heroic people of the Parisian
suburbs. A revolution is a mighty devourer of human energy,
both individual and collective. The nerves give way. Consciousness is shaken and characters are worn out. Events unfold too
swiftly for the flow of fresh forces to replace the loss. Hunger,
unemployment, the death of the revolutionary cadres, the removal of the masses from administration, all this led to such a
physical and moral impoverishment of the Parisian suburbs
that they required three decades before they were ready for a
new insurrection.

The axiomlike assertions of the Soviet literature, to the effect that the laws of bourgeois revolutions are "inapplicable" to a proletarian revolution, have no scientific content whatever. The proletarian character of the October revolution was determined by the world situation and by a special correlation of internal forces. But the classes themselves were formed in the barbarous circumstances of tzarism and backward capitalism, and were anything but made to order for the demands of a socialist revolution. The exact opposite is true. It is for the very reason that a proletariat still backward in many respects achieved in the space of a few months the unprecedented leap from a semi-feudal monarchy to a socialist dictatorship, that the reaction in its ranks was inevitable. This reaction has developed in a series of consecutive waves. External conditions and events have vied with each other in nourishing it. Intervention followed intervention. The revolution got no direct help from the west. Instead of the expected prosperity of the country an ominous destitution reigned for long. Moreover, the outstanding representatives of the working class either died in the civil war, or rose a few steps higher and broke away from the masses. And thus after an unexampled tension of forces, hopes and illusions, there came a long period of weariness, decline and sheer disappointment in the results of the revolution. The ebb of the "plebeian pride" made room for a flood of pusillanimity and careerism. The new commanding caste rose to its place upon this wave.

The demobilization of the Red Army of five million played no small role in the formation of the bureaucracy. The victorious commanders assumed leading posts in the local Soviets, in economy, in education, and they persistently introduced everywhere that regime which had ensured success in the civil war. Thus on all sides the masses were pushed away gradually from actual participation in the leadership of the country.

The reaction within the proletariat caused an extraordinary flush of hope and confidence in the petty bourgeois strata of town and country, aroused as they were to new life by the NEP, and growing bolder and bolder. The young bureaucracy, which had arisen at first as an agent of the proletariat, began now to feel itself a court of arbitration between the classes. Its independence increased from month to month.

The international situation was pushing with mighty forces in the same direction. The Soviet bureaucracy became more self-confident, the heavier the blows dealt to the world working class. Between these two facts there was not only a chrono-logical, but a causal connection, and one which worked in two directions. The leaders of the bureaucracy promoted the proletarian defeats; the defeats promoted the rise of the bureaucracy. The crushing of the Bulgarian insurrection and the inglorious retreat of the German workers' party in 1923, the collapse of the Esthonian attempt at insurrection in 1924, the treacherous liquidation of the General Strike in England and the unworthy conduct of the Polish workers' party at the installation of Pilsudski in 1926, the terrible massacre of the Chinese revolution in 1927, and, finally, the still more ominous recent defeats in Germany and Austria—these are the historic catastrophes which killed the faith of the Soviet masses in world revolution, and permitted the bureaucracy to rise higher and higher as the sole light of salvation.

As to the causes of the defeat of the world proletariat during the last thirteen years, the author must refer to his other works, where he has tried to expose the ruinous part played by the leadership in the Kremlin, isolated from the masses and profoundly conservative as it is, in the revolutionary movement of all countries. Here we are concerned primarily with the irrefutable and instructive fact that the continual defeats of the revolution in Europe and Asia, while weakening the international position of the Soviet Union, have vastly strengthened the Soviet bureaucracy. Two dates are especially significant in this historic series. In the second half of 1923, the attention of the Soviet workers was passionately fixed upon Germany, where the proletariat, it seemed, had stretched out its hand to power. The panicky retreat of the German Communist Party was the heaviest possible disappointment to the working masses of the Soviet Union. The Soviet bureaucracy straightway opened a campaign against the theory of "permanent revolution," and dealt the Left Opposition its first cruel blow. During the years 1926 and 1927 the population of the Soviet Union experienced a new tide of hope. All eyes were now directed to the East where the drama of the Chinese revolution was unfolding. The Left Opposition had recovered from the previous blows and was recruiting a phalanx of new adherents. At the end of 1927 the Chinese revolution was massacred by the hangman, Chiang-kai-shek, into whose hands the Communist International had literally betrayed the Chinese workers and peasants. A cold wave of disappointment swept over the masses of the Soviet Union. After an unbridled baiting in the press and at meetings, the bureaucracy finally, in 1928, ventured upon mass arrests among the Left Opposition.

To be sure, tens of thousands of revolutionary fighters gathered around the banner of the Bolshevik-Leninists. The advanced workers were indubitably sympathetic to the Opposition, but that sympathy remained passive. The masses lacked faith that the situation could be seriously changed by a new struggle. Meantime the bureaucracy asserted: "For the sake of an international revolution, the Opposition proposes to drag us into a revolutionary war. Enough of shake-ups! We have earned the right to rest. We will build the socialist society at home. Rely upon us, your leaders!" This gospel of repose firmly consolidated the *apparatchiki* and the military and state officials and indubitably found an echo among the weary workers, and still more the peasant masses. Can it be, they asked themselves, that the Opposition is actually ready to sacrifice the interests of the Soviet Union for the idea of "permanent revolution"? In reality, the struggle had been about the life interests of the Soviet state. The false policy of the International in Germany resulted ten years later in the victory of Hitler— that is, in a threatening war danger from the West. And the no less false policy in China reinforced Japanese imperialism and brought very much nearer the danger in the East. But periods of reaction are characterized above all by a lack of courageous thinking.

The Opposition was isolated. The bureaucracy struck while the iron was hot, exploiting the bewilderment and passivity of the workers, setting their more backward strata against the advanced, and relying more and more boldly upon the kulak and the petty bourgeois ally in general. In the course of a few years, the bureaucracy thus shattered the revolutionary vanguard of the proletariat.

It would be naïve to imagine that Stalin, previously unknown to the masses, suddenly issued from the wings full armed with a complete strategical plan. No indeed. Before he felt out his own course, the bureaucracy felt out Stalin himself. He brought it all the necessary guarantees: the prestige of an old Bolshevik, a strong character, narrow vision, and close bonds with the political machine as the sole source of his influence. The success which fell upon him was a surprise at first to Stalin himself. It was the friendly welcome of the new ruling group, trying to free itself from the old principles and from the control of the masses, and having need of a reliable arbiter in its inner affairs. A secondary figure before the masses and in the events of the revolution, Stalin revealed himself as the indubitable leader of the Thermidorian bureaucracy, as first in its midst.

The new ruling caste soon revealed its own ideas, feelings and, more important, its interests. The overwhelming majority of the older generation of the present bureaucracy had stood on the other side of the barricades during the October revolution. (Take, for example, the Soviet ambassadors only: Troyanovsky, Maisky, Potemkin, Suritz, Khinchuk, etc.) Or at best they had stood aside from the struggle. Those of the present bureaucrats who were in the Bolshevik camp in the October days played in the majority of cases no considerable role. As for the young bureaucrats, they have been chosen and educated by the elders, frequently from among their own offspring.

These people could not have achieved the October revolution, but they were perfectly suited to exploit it.

Personal incidents in the interval between these two historic chapters were not, of course, without influence. Thus the sickness and death of Lenin undoubtedly hastened the denouement. Had Lenin lived longer, the pressure of the bureaucratic power would have developed, at least during the first years, more slowly. But as early as 1926 Krupskaya said, in a circle of Left Oppositionists: "If Ilych were alive, he would probably already be in prison." The fears and alarming prophecies of Lenin himself were then still fresh in her memory, and she cherished no illusions as to his personal omnipotence against opposing historic winds and currents.

The bureaucracy conquered something more than the Left Opposition. It conquered the Bolshevik party. It defeated the program of Lenin, who had seen the chief danger in the conversion of the organs of the state "from servants of society to lords over society." It defeated all these enemies, the Opposition, the party and Lenin, not with ideas and arguments, but with its own social weight. The leaden rump of the bureaucracy outweighed the head of the revolution. That is the secret of the Soviet's Thermidor.

Louis Fischer

THE MOSCOW TRIALS AND CONFESSIONS

"The trials showed that these dregs of humanity . . . had been in conspiracy against Lenin, the Party and the Soviet state ever since the early days of the October Socialist Revolution. . . . The Trotsky-Bukharin fiends . . . these Whiteguard pigmies . . . these Whiteguard insects . . . these contemptible lackeys of the fascists . . . The Soviet people approved the annihilation of the Bukharin-Trotsky gang and passed on to next business."—Official History of the Communist Party of the Soviet Union, Short Course.

"Stalin does not resort to castor oil to punish Communist leaders who are so stupid or criminal as still to believe in Communism. Stalin is unable to understand the subtle irony involved in the laxative system of castor oil. He makes a clean sweep by means of systems which were born in the steppes of Genghis Khan. . . . Stalin renders a commendable service to Fascism, by cutting down thousands of revolutionists as Fascist spies." Mussolini, on the Moscow Trials and Purges, in Popolo d'Italia (1938), quoted in Freda Utley's The Dream We Lost.

Editor's Note

IN LENINGRAD on December 1, 1934, a shot was fired by a young Communist, Nikolaiev, killing Sergei M. Kirov, a Politburo member. The episode has yet to be definitively explained but the shot became one that was heard throughout the world. This assassination permitted Stalin the opportunity to achieve what had never before been possible for him: the utter eradication of the outstanding leaders of the Communist party, the fathers of the Bolshevik revolution.

The killing unleashed a new and unprecedented period of terror in the USSR, and in time made for an outstanding change in the character of the Stalinist dictatorship. Lenin had long warned that the Party not repeat the tragedy of the Jacobins in wreaking mutual extermination. Now, for the first time, a long list of other "opponents" having been eradicated, the most outstanding leaders of the Bolshevik revolution were to fall victims of the Stalinist state. Harassment suddenly became murder. Slowly, patiently, charges first appearing against some, then unexpectedly against others, Stalin wove all members of the "opposition" into the giant tapestry of extermination. The world soon learned to recognize the procedure as the "Moscow Trials." Without a shred of evidence, the so-called Zinoviev-Kamenev-Smirnov trial of August, 1936, the Radek-Piatakov trial of January, 1937, and others were held, some secret, some public. Countless persons were executed or imprisoned without trial. It is important to remember that only a tiny number of those accused ever came to "trial."

No documentary evidence existed at the trials; there was none. The most unsupported allegations of the defendants supposed trafficking with the Nazis were freely made. It is instructive to note that since the fall of Hitler, the Soviets have been repeatedly asked to open any Nazi archives in their possession on this point. They have steadfastly refused. The only evidence consisted of "confessions"—as in the recent farce trial of Cardinal Mindszenty—which the defendants loquaciously made. As Louis Fischer puts it in this selection: "The trial of the 'Trotzkyist criminals' who allegedly made a pact with the Nazis led ultimately to Stalin's pact with the Nazis."

For a sample of the credibility of the "confessions" follow this verbatim talk in the courtroom between Andrei Vishinsky, Soviet prosecutor, and the famed Soviet leaders Kamenev and Zinoviev:

VISHINSKY: What appraisal should be given of the articles and statements you wrote in 1933, in which you expressed loyalty to the Party? Deception?

KAMENEV: No, worse than deception.

VISHINSKY: Perfidy?

KAMENEV: Worse.

VISHINSKY: Worse than deception, worse than perfidy— find the word. Treason?

KAMENEV: You have found it.

VISHINSKY: Accused Zinoviev, do you confirm that?

ZINOVIEV: Yes.

VISHINSKY: Treason, perfidy, double-dealing?

ZINOVIEV: Yes.

Whatever allegations were made as to occurrences outside of the USSR, investigations have proven them untrue. Yet, during World War II, a large number of persons sincerely and properly cooperating with the Soviet Union in the common effort against Nazism, came to believe that in order to demonstrate friendship it was necessary to ignore historical facts, to overlook the nature of the Soviet dictatorship. The Moscow Trials were not mock trials—became the refrain—they purged the Nazi fifth column. In 1941, after the German invasion of Russia, to ex-diplomat Joseph Davies* "passing through Chicago" on the way home from the June commencement of his old university, there "came a flash in my mind." After a lecture, he was asked: "What about Fifth columnists in Russia?" "Off the anvil, I said: 'There aren't any—they shot them.'" A terrible myth, which still lingers, was in the making.

One of the staunchest friends of the Soviet Union for a decade and a half, although never a member of the Communist Party, was Louis Fischer, the veteran American journalist. His correspondence on Soviet affairs were widely read, his books much discussed. His contacts in the Soviet Union, his long residence, the depth and extent of his allegiance, his sincerity and

* United States Ambassador to the Soviet Union, 1936-38, author of *Mission to Moscow*.

devotion to what he believed admirable won for him many followers. When he finally found it impossible to further suspend judgment in the hope that time would bring changes for the better it is understandable that his measured and long-deliberated verdict should have carried weight with a sizable number of American liberals.

He has described his own political metamorphosis: "From far and near I watched this evolution of the Soviet revolution with mounting concern . . . I never wrote or uttered a word of justification of the Soviet trials and purges. From 1936 on I ceased writing about Soviet internal affairs." He did this because of his belief that the Soviet Union was still "an active factor for world peace." When the Nazi-Soviet pact came, he found it impossible to delude himself for another moment. Recognizing it as the "ugly fruit of the preceding years," highlighting as it did "the chasm between the will of the leaders and the spirit of the people," he turned his pen against the dictatorship. In the last decade Mr. Fischer has been a source of especially impressive and enlightened commentary on the Soviet state. Moderation of judgment, distaste for the extremism of both far left and right, these are traits that characterize his writing and do him credit.

He was born on February 29, 1896 in Philadelphia. After teaching in the schools he began his journalistic career by contributing to the *New York Evening Post* from Berlin. He made his first trip to Russia in 1922 and has specialized in the field of European politics, with special emphasis on the Soviet Union, since. For many years he was the Moscow correspondent of *The Nation*. His books include: *Oil Imperialism;* the two volumes of *The Soviets in World Affairs; Soviet Journey; The War in Spain; Dawn of Victory; The Great Challenge;* and *Thirteen Who Fled* (ed.). This selection, a closely detailed dissection of the Moscow Trials, the crucial event in the disaffection of the author's faith in Soviet Communism, is extracted from the chapter on that subject in *Men and Politics* (1941), his famed autobiography.

The Moscow Trials and Confessions by Louis Fischer

First of all, why the trials?

Since there is no abstract justice under Bolshevism—no absolute sins and, unfortunately, no absolute virtues—it is necessary to ask what the Soviet regime tried to achieve by the trials. Many Bolsheviks have been executed without trials, and the defendants in the trials could have been executed without trials. Why the trials?

The chief defendant in all the three Moscow trials of leading Bolsheviks was Leon Trotzky. Men sat in the dock and made statements and received sentences. Yet Trotzky was the person the court wished to condemn. The edifice of guilt which the state prosecutor André Vishinsky sought to construct was an enormous leaning skyscraper. Its numerous floors and underground cellars were often connected with one another, but sometimes not. Threads from them all ended in the hand of Trotzky. It was a case of remote control.

The scheme, as it emerged from the confessions, was this: The Trotzkyists in the Soviet Union would hasten a foreign attack on Russia. The attackers—Germany and Japan—would help Trotzky and his friends to rule defeated Russia. Trotzky would give the Ukraine to Germany and the Far Eastern provinces and Amur district to Japan. The Germans would also get economic concessions in Russia.

Radek, testifying under the eyes of sixteen co-defendants, the judges of the Supreme Court, the prosecuting attorney Vishinsky, and his assistants, scores of Soviet and foreign journalists, a group of foreign diplomats, and hundreds of Soviet spectators, declared that he had frequently been in touch with Trotzky and received several letters from Trotzky by secret emissaries. "In 1935," said Radek, "the question was raised of going back to capitalism." Vishinsky: "To what limits?"

Radek: "What Trotzky proposed was without limits. To such limits as the enemy might require." The enemy was Germany and Japan. Trotzky, according to Radek, advised a complete sell-out to Russia's foes and to world Fascism.

How was this to be achieved? Trotzky wanted the Soviet leaders assassinated, the accused in the three trials deposed. Kill Stalin, Voroshilov, Molotov, Kirov, Kaganovitch, Zhdanov, and the others. Commit acts of sabotage. Wreck trains and factories. Blow up bridges. Poison soldiers. Give military information to Berlin and Tokio. Crush Bolshevism. Subjugate Russia. Then Trotzky and his accomplices, as puppets of Hitler and the Mikado, would govern this capitalistic, truncated, weakened Russia.

This was not just a paper scheme. Trotzky himself, it was alleged, had discussed the whole matter with Rudolf Hess, Hitler's first assistant. (Molotov saw Hess in Berlin in November, 1940.) They had worked out a plan. Trotzky also had contacts with the Japanese government. In April, 1934, Gregory Sokolnikov—so he reported at the trial—received the Japanese Ambassador in the Commissariat of Foreign Affairs. Sokolnikov was then Vice-Commissar of Foreign Affairs. At the end of the interview the interpreters went out, and the Ambassador asked Sokolnikov whether he knew that Trotzky had made certain proposals to his government. Sokolnikov replied, "Yes." The Ambassador, you see, was trying to find out whether Trotzky was acting on his personal behalf or whether he had strong backing in Soviet Russia.

Think of the members of this anti-Bolshevik, pro-Nazi, pro-Japanese conspiracy! Rykov, Prime Minister of the whole country. Yagoda, head of the mighty GPU. Tukhachevsky and his eight leading generals. The Number Two man in Soviet industry. The President and Prime Minister of White Russia. The Prime Minister of the Ukraine. The Prime Minister of Uzbekistan. The Prime Minister of Tadjikistan. The Federal Commissar of Finance. The Federal Commissar of Agriculture. The Secretary of the Soviet government. The commander of the military guard of the Kremlin. Two assistant commissars of foreign affairs. Several Soviet ambassadors. Hundreds of factory managers. Each one of these had numerous subordinates. Yagoda could put the entire secret police of the nation at the disposal of the plotters. Tukhachevsky was the key-man in the Red Army.

Why did they fail?

Fritz David, a German Communist, defendant in the 1936 Zinoviev-Kamenev trial, admitted in the public hearings that Trotzky had chosen him for the "historic mission" of killing Stalin. David actually got to a Third International congress in Moscow attended by Stalin. He had a Browning revolver in his pocket. But he was too far away to get a good aim, he said.

All right. But Yagoda's men guarded every entrance and exit of the Kremlin and of Stalin's apartment. They were posted at frequent intervals along the road which leads from Moscow to Stalin's country home. They guarded the country home. Yagoda himself, Tukhachevsky himself, Piatakov, and many other accused had carried arms and were regularly in Stalin's intimate company. Why didn't they kill him? There is no answer. At the trials the question was not even asked. Why hire a poor German Communist for a job of assassination when you have the whole Kremlin guard and army chiefs and the secret police?

From Turkey, France, and Norway, Trotzky allegedly gave orders, and in Moscow, Leningrad, Siberia, and Turkestan they were executed by the highest officials of the Soviet government, by men who had signed his deportation order, who had condemned him in speeches and articles, who maligned and swore against him each day. The prosecution thus unwittingly paid a tribute to Trotzky's personality. But—Trotzky has branded as a lie every accusation leveled against him at the trials! He called all the trials gigantic frameups.

There was in Berlin a swarthy young man named Bukhartsev, correspondent of *Izvestia*, as fervent a Bolshevik as I have ever met. In addition to his work as correspondent, he spied on the Nazis and got young American ladies to help him. But at the trial, Bukhartsev testified that he had been a partner in this big pro-Nazi, anti-Bolshevik, Trotzkyist plot to restore capitalism in Russia. In December, 1935, Yuri Piatakov, Soviet Vice-Commissar of Heavy Industry, went to Berlin on official business, to buy equipment. Bukhartsev met him and took him to the Tiergarten, Berlin's central park, where they saw one of Trotzky's undercover men. This man said that Trotzky wished to see Piatakov. He would make all the arrangements. So he got Piatakov a false German passport, chartered a private plane, and Piatakov flew non-stop to Oslo where he talked with Trotzky for two hours. Then he came back to Moscow and reported to Radek and Sokolnikov the details of the conversation. He gave the details to the court. Radek and Sokolnikov confirmed what Piatakov said. He had said it to them at the time.

But Trotzky denied that he ever met Piatakov in Oslo or anywhere else in 1935 or any other year of his exile. The director of the Oslo airport told newspapermen that no airplane from Berlin, in fact, no foreign airplane, landed on his field in December, 1935. The Norwegian family with whom Trotzky was living swore out affidavits to the effect that Trotzky never received a visit from any Russian and never went away from them to meet anybody.

Vladimir Romm, a Soviet correspondent in Geneva and Washington, testified in court that he met Trotzky in Paris by secret appointment. He named the place, the Bois de Boulogne. Date: end of July, 1933. Romm went with Trotzky's son, Leo Sedov, to the park and there they met Trotzky. Trotzky gave Romm instructions for Radek. He also gave Romm a letter for Radek. The letter was pasted in the cover of Novikov Priboi's novel *Tsusima*. Romm brought the letter to Radek in Moscow. Radek in the witness stand confirmed this testimony by Romm and described the contents of the letter.

But Trotzky swore that he never met Romm, never in his life, never even heard of him, and never wrote any letters to Radek from exile. Romm went all the way from Washington to Moscow on a GPU summons to testify at this trial and to incriminate himself. Since the day he appeared in court he has not been heard of again. He expected trouble before he left America and told his American friends so. They advised him not to go. He went because he could not disobey the GPU. It can compel obedience. It has murdered men abroad. I know that because I know of one case in all its gruesome, bloody particulars.

The GPU killed Ludwig. That was the only name by which I knew him. So when the French press announced in September, 1937, that a Czech named Hans Eberhardt has been killed under mysterious circumstances near Lausanne, I thought nothing more of it. Several months later, I learned that Eberhardt's real name was Ignace Reiss, and that he was the Ludwig whom I had known since 1931. I met him in Berlin through German Communists. He was introduced simply as "Ludwig." That was not unusual in such circles, and one asked no questions. Ludwig was a round, jovial Polish Jew with a most keen intelligence. I enjoyed discussing politics with him. He invited me to a café once, and took me to an expensive one. He also dressed well. His conversation, his interests, his manner made me think he worked for the GPU.

When Hitler arrived, Ludwig left Germany. Several times he visited us in Moscow. He was an interesting person and an idealist. In 1935, I met him in Paris. He had made Paris his headquarters. He never told me what he did and I never inquired, but in France he spoke less guardedly and I deduced that he was engaged in military espionage for the Soviet government with special emphasis on Hitler's war preparations. For months he would disappear, and then he telephoned me and we met in the café of the Hotel Lutetia where I lived or in a café on the Champs Elysées. I also met his wife, a brave intelligent woman. She knew the danger he courted every day. He traveled across Europe on false passports, stole across borders, used false names, and lived illegally in Paris. There was always the possibility that a foreign agent of the German Gestapo would shoot him or that the police of some country would arrest him.

During our Paris meetings in 1936, Ludwig spoke very critically of the Soviet regime. Until then he had been completely loyal and devoted. When I returned from America in June, 1937, he called me up and we had a sitting of several hours. The Zinoviev-Kamenev trial in August, 1936, had deeply upset him. On its heels came the Piatakov-Radek-Sokolnikov trial in January, 1937. Stalin was destroying the old revolutionists and, with them, the Revolution, Ludwig stormed. Stalin was using the trials to wipe out all potential rivals and everybody who had ever disagreed with him or agreed with Trotzky. Even Hitler did not commit such atrocities, he said. He regarded the Moscow trials as frameups and the confessions as fakes.

I warned him to be cautious. If he talked that way he could easily be reported. I suspected how perilous it was for an agent of the secret police to turn against his masters. Since he knew many secrets they would try to destroy him. I would have been even more perturbed about this fine person if I had known then, what I learned subsequently, that he was a chief of the Soviet military intelligence work abroad. When such a man goes anti-Stalin he signs his death warrant.

I pleaded with Ludwig to hold his tongue. I also said to him that there was still Spain and that Russia was aiding Spain. "Not sufficiently," he said.

"Still," I urged, "wait till I come back from Spain. Don't do anything rash until we have another talk." His mood made me think he might kick over the traces.

I never had any way of reaching him. I did not have his address or telephone number. But he always managed to know when I arrived in Paris. This time, on my return from Brunete and Madrid, he got in touch with me immediately. "Don't tell me about Spain. They have shot Tukhachevsky, Yakir, Kork, and the others. And Gamarnik committed suicide. Silly. I knew Gamarnik. He would never have committed suicide." All restraint was now gone. He was out-and-out anti-Stalin. He wondered whether Voroshilov would be next.

He talked about his comrades in Moscow. He had worked closely in the GPU with several Polish friends and he realized that whatever he did would react against them. He obviously contemplated some desperate deed, but I had no idea what it might be.

The rest I know from the officially announced findings of the Swiss police and from Victor Serge's book on Ignace Reiss. Ludwig had worked sixteen years for the GPU. On July 17, 1937, he wrote a letter to the Soviet-government full of vituperation against Stalin and denouncing the purges. He was joining Trotzky, he said. He was returning the decoration he had received for distinguished work on behalf of the Revolution. The courage he had displayed in serving the GPU he now displayed in breaking with it. He wrote the letter and delivered it at the Soviet Embassy in Paris.*

---

* [Former Soviet General Walter G. Krivitsky (see preface to his selection in this book) worked closely with Reiss for many years. Just before Reiss' open break Krivitsky attempted to change his friend's mind. "I mustered all the familiar arguments," he has written, "and sang the old song that we must not run away from the battle . . . Stalins will come and go, but the Soviet Union will remain. It is our duty to stick to our post." When the GPU sought to involve Krivitsky in the assassination of Reiss, he too broke with the regime. Ignace Reiss' letter, to which Mr. Fischer refers, is reproduced in Krivitsky's *In Stalin's Secret Service*. Excerpts: "The letter which I am addressing to you today I should have written a long time ago, on the day when the Sixteen (referring to the Kamenev-Zinoviev group, executed in August, 1936) were murdered in the cellars of the Lubianka at the command of the Father of Nations (a Soviet appellation for Stalin). I kept silent then. I raised no voice of protest at the subsequent murders, and for this I bear a large responsibility. My guilt is great, but I shall try to make up for it. to make up for it quickly, and to ease my conscience. Up to now I have followed you. From now on, not a step further. Our ways part! He who keeps silent at this hour becomes an accomplice of Stalin, and a traitor to the cause of the working class and of Socialism.

"From .he age of twenty I have battled for Socialism. I do not want now, on the eve of my fifth decade, to live by the favors of Yezhov (then head of the GPU). Behind me are sixteen years of underground service—this is no trifle, but I still have enough strength to make a new start. . . .

"P.S.: In 1928 I was awarded the Order of the Red Banner for my service

That evening he sat in his hotel room. The telephone rang. He answered. No one spoke. Five minutes later it rang again. He answered. Not a sound. This happened four times. The GPU employees in Paris who had opened Ludwig's letter had had a council of war that evening to decide on their course of action. One of them, a friend of Ludwig, left the meeting, walked down a boulevard, stopped in a pay station, called Ludwig and when Ludwig said "Hello" he hung up. He walked two blocks and telephoned again. Ludwig answered "Hello"; the friend slowly put down the receiver. Then he called again in another pay station, and again. He wanted to make Ludwig uneasy. But he did not dare to speak to him. How did he know whether Ludwig's phone had been tapped by the GPU? If his voice were heard he would be doomed, for he had just come from the meeting which determined the fate of Ludwig. Or perhaps the meeting was a trap. Perhaps the GPU was testing him. Perhaps Ludwig was a party to the trap. If he spoke to Ludwig over the telephone the GPU would know that he revealed its secret. Ludwig understood the meaning of these telephone signals. The next morning he took a train for Switzerland. He assumed he would be safer there.

In Lausanne, an old woman friend, Gertrude Schildbach, likewise a GPU agent, visited him. He had talked to her about the pain which the Moscow trials had caused him and she expressed sympathy and understanding. He wanted to talk to her now. He took her out to dinner. After dinner they walked down a country road. An automobile stopped and the men in it, and Gertrude Schildbach, pushed Ludwig into the car. There they opened up on him with submachine guns. He struggled, and under his fingernails the Swiss police found pieces of Miss Schildbach's hair. Then the murderers threw Ludwig's body into the road and abandoned the car.

I lived in Lutetia until after the second World War com-

to the proletarian revolution. I am returning it herewith. To wear it simultaneously with the hangmen of the best representatives of the Russian workers is beneath my dignity."—*Ed.*]

menced. And every time I passed the café downstairs I thought of Ludwig's body with bullet holes in it lying in a Swiss road.

So Vladimir Romm knew he had to go to Moscow when the GPU in Washington told him to go. If he refused he would suffer the consequences. At the trial Romm described in detail his encounter with Trotzky in the Paris Bois. But Trotzky denied it. Trotzky denied any contact with Rudolf Hess, the Nazi leader. He denied any contact with Japan. Trotzky declared he was opposed to personal terror and assassination. Nor did he wish the defeat of the Soviet Union in war. (He did not want to see Russia defeated in Finland.) And of course he was a Communist, anti-Fascist, and anti-capitalist, and indignantly disclaimed any wish to restore capitalism in the Soviet Union.

It was for the Soviet prosecutor to prove his charges. He submitted no proofs, no documents, no evidence—except the confessions of defendants and witnesses. All the trials were based on the statements which the accused made in the preliminary hearings in prison. The procedure in court consisted in getting each defendant to repeat publicly what he had already said in the secret investigation chambers, and in getting other defendants to corroborate these statements. Not one of the witnesses was a free man. . . .

The men in the dock—not a single woman—had written numerous bright pages in the annals of Bolshevism. Forty years or less, they sacrificed and labored for the cause, many by the side of Lenin, many in the company of Stalin. But now they did not merely blacken their records with admission of treachery and counter-revolution. They assassinated their own characters. They spat on their whole lives and dragged their names through the vilest filth.

Take Rakovsky. An old revolutionist and recognized as such by the world and in Russia, he admitted at the trial that he betrayed the labor movement before 1917. Also, he was a landlord. "Well, of course, I was an exploiter," he exclaimed in the witness stand. He further testified that in 1924, while Soviet Ambassador in England, he signed up as a British spy. Scotland Yard recruited him in a restaurant. Two men just walked up to him and said he had to work for the British intelligence service and he agreed. That is how he described it in court. Then he went into exile as a Trotzkyist, first in Saratov, later in Barnaul. In 1934, he recanted. "This telegram [of recantation]," he said at the trial, "was insincere. I was lying. . . . It was my deliberate intention to hide from the Party and the government my association with the [British] intelligence service ever since 1924, and Trotzky's association with the [British] intelligence service since 1926." After this insincere recantation, the Soviet government sent him on a mission to Tokio. There the Japanese intelligence service recruited him. "I returned from Tokio," he seemed to boast, "with the credentials of a Japanese spy in my pocket." . . .

Bukharin is testifying at the March, 1938, trial. In the dock he was no less witty and scintillating than at his desk or at a mass meeting. Bukharin denied complicity in the assassination of Kirov. He denied plotting to kill Lenin or Stalin. He denied being a foreign spy as the indictment alleged. But he admitted his participation in a revolt of rich peasants in the Kuban region. He did wish to overthrow the Soviet regime and turn it over to Germany and Japan. For all this "I am responsible," he exclaimed, "as one of the leaders and not merely as a cog." Heaven forbid that anyone give him too little discredit! "I do not want to minimize my guilt," he declared in court. "I want to aggravate it." . . .

On another occasion Bukharin had admitted that he contemplated arresting Lenin for twenty-four hours in 1918; however, "as regards assassination, I know nothing whatever."

VISHINSKY: "But the atmosphere was . . ."

BUKHARIN, *interrupting:* "The atmosphere was the atmosphere."

Still another encounter between angry hunter and playful quarry:

VISHINSKY: "I am not asking you about conversations in general but about this conversation."

BUKHARIN: "In Hegel's *Logic* the word 'this' is considered to be the most difficult word. . . ."

VISHINSKY: "I ask the court to explain to the Accused Bukharin that he is here not in the capacity of a philosopher, but a criminal. . . ."

BUKHARIN: "A philosopher may be a criminal. . . ."

VISHINSKY: "Yes, that is to say, those who imagine themselves to be philosophers turn out to be spies. Philosophy is out of place here. I am asking you about that conversation of which Khodjayev just spoke. Do you confirm it or do you deny it?"

BUKHARIN: "I do not understand the word 'that' . . ."

At one time, both gentlemen began to lose their tempers. Said Bukharin to Vishinsky, "I beg your pardon. It is I who am speaking and not you." The Chief Justice called Bukharin to order. But a moment later, Bukharin again reprimanded Vishinsky. "There is nothing for you to gesticulate about," he yelled to the federal prosecutor. Vishinsky got his revenge when he said a moment later, "You are obviously a spy of an intelligence service. So stop pettifogging."

BUKHARIN: "I never considered myself a spy, nor do I now."

VISHINSKY: "It would be more correct if you did."

BUKHARIN: "That is your opinion, but my opinion is different."

VISHINSKY: "We shall see what the opinion of the court is."

The accused were, for the most part, men of big caliber and great intellect and they did not show the least sign of physical torture or of having been drugged or doped. They were keen and quick. They tripped up one another, made brilliant speeches, and displayed good memories. And always they insisted they were traitors and criminals.

Rykov said he worked for the Polish Intelligence Service while Prime Minister of the Soviet Union. Krestinsky said he had been a German spy since 1921, and that he was in Germany's pay while serving as Soviet Ambassador in Berlin. In return for this he received a quarter of a million marks per annum from General von Seeckt, the commander-in-chief of the Reichswehr. "I used to take it to Moscow myself and hand it to Trotzky." (He said this in the preliminary hearings but omitted it at the trial and Vishinsky himself failed to bring out this quaint bit of testimony regarding the German army's financing of Trotzky.) Foreign Trade Commissar Rosengoltz said he had supplied information on the Soviet air force to General von Seeckt in 1922 on instructions from Trotzky. Other defendants heaped equally damaging admissions upon their heads.

In all this symphony of self-denunciation and self-condemnation only one fully discordant note was struck. Krestinsky, former envoy to Germany, former Assistant Commissar for Foreign Affairs, had, at his first interrogation in prison—June 5 to 9, 1937—within a week after his arrest, confessed to every crime of which the preliminary investigator accused him. The public trial started on the morning of March 2, 1938. All the defendants pleaded guilty. Except Krestinsky. He pleaded not guilty.

Prosecutor Vishinsky called Accused Bessonov as the first witness. Bessonov had been Krestinsky's Counselor in Berlin. Under Vishinsky's cross-examination, he declared that he and Krestinsky had engaged in Trotzkyist activity in Germany. Krestinsky, summoned to the side of Bessonov to testify, denied Bessonov's statements. Vishinsky reminded him that in the preliminary secret hearings he had admitted his crimes.

"My testimony of June 5 or 9," Krestinsky affirmed, "is false from beginning to end." He had given false testimony in prison in the first week of his GPU detention. He stuck to it all the time he was in prison. Why? Here is a clue to the secret of the trials.

VISHINSKY: "And then you stuck to it."

KRESTINSKY: "And then I stuck to it because from personal

experience I had arrived at the conviction that before the trial
. . . I would not succeed in refuting my testimony." Now, in
court, he declared he was not a Trotzkyite and not a conspira-
tor or criminal. . . .

Court is dismissed. Krestinsky spends the night in his cell.
The next morning, hearings are resumed. Krestinsky is not
called on that morning. In the evening session, Accused Rakovsky reports on conspiratorial connections he had had with
Krestinsky in the interests of Trotzkyism. Krestinsky thereupon
confirms Rakovsky's declarations. He adds, "I fully confirm the
testimony I gave in the preliminary investigation." But all day
yesterday he had denied that testimony. What had happened?
Vishinsky also wanted to know. He asked Krestinsky the meaning of this sudden shift since yesterday.

"Yesterday," Krestinsky replied, "under the influence of a
momentary keen feeling of false shame evoked by the atmosphere of the dock and the painful impression created by the
public reading of the indictment, which was aggravated by my
poor health, I could not bring myself to tell the truth. . . . In
the face of world public opinion, I had not the strength to
admit the truth that I had been conducting a Trotzkyite struggle all along. . . . I admit my complete responsibility for the
treason and treachery I have committed." . . .

How did the authorities extract the confessions from the accused? The man who knew was Yagoda, the head of the GPU
for many years. He himself had staged numerous public trials
including the trial of the Zinoviev-Kamenev group. Now he
himself was on trial. And he confessed.

Imagine how much Yagoda might have disclosed! But he sat
through the trial bored and listless and was rarely called on to
speak. He did not open his mouth until late on the fifth day of
trial even though others had mentioned him and it is normal
procedure in Soviet courts to ask an accused person to corroborate or reject accusations made against him in the witness
stand. Brought to his feet on the fifth day by Vishinsky he

helped Vishinsky by disputing Bukharin's and Rykov's assertion of innocence in the Kirov murder.

"Both Rykov and Bukharin are telling lies," Yagoda stated.
"Rykov and Yenukidze were present at the meeting of the center where the question of the assassination of S. M. Kirov was
discussed."

VISHINSKY: "Did the Accused Rykov and Bukharin in particu-
lar have any relation to the assassination?"
YAGODA: "A direct relation."
VISHINSKY: "Did you?"
YAGODA: "I did."

Then Yagoda sat down and was not heard from again until
the seventh day of the public trial. On that day, Drs. Levin
and Kazakov, two Soviet physicians, were testifying about their
alleged efforts to kill Maxim Gorky, revered Russian author,
Menzhinsky, chief of the GPU, Kuibishev, a member of the
Politbureau, and Max Peshkov, Gorky's son. Levin, a venerable
man past seventy who had treated Lenin and who was an honored figure in Moscow, as well as Kazakov testified that they
had acted on Yagoda's instructions.

Yagoda said it was true he conspired to kill Gorky and Kuibishev but not Peshkov or Menzhinsky. Vishinsky read from
Yagoda's preliminary evidence in prison: "But he (Levin) said
he had no access to Menzhinsky, that the physician in attendance was Kazakov without whom nothing could be done. I instructed Levin to enlist Kazakov for this purpose."

VISHINSKY: "Did you depose this, Accused Yagoda?"
YAGODA: "I said that I did, but it is not true."
VISHINSKY: "Why did you make this deposition if it is not
true?"
YAGODA: "I don't know why."
VISHINSKY: "Be seated."

Dr. Kazakov in court described in great detail a conference he had with Yagoda in Yagoda's office and he repeated the instructions Yagoda had then given him. In prison, Yagoda had corroborated Kazakov's information. "I summoned Kazakov and confirmed my orders. . . . He did his work. Menzhinsky died," Yagoda had said. But now at the trial Yagoda declared that he had never set eyes on Kazakov before he saw him here in the dock. Vishinsky read out Yagoda's statement in prison.

VISHINSKY: "Did you depose this?"

YAGODA: "I did."

VISHINSKY: "Hence you met Kazakov?"

YAGODA: "No."

VISHINSKY: "Why did you make a false deposition?"

YAGODA: "Permit me not to answer this question."

VISHINSKY: "So you deny that you organized the murder of Menzhinsky?"

YAGODA: "I do."

VISHINSKY: "Did you admit it in the deposition?"

YAGODA: "Yes."

The same questions came up again. Vishinsky said to Yagoda, "At the preliminary investigation you . . ."

YAGODA: "I lied."

VISHINSKY: "And now?"

YAGODA: "I am telling the truth."

VISHINSKY: "Why did you lie at the preliminary investigation?"

YAGODA: "I have already said: permit me not to reply to this question."

Mystery. The man who knew most said least. . . .

A little episode now occurred in court which lifts the veil behind the secret of the Moscow trials and confessions. Doctor

Levin was still in the stand explaining how, on Yagoda's orders, he killed Gorky, Gorky's son, Menzhinsky, and Kuibishev. Any men accused in a Soviet trial may put questions at any time to another accused or to a witness. Yagoda rose. "May I put a question to Levin?" "When Levin finishes his testimony," the presiding Chief Justice replied. Normally, Yagoda could have put his question immediately. Yagoda therefore insists: "This concerns Maxim Gorky's death." "When the Accused Levin finishes, then by all means," the Chief Justice assured him.

Levin continued with his testimony. When he finished, however, the President did not give Yagoda an opportunity to ask his question. Instead, he adjourned the session for thirty minutes. When the court reconvened after this interval, Yagoda was permitted to put his query to Levin. Yagoda said, "I ask Levin to answer in what year the Kremlin Medical Commission attached him, Levin, to me as my doctor, and to whom else he was attached."

Levin did not remember. That was the end of Yagoda's questioning. He did *not* put that question to Levin about the death of Maxim Gorky. He substituted another irrelevant, unimportant question.

What happened in that thirty-minute recess? Obviously, Yagoda promised the authorities not to put the question. . . .

What induced the accused Bolsheviks to enter into a bargain with the authorities?

They were offered the alternative: Confession or Death. Trotzky, who knew many of the accused intimately, and who understood Soviet methods better than anyone outside Russia, said to the American Preliminary Commission of Inquiry— Professor John Dewey, Carleton Beals, Otto Ruehle, Benjamin Stolberg, and Suzanne La Follette—which interrogated him in Mexico in April, 1937, "When anybody has to choose between death at one hundred percent and death at ninety-nine percent when he is in the hands of the GPU, he will choose the ninety-nine percent against the one hundred percent." The defendants in the Moscow trials chose the ninety-nine percent of living death because if they had not confessed they would have been shot immediately.

There was, for instance, Leo Karakhan, former Vice Commissar of Foreign Affairs. At the Bukharin trial, several defendants stated that Karakhan was a German spy and that he conducted all the treasonable negotiations with the Nazis. Then he should have been in the dock with the others. But he was not. He had been shot together with Yenukidze, who, it was alleged by the prosecution and by the defendants, had been the key-man in the entire conspiracy. They were executed in prison on December 19, 1937. That was just when the defendants in the Bukharin-Rykov trial were being cross-examined in the GPU prison for the March, 1938, trial. If Karakhan and Yenukidze had confessed they would have been in the dock. They refused to confess. They were executed. This cannot have been without its effect on the preliminary prison cross-examinations.

Bessonov, one of the defendants in the March, 1938, trial, stated in court that he refused to confess from February 28, 1937, to December 30, 1937, when he was confronted with Krestinsky's confession. But this is incorrect. For Krestinsky confessed in June, 1937, and had finished testifying by October. I am sure it was the execution of Karakhan and Yenukidze on December 19 which induced Bessonov's breakdown on December 30. The publication of the story of the execution in *Pravda* was an unusual expedient. It served to intimidate those who still refused to confess. I can imagine what it meant to Bessonov when a copy of *Pravda* with the news of the Karakhan-Yenukidze execution was introduced into his cell. He must have read it and said to himself, "This is my last chance. If I do not confess now they will shoot me as they have Karakhan and Yenukidze. They are promising me my life if I confess. Maybe they will keep the promise. I have a one percent chance to live if I confess according to dictation."

Or take the case of my dear friend Boris Mironov, whom many foreign correspondents knew as assistant chief of the

Press Department under Oumansky. He was witty and highly educated and very much in love with his wife Celia. We used to visit one another often. Then he was arrested. At the trial, Krestinsky asserted that he had kept in touch with Trotzky through foreign correspondents and that Mironov had arranged all this. What correspondent? Vishinsky asked.

KRESTINSKY: "I cannot tell definitely. He left for America."

Some people thought it was I. But I never had anything to do with it. Moreover, they assumed that there were such activities, and that Mironov engaged in conspiracy. If he had, it would have been natural for him to be brought in as a witness when Krestinsky referred to him. Romm and Bukhartsev who allegedly served similar liaison functions had testified. Why didn't Mironov testify? Because he refused to confess to lies. Mironov is dead. . . .

The Soviet government needed the Moscow trials and confessions, or thought it did, and the accused met the government's need. They behaved in most respects just as the Kremlin would have wanted them to. In a Soviet court the defendant can at one time or another say anything he pleases. But in these trials, the defendants were interrupted on several occasions by Vishinsky when they approached ticklish subjects—Bukharin's dispute with Stalin, for instance—and they never reverted to them. That was part of the bargain.

From Stalin's viewpoint, the ideal result of the trials would have been high praise of Stalin, condemnation of Trotzky, and acceptance by the accused of the accidents, economic difficulties, shortages, and political disturbances which had occurred in the country during the past seven or eight years. This *was* the result.

The dictator is infallible; the dictatorship can make no mistakes. That is the official Stalin credo. But there had been hundreds of train wrecks. "We deliberately staged them," the defendants said. From the beginning of Bolshevik time winter goods had been offered to customers in the summer, and summer goods in the winter. "That is," said Vishinsky at the trial, "the public was offered felt boots in the summer and summer shoes in the winter." "Yes," replied Accused Zelensky, head of the co-operative stores. This, he confessed, was part of the conspiracy. He thus absolved the Soviet government of a shortcoming for which many citizens cursed it. The Commissariat of Finance had adopted certain measures with regard to savings banks in which millions of individual depositors were interested. Commissar of Finance Grinko, accused, declared that he did it deliberately because "it caused irritation among the broad masses of the population." Now the broad masses would understand and no longer blame Stalin for their irritation. Stalin must be without blame. They would blame Grinko, the puppet of Trotzky; whatever went wrong in Russia was Trotzky's doing. The peasants in collective farms had complained that they were underpaid. Grinko testified that Rykov ordered this to sow discontent. There had been a bread shortage. Didn't you do that, Vishinsky probed. Of course, Grinko asserted, I did it with Zelensky. Tractors which served the farm collectives broke down frequently and the peasants always had trouble providing for tractor services. Ex-Commissar of Agriculture Chernov revealed that he did this purposely and put men of his own illegal, rightist, Trotzkyist organizations in charge of the tractors with a view to spoiling the government's relations with the peasants. "As regards stock breeding," he added, "the aim was to kill pedigree breeding stock and to strive for high cattle mortality." That should satisfy the peasants who had complained that beasts in collectives died too fast. There had been a shortage of paper. Ivanov testified that he arranged that on Bukharin's orders. Peasant revolts in Siberia and the Kuban? Bukharin did that too. "The kulaks," said Ivanov, "were in an angry mood." Bukharin exploited this mood. The government had distributed impure seed in the villages. "I did it," affirmed Accused Zubarev. In White Russia, the number of livestock had been disastrously reduced. It was done at the wish of the

Polish Secret Service, several defendants deposed. Thirty thousand horses died of anemia in 1936 in White Russia. "My work," Accused Sharangovich admitted. This admission was then headlined in White Russia's newspapers and radio broadcasts. In a mining district, some children were digging in the dirt and struck some dynamite which killed a large number of them. Shestov took this crime on his shoulders. The accused damaged the cotton crop of Turkestan and the silk production of Uzbekistan, delayed the construction of a giant water-power station in Ferghana, put nails and glass in butter, gave short weight and measure in retail stores, and committed hundreds of similar acts.

All right. The accused have been removed forever from Soviet administration. But the Soviet press in 1939 and 1940 continued to announce arrests for train wrecks, venality in cooperative stores, poisonings. The *New York Times* of December 14, 1940, reported from Moscow that the Soviet newspaper *Soviet Agriculture* charged the "capitalist world" with "trying to send to our country not only spies and terrorists; the enemy is trying to wreck with anything possible . . . seeds infected with pink worms, lemons with larva of the Mediterranean fruit fly, and infected potatoes" . . . and diseased cotton had been shipped into the country. The guilty nations this time were America, England, and the Netherlands. Apparently, Soviet farming had again suffered some setbacks for which a scapegoat and explanation had to be found. These setbacks—and excuses—seem to be a permanent feature of Soviet life. In 1936, 1937, and 1938 the Soviet dictatorship hoped to pass the blame to those who confessed. Stalin must be blameless. . . .

Big Soviet trials have nothing to do with justice. They are forms of super-propaganda. They are not, primarily a product of bad economic conditions. They serve to rewrite history. The Bolsheviks have been very energetic in rewriting history. They serve to alter the political record, to whitewash Stalin, to blacken his enemies, to frighten potential enemies. The trials undertook to demonstrate that the Soviet administration is perfect; the only trouble is that some Trotzkyists are still at liberty.

For these purposes Stalin needed the trials and the confessions. If the accused had been dangerous they could have been removed without public ceremonies. But they were assets to Stalin. The only problem was to induce them to perform in the required fashion. . . .

Above all, the accused, many of them old friends of Trotzky, outbid one another in maligning Trotzky. This was certainly very pleasing to Stalin. Thus Piatakov: "I only deeply regret that he, the main criminal, the unregenerate and hardened offender, Trotzky, is not sitting beside us in the dock." Sokolnikov: "I express the conviction, or at any rate the hope that not one person will now be found in the Soviet Union who would attempt to take up the Trotzky banner. I think that Trotzkyism in other countries too has been exposed by this trial, and that Trotzky himself has been exposed as an ally of capitalism, as the vilest agent of Fascism." Rakovsky, for thirty-four years a devoted friend of Trotzky: "I share the State Prosecutor's regret that the enemy of the people, Trotzky, is not here in the dock with us. The picture of our trial loses in completeness and depth because of the fact that the ataman of our gang is not present here." Rosengoltz: "Trotzky . . . is the vilest agent of Fascism . . . Rakovsky was right when he said that here in the dock it is Trotzky in the first place who is missing. Trotzkyism is not a political current but an unscrupulous dirty gang of murderers, spies, provocateurs, and poisoners. . . . Long live the Bolshevik party with the best traditions of enthusiasm, heroism, self-sacrifice which can only be found in the world under Stalin's leadership." Bukharin: "In reality the whole country stands behind Stalin. He is the hope of the world. He is a creator. . . . Everybody perceives the wise leadership of the country that is ensured by Stalin." That is how Stalin felt about it. . . .

The Soviet government obviously realized that the confessions heavily taxed the credulity even of Soviet citizens who did not hear the counter-arguments. The state prosecutor, and especially the accused, used every opportunity to try to make the confessions appear more plausible. Bukharin, Radek, and many of the accused obligingly devoted long impassioned speeches to an attempt to dispel the doubts about the truth of their confessions. "Please believe us," they cried in appeals directed to the outside world and to their own country. But how could one believe them? While allegedly serving as dupes of Fascism, while allegedly plotting to overthrow the Soviets and assassinate Stalin they had written and spoken in public in fulsome praise of Stalin and behaved as enemies of Fascism and staunch Bolsheviks. Perhaps they were no less hypocritical now. . . .

It was easy to defy the Czarist Okhrana. It was the hated enemy. But when your own Soviet secret police asked you to confess falsely in order to save Stalin's face it broke your heart first and then broke your will.

The spine of many of the accused Bolsheviks had been crushed even before they were arrested. A mild illustration: Michael Borodin, a man of powerful build and striking presence, had been sent by Moscow to China. He quickly became the real master of nationalist China. He twisted provincial war lords around his little finger; the big men of China deferred to his political sagacity. In 1927, he returned to Moscow and became the scapegoat for the failure of Stalin's policy in China. He was put in charge of a Soviet paper-manufacturing trust and, of course, he made a mess of it because he lacked business experience. Then he got another but smaller economic job which he likewise mishandled. This was all part of a deliberate scheme of humiliation. Finally he landed in the editor's chair of the *Moscow Daily News*. Two little Communists were introduced into the office to hamper every step he made and to check and irritate him. Before he could print an editorial he had to consult the Central Committee of the party. He was barred from any initiative. Just as a man may rise and grow when given a big task so he may shrink when he is a dismal misfit in a small one. I was present once in Borodin's office in the *Moscow Daily News* when an American radical, a lad of twenty-three who worked on the paper, came in. Borodin scolded him for falling down on a story. The American argued. Borodin became angry. The American yelled, "You can't talk to me that way." Borodin yelled back. They both waxed hot. Borodin finally threw his hands above his head and shouted, "Get out of here. You're fired." The great statesman who had ruled millions at war and molded big Chinese minds to his will could not manage a cub reporter.

Magnify this many times. Rykov took Lenin's job as Prime Minister and held it from 1924 to 1930. He was under constant attack as an oppositionist, until he was removed December 19, 1930. He was unemployed for several months and then was appointed Commissar of Posts and Telegraphs, notoriously a Soviet job of no political importance. The attacks in the press and at meetings continued. His best friends shunned him. On a vacation in the Caucasus, he slipped into a public celebration on the anniversary of the Revolution. People moved away from him. Nobody talked to him. The orators flayed him. In August, 1936, his name was mentioned in the Zinoviev-Kamenev trial as one of the leading conspirators. On September 27, 1936, he was dismissed from the Post Office. He sat home, did nothing, and waited. He waited for five months. He was not arrested until February 27, 1937, and arrest must have come as a relief from morose suspense. He stayed in prison for a year before his trial opened. After all this he naturally had very gloomy and cynical ideas about what had happened to the Revolution, and rather than feel inspired to help the Revolution by self-flagellation and self-immolation his mood was rather: "Oh, what's the use. If Stalin wants me to confess and say thus-and-so, I'll do it. Why should I die for this?"

When Rykov left the Commissariat of Posts and Telegraphs, Yagoda took his place. The Commissariat of Posts was a sort of halfway house to prison. Soon, accordingly, Yagoda was ousted from it and charged with embezzling funds. Later he was arrested and charged with murder and treason. He and Rykov were defendants in the same trial in March, 1938, and sentenced to death. The trial was staged by Yezhov, who succeeded Yagoda as head of the GPU. But on July 25, 1938, Yezhov was dismissed from the GPU and appointed to head the Commissariat of Water Transport, which is another non-political sideshow like the Commissariat of Posts and Telegraphs. Later Yezhov disappeared.

Stalin's technique of slow-motion destruction demoralized his victims long before they entered their prison cells. No ordinary third-degree would have produced the confessions. It was a third-degree that lasted for years, a third-degree to which the entire country was and is today submitted. The Moscow trials and confessions were merely the sensational, highly-silhouetted shape of an everyday Soviet phenomenon, and it is only against the background of this phenomenon that the confessions can be understood. Millions of Soviet citizens live lies every day to save their lives and their jobs. They make false confessions day in and day out. They write lies, speak lies. They lie to one another and know it. They lie to themselves and get accustomed to it. They lose their illusions and succumb to the sole cynical goal of self-preservation until a better day. The assassination of character and the annihilation of personality is the dictatorship's chief weapon which it never forgets. The further a Soviet citizen is from the center of the regime the less he feels its blows. The peasants are least exposed to it. The workers more. The officials much more. And for the highest officials like Rykov, Yagoda, and Krestinsky the destruction of personality and character took the intensified, telescoped form of trial and confession. The wonder of it is that so few confessed.

The Bolshevik dictatorship has become a personal dictatorship. It was not that in the beginning. In a personal dictatorship, all persons are effaced to save one person's face.

But the effect of the Moscow trials was to undermine confidence in the Soviet regime. For years Yagoda was "the flaming sword of the revolution." He put Zinoviev, Kamenev, and others on trial. Now he himself was in the dock as a traitor. Could he have staged the trials to harm the Revolution? Yagoda was succeeded by Yezhov, and Yezhov became "the flaming sword of the revolution." Then Yezhov disappeared in disgrace from the GPU. Whom could one trust?

During the many years he had tortured Russia as head of the GPU, Yagoda executed, exiled, and arrested millions of men, women, and children. The dead could not be resurrected. But were the cases of prisoners and exiles reviewed after it was allegedly discovered and proved that Yagoda had long been a traitor in league with Fascists? Hadn't he falsely accused and punished innocent people? A few dozen individuals were granted clemency after Yagoda's eclipse. But the vast bulk went on serving their sentences. How did the wives feel whose husbands had been sent away by Yagoda? How did the families feel whose members had been shot by him? They got no redress and no comfort.

Thousands of Soviet authors, journalists, party speakers, and provincial leaders had been purged as "enemies of the people." Then how could the ordinary Soviet citizen know that the man whose article he was reading in the morning's paper or whose speech he was listening to over the radio would not be annihilated tomorrow as an "enemy of the people." Should he believe what he was reading or hearing?

The purges and trials produced a serious crisis of faith in the Soviet Union which continues to this day. Since everybody is a potential spy and traitor then it is best to distrust everybody. This has been ruinous to economic activity and morale. Keep as far as possible from responsibility; do as little as won't hurt you. Be a hypocrite if need be. *Sauve qui peut.* These became the guiding rules of Russian life.

The Soviet masses and intellectuals took refuge in indifference and passivity. The Communist party became more and more of a rubber stamp. Citizens did not care what happened as long as they were left out of it personally. Stalin's pact with the Nazis in 1939? "Well, the hell with it. I'm all mixed up. It's not my business. I'm taking care of myself."

The trial of the "Trotzkyist criminals" who allegedly made a pact with the Nazis led ultimately to Stalin's pact with the Nazis. . . .

Walter G. Krivitsky

STALIN APPEASES HITLER

Editor's Note

THE Nazi-Soviet Pact of August 23, 1939, burst like a bombshell on the democratic world. Supporters of the Soviet cause, usually articulate, grew strangely silent. Inside the Communist parties of the world consternation temporarily raged. As with other periods of "crisis" for the Communist movement, such as the Moscow Trials, a good many members found it no longer possible to believe in the idealism of the Soviet Union and left. Those who remained quickly acclimated themselves to the new "line" and proceeded to repeat it. The pact, as history records, was the signal for World War II; Nazi Germany no longer faced a threat from the east. Indeed, it could now count, as the Polish experience indicated, on an ally. Hitler's army began to move; the war broke out with the invasion of Poland. Hitler pounced on that country from one side. Pincerlike, in a coordinated manner, Russia marched into the territory allotted to it, from the rear.

One of the persons who was demonstrably not surprised by the pact was former Soviet General Walter G. Krivitsky. He had correctly predicted the pact some months before, on April 29, 1939, in an article in the *Saturday Evening Post* that had caused a sensation. Krivitsky's revelations were based on his two decades of important Soviet service. Pointing up the probability of the coming pact, Krivitsky asserted, was a long record of covert and open Soviet policy toward Germany, both before and after the Nazi ascension to power. In the events leading up to the development and implementation of this policy, Krivitsky played an important espionage role. He indicated in his now famous article, one in a widely read series, the continual efforts of the Soviet state—under the leadership of Stalin—to achieve a close working relationship with Hitler's Germany. These views were greeted by Soviet supporters with abuse of the most extreme kind. Communist spokesmen put it up to the American public to decide on the basis of common sense, if no more, what to think of an account which looked forward confidently to a Nazi-Soviet Pact. Was not the Soviet Union the chief foe of the Nazis in the entire world? Many liberals found this argument persuasive, even irrefutable. Then came the pact! Public abuse of Krivitsky diminished noticeably.

Late in 1939, several months after the pact he correctly predicted, General Krivitsky's *In Stalin's Secret Service* appeared. His essay here, "Stalin Appeases Hitler," is chapter one of that book.

In 1948 additional confirmation of many of Krivitsky's allegations regarding Stalin's intentions toward Germany came from an unexpected source: the secret archives of the German Foreign Office, as reprinted by the U. S. State Department in its *Nazi-Soviet Relations, 1939-41*. These documents had been seized by the American and British armies in 1945. They are essential reading for those who maintain faith in the integrity of the Soviet cause. Containing the top *secret* records of the German diplomats covering the closed-door negotiations between Germany and Russia, they present one of the most revealing accounts in recent years of Soviet—and Nazi—amoralism. Beyond dispute they record that the initial overture in this new harmony came from the Russians. In the very first document, Weizsacker, for Germany, summarizes to his Nazi chiefs the following official statement made to him in Berlin by Merekalov, Soviet Ambassador in Germany: "Russian policy had always moved in a straight line. Ideological differences of opinion had hardly influenced the Russian-Italian [Mussolini's Italy] relationship, and they did not have to prove a stumbling block with regard to Germany either. Soviet Russia had not exploited the present friction between Germany and the Western democracies against us, nor did she desire to do so. There exists for Russia no reason why she should not live with us on a normal footing. And from normal, the relations might become better and better."

Moreover, the documents show that the Soviet Union painstakingly collaborated on the schedule for the joint invasion of Poland. For their aid territory was allotted to them into which they later marched. One proposed Soviet stratagem even shocked the Nazis. Listen to this "very urgent, strictly secret" telegram sent to Germany by Schulenburg, the Nazi Ambassador in the Soviet Union on September 10, 1939:

> *I explained emphatically to Molotov how crucial speedy action of the Red Army was at this juncture* [to move into Poland]. . . . *Then Molotov came to the political side of the matter and stated that the Soviet Government had intended to take the occasion of the further advance of German troops to declare that Poland was falling apart and that it was necessary for the Soviet Union, in consequence, to come to the aid of the Ukrainians and the White Russians "threatened" by Germany. This argument was to make the intervention of the Soviet Union plausible to the masses and at the same time to avoid giving the Soviet Union the appearance of an aggressor.*

In other words, the Soviet Union was to participate in the dismemberment of Poland, in cooperation with its Nazi allies, and then be allowed *by* the Nazis to announce for the benefit of world opinion that they were protecting the invaded nation *from* the Nazis!

These are only some of the details in this gold mine of documentary evidence regarding the nature of Soviet "idealism."

One additional quotation, of another kind, perhaps makes clear the entire tenor of Soviet conduct in this period. After operations began, Weizsacker reported this incident: "*At a quiet place in the woods, a thousand Jews were expelled across the Russian border; 15 kilometers away, they came back, with the Russian commander trying to force the German one to readmit the group. . . .*"

All this makes for especially interesting reading in connection with Krivitsky's "Stalin Appeases Hitler."

Walter Krivitsky (Samuel Ginsburg) was born in the Russian Ukraine on June 28, 1899. His political sympathies developed early and at the age of seventeen he was already an active member of the Ukrainian revolutionary army. His adoption of the name of Krivitsky, as with Lenin, Stalin and Trotsky's change of names, was to avoid arrest by the Tsar's police. In 1921 he was appointed a political commissar in the Red Army. Two years later he was sent abroad to Germany to organize secret Communist units. In 1924 he returned to Russia and received promotion to the position of commander of a brigade in recognition of his services. He was next attached to the Third Division of the General Staff. In 1928 he worked in France and Italy as undercover agent. He was twice jailed for his activities abroad, once for five months in Austria in 1934. He was sent abroad again in 1935, this time as Chief of Soviet Military Intelligence for Western Europe. He remained in this position until December, 1937, when he broke with the Soviet Union. He had served the military-intelligence department during all of his adult life. Experiencing increasing disillusion with the Soviet cause, despite his years of hope for a change in the character of the state, he finally broke when an attempt was made to involve him in an assassination move against one of his closest friends, Ignace Reiss, a former Soviet agent who had broken with Stalinism. Krivitsky sent a warning to Reiss but it was of no avail. Reiss was machine-gunned to death in Lausanne, Switzerland.

Krivitsky's break gained considerable attention; it ramified the effect produced by the earlier disclosure that Alexander Barmine, former Red Army General and Chargé d'Affaires at Athens, had refused to return to Russia and had abandoned the Soviet cause. In the U. S. Krivitsky turned over information to the State Department and the Federal Bureau of Investigation on foreign spies. Living in fear of Soviet reprisals, he told an aide for a congressional committee: *"If they ever try to prove that I took my own life, don't believe it."*

On February 11, 1941, the *New York Times* carried a startling front-page story which began: "Washington—Feb. 10.—General Walter G. Krivitsky, former Red Army Chief of Intelligence, was found dead on his bed in a fifth-floor room of the Hotel Bellevue near Union Station early today with a .38-calibre bullet in his right temple." Krivitsky, said the police, had committed "suicide."

A number of unexplained circumstances have persuaded many informed persons to withhold judgment on the "suicide" verdict. One of these persons is Louis Waldman, the late General's attorney, who made an independent investigation of the affair. His findings and views are to be found in the chapter, "Suicide Equals Murder," in his *Labor Lawyer* (1944).

#

Stalin Appeases Hitler *by Walter G. Krivitsky*

DURING the night of June 30, 1934, when Hitler's first blood purge broke out and while it was still going on, Stalin called an extraordinary session of the Politbureau in the Kremlin. Even before the news of the Hitler purge reached the wide world, Stalin had decided upon his next move in relation to the Nazi regime.

I was then at my post in the Intelligence Department of the

General Staff of the Red Army in Moscow. We knew that a crisis was impending in Germany. All our confidential dispatches had prepared us for an outbreak. As soon as Hitler launched his purge, we began to receive constant bulletins from Germany.

That night I was working feverishly with a staff of assistants, summarizing our information for War Commissar Voroshilov. Among the non-members summoned to that meeting of the Politbureau were my chief, General Berzin; Maxim Litvinov, Commissar for Foreign Affairs; Karl Radek, then director of the information bureau of the Central Committee of the Communist Party; and A. C. Artusov, chief of the Foreign Division of the Ogpu.

The emergency meeting of the Politbureau had been called to consider the probable consequences of the Hitler purge, and its effects upon Soviet foreign policy. Confidential information in our possession showed that two extreme wings of Hitler's opponents were involved. There was the group led by Captain Roehm, consisting of Nazi radicals dissatisfied with Hitler's moderate policies. They were dreaming of a "second revolution." The other group was composed of officers of the German army, under the leadership of Generals Schleicher and Bredow. This circle had looked forward to a restoration of the monarchy. It joined hands with the Roehm wing for the purpose of unseating Hitler, each side hoping to emerge triumphant in the end. Our special bulletins from Germany brought the news, however, that the garrisons in the metropolitan centers remained loyal to Hitler and that the main body of army officers was true to the government.

In Western Europe and America, Hitler's purge was widely interpreted as a weakening of the Nazi power. In Soviet circles, too, there were those who wished to believe it foreshadowed the collapse of Hitler's rule. Stalin had no such illusions. He summed up the discussion at the Politbureau as follows:

"The events in Germany do not at all indicate the collapse

of the Nazi regime. On the contrary, they are bound to lead
to the consolidation of that regime, and to the strengthening
of Hitler himself."

General Berzin came back from the Kremlin session with this
dictum of Stalin.

In my anxiety to learn the decision of the Politbureau I had
stayed up all night awaiting Berzin's return. We had a strict
rule that no one, not even the Commissar of War himself, could
take confidential state papers home with him, and I knew that
Berzin would have to come back to the department.

The course of Soviet policy toward Nazi Germany followed
from Stalin's dictum. The Politbureau decided at all costs to
induce Hitler to make a deal with the Soviet government. Stalin
had always believed in coming to terms early with a strong
enemy. The night of June thirtieth convinced him of Hitler's
strength. It was no new course for Stalin, however. It marked
no revolutionary departure in his policy toward Germany. He
only decided to redouble his past efforts to appease Hitler.
His whole policy toward the Nazi regime during the six years
of its existence had lain in that direction. He recognized in
Hitler a real dictator.

The idea prevailing up to the recent Russian-German pact
that Hitler and Stalin were mortal enemies, was pure myth. It
was a distorted picture, created by clever camouflage and the
vapors of propaganda. The true picture of their relations was
that of a persistent suitor who would not be discouraged by
rebuffs. Stalin was the suitor. There was enmity on Hitler's side.
On Stalin's there was fear.

If one can speak of a pro-German in the Kremlin, Stalin has
been that figure all along. He favored cooperation with Germany right after Lenin's death, and he did not alter this basic
attitude when Hitler rose to power. On the contrary, the triumph of the Nazis strengthened him in his quest for closer
bonds with Berlin. In this he was spurred on by the Japanese
menace in the Far East. He had a profound contempt for the
"weakling" democratic nations, and an equally profound re-

spect for the "mighty" totalitarian states. And he was guided throughout by the rule that one must come to terms with a superior power.

Stalin's whole international policy during the last six years has been a series of maneuvers designed to place him in a favorable position for a deal with Hitler. When he joined the League of Nations, when he proposed the system of collective security, when he sought the hand of France, flirted with Poland, courted Great Britain, intervened in Spain, he was calculating every move with an eye upon Berlin. His hope was to get into such a position that Hitler would find it advantageous to meet his advances.

A high point in this Stalin policy was reached late in 1936 upon the conclusion of a secret German-Japanese agreement, negotiated behind the smoke screen of the anti-Comintern pact. The terms of that secret agreement, which came into Stalin's possession in the main through my efforts and those of my staff, incited him to a desperate attempt to drive a bargain with Hitler. Early in 1937 such a deal was actually pending between them. Nobody knows to what extent the recent treaty of August, 1939, was anticipated at that time.

It was two years before Stalin began to disclose to the world his friendly attitude toward Germany. On March 10, 1939, he made his first pronouncement following Hitler's annexation of Austria and occupation of the Sudeten areas, giving his answer to these world-shaking Nazi conquests. The world was astounded by Stalin's friendly overtures to Hitler. It was dumbfounded when, three days later, Hitler marched into Czechoslovakia.

The record of Stalin's policy of appeasement toward Hitler —both the open and the secret record—reveal that the more aggressive Hitler's policies became, the more Stalin pressed his courtship. And the more strenuously Stalin wooed him, the bolder were Hitler's aggressions.

Long before the rise of Hitler, or even of Stalin, Soviet-German cooperation had been dictated by the pressure of events.

A Moscow-Berlin tie had been formed more than ten years before Hitler in the Rapallo pact of 1922. Both the Soviet Union and the German republic were then being treated as outcasts; both were in disfavor with the Allies; both opposed the Versailles system. They had traditional business bonds and mutual interests.

It is now common knowledge that during those ten years there was a secret arrangement between the *Reichswehr*—the German army—and the Red Army. Soviet Russia permitted the German republic to evade the Versailles prohibitions against training artillery and tank officers, and developing aviation and chemical warfare. These things were done on Soviet soil. The Red Army, on the other hand, got the benefit of expert German military knowledge. The two armies exchanged information. It is also common knowledge that trade between Soviet Russia and Germany flourished during that decade. The Germans invested capital and operated concessions in the Soviet Union. The Soviet government imported machinery and engineering personnel from Germany.

Such was the situation when Hitler's menacing figure arose. Some seven or eight months before his ascent to power, in the early summer of 1932, I met in Danzig one of the high officers of the German general staff, a confirmed monarchist who came from Berlin expressly to meet me. He was an old-school military man and believed in the restoration of the German Empire in cooperation with Russia.

I asked this officer for his opinion on Germany's policy in the event Hitler became the head of the government. We discussed Hitler's views as outlined in his book, *Mein Kampf*. The German officer gave me his analysis of coming developments, and concluded: "Let Hitler come and do his job. And then we, the army, will make short work of him."

I asked the officer if he would be good enough to submit his views in writing for me to forward to Moscow, and he agreed to do so. His report created a stir in Kremlin circles. The prevailing view there was that military and economic ties between

Germany and Russia were so deep-rooted that Hitler could not possibly disregard them. Moscow understood Hitler's fulminations against Bolshevism as a maneuver on the road to power. They had their function. But they could not change the basic interests of the two countries, which were bound to make for cooperation.

Stalin himself derived much comfort from the report of the German officer. Although fully alive to the Nazi doctrine of "pressure toward the east," he was habituated to the tradition of collaboration between the Red Army and the Reichswehr, and had a wholesome respect for the German army and its leadership under General Von Seckt. The report of the German staff officer dove-tailed with his own views. Stalin looked upon the Nazi movement primarily as a reaction to the Versailles peace. It seemed to him that all Germany would do under Hitler was to throw off the shackles of Versailles. The Soviet government had been the first to hammer at them. Indeed, Moscow and Berlin had originally been drawn together by their common opposition to the rapacity of the allied victors.

For these reasons, Stalin made no effort after the rise of Hitler to break the secret Berlin-Moscow tie. On the contrary he tried his best to keep it in force. It was Hitler who, during his first three years, gradually dissolved the intimate link between the Red and the German armies. But this did not deter Stalin. He only became more assiduous in the pursuit of Hitler's friendship.

On December 28, 1933, eleven months after Hitler became chancellor, Premier Molotov, speaking before the Congress of Soviets, asserted Stalin's adherence to the former German policy:

"Our relations with Germany have always occupied a distinct place in our international relations . . . The Soviet Union has no cause on its part for any change of policy toward Germany."

The following day, before the same Congress, Foreign Commissar Litvinov went even further than Molotov in pleading for an understanding with Hitler. Litvinov described the program outlined in *Mein Kampf* for the reconquest of all German territories. He spoke of the Nazi determination, "by fire and sword, to pave the way for expansion in the east, without stopping at the borders of the Soviet Union, and to enslave the peoples of this Union." And he went on to say:

> We have been connected with Germany by close economic and political relations for ten years. We were the only great country which would have nothing to do with the Versailles Treaty and its consequences. We renounced the rights and advantages which this treaty reserved for us. Germany assumed first place in our foreign trade. Both Germany and ourselves have derived extraordinary advantages from the political and economic relation established between us. (President Kalinin, of the Executive Committee: "Especially Germany!") On the basis of these relations, Germany was able to speak more boldly and confidently to her victors of yesterday.

This hint, emphasized by President Kalinin's exclamation, was designed to remind Hitler of Soviet Russia's help in enabling him to challenge Versailles victors. Litvinov then made the following formal declaration:

> With Germany, as with other states, we want to have the best relations. The Soviet Union and Germany will gain nothing but benefit from such relations. We, on our side, have no desire for expansion, either in the west or the east or in any other direction. We would like to hear Germany say the same thing to us.

Hitler did not say it. But that did not deter Stalin. It encouraged him to a more strenuous courtship of the Nazi regime.

On January 26, 1934, Stalin himself, addressing the Seventeenth Communist Party Congress continued the drive for an appeasement of Hitler. Hitler had then been in power exactly one year. He had rebuffed all of Moscow's political advances, although he had entered into a trade deal on favorable credit terms with Soviet Russia. Stalin interpreted this as a sign of political good will. He referred to those Nazi elements which favored a return to "the policy of the ex-Kaiser of Germany, who at one time occupied the Ukraine, undertook a march against Leningrad, and transformed the Baltic countries into an encampment for this march." There had been a change, he said, in German policy, which he attributed not to the theories of National Socialism, but to a desire to avenge Versailles. He denied that Soviet Russia had changed its policy toward Berlin because of "the establishment of a Fascist regime in Germany," and stretched out his hand to Hitler with these words:

> Of course we are far from enthusiastic about the Fascist regime in Germany. But Fascism is not the issue here, if only for the reason that Fascism, in Italy for example, did not prevent the Soviet Union from establishing good relations with that country.

Stalin's outstretched hand was ignored in Berlin. Hitler had other ideas on the subject. But Stalin would not be discouraged. He only decided upon a change of method. Viewing the Nazi agitation for an anti-Soviet bloc as a maneuver on the part of Hitler, he resolved to respond to it with a counter-maneuver. Henceforth, the Soviet government would appear as an upholder of the Versailles system, would join the League of Nations, would even associate with the anti-German bloc. The threat involved in such a course, Stalin thought, would bring Hitler to his senses.

Stalin picked a brilliant journalist to pave the way for this somersault. It must be remembered that an entire Soviet generation had been brought up in the belief that the Versailles Treaty was the most pernicious instrument ever drawn up, and that its authors were a band of pirates. It was no simple task to dress up the Soviet government in the costume of a defender of Versailles. There was only one man in the Soviet Union who could do this publicity stunt adequately both for domestic and foreign consumption. That was Karl Radek, the man who subsequently played such a tragic role in the great trial of January, 1937. Stalin picked Radek to prepare Russian and world opinion for his change of tactics.

I saw a great deal of Radek in those days—the early spring of 1934—at the headquarters of the Central Committee of the Communist Party. The Inner Circle in Moscow was then buzzing with talk about Radek's assignment to prepare a series of articles forming a build-up toward the coming turnabout in Kremlin policy.

The articles were to appear in both *Pravda* and *Izvestia*, the leading Communist and Soviet organs. They would be reprinted throughout the world and carefully studied in all European chancelleries. Radek's task was to whitewash the Versailles peace, to herald a new era of friendship with Paris, to persuade Soviet sympathizers abroad that such a stand was harmonious with communism, and at the same time to leave the door open for an agreement with Germany.

I knew, because of my frequent calls at Radek's office, that he was in daily consultation with Stalin. Sometimes he would dash over to Stalin's office several times a day. Every phrase he wrote was subject to Stalin's personal supervision. The articles were in every sense a joint labor of Radek and Stalin.

While these articles were in preparation, Commissar Litvinov was keeping on with efforts toward an agreement with Hitler. In April, he proposed to Germany a joint undertaking to preserve and guarantee the independence and inviolability of the Baltic states. Berlin rejected the proposal.

The Radek article was hailed widely as foreshadowing a Soviet turn toward France and the Little Entente, and away from Germany. "German Fascism and Japanese imperialism,"

wrote Radek, "are in a struggle for a redivision of the world—
a struggle directed against the Soviet Union, against France,
Poland, Czechoslovakia, Rumania and the Baltic states; against
China and the United States of America. And British imperial-
ism would like to direct this struggle exclusively against the
Soviet Union."

At this time I had quite a conversation with Radek. He knew
that I was familiar with his assignment. I made some remark
about our "new policy" and spoke of the impression it was creating in uninformed circles.

Radek let loose a flood of talk: "Only fools can imagine we
would ever break with Germany. What I am writing here is one
thing—the realities are something else. No one can give us what
Germany has given us. For us to break with Germany is simply
impossible."

Radek continued to discourse along lines only too familiar
to me. He spoke of our relations with the German army, which
was very much in the saddle even under Hitler, of our relations
with big business in Germany—and was not Hitler under the
thumb of the industrialists? Surely Hitler would not go against
the general staff, which favored cooperation with Russia.
Surely Hitler would not cross swords with German business
circles, who were doing a large trade with us. These two forces
were the pillars of German-Soviet relations.

He denounced as idiots those who thought that Soviet Russia
should turn against Germany because of the Nazi persecution
of Communists and Socialists. True, the Communist Party of
Germany was smashed. Its leader, Thaelmann, was in prison.
Thousands of its members were in concentration camps. But
that was one thing. It was something else when one considered
the vital interests of Soviet Russia. Those interests demanded
a continuation of the policy of collaboration with the German
Reich.

As for the articles he was writing, what did they have to do
with the facts? It was all a matter of big politics. It was a nec-

essary maneuver. Stalin had no idea of breaking with Germany. On the contrary, he was seeking to draw Berlin closer to Moscow.

All of this was elementary to those of us who were on the inside of the Kremlin policy. None of us dreamed, in the spring of 1934, that a rupture with Germany was possible. We all regarded the Radek articles as Stalinist strategy.

Litvinov went off on a tour of the European capitals, ostensibly in the interests of the so-called Eastern Locarno pact which was to insure, by mutual agreement of all the governments concerned, the existing boundaries of the nations in Eastern Europe. He visited Geneva. His visit filled the world with rumors of a coming Franco-Russian *rapprochement,* crowning the work begun by Radek's articles. At the same time, Stalin continued doggedly to assert at the Politbureau: "And nevertheless, we must get together with the Germans."

On June 13, 1934, Litvinov stopped in Berlin to confer with Baron Konstantin von Neurath, then Hitler's Foreign Minister. Litvinov invited Germany to join in his proposed Eastern European pact. Von Neurath firmly declined the invitation, and bluntly pointed out that such an arrangement would perpetuate the Versailles system. When Litvinov intimated that Moscow might strengthen its treaties with other nations by military alliances, Von Neurath replied that Germany was willing to risk such an encirclement.

The following day, on June fourteenth, Hitler met Mussolini in Venice for luncheon.

Stalin was not discouraged by this latest rebuff from Berlin. Through the Soviet trade envoys, he had all along endeavored to persuade the leading German circles of his sincerity in seeking an understanding with Hitler, allowing them to intimate that Moscow would go a long way in making concessions to Germany.

At the same time, Stalin tried to induce Poland to define her policy to the disadvantage of Germany. Nobody knew at that time which way Poland was going, and a special session of the

Politbureau was called to consider this problem. Litvinov and Radek, as well as the representative of the Commissariat of War, took the view that Poland could be influenced to join hands with Soviet Russia. The only one who disagreed with this view was Artusov, the chief of the Foreign Division of the Ogpu. He considered the prospects of a Polish-Soviet accord illusory. Artusov, a bit rash in thus opposing the majority of the Politbureau, was cut short by Stalin himself: "You are misinforming the Politbureau."

This remark of Stalin traveled fast in the inner circle. The "dare devil" Artusov was regarded as already a finished man. Subsequent events proved Artusov right. Poland joined the German fold, and that may have saved Artusov for a while. He was a Swiss who had taken up residence in Czarist Russia as a French teacher. He had joined the revolutionary movement before the World War and the Bolshevik Party in 1917. Of small stature, gray-haired, wearing a goatee, a lover of music, Artusov had married a Russian woman and raised a family in Moscow. In 1937 he was arrested and executed in the great purge.

The fiasco with Poland increased Stalin's conviction of the need of appeasing Hitler. He used every avenue to convey to Berlin his readiness for an amicable arrangement. Hitler's blood purge of June thirtieth immensely raised him in Stalin's estimation. Hitler had demonstrated for the first time to the men in the Kremlin that he knew how to wield power, that he was a dictator, not only in name but in deed. If Stalin had doubts before as to Hitler's ability to rule with an iron hand, to crush opposition, to assert his authority even over potent political and military forces, those doubts were now dispelled. From now on, Stalin recognized in Hitler a master, a man able to back up his challenge to the world. This, more than anything else, was responsible for Stalin's decision on the night of June thirtieth to secure at whatever cost an understanding with the Nazi regime.

Two weeks later, on July fifteenth, Radek, writing in the official Soviet organ *Izvestia,* attempted to raise before Berlin the bugaboo of Moscow's alignment with the Versailles powers. He ended, however, with this contrary note:

"There is no reason why Fascist Germany and Soviet Russia should not get on together, inasmuch as the Soviet Union and Fascist Italy are good friends."

Hitler's warning, conveyed through Von Neurath, that Germany was willing to risk encirclement was what sent Stalin off on a move for counter-encirclement. At this time, the close relations between the Red Army and the German army were still in existence. The trade relations between the two countries were very much alive. Stalin therefore looked upon Hitler's political course toward Moscow as a maneuver for a favorable diplomatic position. Not to be outflanked, he decided to respond to it by a wide maneuver of his own.

Litvinov was sent back to Geneva. There in late November, 1934, he negotiated with Pierre Laval a preliminary joint agreement envisaging a mutual-assistance pact between France and Russia, purposively left open for other powers to join. This protocol was signed in Geneva on December fifth.

Four days later, Litvinov issued the following statement: "The Soviet Union never ceases especially to desire the best all-around relations with Germany. Such, I am confident, is also the attitude of France towards Germany. The Eastern European pact would make possible the creation and further development of such relations between these three countries, as well as between the other signatories to the pact."

To this maneuver Hitler did at last respond. Large credits were opened to the Soviet government. Stalin was tremendously encouraged. The financial interests of Germany were, in his judgment, forcing Hitler's hand.

In the spring of 1935, while Anthony Eden, Pierre Laval and Eduard Beneš were visiting Moscow, Stalin scored what he considered his greatest triumph. The Reichbank granted a long-term loan of 200,000,000 gold marks to the Soviet government.

On the evening of August 2, 1935, I was with Artusov and

the other members of his staff at the Lubianka offices of the Foreign Division of the Ogpu. It was on the eve of Levanevsky's take-off on his famous first flight across the North Pole from Moscow to San Francisco. We were all waiting for a car to take us to see Levanevsky and his two companions start for America. While we were waiting and looking up papers in the safes, the subject of our relations with the Nazi regime came up. Artusov produced a highly confidential report just received from one of our leading agents in Berlin. It was prepared in answer to the question worrying Stalin: What and how strong are the forces in Germany favoring an accord with the Soviet Union?

After an exceptionally interesting review of the internal economic and political conditions in Germany, of the elements of possible discontent, of Berlin's relations with France and other powers, and of the dominant influences surrounding Hitler, our correspondent arrived at this conclusion:

"All of the Soviet attempts to appease and conciliate Hitler are doomed. The main obstacle to an understanding with Moscow is Hitler himself."

The report made a profound impression upon all of us. Its logic and facts seemed unanswerable. We wondered how the "big boss" took it. Artusov remarked that Stalin's optimism concerning Germany remained unshaken.

"Do you know what the boss said at the last meeting of the Politbureau?" Artusov observed with a wave of the hand. And he quoted Stalin:

"Well, now, how can Hitler make war on us when he has granted us such loans? It's impossible. The business circles in Germany are too powerful, and they are in the saddle."

In September, 1935, I left for Western Europe to take up my new post as Chief of the Military Intelligence there. Within a month I flew back to Moscow. My hurried return trip was caused by an extraordinary development.

I discovered, in taking over our Intelligence network, that one of our agents in Germany had come upon the trail of secret negotiations between the Japanese military attaché in Berlin,

Lieutenant General Hiroshi Oshima, and Baron Joachim von Ribbentrop, then Hitler's unofficial minister for special foreign relations.

I decided that these negotiations were a matter of such paramount concern to the Soviet government that they required exceptional attention on my part. To watch their progress would be no routine affair. I needed for the task the boldest and best men at our disposal. For this purpose I returned to Moscow to consult headquarters. I came back to Holland armed with all the necessary authority and means to pursue to the bitter end the quest for information on the Oshima-Ribbentrop conversations.

These conversations were carried on outside ordinary diplomatic channels. The Japanese ambassador in Berlin and the German Foreign Office were not involved. Von Ribbentrop, Hitler's envoy extraordinary, was handling the matter privately with the Japanese general. By the end of 1935, the information in my possession showed beyond a shadow of doubt that the negotiations were progressing toward a definite objective. We knew, of course, that that objective was to checkmate the Soviet Union.

We also knew that the Japanese army had for years been anxious to secure the plans and models of Germany's special anti-aircraft guns. The Tokyo militarists had shown themselves willing to go to any lengths to obtain from Berlin all the latest technical patents in weapons of warfare. This was the starting point for the German-Japanese negotiations.

Stalin kept in close touch with developments. Apparently Moscow decided to try to spike the negotiations by publicity. Early in January, 1936, reports began to appear in the Western European press that some kind of secret agreement had been concluded between Germany and Japan. On January tenth, Soviet Premier Molotov referred publicly to these reports. Two days later, Berlin and Tokyo denied that there was any substance in the rumors.

The only effect of the publicity was to increase the secrecy of

the negotiations and to force the German and Japanese governments to devise some mask for their real treaty.

Throughout 1936, all the world capitals were astir with
public and private reports of the German-Japanese deal. Diplomatic circles everywhere buzzed with exciting speculation.
Moscow pressed hard for documentary proof of the agreement.
My men in Germany were risking their lives, in the face of almost insuperable difficulties. They knew that no expense was
too high, no hazard too great.

It was known to us that the Nazi secret service was inter-
cepting, and had in its possession, copies of the coded messages
exchanged during the negotiations between General Oshima
and Tokyo. Late in July, 1936, I received word that the complete file of this confidential correspondence had at last been
secured in photostatic form by our men in Berlin. The channel
thus opened would provide us with all future messages from
Oshima to his government and back.

The strain of the following days, when I knew that this
priceless material was in our hands, but had to await its safe
arrival from Germany, was nearly unbearable. No chances
could be taken and I had to wait patiently.

On August eighth, word came through that the carrier of
the correspondence had crossed the German frontier and was
due in Amsterdam. I was in Rotterdam when the message arrived. I got into my automobile, accompanied by an aide, and
made a dash for Amsterdam. On the way we met our agent,
who was speeding to deliver the material to me. We stopped on
the highway.

"Here it is. We've got it," he said, and handed me some rolls
of film—the form in which we usually put all our mail.

I went straight to Haarlem, where we had a secret photo-
graphic developing room. The Oshima correspondence was in
code, but we had in our possession the Japanese code book. I
also had, awaiting us in Haarlem, a first-class Japanese-lan-
guage expert, whom we had scoured Moscow to find. I could
not keep Moscow waiting for the arrival of the documents by

courier, and I could not send coded messages from Holland. I had one of our men get ready to fly to Paris at a moment's notice, to send off a long message to Moscow.

I saw, as it was being decoded, that I had before me the entire sheaf of Oshima's correspondence with Tokyo, reporting step by step all his negotiations with Von Ribbentrop, and also the suggestions conveyed to him by his government. General Oshima reported that his negotiations were being conducted under the personal supervision of Hitler, who frequently conferred with Von Ribbentrop and gave him instructions. His correspondence revealed that the purpose of the negotiations was the conclusion of a secret pact to coordinate all the moves made by Berlin and Tokyo in Western Europe as well as in the Pacific. No reference to the Communist International, and no suggestion of any move against communism, was contained in this correspondence covering more than a year of negotiations.

Under the terms of the secret agreement, Japan and Germany undertook to regulate between themselves all matters relating to the Soviet Union and to China, and to take no action either in Europe or in the Pacific without consulting each other. Berlin also agreed to place its improvements in weapons of war at the disposal of Tokyo and to exchange military missions with Japan.

At five o'clock one afternoon, my courier took off for Paris with my coded message. I returned home and took a rest for several days. From then on, all correspondence between General Oshima and Tokyo flowed regularly through our hands. It revealed finally that a secret pact had been drawn up and initialed by General Oshima and Von Ribbentrop. The pact was so worded as to extend the field of cooperation between Japan and Germany to include interests beyond China and Soviet Russia.

There was but one problem to settle: How to camouflage the secret agreement; Hitler decided to draft the anti-Comintern pact as a device for misleading world opinion.

On November twenty-fifth, in the presence of all the envoys

of the foreign powers in Berlin, with the exception of the Soviet Union, the anti-Comintern pact was signed by the official representatives of the governments of Germany and Japan. The pact is a public document consisting of a couple of brief clauses. Behind it lies concealed a secret agreement, the existence of which has never been acknowledged.

Stalin was, of course, in possession of all the proofs of this which I had uncovered. He decided to show Hitler that the Soviet government knew all about it. Foreign Commissar Litvinov was assigned to spring the surprise upon Berlin. On November twenty-eighth addressing an extraordinary session of the Congress of Soviets, Litvinov said:

> Well-informed people refuse to believe that in order to draw up the two meager articles which have been published of the German-Japanese agreement, it was necessary to conduct negotiations for fifteen months; that these negotiations should have been entrusted to a Japanese general and a German super-diplomat, and that they should have been conducted in extraordinary secrecy and kept secret even from German and Japanese official diplomacy. . . .
>
> As for the German-Japanese agreement which has been published, I would recommend to you not to seek for any meaning in it, since it really has no meaning. It is only a cover for another agreement which was simultaneously discussed and initiated, probably also signed, and which was not published and is not intended for publication.
>
> I assert, realizing the full weight of my words, that it was to the working out of this secret document, in which the word communism is not even mentioned, that fifteen months of negotiations between the Japanese military attaché and the German super-diplomat were devoted. . . .
>
> This agreement with Japan will tend to extend any

war which breaks out on one continent to at least two, if not more than two, continents.

Needless to say, there was consternation in Berlin.

As for my own share in this affair, Moscow hailed it as a triumph. I was recommended for the Order of Lenin. The recommendation was approved all along the line, but got lost sight of at the time of the Red Army purge. I never received it.

An American sequel to the German-Japanese secret pact came to my attention when I was already in the United States. In January, 1939, Hitler appointed his personal aide, Capt. Fritz Wiedemann, consul general at San Francisco. Fritz Wiedemann had been Private Hitler's commanding officer in the World War and is one of the Fuehrer's most intimate and trusted collaborators. The appointment of such a figure to a seemingly minor post on the Pacific suggests the significance of the German-Japanese secret agreement. Hitler included in his plans even the possibility of joint maneuvers with Japan in the Pacific.

Lieutenant General Oshima was elevated from military attaché to Japanese ambassador to Germany in October, 1938, and presented his credentials to Hitler on November twenty-second, last.

Now, what was the effect of the Berlin-Tokyo pact upon the Kremlin's foreign policy? How did Stalin react to Hitler's enveloping operation against the Soviet Union?

Stalin continued his two simultaneous courses of action. The series of maneuvers he executed on the surface is a matter of open record. He strengthened his association with France by a special treaty and pressed for an alliance. He entered into a mutual-assistance pact with Czechoslovakia. He launched the united-front campaign throughout the anti-Fascist world. He had Litvinov inaugurate the crusade for collective security, designed to align all the great and small powers in the defense of the Soviet Union from German-Japanese aggression. He intervened in Spain in order to forge a closer link with Paris and London.

But all these surface moves were designed only to impress Hitler, and bring success to his undercover maneuvers which had but one aim: a close accord with Germany. No sooner was the German-Japanese pact signed than Stalin directed the Soviet trade envoy in Berlin, his personal emissary, David Kandelaki, to go outside the ordinary diplomatic channels and at whatever cost arrive at a deal with Hitler. At a meeting of the Politbureau held at this time, Stalin definitely informed his lieutenants: "In the very near future we shall consummate an agreement with Germany."

In December, 1936, I received orders to throttle down our work in Germany. The first months of 1937 were passed in expectancy of a favorable outcome of Kandelaki's secret negotiations. I was in Moscow when he arrived from Berlin, in April, accompanied by the Ogpu representative in Germany. Kandelaki brought with him the draft of an agreement with the Nazi government. He was received in private audiences by Stalin, who believed that he had at last achieved the goal of all his maneuvers.

At this time I had occasion for a long conference with Yezhov, then head of the Ogpu. Yezhov had just reported to Stalin on certain operations of mine. Yezhov had been a metal worker in his youth, raised in the Stalin school. This dreaded marshal of the great purge had a simple mind. Any question of policy he took up with Stalin at once, and whatever the big boss said, he repeated word for word, and then translated into action.

Yezhov and I discussed various reports in our possession as to discontent in Germany, and possible opposition to Hitler from the old monarchist groups. Yezhov had discussed the same subject that very day in his conference with Stalin. His words were practically a phonographic record of the boss himself:

"What's all this drivel about discontent with Hitler in the German army?" he exclaimed. "What does it take to content an army? Ample rations? Hitler furnishes them. Good arms and equipment? Hitler supplies them. Prestige and honor? Hitler provides it. A sense of power and victory? Hitler gives that, too. The talk about army unrest in Germany is all nonsense.

"As for the capitalists, what do they need a Kaiser for? They wanted to put the workers back in the factories. Hitler has done it for them. They wanted to get rid of the Communists. Hitler has them in jails and concentration camps. They were fed up with labor unions and strikes. Hitler has put labor under state control and outlawed strikes. Why should the industrialists be discontented?"

Yezhov continued in the same vein: Germany is strong. She is now the strongest power in the world. Hitler has made her so. Who can doubt it? How can anyone in his senses fail to reckon with it? For Soviet Russia there is but one course. And here he quoted Stalin: "We must come to terms with a superior power like Nazi Germany."

Hitler, however, again rebuffed Stalin's advances. By the end of 1937, with the collapse of the Stalin plans in Spain and the Japanese successes in China, the international isolation of the Soviet Union became extreme. Stalin then took, on the surface, a position of neutrality between the two major groups of powers. On November 27, 1937, speaking in Leningrad, Foreign Commissar Litvinov poked fun at the democratic nations for their handling of the Fascist nations. But Stalin's underlying purpose remained the same.

In March, 1938, Stalin staged his ten-day super-trial of the Rykov-Bukharin-Krestinsky group of Bolsheviks, who had been Lenin's closest associates and who were among the fathers of the Soviet Revolution. These Bolshevik leaders—hateful to Hitler—were shot by Stalin on March third. On March twelfth, with no protest from Russia, Hitler annexed Austria. Moscow's only reply was a proposal to call a parley of the democratic nations. Again, when Hitler annexed the Sudeten areas in September, 1938 Litvinov proposed concerted aid to Prague, but made it conditional upon action by the League of Nations. Stalin himself remained silent during the whole eventful year of 1938. But signs have not been wanting since Munich of his continued wooing of Hitler.

On January 12, 1939, there took place before the entire diplomatic corps in Berlin the cordial and demonstrative chat of Hitler with the new Soviet ambassador. A week later an item appeared in the London *News Chronicle* reporting a coming *rapprochement* between Nazi Germany and Soviet Russia. And this item was immediately and prominently reprinted, without comment and without refutation, in Stalin's mouthpiece, the Moscow *Pravda*.

On January twenty-fifth, W. N. Ewer, foreign editor of the London *Daily Herald*, leading British Labor paper, reported that the Nazi government was "now almost convinced that in the event of a European war the Soviet Union would adopt a policy of neutrality and non-intervention" and that a German trade delegation whose "objects are political rather than commercial" was on the way to Moscow.

Early in February it was disclosed that Moscow had made a deal to sell its oil only to Italy and Germany and nations friendly to the Rome-Berlin axis. For the first time in its history the Soviet government had stopped the sale of oil to private foreign corporations. This new policy would provide supplies vital to Italy and Germany in case of war with Great Britain and France.

Then, on Friday, March 10, 1939, Stalin at last spoke up. It was his first word since the annexation of Austria and the Sudeten lands by Germany, and he displayed such remarkable good humor toward Hitler that it came as a shock to world opinion. He excoriated the democracies for plotting to "poison the atmosphere and provoke a conflict" between Germany and Soviet Russia, for which, he said, there were "no visible grounds."

Three days after Stalin's speech, Hitler dismembered

Czechoslovakia. Two days later, he extinguished Czechoslovakia altogether. Of course, this was the result of Chamberlain's policy of appeasement. The world did not then realize that it was also the result of Stalin's policy of appeasement. Secretly Stalin had been playing the Rome-Berlin axis against the London-Paris axis all along. He does not believe in the strength of the democratic states.

To Stalin it was clear that Hitler had undertaken to solve the entire problem of Central and Southeastern Europe, to bring the peoples and resources in those areas under his political and economic domination, and to extend there his military base for future operations.

Stalin has seen Hitler in recent years reach out and get a foothold for a leap in almost every direction. He has dropped an anchor in the Pacific, and put his hand in South America. He is coming within striking distance of the British Empire in the Near East. And he has, with the aid of Mussolini, driven a stake in colonial Africa.

Stalin wants to avoid war at any cost. He fears war most. If Hitler will assure him peace, even at the price of important economic concessions, he will give Hitler a free hand in all these directions.

Granville Hicks

COMMUNISM AND THE AMERICAN INTELLECTUALS

Editor's Note

THE literature contributed to contemporary political knowledge by ex-Communists is considerable. That it is instructive and permissive of a more incisive understanding of the Soviet state hardly seems questionable at this late date. But to the close student the accounts of the ex-Communists treat one sector scantily—broadly speaking: *themselves*, the psychological histories of the disaffected. This in no way detracts from the value of that about which they can and have spoken authoritatively. Above all, many of them have emerged from their experiences as more enlightened crusaders for human decency, and they perform for us the invaluable service of taking us behind the thought barricades. Let it be clear that these writers have not willingly ignored or derogated the quite separate task of turning their analytic powers introspectively. What were the lures they first felt? What services did they think they were performing? How did they rationalize their ideals with the actualities of the cause they supported? These are some of the questions that have been answered only generally. One reason may have been the fear that self-probing might be misunderstood as immodesty, also that indefinite knowledge of their own psychological conflict might be confused—by some, intentionally—with their definite knowledge of certain physical realities. "Stick to the facts" is doubtless excellent advice, and it has especially been

385

applied, and rightly, by many of those who wrote about what they knew of the USSR. But pushed too far, it may have deprived us of much in rich subjective reactions.

Our gratitude then for accounts which attempt this not unpainful task of self-investigation ought to be manifest. And when the narrative concerns itself with the inner political life of a sensitive former *American* Communist—a much untilled area—it grows still greater in value. Such an account is Granville Hicks's selection. As the author reminds us, he has seen the Communist movement from the useful vantage point of one observing it as he approached, as a member, and as one leaving it. His study of this subject, as of others, has not yet ceased. Such an investigation of one's own impulses and motivations calls for a deft, honest, and perhaps rebellious nature, a nonconformity that is not solely a matter of politics but of temperament as well. One must not be halted in such a task by anticipations of adverse reactions from a less-involved reader who perhaps awaits a document essentially concerned with contrition. As an ex-Communist it would be as difficult to pigeonhole Mr. Hicks now as it would have been in earlier periods of his life. In many areas he has found it worthy to adhere to older notions: his attitude, if we read it correctly, is that one doesn't helpfully throw out the baby in the celebrated and necessary duty of bath-emptying. Mr. Hicks joined the Communist Party in the desire for an increasingly better society; he learned that in this he was certainly on the wrong track. But he does not forget his goal. His writings are not breast-beatings but a continued search for a more correct path.

Granville Hicks was born in New Hampshire on September 9, 1901. When he was seven his family moved to a "bleak, treeless suburb of Boston." His boyhood, he has said, was an unhappy one. At age 11: "Not only had I picked up the rudiments of intellectual snobbishness; in moral matters I was a dogmatic and inflexible little boy." High school was somewhat better but in a negative sense. "If a scholar was still less highly regarded than a football player, he was not positively scorned." He decided to go to Harvard. A cousin of his, who had worked his way through, reliably told him that Harvard was the place for a poor boy. Hicks did well scholastically and managed to support himself by scholarships. For social life and self-expression he turned to the youth group of the Universalist church. His faith at the time consisted of what he refers to as a little trinity: the scientific mind, the social mind, and the open mind. When he was graduated, he remained without a clear occupational goal. He had an offer from a small college to teach English but the "evangelical mind won." He enrolled at Harvard's Theological School. Here, for two years, he studied the history of religions, church history, and other related subjects. He left with great respect for the scholarship and character of his teachers. He also knew that he did not want to be a minister— he no longer felt that the church was an effective instrument for what he believed in. He became an instructor at Smith College, where he spent three happy and fruitful years. His essay here concerns the next years. Those interested in pursuing further details of Mr. Hicks's political development are referred to his *Small Town*, especially to Chapters 2 and 10, "The Natural History of an Intellectual," and "The Larger Society." Mr. Hicks has also taught at Rensselaer Polytechnical Institute and at Harvard University. For five years he was a member of the editorial staff of the *New Masses*. He is the author of *The Great Tradition; John Reed; I Like America; Figures of Transition; The First to Awaken;* and two novels.

This selection is extracted from a long essay in *Whose Revolution?* (1941), edited by Irving DeWitt Talmadge. Two omitted sections deal with the subjects, "The Strength of Communism," and "Who Were the Communists?"

Communism and the American Intellectuals
by Granville Hicks

THE past ten years of my life divide into four years as a fellow-traveler of the Communist party, four years as a member, and two years as an ex-member. I have seen how the party looks when one is moving towards it, when one is in it, and when one is going away from it. I have tried during the past two years to look back without bitterness and learn what I could. And what I have learned may not be without significance, since the story of Communism in the 'thirties is an integral part of the intellectual history of America . . .

The United Front

The high enthusiasm of the election campaign of 1932 rapidly declined. The first acts of the Roosevelt administration, though criticized by the Left as inadequate, reduced the sense of pressure, of the immediacy of collapse. The depression was not over, but the crisis was.

The persons who foreswore their allegiance to Communism in 1933 and 1934, however, did not as a rule embrace the New Deal: either they abandoned politics altogether or they turned to some other Marxist faction. It was as if, with the diminution of pressure, they could permit critical faculties to function again, and petty quibbling and mere vanity were involved as well as what we must now recognize as sound judgment. Some intellectuals, on the other hand, following an equally complicated and obscure emotional pattern, remained loyal, and these drew closer to the party.

If tension decreased in America after Roosevelt's inauguration, the triumph of fascism in Germany kept us from any sense of security. Fascism, according to the thirteenth plenum of the Executive Committee of the Communist International, was "the open terrorist dictatorship of the most reactionary, most chauvinistic, and most imperialistic elements of finance capitalism." We fellow-travelers accepted that definition, for we knew that Hitler could not have come to power without the direct support of German monopolists and the encouragement of British and American financiers. And I think that in 1933 we were largely right, though we failed to understand the laws of fascist development.

Fascism so violently dramatized everything we hated, it so completely expressed the barbarism that we had found implicit in a decadent capitalism, it was so horrifying and immediate a menace, that most of us felt a renewed loyalty to the revolutionary cause. That capitalism could evolve into fascism was the final demonstration that it must be abolished. And we thought it no accident that Hitler had struck first against the Communists, for they had been his most militant enemies. Indeed, we fellow-travelers believed the Communists when they claimed to be the only effective fighters against the fascist threat.

But increasingly it seemed to us that, as the character of the struggle had changed, new methods must be found for the new phase. There was more and more talk about an alliance of all anti-fascist forces, but nothing happened because of a debate, which appeared to us almost medieval in its subtlety, about the "belowness" or the "aboveness" of the united front. The Communists, in fact, took the occasion of the destruction of both parties in Germany to renew their attack on socialism as the chief enemy of the working class. I believed—most of the time at least—that the socialists were objectively social-fascists, but I never doubted that they were anti-fascist in intention, and I was sure that the name-calling did no good and much harm.

On February 16, 1934, the Socialist party held a meeting in Madison Square Garden to protest the Dollfuss *putsch* in Austria. Communists marched in a body to the meeting, booed

LaGuardia and Woll, who were on the platform, and created such a disturbance that the meeting ended in violence. By accident I heard the riot over the radio and was heartsick at the discrediting of the whole revolutionary cause. But what was I to do? By this time I was an editor of the *New Masses* and close enough to the party to speak out in party circles, but it was obviously a question whether pressure from outside would not be more effective than pressure from inside—which seemed to get nowhere, though many members privately agreed with me. The dilemma was sharpened because an open letter of protest was sent to the party, and two or three persons who stood in about the same relationship to the party as I did signed it. At least half of the signers, however, were, or were on their way to becoming, Trotskyites, though they represented themselves as injured well-wishers, and several of the others had repeatedly shown themselves indifferent or hostile. I thought and still think that, however honest certain of the signers were, the letter itself was a device to discredit the party. Public criticism, then, could only aid those whose faults seemed to me much worse than the party's, and I had to content myself with private protest. It was not the first or the last time that I had this choice to make.

I have given a false impression if I have not suggested that I myself was intensely sectarian in this period, not so sectarian, of course, as the official party line, but dogmatically convinced that salvation lay solely with the Communist party. I think it unlikely, however, that I should have joined the party if it had not changed: I might have remained a fellow-traveler or I might not, but I should not have become a member. The change did not come quite so suddenly as is usually supposed. Long before the seventh congress of the Communist International in August, 1935, Communists in this country were feeling their way toward new attitudes. John Dos Passos, defending his signing of the letter of protest, spoke of his "growing conviction that only a drastic change of policy and of mentality can save the radical movement in this country from the disastrous defeats suffered in Italy, Germany, Austria, and Spain." Fellow-travelers and even party members shared that conviction, and it seemed to me that there was less and less of what Dos Passos described as "unintelligent fanaticism."

That is why I and others like me did not doubt the sincerity of the transformation that took place at the seventh congress. Naïve as we probably were, we might have doubted it if we had not seen so clearly that circumstances demanded the change and that the American party was overripe for it. The International, we thought, had at last learned the lesson of the rise of fascism, and we were glad. The new line fitted our conception of the international situation by recognizing fascism as the chief enemy. At home it permitted us to cooperate with the insurgent forces in the labor movement and the progressives in the New Deal. It was what we wanted, and it seemed to us a great step ahead for the revolutionary movement.

Now the change that had been slowly going on in the party became rapid. The superficial manifestations were often amusing, and we laughed at the way some of the ardent comrades hastened to equip themselves with marriage certificates, conventional clothes, and a new vocabulary. As Max Lerner observed, the Communists, having always been extremists, were now becoming extremely moderate. But the change went below the surface, not only because the new line brought in new members but also because it released qualities in the old members that had been suppressed. Veterans of all the factional fights, who had read nothing but the Marxist classics and the *Daily Worker,* dutifully began to read American history and literature, and were surprised to find that they were learning something. Some of the older comrades were disgruntled, but most of them were glad to relax and be human, and it was a surprise to themselves as well as to others to discover how human they could be. Mother Bloor, at a birthday party in her honor, is reported to have said, "Thank God I have lived to see a little sentiment in the Communist party!"

Immediately our whole relationship to the party was

changed. As I have said, we knew that we were deficient in the Bolshevik virtues, and the party knew it too and did not encourage us to join. But after the summer of 1935 the party wanted us, and wanted us for what we were, middle-class intellectuals. Of the score of intellectuals I have been thinking about as I wrote this narrative, perhaps half had been alienated from the party by this time. Most of the others became members within the next year or two.

We changed, too. Our sectarianism had always been both an intellectual and a temperamental strain, and we responded quickly to the new environment. I suppose now that the party leaders knew they would lose many of us when the next turn came, but that did not keep them from using us for all we were worth. I, for example, having received some newspaper publicity at one time or another, was pushed forward as an example of the new type of Communist: soundly American, incurably middle-class, idealistic, given to correct grammar, kind to my family. And the farther away I got from the old sectarianism, the worse it seemed to me. Thus it happened that the book I wrote at this time, *I Like America*—the one book of mine, by the way, widely circulated by the party—contains only two or three pages, those dealing with the Soviet Union and with the party itself, that I could wish expunged. It is also true that I could not now achieve quite that note of optimism, but that is a different story, and I am not ashamed of having once been more hopeful than at present I can bring myself to be.

From 1935 to 1939 the party grew steadily, and even more in influence than in members. For what we did during this period I think we need not apologize: the building of the democratic front in support of Roosevelt, the creation and strengthening of white-collar unions, the work in the CIO, the boycott of Japan, the advocacy of collective security: there is not one of these things that I would not do again.

But I would not do them under the leadership of the Communist party, and that is the tragedy for all of us who were in the party or worked with it. We never suspected that by a dozen words Joseph Stalin could destroy everything we had done. We would have denied, of course, that Stalin would ever want to speak those words, and we did deny it, steadfastly, right down to the eve of the Soviet-Nazi pact. But we also would have denied that anything Stalin did could destroy the achievements of our democratic front. And we were wrong.

Why were we so stupid? In particular, why did we not take warning from the Moscow trials? Here I can speak only for my-self. My private view of the purges was that most of the men were guilty of the crimes with which they were charged, but I thought that their defections were evidence that something was wrong in the Soviet Union. That was the position around which I wavered, sometimes more convinced of the wrongness of the trials, sometimes less. But I subordinated the question of the guilt of the victims and the fairness of their treatment to another question. "If," I asked myself, "the worst that is claimed by the Trotskyites about these trials is true, what dif-ference will it make to me?" And this was the answer I gave: "Even if the trials are complete frame-ups, it still remains true that Russia is on our side in the struggle against fascism. More-over, the good work we are doing over here has no connection with what is happening in Moscow." This second point was for me much the more important. I went through plenty of bad moments during the trials, but I was determined not to let my distress interfere with my contributions to the democratic front. In fact, I was smug and superior towards those who had noth-ing better to do than to try to exonerate Trotsky while I was raising money for Spain and helping to build the labor move-ment. Thus I took the hurdle of the trials as I had taken that of the Madison Square Garden riot, never suspecting there would be a higher hurdle that would trip me up. . . .

Thoughts After the Pact

We were a good lot, but rather blind. For we had not seen that it was the Russophile bureaucrats who had control. Thou-sands of us had come flooding into the party, and we flattered ourselves that we had changed it. Sometimes it occurred to us that we had done just about what Wilson* had called for: we had taken Communism away from the Communists, from Communists, that is, of the kind he was objecting to. And we were as wrong as we could be.

In a debate in Boston in the spring of 1939 I quoted from the constitution of the Communist party the paragraph on the defense of democracy. "Father Curran no doubt will tell you," I said, "that this is a trick, that we don't really believe it. Be reasonable. How far would a party get if it told people one thing when it asked them to become members and something else when they had become members? Even if our leaders had some design contrary to that statement in the party constitution, they would be helpless against the members of the party." I believed that, and I was wrong.

In the confusing weeks after the Soviet-Nazi pact I realized that I could not follow the party's new line, but even then I was tempted to put the blame on a leadership that had always seemed to me lacking in initiative and intelligence. It was only some months afterward that I understood how fantastic it had been to imagine that any Communist leader would oppose, or even criticize, anything the Soviet Union did. I learned two things that perhaps I should have known before but didn't: Moscow cracked the whip, and the bureaucrats controlled the party.

Though the leaders obviously were not forewarned, though Moscow had permitted them to go on denying the possibility of a Soviet-Nazi pact down to the moment when it was signed, though they were compelled to make fools of themselves as well as to tear down what they had spent four devoted years in building up, they took their medicine. I cannot answer for their private thoughts, which I suspect were bitter, but they publicly competed with each other in asininities in order to prove their blind loyalty to the USSR. I came to see that any talk of principles—Marxist-Leninist principles quite as much

* [Edmund Wilson, noted anti-Communist literary critic.—*Ed.*]

as democratic principles—was eyewash. The leaders had, in the first place, organizational loyalty: they could no more conceive of life outside the party than a New York City ward-heeler could imagine life apart from Tammany. And above that they had loyalty to the Soviet Union: having spent twenty years in its defense, they accepted orders as unquestioningly as officers of the regular army, and when there were no orders they were grateful for hints.

No one will ever know how many members left the party in the months after the pact, but, though badly damaged, it survived the aboutface. The same loyalties, in a different degree, held the rank-and-file as held the leaders. After my resignation a party official said to me in an open letter, "To me it always appeared that you had an inner lack of conviction that the Soviet Union really symbolizes Socialism Victorious." He was right so far as I was concerned, but there were many members, even among the intellectuals, to whom he could not have objected on that ground. It was an intellectual who asked me, "Don't you know in your soul that Stalin and Molotov are comrades?" I had no such transcendental assurance, but certain of my friends did.

In the same way many members of the rank-and-file, though of course their whole existence was not bound up with the party, could not see what meaning life would have apart from it. I had not fully realized the emotional quality that membership had for certain persons until they started writing me at the time of my resignation. Here, for example, is a young woman speaking:

> So it all comes to this: that your whole life previous to this time, all you underwent for the party, all the privations you seem willingly to have suffered when you could have had any post you wanted anywhere in the country, all this has gone up in a puff of smoke and lost its meaning. What for? You might just as well have taken it nice and easy and saved yourself the trouble. It might just

as well never have happened. What a pity, to find one's
life suddenly without meaning. What is left for you
now? You have maintained your precious integrity. I
suppose you can sit and contemplate it like some unbelievable Buddha. But unless you have guts enough to
admit a mistake, you have taken the first step downward on a path which leads to a swamp. Now you are
reduced to the rank of one of the pack who snarls at
the heels of the leadership of our party. What a position
to be in! I think it won't be so good for your integrity,
Mr. Hicks. Has Mr. Hearst come to you yet with a good
offer for your story, the story of "How I Preserved My
Integrity from the Communist Party"? If he hasn't,
don't worry; he'll be around.

On the morning of March 12, 1938, one A. P. Rosengoltz made the following statement: "Woe and misfortune will betide him who strays even to the smallest extent from the general line of the Bolshevik party. I want
you to believe me, to believe in the sincerity of the words
which I now utter." You can believe him, because a few
mornings later he was shot for high treason in the Soviet
Union. I guess you haven't read the account of those
trials. If you start on page 714 of the last one and read
just the final pleas of these men, you might still be able
to draw a lesson from it before it is too late.

That particular religious fervor was more common than I
would have supposed, but it was not the general rule. Many of
my friends were at first overcome by the pact, and they had
inner conviction neither of the comradeship of Stalin nor of
the sacredness of the Bolshevik line, but they were not forced,
as in effect I was, to take an immediate stand, and they waited
to see what would happen. A few of them were expelled for
their hesitations by zealous branches, but the party as a whole
recognized the expediency of tolerance. As the autumn of 1939
went by, they began to feel that, if their hope in the Soviet Un-

ion had been dimmed, there was no greater radiance any-where else. In a desperate world even a rather bad Soviet Un-ion was something to cling to. As for the party, it was not quite what they had thought it to be, but it was still the only mili-tant revolutionary organization. Some of them held on with difficulty, consoling themselves with private explanations and waiting for what has now happened, war between Germany and the Soviet Union, but others found it easy, when time had dulled the shock of the pact, to go back to their old habits.

I can understand all this, and it would not occur to me to question the sincerity of those who stood by the party, but that does not mean I think they are right. On the contrary, I have been driven by events since the pact and by a reconsideration of the theory and practice of the party to a position very differ-ent from theirs. I left the party because I disagreed with its policies: on the pact itself I reserved judgment; but not indefi-nitely. The partition of Poland, the seizure of the Baltic Repub-lics, and the invasion of Finland, all demonstrated to me that the only kind of Communism the Soviet government was inter-ested in was the kind that could be spread by the Red Army. I concluded that that government was, for all practical purposes, a bureaucracy interested in the preservation and extension of its own power. I reviewed the history of the Soviet Union and re-read Lenin to see how this had happened, and decided that the tendency was inherent in Leninism and in certain aspects of Marxism itself.* I came to the conclusion that there could be no shortcuts for the believer in democracy. I still believed that capitalism was decaying and that some form of socialism must take its place, and I continued to recognize the ruthless-ness with which the beneficiaries of the existing order de-fended it, but I repudiated any idea that we could get more democracy by giving up what we have. I rejected, in short, the whole theory of the dictatorship of the proletariat and Lenin's conception of the monolithic party.

I was driven to these conclusions not merely by my reflec-

* "The Blind Alley of Marxism," *Nation*, Sept. 28, 1940.

tions on Communism but also by the dramatic demonstration of fascist efficiency. If on the one hand I was forced to see that the new social order in Russia was dominated by a power-grasping bureaucracy, on the other I had to admit that the power-grasping bureaucracy in Germany had created a new social order. There were, I recognized, striking differences between the two regimes, but the significant fact was that, starting from wholly different premises, they had come closer and closer together.

I began to see, in other words, that fascism was the revolution. Marx had been right in his prediction of the collapse of capitalism. He had been right in saying that the very nature of the means of production in an advanced industrial economy would demand large-scale planning and control by the state rather than by individuals. But he had been wrong in maintaining that only the proletariat could make the revolution and perhaps in maintaining that the proletariat could make it at all. He had been wrong in making the public ownership of the means of production his chief aim, for fascism had shown that, if the bureaucracy could control production, it did not matter who owned the factories. Above all else he had been wrong in his assumption that the revolution would carry over and extend the cultural and humanitarian achievements of the nineteenth century, for fascism repudiated them openly and Soviet Communism in practice.

Fascism, I began to say to myself, is what happens—or at least what is very likely to happen—when capitalism breaks down. Monopoly capitalism lends itself easily to bureaucratic control. Moreover, it is immeasurably easier for a tyrannical government to adopt a planned economy than for a democratic government to do so. When capitalism becomes insufferable to its victims, or when, as is perhaps more likely to happen first in the world as it is, a capitalist nation cannot compete with its fascist rivals, fascism is the natural—but, I trust, not the inevitable—development.

I am talking about the conclusions to which I came, and

I am not trying to give evidence for them. The theory is not peculiar to me, and evidence for it can be found elsewhere. My reaction to these conclusions, however, is part of the story. The choices were simple: I could accept fascism as the revolution, saying, as some of my friends say, that this is the way history is going and there is nothing for us to do but regretfully to acquiesce; or I could make up my mind to go on fighting fascism in the hope that, if we could defeat this immediate onslaught, we could find ways of shaping history. I chose the latter course.

In Search of a Moral

The lessons of this story are, I fear, largely negative. I am sorry, but one of the things I have learned not to do is to pretend that I have a solution for the world's problems when I haven't. Last winter I was carrying on a debate by mail with an acquaintance of mine, who finally declared that he hadn't changed his mind on politics in the past twenty years. I lost interest. I have no respect for persons who haven't changed their minds at least once in the past decade, and I am afraid of persons who know exactly what ought to be done.

In Arthur Koestler's *Darkness at Noon* Commissar Rubashov, awaiting trial and death, reflects on the character of Communist theory and practice. He can find no flaw in the logic: if your purpose is right, your means must be. This is not, Koestler knows, the first time men have so reasoned, and at the beginning of one section he quotes the Bishop of Verden, who said in 1411: "When the existence of the Church is threatened, she is released from the commandments of morality. With unity as the end, the use of every means is sanctified, even cunning, treachery, violence, simony, prison, death. For all order is for the sake of the community, and the individual must be sacrificed to the common good." But the bishop at least had the consolation of believing that he was carrying out God's will, whereas Rubashov knows that he obeys the will of "No. 1." And what he comes to doubt is not so much the infallibility of Stalin as the infallibility of man.

"We have thrown overboard all conventions," he writes in his diary; "our sole guiding principle is that of consequent logic." But the experiment had failed; so far at least there was no end in sight to justify the means that had been used. "For forty years he had fought against economic fatality. It was the central ill of humanity, the cancer which was eating into its entrails. It was there that one must operate; the rest of the healing process would follow. . . . The only solution was the surgeon's knife and his cool calculation. But wherever the knife had been applied, a new sore had appeared in place of the old." He began to wonder: "Perhaps it did not suit mankind to sail without ballast. And perhaps reason alone was a defective compass, which led one on such a winding, twisted course that the goal finally disappeared in the mist."

Many intellectuals have had doubts like Rubashov's, and some have concluded that the only hope is a return to religion. Man recognizes his insufficiency, they argue, only when he admits the greatness of God. As one neo-Protestant puts it, if men don't believe in hell after death, they'll get a hell of bombs on earth. But some of us remember that men had plenty of hell on earth while they still believed in hell in the hereafter. We agree that a belief in the limitlessness of human powers brings disaster—Herman Melville might have taught us that lesson—but we cannot conclude that there is therefore an omnipotent and beneficent God in whom man should put his trust. Our discovery concerns man, not God.

Our practical problems, of course, remain, and they will not wait forever—or even very long—for men to solve them. More or less bad men will go on making history, more or less badly, and practical decisions will always involve supporting bad men against worse. As a matter of fact, Rubashov's new party in their monk's cowls, preaching purity of means, could ruin the world almost as effectively as the old party with its dogma of human infallibility and the justifying end. There is neither one way of ruin nor one way of salvation, and perhaps, as there is no absolute salvation, there is no absolute ruin, though what we are facing is near enough to it for our purposes.

Those of us who have lost a series of certitudes have become suspicious of all certitude. That is what I meant when I said that the lessons of this story are mostly negative. When I first got out of the party, I missed the sense of being constantly active in a good cause, but I have learned that doing something for the sake of doing something creates one of the most dangerous of illusions. This is not a counsel of passivity. I believe in action, and, if I emphasize understanding, it is for the sake of action. Action should grow, however, not out of faith in the inevitability of socialism or anything else, but out of wisdom with regard to the issues and humility with regard to the outcome.

Though troubled about the future, I am in no fundamental sense a pessimist. We have seen good turning into evil, and the spectacle is so cruel a shock to our sensibilities, which are post-Victorian in spite of everything, that we have loudly re-asserted our own version of the doctrine of original sin. We have done well to recognize that our ancestors were not wholly fools on the subject of human nature, but there is more to learn than that. Rubashov forgot that his whole life was an act of self-abnegation that could never be explained in terms of his consequent logic. In other words, he chose to deny in himself what he found it necessary to ignore in others. If the experiment failed, it may have been because men were too good as well as too bad for it. That, at least, is a basis for hope.

III. The Third Decade

T H E   E N D   P R O D U C T

(1940-1950)

Part Three

———

THE third decade is that of only yesterday. Its daily events lie well within the active memory of all but the youngest. England was at war with Nazi Germany as the decade began, the Soviet Union in alliance with Hitler's Government. The alliance came to an end at Nazi Germany's choice and Soviet Russia unwillingly entered World War II. The attack on Pearl Harbor in December, 1941, embroiled America in a war from which there was no escape, and from which it had not attempted to escape, having rightly involved itself by extending aid to England which had become the last bastion of democracy in Europe. A certain irony, however, was not absent from the situation.

For two decades the Soviet Government had taught that the parliamentary democracies of England and the United States were joined in a conspiracy to overthrow the Soviet Government. Soviet "defense" tactics included an international espionage agency, with operatives in every country of the world, a political fifth column to agitate in the democratic countries, to influence their policies, and to hamper them in any manner possible. But it had been the Communists who had signed the pact with the Nazis, not England which had gone to war prior to attack. And later when the overthrow of the Soviet regime was most possible, at a time when the Nazis were advancing in Russia almost as quickly as they could move, the democracies came immediately to Russia's aid, an assistance rendered despite the Soviet-Nazi division of Poland, despite the security on the Eastern front that the pact had allowed Germany, a pact that was the immediate cause of World War II.

Stalin was the only chief of state who failed to address his people when his government entered the war. The reasons for this silence were not difficult to fathom. The ally of yesterday had attacked Russia; the enemies of yesterday, a long yesterday, the countries in which Communists had been ordered to declare strikes and sabotage war production by such maneuvers, had come to Russia's aid. When Stalin did speak, on July 3, 1941, his comments were accordingly not without interest.

What was his explanation for previous policy, for the pact with the Nazis, for a friendship so great that Stalin had spoken of it as being "cemented in blood?" Germany, he now reported, "suddenly and treacherously violated the Non-Aggression Pact she had concluded in 1939 with the USSR. . . . Naturally, our peace-loving country, not wishing to take the initiative of breaking the pact, could not resort to perfidy."

What had Russia gained from the pact? "We secured our country peace for a year and a half, and the opportunity of preparing its forces to repulse fascist Germany should she risk an attack on our country despite the pact. This was a definite advantage for us and a disadvantage for fascist Germany."

This became the refrain of the Communist parties throughout the world and of countless liberals, conservatives and others; the pact had been necessary, it had won Russia time.

Why then were the Nazis advancing so rapidly? Why was not Russia prepared? "This is chiefly due," said Stalin, "to the fact that the war of fascist Germany on the USSR began under conditions favorable for the German forces. The fact of the matter is that the troops of Germany, as a country at war, were already fully mobilized . . . whereas Soviet troops had still to effect mobilization and move up to the frontier."

Claim number one: the pact had bought time for Russia, allowing it to prepare. Claim number two: the Nazis had attacked "suddenly and treacherously"; its armies were mobilized, Russian armies were not. In direct contradiction one explanation with the other, both became successful propaganda claims simultaneously.

Having failed to answer satisfactorily his own question: "How could it have happened that our glorious Red Army surrendered a number of our cities and districts to fascist armies . . . ?", Stalin reminded his listeners that all was not black, that they could count on the help of England and America, their new "loyal allies." He referred to the "historic utterance" of Winston Churchill and the declaration of aid from the American government. These, he said, can only "evoke a feeling of gratitude in the hearts of the peoples of the Soviet Union . . ." He warned, significantly and somewhat nervously: "We must bear in mind that the enemy is crafty, unscrupulous, experienced in deception and the dissemination of false rumors. We must reckon with all this and not fall victim to provocation. All who by their panic-mongering and cowardice hinder the work of defense, no matter who they are, must be immediately haled before the military tribunal."

He did not fail to assert that "the enemy's finest divisions and finest air force units have already been smashed and have met their doom on the field of battle . . ."

On November 6, 1941, when Stalin spoke again, the "doomed" Germans were still advancing, and with mysterious speed.

"Today," Stalin said, "as a result of four months of war, I must emphasize that this danger—far from diminishing—has on the contrary increased. The enemy has captured the greater part of the Ukraine, Byelorussia, Moldavia, and Estonia, and a number of other regions, has penetrated the Donbas, is looming like a black cloud over Leningrad and is menacing our glorious capital, Moscow."

One development did not fail to impress all observers. In its direst moment, the Soviet regime was failing to place its propaganda stress on Soviet Communism. Here, if ever, was an opportunity for the leaders of the Communist state to indicate the truth of what Soviet propagandists had been proclaiming for two decades. The Communist state, beloved by the people, was in the most extreme danger. The enormous contributions to the Russian people should have furnished many noble slogans, *the* slogans of resistance. Fight in defense of the *Communist* way of life! Fight for the unsurpassed conditions furnished you by the *Communist* system! These were the logical battle cries.

But these aspects received only token and intermittent mention. Stalin spoke of the "perfidious military attack on our *fatherland*." In his second address he invoked the names of the tsarist heroes, Suvorov and Kutuzov. The war was now the "patriotic war of liberation." Ideology began to disappear from the scene; Russian nationalist sentiment replaced it and was soon fanned without restraint. Tsarist Russia had come back to life!

As Isaac Deutscher has said in his *Stalin* (1949):

"Commenting in November, 1942, on a decree which abolished 'socialist competition' in the army, *Pravda* bluntly stated that the soldier had no Socialist obligations whatsoever and that his job was simply to serve his fatherland, as his forebears had done. The army regulations of Peter the Great were recalled as a model for imitation. Guards regiments and guards divisions—their very names recalled Tsarist days—were created. Orders of Suvorov and Kutuzov were instituted. Cossack formations, once despised as symbols of Tsarist oppression, were brought back to life . . . ," etc., etc.*

On November 7, 1941 Stalin himself had said: "Let the manly images of our great ancestors—Alexander Nevsky, Dmitri Donskoi, Kusma Minin, Dmitri Pozharsky, Alexander Suvorov, Mikhail Kutuzov—inspire you in this war!"

What could be clearer? Soviet Communism was demonstrating that it did not, in its greatest moment of necessity, dare ask the people to fight for Soviet Communism. Stalin made another statement, one that might have—but didn't—confound those who thought that the Soviet regime was conducting a war that would indicate the superiority of ideological systems.

"The present war," said Stalin, "is a war of motors. He who will have the overwhelming superiority in the production of motors will win the war. If we combine the output of the motors of the United States, Great Britain and the USSR, we will have a superiority of motors of at least three to one as compared with Germany."

It is a statement to remember. Soviet Communism would win because of the aid of American and British "motors." The motor of Soviet ideology had stalled in its most crucial moment.

Behind this fear-laden backdrop was transpiring one of the most dramatic upheavals of our time. It is suggestive of the

---

* "The words 'communism' and 'Soviet' disappeared. Instead everything was spoken of as 'Russian.' Marxism was forgotten. Communism versus Fascism was forgotten. Everything carried the 'Defend Russia' theme." (*The Iron Curtain* by Igor Gouzenko.)

state of Western knowledge of Soviet reality that nearly all persons in the "outside world" were led to believe the exact opposite of what was actually happening. Those were the years in which one heard that the USSR was the only country in the world without a fifth column; indeed—so went the myth—this was so because the Moscow Trials had destroyed the Nazi fifth column; such historical "facts" were relentlessly circulated by the radio, newspapers, magazines and a really unforgettable movie, *Mission to Moscow*. A reputable American publisher stated matter of factly on the cover of a cheap edition of Joseph Davies' book of that name: "On the basis of evidence and impression accumulated by Mr. Davies at the time and on the spot, it is now clear that these trials scotched Hitler's fifth column in Russia." The retrospective myth was working overtime.

Suddenly, as hostilities drew to a close, the myth exploded violently. Five so-called autonomous Soviet Republics (Volga-Germans, Chechen-Ingushs, Kalmyks, Crimean Tatars and Karachayevians) were declared "disloyal" *en masse* to the Communist state, and brutal deportations of the remaining populations to remote, barren spaces was the punishment. The nation which supposedly had been cleansed of a "fifth column" during the Moscow Trials—and in the orgies of killing that had preceded and followed that period—was suddenly declared in this way—*by the Soviet state itself!*—to have suffered from "treason" on a scale unknown to any country in the war.

But this was only part of the actual story. As Soviet citizens and prisoners of war began to flood Europe in enormous numbers, as the Soviet Government began a desperate campaign to retrieve its nationals who were unwilling to return to their "fatherland," the wartime reality behind the Soviet backdrop grew more and more revealing.

In the last years the deeply significant story of the Russian people has become starkly clear in outline; it is only the diligence of Soviet efforts in cutting off the USSR from the rest of the world that prevents the story from being completely learned. During the first Nazi advances there had been large-scale troop desertions to the Germans. In some areas the invading armies were greeted as "liberators." Russian crowds thronged their path; Russian soldiers surrendered without fighting. A people cut off from outside reality for many years, lulled into a false sense of security by conciliatory Soviet propaganda towards the Nazis during the pact, tending at other times to disbelieve what state organs said about the Nazis, as it disbelieves such official sources on other questions, hating the regime with an implacable ferocity, masses of Russians looked upon even the Nazis as "liberators"—a tragic notion but nevertheless widespread. One cannot calculate what the response might have been among millions of other Russians if the invading army had not been that of the Nazis. For most Russians the choice was one of the cruelest that history has ever seen fit to put before a people.

American knowledge of this important subject of mass alientation has been supplemented by the captured archives—the secret not the propaganda files—of the Nazi's Operation Barbarossa, the code name for the invasion of Russia. These documents make clear that the Germans were astounded at the reception their forces received when they first invaded the USSR. Especially interesting are the figures in the files of the German Foreign Armies (East) Department on Russian prisoners. Here are some of them, as provided by Wallace Carroll, former director of the Office of War Information in Europe:

> "June 29-July 7 [1941], pocket of Bialystok and Minsk, 320,000 prisoners; July 16, battle of Smolensk, 300,000; August 5-8, battle of Uman, 103,000; September 24, battle of Kiev, 665,000; October 18, double battle of Bryansk and Vyazma, 665,000." *

* *Life*, December 19, 1949. This important article contains a highly revealing summary of the German documents. As such it reinforces the articles, with similar findings, which have preceded it on the subject. Mr. Carroll comments: "It should be noted that these mass surrenders of more than two million men took place at a moment when the Soviet forces were fighting on their own soil

To which should be added:

> "It is little known abroad that a Soviet prisoner of war is considered a criminal by the very fact of having fallen into enemy hands. Since many of the prisoners had been drafted by the German armed forces into labor battallions and military formations, every prisoner returning home is being screened and, unless he can show why he failed to die fighting rather than surrender, he is sentenced to a term of forced labor. This procedure, unbelievable at first, has now been confirmed by a multitude of reports from Russia as well as from individuals who managed to escape back to Germany or France. . . . Along with prisoners of war, Russian laborers, men and women dragged by the Germans from the occupied areas into forced labor, are undergoing the same process of screening, and many are sentenced to deportation." (David J. Dallin, "Concentration Camps in Soviet Russia," special supplement, *The New Leader*, March 29, 1947.)

Why then did Hitler lose in Russia? This phase is more widely known. Happily, he was the source of his own doom. With an arrogant confidence and bestiality that was characteristic of the entire edifice of Nazism, his armies were instructed not to grant those concessions to the population that might have gained their support. The Nazi armies, in his belief, were invincible; they need concede nothing. The record of the Nazi armies in Russia were soon identical with the Nazi record elsewhere: wholesale slaughter, burning of

---

against a nation which they knew to be an aggressor." Also: "Before long, some divisions listed in the order of battle as German divisions actually had as many Russians on their rolls as they did Germans. By midsummer, when the Germans were advancing on Stalingrad, they had half a million Soviet citizens in their ranks."

villages, policies of race superiority, pillage. The war suddenly changed in coloration. The Russian people fought, as they had fought in earlier times, for their homes, their families, their very lives. Thus, the Soviet stress on nationalist rather than Communist propaganda, the "patriotic war of liberation," the fight for the "fatherland," the emphasis on tsarist heroes. After the war the nation that was "free of a fifth column" began the newest of fearful purges: the disbanding of the Republics for "disloyalty," mass deportations to remote areas, the frequent jailing of returned prisoners of war and DPs, the shakeup of the military, many wartime heroes falling by the wayside, the cultural purges, the scientific purges, the economic purges, a "cleansing" that extended into all fields of Russian life.

Alexander Barmine, in a discussion of the "treasonous" role of millions of Russians during the war, summed up the entire matter succinctly:

> "The forgotten fact is that Stalin, with the outbreak of war, was obliged to fight his own people first. That is one reason why the Germans took so much territory in the first eighteen months. . . . One of the central tragedies of this tragic era is this: that the Bolshevik regime undeservedly got the credit for the self-sacrificing heroism of the Russian people in the war—and that the Russian people are now undeservedly getting the blame for the horrors of the regime's policies after the war." ("In Defense of the Russian People," *Saturday Evening Post*, September 4, 1948.)

*   *   *

It is outside the orbit of this book to describe the political alchemy by means of which the "loyal allies," as Stalin described the democracies, again became "imperialists." Nor is it our task here to enter into a country by country analysis of how Nazi domination of many European nations has been replaced by Communist domination, nor can we discuss the tragic victory of the Stalintern in China. The repetitious pattern of appeasement had again produced the same fruits. But if the beginning of the fourth decade is witnessing the crystallization abroad of everything that the Soviet regime has represented from the start at home—a catastrophic verification of what had been taught unavailingly by three decades of rebels against Soviet tyranny—it also has brought more hope than had existed before. The free nations of the world seemed increasingly aware of what the Soviet system really meant; in the same painful process that had characterized the gaining of knowledge about Nazism, knowledge was being won about the Communist state. What in the United States was still a matter for "debate" could be learned by many an anguished European by a glance at the guard on his street corner. In 1950, however, the democratic counterfight had already started—fumbling and hesitant, but there was common recognition that the stakes were the survival of the democratic systems and possibly of mankind itself. It was clear that hard-gained liberties would not be easily surrendered.

There were voices being carried to the Russian people over the airwaves, over the Iron Curtain, and they were telling the Russians that free men did not hold them accountable for the crimes of their enslavers, that free men knew that the Russian people were the first victims of Communist tyranny. They were telling the Russian people, over the attempts of the Russian tyrants to prevent the transmission of the message, that they had allies, and they knew that the Russian people were anxious to transmit back their statements of friendship. The fact that the Communist state did what it could to prevent communication, both ways, was more articulate than a hundred indictments.

As a representative of the Russia that had stood for freedom, the British Broadcasting Corporation made it possible for Alexander Kerensky to speak to his countrymen for the first time in three decades, as our own Voice of America was making it possible for others. Kerensky told the Russian people of those in the free nations who had only friendship for them and who were desirous of peace. He said:

> "The hundreds of thousands of new immigrants of a new generation, educated by the Soviets, brought with them to the West the real feelings, thoughts and hopes of the silent but feverishly thinking Russian people. It is this unofficial Russia that the democratic West met in camps for ex-prisoners of war, especially for DPs. This Russia did not turn out to be the land of born slaves. Nor did it turn out to be a happy land, building up its prosperity under the wise leadership of the leader of 'socialism.' It turned out that Russia was a country whose enslaved inhabitants worn out by poverty and terror are looking for freedom and for a right to lead a life in truth, in peace and friendship with other peoples and other countries. . . . Believe me, a free Russia governed by its peoples will not have to force its citizens by means of terror to live in abject poverty so that the great wealth of the country could be squandered on a gigantic military machine. Who needs this military machine, and for what reason? . . . Stirring up hatred between peoples throughout the world, Communists push the world towards a new catastrophe. This is the devil playing with fire! This fire once lit can certainly burn Russia if not the whole civilized world."

*   *   *

In 1848 Karl Marx and Friedrich Engels wrote: "A Spectre is haunting Europe—the spectre of Communism." A century later, in a way they could not have foreseen, the totalitarian state that was the result of three decades of suppression and terror was threatening the entire world. Our last section is concerned with this grotesque End Product.

Ignazio Silone

THE END OF A CONCORDAT

Editor's Note

THIS pithy summary of some of the factors that have alienated a most distinguished international crop of intellectuals from the Soviet cause speaks volumes for the general recognition, that had to come, of the disparity between slogan and actuality in the USSR. Silone, Italy's best-known contemporary novelist, once summed up this cleavage in a pregnant phrase: *juridical cretinism.* This distressing phenomenon, he explained, "consists especially of the habit of considering the laws of a country as the exact representation of the social relations obtaining among the citizens of that country." ("A Letter to Moscow," *International Review,* November, 1936.) In other words, when the time is near for purges and "trials," proclaim a Constitution. Those who are so disposed will ignore the repression and console themselves with the document.

Between the years of 1921-27, approximately the period of NEP, Silone had frequent occasion to visit the Soviet Union as a member of the Italian Communist delegation. A man bred among peasants, thoroughly devoted to a humanist view, Silone was gradually to penetrate the myths that continued to impress so many of his associates in the Communist movement for so long. A man also of action as well as perception, he renounced the Soviet state. He did not, however, abandon his belief in socialism. In an essay in 1950 he reaffirmed this stand ("to which I think I can say that my entire life bears testimony"), and stated that he viewed socialism as an "extension of the ethical impulse from the restricted individual and family sphere to the whole domain of human activity, a need for effective brotherhood. . . . I do not conceive Socialist policy as tied to any particular theory, but to a faith." (In *The God that Failed*.)

He was born in Italy in 1900. His father was a landowner and he came to know intimately the life of the peasants. His understanding of their temperament—cagy, elemental and at times verbosely philosophical, hearteningly human—is manifested in all his novels. *Fontamara* is a classic folk tale in the modern idiom. He studied in his native town and in various Catholic institutions. An earthquake brought death to his mother and five brothers when he was in his teens. He became politically active in a peasant league and in left-wing groups. Later he edited several labor publications which were soon suppressed by the Fascists when they came to power. Thus, Silone began an underground life. His brother, the only remaining child in the family besides himself, was beaten to death by the Fascists. For a number of years he evaded Mussolini's police who hunted him throughout Italy. In 1930 he broke with the Communists, as the Soviet experience continued to grow worse with time. In the following year he escaped from Italy to Switzerland, and spent the war years in that country. Since then he has returned to Italy. His public life has been an effective demonstration of the dedication of an individual against the major totalitarianisms of our time. His novels *Bread and Wine*, the *Seed Beneath the Snow*, and other works, are known to an international audience.

This selection, written after the Nazi-Soviet Pact, appeared in *Il Mondo*, and has been translated for this book from a manuscript furnished by Mr. Silone.

The End of a Concordat by Ignazio Silone

Stalin's policy has finally revealed the bureaucratic nature of the Russian state, in a light so vivid that anyone with eyes can see it clearly. I say bureaucratic, not soviet, for the obvious reason that since 1919 the Soviets have abandoned their function as representatives of the people. On the other hand, it would be equally inaccurate to call the present Russian system a dictatorship of the Bolshevik party, because after 1927 the Russian party lost all the characteristics of an autonomous organization, and therefore of a party. To make this fact apparent to some of the writers of the left, however, is difficult indeed: I know certain leftist intellectuals whose eyes seemingly function only as an excuse for them to wear glasses. I would like to ask any of my friends who can do so, to explain to me what writers like Bert Brecht, Ludwig Renn, and Anna Seghers (to name only a few of the intelligent Communist writers) think of Stalin's policy? Why has intellectual rectitude never been so rare a commodity? Must I attribute the silence of these writers to cowardice? or to ignorance? or to a vain hope that Stalin's bureaucracy will end by swinging left? or to a type of pride (wholly misplaced) which restrains them from "abandoning the sinking ship like rats"?, or, finally, solely to their material difficulties of the moment? I take these difficulties into account. And they bring back to mind the hard struggles I fought with myself, during the period from 1927 to 1930, before resolving to abandon the Communist party.

The strength of the Communist party, its "superiority" with respect to other parties (except, perhaps, the Fascist party), is that it does not limit itself to obtaining from its members attendance at meetings and the exercise of the franchise: it is not satisfied with having merely a share in their activities, it demands their entire life. In this respect it is not exactly a party, but rather an *Order*. To a good Communist the party is more than a political organization: it is his family, his church, his only social reality; or—what is the same thing—a substitute for all these. Such it is especially for those threatened with expulsion. In the chains which bind together the party members no link is stronger than the ideological: the party may change its tactics or its program, may say today the opposite of what it said yesterday; it matters not: "the party is always right." Only the thought of being expelled fills the loyal Communist with terror. The party is his world: to lose it, or to see it crumble, would be for him worse than hellfire. It is this which is the strength of the Communist party, as of the Fascist party; but it is also its weakness. Anyone whose eyes are not merely ornamental will acknowledge the astonishing result; the Communist party has today become the safest refuge for the emptiest stupidity.

The consequences are particularly ruinous for the intellectual in the service of communism. Since the day when Stalinism began to darken every expression of Russian life beneath the wing of its bureaucratic dictatorship Russia has not produced a novel worth reading or a film worth seeing. The pseudo-realism of today's official Russian literature reminds me of the art of retouching, esthetic ideal of a decadent social class which tries to preserve the illusion of a lost youth by resorting to the "artistic" photograph. Many years ago Lenin made clear the dangers of the "childhood diseases" of communism; today any-one with a head on his shoulders must recognize the symptoms of senile idiocy. Sad destiny, to pass from childhood to senility without ever having enjoyed the age of virility!

The slogans "defense of civilization" and "social humanity," though adopted in bad faith, served to attract to Stalinism many top-ranking artists and writers of the Western world. From the very beginning I stood out against the equivocal obligation which they undertook, and all my predictions have been sadly confirmed by the course of events. It was not difficult to foresee that men of the integrity of André Gide, Aldous Huxley, Dos Passos would be unable to play for long the fool's part in the comedy in which they were called to participate. The error lay at the point of departure. *Concordat*—that is the word which to me most happily defines the relationship between the bureaucratic Russian state and the intellectuals of the democracies.

A concordat, as everyone knows, is a debatable compromise by means of which a weak political power and a decadent spiritual power recognize each other, share each other's authority, and promise each other mutual aid. Thus Roman Catholicism enriched itself materially while betraying its spiritual mission. In a concordat it is always the spiritual power which is sacrificed. The bureaucratic Russian state, moving ever further away from true sovietism and communism, felt the need to substitute a spirituality borrowed from the Western world for the vanished light of "Leninism": it wished to be recognized by the Western elite as the realization of the noblest aspirations of humanity, the legitimate heir to the humanist tradition, the state with the most liberal and democratic organization the world had ever known. In exchange, besides material benefits, it offered artists and writers—until then saddened by their isolation—contact with the masses, and the illusion of being at the head of history's most progressive movement. The value of a work of art was determined by the degree to which it accepted the Stalinist concordat. A novel, a painting, a sculpture or a piece of music, was acclaimed by the party press as a masterpiece of art, or condemned and ignored, according to the political faith of its creator.

At their "congresses" the intellectuals could protest against Fascist censorship, the concentration camps of Germany and Italy, the suppression of educational freedom and the religious persecution in those countries, but, thanks to the concordat, they had to close their eyes to the fact that all these things existed in Russia, and to an even greater degree than in the other countries. They could complain of the fate of Ossietzky, but they had to ignore that of Serge. This was sufficient to give a

VERDICT OF THREE DECADES

strange taste and a doubtful effect to the eloquent vindications of human dignity, of liberty of conscience, and of democratic rights which issued from these congresses. The bargain was so obvious and so shameful that it is impossible to excuse the intellectuals who were party to it, even on the grounds of political inexperience. It was also justifiable to suspect the anti-fascism of certain refugee German writers, beloved of Stalin. One may reasonably ask oneself if their anti-Hitlerism was no more than a reaction to the German racial laws; the fact is that some of them made no effort to conceal their admiration for Mussolini—until he too became anti-Semitic. At any rate, the Russo-German pact, with its salutary effects, has put an end—and a rather inglorious end—to the collaboration between the Russian state and the intellectuals of the left. The majority quickly consoled themselves, and found no difficulty in substituting Roosevelt or Churchill for Stalin.

But there are men of the type I described at the beginning of this article, for whom the about-face of the Russian state represents a very different tragedy. Possibly they consider themselves betrayed; if so, it was a case of self-betrayal. Not the least factor in the ruin of the Communist parties has been the conformity of their intellectuals. Great is the wrong for which they must answer to the poor workers whom they have helped to deceive! Let us at least hope that the breaking of the concordat between the Stalinist bureaucracy and the majority of the leftist intellectuals will do some good, will at least serve as a warning to the young writers and artists who are seeking a path to the future. It is proper in this connection to state once again certain truths, by no means new but which this most recent experience has imbued with new vitality.

The marriage of art and revolution cannot be arranged through the subjection of the artist to a political party. A work of art is the fruit of the experience and the intimate life of he who creates. It cannot be an instrument of propaganda. The history of art is the history of the spirit finding a means of expression. Collaboration with the Communist party can give the artist the feeling of standing side by side with the oppressed class, but this too is an illusion, for the heavy blows suffered by the Communist parties in the last fifteen years, the cynical amorality with which they have justified their sudden changes of direction, can be explained only by a progressive alienation from the lowest levels of the working class. A party which has truly linked its fate with that of the people cannot profane its battle cries, cannot pass from bitter anti-fascism to a pact with Hitler, cannot invoke peace and wage war. From the corruption of a bureaucracy parasitic upon the working class will be born a Red nihilism, degenerate sport of the nihilism of which Nietzsche spoke. To remove himself from this bureaucracy is indispensable for the artist who would create a living work of art, as it is for whoever seeks the social truth which moves and lives amongst the oppressed. One must not fear isolation. The artist is never alone: his heart beats with that of millions whom he has never seen. Falsehood alone separates man from his brothers. The worth of an artist lies in the service he renders to the cause of truth.

Jerzy Gliksman

I N P R I S O N

Editor's Note

ONE of the factors that militates against publicizing specific excesses of a dictatorial regime is that one episode, however startling, is soon followed by others and the very act of concentrating on acts of brutality as they occur ironically helps to obscure earlier developments. The tragic case of Alter and Erlich, therefore, has already been all but forgotten. The facts are these: Victor Alter and Henryk Erlich, internationally known socialist leaders in Poland, were arrested in 1939 by the invading Soviet armies. Polish patriots, democratic spokesmen, distinguished in Jewish circles, fighters against poverty and injustice, they were soon arrested by the Soviet administration and sent to the Butirki Prison in Moscow. The charges against them, made by the highest officials of the Soviet secret police, ran from attempted acts of sabotage to collaboration with fascists; in short, not unfamiliar charges. That these allegations were absurd when leveled against leaders of anti-Nazi opinion in Poland, against two men, furthermore, who as Jews and democrats had opposed Nazism since its inception—these absurdities did not diminish at all the ferocity of the Soviet "charges." It is instructive of the caliber of Alter and Erlich to note that neither of them could be compelled to sign a "confession." In time both were sentenced to death. But this, horrible as it was, was not to be the end of their story.

Their sentences were suddenly and strangely reduced to ten years at forced labor, and after the agreement with Poland, which called for amnesty of Polish prisoners, both were released. The Soviet Union had need of them. Since the major conviction of the two men was the necessity for total war to be waged against Nazi Germany, and since the Nazis had marched against Russia, their aid was enlisted by the Russians in the battle against Nazism. To some, all that seemed to have happened was that the Soviet Union had originally made a mistake in regard to the Polish leaders, a mistake it was now trying to rectify, and understandably there were no recriminations.

At this high point of good feeling, the Soviet Union acted once more and without warning. Alter and Erlich suddenly disappeared. Inquiries brought only the information that they had been arrested again. Early in 1942 the NKVD ominously declared that the two men were Soviet citizens; Polish protests on this point were ignored. The matter was now so clear, and so frightful, that world labor intervened, as did individually many of the most distinguished men of science, art, letters, and politics, persons of the stature of Albert Einstein and Eleanor Roosevelt. The Soviet Union retained its silence in the face of all of these requests and demands that the two men be freed. One telegram finally received a reply in February, 1943. Molotov brazenly ordered Ambassador Litvinov to inform William Green, president of the American Federation of Labor, that Alter and Erlich had manifested hostility for the Soviet regime and had made "appeals to the Soviet troops to stop bloodshed and immediately to conclude peace with Germany." They had been rearrested and once again sentenced to death. Casually, Molotov concluded: "This sentence has been carried out in regard to both of them." Later an even more ghastly detail was learned: the two men had been killed as early as December, 1941, soon after their arrest; at the time that the Soviet Union seemed calmly to consider the many appeals for their release, they were already dead! (See *The*

Dark Side of the Moon [New York, 1947], a book, incidentally, which most ably and comprehensively chronicles what happened to Poland in the fateful years of 1939-45.)

The tragedy of Alter and Erlich is especially relevant to a reading of the present selection. Not only does it symbolize the brutal period of Jerzy Gliksman's departure into the Soviet cauldron, there is still a closer relationship: Gliksman was Victor Alter's half brother. Less known than Victor, he managed finally to survive and to be able to tell the story of his experience.

The events leading up to Gliksman's arrest are not unlike those faced by many other Poles during the recent period. When war broke out in 1939, Gliksman, like many other Polish patriots, remained in Warsaw until the Nazi armies were nearly upon the city. Having hoped to organize resistance to the Nazis after the Polish government had fallen, these Poles finally started a desperate retreat to the east, to Russian-occupied Poland. They did not know what to expect from the Russians, but they had hopes; they thought that they might at least reach sanctuary. ("What could they possibly have against me?" Gliksman reasoned. "I had been a socialist all of my life, and I had never shown any enmity toward the Soviet Union; on the contrary, I used to defend it against all kinds of charges.") Gliksman, who had been a lawyer, and the others who fled, men of all occupations, soon learned differently. Arrested, Gliksman was soon released after humiliating treatment; the Soviet police expected to use him as a decoy to lead them to other socialists. He lived uneasily in this half-world of horror until March, 1940, when he was arrested again by Soviet border guards as he tried to enter Lithuania. For many months he languished in jail awaiting his "trial," and was finally sentenced to five years at forced labor in a *lager* (Soviet "corrective" labor camp). That this did not become in effect a death sentence was due to his unexpected release in accordance with the Sikorski-Stalin agreement in mid-1941.

Before 1939 there was a widespread view, born out of many mixed motives, that the methods and systems of justice characteristic of Communist rule were somehow rooted in Russia; they were not for export. Soviet brutality was explained in terms of "local conditions." The fact that policies of terror stemmed from a basic principle of Communist ideology—that all means are necessary and justified in the building of the monolithic society —was a fact too horrible for many to accept. In 1939 there occurred for the first time the successful imposition of the "mind and face of Bolshevism" outside of Russia, and many mistaken notions had to be revised. What happened to Polish democrats, liberals, conservatives, socialists, was a brutal portent of the dictatorial disease that was later to afflict many parts of Europe, a disease that the Communist culture-bearers are continuing to spread. This selection provides us with a glimpse into the instructive aftermath of the Russian invasion of Poland. We have chosen a description of the earlier, and "happier," period of Jerzy Gliksman's incarceration, when he spent months in an NKVD prison in Soviet-occupied Poland waiting for a hearing. That the callousness that he encountered was not exceptional, but integral to Communist "humanism," he learned again at first hand when he was sent to Siberia, a road trod by a million Poles, where he spent a year at forced labor. For an account of this later period the reader is referred to his *Tell the West* (1948), from which this selection is taken, an extremely enlightening report on what life is reduced to for millions of persons in Soviet camps.

#

In Prison by Jerzy Gliksman

If the inmates of Soviet jails were asked to select the worst feature of their imprisonment, they would undoubtedly name the lack of air to breathe as the most terrible. We found the poisoned air in our cell worse than the hunger, the filth, and the lice; worse even than the occasional beatings.

The *kartser* and some of the night interrogations were, perhaps, more cruel than the lack of fresh air, but not all prisoners were subjected to these special questionings, and not all were put into solitary confinement. Yet almost all who chanced to be interned in Soviet prisons had to suffer the unbearably stuffy air in the exceedingly overcrowded rooms.

When I first came into the cell, the windows were kept open day and night and the air was, therefore, endurable.

To prevent us from observing the goings-on in the courtyard, we had to close the windows several times during the day. The panes were covered with thick, white, opaque paint.

The forbidden sights in the courtyard were the prisoners of other cells. The admission of new prisoners as well as the transfer of old ones took place in the yard, as did the prisoners' exercises.

Sometimes, however, we did manage to break the rule forbidding us to peep into the yard. Since the windows were high, we formed, whenever the need arose—and if the guard happened not to be looking—a "human pyramid." The one on top observed the courtyard through a hole scratched in the paint with a small piece of glass.

Thus Druker, the graduate from the Warsaw Jewish Teachers' Seminary, once saw his younger brother being led through the courtyard. They had been arrested together, separated immediately, and for several months had not known of each other's whereabouts.

In the same way, Dr. Polonis, former head physician of the Oshmiana hospital, saw his wife and two small daughters being brought into prison. The family had intended to flee to Lithuania, and the doctor had hoped that his wife and children, at least, would be saved. It turned out, however, that they were locked up in the women's section of the prison.

A friend of mine, Bronek Bloch, a Warsaw student, thus saw his cousin Edek, the son of the Warsaw Jewish Bund leader Nathan Szafran. Edek and Bronek had both been captured at the border while attempting to reach their families in Vilna.

Bronek was worried about his cousin, who was at the time only fifteen years old. After his arrest, Edek was placed in a special prison cell for juvenile prisoners.

On this occasion I, too, looked into the yard. It was heart-breaking to watch the fifty or sixty "juveniles." Most of them were young boys, the oldest perhaps sixteen, several not more than thirteen or fourteen.

Several days later one of the "look-outs" told me that a group of about a hundred women was walking in the yard. Among them I recognized Perel, the wife of Herman Kruk, a well-known cultural leader and the director of the largest workers' library in Warsaw, who was later murdered by the Gestapo. Perel and I had both been arrested at the same time while trying to cross the border and reach Vilna.

Our peeping into the yard was considered a great crime and whenever one of the prisoners was caught red-handed, he was severely punished by the guards.

With the beginning of spring we were struck a heavy blow. Our prison officials decided that we were not sufficiently isolated from the outside world; that the paint-covered window panes did not bar us adequately from viewing the activities in the courtyard; and that prison regulations were thereby being violated. For these reasons one of the most wretched decrees in our prison life was issued.

One morning several guards brought a carpenter into our cell. This man proceeded to cover both our windows with wooden planks while the guards took care that he neither looked at us nor talked. From our room the carpenter went to repeat his work in other cells, and all day long we could hear his hammering as well as the vainly protesting voices of the prisoners. As far as we were concerned, the shutting of the windows was nothing short of a disaster. We now felt ourselves to be in a subterranean dungeon. No longer were we able to see the sky, no longer could we benefit from the meager rays of the sun. Now there was no daylight at all in our cell, and the electric bulb had to be lit day and night.

These, however, were not the most important considerations. Much more vital was that the only source of fresh air for almost a hundred human beings in our cell was now gone.

In the daytime as well as at night we were now unable to breathe freely. Here I understood what was meant by "heavy air." Never before had I experienced anything of the kind.

The stuffiness and stench of the air in the cell were most noticeable when one entered it from the outside after returning from the latrine, from an interrogation, or from the "exercises." The first few instants after entering, a prisoner would be unable to breathe at all. Then, after a while, one's lungs adapted themselves to the foul air, but even then one's breathing remained panting and unnaturally shallow. One had the impression that all inmates were asthmatic, or that all had just finished running. Some of the prisoners, particularly the sick, breathed with their mouths wide open, like fish out of water.

The weather outside was still chilly, but the heat inside the cell was such that we all sweated profusely. Most of the prisoners undressed to their underwear and some, who cared little, remained almost entirely naked and barefooted. Our underwear was always soaking wet—not just damp, but literally drenched through.

The only advantage of our sweating was that our lice were unable to bear it. Lice apparently cannot endure perspiration, and we got rid of many of them.

The guard officers now made it a habit to appear at the regular *poverkas* with perfumed handkerchiefs, which they held to their noses, trying to filter the foul air in which we had to live. The inspections were now quickly over, and the officers would escape from the cell as if pursued by the plague.

There still remained narrow cracks between the planks covering our windows. These were too narrow to enable us to see through, but they were nevertheless the only tiny source of fresh air in the cell. The space immediately under the windows was consequently slightly more airy than the rest of the room.

All places on the floor under the window were now occupied by the criminals and their "invited guests" from among the other prisoners, whom the criminals happened to like for one reason or another. Several times I, too, was honored by permission to sit under the windows. I paid for that privilege by telling them stories which they liked.

The shutting of the windows also brought about a basic change in our sleeping habits. Almost the entire upper floors of the berths, where the heat was most acute—worse than at the top shelf of a Turkish bath—were vacated. Some people remained on the lowest tier of the sleeping shelves, but most prisoners took to the floor.

We were now even more cramped on the floor than we had been on the berths. When we tried to go to sleep the first evening after the shutting of the windows, only part of the sleepers found it possible to stretch out; some had to lie with their legs bent, while others found no room at all.

After several hours of wrangling and fighting which the guards pretended neither to see nor hear, we finally, late at night, evolved a system which, with difficulty, provided everybody with room in which to lie down. We stretched out in two tightly packed rows, every two prisoners head-to-foot, the feet of one row near the heads of the other, and vice versa.

This system made use of every available inch. It is hardly possible to imagine, however, what it meant to have a pair of unwashed and perspiring feet near one's nose all night. Our hot bodies constantly bumped against one another, and unconsciously—some of us purposely—we shoved and kicked one another.

Several weeks passed during which the dictum that one could get used to anything was proved false. We all weakened considerably. Several of us fell ill.

One day in July, events took an even more serious turn. The outside temperature must have been exceptionally high. In the cell we were completely drenched from our own perspiration. It was the worst day we had yet experienced. Several sick prisoners fainted.

And just then thirteen new prisoners were pushed into our cell.

This proved to be the last straw. The mood prevailing in the cell was one of irritation. The guard anxiously looked into the room several times, and the inmates dared to taunt him with jeering remarks. There was trouble in the air.

At bedtime, when we had to squeeze even more tightly together to make room for the new arrivals, it came to open rebellion.

It is difficult to ascertain when, exactly, the open defiance started, or who were its initiators. Sukhanov, the former Red Army lieutenant, as well as other Soviet prisoners, warned us that our actions were futile. It would not help us in the least, they claimed, and it might have disastrous results. When they realized that their advice would not be heeded, they crawled under the berths, thoroughly frightened.

We hardly cared one way or the other. Let them do to us whatever they pleased! We felt that to continue living in these conditions was worse than death and that we had nothing to lose.

We began beating loudly on the door and yelling at the tops of our voices, so that we could be heard throughout the entire prison.

"Air!" we screamed, "give us air! Open the windows! We are choking to death! We demand the warden!"

The guard attempted to quiet us from across the door, pleading at first, then threatening and cursing in the Russian manner—but to little avail. Nobody paid any attention to him. The cell seemed to be seized by hysteria; people shouted, wailed, cried. The few maniacs in our cell became particularly excited and howled wildly. One of them began beating his head against the walls, the door, and the floor. He was soon bleeding profusely. Others had fits, or laughed uncontrollably. We were all close to insanity.

All this lasted for perhaps an hour. Then the door of our cell flew open with a bang, and the highest prison official accompanied by several officers and soldiers with drawn pistols ran into the room.

Silence suddenly fell upon the cell. The commandant's face contracted with disgust at the foul air. He put a handkerchief to his nose and moved closer to the door. He was a short, thin, young Russian with wiry blond hair, and he wore the insignia of a major in the NKVD. He looked us silently over for a while.

"Well," he drawled slowly, "who was making such a racket here, disturbing the quiet of the night in prison?"

Several voices answered immediately.

"We were all shouting," they ventured, "all of us, all."

The commandant seemed to become just a bit angry at that.

"We do not recognize such a thing as 'all,'" he said. "You will have to name the culprits, the leaders of the rebellion . . . *Starosta* (elder) of the cell! Step forward and give the names of the rebels!"

The noise broke loose again. Several prisoners crowded around the commandant shouting wildly that it was impossible to stand it any longer; that they would choke to death; that he could see for himself how things were. Let the windows at least be partially opened, some said, let some of the prisoners be taken out, and so on . . .

The commandant raised his hand and all became quiet. He then addressed us with an air of calmness and with an ironic smile.

"You will gain nothing by your rebellion," he said. "One does not yell in a Soviet prison. Ask the Soviet people among you, they will tell you. If you will not calm down immediately, I have sufficient means . . ." He pointed at the NKVD-men with the drawn pistols. "And should you persist, all I have to do is to press a button in my office and a military detachment with a machine gun will be here immediately. I do believe, however, that you ought to quiet down without it. Now, when the world is trembling at its foundations and historic events are taking place in Europe, you are making a fuss about some air! You ought to be ashamed of yourselves! A Soviet prison must be quiet! Understand?"

Whether as a result of the commandant's threats or, perhaps, because of his hint concerning the "historic events in Europe" (Summer 1940) of which we were then completely ignorant, our spirits fell. The rebellion appeared to be quenched.

The *starosta* stepped forward and assured the commandant in a subservient voice that we would quiet down immediately; and that all we were asking was to keep the door to the corridor open for a few minutes, so that we might breathe more freely.

The commandant pretended that he would have none of it. According to regulations, he said, the door had to be kept shut. And the "rebels" would have to be punished.

After a while, however, he became more gentle.

"I know," he told us in an almost sympathetic voice, "that it is difficult for you here, but there is nothing I can do about it. Conditions are the same everywhere. I hope that a great many of you will shortly leave the prison. You will be sent to the polar bears. And there you will have air in sufficient quantities—more than enough, as a matter of fact. You will certainly also not be too warm."

A deadly calm fell upon the prisoners. Leaving the room and obviously pleased with his victory, the commandant whispered something to the guard, who left the door to the corridor open for a full quarter of an hour. No one was punished for the incident.

The Russian prisoners, Soviet people all, were amazed.

II

A small, soiled notice, *Regulations for Prisoners,* was pasted on cardboard and hung in one of the corners of our cell. Hardly anybody bothered to read this notice. I, however, read it through with great care, and I remember its contents exactly.

The majority of the rules concerned matters which the prisoners were forbidden to do, but there were also a few regulations setting forth the prisoners' rights.

According to regulations, every prisoner was entitled to his own cot or berth, to bedding, a stool to sit on, clean underwear every two weeks, soap for his bath, etc.

The prison rules were even concerned about the prisoners' morale. Once a week the inmates were to be allowed books from the prison library. The prison authorities were also to provide their charges with chess-sets, checkers, and dominoes.

We looked at these printed rules and only smiled sadly.

The *Regulations* also provided for prisoners to have opportunities to "place orders in the prison store." Whoever had money deposited with the prison administration was to be allowed to buy various articles whose total value was not to exceed 75 rubles a month. Purchases were to be done through the guards.

This privilege was purely theoretical. We were repeatedly told that the prison store was empty. In the year that I spent in various Soviet prisons I was only able to buy food twice. Once it was half a pound of blood sausage (sausage made of cereal and blood), the other time a quarter of a pound of liverwurst.

The prison store was, however, of great importance to the smokers in the cell, for from time to time they could there obtain a bit of *makhorka,* the cheapest kind of coarse tobacco, at official government prices.

But even *makhorka* could only be obtained very seldom and in extremely small quantities. At best 2 ounces monthly per person would be obtainable. And on most occasions only a small part of the prisoners, those chosen by the guards, would receive the tobacco. The chosen few were not necessarily smokers, and if not, did a brisk business with the stuff. For tobacco was also a marketable commodity in our cell, and a very expensive article at that.

Luckily, I myself do not smoke. Most of the men in our cell, however, did smoke, and some were even very heavy smokers. Such prisoners suffered from the lack of smoking tobacco nearly as much as from the lack of food, and their craving for nicotine caused them to exchange their wretched piece of bread for a cigarette.

The collective smoking of a single cigarette was quite a common occurrence. In such a case the partners watched one another to prevent too deep a draw by one of the co-smokers. One could also buy one or two draws in the "open market."

The heavy smokers would occupy the first places in the latrine queue every morning. If our cell was taken to the toilet before the others, they stood a chance of finding tiny butts on the muddy latrine floor, left there during the night by the guards. Upon entering the latrine these prisoners would scramble for the minute fragments, even fight over them. Back in the cell these filthy remnants were dried and made into new cigarettes, and sometimes a bit of dried grass which somebody was lucky enough to bring from the prison yard would be added to this kind of tobacco. Even well-bred people whose tastes had once been refined, and who had before been extreme in their cleanliness, did not hesitate to smoke such filth, considering themselves fortunate to be vouchsafed such a treat.

Another difficulty was to obtain a light. It frequently happened that after securing smoking tobacco there was no match. The guards themselves were often out of matches.

It would also happen that even after both tobacco and a match were available, paper to roll the cigarette could not be obtained. The guards were especially watchful not to let the tiniest scrap of paper fall into our hands. We learned later that this is a general rule in all Soviet prisons, designed to prevent the writing of illegal messages. The guards would throw the store tobacco into a cap or a handkerchief, retaining the original thick, brown paper wrapping of the *makhorka*. Questioned as to how we were to smoke without paper, the guards had nothing to say.

One morning I noticed that the visor of my cap was soft and cut open. It turned out that at night, while I was asleep, somebody had stolen the piece of cardboard that had kept the visor stiff. Other caps had been similarly dealt with, and smoked in "cigarettes."

These cigarettes made of filthy refuse rolled into cardboard served to contaminate even more the normally foul air in our cell. It was worst for the sick. But when somebody remonstrated with the smokers about it, they became irritated, and heated arguments ensued. Addiction to tobacco was stronger than human sentiment.

According to the rules, one of the privileges of the prisoners was a half-hour daily walk—the exercises. But the application of this rule was also greatly curtailed.

These *progulkas* took place very irregularly. At times we would be taken out for our walk three or four times a week, while sometimes long weeks passed virtually without exercise. And the duration of our walks was, in fact, not more than ten to fifteen minutes at a time.

The guards sometimes tried to dissuade us from taking our walk by telling us that it was raining, or that the latrines in the courtyard were just being cleaned. But they were never able to persuade us to give up our chance of stepping out into the air, even in the most violent downpour. Everybody ran, all wanted to be first out of the cell and last to return to it.

Sometimes we noticed that some cell inmate was not preparing to take his exercises. This was a sign that he was feeling so weak as to be unable to leave; or that he was suffering from extreme moral depression and dejection and no longer cared about anything. In such cases friends of the individual would carry him into the yard by force, so that he should not lose the opportunity of filling his lungs with fresh air.

The walks took place in the prison yard. For that purpose part of it was screened off with planks so as to prevent other prisoners who happened to be led through the courtyard from seeing the ones taking exercises, and vice versa.

The area thus marked off was very limited, so that we had to walk round and round in a small circle.

We had to walk alone—or sometimes in pairs—one behind the other, with lowered heads and our arms folded to the rear. We were not allowed to turn around, to talk to one another, to pick up anything from the ground, and so on.

The prisoners themselves watched one another for failure to comply with these regulations strictly, for if the guards noticed anyone breaking a rule, the entire group was immediately led back to the cell.

Despite all these restrictions every *progulka* was for us truly a time of joy. When the wind chanced to bring the smell of the woods or the fragrance of a river into the prison enclosure, we felt happy indeed.

One detail of our exercising stands out in my memory. In one of the prisons in which I was detained, part of the front turret could be seen from the exercise area. A red flag fluttered in the breeze over the turret. Painfully I used to think what was being done here in the name of Socialism.

III

To all the bitterness of our prison life, all the hardships we had to endure, another matter must be added: the utter uncertainty as to our future.

Were we to be treated as Russian prisoners were treated in the land of the Soviets, or would we, as citizens of a foreign country and as refugees, be freed, or be interned in the prisons or, perhaps, in special refugee camps for the duration of the war?

For many months we received no answer to these questions. It was only during the rebellion of the prisoners over fresh air that the commandant at last hinted to us that in the near future we would be taken "to the polar bears."

We immediately understood what he meant. His words de-

pressed us greatly. We knew that one could still hope to be
freed from prison, but that there was no way back from the
Soviet concentration camps in the Russian interior.

Zlatin, the warden's assistant, was present during the commandant's talk about the "polar bears." He noticed the impression these words made on the prisoners and he grew to like the
topic. He would come to our cell from time to time and take up
the theme again and again.

"Well, boys," he would say, "it's not far off now. Before long
you will become productive people again. You know what I
mean: hoo-hoo-hoo-hoo."

So saying he would imitate with his arms the pushing of
heavy wheelbarrows.

"Hoo-hoo-hoo-hoo," he always greeted us whenever he entered or was about to leave our cell. And he observed with great
curiosity the effect of his joke on the prisoners, the fear that appeared on all faces. "Hoo-hoo-hoo-hoo"—it hammered in our
minds.

Zlatin remains in my memory in connection with another
incident.

Once during a cell inspection I approached Zlatin. "According to the *Regulations for Prisoners*," I told him, "we are permitted to write once a month to our families. Many months
have passed and we have never been allowed to enjoy this
privilege. Please permit me to let my wife and child know that
I am alive."

The Russian prisoners smiled ironically, and Zlatin rebuked
me curtly and sharply.

"Quit your fooling," he told me earnestly; "forget your wife
and your child. After all, in a short time you will . . . hoo-hoo-
hoo-hoo. . . ." Here he burst out laughing. "If you ever live to
be free, you'll find yourself another wife in Russia, a Soviet
one . . . And you will have other children.

"And if your wife is young and good-looking," he continued
after a while, "she will also find herself another husband—if
she hasn't been clever enough to do it already. And you, boys,"

Zlatin addressed the entire cell, "better think about hoo-hoo-hoo-hoo than about foolishness."

This advice about "another wife" and "other children" we heard frequently from the prison officers, and every time it awoke in us the same bitter feelings.

The fear and anxiety concerning our own future was deepened by our complete ignorance as to events in the outside world.

We never saw a newspaper. We had no radio. Neither the guards nor the investigating officials ever as much as hinted about news from the outside.

Although we could not know what he had meant, the commandant's remark about "historic events in Europe" and "the world trembling at its foundations" persistently stuck in our memories.

The "politicians" in the cell ventured the wildest guesses in explanation of the commandant's words. We all lived in constant expectation of something that would open our eyes to the meaning of his remark.

One night we heard a commotion in the corridor, and we were astounded when the powerful electric bulb, which was normally lit day and night, was extinguished. For the first time in many months we remained in darkness. However, when several hours thus passed without anything further happening, we went back to sleep.

We were suddenly awakened from our uneasy sleep by the sound of numerous locomotive whistles at the railroad station and by the penetrating wailing of sirens. The noises resembled the anti-aircraft warnings which we had heard during the German bombing of Warsaw at the beginning of the war. And soon we could indeed hear the roaring of planes overhead.

All prisoners in the cell were instantly aroused.

A former Polish police officer from Vilna, Sadowski, whispered happily, "It is beginning. The Germans have started marching against the Russians, and we shall soon be free."

"No," Ritterman said softly, "Russia has a pact of friendship with the Germans, and has perhaps entered the war on their side. These must be French or British planes. The Allies will free us . . ."

It now began thundering all around us. We heard the thud of explosions as well as the heavy rumble of anti-aircraft artillery. Through the narrow cracks in the windows we could make out the beams of searchlights scanning the sky.

"Thanks for such 'liberation,' " said Kruk, the former chief prison warden. "Before being 'freed' we shall all be killed in the rubble and ruin of the prison. Don't forget, the prison is not more than a hundred paces from the railway station. We shall be burned alive, I tell you."

"*Nitchevo*," interrupted Petya Vodorin, an intelligent Soviet metal worker. He was a young and handsome lad who was well-liked by everybody in the cell. "It doesn't matter," he repeated. "Better to die from a bomb than to rot without end in the prisons!" For this boy life already had no great value.

But other prisoners started beating at the door. There was, however, no answer from the corridor.

"The guards have escaped and left us to our fate," somebody called out. "We are lost."

The roaring of the planes, the thuds of the bombardment, and the rattle of artillery lasted for more than an hour. Then everything became quiet.

Nobody in the cell, however, went back to sleep. We thought of many explanations, each more fantastic than the other.

Only the imprisoned Soviet lieutenant Sukhanov said that he thought the affair was due not to real bombs and anti-aircraft guns but military exercises.

And it turned out that he was right.

Russia's entry into the war was only to take place a year later.

In any case, we were all thoroughly convinced that our fate was closely tied to the fortunes of the war. After all, our very detention had been a result of the historic events in September, 1939, when Poland had become the first victim of the European war. We were therefore certain that our future likewise depended upon developments on the fighting fronts, and most of us were highly optimistic regarding a quick and decisive Allied victory which, in our estimation, would restore Poland's independence, free us from prison, and allow us to return to our homes.

We were therefore particularly anxious to learn the military news, to see how close we were to our liberation.

We questioned every new prisoner pushed into our cell with the utmost curiosity, inquiring searchingly about all he knew. For the most part, however, these people came to us not from the free world outside but from another cell, or, at best, from another prison—people who, like ourselves, had remained in complete isolation for many months and were as ignorant of war developments as we were.

Once a Byelorussian peasant was brought into our cell. When we learned that he had been arrested only a few weeks ago, we showered him with questions.

"What's new on the front lines?" one asked.

"How about Hitler?"

"Is Russia in the war, and on which side?"

The peasant was hardly able to get his wind. "Yes," he stammered, "they are all fighting. But I cannot make it out . . . I know nothing."

It was hard to tell whether he was afraid to talk and therefore pretended to be an imbecile, or whether he was really as simple as he seemed. In any case, our curiosity remained unsatisfied.

Day after day passed in this way, in constant tension and vain expectation. Deep in our hearts, because we wanted to believe them, we gave credit to the optimists among us who claimed that our rescue was close at hand.

And then, at long last, we did receive some news.

One morning, after we returned from the latrine, my friend

Ritterman approached me and a few others with a mysterious air.

"Boys," he told us, "we are going to have news."

"News? What news? When? How?"

Ritterman's bearing was reserved and conspiratorial. Finally, however, he consented to divulge his secret. He had found a small piece of Russian newspaper in the latrine, smaller than a postcard, which one of the guards had apparently used. He had managed to put the scrap of paper in his pocket unnoticed.

We were burning with curiosity, but we had to wait several hours for an opportune time when neither the guards nor our fellow prisoners were likely to observe our doings.

At long last the four of us, all trusted friends—Ritterman, Hofman, Singer, and myself—crawled under the berths to read our "newspaper." I smoothed it out with trembling hands.

We were filled with apprehension lest it prove to contain items of no interest—a short story, perhaps, or a non-topical column. But no, our luck was with us! We held in our hands a tiny section from the last page of the Moscow *Pravda*, the part where cabled foreign news was usually printed.

Excitedly we began scanning the foreign dispatches.

The first item concerned the inclusion into Russia of the Baltic States—Latvia, Lithuania, and Estonia. At that particular moment this was of lesser importance to us, and we skipped it.

Another item informed us that the *Russian* Army had taken Northern Bukovina and Bessarabia from Rumania.

The "Russian" Army? Not "Red" and not "Soviet"? What kind of sweeping changes had taken place in Soviet Russia?

Never mind this, however; this was not *the* important thing now. We quickly proceeded.

At last, a wire from Paris: "The German City Commander of Paris decreed . . ."

We could not believe our own eyes and started reading the notice once again: "The German City Commander of Paris . . ."

We were as if struck by lightning. Hitler victorious! The

world then was perishing! No longer was there likelihood of our liberation! Russia was in alliance with triumphant German fascism. Our fondest hopes were crushed.

We were hardly able to hold back our tears.

Rudolf Hilferding

STATE CAPITALISM OR TOTALITARIAN STATE ECONOMY

Editor's Note

WHAT is the economic system of
the Soviet state? That important question has been the subject
of considerable speculation on the part of economists throughout the world. That it is not capitalism, as routinely defined, is
evident. Neither, socialists contend, is it any form of democratic socialism, a form of government that doctrinally strives
for wider democratization of state and life, not less. In recent
years it has been increasingly popular to define the Soviet system as a form of state capitalism. In this celebrated essay,
Rudolf Hilferding, an internationally famous Marxian econ-
omist and one of the leading theoreticians of German Social
Democracy, tells why he differs with that depiction. He finds
the present Russian state to be a form of totalitarian state economy. This essay was originally written for the *Socialist Courier,*
an anti-Communist Russian-language magazine now published
in New York; it appeared in the May, 1940, issue. Parts of this
essay have been widely quoted in economic and other journals,
but this translation—which appeared in *Modern Review*—is,
to the best of my knowledge, the first complete English text.
Mr. Hilferding originally wrote this essay as a reply to the view
advanced by a British socialist, R. L. Worrall, in the London
Left, that the economic system of the Soviet Union is actually
state capitalism; the essay has since come to serve a more permanent purpose. Since the author was an important Marxist,

it may be idle to note that most readers will not be in complete agreement with his views; it will nevertheless repay them to give a close reading to the incisive comments contained in this economic statement regarding the Soviet system.

Rudolf Hilferding was born in Vienna in 1877. He joined the socialist movement as a student and became an active follower of Victor Adler, the founder of the Austrian Social Democratic Party. At the age of twenty-five he was already a noted contributor to Karl Kautsky's *Neue Zeit*—his chief writings were on Marxian economics. In 1906 he was called to Berlin to lecture at the party school, and for the next eight years was foreign editor of *Vorwarts*. In 1910 he published his major economic work, *Das Finanzkapital*, which Lenin utilized heavily in developing his theory of imperialism. When World War I broke out Hilferding was one of the Social Democratic deputies in the Reichstag who voted against war credits. In 1923 he served as Finance Minister under Stresemann, and again held the rank of minister in the cabinet of Hermann Muller in 1928-29. He was forced to relinquish the latter position as the result of pressure exerted by Reichsbank President Schacht. Hilferding wrote prolifically and also edited at different times *Die Gesellschaft* and *Freiheit*. In March, 1933, he escaped the Nazis by fleeing to Switzerland. Later he went to Paris and in 1941 was handed over to the Gestapo by Vichy. He was murdered in a Paris prison by Gestapo agents several days later.

#

State Capitalism or Totalitarian State Economy
by Rudolf Hilferding

THE concept of "state capitalism" can scarcely pass the test of serious economic analysis. Once the state becomes the exclusive owner of all means of production, the functioning of a capitalist economy is rendered impossible by destruction of the mechanism which keeps the life-blood of such a system circulating. A capitalist economy is a market economy. Prices, which result from competition among capitalist owners (it is this competition that "in the last instance" gives rise to the law of value), determine what and how much is produced, what fraction of the profit is accumulated, and in what particular branches of production this accumulation occurs. They also determine how in an economy, which has to overcome crises again and again, proportionate relations among the various branches of production are reestablished whether in the case of simple or expanded reproduction.

A capitalist economy is governed by the laws of the market (analyzed by Marx) and the autonomy of these laws constitutes the decisive symptom of the capitalist system of production. A state economy, however, eliminates precisely the autonomy of economic laws. It represents not a market but a consumers' economy. It is no longer price but rather a state planning commission that now determines what is produced and how. Formally, prices and wages still exist, but their function is no longer the same; they no longer determine the process of production which is now controlled by a central power that fixes prices and wages. Prices and wages become means of distribution which determine the share that the individual receives out of the sum total of products that the central power places at the disposal of society. They now constitute a technical form of distribution which is simpler than direct individual allotment of products which no longer can be classed as merchandise. Prices have become symbols of distribution and no longer comprise a regulating factor in the economy. While maintaining the form, a complete transformation of function has occurred.

Both the "stimulating fire of competition" and the passionate striving for profit, which provide the basic incentive of capitalist production, die out. Profit means individual appropriation of surplus products and is therefore possible only on the basis of private ownership. But, objects Mr. Worrall, did Marx not consider accumulation as an essential ear-mark of capitalism and does not accumulation play a decisive role in the Russian economy? Is that not state capitalism?

Mr. Worrall has overlooked one slight detail; namely, that Marx refers to the accumulation of *capital*, of an ever-increasing amount of the means of production which produce profit and the appropriation of which supplies the driving force to capitalist production. In other words, he refers to the accumulation of value which creates surplus value; i.e., a specifically *capitalist* process of expanding economic activity.

On the other hand, the accumulation of means of production and of products is so far from being a specific feature of capitalism that it plays a decisive part in all economic systems, except perhaps in the most primitive collecting of food. In a consumers' economy, in an economy organized by the state, there is not accumulation of values but of consumers' goods—products that the central power wants in order to satisfy consumers' need. The mere fact that the Russian state economy accumulates does not make it a capitalist economy, for it is not capital that is being accumulated. Mr. Worrall's argument is based on a gross confusion between value and use value. And he really believes that a socialist economy could do without accumulation!

But what then (and here we come to the basic question) is that central power that rules over the Russian economy? Trotsky and Worrall reply: "Bureaucracy." But while Trotsky refuses to consider the bureaucracy as a class (according to Marx a class is characterized by the place it occupies in the process of production), Worrall makes an amazing discovery. Soviet bureaucracy in its structure (which unfortunately he does not analyze) differs "basically" from any other bourgeoisie, but its function remains the same—the accumulation of capital. The fact that, despite great structural differences, the function can remain unchanged is, of course, a miracle that cannot occur in nature but seems (according to Worrall) possible in human society.

In any case, Worrall accepts this as evidence that Russia is dominated by a bourgeois class and thus by state capitalism. He clings obstinately to his confusion of capital and the means of production and seems unable to conceive of any form of accumulation other than capitalist accumulation. He fails to understand that accumulation (i.e. the expansion of production) in any economic system is the task of the managers of production; that even in an ideal socialist system this accumulation can result only from the surplus product (which only under capitalism takes the form of surplus value), and that the fact of accumulation in itself does not prove the capitalist nature of an economy.

But does the "bureaucracy" really "rule" the economy and consequently the people? Bureaucracy everywhere, and particularly in the Soviet Union, is composed of a conglomeration of the most varied elements. To it belong not only government officials in the narrow sense of the word (i.e. from minor employees up to the generals and even Stalin himself) but also the directors of all branches of industry and such functionaries as, for example, the postal and railway employees. How could this variegated lot possibly achieve a unified rule? Who are its representatives? How does it adopt decisions? What organs are at its disposal?

In reality, the "bureaucracy" is not an independent bearer of power. In accordance with its structure as well as function, it is only an instrument in the hands of the real rulers. It is organized as an hierarchy and subordinated to the commanding power. It receives but does not give orders. Any functionary, as Trotsky justly puts it, "can be sacrificed by his superior in the hierarchical system in order to decrease any kind of dissatisfaction." And these are the new masters of production, the substitute for capitalists! Stalin thoroughly exploded this myth when, during the last purges, he ordered shot, among others, thousands of industrial managers.

It is not the bureaucracy that rules, but he who gives orders to the bureaucracy. And it is Stalin who gives orders to the

Russian bureaucracy. Lenin and Trotsky with a select group of followers who were never able to come to independent decisions as a party but always remained an instrument in the hands of the leaders (the same was true later with the fascist and national-socialist parties) seized power at a time when the old state apparatus was collapsing. They changed the state apparatus to suit their needs as rulers, eliminating democracy and establishing their own dictatorship which in their ideology, but by no means in practice, was identified with the "dictatorship of the proletariat." Thus they created the first *totalitarian state* —even before the name was invented. Stalin carried on with the job, removing his rivals through the instrument of the state apparatus and establishing an unlimited personal dictatorship.

This is the reality which should not be obscured by construing alleged domination by a "bureaucracy" which is in fact subordinate to the government to the same extent as are the rest of the people. This is true even though some modest crumbs from the master's table may be doled out to it—without, of course, a guarantee that other crumbs are to follow and at the price of constant danger to their very lives. Their material share does not constitute any important portion of the social product. Nevertheless, the psychological effect of such a differentiation may be quite considerable.

Important economic consequences flow from this fact. It is the essence of a totalitarian state that it subjects the economy to its aims. The economy is deprived of its own laws, it becomes a controlled economy. Once this control is effected, it transforms the market economy into a consumers' economy. The character and extent of needs are then determined by the state. The German and Italian economies* provide evidence of the fact that such control, once initiated in a totalitarian state, spreads rapidly and tends to become all-embracing as was the case in Russia from the very beginning. Despite great differences in their points of departure, the economic system

---

* Writing in 1940, Hilferding is referring to the German Nazi and Italian Fascist economies at this point.—*Ed.*]

of totalitarian states are drawing close to each other. In Germany, too, the state, striving to maintain and strengthen its power, determines the character of production and accumulation. Prices lose their regulating function and become merely means of distribution. The economy, and with it the exponents of economic activity, are more or less subjected to the state, becoming its subordinates. The economy loses the primacy which it held under bourgeois society. This does not mean, however, that economic circles do not have great influence on the ruling power in Germany as well as in Russia. But their influence is conditional, has limits and is not decisive in relation to the essence of policy. Policy is actually determined by a small circle of those who are in power. It is their interests, their ideas as to what is required to maintain, exploit, and strengthen their own power that determines the policy which they impose as law upon the subordinated economy. This is why the subjective factor, the "unforeseeable," "irrational" character of political development has gained such importance in politics.

The faithful believe only in heaven and hell as determining forces; the Marxist sectarian only in capitalism and socialism, in classes—bourgeoisie and proletariat. The Marxist sectarian cannot grasp the idea that present-day state power, having achieved independence, is unfolding its enormous strength according to its own laws, subjecting social forces and compelling them to serve its ends for a short or long period of time.

Therefore neither the Russian nor the totalitarian system in general is determined by the character of the economy. On the contrary, it is the economy that is determined by the policy of the ruling power and subjected to the aims and purposes of this power. The totalitarian power lives by the economy, but not for the economy or even for the class ruling the economy— as is the case of the bourgeois state, though the latter (as any student of foreign policy can demonstrate) may occasionally pursue aims of its own. An analogy to the totalitarian state may be found in the era of the late Roman Empire, in the regime of the Praetorians and their emperors.

Of course, from a social democratic viewpoint the Bolshevik economy can hardly be called "socialist," for to us socialism is indissolubly linked to democracy. According to our concept, socialization of the means of production implies freeing the economy from the rule of one class and vesting it in society as a whole—a society which is democratically self-governed. We never imagined that the political form of that "managed economy" which was to replace capitalist production for a free market could be unrestricted absolutism. The correlation between the economic basis and the political structure seemed to us a very definite one: namely, that the socialist society would inaugurate the highest realization of democracy. Even those among us who believed that the strictest application of centralized power would be necessary or inevitable for the period of transition, considered this period only temporary and bound to end after the suppression of the propertied classes. Together with the disappearance of classes, class rule was also to vanish —that class rule which we considered the only possible form of political rule in general. "The state is withering away . . ."

But history, this "best of all Marxists," has taught us differently. It has taught us that "administering of things," despite Engels' expectations, may turn into unlimited "administering of people," and thus not only lead to the emancipation of the state from the economy but even to the subjection of the economy to the state.

Once subjected to the state, the economy secures the continued existence of this form of government. The fact that such a result flows from a unique situation primarily brought about by war does not exclude a Marxist analysis, but it alters somewhat our rather simplified and schematic conception of the correlation between economy and state and between economy and politics which developed in a completely different period. The emergence of the state as an independent power greatly complicates the economic characterization of a society in which politics (i.e. the state) plays a determining and decisive role.

For this reason the controversy as to whether the economic system of the Soviet Union is "capitalist" or "socialist" seems to me rather pointless. It is neither. It represents a *totalitarian state economy*, i.e., a system to which the economies of [Nazi] Germany and [Fascist] Italy are drawing closer and closer.

Solomon M. Schwarz

TRADE UNIONS IN SOVIET RUSSIA

Editor's Note

IN NO country where totalitarianism has triumphed have trade unions remained free. One might well take the existence of free trade unions (along with other free institutions, education, religion, legislative systems) as a test of the freedom of any given state. It is significant, as this selection makes abundantly clear, that the Soviet Union cannot withstand such a test. The "new democracy," it might be said, seems to consist only of the loss of all the old freedoms. In view of the fact that Communists abroad always represent themselves as the staunchest fighters for free trade unions, the facts about trade unions in Soviet Russia become especially embarrassing. The present selection heightens that embarrassment by its calm, rigorous marshaling of the facts. The writer is a widely respected authority on Russian economic and political history. He has long specialized, among other subjects, in the area of Russian trade unions and labor.

Solomon M. Schwarz was born in Russia in 1883. He has been active in the Russian socialist and labor movements since the 1905 Revolution, and has studied at various universities both in Russia and Germany. Since being expelled from the USSR in 1922, he has published an important series of books on the Soviet Union in four languages and numerous articles in many academic and political journals on economic questions. In the United States, where he has lived since 1940, he is perhaps best known for his co-authorship of the standard work, *Management in Soviet Russian Industry and Agriculture.* He has been associated with the International Labor Office, the International Institute for Social History (Amsterdam), the Hoover Library on War, Peace, and Revolution, and the New School for Social Research. He recently completed a major work on Russian trade unions and labor that was many years in preparation, and is currently at work on an extended study of Russian nationalities policy. This selection originally appeared in 1948 in the *International Free Trade Union News,* a publication of the Free Trade Union Committee of the American Federation of Labor.

Trade Unions in Soviet Russia by Solomon M. Schwarz

IN THE Soviet Union a much larger number of workers, both manual and white-collar, are organized in trade unions than in any other country, although official union membership figures have not been published for a long time. *Trud,* official Soviet trade union organ, reported on February 19, 1947, however, that 84 per cent of all manual and white-collar workers employed in industry, transport, building trades and agriculture are members of trade unions. It can be assumed that the percentage of unionized workers in other occupations is not much lower. Since the total number of manual and white-collar workers in the Soviet Union passed the 30,000,000 mark in 1946 and continues slowly to increase, the total membership of Soviet trade unions at the present time can be estimated as between 25,000,000 and 26,000,000—a figure greater than the combined union membership of the United States and Great Britain, the two countries with the strongest trade union movements.

In view of this seemingly tremendous growth of the Soviet trade union movement, it is particularly noteworthy that trade unions do not play a conspicuous role as an independent force in the economic, political and social life of the nation. This fact cannot be denied by anyone who has studied the course of the Soviet Union with attention.

I

The role of the Soviet trade unions is strictly auxiliary. According to the basic principle of Communist trade union policies—which has, in effect, become a law in the Soviet Union —the trade unions are a "transmission belt" designed to connect the Communist Party with the mass of the workers, and to give the dictatorship of the Communist Party over the country and the working class the appearance of a "dictatorship of the proletariat." The concrete tasks assigned to the unions may change from time to time, but the fundamental concept of the "transmission belt" remains unchangeable.

In his *Problems of Leninism,* Stalin expressed this idea in the following manner:

> . . . *The Party realizes the dictatorship of the proletariat. It does so, however, not directly, but with the help of the trade unions, and through the Soviets and their ramifications. Without these "belts," anything like a firm dictatorship would be impossible. . . .*

Here in the Soviet Union, in the land of the dictatorship of the proletariat, the fact that not a single important political or organizational question is decided by our Soviet and other mass organizations without directions from the Party must be regarded as the highest expression of the leading role of the Party. *In this sense,* it could be said that the dictatorship of the proletariat is *in essence* the "dictatorship" of its vanguard, the "dictatorship of its Party, as the main guiding force of the proletariat." (J. Stalin, *Problems of Leninism,* New York, 1934, pp. 33-34.)

In order that the Soviet trade unions may fulfill this task, their complete domination by the Communist Party is indispensable. During the early years after the October Revolution, the Communist Party frequently used the method of direct intervention by the police in order to establish its control. Communist Party domination in a number of unions, including the national printers' union as well as several of its local unions, the Moscow union of chemical workers, many unions of white-collar workers and other unions, could be established only by the direct help of the political police—the Cheka. By 1922 the process of subjecting the unions to Communist control had been completed everywhere. Since that time, Communist domination of the unions has been guaranteed by "normal" methods and a certain outward semblance of elections has been maintained.

The technique of Soviet trade union elections was extremely simple for many years. Communist Party control was guaranteed by the strict observance of the "open vote" principle. If an open and organized opposition against the Communist Party had been possible in Russia—and within its unions—even the open vote would not have always assured the victory of the Communist Party, in spite of all the pressure brought to bear upon the people. This was shown by the experience of the early years of the Revolution. However, combined with the ruthless suppression of any kind of opposition, open elections, in effect, very soon became a compulsory vote for the only existing and officially sponsored candidate or list of candidates—a farce which discredited the very idea of elections.

For a long time, the open vote remained an official article of faith. The secret vote was characterized as a counter-revolutionary concept which, in a "classless society," could be defended only by "enemies of the working class," "enemies of socialism" and "enemies" pure and simple. However, the official concept was abandoned in the middle 1930's.

II

The middle 1930's were a period of vacillation in the leading circles of the Communist Party. At the beginning of 1935, these vacillations resulted in the unexpected decision to democratize the Soviet Constitution and, particularly, to introduce universal, equal and direct suffrage and the secret ballot. This had been conceived as a step towards a certain relaxation of the dictatorial regime. However, the vacillations which had caused that measure soon came to an end, and the leadership of the Communist Party decided that the dictatorial regime should not be weakened but, on the contrary, intensified to the utmost.

Still, it was impossible to go back on the democratic suffrage —and, in particular, the secret ballot—which had been solemnly promised and unanimously approved by a Soviet Congress. The Soviet legal experts, therefore, had to solve the problem of how to retain formally the secret ballot while reducing its practical importance to zero. These experts found an ingenious solution by devising a complicated method of nominating candidates which had no precedent anywhere and enabled the Communist Party to maintain its boundless domination, in spite of the introduction of the secret ballot. The trade unions eagerly adopted this election system and eventually perfected it.

Since 1937, voting in union elections has been secret. However, in the preliminary meetings, at which candidates are nominated, all present have the right to raise objections against any candidate—even without giving any specific reason. In that case, the question as to whether the person against whom objections have been raised should remain on the list of candidates is decided by open vote. Under the conditions prevailing in the Soviet Union, this is obviously sufficient to insure absolute Communist control of the election procedure. In addition, the Communist Party leadership has devised a number of supplemental election rules in order to be able to cope with any possible "accident" that might occur.

Both the old system of open elections and the present system of pseudo-secret elections were based upon the assumption—which, obviously, has never been publicly voiced—that in a really free election the workers would probably vote not for the Communist or Communist-sponsored candidates but for those whose conception of the interests of the worker differs from that of the Communists. The Communist Party thus not only silently admits the distrust of the majority of the workers; it also reveals its awareness that the Soviet workers, if permitted to act freely, would demand that their trade unions pursue objectives quite different from those which are now imposed upon them by the Communist Party. Given the necessary freedom, the workers might adopt new trade union policies and even attempt, contrary to the wishes of the Communist Party, to influence the general policies of the nation.

It is noteworthy that such apprehensions were widespread among leading Communists even in the 1930's when Soviet trade unions, according to the Communist theory prevailing at that time, had a conception of their tasks which was basically similar to that of trade unions in all other countries. At that time, Communist theory likewise recognized that one of the fundamental tasks of the Soviet trade unions is to defend the interests of the manual and white-collar workers in their relations with those who hire and employ them. Obviously, the defense of the interests of the Soviet manual and white-collar workers in their relations with management was approached in a manner different from that which prevails in capitalist countries.

Since a gigantic portion of Soviet economy is state property and the state is considered a "workers' state"—this was constantly harped on by official theoreticians during the first decade of the Soviet regime—the trade unions were given the task of increasing production and furthering the development of the national economy as a whole. In practice, the latter task frequently—and, as years went on, in an ever-increasing measure—superseded that of defending the workers' interests. However, at that time the Soviet trade unions tried, in principle, to fulfill, at least outwardly, the usual tasks which are assumed by unions in other countries. In 1922 Lenin gave a clear definition of that conception of the role of trade unions in the Soviet state. He said: "A certain antagonism of interests between the mass of the workers and the managers of state enterprises or agencies" is "inevitable" in regard to "working conditions in the factories owned by these enterprises or agencies." He concluded: "As far as socialized enterprises are concerned, trade unions have, consequently, the unquestionable duty to defend the interests of the workers and to further, as far as that is possible, the improvement of their living standards."

Actually, even during the 1920's, the trade unions practically subordinated the defense of the interests of their members in large measure to the interests of production; the right to strike, while not formally abolished, was in fact very early removed from the trade union arsenal, and the trade union leadership sharply condemned the very idea of striking. However, in comparison with the trade union situation as it developed during the 1930's, the first decade of the existence of Soviet trade unions may appear in retrospect as a period during which the trade unions experienced a certain upsurge in vitality, even though this phase was peculiar and only relative.

III

In 1929 this conception—which at that time became known by the semi-polemical designation of "the defense theory of the trade union movement"—was sharply condemned by the Central Committee of the Communist Party as "opportunistic" and "trade unionistic," and the entire trade union machinery, from top to bottom, was subjected to a drastic purge which was carried out under the supervision of the party's Central Control Commission.

The broad stratum of Communist trade union officers which had grown up during the first decade of the Revolution was completely expelled from the unions at the behest of the Central Committee of the Communist Party. Michael Tomsky, the most widely recognized leader of Soviet trade unions and eminent even outside Russia, was banished forever from trade union work in the summer of 1929. Not later than December, 1928, Tomsky had been unanimously elected a member of the Central Council of Trade Unions at the Ninth National Convention, and had been unanimously named by the Central Council as its chairman.

After the elimination of Tomsky, the leading posts in the Soviet trade unions were filled throughout with new incumbents, mostly former Communist Party secretaries, the majority of whom lacked any important trade union experience. Among them was Nikolai Shvernik who, from that time on, served for more than a decade as the figurehead of the Soviet trade unions.

The unions were ordered to adopt a new attitude strictly oriented towards "production." Their activities were totally subordinated to the aim of increasing the productivity of labor; according to the new theory, this was eventually to result in an automatic increase in the living standards of manual and white-collar workers.

In order to carry out these new trade union policies, Communist Party control of the unions was intensified to the degree of completion. These measures resulted in a rapid decline of the Soviet trade union movement. Although the decline has not affected union membership figures and union organization continues to comprise almost all Soviet wage-earners, the internal life of the unions has come to a virtual standstill. The unions have become a mere apparatus; even conventions are no longer held. From 1918 to 1928 there were eight nation-wide union conventions. After the turn in union policy in 1929 one

convention was held—the Ninth Trade Union Convention in
1932. In the more than fifteen years since that time no convention has taken place*—an open violation of the constitution
of the unions. For years the Central Council of Trade Unions
has been headed by officers who were never elected by a convention—likewise in open violation of the constitution of the
unions.

During the early years after the 1929 turn in policy, the
trade unions, through sheer inertia, preserved some "trade
unionist" characteristics, such as the conclusion of collective
agreements and participation in the supervision of the hiring
of manual and white-collar workers. However, these characteristics began to wither away very rapidly. As early as the beginning of the 1930's the official Employment Offices, in whose
organization the unions had played a prominent role, were
abolished. The hiring of workers became an exclusive preroga-
tive of management. Soon the role of the unions in the determination of wages was equally reduced to zero and the right
to decide on wage problems was handed over to the managers.
At the meeting of the Central Council of Trade Unions in the
summer of 1933, the trade union leaders gave the following explanation of this evolution:

> No one other than economic officials can be primarily
> responsible for the wage scales, fixing of production
> quotas, piece-rates, etc. Today the idea is rooted in the
> consciousness of some comrades in the factories that the
> trade union has to have equal say with the economic
> agency in fixing wages. This is a "leftist" and opportun-

* [The Tenth Congress, the first since 1932, finally met in Spring, 1949.
Wage-hour questions were virtually ignored; stress was placed on the need for
increased productivity. *Pravda* summarized the work of the Congress: "Soviet
trade unions have been, are, and shall be faithful and active executants of the
policy of the Bolshevik Party." (Cf. Solomon Schwarz in *The New Leader*,
September 10, 1949.)—*Ed.*]

istic deviation, an attempt to destroy the one-man leadership and to interfere with administration. This must
be ended. (*Trud*, July 8, 1933.)

As a result, the practice of collective bargaining was rapidly
and completely abandoned. In the Soviet Union collective
agreements were usually negotiated for one year, with the negotiations taking place at the end of the calendar year. At the
end of 1933 the Central Committee of the Communist Party
issued an order that new collective agreements were not to be
negotiated and that the existing contracts were to be extended
for another year. At the end of 1934 even that formality was
omitted; only in a few fields, such as commerce, water transport, lumber cutting and lumber rafting, were collective agreements concluded by special order of the government. At the
end of 1935 even these contracts had expired and collective
agreements simply disappeared in the Soviet Union.

In the spring of 1947 collective agreements were reintro-
duced in the Soviet Union. Actually, however, only the outward appearance of collective bargaining has been restored.
The collective agreements of 1947 differ in their essentials from
collective agreements in other countries, and even from those
negotiated in the Soviet Union before 1933. A survey of recent
developments in the Soviet trade union movement will serve
to explain this.

IV

In the middle 1930's the decline of the Soviet trade unions
was so pronounced that the Communist leadership began to
fear that the "transmission belt" might be wearing out. During the last weeks of 1935 the Soviet press began to speak
openly of a "crisis in the trade union movement." In the spring
of 1937 a plenary meeting of the Central Council of Trade
Unions was convened after a lapse of almost two and one-half
years. At that meeting, Nikolai Shvernik, first secretary of the

Central Council (today he is chairman of the Presidium of the Supreme Soviet or, so to speak, President of the U.S.S.R.), spoke sharply on the difficult situation of the trade unions.

As a means of revitalizing the unions, this plenary meeting decided to re-establish the elective character of trade union organs, to reintroduce collective bargaining and to convoke the Tenth Trade Union Convention for October 20, 1937. However, these decisions were soon forgotten, nothing was changed and the decline of the Soviet trade union movement continued. At the same time, the machinery of the Communist Party was greatly expanded and the Communist Party began to intervene on an increasing scale in all internal relations in industrial enterprises and in all problems of the organization of production; as a result, even in this field the trade unions were pushed into the background. The "transmission belt" was wearing out and, in addition, was no longer needed in the same measure as before.

The war brought an immediate change in the situation. After the U.S.S.R. entered the war, a great number of problems relating to the living conditions of the workers, such as housing, food and care of soldiers' families, disabled veterans and children of working mothers, became extremely urgent. It should be noted that in the Soviet Union there has long existed a tendency to seek a solution for such problems within the framework of the enterprise—the place of employment—as a means of strengthening the ties between the workers and the enterprise. Even before the war the unions had had considerable experience along such lines. When the U.S.S.R. became engaged in actual hostilities, the unions were directed to extend their activities to all these fields. The result was to revitalize the unions and, simultaneously, to confirm their role as a "transmission belt."

During the war, other new factors made their appearance which also contributed to interest the Communist Party in the revitalization of the unions. In most countries of continental Europe the trade union movement was almost destroyed during the war. For all practical purposes the International Federation of Trade Unions—the I.F.T.U.—went out of existence. After the war, the trade union movement had to be reconstructed, and in many countries the post-war situation created favorable conditions for a growth of Communist influence in the unions. The Soviet trade unions actively participated in the creation of the new World Federation of Trade Unions —the W.F.T.U. As a result, the Communist Party of the Soviet Union has obtained increased opportunities for influencing the labor movement outside Russia. Thus, international perspectives opened up for using the Soviet unions as a "transmission belt."

It is this situation which serves to explain why the Soviet trade unions resumed the practice of collective agreements. Outside the Soviet Union those whom the Communists want to influence have never been able to understand how the Russian unions could possibly function without collective agreements. The pro-Soviet press either carefully concealed the absence of collective agreements or told its readers how widespread such agreements were in the Soviet Union, what tremendous influence Russian trade unions exerted in determining wage scales, and similar fictions. When closer relations were established between Soviet and non-Russian trade unions, it became increasingly difficult to maintain this legend.

The return to collective agreements eliminates these difficulties. However, that was not the only reason—perhaps not even the principal one—for the restoration of collective agreements in the Soviet Union. During the war the Soviet workers readily accepted privation in order to save their country from a terrible menace. They also acquiesced in the severe discipline which was established in the factories. After the war there is, on the contrary, much less readiness for continued acceptance of such conditions. Accordingly, camouflage with the help of trade unions has again become essential—and collective agreements are a particularly good form of protective coloration.

It is scarcely necessary to explain at this point that collective agreements everywhere originate as instruments for the defense of the interests of the workers as a whole. Agreements between the individual worker and employer—which, in most cases, practically mean that the worker is forced to submit to the terms unilaterally fixed at the will of the employer—were superseded by agreements on the working conditions and, especially, on wages which the trade union negotiates with an employer or group of employers in order to obtain definite guarantees for the workers. Under the "defense theory of the trade union movement" this was also, in principle, the practice of collective bargaining in the Soviet Union.

But the collective agreements which are now negotiated in the Soviet Union have completely different aims. The purpose of a collective agreement—as the Soviet press insists on repeating—is "to guarantee that the production plan of the government is fulfilled and surpassed." Everything is subordinated to that aim. Collective agreements do not even deal with the question of wage scales but concentrate upon increases in the productivity of labor. A rise of the wage level is envisaged solely as an eventual "consequence" of such increased productivity. However, even such wage increases are not at all sure. Simultaneously with the conclusion of collective agreements a vigorous campaign has been organized in order to increase the norms of output—that is, to reduce the pay for piece-work. These norms are to be based on the output of the so-called "progressive" workers, the Stakhanovites. The intention is to achieve an increase in the productivity of labor under conditions which subject the wage level to intense pressure. Since such wage policies are bound to provoke dissatisfaction among the workers, it would be difficult to cope with the situation without the "transmission belt." Moreover, the "transmission belt" must also be constantly supervised. As *Pravda* of March 14, 1947, put it:

> The trade unions enter a new period of their activities, and in this important period, the Party organizations

must give them the necessary help, incessantly watch
the preparations for the conclusion of collective agreements and strengthen the entire organizing and educational work of the unions. . . . In this respect, the directing and leading role of the Party organizations is
particularly important.

Kirill Alexeiev

THE REAL ENEMIES OF THE RUSSIAN PEOPLE

DR. STOCKMANN: *They have called me an enemy of the people; so an enemy of the people, let me be!*
MRS. STOCKMANN: *You will never be that, Thomas.*
DR. STOCKMANN: *Don't swear to that, Katherine. To be called an ugly name may have the same effect as a pin-scratch in the lung. And that hateful name—I can't get quit of it. It is sticking here in the pit of my stomach, eating into me like a corrosive acid. . . .*

IBSEN, An Enemy of the People

Editor's Note

To FLEE from the country one loves is not an easy thing to do. To know that it may never be possible to return, to know that all one can anticipate is vilification, the need for hiding, the constant threat of physical injury to oneself and one's family, especially if one's family is being held hostage—these are almost unbearable considerations. Yet, and precisely for these reasons, there have been those, advanced in the Soviet scale, who have fled from the Russian state when the rare opportunity appeared. They need to be understood, these men and women. One of the heartening by-products of the Soviet tyranny has been the emergence of those who have chosen, in full knowledge of what it meant, to stand alone. As Dr. Stockmann in Ibsen's play finally learned: "It is this, let me tell you—that the strongest man in the world is he who stands most alone." Those, of this kind, who fled the Soviets did not *prefer* the haunting life their flight made inevitable; they did not rejoice to stand aside, to renounce the

468

privileges and rewards their favored positions might have earned from the regime. It is interesting, indeed, to note that many who sought sanctuary elsewhere were men highly placed in the Soviet system. If they had been less well thought of, the possibility for escape would never have appeared. In a universal dictum, the Communist rulers have labeled them "enemies of the people." There is undoubtedly a psychological insight to be gained from the self-conscious vigor with which this epithet springs to the tongues of the Soviet rulers.

Among the Soviet officials who have fled have been: Alexander Barmine, former Soviet general; Victor Kravchenko, Soviet purchasing official; Feodor F. Raskolnikov, ex-Soviet Minister to Bulgaria and an "Old Bolshevik," who "died" mysteriously; Walter Krivitsky, former Chief of Soviet Military Intelligence in Western Europe, who "committed suicide" in Washington; Ignace Reiss, Soviet intelligence agent, machine-gunned in Switzerland; Igor Gouzenko, Soviet secret cipher clerk in Canada. All of them, and others, have been identified as "enemies of the people." That these men chose not only to seek freedom, some with tragic ends, but that they also dedicated themselves to telling the truth about the dictatorship in their native country, with all the risks the choice involved, is something that must cause the members of the Politburo considerable consternation. We can only be grateful for their courage in helping to illuminate a "dark" subject. These men, to my mind, are to be greeted with all the admiration justly earned by those who fled Germany to tell us what the Nazi ascension to power meant for Germany and for the world. Were not those early German refugees also greeted by a large public with derision? The Russians who fled are not enemies of the Russian people; those of them who have access to the conscience of the Western world are among its few hopes. One thinks of the hopeless woman in a Soviet camp and what she said to Jerzy Gliksman when she learned that, as a Polish citizen, he might be released. Gliksman asked if there were anything he could do for her, anyone he could appeal to in her behalf. " 'You can do one thing for us, and one thing only,' were her last words to me. 'Should you really succeed in getting abroad—and I most sincerely hope that you will—tell all you know about us. . . . Tell the West. . . .'"

One man in the Soviet employ who managed to "tell the West" was Kirill Alexeiev, former commercial attache of the USSR in Mexico, and an engineer by profession. His story here is a simple one, little more than what he experienced and witnessed in the Soviet Union, what he had been told about the United States and what he learned for himself. It is a brief, plainly told tale and for that reason it is doubly impressive. It tells us who really are "the enemies of the Russian people." It is a representation of a story, the major facts of which might be told by millions of Russians if the opportunity were presented to them. The text of Mr. Alexeiev's public statement is reprinted as it appeared in *The New Leader* in 1947.

\#

The Real Enemies of the Russian People by Kirill Alexeiev

IN APRIL of 1944, I was assigned by the Soviet Government to a job in Mexico, and until September of 1946 worked as Commercial Attache at the Soviet Embassy.

I graduated from the Moscow Mining Academy, and continued as "assistant" at the Academy for the prescribed period. After that I designed and constructed one of the most important war industry plants in the Soviet Union, and later worked as chief engineer in large munition factories. Finally, I was chief engineer of a Trust uniting a group of the most important plants of the aviation industry.

Living now in the United States with my wife and two children, I consider it my duty to state publicly that I am opposed to the Soviet regime, and explain the reasons of my antagonism. Life abroad has opened to me the true meaning of what I saw in the Soviet Union.

The Soviet Government's domestic policy is based on the principle of complete isolation of the Russian people from the democratic nations, especially the USA. The government persistently tries to inculcate the spirit of animosity toward everything foreign. On the other hand, Soviet agents abroad conduct a fervent propaganda in favor of the Soviet system, and disseminate false information about flourishing conditions of life in the land in which "Socialism" has been achieved; thus they try to win the sympathy of the democratic nations, essential to the Soviet regime.

During my sojourn abroad, I have realized the monstrosity of the lies spread in the Soviet Union about "the beastly exploitation of workers in the capitalist countries." Such stories are told the Russian people for the purpose of arousing their indignation against the democratic regime of the USA.

All my life I have loyally worked for the Russian people, whom I love and to whom my attachment is very deep. But it has become clear to me that my work, like that of the whole Russian people, is beneficial to the Soviet regime, and not to themselves.

No nation is more exploited, or rather enslaved, than the Soviet nation. According to Soviet propaganda, workers' strikes are brutally suppressed in the US, while in the Soviet Union nothing of this kind can happen. In reality, the American worker strikes to protest against the existing conditions and to obtain higher wages. But he is not faced with the gruesome problem of saving his children from starvation, a problem that has haunted the Soviet worker since the inception of the Soviet regime. It is true that strikes hardly ever occur in the USSR, but the reason is that the least protest entails cruel suppression by the NKVD.

In spite of this, workers driven to despair sometimes, though very rarely, risk a strike. Before the war, I witnessed a strike at the Krasnourelski copper smelting plant, in which workers stayed away from work, exhausted by the "Stakhanovite" sweating methods. For a whole month they had received no bread (their staple food, since nothing else could be obtained), and, with wages miserly as they were, could not afford to buy bread on the market. But the plant did not stop work. Prisoners were promptly brought from concentration camps, and the strikers were taught a brutal lesson by the NKVD. This example of "Free socialist labor," of course, has never come to the knowledge of foreign workers; I had to refrain from talking about it even with my closest friends.

Millions of guiltless men and women have been put into concentration camps, and provide the state with unpaid manpower, working under conditions unheard of even in the history of the most despotic regimes. I happened to see these prisoners work before and during the war.

And a friend of mine, a mining engineer, who worked in Norilok, a place in the Arctic North, spoke of them with tears in his eyes. Among them the daily toll of death from overstrain and hunger went into the hundreds. When an accident occurred in the mines, the rescue of workers was prohibited so that they were buried alive, no care was taken of the sick, and the least attempt to protest was suppressed by execution and loosing of bloodhounds. This is how Stalin builds his land of "Socialism" where, to quote his words, "labor is a matter of honor, of valor and heroism."

Of my very close friends, honest and efficient men, many perished guiltlessly. One of them, P. A. Abroskin, arrested in 1938, has disappeared since; his wife and 7-year-old daughter also vanished, leaving no trace. The world-renowned professor of metallurgy, V. A. Pazukhin, who had spent his life in honest work, died in the prime of life, in 1941, in a concentration camp. Others, millions of them, including prominent experts, whose names I cannot disclose, are now perishing in camps.

But the NKVD—Stalin's right arm (his left arm is the Communist Party)—holds sway not only over jails and concentration camps, but also over all Russian workers and intellectuals. Actually, the entire Soviet Union is a concentration camp where the fate of everyone depends on the perfidy of the NKVD.

During my work at the Stepniak gold mines, I saw the toiling Russian people in Kazakstan driven to desperation. I saw ruined families whose guiltless fathers had been sent to camps, and wives and children were doomed to perdition. I saw corpses of men who had died in deserted mines, and dead bodies of children abandoned by their desperate mothers who had not the heart to see them die slowly from starvation. As a student, I drank and spoke with a fellow student, Kutsenko, a former resident of the Ukraine, the bread basket of Russia, who went through all the horrors of collectivization and avoided starvation only by feeding on dead human bodies. This man was now obliged to extol the Soviet system.

In 1941, before the war broke out, I was in the Ukrainian town Norozovsk. I visited an engineer, Kremenchugski, who worked in a mechanical plant. He presented to me his 5-year-old son who did not know what sugar was.

All these things happened at the time when the Communists exulted in the victory of "Socialism," deceiving the foreign workers and the whole world, and carefully concealing the horrid truth.

NKVD in homes, NKVD in factories, kolkhozes, sovkhozes, NKVD like an ill-boding ghost shadow, everybody, everywhere. The elemental human urge to live and keep the family alive compels the Soviet people to resign themselves to this constant horror, and even to work for the NKVD.

It was hardly of his own free will that Prof. S. P. Alexandrov (known in America), a prominent expert in metallurgy and former director of the Institute of Non-Ferrous Metals, accepted in 1936 the job of chief engineer of the GULAG (Department of Concentration Camps). Alexandrov has been set free, and is now in the Soviet diplomatic service. I also knew A. Gromyko, at that time one of the numerous teachers of "political literacy."

Even men belonging to the closest entourage of the dictator do not feel safe. They are the arbiters of the fate of millions of the Russian people, but they know that their own destiny is at the mercy of the supreme ruler.

This is why the great majority of the Russian people hate the Soviet regime. And this is why it is hated also by the great majority of Communists, even by men closest to the government.

And this is the reason why I cannot return to my homeland and doom my family, which has become accustomed to breathe the fresh air of freedom, to a life under the hell of dictatorship. But I feel sure that in this country they will become free human beings, and I firmly believe that my family and I will be given an opportunity to start a new life here.

Peter Meyer

THE SOVIET UNION: A NEW CLASS SOCIETY

Editor's Note

THE author of this selection has won a reputation for scholarship on the Russian question by his many impressively informed articles on the subject in various American publications in recent years, and in European periodicals during the 1930s. He is compelled to write under the pen name of Peter Meyer for reasons familiar to many Europeans in these days of widespread Russian "liberation" of many lands. This brilliant factual treatment and summation of the disparity between Soviet myth and reality in the economic field —abundantly documented as it is—speaks articulately for itself.

The subject of whether Russia is a "socialist" state is of far more than academic importance. In non-Communist Europe, in as yet unconquered Europe, it is Russia's prime propaganda weapon in the "cold war." The idyllic Communist picture is that of an equalitarian society, no privileges for anyone, high wages and unrivaled living conditions for Russian workers, and so on. A last line of defense for hard pressed pro-Communists is to admit that the Soviet state is a political dictatorship but at the same time to insist chimerically that it is an "economic democracy." This essay, with its therapeutic familiarity with Russian source materials, ought to come as an "eye opener" for such persons, that is, if their pro-Communism is based on lack of information and knowledge and if they retain sufficient integrity to recognize fact as fact.

It is not surprising that "The Soviet Union: A New Class Society," which appeared in the March and April, 1944, issues of *Politics,* should have been widely quoted since its publication; it is prominently cited in Arthur Koestler's famed discussion of the Soviet system in his *The Yogi and the Commissar.*

Readers interested in an even more detailed discussion of the real Soviet economic record will find much startling material in Manya Gordon's consummately documented and comprehensive *Workers Before and After Lenin* (1941), and in the additional sources indicated by Mr. Meyer and Manya Gordon.

#

The Soviet Union: A New Class Society by Peter Meyer

AT LEAST one claim of Stalinist propaganda is thoroughly justified: no one can understand contemporary history, let alone intervene effectively in it, without clarity as to the nature of present-day Soviet society. Enlightenment will not come—to sincere socialists or liberals, at any rate—from the rate of the Red Army's advance or retreat, nor from whether Stalin and Molotov happen to be dividing up the world with Hitler and Ribbentrop at the moment, or with Churchill and Roosevelt. It will come only through an attempt to answer such questions as whether Russia is now a land of freedom or slavery, whether social equality or inequality predominate there, whether it is a progressive or a reactionary country. Or—if we want to be more modest—whether Russia is evolving, through its inner laws of development, toward freedom or toward slavery, equality or exploitation, harmony or contradictions.

To answer such questions, we must know what social classes compose the Russian population today, what are their relations to each other and to the system of production, and by whom and in whose interests are society and the State managed?

There is no shortage of answers. The official Communist thesis insists that socialism, the lower phase of communism, has already been realized in Russia, and, furthermore, that the Soviet Union is a society that is at once classless and ruled by the working class. The orthodox Trotskyists counter that Russia is a Workers' State in spite of the fact that the workers do not rule there but are, on the contrary, grievously exploited. In many circles, totalitarianism, dictatorship, Bonapartism are talked of—but these much misused terms do not explain the economic and social structure of a society. Others fall back on the term "State capitalism," but usually fail to indicate to what extent "State capitalism" is still capitalism and in what sense the rulers of Russia can be considered capitalists. Others talk of a "transition period," but the question is precisely: transition towards what—socialism, capitalism or some *tertium quid?*

Most of the above theories are variants of the two fundamental theories, which regard Russia as in essence (1) socialist, or (2) capitalist. Let us begin by considering these.

The first thing that strikes one is that most of the arguments on both sides are negative. Those who hold that Russia is basically socialist or moving in that direction, point out that the capitalists have been expropriated, that there is no bourgeoisie, that private ownership of the means of production has been eliminated, that goods are no longer produced for private profit, and that the laws of free exchange and therewith the Marxist laws of value and surplus value no longer dominate the economy. There is no more capitalism, *therefore* Russia is "essentially" socialist; the bourgeoisie have been liquidated, *therefore* it is a Workers' State. It has precious little resemblance to our own conception of socialism, the Trotskyists will admit, and so it is a "degenerated" Workers' State—but nonetheless a Workers' State.

Those who regard Russia as capitalist point out the great social inequalities, the class contradictions, the lack of that democracy and freedom without which socialism is inconceivable, the failure of the repressive apparatus to wither away (putting it mildly). This indeed is not socialism, *therefore*—it is capitalism. And since it has precious little resemblance to our —and Marx's—conception of capitalism, it is, to be exact, State capitalism, of a new and degenerate variety it is true, but nonetheless "essentially" capitalism.

If one assumes *a priori* that all possible social systems today must be *either* capitalist *or* socialist, then the above "therefores" are valid and one of the two sides is right. The assumption is, however, unwarranted, and the actual state of affairs in Russia would refute it if nothing else did.

Human thought is conservative and always tries to trim new facts to fit old patterns. There is something to be said for this procedure on the score of economy of effort, but only if the old categories fit the data. Brushes, as Engels once observed, are hair-bearing creatures but they will never acquire mammary glands through being subsumed under the genus, mammalia. The dogma of the excluded third gets us into a dilemma when applied to Russia, forcing us to term "socialist" a society which is an insult to every conception of socialism, or to postulate a kind of capitalism without capitalists, market relations, private property or private profit. Only if this dogma is abandoned, do avenues of really fruitful investigation open up. It begins to appear then that both sides are right in their negative propositions, and that both are wrong when from these they make a break-neck leap, with their ominous "therefores," to their conclusions. Perhaps there is neither capitalism nor socialism in Russia, but a third thing, something that is quite new in history.

The point of departure for our investigation will be conditions as they are. The question of how they came to be what they are must be left for a separate study. Most of the data used will be from the period previous to Russia's entry into the war, for two reasons: (1) the dim-out which for many years has veiled information about Soviet Russia has become a blackout since Russia has become an ally of this country; (2) this procedure obviates the objection that the conditions described are merely the temporary, abnormal effects of war.

The "Socialized" and the Private Sectors

To begin with, all the decisive means of production are in the hands of the State. This is completely true of the urban and industrialized sector. The 54,600,000 workers and the 29,700,-000 "employees" (including dependents) shown by the 1939 Soviet census, amounting to almost 50 per cent of the total population, are in their overwhelming majority employees of the State or of institutions controlled by it.*

The case is somewhat different for the peasants. Families included, there are 75,600,000 members of collective farms (almost 45% of the total population) and 3,000,000 individual farmers (not quite 2% of the total population). By the end of the Second Five Year Plan, there were 2,500,000 collective farms, embracing 94% of the farms and practically all (99.6%) of the land. This land is the property of the State and cannot be disposed of, having been given to the collective farms for their "eternal use" since 1935. The State prescribes to these farms exactly what they are to produce and what they are to deliver at what prices, and also closely regulates their internal structure.** Some two-thirds of agricultural production is used by agriculture itself for productive and consumption purposes. Of the third that goes to the city, the State acquires 85% by means of various forms of forced delivery and so-called "decentralized buying." The remaining 15% of this third, or some

---

* The so-called consumers' cooperatives belong among these. All they have in common with real co-ops is their name. They are actually mere State distributing organizations.

** It [the State] has in its hands such levers as wages, prices, taxes, budget and credit. The completely disproportionate income of a series of central Asiatic cotton collectives depends much more upon the correlation of prices established by the government than upon the work of the members of the collectives."—Leon Trotsky, *The Revolution Betrayed*, p. 133.

5% of the total raw products in kind, is placed on the "free collective-farm market." [1] To be sure, the monetary share taken by the free market is much greater, since prices are a good deal higher there, and the 15% which Soviet statistics (1938) estimate as its share is probably too low. Nevertheless, the exchange of goods between city and country is handled predominantly by the State.

There are also two sectors within the collective farm itself: its collective economy and the small private economy of the individual member, to whom the law of 1935 granted the following private property: a house, one to two and a half acres of ground, one cow, two calves, one sow with its litter, ten goats or sheep, and an unlimited number of fowl and rabbits. The collective farms sell 15% of the total products placed on the collective-farm market, their members sell 45% of them out of their wages in kind, 30% out of their individual shares, and the individual farmers sell 10%.

One can sum up by saying that the means of production in the city belong almost altogether to the State; that agricultural production, in spite of the existence of a not insignificant private sector within the collective farm and the survival of some individual farmers, is largely collectivized; and that the State directly controls all exchange of goods with foreign countries and inside the city, and most of the exchange between city and country.

All this has to be placed in evidence because some critics consider the concessions made to the peasants after the great wave of collectivization in the early Thirties, to be a return to the New Economic Policy (NEP) and to the general supremacy of market relations. But there can really be no question of that. The concessions of 1935 (eternal use of the land by the collective farms, the sanctioning within them of the dwarf economies of their individual members, and the open collective-farm market) went in the same *direction* as the retreat of 1921, but for a *much shorter distance* and from *far more ad-*

* [References will be found at the end of this selection.—*Ed.*]

vanced positions. There were 20,000,000 independent peasants during the classic NEP; Russia was an overwhelmingly agrarian country; industry was ruined and weak; market relationships dominated the exchange between city and country; private commerce was allowed to act as an intermediary; capitalists could compete with the State to a limited extent even in industry. Under the present "Neo-NEP" the peasants are organized in collective farms, which are much more effectively under the State's control; Russia is industrialized; there are no private agencies of exchange; exchange between city and country is regulated predominantly by the relationships of a planned economy—which is why a repetition of the "grain strike" of 1928 is impossible during the present war.

During the NEP it was still an open question whether the "private" or the "socialized" sector would win. Today the struggle has been decided in favor of the State. We have yet to see whether that has anything to do with the victory of socialism.

Standards of Living of the People

Let us next investigate the standard of living of the broad masses of the urban population. This is no easy task. "No statistics of any kind are issued dealing with prices, currency, housing, cost of living and a number of other phenomena, which are indispensable to a true evaluation of any economic system." [2] The Soviet Union is the only civilized state in the world that has not for years published a standard-of-living index. In 1930 the Gosplan and the Statistical Bureaus were purged, and it was announced that statistics were a "weapon in the fight for Communism." This weapon is used to keep the population's standard of living a secret.

We possess data indeed as to the average money wages (all wages from those of day laborers to those of the highest directors lumped together) and they show an impressive advance: from 37.5 rubles in 1924/25 to 94 in 1931, 130 in 1933, 188 in

1935,[3] 245 in 1937,[4] and 289 in 1938.[5] The last estimates of
the pre-war period again and again mention 300 rubles as the
average gross monthly wage.

But we are interested in *real* wages. *Planovoie Khoziaistvo*
in 1938 gave some facts as to how much food an average family of St. Petersburg textile workers consumed per week in 1908
under the Czar. Using this as a basis, we find that wages and
living costs have run the following course under Stalin:[6]

	1913		1929	1937
Cost of 1 week's food	3.40	(rubles)	5.90	49.60
Index of food prices	100		172	1449
Average monthly wages ...	25	(rubles)	66	245
Index of real wages	100		154	68

The figures speak for themselves. In 1929 the average standard of living of the Russian wage-earner was 54% higher than it
had been before the Revolution. By 1937, it was 32% *lower,*
and less than half the 1929 level.*

Manya Gordon estimates that the price of food consumed by
workers' families was eighteen times as great in 1937 as in 1913.
In her richly documented *Workers Before and After Lenin*
(p. 159), she compares 1937 food prices not with the *average*
but with the *minimal* wages of the *worst paid* workers (10
rubles in 1914, 105 in 1937 after the deduction of taxes) and
comes to the conclusion that the workers' standard of living
had sunk by more than a third since the Czar's time.

Since all these figures can only be approximate, because of
the lack of all official indices of living, it may be well to cite
still another source. In 1939 and 1940 the American Embassy
ascertained the prices in Moscow retail stores.[7] Their correctness was never disputed by Soviet authorities; single details
were repeated by the Soviet press in scattered items. Using the

---

* The 1929 level was somewhat lower than estimated here, since only food
is taken into account. In 1929 food was cheap, clothing and other manufactured
products expensive.

Embassy's price scale, and taking the typical consumption of a worker's family as reported by a Russian publication in 1926, we can construct the following indices:[8]

	1913	1928	1940
Index of Prices	100	187	2248
Index of Money Wages	100	233	1383
Index of Real Wages	100	125	62.4

These estimates are given for the capital city, whose population receives favored treatment in every respect. They do not take into account, furthermore, the much higher prices on the "free market," where the worker often has to buy when he cannot get necessities at the State stores.

Poverty and Luxury

If all this is correct, one may say, then a state of real hunger must exist in Russia. The conclusion is correct: it does exist.

The terrible effects of this hunger are suggested by Soviet census statistics. The census of December, 1926, reported a population of 147,000,000. In 1930, an official government estimate put the population at 157,500,000. On January 1, 1934, Molotov reported a figure of 168,000,000. Stalin himself declared, on October 1, 1935, that the normal yearly increase was three millions, which was about that of the NEP period. At this rate, the census of January 6, 1937, should have shown 177,000,000 inhabitants. No one knows what it did show, for the results were never published, and the directors of the statistical bureau were liquidated as Trotskyist saboteurs. A new census was undertaken in January, 1939, by new and "dependable" personnel. By this time, at Stalin's rate of three million increase a year, there should have been at least 183,000,000 inhabitants. But the official figures show only 170,500,000 souls. Twelve and a half millions had simply disappeared. Many factors may be involved in this cruel deficit: a fall in the birth rate due to want, an increase in infant mortality, above all the terrible famine of 1932 when at least four million peasants died of starvation because of the brutal tempo and the ruthless methods with which Stalin pushed through the forced-collectivization program. Another factor may have been the great purges of 1937-1938, where the death roll may have run into the hundreds of thousands. Of one thing at least we may be certain: scientific birth control was not involved, since this had become an illegal privilege strictly limited to the upper ranks of the bureaucracy after the prohibition of abortions in 1936.

There is no space here to go into detail about the subhuman living standards of the great Russian masses. Those interested will find copious documentation in the works of Hubbard, Yvon, Ciliga, Serge, Manya Gordon, Trotsky and others. "Life is better and happier now," said Stalin in 1936. The question is: whose life?

The French worker, Yvon, who lived in Russia for almost fifteen years and wrote one of the best books about the Soviet Union, gives us the answer, as of 1936:

"The restaurants are open again, and the Soviet press is filled with advertisements, for the benefit of those with plenty of cash, such as have not been seen since the times of the *ancien regime*. These ads give the addresses and phone numbers of de luxe night clubs, praise the quality of their jazz, and invite the customers to spend gay nights there. Dancing, champagne, the rarest liquors. Other ads offer fancy perfumes for the ladies at 200 rubles a tiny bottle (*Izvestia*, Feb. 4, 1936) and dolls for children at 95 rubles each (*Izvestia*, Feb. 2, 1936) . . . One enterprising restaurant—the workers' fatherland must 'catch up with and overtake' capitalism!—offers to organize banquets, official or private, for which it will deliver everything, including the servants. A simple phone call—and the lackeys of the State will serve you up a dinner in your own apartment at 200-300 rubles a plate." [9]

We have the word of more than one enthusiastic Friend of the Soviet Union that these gala banquets have continued even throughout the grim years of the war.

"There are special villas for high specialists, technicians, writers and scholars," continues Yvon. "New apartments have not only the most luxurious appointments, but also special servants' rooms—of 6 square meters, as against the 12 to 24 meters allotted for the master's quarters. (*Izvestia,* March 9, 1936.)" [10]

Perhaps the most revealing fact of all, however, is that between 1932 and 1936 the production of luxury goods increased much faster than the production of cheap consumer's goods. Production of perfumes increased 270%, of phonographs 450%, of cameras 1750%, of silk goods 2220%; while cotton fabrics went up only 44% in the same period.[11] The sales tax on necessities, also, is much higher than on luxuries: 100% on cotton goods, 300% on bread, and only 50% on silk.[12]

Wages and Salaries

The silence of official Soviet statistics becomes positively death-like when we come to the delicate question of wage differentials. "So far as I know," writes Hubbard in *Soviet Labor and Industry* (p. 170), "the Soviet Government has never allowed the publication of figures giving the total number of relative proportions of workers in different wage groups." And the same author writes in his *Soviet Trade and Distribution* (p. 369): "The wage tables give no hint at all regarding the differences between the remuneration of different sorts of labor. From occasional references in newspapers and publications it is clear that the difference between the highest and lowest industrial wages is exceedingly large."

Just how large? According to Yvon, a housemaid in Moscow received toward the end of 1937 fifty to sixty rubles a month plus free board and lodging; the monthly wages of workers were between 110 and 400 rubles, usually 150 to 250 rubles; minor officials received 110 to 300 rubles, usually between 130 and 225 rubles; middling officials and technicians between 300 and 1000 rubles a month; the "responsible ones" from 1500 to 10,000 rubles, but often as much as 20,000 and 30,000 rubles monthly.[13]

Other sources confirm this picture. Only a single illustration will be given of the distribution of the wage-earners in the various wage categories. Of 1535 employees in a Donetz Basin mine in 1935, sixty made 1,000 to 2,500 rubles monthly, seventy-five between 800 and 1,000 rubles, four hundred 500 to 800 rubles, and the remaining one thousand averaged 125 rubles each per month.[14]

It was no exaggeration at all when Leon Sedov observed: "There is hardly an advanced capitalist country where the difference in workers' wages is as great as at present in the USSR . . . One could show without difficulty that the wages of the privileged layers of the working class are 20 times higher, sometimes even more, than the wages of the poorly paid layers . . . Ostrogliadov, the head engineer of a pit, gets 8600 rubles a month; and he is a modest specialist, whose wages cannot, therefore, be considered exceptional. Thus, engineers often earn from 80 to 100 times as much as an unskilled worker." [15]

Nor did Trotsky exaggerate in any respect when he wrote: "In scope of inequality in the payment of labor, the Soviet Union has not only caught up to, but far surpasses the capitalist countries." [16] In 1936 *The New Republic* estimated that the salaries of the highest directors of the Chile Copper Company bore a ration of 41 to 1 to the average wage of its workers. In the Curtis publishing house the ratio was 51 to 1. Our Ostrogliadov is not left behind, for his salary of 8600 rubles is almost 48 times as high as the average Russian wage in 1935. According to *The New Republic*, Mr. H. F. Sinclair of Consolidated Oil in 1935 received 82 times as much as the average wage in his company. Yet salaries are paid in the Soviet Union which are 100 times higher than the average wage and 300 times higher than the minimal wage.

It might be rejoined that the directors of capitalist concerns receive other income than their fixed salaries. This is quite true; but it is also true of Soviet directors. Since the Decree of April

19, 1936, a directors' fund has existed in every Soviet concern, into which 4% of the earnings provided for by the Plan is paid and 50% of the earnings in excess of the Plan. Since prices are fixed from above, "earnings in excess of the Plan" can only be attained at the expense of the workers. Let us give a typical example of how this directors' fund is distributed. In 1936 a factory in Kharkov distributed 60,000 rubles from its directors' fund in the following manner: 22,000 rubles to the director, 10,000 rubles to the Party secretary, 8,000 rubles to the head of the production office, 6,000 to the head of the clerical staff, 4,000 to the chairman of the union, 5,000 to a section superintendent, and 5,000 rubles to all the others put together.[17]

But there are many other ways in which incomes differ. Very much to the point is the following from Yvon's book: "The position of the new masters is incomparably superior to that of the other strata of the population. They receive ten to twenty times as much income as the workers.[18] They get the best apartments and the right to larger dwelling space; furnishings are often free; watering places and first-class beaches are at their disposal . . . They travel in 'soft' or 'international' trains (the Soviet terms for first-class and parlor cars); official business is a frequent pretext for free tickets. And then they have first call on 'secret funds,' the use of which is permitted to help important people out of difficulties. In case of sickness, they receive the best care in first-class hospitals, naturally at no expense to themselves . . . Cars and chauffeurs or carriages and drivers are free and replaceable, since they are attached to the job and not to the job-holder, who has a larger and larger use of them. The opportunities for personal savings are very few, but savings are no longer necessary where one's job is a better guarantee of a high standard of living than a bank account." [19]

In the collective farms too there are very different levels of payment for work. Wages are paid by so-called "working days," which are not real working days but fictive unities. The full working day of a helper is worth half a "working day," that of a tractor-driver five "working days." Even more "working days" can be earned in a single day by exceeding the fixed quotas of production. Laborers are paid only for days actually spent at work, while every day is an official working day for managers and secretaries. Thus, in 1929 only 25% of the collective-farm members earned more than 300 "working days" for the whole year; the average was 150 "working days." The value of a "working day" varies within limits of 1 to 3 in products and of as much as 1 to 10 in money.[20]

Material changes usually reflect themselves in ideology, and the history of Russian opinion as to equality of income—and equality in general—is a beautiful example of that. In *State and Revolution,* Lenin considered the chief guarantee of the proletarian character of the State power would be the fact that no public official could receive higher pay than a qualified worker. Soon after the Revolution, higher salaries were granted bourgeois specialists so that their knowledge could be used to raise production and train proletarian specialists willing to work out of idealism. But the so-called Party maximum continued to apply to Party members; even though occupying the highest positions they could not draw higher pay. The privileged stratum then in process of birth supplemented its income by "journalistic activity" royalties, various kinds of bonuses, and payments in kind such as official dwellings, official autos, etc., etc. That its ideology was already changing then can be seen by the general cry of rage that went up when the unfortunate Zinoviev wrote an article in 1925 in which he sought the "philosophy of the age" in the idea of equality. At that time the unions could still uphold the idea of equalization of income as a far perspective. Inequality already attained great proportions by the time of the first Five-Year Plan, expressing itself not so much in money incomes as in special stores and restaurants for the upper ten thousand where everything which the rest of the population lacked could be obtained. In the June of 1931 Stalin made his famous speech against *"uravnilovka"* or equality of pay. Every effort towards equality of income since then has been a "petty-bourgeois deviation." After the rise of the Stakhanov movement and the lifting of rationing the differences became unrestrainedly expressed in money incomes as well. With the results seen above.

"It would be probably necessary to conclude," wrote Trotsky, who still continued to regard Russia as a Workers' State, "that 15%, or say, 20% of the population enjoy not much less of the wealth than is enjoyed by the remaining 80 to 85%." [21]

We can sum up by saying that the differences of income in Russia are quantitatively in no way inferior to those in capitalist countries. They can no more be explained by differences in amount of work performed, skill, and so forth than can the differences between bourgeois and proletariat. They have long ago reached a stage where the poverty of the broad masses stands sharply contrasted to the luxury of the upper ten thousand. They go hand in hand with differences in rank and prestige; and they increase instead of diminishing. Nor are they felt as an evil by reigning official opinion, but are glorified by it. Equalization is not only not the official policy, but its very propagation is forbidden and viewed as a deviation, that is, as a crime against the State.

Those Who Dispose and Those Who Are Disposed Of

The *Small Soviet Encyclopedia*, 1939 edition, defines the concept "class" by quoting Lenin: "Classes are great groups of persons who are differentiated by their positions in the historically determined system of social production, by their relations to the means of production, by their roles in the social organization of work, and consequently by the manner and extent of their participation in social wealth. Classes are human groups of such a kind that some can appropriate to themselves the fruits of others' labor, thanks to their different positions in the social economy." The encyclopedia comments that the first two (position in the system of production and relation to the means of production) of the three characteristics mentioned are primary and that the third characteristic (difference of income) is their result. [22]

The above definition is fairly generally accepted among Marxists, and it has been quoted from an official Soviet source only for the sake of piquancy. Taking it as his point of departure, Trotsky in 1936 wrote in an article on the Soviet Constitution that although there was a tremendous difference between the incomes of a charwoman and a Soviet marshal, their relations to the means of production were essentially the same. And in spite of the fact that Trotsky himself made several tentatives towards a correction of this theory, he never explicitly revised it.[23]

At first glance the observer schooled in Marxism will certainly be struck by the thought that differences of income so great, so systematic and so much on the increase as those in the Soviet Union could not come about without differences in the roles played by their recipients in the processes of production —there must be fire behind so much smoke. Besides, it is also known that differences in social ascendency between the privileged and the disinherited in Russia preceded differences in consumption. To make it appear as though the differences in consumption arose first and began only subsequently to infiltrate the spheres of production is downright misleading. But let us examine the facts themselves. What positions do the individual strata of Russian society occupy in the processes of production? How do their relations to the means of production differ?

Every Russian worker has to have a work book. During his entire time of employment it is kept by the management. No one, since 1938, is allowed to accept employment without a work book or employ a worker without one. All "work offenses" and punishments, especially disciplinary dismissals, are entered in this book.[24] One day's absence from work without an excuse or a lateness of more than 20 minutes was until 1940 legal ground for dismissal.[25] As long as rationing prevailed, dismissal brought with it the loss of one's ration card, and later on even the forfeiture of the right to dwelling space. But those happy days are no more. Since 1940 no Soviet worker can leave his job without special permission from his manager, which may be given only when the worker submits a medical certificate pronouncing him unfit for work and when no other work can be found for him in the establishment.[26] Anyone leaving his job without permission is given two months in jail. The punishment for temporary absence or lateness (20 minutes are enough) is forced labor up to six months, performed, if possible, at the same establishment, but under guard and at a reduction of 25% in wages. All disciplinary cases, according to this same law, must be decided within five days, and by a single judge without the usual government counsel. Judges who show leniency in such cases[27] and managers who do not bring offenders to court[28] are threatened with heavy penalties.

These measures apply "to all state, cooperative and public establishments" and all their employees. They were later extended to the motor-tractor stations,[29] craftsmen's associations,[30] and other establishments. In the Fall of 1940 the Soviet press published a flood of letters from women of the more privileged circles, asking that the same measures be extended to housemaids, about whose "laziness" and "negligence" they complained in a tone which in civilized capitalist countries has survived only in comic sheets.

According to another decree,[31] all individual work contracts of employees have been cancelled. Employees can be assigned to any establishment in no matter what part of the USSR.

From 800,000 to 1,000,000 young boys are conscripted annually for labor service. After a training lasting from six months to two years they are obliged to work four years wherever they are sent.[32] They cannot leave their places after the four years are up without official permission as long as the obligatory labor service law remains in effect.

The same law introduced a work week of six days of eight hours each, replacing the former five-day week of seven hours each.[33] The working day for young people over sixteen was raised from six to eight hours; a later decree made them liable to over-time and night work. A special law reduced the number of holidays to five a year;[34] another one forbade the shortening of work on Saturday.[35] At the same time that working hours were lengthened it was expressly directed that monthly wages remain the same; all hour, piece-work and job rates were revised in such a way that they gave no greater monthly return to the worker than under the shorter working hours.

Most of the work in industry is done as piece work. Work quotas or norms are fixed by the management. Bonuses are granted for additional work; deductions are made for failure to fill the quotas, which are often revised upward without consulting the workers[36]—of whom 22 to 32% are unable to fulfill the norms.[37]

The foremen are responsible for the workers placed under them. They have the right to hire and fire, to assign work, to threaten disciplinary measures, and to distribute rewards according to their own judgment. But they are responsible to their superiors in matters of work discipline.[38]

The workers can exert no influence on their rates of pay and conditions of work. "The wage scale must be left entirely in the hands of the heads of industry. They must establish the norm." [39] The so-called trade unions work in the same direction. "Their primary purpose is to direct the fight for the completion and over-fulfilment by every worker of his prescribed norm of work." [40] "The proper determination of wages and the regulation of labor demand that the industrial heads and the technical directors be immediately charged with responsibility in this matter. This is also dictated by the necessity of establishing a single authority and ensuring economy in the management of enterprises . . . [The workers] must not defend themselves against their government. That is absolutely wrong. That is supplanting the administrative organs. That is Left opportunistic perversion, the annihilation of individual authority and interference in the administrative department." [41] "In 1932 the central committee of the machinists' union called to the attention of the government the fact that in several machine works

higher wages were being paid than the budget called for. The
union took steps to turn the matter over to the government prosecutor for bringing criminal charges against the factory directors." [42]

The Soviet Bill of Rights

Let us take a look at one more aspect: the legal protection of
property from the workers and the collective-farm peasants.
Theft of the "collective property" of the state or of a collective
farm is punishable by ten years' imprisonment or death.[43] Children over twelve come under this law; according to a special
decree, the penalties for theft and wrecking, among other
crimes are to be applied to them in the same way as to adults
and by the same courts.[44] Yvon cites examples from Soviet newspapers of how two peasants were sentenced to ten years' imprisonment for stealing four kilograms of grain from their collective farm, and how other collective-farm members were even
condemned to death, in accordance with this law, for the illegal
use of a horse and a rowboat belonging to their collective
farm.[46] In both cases the sentences were mitigated by higher
courts. But how many have not been?

This is the kind of freedom the Russian worker enjoys while
at work, but he has just as little freedom of movement in other
respects. Since 1932 every Soviet citizen must have a domestic pass.[46] He cannot leave his place of residence for more than
twenty-four hours without having his pass inspected by the
police. One cannot live in a big city or within a radius of 50
to 100 kilometers of it without special permission. Its forfeiture
means Siberia.[47] Travel abroad is practically forbidden—except
to bureaucrats on official missions. Aside from them, almost no
other Soviet citizens have been encountered outside Russia
in the last fifteen years. To ask for permission to travel abroad
is equivalent to accusing one's self of high treason. Illegal attempts to go abroad on the part of a civilian are punishable by
ten years in jail or by death, on the part of one liable to military
service by death alone. The adult members of one's family are

imprisoned for five to ten years if they knew of the trip, and are deported to Siberia for five years if they did *not* know of it.[48]

I do not think it necessary to mention political rights and freedom here. There are absolutely none—except the liberty to assent enthusiastically to official policy and praise Stalin. Any expression, even the mildest, of opposition, or of doubt too, is punished, very often by death. Simply to remain silent during an official panegyric is perilous; to abstain from voting in connection with an official resolution of praise is considered a crime against the State. There is a universal obligation to inform against others, even one's closest relatives. Failure to denounce a "state criminal" is complicity and is severely punished.

Those refusing to recognize these generally known facts have only to instance one example—just a single solitary one!—within the last ten years of any one in the Soviet Union who criticized its regime—Stalin, that means—whether by word or by writing, whether mildly or severely, without being punished as soon as the authorities learned of it. And let him remember that on August 21, 1939, one hundred and eighty million Soviet subjects were unanimously and enthusiastically in favor of collective security, the Popular Front, and a democratic war against Germany, and that two days later they were just as unanimously and enthusiastically for the Hitler-Stalin pact and against the English and French imperialist war. One hundred and eighty million people, and not a single voice was raised in opposition or even in doubt at such an abrupt about-face; unanimous enthusiasm for the new turn, without a single small exception—that must have been a miracle compared to which those in the Bible were nothing but juggler's tricks—or else it must be that there is not a single iota of political freedom in the USSR.

But this lack of political liberty is, as we have seen, only another aspect of the enslavement involved in the processes of production, and it leads us back to the question of classes.

Main and Intermediate Classes

There are two main classes in Soviet society. The "place in production" and the "relation to the means of production" of one class consists in its absolute lack of individual or collective power over the means of production. It has no voice as to what is to be produced, and how and where; how production is to be organized, its products distributed, and their prices fixed.* Its members cannot participate in the determination of their conditions of work and their pay. They must work, obey, and live in poverty. Far from being masters of the means of production, they are their appendages in a far more literal sense than are their fellows in the bourgeois democracies. Their incomes are confined to the most essential and elementary articles of subsistence, and often amount to less than that, even though they support the whole of society by their labor. They are the exploited.

There is another class of people, who control the means of production. They decide what is to be produced, and how and where; what prices, wages, bonuses, and rewards are to be paid, and how social products are to be distributed. Their power of command over the means and processes of production and their power to dispose of its products is unlimited from below, but subordinated to every higher authority in their own class. Under this collective, hierarchical organization they control

* "It is self-evident that the workers themselves have no voice in the decision how accumulated capital shall be invested, this has from the very first been a function only of the Government." (Hubbard, *Soviet Trade*, pp. 321-322) "In actual fact the *kolchozniki* have little voice in the organization of their own farm. Not only are the main activities of the farm, the crops to be planted, the livestock to be raised, the technical method to be employed, laid down by the Plan, but the scale of remuneration and the form in which the remuneration is paid is governed by law . . . Once allotted to brigade the *kolchoznik* has to obey the orders of his *zvenovod*, who is under the brigadier, who is responsible directly to the president." (Hubbard, *The Economics of Soviet Agriculture*, pp. 165-166) "The president of a *kolchoz* is usually a Party functionary and not a farmer, and in fact, very few presidents are local men, or men of local origin . . . Professional presidents . . . to-day rule most of the 240,000 *kolchozy*." (Ibid. p. 162)

the means of production monopolistically—i.e. to the exclusion of all other, non-privileged strata of society. They thereby decide as to the distribution of the national income and arrogate the lion's share to themselves. They are the exploiters.

We know now why the marshals, the Party secretaries, and the "Red executives" "live better and more happily": they belong to the class that controls the means of production. The servants and workers live in poverty because they belong to a class that has absolutely no power over the means of production. The differences in "the sphere of consumption" are the results of differences of position in the processes of production. Political power belongs to the same class to which economic power belongs: both are only the different sides of a single fundamental social relation, that of exploitation and oppression.

The relations between the two classes are those of commanding and obeying, of exploiting and being exploited. To that degree they resemble those of all other class societies, including the capitalist.** The differences begin further on. The capitalists control the means of production by right of private property; the Russian ruling class by right of social administration. Each of the bourgeoisie—at least under classical capitalism—controls "his" means of production individually; the Russian ruling class commands the means of production collectively, through a hierarchical organization. In a capitalist society the worker can choose which capitalist to sell his labor power to—but he has to sell it to one or another, otherwise he cannot live. In Russia the labor power of all workers belongs, to start

---

** "The basic classes of a given society are two in number: on the one hand, the class which commands, monopolizing the instruments of production; on the other hand, the executing class, with no means of production, which works for the former. The specific form of this relation of economic exploitation and servitude determines the forms of the given class society. For example: if the relation between the commanding and the executing class is reproduced by the purchase of labor power in the market, we have capitalism. If it is reproduced by purchase of persons, by plunder or otherwise, but not by the purchase of labor power alone, and if the commanding class gains control of not only the labor power but also of the body and soul of the exploited person, we have a slaveholding system." (Nikolai Bukharin, *Historical Materialism*, English edition, New York, 1926, p. 282.)

with, to the collectivity of the exploiters. Under the capitalist system the worker sells his labor power temporarily and on the social average is paid its value, while the capitalist appropriates its surplus value: the line between value and surplus value being determined on the free labor market by automatically effective economic laws. In the Soviet Union labor power belongs to the state without being purchased by it: the line between the worker's share and the surplus product is not determined by laws of value. It is pressed down from above by the exploitative appetites of the bureaucracy, which are practically unlimited, and is kept up from below—very unevenly—by the danger of the working class's extinction.*

It will be objected perhaps that we have simplified the picture. There are not just ruling bureaucrats and workers. Certainly we have simplified; it was a question first of all of the *fundamental* and *new relationships* which are typical of this society.

After one hundred and fifty years of existence, no capitalist society can be found anywhere that consists just of capitalists and proletariat. Besides these fundamental classes there are intermediate classes peculiar to capitalism and large remnants of pre-capitalist classes.

There are similar phenomena in the Soviet Union. The independent peasants and craftsmen belong pre-eminently to the remnants of pre-Soviet classes. They are close to the type of "simple producers of goods" in capitalist society, but their control of their means of production and of their products is much more limited.** Their number is relatively small and their role in the whole of the processes of production insignificant. The collective-farm peasants, who form the overwhelm-

---

* It is self-evident that in any class society the oppressed classes must be nourished somehow and be able to reproduce itself; and that the ruling class receives the surplus product above the subsistence level. The specific method, however, by which the surplus product is appropriated differentiates the various class societies.

** The "simple producer" of goods is, in Marxist terms, a producer who owns his instruments of production, works for the open market, and hires no one else's labor.

ing majority of the agricultural population, are a mixed type. In so far as they work for "wages" in the "socialized" sector of the collective farm and have to deliver their products to the state, they belong to the "proletariat" of Soviet society and their situation is analogous to that of the industrial worker; in so far as they work their individual parcels of land and sell their products on the open collective-farm market, they are "simple producers of goods." They can be termed partly "Soviet proletariat" and partly simple producers of goods.

In addition there are middle strata which belong organically to Soviet society and play approximately the same social role within it as do the petty bourgeoisie and the "new middle class" in capitalist society. These are the workers' aristocracy (Stakhanovtsi) and the middling technicians and officials. They receive larger incomes than the workers but much smaller ones than the high bureaucrats. They function as pushers and speed-up men in the processes of production, as social props of the bureaucracy and as a reservoir from which the ruling class renews itself.

The Closing of Class Frontiers

The favorite rejoinder of Stalinists and their willing and unwilling friends to the theory of class rule in the Soviet Union is to point out that there are "unlimited opportunities to advance oneself" there. The American fable is that "every boy can become president," and by the same logic every Soviet soldier carries a marshal's baton in his knapsack.

There is a certain amount of truth in this, or rather, there was in the initial stages of Soviet society. But even then it was no proof that classes did not exist. In this country, too, bootblacks have become millionaires but no reasonable person has ever thought to deny that it is a class society.

And class frontiers in Soviet society, which were at first relatively open and elastic, have closed themselves with bewildering speed. There are still many workers' and peasants' sons in the contemporary generation of bureaucrats, for this ruling class came into being by differentiation of the working and peasant classes. But the bureaucrats of tomorrow will be preponderantly the children of bureaucrats, and the whole policy of the ruling class is slanted in this direction. It is becoming the rule more and more that the son of a worker becomes a worker, while the son of a bureaucrat, or, at most, of some one belonging to the middle stratum, becomes a bureaucrat.

There are three ways in which privileges are handed down: by inheritance, by the monopoly of education, and by patronage. Inheritance is the least important. To be sure, the right to inheritance has been restored, and the USSR is the only country today in which the right to the unrestricted disposal of property through a last testament is guaranteed by the constitution itself. But you can only will away what you own: furniture, works of art, summer villas, cash, bank deposits, government bonds—all of which have an enormous value amidst the general poverty—but you cannot hand down factories and shares of stock.

The privileged person, however, can have his children educated. And he *alone* can do that. "As far as students are concerned," writes Yvon, "the economic factor is often the most important of all, and the son of a rich father has a great advantage over those whose means are always very limited." [49]

Since this was written there have been many more developments in the same direction. In 1935 the Soviet press recorded with great jubilation the fact that more than 50% of the students were having their way paid by their parents—whereas just after the Revolution the majority of them had been supported by various public institutions. In many places there are special schools for the children of bureaucrats, beginning with the *crèches*. In 1940 tuition fees for the last three years of secondary school and for all universities and colleges were re-introduced;[50] the example was soon followed by all technical, normal, agricultural, medical, and other secondary schools.[51] The tuition at secondary schools amounts to 150 to 200 rubles, at colleges to 200 to 500 rubles. Scholarships are granted only for

the highest marks—two thirds "excellent," the remainder
"good." Tuition fees for the first semester after the introduction
of this law had to be paid within four weeks; those who were
unable to provide the money were expelled. Thus 600,000 students had to leave school.

The establishment of the Suvorov military academies with
preferential openings for officers' sons is another step in the
same direction. All that is lacking is the introduction in the
Kremlin Court of a corps of pages on the Czarist model.

As regards the third way of handing privileges on, Yvon tells
us: "Diplomas are indispensable but they are not the whole
story. The jobs for which they qualify one vary in desirability,
and it is becoming more and more difficult to succeed without
connections. A man in a position of authority can then be of
immeasurable help to his son. He does not start him off in his
own department but in a colleague's, because that attracts less
notice. Once one has a foot in the stirrup, a few good hand-
holds will gain succession to a place worth as much as the inheritance of money from a capitalist." [52]

These facts take the wind out of another favorite argument. The bureaucracy, some say, consumes indeed a disproportionate share of the fruits of production, and at the expense
of the workers, but in the final analysis the greatest part of new
production is consumed neither by workers nor bureaucrats,
but is accumulated. And whom do the newly built factories,
roads—and guns—serve if not the people? Of course, the people are exploited, but the accumulation is for the good of the
whole. But under capitalism the product of new factories and
the use of new means of transportation contribute *in the same
way* to the good of the "whole people." The capitalists do not
eat up all the margarine and all the spaghetti that come from
the new factories, and they do not ride all by themselves in the
new subways; nor do they shoot each other up with the guns.
The Russian ruling classes proceed with accumulation by
building new plants in which they and their descendants can

go on exploiting workers. If Russia were to belong to a *single* great capitalist corporation, she would do just the same.

Contradictions and Disproportions

But perhaps Soviet society—despite differences in income—can develop harmoniously? Let us picture to ourselves that the productivity of labor will grow, and with it the quantity of products, workers will receive better wages, the bureaucrats higher salaries; enough will remain, however, for purposes of accumulation, and new factories will increase productivity even further—everything will be for the best in this best of all possible worlds.

Unfortunately this picture does not correspond to the facts, as we have seen. Why?

In a totalitarian society in which the workers have no rights, the path of least resistance is to depress their standard of living and place on their shoulders the burden of supporting the upper class and providing for accumulation. The position of every member of the ruling class, his prestige, his advancement, his salary, his job, and sometimes even his life depend on whether he fulfils and overfulfils the Plan and on whether he attains and exceeds the prescribed yield of profit. Buying and selling prices are dictated from above, but he can lower wages and increase working hours and tempo. The whole social system is conducive to the wasteful exploitation of labor—as it is, for that matter, wherever labor is not free. Hubbard writes reproachfully that the death of millions of people in the famine of 1932 "must be regarded as a loss of capital to the nation." [53] But the bureaucracy cannot help itself. The over-accumulation and the relative over-consumption of the upper ten thousand are complemented by the undernourishment of the broad masses, which makes for a lower productivity of labor; which in turn diminishes the quantity of social products to be disposed of. This sharpens the struggle over the distribution of products. The crisis is solved by the bureaucracy in the usual way: in order to maintain and increase the tempo of accumulation so that the incomes of the rulers will not suffer, the masses' standard of living is simply depressed further—after all, they cannot defend themselves. And so the vicious circle begins anew.

The underconsumption of the masses is one source of contradictions. But there is no lack of other disproportions. Errors of planning are inevitable. In every modern society there exists some method of regulating the apportioning of the means of production and labor power among the various branches and processes of productive activity. Under capitalism this is taken care of—for better or worse—by the mechanism of prices and profits, and mistakes are corrected in the end by economic crises and losses. The mechanical laws of economy express themselves by economic catastrophes; they function, as Marx has strikingly observed, the way the laws of gravity do when a house collapses on your head. In a socialist society this blind control would be replaced by the conscious democratic supervision by the masses in conjunction with a completely public rendering of accounts. But under the exploitative rule of the bureaucrats the old methods of regulation lose their effectiveness, and new and democratic methods are inconceivable, for they would expose exploitation. *Therefore* the most elementary economic facts are kept secret. But not only that: regulation and criticism "only from above" are no substitute for public control. If orders from above may not be criticized even when they are senseless and impossible to carry out, then their carrying out has to be faked. The despotic system forces everybody to lie. Not a single figure of fact is reliable. At a conference of the Communist Party in February, 1941, Malenkov, secretary of the central committee, told how four different reports as to the supply of raw material in a factory were given simultaneously: one by the head of the supply department, one by the chief accountant, one by the director of the plant and one by a committee of inspection.[54] Four different totals resulted and they differed by several hundred per cent. And yet the inventory of raw material in a plant is the easiest statistical task of all. What happens when prices too are taken into reckoning and when there is a rather unstable monetary standard to be manipulated? Malenkov mentioned this case as a typical one, and we begin to understand how even in a census the bureaucracy can make errors involving figures that run into millions.

Errors of planning are inevitable even with the best statistics. But under conditions such as these they become the rule. Once a mistake has been made under this system it grows into something enormous. Yvon writes: "The possible scale of error is one of the most negative phenomena in the life of the country . . . The possession of almost unlimited power over society lends itself most easily to senseless decisions, which are carried out nevertheless." [55]

Anyone acquainted with the numerous examples of erroneous investments and senseless planning decisions reported in the Soviet press or by foreigners has to admit that the expenses of bureaucratic mis-economy are in no way less than those of capitalist competition.

But besides that, there is also direct parasitism. The unproductive administrative and oppressive apparatus of contemporary Soviet society is one of the costliest in the world in relation to national income.

Now and then some crass examples of this parasitism come to light. In the spring of 1941 it was officially ascertained that there were 50,000 persons in the administrative apparatus of the collective farms of the Rostov district alone who, even by the standards of the bureaucratic State executive, were altogether superfluous. Simultaneously it was discovered that there were several hundred special executives' aides in the factories of Moscow whose sole task in life was to hire new workers. And it was estimated that each aide hired on the average only one new worker a day. The above-mentioned Malenkov told the Party conference of the following case: the Ural state copper works sold the state trust for non-ferrous metals some worn-out equipment for 100,000 rubles; unaware of this, another director of the same copper works bought the equipment back from the trust for 111,000 rubles—and both directors received bonuses, one for a good sale, and the other for a cheap purchase. These are no isolated cases, for a special law was promulgated forbidding such dealings in worn-out equipment.[56] Further examples can be piled up *ad infinitum.*

Thus the bureaucracy can maintain itself only at great social expense. Disorganization, disproportions, and parasitism restrict the development of productive forces and lower the living standards of the masses. Yet a planned economy has one great advantage: in an emergency, all available resources and manpower can be concentrated on *one* job, disregarding all others.

Here we have the clue to the effective resistance Soviet Russia has been able to offer to Nazi invasion. For it is in war that such concentration of effort is most essential. No private property interests, no legitimate rights of labor are permitted to interfere with the war effort in the Soviet Union. Branches of production that are unproductive and unprofitable according to peacetime norms can be maintained almost indefinitely, their losses spread out over the whole national economy. Entire industrial areas can be shifted about, regardless of cost, for reasons of military strategy. New inventions, technical and social experiments can be tested and introduced on a big scale. Manpower can be sent wherever it is most needed, and forced to work under terrible conditions; sacrifices can be imposed on the population such as the most extreme Rightists of America dare not even dream of.*

But this concentration of all power and all resources in a single group of rulers explains not only the Russian successes in war. It also suggests how the bureaucracy in peacetime,

---

* It might be added here that the inequalities we have seen in Soviet civilian life are to be found also in the much-advertised "people's" Red Army, and on an even greater scale. A Red Army private gets 10 rubles a month, a lieutenant 1,000 and a colonel 2,400. American army pay is positively equalitarian in comparison: $50 for a private, $150 for a lieutenant, $333 for a colonel. (See *N. Y. Times,* Aug. 23, 1943)

despite all internal disproportions, mismanagement and social conflicts, was able to maintain its power. Whatever the losses, all the resources of a colossal empire have been at the disposal of the bureaucracy to cover them up, tide the system over the crisis.

State and Economy

Having sketched the social stratification of Soviet society and its contradictions, we wish to deal for a moment with the relation between the State and economy.

The Marxists always used to take pride in revealing the actual social relations behind legal fictions and ideological wrappings. Therefore it is all the more remarkable that many writers who have been through the Marxist school should believe that the means of production in Russia belong to "all" or to the "working class," because it says so in the statute books. The means of production in Russia belong, not to everybody, but to the State. According to Marxist doctrine, the State is the ruling classes' organization of the forcible oppression of the oppressed classes, and its existence and constantly increasing strength should alone have been enough to warn Marxists that a class society was involved. Trotsky once wrote that the means of production in Russia belonged to the State and the State belonged to the bureaucracy. There is more wisdom in this sentence—which Trotsky himself later dismissed unfortunately as a mere bon mot—than in all the Trotskyite literature about a "degenerated workers' State." *

* The whole Trotskyite argument that Russia is a workers' state stands and falls on the thesis that the statification of the means of production means *eo ipso* a workers' state, no further investigation being necessary. This flies in the face of reality no less than of the entire Marxist tradition. Engels had already made fun of the notion by saying that the first socialist institution must have been the regimental tailor, if it was true that every state enterprise had something socialist about it. The Russian state is a workers' state essentially, say the Trotskyites, because it retains the economic foundation of socialism. This foundation is the statification of the means of production. If one were to object modestly that statification in itself is not a socialist measure, since an exploiters' state can statify too, the Trotskyists will answer that statification *by a workers' state* is necessarily a socialist measure. Thus it is revealed that Russia is a workers'

Several authors have already pointed out that in a statified economy everything depends upon whose hands the State power rests in.* If in the hands of the broad, democratically organized masses of the producers, then the means of production are also in their hands and we have socialism or are well on the way to it. But if the State power is found in the hands exclusively of a privileged special stratum, then the latter rules over the means of production too and we have a class society.

The conclusion is that socialism is impossible and inconceivable without democracy. Democracy is not an accidental and superfluous ornament on the structure of the socialist economic order, but its effective basis, its essence.

But it would not be correct to claim that once the means of production have been statified, economic laws are no longer effective, that politics have replaced economics, and so forth. Political oppression is only the reverse side of economic exploitation. And the State defends the class relations existing in the economy.

The despotic dictatorship of the bureaucracy is not an accidental superstructure or excrescence on a socialist economy. It is the adequate and legitimate political expression of the economic fact that the bureaucracy exploits the broad masses. One can say indeed that the bureaucracy rules the factory because it rules the State, but one can turn the statement around with equal justice. Two sides of one fundamental class relationship are involved. It would be correct to say that nothing is lacking to socialism in Russia except the introduction of producers' democracy; but far from meaning simply a "purely political" overturn of the "superstructure," its introduction would mean at the same time a *social* revolution. A revolution could not overthrow the bureaucracy politically without depriv-

state because it retains a socialist foundation, but that this foundation is socialist only because Russia is a workers' state. Or to put it more briefly: Russia is a workers' state because it is a workers' state. Either you believe that or else you are a philistine, petty bourgeois, and renegade. . . .

* Max Shachtman has done this particularly well in various numbers of the *New International*.

ing it of its economic power. It could not introduce democracy without replacing the production relationships of obedience and exploitation by those of freedom and equality, of voluntary cooperation. It would have to transfer the social means of production from the hierarchical collective ownership of the bureaucracy to the democratic collective ownership of the producers. Without that socialism cannot be attained in Russia.

References

1. Leonard E. Hubbard: *The Economics of Soviet Agriculture*, London, 1939, p. 207.

2. Leonard E. Hubbard: *Soviet Trade and Distribution*, London, 1938, p. 368.

3. Ibid., p. 269.

4. Leonard E. Hubbard: *Soviet Labor and Industry*, London, 1942, p. 164.

5. "Stalin's New Deal for Labor" by M. Florinsky (*Political Science Quarterly*, March, 1941).

6. Cf. Hubbard's *Soviet Labor*, p. 164. Hubbard gives the monthly wages for 1929 as 77 rubles, but he has made an error, having taken the figure for 1930.

7. *Monthly Labor Review*, November, 1939; May, 1940; August, 1940.

8. Cf. "An Analysis of Russia Economy" by F. Forest (*New International*, January and February, 1943).

9. M. Yvon: *L'URSS, telle qu'elle est*, Paris, 1938, pp. 212-213. A shorter version was also published entitled, *Ce qu'est devenue la revolution Russe*. This was translated and issued as a pamphlet by the International Review, New York City, under the title: *What Has Become of the Russian Revolution*, in 1937.

10. Ibid., pp. 204-205.

11. Hubbard, *Soviet Trade*.

12. Cf. F. Forest, supra, pp. 17-18, Jan. 1943.

13. Yvon, *L'URSS*, pp. 215-218.

14. *Trud*, Moscow, Jan. 20, 1936.

15. Leon Sedov in the *New International*, February, 1936.

16. Leon Trotsky: *The Revolution Betrayed,* p. 125.

17. *Za Industrializatsiiu,* April 29, 1937 (quoted by Yvon, pp. 110-111).

18. This refers to the more modest specialists, not to the top men.

19. Yvon, p. 163.

20. Hubbard, *Soviet Agriculture,* p. 164-179.

21. Trotsky, supra, p. 142.

22. *Malaia Sovietskaia Entsyklopediia,* Moscow, 1939, V. 3, p. 887.

23. Cf. Trotsky, *Revolution Betrayed,* pp. 238-245.

24. Decree of Dec. 21, 1938.

25. Decree of Dec. 29, 1938.

26. Decree of June 26, 1940. The decree of Oct. 11, 1940, made another exception for the wives of army men following their husbands to other localities.

27. Decree of July 24, 1940.

28. Decree of June 26, 1940.

29. Decree of July 17, 1940.

30. Decree of July 22, 1940.

31. Decree of Oct. 19, 1940.

32. Decree of Oct. 2, 1940.

33. Decree of June 26, 1940, and of July 3, 1940.

34. Decree of July 12, 1940.

35. Decree of July 27, 1940.

36. Cf. Manya Gordon, p. 171; and Yvon, p. 117.

37. Statement by Shvernik, head of Soviet Trade Unions, April 16, 1941.

38. Decree of May 27, 1940.

39. Andreiev in *Pravda,* Dec. 29, 1935; cf. Gordon, p. 104.

40. *Trud,* July 8, 1933; cf. Gordon, p. 103.

41. Statement by the trade union leader, Weinberg, in *Trud,* July 8, 1933; cf. Gordon, p. 105.

42. *Trud,* Feb. 16, 1932; cf. Gordon, p. 103.

43. Decree of Aug. 7, 1932.

44. Decree of April 7, 1935.

45. *Pravda*, April 28, 1934; cf. Yvon, p. 256.

46. Vyshinsky, *Outline of Justice in the USSR*, p. 30; cf. Yvon, p. 256.

47. Decree of December, 1932.

48. Decree of June 6, 1936.

49. Yvon, page 171.

50. Decree of October 3, 1940.

51. Decree of October 12, 1940.

52. Yvon, page 171.

53. Hubbard, supra, page 180.

54. Report in *Pravda*, February 20, 1941.

55. Yvon, page 22. There are many examples of this.

56. Decree of February 10, 1941.

Arthur Koestler

EIGHT FALLACIES OF THE LEFT BABBITT

"His large head was pink, his brown hair thin and dry. His face was babyish in slumber. . . . Babbitt was again dreaming of the fairy child, a dream more romantic than scarlet pagodas by a silver sea." Babbitt *by Sinclair Lewis.*

Editor's Note

THE task Arthur Koestler has set himself in this selection he finds not pleasant but necessary. Better than anyone else, the ex-Communists know of the immense reservoir of good will that has been imprisoned in the walls of Stalinist allegiance—sincerity, energy, conviction, dedication, noble hopes being exploited to bring about opposite ends. It is a mistake, a defeatist act of tragic proportions, to consider all those psychologically entranced by the Communist pipers to be villains, men of unmitigated evil. Partly as tragic as the brutality of the Soviet regime is the cynical exploitation it has made and is making of men and women whose only repayment frequently for their contributions is their pathetic belief that they are helping to build a better world. These men and women, those who are still accessible, must be reached, they must be aided to understand what the Soviet state actually stands for and the extent of the evil their good intentions help to bolster. There are others, a large number, in the Communist camp, who are less naive, less well intentioned. They are not the subject of our present concern.

The "Babbitts of the Left," are strikingly like their opposite numbers of the Right. Both are bound in by conventions (although of vastly different kinds), both are uncritical, both allow themselves to be led, to be blown wherever the dominant winds of their camps carry. That the Left Babbitt follows a puppet-like conformity in the name of rebellion does not alter the similarity. In conversations with the Left Babbitt one becomes aware of a political catechism. There is a unanimity of response in these conversations—no matter how far apart in setting they may be—that is the counterpart of the monolithic attitude-forming machines of which they are the product. In this selection Mr. Koestler deals with eight of these widely held "fallacies."

It is not accidental that it should be Arthur Koestler who deals so illuminatingly with this subject. Few writers have consistently thrown more light on the Communist experience. In the large literature of disillusion his *Darkness at Noon*—a book that must be read as a whole—is already a classic. It is significant that when this suggestive novel of the Moscow Trials, which grew out of the author's acquaintance with several of the defendants and his close study of the subject, was published in France for the first time after the end of the war it was hailed not only as a literary but as a *political* event of considerable importance. Those interested in what may well be the best short (one hundred page) account denuding the Soviet myth are referred to the last half of Mr. Koestler's *The Yogi and the Commissar*.

Arthur Koestler was born in Budapest in 1905. He was educated in Vienna and then spent several years in the Near East. He later became a correspondent for the Ullstein chain and sent dispatches from Paris, Berlin, and the Middle East. A former Communist, he belonged to the movement for seven years, from 1931-38. He has twice been a prisoner of concentration camps: in Spain, where he was sentenced to death by Franco officials until influential British citizens effected his

release; and in France at the time of the German advance in
1940. He is the author of *Dialogue with Death; The Gladiators;
Arrival and Departure; Thieves in the Night; Insight and Outlook; Promise and Fulfillment;* and many newspaper and magazine articles.

This selection was chosen, in addition to the value of what it
has to say and says so well, because it was directed at Americans. In 1948 Mr. Koestler gave a series of lectures in the
United States, which he visited for the first time, for the benefit
of the International Rescue and Relief Committee. He had first
become acquainted with the work of this organization during
his stay in the concentration camp at Vernet. At the time he
was one of the hundreds of anti-Nazi intellectuals who had
sought asylum in France, the majority of them soon being
rounded up by Vichy. Koestler witnessed the work of the IRRC
in rescuing numbers of his fellow prisoners and he became a
strong supporter of the organization which had been started
by a group of well-known American liberals in 1933. This selection is the text of Mr. Koestler's remarks during his American
speeches.

#

Eight Fallacies of the Left Babbitt by Arthur Koestler

Before I started out on this my
first visit to the U. S. my friends in Europe warned me: "You
won't find a common language with the Americans. They live
on the moon."

The first few days over here convinced me that this is not
true. I do feel a growing awareness of the threat over Europe

in this country. The only question is whether it is growing rapidly enough to catch up with the speed of the drift to catastrophe in Europe.

For the war hysteria of which a considerable number of people seem to suffer here is, of course, not a sign of mature awareness. Nor is the mentality of appeasement. I shan't waste your time and mine proving that appeasement doesn't lead to peace but to war; if you haven't found that out yet, I suggest you re-read the arguments against the tactic of appeasement in the old 1933 to 1939 files of liberal and radical magazines—from the *New Republic* to *The New Statesman and Nation.* You will find there explained with a brilliant logic that appeasement of an aggressive, expanding power creates a fog in which neither of the two partners knows where he is; the aggressor, having grabbed positions A, B and C, hopes to get away with grabbing D—and why shouldn't he hope so with all the encouragement he receives from the appeasers in the opponents' camp? But unfortunately position D—Poland in 1939 and maybe Italy today [mid-1948]—has meanwhile come to be regarded by the defensive partner as a *casus belli,* and so the world slides into war—I didn't say it goes to war, I said it slides into war—without either of the two partners wanting it. In other words, appeasement means playing poker; a firm, clearly outlined, principled policy means playing chess.

These are platitudes, the type of platitude which every reader of the *New Republic* or *The New Statesman and Nation* knew by heart in the 1930s. Today they have forgotten it, and arguing against them means regressing to the kindergarten level. I hope that in this meeting we shall remain at least on the level of the primary school. So I shall take it, henceforth, for granted that war hysteria and appeasement are two equally deadly dangers, like Scylla and Charybdis, and that the liberals' extremely precarious task today is to navigate like Ulysses between the two.

Unfortunately our liberal Ulysses of today hardly deserves

the title "nimble witted" which Homer bestowed upon his
hero. When the sorceress calls from the East and her fellow travelers are turned into pigs, he can hardly resist the temptation of sharing their fate. For it is not easy to be a liberal today. It is not easy to navigate between the Scylla of the Hearst
press, of war hysteria and of Red-baiting, and the Charybdis
of the Munich *cum* Pearl Harbor which Mr. Chamberlain—
sorry, I mean Mr. Wallace—would prepare for us.

Allow me as an aid for this perilous task of navigation to
point out some of the logical fallacies and emotional eddies in
which liberals and leftists frequently get shipwrecked. I have
listed for myself eight of them—the eight main fallacies of
what you may allow me to call left Babbittism. Here they are:

First is the *confusion of Left and East.* Some sections of the
reactionary press are unable or unwilling to distinguish between liberals, New Dealers, Social Democrats and Stalinites;
they are all damned Reds. Naturally we are indignant at this
poisonous imbecility. But don't forget that the Left itself is
partly responsible for this confusion. The left Babbitt assumes
that there is a continuous spectrum stretching from pale pink
liberals to deeper red socialists and so on to purple Communists
of the extreme left. His idea is based on the confusion of the
political direction "left" with the geographical direction "east."
It is time that he got it into his head that Moscow is not to his
left but to his east. The Soviet Union is not a socialist country,
and Cominform policy is not socialist policy. In 1939-41, for
instance, French Socialists fought the Nazis on the battlefield
and underground, while the Communists in France and here
collaborated with the Germans against us.

So let us bear in mind that "East is east and Left is left" and
if the twain sometimes still meet, the meeting is purely coin-
cidental. The tragic decline of the Social Democratic movements in France, Italy and the rest of Europe is first and
foremost caused by their failure to denounce Stalinism as a
movement which discredits socialism—as the rule of the Borgias
discredited Christianity. That is why liberals and social demo-

crats in Europe are being swept away like straw in a hurricane.

The second fallacy of the Babbitt of the Left is what we may call the *soul-searching fallacy*. The other day there was a press conference where I mentioned that the people on the Continent, the frightened people in Italy and France, look upon you Americans as their only hope of salvation, salvation from the economic point of view through ERP; salvation from the military point of view in case of an open or disguised Russian aggression on the Czech pattern. Thereupon one of the journalists present said, "Do you really believe that we can help Europe with our dirty hands?" I said, "What do you mean by 'dirty hands'?" He said, "Well, I mean our policy in Greece and in Palestine and backing up Franco and the way we treat Negroes and Jews. We are dirty all over, and if we pose as defenders of democracy it is just hypocrisy."

The answer to this fallacy is to project the argument back to 1938. Then it would run as follows: "We have no right to fight Hitler's plan of sending six million Jews to the gas chambers so long as there are restricted hotels in America and so long as Negroes do not have absolute equality here. Our hands are dirty—so instead of using them to fight racial persecution let us first wash them clean and polish our nails. Once American democracy has become a perfect democracy, then and then only shall we have a right to defend what remains of Europe. And if Europe goes to the dogs before we have finished putting our own house in order, that's just too bad and cannot be helped."

Third and closely related to the soul-searching fallacy is the *fallacy of the false equation*. Its European version is "Soviet totalitarianism is bad. American imperialism is equally bad. There is nothing to choose between them, so let us stay in no man's land and found another 100% purist soul-searching sectarian little magazine until we are drowned in the deluge." To prove that the American system is "just as bad" as the Russian system, to make the two sides of the equation balance, your left purist has recourse to subconscious little subterfuges. He

equates the Hollywood purges with the Moscow purges. The
physical assassination of thousands of the elite of the Russian
Revolution and the dismissal from their jobs of nine film script
writers constitutes for him a perfect equation. Variations of this
attitude are equally frequent in this country. The American
fellow-traveler has never lived under a totalitarian regime,
so when he draws comparisons he mostly doesn't know what he
is talking about. His conscience is in revolt against the "black
belt" of Chicago, the appalling slums in which the workers of
the packing industry live like rats. I spent only a few hours in
Chicago, but most of them I spent in the "black belt" and at the
local headquarters of the packing-house workers on strike. I
was appalled by what I saw and heard and smelled. So don't
think I am a naive tourist, a romantic admirer of your system.
But now compare your treatment of racial minorities at its worst
with the Soviet treatment of the minorities of the Crimean
Republic, the Chechen Republic, the Volga-German Republic,
whose total populations, men, women and children, were deported to the Arctic because they had proved, as the official
Soviet communiqué about the Crimeans stated, "unreliable during the war"—even the babes in their cradles were unreliable
and had to go to Siberia. In Chicago I saw men on strike and
sympathized with them. In Russia strikes, or incitement to
strike, are qualified as high treason and punished by the maximum penalty. In American elections political machines may
distort the people's will. In Russian elections 99½% vote for the
one official list—the remaining ½% presumably being in bed with
influenza. Thus the fallacy of the false equation equates an
imperfect democracy with a perfect totalitarian regime; its
philosophy boils down to the simple maxim that there is nothing to choose between measles and leprosy.

Fallacy number four is the *anti-anti attitude*. It runs as follows: "I am not a Communist. In fact, I dislike Stalinist politics, but I don't want to be identified with anti-Communist
Red-baiting, with the Hollywood purges and the Hearst press.
Hence I am neither a Communist nor an anti-Communist, but

an anti-anti-Communist." If W. R. Hearst says that twice two is four, I shall automatically hold that twice two is five or at least 4½. The 2 x 2 = 4½ mathematicians are usually Wallace voters.

Don't laugh, for the roots of this fallacy are very deep in all of us, myself included. I remember how painful it was when an old dodderer in a London club walked up to me and said with a friendly tap on my shoulder, "Well, well, young man, I am glad that at last you have come around to see reason. I myself knew 25 years ago what Bolshevism means, and it's never too late to repent."

You can't help this sort of thing; you can't help people being right for the wrong reasons. In the last war we fought in the name of democracy in an alliance with Dictator Metaxas of Greece, Dictator Chiang Kai-shek and Dictator Stalin. And rightly so, because at that time Nazism was the main menace to the world, and politics is based on forming alliances. But there is a fundamental difference between a wartime alliance and political identification with one's allies. Being allied to Chiang didn't mean that we accepted the Chinese regime in England or America. Being against our will in one camp with the Hearst press against the totalitarian menace from the East doesn't mean that we identify ourselves with Mr. Hearst's ideology. This fear of being in bad company is not an expression of political purity; it is an expression of a lack of self-confidence. If you are sure of yourself—politically and ideologically—you will no longer be frightened to say that twice two makes four even if Colonel McCormick says the same.

Fallacy number five is the *sentimental fallacy*. For years we were allied to Communists in the antifascist struggle, and now when we have to part company some roots of past loyalty, of a sentimental conservatism remain in us which are very difficult to eradicate. Our bedfellows of yesterday do not, of course, share this emotional squeamishness. Over the slightest disagreement they will denounce us as fascists, spies and traitors. These emotional ties are one-way ties and it is essential to bear in

mind that they are entirely irrational and conservative in nature.

Fallacy number six may be called the fallacy of *Caligary
logics*. *The Cabinet of Dr. Caligary* was the first film which
might be called surrealistic, made about 25 years ago. The
fellow traveler, the fellow traveler's fellow traveler, the crypto-
fellow traveler and so on, live in a world of surrealistic logic
where all facts are seen reflected in curved distorting mirrors.
Example: the fellow traveler will tell you, "You criticized the
Stalinist regime, but in Stalingrad the heroic Red Army defeated the Germans and thereby proved the superiority of the
Stalinist regime over every other regime."

You answer, "If the military defeat of the Germans by the
Russians in 1943 is to be regarded in itself as a proof of the
superiority of the Stalinist regime, then the military defeat of
the French by the Russians in 1812 must be regarded as a
proof of the superiority of the czarist regime and of the system
of serfdom over the ideology of the French Revolution."

The Caligary logician will thereupon answer you indignantly, "It is typical of your perverted mind to compare Stalin
with the czar."

Fallacy number seven is the fallacy of the *perfect cause*. It
is related to number two, the soul-searching fallacy. Only absolutely clean hands have a right to reach out to protect and
save what remains of Europe. Only an absolutely perfect cause
is worth fighting for. And the search for the perfect cause becomes an excuse for inactivity, for staying put in the homeless
radical's no man's land.

History knows no perfect causes, no situation of white against
black. Eastern totalitarianism is black; its victory would mean
the end of our civilization. American democracy is not white
but gray. To live, even to die for a perfect cause is a luxury permitted to few. In 1942 or '43 I published an article* which

---

* ["The Fraternity of Pessimists," *New York Times Magazine*, November,
1943; also included in Koestler's *The Yogi and the Commissar*, New York,
1945.—Ed.]

began with the words, "In this war we are fighting a total lie in the name of a half-truth." The total lie was Hitler's New Order. The half-truth was our democracy. Today we face a similar emergency and a similar predicament. Once more the choice before us is merely that between a gray twilight and total darkness. But ask the refugees who manage to escape, at the risk of their lives, from behind the iron curtain into our gray democracy, whether this choice is worth fighting for. They know. You don't.

The last fallacy, number eight, is the *confusion between short-term and long-term aims.* It is the most dangerous of all. By long-term aims I mean the age-old struggle for reform, for social justice, for a more equitable system of government. By short-term aims I mean the necessity of fighting an immediate emergency. The danger of confusion is twofold. Your leftist Babbitt may refuse to fight against the short-term emergency until he has finished the job of creating a perfect government in his country, in 100 years or so. The opposite danger is to become so obsessed with the immediate emergency, that all principles of the long-term struggle are thrown overboard. Ex-Communists and disappointed radicals are in a particular danger of toppling over to the other extreme. It is essential that we should keep in mind that there are two distinct levels involved in our struggle; that to defend our system against a deadly threat does not imply acceptance of everything in this system, does not imply the giving up of the long-term fight to improve it; and vice versa, that our criticism of the shortcomings of this system does not free us from the obligation of defending it, despite its ambiguous grayness, against the total corruption of the humanitarian ideal.

This talk was mainly addressed to the Left. I may have been harsh to the left Babbitt; it was a brotherly harshness. To the Babbitt of the Right I have nothing to say; we have no language in common.

The power-vacuum which two world wars have created in Central and Western Europe, has inescapably linked your fate

with that of the European continent. I feel the enormous burden which is falling on your shoulders. For there will either
be a *Pax Americana* in the world or there will be no pax. Never
has such a burden and such a responsibility been borne by any
single nation in history. It is the more unfair to you as yours is
an adolescent civilization, with adolescent enthusiasms and
adolescent pimples. The task of the progressive intelligentsia of
your country is to help the rest of the nation to face its enormous responsibilities. The time for sectarian quarrels in the
cosy no man's land of abstract radicalism is past. It is time for
the American radical to grow up.

Bertram D. Wolfe

SOME WONDERS OF THE RUSSIAN TONGUE

Editor's Note

ONE of the pleasures of childhood is the defiant refrain: "Sticks and stones can break my bones, but words will never harm me." Not even an habitual windmill-tilter would take the trouble to dissect this feeble and fallacious faith, however wide a following it has gained among adults. In the realm of totalitarian politics, dogma, and administration, the evil uses to which the Word has been put, the catastrophic hurt it is capable of wreaking is written in not a few bloody pages of history, especially recent history. Sidney Hook has labeled the matter correctly when he speaks of the modern "degradation of the word." Despotism can be re-packaged semantically as "new democracy," "higher democracy." Not keeping one's word—a trite and easily understood matter—is marketed under a dozen slogans of idealism. Concentration camps are social rehabilitation centers; guiltless persons may be found culpable for "unconscious deviations." The goal of the totalitarian state is to strip reality of ascertainable meanings, to rid language of the quality of independent utility. One no longer sees what is before him; vision is transmuted by explanation, giving way to "juridical cretinism." One is told what one sees. From this stage it is just a short step to doing what one is told to do.

In this brief selection, which appeared in *Modern Review* in 1947, Bertram D. Wolfe focuses on that most innocent of documents, the Soviet dictionary. By an informed reading he makes a number of discoveries and provides us with an unexpected additional view into the Soviet state.

Bertram David Wolfe was born in Brooklyn, New York, on January 19, 1896. He was graduated from City College in 1916 and later attended the University of Mexico. Returning to the United States he took his M.A. at Columbia in 1931. He taught in both New York and Mexico City. From 1925-29 he served as director of the Communist Workers School in New York. After his disaffection, he continued to develop his own notable scholarly aptitudes and has won considerable recognition as an historian, journalist, political analyst and cultural critic. Among his books are: *Portrait of America; Portrait of Mexico; Civil War in Spain; Diego Rivera: His Life and Times* and *Deathless Days.* Most recently he gained widespread critical praise for *Three Who Made a Revolution,* a triple biography (Lenin, Trotsky, Stalin) and history of especially high order. It was ten years in preparation and will be completed in two forthcoming volumes.

#

Some Wonders of the Russian Tongue
by Bertram D. Wolfe

I AM one of those hapless mortals who is condemned to read what Turgeniev once called "the great, powerful, truthful and free Russian tongue," with the aid of a dictionary. Next to the telephone book there would appear to be no more dismal consecutive reading than a dictionary. Gone are the days when a crotchety lexicographer could indulge his feelings as Dr. Johnson did when he defined *oats* as "food for horses, and, in Scotland, for humans." Modern dictionaries are collective, cumulative, standardized compilations, informative but uninspired and uninspiring. At least, so I thought until I began to consult the highly useful abridged *Russko-Angliiski Slovar,* published by *Ogiz-Gis,* or, by the State Publishing House for Foreign and National Dictionaries.

Naturally, I did not set out to read the dictionary from *abazhur* to *yashchik* as consecutive reading. No, I perused Russian books and papers, and, in moments of confusion, turned to this little compendium for help and enlightenment. It is a good dictionary for its size—none better—and it rarely failed me. Only gradually did I become aware of the fact that other words on the page might be more interesting than the one I was seeking.

For most words there was the Russian, and then, without more ado, a single English equivalent, e.g. *"ventilyator, ventilator"* or *"verblyud,* camel." No less natural was it to find occasional words like *"velikii,* great," first defined and then illustrated by the expression, *"velikie derzhavy,* great powers," or even to find that *"vera,* faith," was illustrated with the expression "faith in the revolutionary cause" without any hint that there might also be a faith denominated as religious.

It was when I stumbled across the word, *"pyad,* span or inch," that I first began to note the unexpected qualities of this usually so laconic book. For after the word "inch" I found, *"Ni odnoi pyadi chuzhoi zemli ne xotim; no i svoei zemli ne otdadim nikomu* (Stalin)" and after that, in English: "We do not want a single foot of foreign territory; but we will not surrender a single inch of our territory to any one (Stalin)." Thus not only was foreign territory inexplicably measured in feet and domestic in inches, but the tiny, simple seeming word, *inch,* occupied not one line but eight in this usually so laconic and tightly abridged dictionary.

Anxiously I glanced at the date of publication (1942) and wondered how, after the annexation of half of Poland, part of Finland, and all of Bessarabia, Lithuania, Latvia and Esthonia, a dictionary published in Moscow could still be renouncing every single foot of foreign territory. I hastily turned to the letter L and on page 111 found "*Litovskaya Sovetskaya Sotsialisticheskaya Respublika,* the Lithuanian Soviet Socialist Republic," whence I concluded that this particular foot of ground had not been rejected. Still I felt an inexplicable conflict between the definition of *pyad* and that of *Litovskaya* until I noted that besides the publication date 1942 (which accounts for the second) there was also the note "printed from plates of 1939" which accounted for the retention of the first. I breathed easier, but somebody may yet get purged for this failure to keep uptodate in definitions . . .

After that, I could never resist the temptation to stray from the word I was seeking, usually so coldly and briefly defined, to any other on the page that happened to have a lot of type after it. My habit of straying from the strait and narrow path was often surprisingly rewarded, for this proved to be a dictionary in which some select words gave you not only definitions but something to think about.

Thus if "*voina,* war" on page 30 was followed by "imperialist war" and "civil war" but not by "Great Patriotic War," you could blame it on the "plates of 1939," and ponder on the change of fashions in the meanings and affective overtones of words, and the mutability of pacts and attitudes towards war. Or, if "*smertnost,* mortality" was bloodily illustrated by "*smertnaya kasn,* capital punishment" and "*smertnyi prigovor,* death sentence," it inspired reflections on what progress has been made since the Soviet Union abolished the death penalty in 1947, in order to lessen the opposition of other countries to returning Russian refugees. And reflections, no less, on the superior economic uses to the state of working prisoners to death in concentration camps rather than wasting a bullet on them along with their potential labor power.

But it is time to let the dictionary speak for its inimitable self, in words culled at random, since I have still not started to read it from *abazhur* to *yashchik.* On page 79 under "*znamya,* banner" the reader will find in both languages "to hold aloft the banner of Lenin and Stalin," which surely should help him to use the word properly. Under "*nezavisimo,* independently" on p. 140, there is a lengthy aid to proper use: "the equality of the rights of the citizens of the USSR, independently or irrespective of their nationality or race, is an indefeasible law," which mouthful gives *nezavisimo* ten lines instead of one. This business of "rights" moreover seems to have bothered the lexicographers for on p. 136 under "*natsionalnost,* nationality," we again find the same statement about the "indefeasible law" in all its amplitude. And on p. 200 under "*podlinnik,* original" and "*podlinnyi,* genuine" we find the genuine exemplification in the sentence: "genuine democracy is carried out in the USSR." I wondered about the English words "carried out" until I was brought up short by the added expression, "*s podlinnym verno,* checked and found correct." And, unexpectedly, under "*neprelozhnyi,* immutable," there is the illustration: "the equality of rights of the citizens of the USSR is an immutable law." To silence doubt, follow the words, "*neprelozhnaya istina,* indisputable truth."

Perhaps the climax in lengthy illustration of the definition of a short word comes with "*pravo,* right." No Soviet dictionary could let it go at that. There are 22 lines of exemplification, including such rights as "the right to vote" (but not to choose between candidates or tickets), "the right of self-determination," "the right of asylum," "the right to work in the USSR is ensured by the socialist organization of national economy," and "citizens of the USSR have the right to rest and leisure which is ensured by the institution of annual vacations with pay." How touching to have so many exemplifications of the words must go badly defined and unexemplified!

But not every word, for on the selfsame page, as if the alphabet itself or the paging were the work of a diversionist or wrecker, is the word which droppeth as the gentle rain from heaven, "*poshchada,* mercy" with the truly startling exemplification by the sentence "no mercy for the enemies of the people!" (exclamation point in the original). And when it began to seem to me in my simplicity that that was a poor exemplification of the word "mercy" I found my answer under the simple word "*tot*," meaning "that," which was followed by the disconcerting "*tem samyn vy prisnaete svoyu oshibky,* by that you confess your mistake." Lest I demur further, the dictionary added severely "*tem khuzhe,* so much the worse for you." *

* [Speaking of words, Lenin himself contributed a few useful ones that are the predecessors of Walter Winchell's expressive "communazi," and that deserve to be better known. Lenin's words: "com-lies" and "com-boasts," or Communist lies and Communist boasts. "The quaint expression 'com-boasts' had a great success," one commentator has written, "so well did it fit the facts." Here is how the father of Bolshevism used the other word. "Every day," Lenin said, "we hear, I especially on account of my position, so many glib Communist lies, so many com-lies, that it's enough to make me sick, violently so, sometimes." (Cf. Souvarine's *Stalin,* pp. 302-3.)—*Ed.*]

Igor Gouzenko

THE "NEIGHBORS" IN CANADA

Editor's Note

AT THE present time a young man, his wife, and small children are living quietly in Canada. Their situation is unusual in that they are constantly guarded, they have had to select new names, security regulations prohibit the printing of their photographs or details of their whereabouts, their children do not know, and cannot yet be told, their parents' real names, country of origin, or of the events leading up to this fearful seclusion. A strange existence for persons living in Canada!

By his disclosures Igor Gouzenko has won the gratitude of Canada and of the Western world. He has not yet found the peace he sought. Admired by many for his extraordinary courage, his name has been reviled by Communist supporters in many countries. The Soviet Union has good reason to hold him in everlasting enmity. His actions, which began on the evening of September 5, 1945, were to lead to a public revelation which startled the entire world. What Gouzenko proved was that the Soviet Union had at work several parallel espionage networks in Canada and additional spy-rings in other countries. Unlike others who fled from the Soviet employ armed solely with the determined hope of convincing the world, regardless of penalties to themselves, of the existence of Soviet agents abroad, Gouzenko was able to bring the proof along with him.

What was his role and how did he happen to be in a position to make this disclosure? Igor Gouzenko was born in Russia in 1919. It is therefore significant to note that he is entirely the product of the post-revolutionary era. Like other Soviet youngsters he looked forward to a career in the service of the state. At sixteen he was a member of the *Komsomols*, or Young Communist League. In time, after considerable training at the Moscow Architectural Institute, at the Kuibishev Military Engineering Academy of Moscow, and later at Intelligence Headquarters in Moscow, he came to hold the rank of lieutenant in the Red Army. He received special training preparatory to his being sent as an espionage aide to Canada. He was thoroughly investigated and re-investigated. In June, 1943, he arrived in Ottawa, ostensibly as a "civilian employee" of the Soviet Embassy. If questioned, he was instructed to say that he was a translator and secretary. His military-intelligence background was kept secret and he took up his actual job of secret cipher clerk for the Soviet Military Attaché, Colonel Zabotin. Gouzenko has explained that all Soviet espionage agents are equipped with "legends," completely fictitious personal histories to cover traces of their actual assignments. His work consisted of deciphering espionage and other messages from Moscow for the military attaché and of enciphering Zabotin's telegrams to Moscow, to "The Director." These "messages" were also transmitted by secret courier, photographically and in other ways. In time Gouzenko became head secret cipher clerk. He was thus kept closely in touch with Soviet espionage activities in Canada.

Shortly before he was scheduled to return to the Soviet Union, he began making preparations for his flight. Life in Canada he had seen to be so very different from what he had been led to expect that he no longer wanted to return to the USSR. He was particularly anxious not to place his pregnant wife and small son within the borders of the Soviet Union from which they would not be able to escape. He therefore decided on those documents, to and from Moscow which related to espionage in Canada, that he would take with him. He knew that he was likely to meet with a bewildered response from Canadian authorities regarding espionage in their midst, conducted by a country to which they had sent considerable wartime assistance and with which they enjoyed "friendly" relations. On September 5, 1945, Gouzenko left the embassy with 109 (!) documents in his possession.

So bizarre was his fear-laden story to the Canadian mind that he was placed, without his knowledge, under surveillance —and his story was listened to and documents examined only after the NKVD, the Russian secret police, were apprehended breaking into his apartment in a frantic search for the missing documents. On the fateful day of his break, while he wandered forlornly from newspaper to ministry in vain, with time running short and with a death reward from the NKVD in store, he asked his wife, Anna, what she would do until he returned. With a startling prosaic heroism, she answered: "I have a big washing to do. Don't worry about me, Igor." The subsequent public developments, as we know, electrified the Western world. Involuntarily, thousands of well-meaning persons professing friendship for our "wartime ally" had to accept the grim and incontrovertible documentary evidence of the international Soviet espionage network. Colonel Zabotin immediately fled from Ottawa—without notifying the Canadian authorities to which he was accredited—and sailed from New York on the Soviet ship *Alexander Suvorov* which sailed clandestinely at night without complying with port regulations.

What makes the Gouzenko case important for us? First the documents established beyond dispute the existence in the Western hemisphere of several parallel Soviet espionage rings. They established, in addition, links with agents in the U. S., London, and elsewhere. The case resulted in prison sentences, after extensive hearings and trials, for a number of persons. Also, it demonstrated that during a period of "friendly" relations, when Canada and the U. S. had aided Russia in its most desperate hour with vast shipments, the Soviet agents nevertheless repaid this cooperation with espionage. Their objective, it should be stressed, included postwar military defenses, the atom bomb, and other technical developments. This will be seen in the sample of Soviet espionage documents that follow.

The full data, photostats of documents, messages to and from Moscow, hearings given to those named as Soviet spies and accomplices, data on their "motivations," Soviet dossier identifications of espionage agents, details of the Soviet recruitment system, and many other related subjects are contained in the 733-page *Report of the Royal Commission,* a model investigation of its kind. There is no substitute for the report; for an understanding of the Canadian case, it must be read in full. The following short extracts from that painstakingly compiled work are designed to give its flavor. Its contents can only be minutely indicated.

Following Gouzenko's short statement here, there appear some samples of the documents he took with him, and a brief analysis by the commission of the value of the material obtained by Soviet agents. Particularly interesting in the last section is Moscow's awkward and blustering statement to Canada. It is a masterpiece of squirming when caught in the act. One cautionary note ought to be added: some Stalinists have concocted the remarkable defense, after first denying of course that an espionage ring existed, that a ring did exist but that nothing of great importance was obtained and that therefore the entire matter is unimportant. That, indeed, is the attitude of the Soviet statement. The reasoning is curious. First, as the commission states, valuable material *was* obtained. Second, the fact that Gouzenko's disclosures caused the ring to be broken up in time hardly reflects credit on the Soviet Union. If this had not happened, it is reasonable to assume that espionage successes would have been greater in the future. In addition, Gouzenko was able to provide information only on one of the

Soviet networks; there are known to have been several, nine in Canada alone. Gouzenko, also, submitted documentary material on a relatively short period—the ring preceded his appearance in Canada. Finally, the damage while not decisive —through no virtue of the Soviet Union—was considerable. Samples of uranium, together with other items, were shipped to Moscow. What part these shipments and related ones from other networks abroad played in the events leading up to the more recent announcements of Soviet production of atomic materials cannot be determined.

One known supplier of uranium samples was Dr. Allan Nunn May (cover name: "Alek") who was implicated by the Soviet espionage documents. He pleaded guilty and was sentenced to ten years' penal servitude. In his written statement, Dr. May, a British nuclear physicist, confessed: "At one meeting I gave the man microscopic amounts of U.233 and U.235 (one of each). The U.235 was a slightly enriched sample and was in a small glass tube and consisted of about a milliogram of oxide. The U.233 was about a tenth of a milliogram and was a very thin deposit on a platinum foil and was wrapped in a piece of paper." The "man," whom Dr. May declined to name, was identified by Gouzenko as Lieutenant Angelov, Assistant to the military attaché.

The title, "The 'Neighbors' in Canada," binding the following extracts has been added by the editor. "The Neighbors" was the espionage code name for the NKVD in Canada. Readers interested in a personal account of Igor Gouzenko, including informative material on life in the USSR, are referred to his book *The Iron Curtain* (New York, 1948).

The *"Neighbors"* in Canada by Igor Gouzenko

I, IGOR GOUZENKO wish to make the following statement of my own will:

Having arrived in Canada two years ago, I was surprised during the first days by the complete freedom of the individual which exists in Canada but does not exist in Russia. The false representations about the democratic countries which are increasingly propagated in Russia were dissipated daily, as no lying propaganda can stand up against facts.

During two years of life in Canada, I saw the evidence of what a free people can do. What the Canadian people have accomplished and are accomplishing here under conditions of complete freedom—the Russian people, under the conditions of the Soviet regime of violence and suppression of all freedom, cannot accomplish even at the cost of tremendous sacrifices, blood and tears.

The last elections which took place recently in Canada especially surprised me. In comparison with them the system of elections in Russia appear as a mockery of the conception of free elections. For example, the fact that in elections in the Soviet Union one candidate is put forward, so that the possibilities of choice are eliminated, speaks for itself.

While creating a false picture of the conditions of life in these countries, the Soviet Government at the same time is taking all measures to prevent the peoples of democratic countries from knowing about the conditions of life in Russia. The facts about the brutal suppression of the freedom of speech, the mockery of the real religious feelings of the people, cannot penetrate into the democratic countries.

Having imposed its communist regime on the people, the Government of the Soviet Union asserts that the Russian people have, as it were, their own particular understanding of freedom and democracy, different from that which prevails among the peoples of the western democracies. *This is a lie.* The Russian people have the same understanding of freedom as all the peoples of the world. However, the Russian people cannot realize their dream of freedom and a democratic government on account of cruel terror and persecution.

Holding forth at international conferences with voluble statements about peace and security, the Soviet Government is simultaneously preparing secretly for the third world war. To meet this war, the Soviet Government is creating in democratic countries, including Canada, *a fifth column,* in the organization of which even diplomatic representatives of the Soviet Government take part.

The announcement of the dissolution of the Comintern was, probably, the greatest farce of the Communists in recent years. Only the name was liquidated, with the object of reassuring public opinion in the democratic countries. Actually the Comintern exists and continues its work, because the Soviet leaders have never relinquished the idea of establishing a Communist dictatorship throughout the world.

Taking into account least of all that this adventurous idea will cost millions of Russian lives, the Communists are engendering hatred in the Russian people towards everything foreign.

To many Soviet people here abroad, *it is clear that the Communist Party in democratic countries has changed long ago from a political party into an agency net of the Soviet Government, into a fifth column in these countries to meet a war,* into an instrument in the hands of the Soviet Government for creating artificial unrest, provocation, etc., etc.

Through numerous party agitators the Soviet Government stirs up the Russian people in every possible way against the peoples of the democratic countries, preparing the ground for the third world war.

During my residence in Canada I have seen how the Canadian people and their Government, sincerely wishing to help the Soviet people, sent supplies to the Soviet Union, collected money for the welfare of the Russian people, sacrificing the lives of their sons in the delivery of these supplies across the ocean —and instead of gratitude for the help rendered, the Soviet Government is developing espionage activity in Canada, preparing to deliver a stab in the back of Canada—all this without the knowledge of the Russian people.

Convinced that such double-faced politics of the Soviet Government towards the democratic countries do not conform with the interests of the Russian people and endanger the security of civilization, I decided to break away from the Soviet regime and to announce my decision openly.

I am glad that I found the strength within myself to take this step and to warn Canada and the other democratic countries of the danger which hangs over them.

(sgd) Gouzenko.

I have read the foregoing translation which was made from my original statement in Russian, and have found it to be correct.

October 10th, 1945.

(sgd) Gouzenko.

* * *

The following selection of extracts from the documents illustrates the variety of subjects on which material was sought:

Supplement to No. 11923

N 11931
22.8.45

To Grant

Take measures to organize acquisition of documentary materials on the atomic bomb!

The technical process, drawings, calculations.

Grant
22.8.45.

Director,
22.8.45.

. . . Try to get from him before departure detailed information on the progress of the work on Uranium. . . .

. . . Badeau asks for permission to change to work on uranium. There is a possibility either by being invited or by applying himself, but he warned that they are very careful in the selection of workers and that they are under strict observation. . . .

ASSIGNMENT No. ———

Assigned personally 25.8.45

1. Answer last letter regarding the new radio tubes, radio-locators (both for $\Lambda = 1, 2, 3$ cm) and the other questions indicated in that letter.
2. Try to find out any particulars about the "Electron Shells."
3. For the next time bring the following books: LG 13853; GL 14017 and P(RAD) 13920.

   P.S.—burn after reading.

ASSIGNMENT No. 2

Assigned 6.7.45 directly . . .

1. To give the basic description of the features of the contrivance transmitting and receiving radio tubes for $\Lambda = 3$ and $\Lambda = 1$ cm. and their technical manufacture.
2. The same with respect to tube "4j-33."
3. New work in the field of radio locators for antiaircraft artillery and aeroplanes with $\Lambda = 3$ and $\Lambda = 1$ cm.
4. What are the features of the "T-R Switch" on wave $\Lambda = 3$ cm and $\Lambda = 1$ cm.

5. The types of radio antennae for $\Lambda = 3$ and $\Lambda = 1$ cm.

6. What are they engaged in on the second floor at the "Boyd Station," there is a supposition that they study infra-red rays and develop cm. radio installations.

7. To give a more detailed technical description of "an/aps-10." . . .

2. Also to give us documentary material for photographing.

3. If there is no opportunity in fulfilling certain requests, no special activity to be displayed.

4. After reading this material burn it.

266

To the Director,

We have received from Badeau 17 top secret and secret documents (English, American and Canadian) on the question of magnicoustics, radio-locators for field artillery; three secret scientific-research journals of the year 1945. Altogether about 700 pages. In the course of the day we were able to photograph all the documents with the help of the Lecia and the photofilter. In the next few days we will receive almost the same amount of documents for 3 to 5 hours and with one film we will not be able to cope with it. I consider it essential to examine the whole library of the scientific Research Council.

Your silence on my No. 256 may disrupt our work on photographing the materials. All the materials I am sending by regular courier.

Grant

27.8.45

N 11273
11.8.45.

To Grant.

It is very important to receive information on the following questions:—

(a) To confirm the official data about the transfer of American troops from Europe to the USA and to the Pacific, also the headquarters of the 9th army, 3, 5, 7, 13 armoured Corps,

18 ADK, 2, 4, 8, 28, 30, 44, 45, 104th Infantry Divisions and 13th Tank Division. To establish the dates of their transfer.

(b) Dislocation of the headquarters of the 8, 16 Armoured Corps, 29, (75), 89th Infantry Divisions, 10th Tank Divisions, 13th and 17th ADD. Also about the dislocation of the Brazilian Infantry Division. . . .

8.8.   The Director.

Grant
11.8.45
To make known to Brent

11295
14.8.45

To Grant.

. . . It is desired to obtain the following information:—

1. 37 methods 2507 and technical processes of the production of war supplies, VV and powders.
2. Deciphering of laminated BB, the production of T. H. and H. S. (composition, purpose, technology and specific qualities).
3. The application of picrate and nitrate-gushnidina. I repeat: picrate and nitro-gushnidina.
4. The technique of producing detonating capsules and igniting capsules. Wire to whom do you consider it possible to give this task.
   If Bacon still continues to work in the Artillery Committee, this task should be assigned to him.

9.8.45   Director.

Grant
14.8.45

ASSIGNMENT No. 3 of "1.8.45"

1. Requirements which a person living as an "illegal" must meet (nationality, citizenship, occupations, education, knowledge of languages, family and financial conditions etc.)

2. Ways of legalisation (organization of a commercial under-taking, joining a business firm as a partner, what kind of firm, joining as a member any office, joining the army as a volun-teer, accepting employment.)

3. Documents which an "illegal" must possess (passport, differ-ent kinds of certificates, references, recommendation letters, etc.)

4. More expedient methods to slip into the country.

5. To provide for secure living quarters and financial means during the period when the "illegal" gets acquainted with the local set-up and conditions. . . .

6. Methods of work of the counter-espionage. The organization of the Federal and provincial counter-espionage services.

*   *   *

Evaluation of Material Delivered

Questions which naturally arise are how much information was obtained by the Russians by means of the illicit operations described in this Report, and what was the importance of that information.

It is impossible to say how much information was obtained, or of what it all consisted. These operations have been going on for a number of years, and the evidence does not by any means disclose the full extent of the information given, even within that one of the networks which we have been able to investigate in some detail. Enough is disclosed, however, to show that a very great deal of secret information from a number of Depart-ments and Agencies of Government was regularly finding its way to the Russians.

The statement handed by Mr. Lozovski, the Soviet Deputy Commissar of Foreign Affairs, to the Chargé d'Affaires of the Canadian Embassy at Moscow on February 21, 1946, which is set out fully in Section IX, contains the following:—

"In this connection, after appropriate investigation, the Soviet Government consider it necessary to make the following statement:

"Soviet organizations have become aware that in the latter periods of the war certain members of the staff of the Soviet Military Attaché in Canada received, from Canadian nationals with whom they were acquainted, certain information of a secret character which did not, however, present great interest for the Soviet organizations. It has transpired that this information referred to technical data of which Soviet organizations had no need in view of more advanced technical attainment in the U.S.S.R., the information in question could be found in published works on radio location, etc. and also in the well known brochure of the American J. D. Smyth, 'Atomic Energy.'

"It would, therefore, be ridiculous to affirm that delivery of insignificant secret data of this kind could create any threat to the security of Canada.

"None the less, as soon as the Soviet Government became aware of the above mentioned acts of certain members of the staff of the Military Attaché in Canada, the Soviet Military Attaché, in view of the inadmissibility of acts of members of his staff in question, was recalled from Canada."

While it admits the operation of the Military Attaché, this statement is also significant because of its attempt to minimize the importance of the information and data obtained.

We did not consider it part of our duty to inquire whether there is in fact "more advanced technical attainment in the U.S.S.R.," but we are impressed by the elaborate nature of the organization set up by Russians to obtain information, and by the lengths to which their agents were prepared to go in the furtherance of that purpose.

We can say that our investigation has satisfied us that none of the secret information and data which the evidence shows was handed over could, at the time it was handed over, be found in any published works. If it could, it would not be secret as the Russian statement admits it was. The Smyth report is dealt with in Section VIII.

The witnesses who appeared before us were not able to speak with any authority about what the Russians knew or had achieved along scientific lines because they were unanimous that the Russians told no one what they knew or what they were doing. As one witness put it, the Russians "took everything and gave nothing out." It is clear that the information sought was considered of the greatest importance by the Russian espionage leaders, and that alone might be a fair test on the question of value.

But the evidence is that some of the information supplied standing alone would appear to have little, if any value. This, however, does not mean that it was in fact valueless. The evidence indicates that there were agents working along the same lines in the United Kingdom, the United States, and elsewhere. The Russians would know from their agents in Canada that information was being pooled: by getting some information on a subject here, some in England and some in the United States, and then assembling it, a very large body of data could be built up. It is therefore impossible to say that any information handed over, no matter how trivial it might appear by itself, was not of some value.

Furthermore the fact that work carried to a certain stage in one country, would be carried a stage further or to completion in another, would mean that for adequate evaluation the material obtained in one place would have to be checked against that obtained in another.

However much secret and valuable information was handed over. Some of it is so secret still, that it can be referred to only obliquely and with the greatest care, and this is especially so in the case of certain secret information shared by Canada, the United Kingdom, and the United States.

From the beginning there was the closest co-operation in scientific research between Canada, the United Kingdom and, later, the United States. While some secrets were not fully shared, as in the case of some details concerning the atomic bomb, the results of continuing research work by scientists in one country was in almost all cases at once communicated to their opposite numbers in the other two. Work carried to a certain stage in one would be further advanced in another; and experimentation and research did not stop when a reasonably satisfactory result appeared to have been achieved but further improvements were sought and frequently made.

As to the question of atomic energy and the work done by nuclear physicists, we are able to say in the first place that on the evidence before us no one in Canada could have revealed how to make an atomic bomb. There was no one in Canada who had that information. In the second place there is no suggestion in the evidence that anyone who had any information on the subject made any disclosures except May.* As to May, he did have certain information that would be of value to the Russians. He was in a position to get, where we do not know but possibly in Montreal, samples of Uranium 235 enriched and Uranium 233; he did get them and did deliver them to Lt. Angelov.* These samples were considered so important by the Russians that upon their receipt, Motinov* flew to Moscow with them. May also possessed considerable knowledge of the experimental plant at Chalk River, Ontario, which was described as "unique." In addition to May's work in Canada, he also did some work in the United States in collaboration with American scientists, but the evidence before us is that in such work also he could not properly have obtained the full story. How much of his information he handed over we are not able to say, but what he is known to have given, as shown by the documents and by his own written statement, we are told would be of considerable help to the Russians in their research work. May, in his written

* ["Alek" identified in the Report as Dr. Alan Nunn May, British nuclear physicist; "Baxter" as Lt. Angelov, Assistant to Soviet Military Attaché, Ottawa; "Lamont" as Lt. Col. Motinov, Soviet Embassy, Ottawa.—*Ed.*]

statement, did not particularise about the extent of the information he gave, but stated in effect that it was more than has since appeared (i.e. in the *Smyth* Report). He said that he gave his "contact" a "written report on atomic research as known to me. This information was mostly of a character which has since been published or is about to be published."

Next to the atomic bomb it would appear to us that the development of Radar was perhaps the most vital work accomplished by the English-speaking Democracies in the technical field during the period in question. British scientists had already done valuable pioneering work before 1939, but the improvements made since then have been considerable and many of these are still in the Top Secret category. Information of the greatest importance in this field was communicated to the Russians by agents.

The work done in connection with anti-submarine devices, Asdic, is as important as the work done on Radar—some authorities say that it is more important. Much of it is still in the Top Secret category. The information before us leads us to the conclusion that much, and very possibly all, of the information available in Canada on this subject has been compromised. It would at least be unwise to assume anything else.

The advances made in Canada by Canadians in developing and improving explosives and propellants were outstanding. Canadian scientists were given very full information on the work being done in the same fields in the United Kingdom and the United States. The very names of many formulas are still supposed to be secret: the production methods even more so. But the names and much of the secret information were given to the Russians as well as continuing information about trials, experiments and proposed future research. This information was of great value.

Another development in which Canada played a leading role is the "V.T. Fuse," the name being a code name. "This is the fuse that knocked the Japanese Air Force out of the air," and it was used against the Germans in the latter part of the European

War. The wiring details and the details of manufacture are still classified as secret. This fuse was developed in Canada. "We started to work in 1943," said a witness, "and developed it to the place where we had to put it into manufacture; but we had no place to manufacture it so we gave this secret to the Americans, and they, with their own knowledge and ours, produced this fuse. Canadians have been in on this right from the very beginning." One of the agents upon whom we are reporting had the wiring diagram of this fuse. There are certain details of the manufacture which were known only to the Americans; and the United States of America is, we are told, the only country that can build the fuse at the present time. This fuse is the "electro bomb" referred to in some of the Russian documents. None of the armaments sent to Russia during the war included this fuse.

In conclusion, therefore, we can say that much vital technical information, which should still be secret to the authorities of Canada, Great Britain and the United States, has been made known to the Russians by reason of the espionage activities reported on herein. The full extent of the information handed over is impossible to say; as we have already pointed out, these operations have been going on for some time. We should emphasize that the bulk of the technical information sought by the espionage leaders related to research developments which would play an important part in the *post-war* defences of Canada, the United Kingdom, and the United States.

Much of the information . . . comes in a different category from the technical and scientific information dealt with above. This second category may be described briefly as economic information. It included information on production, location of industries, transportation, and planning. It included also information regarding a wide variety of financial matters and matters pertaining to international trade and commercial policy. It is sufficient to say here that the amount of material in this category which was handed over was very great indeed . . . Regarding evaluation of this material, we will say only that this information appears to have been such as would be designed to facilitate detailed estimates of Canada's post-war economic and military potential. Parts of this information could also be useful in connection with possible sabotage operations.

There is a further category of information which we should mention briefly. In addition to material on technical, scientific and economic subjects, the espionage leaders also sought—and obtained from agents in the cipher division of the Department of External Affairs and in the registry of the Office of the United Kingdom High Commissioner at Ottawa—political information. Much of the political information obtained was classified as Top Secret and related not only to the policies of the Canadian Government but to those of the Governments of the United Kingdom and the United States. The value of information of this type needs no particularization.

Again, Canadian citizenship documents such as passports, naturalization certificates, and marriage or birth certificates were sought for illegal purposes and in some cases obtained. Such documents were sought not only for use in Canada but also, as illustrated for example by the Witczak passport case dealt with in Section V of this Report, for use in the United States. Sam Carr accepted in 1945 an assignment to facilitate the entry of other planted agents into Canada in the future, and it is clear that this type of operation, which was not a new development, was intended to be used more extensively in the future. Such planted agents could in time be used not only for espionage but for sabotage, leadership of subversive political groups, and other purposes. It is unnecessary to comment on the possible gravity of these operations.

The other aspect of this whole matter should not be lost sight of. Of paramount importance is the fact that Canadians were willing to give secret information no matter what its importance, and were carrying out their agreements. Some gave all they had or all they could get; others apparently gave only some of what was in their possession; some had not much to give but were in positions where they would, in the future, have been able to give more and they would undoubtedly have done so. The most important thing is the agreement of certain Canadian Communists to work under foreign orders in a conspiracy directed against their own country.

David J. Dallin

THE NEW RELIGIOUS POLICY

Editor's Note

The present selection is an informative antidote for many of the confusions in regard to the question of religion in Russia. It deals with this complex subject comprehensively and yet succinctly. Written in 1944, at the height of the din about Soviet Russia's "new religious policy," it provides a clear guide to an understanding of that policy, as well as more recent Soviet reversions to type—especially in the satellite countries—actions and repressions which must have come as a severe surprise to those who had been "re-won" on this issue by wartime Soviet propaganda.

David Julievich Dallin was born in Rogachow, Russia, on May 24, 1889. He is widely recognized as one of the most authoritative students of Russian affairs. He studied at the Universities of St. Petersburg and Berlin and later took his doctorate at the University of Heidelberg. He was arrested for political activity in 1909 and spent the years 1911-17 in exile. He returned to Russia after the Revolution and served as an opposition deputy in the Moscow Soviet. In 1921 he was again forced to leave his native land. He later lived in Germany, Poland and France, and for a number of years has made his home in the United States. His many books on the Soviet Union (and many articles) furnish an enlightening guide to the political and social systems of that country. He is the author of *Wages and Social Movements; After Wars and Revolutions; Soviet Russia's Foreign Pol-*

THE NEW RELIGIOUS POLICY—David J. Dallin 547

icy; Russia and Postwar Europe; The Big Three; Forced Labor in Soviet Russia (with Boris I. Nicolaevsky); *Soviet Russia and the Far East;* and the *Rise of Russia in Asia.* This selection is taken from his *The Real Soviet Russia* (1944).

\#

The New Religious Policy by David J. Dallin

W<small>HEN</small> the Calvinist King of France, Henry IV, found himself hard pressed in his conflict with the French Catholics and it appeared difficult to take Paris, Henry, that prototype of political "realists," declared that *"Paris vaut bien une messe"* ("Paris is worth a mass"): he embraced Catholicism and the capital opened its gates to him. Was it worth sacrificing ponderable interests for the sake of vague ideology? asked the realistic king.

There are many people who imagine that something similar is now happening in Russia in the field of religion. They read of brilliant church services in Moscow, of the reopening of closed churches, of the election of a patriarch, of the government agreeing to the restoration of churches wrecked at the front, of the solidarity of the Orthodox clergy with the government in all questions concerning the war—and they imagine that "the great realist in the Kremlin" is emulating the policy of his French prototype, and that before long Russia will have either complete freedom of religion or that the Orthodox Church will be restored to the position it occupied before the revolution in 1917.

Moscow, on the other hand, does all it possibly can to strengthen the impression that there is a genuine restoration of religious freedom. In conceding an inch to the church Moscow seeks to make the world believe that it is granting a mile. Nothing pleases Moscow more than the belief cultivated by the foreign press that Russia is returning to her traditional roads:

"Bright with candlelight and the splendor of clerical garb, the church presented a magnificent spectacle, perhaps as magnificent as it has ever witnessed. It was like a page from ancient Russia. . . ."

A page from ancient Russia! As though by accident the author of this report from Moscow, Maurice Hindus, uses a phrase which Moscow was eager to have used. It wants to spread the belief among all inside and outside the country who prefer the old Russia to the new that "a page of ancient Russia" has turned up again amid the Soviet metamorphoses, that Russia has turned her back on her Communist ways, substituted bishops for Marxists, conservatives for revolutionists, and transformed her government from an instrument of world revolution to a bulwark of world stability.

The history of the religious policy of the Soviet Government exposes the error of this conception, so widely current because human beings are so prone to forget the recent past. The true meaning and character of the evolution Russia has undergone on this question may be clearly discerned in the tortuous history of Soviet religious policy.

Russia has experienced no less than three violent outbursts of the antireligious movement, of persecutions and the closing of churches, in the twenty-seven years of the Soviet regime. And three times, after each outburst, came periods of relief, of moderation, of compromise.

The first big wave of antireligious persecutions, which had already begun during the civil war, struck the church in the period of the NEP, 1921-23. While some concessions were being made to private economy and many observers had imagined that a return to "ancient Russia" was impending, the "revolutionary offensive" continued in the sphere of religion. Arrests and executions of priests assumed a mass character. "Freedom of conscience" as guaranteed by the Soviet constitution had no real significance beyond propaganda aims. Paragraph 13 of the first Soviet constitution provided:

"The church is separated from the state, and freedom of religious and of antireligious propaganda is recognized for all citizens."

"All citizens" (not only the workers) were accorded the right of religious propaganda. Yet the years following adoption of the constitution were a period of ruthless persecution of religion. Religious propaganda was rigorously suppressed.

The constitution, adopted in 1924, and drafted with great care on the basis of previous experience (Stalin participated actively in the drafting), separated the school from the church but reaffirmed the phrase concerning the rights of citizens to religious propaganda. Paragraph 4 declared:

"To assure the workers of true freedom of conscience the church is separated from the state, and the school from the church, and freedom of religious and antireligious propaganda is recognized for all citizens."

In explanation of the Soviet Government's policy on questions of religion, Stalin declared in his interview with an American labor delegation in 1927:

"The party cannot be neutral in respect to religion, it wages an antireligious propaganda against all religious prejudices because it stands for science . . . There are cases of party members interfering with the full development of antireligious propaganda. It is good that such members are expelled."

The persecutions in the first period of Soviet antireligious policy reached their zenith in 1923. The execution of the Catholic priest Budkiewicz provoked an international conflict, with particularly serious consequences to Soviet Russia's relations with England. The Soviet Government found it wise to make concessions. Its religious policy experienced a shift. The persecutions were moderated and the remaining open churches were permitted to function.

The antireligious movement was halted in part. The Union of Militant Godless, founded in that period, continued to function, supported by the Komsomol, and the distribution of antireligious literature continued, but the persecution of priests was considerably alleviated.

By that time the basic feature of the subsequent antireligious movements—from the end of the 'twenties to the war—had become crystallized. These movements ceased to be as popular and spontaneous as in the first ten years of the revolution and assumed in all their alternating outbursts and recessions an artificial character. The population, especially the youth, continued to display a lively interest in religious and antireligious problems; supporters of religion declined in number. But the original fervor ("we will climb up to heaven and disperse all the gods") had abated, the sensational digging up of relics of saints was over. The international effect of Soviet religious policy moved the government, for its part, to put on the brakes on antireligious stunts.

The principal center of the antireligious movement was in the GPU, which had a special division concerned with religious problems whose task it was to accelerate or moderate the pressure, as need required. In more recent years the Union of the Godless worked in close contact with and under the direction of the GPU.*

The moderation of religious persecutions in the middle and late 'twenties gave rise to the same kind of discussions and hopes that now prevail. The Metropolitan Sergius, the acting patriarch (later chosen patriarch), who died in 1944, addressed the following manifesto to believers in July, 1927:

"We inform you that in May of this year, upon my instructions and with permission of the authorities, a Patriarchal Synod has been established by the administration of the Patriarch's Office.

"We hope that this legalization will gradually be expanded to the lower church administration.

"The joys and successes of the Soviet Union are also ours."

* The official book on *The Komsomol and Antireligious Propaganda* contains many observations like the following: "Cells of the Union of the Godless frequently confine their activity to distributing membership cards in the Union of the Godless. Godless members of the Komsomol have become too tame."

But in 1929-30 came collectivization, and the attitude of the government toward the church experienced a radical change. The local church constituted an important element in village life, and the attitude of the clergy toward the collectivization was known to be hostile. The entire course of internal policy swung to the left, and many promises previously given were wiped out in a moment. Mass closings of churches were resumed, many priests were exiled, wholesale arrests were under way everywhere. The persecutions were soon extended to the cities; in 1932 priests were exiled from the cities in batches as "nonworking elements." The severe repressions continued for several years. The aforementioned Paragraph 4 was revised as follows by the Congress of Soviets of the RSFSR in 1929:

"In order to assure the workers of true freedom of conscience, the church is separated from the state and the school from the church, and freedom of religious worship and of antireligious propaganda is recognized for all citizens."

From now on there was to be freedom only for antireligious propaganda but not for religious propaganda. Believers were accorded only "freedom of religious worship," which meant the right of priests to perform services but no more.

In July, 1930, the Communist Party Congress decided to intensify the antireligious propaganda.

How difficult was the position of the representatives of the church, and how great were the concessions they were obliged to make for their self-preservation may be seen from the interview given by the Metropolitan Sergius in February, 1930, and published by the entire press under the signatures of two metropolitans, two bishops, and two other prelates:

"QUESTION: Is there persecution of religion in Russia?

"ANSWER: There never were persecutions of religion in Russia. . . . True, some churches were closed, but this is not done on the initiative of the government but by will of the population, in some instances even by decision of the believers themselves.

"QUESTION: Is religious propaganda permitted in the USSR?

"ANSWER: Religious services and sermons are not forbidden. The teaching of religion is permitted."

The next question concerned repressions and cruelties practiced against priests.

"ANSWER: All this is pure invention, slander. We have had no limitations placed upon the administrations of our church organs to date." *

Only in 1934-35, after collectivization had been completed and the international situation required that the Soviet Government embrace the policy of collective security and support of the League of Nations, did the government again moderate its church policy. Mass persecutions ceased. Antireligious processions were forbidden. It was permitted to light Christmas trees, to manufacture wedding rings, etc.

Once more official pronouncements declared: "We do not persecute religion by any means. We demand from church parishioners that they refrain from interfering in politics. The old clergy, bound to the old regime, would not abandon its struggle against the Soviet power, and it was necessary for us to resort to repressions. But now they have apparently turned their faces in our direction—and the church is free." This was almost literally a repetition of the arguments used in the 'twenties, which had been followed by new outbursts of repressions.

Meanwhile, the new constitution, drafted in 1936, in this period of religious liberalism, did not signify a return to Lenin's formulas. It again excluded religious propaganda: "Freedom of religious worship and freedom of antireligious propaganda is recognized for all citizens."

On the other hand the new constitution abolished the civil disabilities imposed upon "nonworkers," which had applied also

---

* The details of this interview, historic in its way (published in *Izvestiga,* February 16, 1930) are told in William Henry Chamberlin's *Russia's Iron Age,* Chapter XXI.

to priests. The right of franchise in elections to the Soviets (even the right, on paper, of being elected) was accorded also to priests. However, the significance of these constitutional reforms was negligible.

At the end of 1937 came a new wave—the third—of persecution of religion. This was the period of the great purge. More than ten thousand religious parishes were closed according to Professor N. S. Timasheff.* Severe repressions descended upon priests, with arrests, exile, imprisonment in concentration camps, and even executions. The old trite accusations of espionage, industrial sabotage, and all the other crimes attributed at that time by the NKVD to many others were directed also against priests.

In 1939, with the conclusion of the purge, the repressions against priests ceased. Another period of tolerance ensued. It continued until the outbreak of the war with Germany.

In 1940 the observance of Sunday was restored with the reestablishment of the seven-day work week. While there were some repressions of priests in the new regions annexed to Russia, the general policy was a cautious one.** To avoid misunderstanding, the Central Committee of the Communist Party was now moved to remind its members that they were forbidden to practice religion.

And so the history of the period of 1918-41 follows a tortuous line. Periods of severe repression alternated with spans of relative tolerance. For the religious policy was only part of the general internal policy with its ups and downs. But with the end of each span of repression, the surviving representatives of the church would begin to console themselves with the hope that a profound evolution had taken place in the ideology of the government, and that the new rights accorded to the church would remain inviolate.

It is to be observed that at no time did a turn favorable to

* *Religion in Soviet Russia.*
** The Swiss press reported that in Bessarabia priests were ordered in December, 1940, to move into the interior of Russia. In Riga churches were closed at Christmas, 1940.

religion win all the ground lost by the church through previous repressions. Only a few of the closed churches were permitted to reopen and exiled priests were not given their liberty. A new generation of priests was not permitted to develop, and in many instances laymen, and occasionally women, served as substitutes for the clergy. The right to publish the Bible was not restored, nor was it permitted to import it from abroad, even if it was sent free.

At the time of Hitler's invasion of Russia, after twenty-four years of the Soviet regime, Russia had:

> 28 bishops—a decrease of 75 per cent since 1917.
> 5,665 priests—a decrease of 90 per cent since 1917.
> 3,100 deacons—against 15,210 in 1917.
> 4,225 churches—against 46,457 in 1917.
> 37 monasteries—against 1,026 in 1917.

Regarding the attitude of the population toward religion, Soviet sources noted before the war that about two thirds of the village population and approximately one third of the city population, *i.e.*, about half of the population, considered themselves as adhering to various churches. These figures are from a census taken in 1937. Because they showed a surprisingly persistent devotion to religion, they served as the motive for a new antireligious campaign, begun in 1937 and halted at the beginning of 1939. *

The war brought great relief for religion and the church.

The principal reason for the new reforms lay in the religious sentiments preserved by the population, particularly in the villages. It was possible to ignore them when the government had to do with collectives and purges, but when the peasants were mobilized for a life and death struggle it was necessary to take a "step backward" and to adapt the policy to the needs of "backward elements." The present situation, involving as it does great popular activity, particularly in matters concerning the war, has compelled a retreat from the straight Communist line on the ideological front. The concessions granted during the war were specifically a compromise with the Russian peasantry. This was the first and most important of the reforms.

The first but not the only one.

Much of what has taken place in the relations between the government and the church in the period from 1914 to 1944 has become known abroad; what remains unknown is the actual character of these relations, which have developed on the principle of *do ut des*. The government made one concession after another to the church. But for every concession received the church was obliged to pay immediately with political moves favorable to the government; at times this assumed a quite overt character.

For a number of years Hitler's government had encouraged the activities of Orthodox prelates and priests resident in Germany and consisting almost exclusively of émigrés from Russia. Hitler appropriated money for the construction of an Orthodox cathedral in Berlin; nineteen Orthodox churches received government appropriations for repairs. All this was by way of preparation for the great political campaign which developed immediately after the invasion of Russia by German troops.

In the occupied regions a number of Orthodox priests declared their support of Germany and prayed for the success of the German arms. Some high dignitaries of the church went over to the German side. Attention has already been called to the Riga conference of church leaders in occupied territories and the blessing they conferred upon the German army.

The Germans paid particular attention to the church in the

---

* Because many feared to answer the question "believer" or "nonbeliever" in the census, little value must be attached to the final figures. The Soviet press has contended that believers had little genuine faith. The *Komsomolskaya Pravda* received the following letter in 1937 from a person who had taken the entire course of antireligious propaganda:

"We repudiate the writings about God and we assert that there was not and there is not any such person. This fact has been established on the basis of scientific data concerning the origin of man as well as the origin of the universe. But what interests me is another thing: Do sorcerers and conjurers really exist and what is the power they possess by which they corrupt people and transform them into swine, dogs, etc.? You may, perhaps, deny this, but these are facts."

Ukraine. By conferring favors upon it they sought to wean it away from Moscow, and in this respect they had some success. Their second aim was to obtain support of the church against the Vatican; in this respect they were not so successful. Not until the end of 1942 did the Germans become rather cool toward matters concerning the Orthodox and Ukrainian churches.

The pro-Hitlerite policy of the Orthodox clergy in the occupied regions of Russia was an important factor in determining the policy on religion pursued by the Soviet Government during the war. It was wise to come to the "defense of religion" in the struggle with heathen Hitlerism. German propaganda sought to create a great European bloc against "Godless Bolshevism," and Moscow replied with a counterblow: defense of religion against the heathen, revival of the patriarchate, and restoration of churches destroyed by the Germans.

One of the motives for a change in Soviet religious policy was the effect which the antireligious policy as pursued over a long period had created in neighboring allied and enemy countries. The religious beliefs of the populations constituted an obstacle to the policies recommended by Moscow for the various national movements (in which Communists were to play the directing part). In Yugoslavia members of the Orthodox Church constituted half the population (more than half among the Serbs); in Bulgaria they were two thirds; in Rumania, two thirds, in Greece, 99 per cent. The "All-Slav Meetings" in Moscow were appealing to the national sentiments of the Slav peoples; Orthodox religious leaders were in a position to appeal also to non-Slav peoples, such as the Rumanians and Greeks. It was natural, therefore, to combine the All-Slav propaganda with Orthodox propaganda. In June, 1943, a group of six bishops, headed by the Metropolitan Nikolai, made their appearance at a solemn meeting of the All-Slav Committee in Moscow.

Moreover, there were a number of political problems presenting a source of disagreement between Russia and her allies on which an authoritative nongovernment voice, the voice of public opinion, expressing itself in support of Russia would be more effective than the Kremlin's. On the question of the second front, for example, the Orthodox Church spoke out with determination in support of the government's position. Many other such questions may arise in the future.

Immediately after the beginning of the Soviet-German war the highest church authority in Russia, the Metropolitan Sergius, declared his support of the war in the name of the church. At a solemn service in Moscow, on June 29, 1941, he prayed for success of the Russian arms.

In September of the same year the *Godless* and the *Antireligionist* ceased publication. In America and other countries this was interpreted by some as the consequence of intervention by President Roosevelt through Averell Harriman, who at that time made his first visit to Moscow as an official representative. Harriman did talk about the matter to Stalin. But as indicated above, there were many other extremely important reasons for a change in Soviet religious policy.

On the anniversary day of the November revolution the Metropolitan Sergius hailed Stalin as "the divinely appointed leader of our armed and cultural forces leading us to victory." Metropolitan Nikolai of Kiev wired Stalin wishing him a long life. A week later came the sensation of his appointment as a member of the Commission of Inquiry into German Atrocities. The churches participated in war-fund drives.

Very soon, in February, 1942, the Metropolitan Sergius, who had been evacuated from Moscow to Ulianovsk (the former Simbirsk) issued a manifesto against the Orthodox priests who had gone over to Hitler and were forming an "independent" church in the Ukraine. He pointed out that the leader of this movement, Bishop Polikarp Sikorsky, had previously pledged allegiance to the Soviet Government. The Metropolitan Sergius threatened the renegades with excommunication and called upon the Orthodox faithful to repudiate them.

Then followed another sensation. The church leaders—for the first time since the revolution—published a book in Russia on religion entitled *The Truth About Religion in Russia*. Expensively printed, despite the difficulties experienced by the printing industry in wartime, and richly illustrated, this book sought to prove that religion was free and that, in general, there had never been any persecution of religion in Russia on the part of the government. Any unpleasant developments that had occurred had been due to the activities of the Union of the Godless and not of the government! (As already indicated, this loyal interpretation had been used as a defense mechanism by the clergy since 1930.) Despite its loyalty and patriotism, however, this book was not distributed through book stores. It was circulated only among Soviet grandees and institutions abroad. It is worth noting that it was printed in the printing shop which used to print the *Godless.* Apparently the NKVD division which had previously directed the antireligious propaganda was now directing the proreligious activity behind the scenes. No doubt the very same persons did both jobs.

On Good Friday, 1943, the Metropolitan Sergius read over the radio an address to the Orthodox population of all countries, but directed particularly to the Serbs, Czechs, and Greeks. Naturally, it had previously been approved by the government.

The biggest moment in the history of the Orthodox Church came in September, 1943. The government permitted the election of a Patriarch. On September 4, 1943, Stalin, in the presence of Molotov, received the 76-year-old Metropolitan Sergius, who was accompanied by two other metropolitans. This was followed immediately by announcement of the restoration of the Synod, composed of six men, and of the election of Sergius as Patriarch. The day after his reception by Stalin the new Patriarch demanded a second front, addressing the following sharp remark to Russia's allies:

"We Russians are the world's most patient people, but the cup of our patience is overflowing."

At the same time a conclave of nineteen metropolitans, archbishops, and bishops made public a manifesto declaring:

"There are individuals found among the clergy and laymen who, forgetting the fear of God, have dared to build their own welfare upon the misfortune of all. They meet the Germans as welcome guests, enter their service and sometimes go so far as direct treachery, betraying their brethren to the enemy, as, for example, guerrillas and others who are sacrificing their lives for their country.

"Everyone guilty of treachery to the common cause of the church and desertion to the side of fascism as an enemy of God's crucifix will be deemed excommunicated; and if he be bishop or priest he will be unfrocked. Amen!"

The Patriarch was given the use of one of the finest houses in Moscow, formerly occupied by an official German delegation. Churches began to be restored, particularly in territories cleared of the Germans. Churches previously reopened under the Germans continued to function. The Alexander-Nevsky Monastery was restored; Troitsko-Sergiev partly so. The former, where Suvorov was buried, experienced a flow of visitors, and military men were ordered to kneel before his grave.

At the beginning of 1944 training of new priests was permitted. Establishment of the Orthodox Theological Institute was authorized, as were various theological courses. Contrary to the new practice in universities, tuition is free, but students must not be below eighteen years of age.

Finally, in order not to compromise the church with a connection with the NKVD, a separate government Committee on Affairs of the Orthodox Church was set up to act as a liaison between the church and the government. In June, 1944, the Soviet Government decided to create an official committee dealing with the affairs of all churches.

Support of the clergy became necessary also in the struggle with the Vatican, which continued to play a very important role in the European war.

The Vatican's moral influence was thrown entirely on the anti-Hitler side of the scales, particularly after 1939, when Catholic France, Poland and Czechoslovakia fell under German domination. But, unlike other anti-Hitlerite powers—Britain and the United States—the Vatican, as a spiritual power, could not think of collaboration with the Soviet Government without a radical change in Soviet religious policy. The Vatican could not simply forget, as did the temporal powers, the activities of Communism in all countries, the religious persecutions which had held sway in Russia only five years before, the fate that had been inflicted upon Catholic priests in Spain, and similar events.

For this reason the Vatican remained not only an anti-Hitlerite but also an anti-Communist power. It could afford the luxury of such consistency because it had no armies and navies of its own, did not concern itself with strategy, and was not trying to solve problems of first and second fronts. Foreseeing the defeat of Germany, the Vatican feared the spread of Communist, antireligious movements in Europe, and adopted, therefore, a very cautious attitude on the question of collaboration between non-Communists and Communists in liberated territories. The Vatican had thus become a great anti-Soviet force during the war, during the very period when the Soviet Government had hoped to expand its political and intellectual influence in Europe.

To stand in its old position of unstable legalistic "freedom of conscience" was not wise for the Soviet Government. It was necessary to bring into action another religious power against the Vatican, a power that would wield greater influence in the Christian world in matters of religion than could the Soviet Government. The Orthodox Church, and particularly the figure of the Patriarch, stood out as the proper authority for this purpose.

With improvement of relations between Soviet Russia and her allies (after the Moscow and Teheran conferences) at the end of 1943, the Vatican appeared as Moscow's sole serious opponent in the anti-Hitlerite camp.

On February 1, 1944, *Izvestiya* again assailed the Vatican. "The Vatican's foreign policy—wrote the official organ—has earned the hatred and contempt of the Italian masses for supporting fascism. The disgraceful role the Vatican played in

Hitler's and Mussolini's Spanish adventure is widely known. The Vatican emerged in the role of a supporter of armed intervention."

The foreign policy of the Soviet Government was thinly veiled behind an apparently theological dispute which otherwise would seem incomprehensible in wartime. Patriarch Sergius attacked the very principles of the Papacy, in April, 1944. "The uninterrupted presence of Christ in the church," the Patriarch wrote in his *Journal of Moscow Patriarchate*, "and the spiritual marriage between Christ and the church make inconceivable the concept of an intermediary between the two such as a vicar on earth." He concluded with a hint of a political nature: "I could conceive of a union of churches around some chief who could not be a vicar of Christ but a bishop of some world capital."

In 1944 a new feature appeared, however, in the attitude of the Soviet Government to the Catholic world. The territories with a prevailing Orthodox population were reoccupied by the Red Army in the first months of that year, and the Soviet troops stood at the gates of Catholic countries: Lithuania, Poland, Czechoslovakia. In the Balkans and in Austria the influence of the Catholic church is strong, too. Achievement of the war aims of a zone of Soviet influence in eastern Europe, and especially a favorable solution of the Polish problem, required collaboration, at least at the beginning, with the Catholic forces in these countries.

Therefore the attacks on the Vatican were supplemented now by conciliatory political moves. On the invitation of Stalin, Father Orlemanski of Springfield, Massachusetts, made his trip to Moscow; the Italian Communist leader Ercoli went to a mass in a Catholic church, and other similar maneuvers were to be expected in the near future. A kind of agreement, at least a wartime truce, with the Vatican was becoming necessary, and Moscow would be ready to make certain concessions to achieve it.

Soviet church reforms followed in quick succession. Solemn

services attended by thousands, and numerous declarations by church leaders, created the impression that the Soviet Government had entered upon the road of complete religious liberty, even of encouragement of religion. But this was far removed from the facts.

When the Archbishop of York, known for his liberal views, visited Moscow in October, 1943, he attended a solemn service and spoke at length with the Patriarch and his associates. Upon his return to London he declared: "The Russian Patriarch and his colleagues were most anxious to make it plain that they had complete freedom of worship within their churches."

"Within their churches" meant that the priests and parishioners were not disturbed by the police or by Godless agitators during services. This and this alone constituted their freedom. But, added the Archbishop of York, "very many churches are still closed or secularized."

As if to emphasize Communist principle and devotion to old positions, President Kalinin wrote in June, 1943, that the government continued as before, to regard religion as "a misguiding institution."

This statement is confirmed by the following figures on the number of churches in Moscow, where the church enjoys greater freedom than in the provinces: in 1900 there were 351 churches in Moscow; in 1934 there were 40 churches functioning; in 1938, 25; in 1939, 15. In the spring of 1943 this number rose to 30, and at the end of the year there were about 50. Thus three times as many churches were open as on the eve of the war, but the number was many times less than before the revolution.

The situation in the provinces was even more difficult. Every local church parish, however small, provokes fear and distrust on the part of the authorities. Every parish lives its own life and must, perforce, exhibit differences of opinions on various questions. It is not so much the sermons that can be dangerous for the regime as the conversations of the parishioners among themselves and in their collective life. A police government is bound to fear that a church parish may be transformed into a cell of discontent and opposition. Its autonomy is a dangerous thing, however efficient may be the system of espionage operating within.*

For this reason, and not only because of the shortage of priests, the number of open churches remains small. The freedom of religion granted during this war may not last long. It is but another move in the tortuous history of Soviet religious policy.

It has also become clear that separation of church and state has no basis in fact under a political regime such as exists in Russia. Under Soviet conditions, the church cannot develop its activities if the state does not assist it: under such circumstances the restoration of churches without the help of the state's economic organs is impossible. It is impossible to obtain the ornaments and habiliments necessary for services without the cooperation of government agencies. The printing of books and magazines in Russia requires not only money but also the active collaboration of various government agencies. The Synod, the Patriarch, the Theological Institute, and the rest can be housed only with the assistance and at the will of the government.

For this reason the church is not actually separated from the state in Soviet Russia. Living by the grace of the government, the church faces the risk of losing its new privileges at any moment; hence it is compelled to cooperate fully with the government politically, and at times church leaders find themselves in an undignified position. The church leaders, who also

---

* In an interview with a representative of the Religious News Service (August 11, 1944), Georgi Karpov, head of the Soviet Committee on Orthodox Affairs, declared that there were "no barriers to church expansion" any more. He did not, however, give the number of newly opened churches, after a year of his Committee's activity. He mentioned the following legal reasons for rejecting petitions for the opening of new churches: first, where there is no church building available (private houses have been used for church services in the last decades in Russia); second, "when people in a small hamlet already having two or three churches want another." This alleged abundance of churches and unreasonableness of the believers seem curious.

are "realists," accept many compromises in order that the churches may be permitted to function. But at the same time they swallow many bitter pills.

The church does not play a great role in the social life of Russia today. But the history of religion and of religious policy illustrates glaringly the nature of the political system and the conditional character of the political shifts.*

* [A most distressing recent development in the religious and ethnic field has been the emergence of a new official anti-Semitism. This area is one in which the Communists were universally accorded respect for not emulating the policies of Jew hatred which served Tsarism as so useful a "divide and conquer" method. The literature on this depressing subject is far heavier than most persons realize. Among other accounts, see: "The New Anti-Semitism of the Soviet Union" by Solomon M. Schwarz, *Commentary,* the magazine of the American Jewish Committee, June 1949; "Soviet Russia and the Jews" (pamphlet, 1949), by Gregor Aronson, published by the American Jewish League Against Communism; Chapter 14 of Igor Gouzenko's *The Iron Curtain;* "Has Russia Solved the Jewish Problem?" by Harry Schwartz, *Commentary,* February 1948; Chapter 12 of Walter Bedell Smith's *My Three Years in Moscow.* "Jews Behind the Iron Curtain" (pamphlet, 1949), is an informative and comprehensive survey on the satellite nations prepared by Emmanuel Patt for the Jewish Labor Committee. Antedating the current campaign is the dismal story of the systematic Soviet devastation of Jewish culture and cultural institutions. The Hebrew language, for example, has long been forbidden. Zionism, as are all non-Communist political activities, has long been verboten, and Communist persecution of Zionists has been without parallel in any country with the exception, of course, of Nazi Germany. Julius Margolin, a Zionist leader who spent five years as a prisoner in Soviet concentration camps, has sadly stated what every Russian Jew knows: *"An entire generation of Zionists has died in Soviet prisons, camps and exile."* (An extended statement by Dr. Margolin will be found in the special supplement to *The New Leader* of March 29, 1947.) On the cultural plight of the Soviet Jews, see Jacob Lestshinsky's articles in *Jewish Frontier,* December 1948, and in *The New Palestine,* October 4, 1946. For the latest dismal report on Birobidjan, the so-called "Jewish National State" in the USSR, see "Veil Is Lifted From Soviet Jewish State; Living Conditions Primitive, Many Work 16-Hour Day," in the *New York Herald Tribune,* November 9, 1949, by Joseph Newman, former Russian correspondent of that paper.—*Ed.*]

Sergei Eisenstein

M E A   C U L P A

Editor's Note

IN SPEAKING of art, science, and
scholarship, Soviet officials are fond of utilizing military language. The terminology is appropriate. For many years a war
has indeed been waged against Soviet culture. The first stage
called for the demolition of all independent thought, the second for its resurrection, stripped of creative content, as a
"weapon" on the side of the masters of the Soviet state. Art, in
its primary and essential purposes, is destroyed; art as an implement of the dictatorial state, as an important means of dis-
seminating official views, is given a high place. Artists who
aspire to creative pursuits are broken in spirit, barred from
cultural media, and dealt with in less decorous ways. "Artists"
who turn into production directives of official bureaus are well
rewarded. Whatever disappointments the Soviet state may
have suffered in bringing the nation's industry and agriculture
under its sway, it has been impressively successful in collectiv-
izing art and artists.

In an earlier day, one could speak tellingly of "artists in uniform"; in our day Soviet art has become an adjunct of forced
labor. The entire apparatus of political repression has been
bodily transported into the realm of creative activity. "Confessions," charges of sabotage, recantations—all these are
threaded into the pattern of Soviet indictments and artistic
capitulation. The Western world has observed with astonish-

ment the recurrent spectacle of writers, musicians, economists and historians, scientists, all being obliged to ape defendants in the Moscow Trials. Not a field has been excluded.

"We recall," Irving Talmadge has written, "the literary soirees, the 'vecherinkas,' in Moscow in the early 1930s. The art discussions in those days. We remember many of the participants. The famous regisseur, Vsevolod Meyerholdt, founder of the Meyerholdt Theater; the eminent critic, A. Voronsky; the brilliant journalist, Karl Radek; the dramatist, Sergei Tretiakov, author of *Roar China;* the editor of the *Novy Mir,* Ivan Gronsky; the novelist, Boris Pilnyak; the director of the Kamerny Theater, Tairov. All of them, and scores of others—names well-known at home and abroad—have since perished in the purges. 'Liquidated' is the official term."

Few Soviet artists have been able to rival the almost universal esteem in which the achievements of Sergei Eisenstein were held. At one time, the work of Eisenstein and some others instilled in many persons, spread over the globe, hope in the future of Soviet culture. The Communists themselves exploited this vein heavily. How could one fail to sanction the present regime when it was productive of such accomplishments? Political repression, the terror of the secret police, internal purges, an "undistinguished" foreign policy, miserable living standards —all these were temporary. Sergei Eisenstein was a straw in the wind; his work was a portent of the new society, the new world, the Soviet Union was to bring into being. Undoubtedly many who accepted this formulation were sincere. They were patient. Time would bring enormous changes.

It has. The cultural toll recorded above by Mr. Talmadge is but a token listing; it does not indicate, dreadful as it is, the total denudation of Soviet art.

What about Sergei Eisenstein? What was his fate? In order to appreciate his fate it is necessary to be aware of his accomplishments. Eisenstein was one of the most notable pioneers in the development of the modern motion-picture form. His

October, Potemkin, Ten Days That Shook the World helped
indicate a new cultural frontier by their remarkable contributions to a new art form: Eisenstein's technical innovations, his
use of "montage," his deft development of the screen as creative image and movement, movies as more than the transfer
of other art forms to celluloid. In the history of the motion picture Eisenstein's contributions must be listed as many.

In 1930 Eisenstein visited the United States. After working
on several abortive projects here he returned to the USSR. His
admiration for the U. S. is known to have been considerable
and he soon began to fall from the high favor in which he had
previously been held by the authorities. Integrity in a Soviet
artist is ultimately a liability; coupled with an international
following, it is an invitation for harassment. Eisenstein again
applied for permission to visit the U. S. but this time it was
not forthcoming. He turned therefore to his work and continued to develop vast plans for future films. After an unprecedented record of advance, his following films were banned!
From this point on, his frustration becoming mountainous,
Eisenstein became more tractable. There was no alternative:
one needed to comply. The once independent spirit of this
artist now began to show signs of deterioration. He produced
Alexander Nevsky, which has been described as a "poster-like
kind of patriotism," a sample of the kind of nationalistic, historical propaganda of which the Soviet Union has become so
enamored. But even this capitulation was not sufficient to
bring Eisenstein back into the fold. The period which had produced his rebellious technical experimentation was gone. The
state had use now for only the most literal kind of art by fiat,
art which glorifies the present rulers, which rewrites history,
which never despairs of talking, talking, talking, telling the
people over and over again of Soviet military victories, of the
American and British spies in their midst, of the great, wise
Stalin. Broken, sterile, his pictures unreleased, even his conformist projects found unsatisfactory, Eisenstein produced two

more films. These were *Great Life* and *Ivan the Terrible*, and they were to throw him into new official "disgrace." Even the utterly conformist artist is not safe!

Eisenstein's selection here, his "mea culpa," which first appeared in the Soviet *Culture and Life*, is one of the most debased documents imaginable. The extent of its debasement will be evident to the reader to the extent that he is familiar with Eisenstein's notable past, his achievements, the reputation he enjoyed in Russia and abroad. But even if one had never heard of Eisenstein the document speaks for itself. The reader is revolted by the rock-bottom servility of him who is compelled to write such a statement. One need not characterize the regime that finds it necessary to dictate such "confessions." The literature of the Soviet Union is rife with such breast-beatings by innocent persons—by no means the most contrite, Eisenstein's "mea culpa" provides an insight into all of them.

What exactly does Eisenstein recant in his "mea culpa"? His portrayal of Tsar Ivan, far from hostile, was not sufficiently eulogistic! The Communists who "liberated Russia from despotic Tsarism" now find such a view intolerable. The *oprichniki* —murderous minions of the Tsar—are to be presented, according to the new Soviet view, as heroes. "In the film," states Eisenstein, "the progressive *oprichniki* were presented as a gang of degenerates, something like the Ku Klux Klan. The Central Committee justly condemned this rough misrepresentation of historical fact." How should Ivan be presented? Eisenstein repeats what he has been told. "Is it not so that the center of our attention is and must be *Ivan the builder, Ivan the creator of a new, powerful, united Russian power,* Ivan the inexorable destroyer of everything that resisted his progressive undertakings?" And then that strange lapse, that strange stirring of conscience, the sentence in this confession that Freud might fruitfully have studied: *"The sense of historical truth betrayed me. . . ."* Finally, the conclusion of the destroyed artist: "We must master the Lenin-Stalin method of perception of real life and history. . . . This is a guarantee that in the nearest future our cinematography will again create highly ideological artistic films worthy of the Stalin epoch." Broken in spirit, broken in health, weary, Eisenstein died in 1948.

\#

Mea Culpa by Sergei Eisenstein

IT IS difficult to imagine a sentry who gets so lost in contemplation of the stars that he forgets his post. It is difficult to imagine a tankist eagerly reading an adventure novel while going into battle. It is difficult to believe there could be a foundryman who, instead of giving all his attention to the mass of molten metal flowing into prepared forms, turns aside from his work to contemplate a pattern of his own phantasy. They would be a bad sentry, a bad tankist and a bad foundryman. Each would be a bad soldier.

In our Soviet Army and in our Socialist production there are no bad soldiers.

It is even more difficult to realize that during the stern accounting caused by demands of our Soviet reality such bad and unworthy soldiers were discovered in the front lines of literature and art.

Reading again and again the resolution of the Party Central Committee about the film *Great Life,* I always linger on the question which it put forth: "What can explain the numerous cases of production of false and mistaken films? Why did such known Soviet directors as Comrades Loukov, Eisenstein, Pudovkin, Kozintsev and Trauberg create failures while in the past they have created films of high art value?"

I cannot let the question go unanswered. First of all we failed because at a critical moment in our work we artists forgot for a time those great ideas our art is summoned to serve. Some of us forgot the incessant struggle against our Soviet ideals and ideology which goes on in the whole world. We lost for a time comprehension of the honorable, militant, educational task which lies on our art during the years of hard work to construct the Communist society in which all our people are involved.

The Central Committee justly pointed out to us that the Soviet artist cannot treat his duties in a light-minded and irresponsible way. Workers of the cinema should study deeply whatever they undertake. Our chief mistake is that we did not fulfill these demands in our creative work.

Like a bad sentry we gaped at the unessential and secondary things, forgetting the main things, and so abandoning our post. We forgot that the main thing in art is its ideological content and historical truth. Like a bad foundryman, we lightmindedly allowed the precious stream of creation to be poured out over sand and become dispersed in private, unessential sidelines. This brought us to vices and mistakes in our creations.

A stern and timely warning of the Central Committee stopped us Soviet artists from further movement along this dangerous and fatal way which leads towards empty and nonideological art for art's sake and towards creative degradation.

The resolution of the Central Committee reminds us with new force that Soviet art has been given one of the most honorable places in the decisive struggle of ideology of our country against the seductive ideology of the bourgeois world. Everything we do must be subordinated to tasks of this struggle.

In the second part of *Ivan the Terrible* we committed a misrepresentation of historical facts which made the film worthless and vicious in an ideological sense.

We know Ivan the Terrible as a man with a strong will and firm character. Does that exclude from the characterization of this Tsar the possibility of the existence of certain doubts? It is difficult to think that a man who did such unheard-of and unprecedented things in his time never thought over the choice of means or never had doubts about how to act at one time or

another. But could it be that these possible doubts overshadowed the historical role of historical Ivan as it was shown
in the film? Could it be that the essence of this powerful 16th
Century figure lies in these doubts and not in his uncompromising fight against them or unending success of his state activity.
Is it not so that the center of our attention is and must be *Ivan
the builder, Ivan the creator of a new, powerful, united Russian
power*, Ivan the inexorable destroyer of everything that resisted
his progressive undertakings?

The sense of historical truth betrayed me in the second part
of *Ivan the Terrible*. The private, unimportant and non-charac-
teristic shut out the principal. The play of doubts crept out to
the front line and the wilful character of the Tsar and his historically progressive role slipped out of the field of attention.
The result was that a false and mistaken impression was created
about the image of Ivan. The resolution of the Central Committee accusing me of a wrong presentation which disfigures
historical truth says that in the film Ivan is presented as "weak-
charactered and lacking in will, a kind of Hamlet." This is
solidly grounded and just.

Some historically wrong impressions of the epoch and reign
of Ivan the Terrible which were reflected in my film were
widely current in pre-Revolutionary literature. This was especially true of the film's presentation of the Tsar's bodyguards
(*oprichniki*). Works of classics of Marxism on questions of
history have illustrated and made available to us the historically correct and positive evaluation of Ivan's *progressive lifeguards*. In the light of these works it should not have been
difficult to overcome the false presentation of the lifeguards in
writing of Traitor-Prince Andrei Kurbsky. It should have been
easy to unveil tendentious descriptions of Ivan's activity which
were left us by historian spies of the Western Powers, Taube
and Kruse or the adventurer Henry Shtaden. But it was much
more difficult to overcome in one's own self the remnants of
former purely imaginary presentations left over from childhood
reading of such books as Alexei Konstantinovich Tolstoy's

novel *Silver Prince*, or the old novel *Koudeyar*. [This Tolstoy, related neither to playwright Alexei or novelist Leo, died in 1875.]

As a result, in the film the progressive *oprichniki* were presented as a gang of degenerates something like the Ku Klux Klan. The Central Committee justly condemned this rough misrepresentation of historical fact.

On the basis of the Central Committee's resolution, all workers in art should make a most important conclusion as to the necessity of putting an end to light-minded and irresponsible attitudes toward their work. We must fully subordinate our creations to the interest of education of the Soviet people, especially youth, and not step aside one jot from this aim.

We must master the Lenin-Stalin method of perception of real life and history to such a full and deep extent as to be able to overcome all remnants or survivals of former notions which, although they have been banished from our consciousness a long time, are obstinately and maliciously attempting to infiltrate into our works as soon as our creative vigilance is weakened even for only a single moment.

This is a guarantee that our cinematography will be able to eliminate all ideological and artistic failures and mistakes which lie like a heavy load on our art in this first postwar year. This is a guarantee that in the nearest future our cinematography will again create highly ideological artistic films worthy of the Stalin epoch.

All we workers of art must interpret the hard and just criticism of our work contained in the decision of the Central Committee as an appeal to the widest and most ardent and purposeful activity, an appeal to us masters of art to fulfill our duty before the Soviet people, state and party by creation of highly ideological artistic films.

H. J. Muller

THE DESTRUCTION OF SCIENCE IN THE USSR

Editor's Note

ONE of the by-products of totalitarianism is a politicalization, *i.e.*, debasement, of science. Under the aegis of the Soviets a new name has recently emerged in international science, that of Lysenko. The *mores* of fair play would seem to prescribe that opponents of a point of view accord respect to their antagonist even when disagreement is expressed. To do this, however, in the case of "Lysenkoism"—as this selection makes clear—would be to make a mockery of contemporary science. The new doctrine can, of course, be refuted scientifically—indeed, with ease. Its deeper significance, however, is as still another symptom of an omnipotent dictatorship, not as a scientific "error." The phenomenon it points up is but another step in the destruction of free institutions.

In this selection, Lysenkoism and the context in which it appears are dissected by one of the most qualified authorities in the world of science: Professor H. J. Muller, internationally distinguished Nobel Prize geneticist. Analyzed is the background of political science in the USSR which has allowed the Central Executive Committee of the Communist Party to promulgate the doctrine of Lysenkoism as the "official" Russian version of the science of genetics. Included in Professor Muller's account is a startling appraisal of the "ideas" of

Trofim Lysenko, the Communist-elevated peasant-turned plant-breeder. The reader would do well to keep in mind that the Soviet state has depicted the genetic principles accepted by scientists in all other countries as "foreign bourgeois deviations." It is to Professor Muller's credit that in the face of this newest Soviet onslaught, he is not merely content to expose—a most necessary job—the fraudulence of the Soviet view but stresses the heightened need for Americans, and citizens of all other countries, to increase their vigilance in protection of free science in their own and in all nations of the earth. Enemies of independent science—as with enemies of all free institutions—are enemies of democracy no matter in which country they reside.

Professor Muller's credentials for a discussion of this sort would be of the very highest order if one were to note no more than the recognition and acclaim his lifework have won for him as a scientist and geneticist. But there is more which ideally equips him for a probing of this kind. From 1933 to 1937 he was senior geneticist at the Institute of Genetics in Moscow; he has known the leading Soviet geneticists as co-worker and friend. In the same years he was also a member of the staff of the Moscow Medicobiological Institute. He is therefore thoroughly conversant with the scientific terrain involved, in principle and in locale.

Hermann Joseph Muller was born in New York City on December 21, 1890. He received his B.A., M.A., and Ph.D. from Columbia University. Later he took a D.Sc. at the University of Edinburgh. He has taught and conducted research at Rice Institute, the University of Texas, the University of Edinburgh, and Amherst College. His work in genetics has won for him a Nobel laureate in physiology, presidency of the Genetics Society of America, and presidency of the Eighth International Congress of Genetics at Stockholm. At present, he is professor of zoology at Indiana University. He is the author of *Out of the Night, The Mechanism of Mendelian Heredity* (with others), and many technical papers and lectures on scientific subjects.

This selection originally appeared as two articles in the *Saturday Review of Literature* in December, 1948.

In publicly resigning some time ago from the Academy of Sciences of the USSR, to which he was elected a corresponding member in 1933, he listed a series of anti-scientific acts by the Soviet state. "These disgraceful actions," he stated, "show clearly that the leaders of your Academy are no longer conducting themselves as scientists, but are misusing their positions to destroy science for narrow political purposes, even as did many who posed as scientists in Germany under the domination of the Nazis. In both cases the attempt was made to set up a politically directed 'science' separated from that of the world in general, in contravention of the fact that true science can know no national boundaries. . . ."

#

The Destruction of Science in the USSR by H. J. Muller

THE wilful destruction of science in the USSR by politicians is a tragedy of the greatest significance. It is quite evident that the Soviet politicians, being uneducated in modern natural science, and having proved themselves unwilling or unable to grasp the exacting technicalities involved in genetic reasoning, have through motives of their own taken a dislike to its conclusions, and have accordingly maneuvered to have it cast into limbo. This aim they have accomplished by the use of the same combination of flagrant misrepresentation and calculated brutality which has marked their dealings with their political opponents. Hardly four months ago, as a case in point, the Central Executive Committee of the Communist Party of the Soviet Union officially repudiated the entire science of genetics and approved in its stead a group of superstitions that hark back to ancient times.

This amazing act is of the greatest significance not only for geneticists, nor for scientists alone, but for everyone. For despite the pretenses of Communist officials and their followers, this matter is not a controversy between scientists or a dispute over the relative merits of two scientific theories. It is a brutal attack on human knowledge.

And, ironically, the great majority of the geneticists who have been purged were thoroughly loyal politically; many were even ardent crusaders for the Soviet system and leadership, as the writer well knows through personal contact with them.

Unhappily, it is necessary to confess that there no longer seems any chance of saving the core of biological science, in that section of the world, short of a political overturn. Nor could what has been lost be restored in one generation. All that we can now hope to do is to conduct an autopsy, in the hope of discovering ways to check the already dangerous spread of infection to countries outside the Soviet sphere, and to make clear to the people of those countries the important lessons for civilization and humanity involved in it.

What has happened to genetics during the past few months in the USSR is only the dramatic culmination of a campaign which has been ruthlessly waged against this section of science and the workers engaged in it for more than a dozen years. In 1935 genetics had reached a very high state of advancement in the USSR, and many eminent scientists were working in it. In that year the Soviet Communist Party, unable to find a single reputable scientist willing to take part in its attack on genetics, began systematically to build up the reputation of an alleged "geneticist," a peasant-turned-plant-breeder named Trofim Lysenko. Lysenko had achieved some dubious success in applying, by trial-and-error proceedings an early American discovery about pretreating seeds in order to influence the time of maturation of certain crops; but this gives him no more claim to being a geneticist than does the treatment of dogs for worms. To a scientist, Lysenko's writings along theoretical lines are the merest drivel. He obviously fails to comprehend either what a controlled experiment is or the established principles of genetics taught in any elementary course in the subject.

The role of USSR's second great so-called "geneticist" was assumed by a suave and unscrupulous juggler of words, the dialectical materialist "philosopher," I. Present. His authoritarian sophistries have been calculated to lend an aura of profundity that at the same time confuses and impresses the earnest lay disciple of the Party Line. However, like Lysenko's work, his writings are thoroughly unscientific in method, and fail to stand up under either theoretical analysis or the test of objective results. These two careerists have been represented to the public as bona fide scientists. They have been pushed forward, ahead of conscientious experimentalists, as proponents of what is supposed to be a valid scientific theory, but is actually a naive and self-contradictory party dogma. Although taking the name of Darwinism, or, more specifically "Michurinism," this dogma actually represents a reversion to a pre-Darwinian era all but forgotten by modern scientists.

That Lysenko and Present are not, as they are made to appear, self-constituted leaders of the rebellion against science, but are merely the tools of the highest political power, is shown by a number of telling facts. For one thing, long before Lysenko and Present had risen to their present eminence, not a few geneticists of high standing were individually martyrized on various pretexts. Only a deep-seated antagonism to genetics on the part of the higher authorities can explain why, in 1933 or thereabouts, the geneticists Chetverikoff, Ferry, and Ephroimson were all, on separate occasions, banished to Siberia, and Levitsky to a labor camp in the European Arctic, or why, in 1936, the Communist geneticist Agol was done away with, following rumors that he had been convicted of "Menshevik idealism" in genetics.

Again, in 1936, the Medicogenetical Institute, which with its numerous staff of biologists, psychologists, and more than 200 physicians constituted a shining example, unmatched anywhere in the world, of the possibilities of research in human genetics, was vilified and misrepresented in *Pravda*, and then dissolved. One of the charges made against the Institute was that it had been attempting to exalt heredity as against environment. Everyone conversant with the Institute's work knows that actually it had been entirely objective in its gathering of data, but that in its interpretations it had leaned as far as possible—if not even too far—in the environmentalist direction. Under pressure Solomon Levit, founder and director of the Institute, made a "confession" of scientific guilt, which he later admitted to the writer was entirely false and given only because loyalty to the Communist Party demanded it. Immediately afterwards he was abstracted from the scene, and has not been heard from since.

Both Agol and Levit spent the year 1931-32 in Texas, working on Rockefeller Foundation fellowships under the writer's direction. They were able then to express themselves freely in private conversation without fear of reprisals. Yet the writer can vouch that both of them went out of their way on every occasion to defend the Soviet regime, the policies and person of Stalin, and the orthodox philosophy of dialectical materialism, and that they made rather a nuisance of themselves in magnifying the importance of environmental influences even where the pertinent evidence was weak or absent. In short, they were convinced Stalinists but, being scientists with dangerous knowledge and data, the government sacrificed them.

Further evidence of the machinations of the Party to build up the reputation of Lysenko, Present, and their hangers-on, may be found in an affair that occurred in December 1936. A carefully prearranged and widely publicized "genetics controversy," was held in Moscow before a packed auditorium of invited spectators, with Lysenko appearing as the main speaker for what may be called the prosecution. It was obvious that the Party administrators, who presided over the session, paid no attention to the painstaking scientific arguments of the geneticist defendants, but rejoiced at every crude slander dropped by the attacking clique. The scientifically-educated portion of the audience sided completely with the geneticists; however, the administrators and the organs of publicity, though they did not yet dare to damn them completely, thundered dire warnings. The addresses of this congress were heavily expurgated when printed in book form; yet within a few months even this emasculated volume was placed on the banned list.

Still more evidence of the Party's hostility to genetics is offered by the case of the Seventh International Congress of Genetics, that was scheduled to be held in Moscow during the summer of 1937. This meeting was called off after the Party had first toyed with the idea of allowing it to be held with the provision that all papers on evolution and human genetics be omitted—in spite of the fact that many foreign geneticists had intended in their papers to attack the Nazi racist doctrines! In 1939, when Edinburgh finally acted as host to the Congress, all forty Soviet geneticists who had submitted papers to it were at the last moment refused permission to attend. At the same time the world-renowned and widely-beloved president of the Congress, Nicolai Ivanovich Vavilov, the Soviet's leading bona fide geneticist, sent to Edinburgh a discourteous letter of resignation, which, according to information in my possession, had been written for him.

During 1939 another public "genetics controversy" was staged in Moscow, and this time the now exalted Lysenkoists were made to appear as the clear-cut victors, while Vavilov and the other real geneticists were publicly shamed. At about this time, Vavilov's important posts as president of the Lenin Academy of Agricultural Sciences, head of the Institute of Plant Production, and head of the Institute of Genetics were turned over to Lysenko. In 1940, during the period of the Soviet-Nazi liaison, Vavilov was arrested and sentenced to death on the charge of being a British spy. After the Nazi attack on the USSR, he was sent to Magadan in far northeastern Siberia, where he died in 1942. It is reported that after his death his invaluable collection of thousands of economically important agricultural plants, together with its great reservoir of genes, which he and his fellow-workers had painstakingly collected all over the world, was allowed to disintegrate.

Meanwhile, the Soviet attack on other geneticists and the science of genetics in general continued. Owing to war conditions, the imposition of internal secrecy, and censorship on news leaving the country, it is impossible to learn the real causes of the death of such distinguished geneticists as Karpechenko, Koltzoff, Serebrovsky, and Levitsky. Certain it is, however, that from 1936 on Soviet geneticists of all ranks lived a life of terror. Most of those who were not imprisoned, banished, or executed were forced to enter other lines of work. The great majority of those who were allowed to remain in their laboratories were obliged to redirect their researches in such a way as to make it appear that they were trying to prove the correctness of the officially approved anti-scientific views. During the chaotic period toward the close of the war, some escaped to the West. Through it all, however, a few have remained at work, retained as show pieces to prove that the USSR still has some working geneticists.

Late last year these remaining geneticists, and those biologists in related fields who still had the temerity to support the genetic viewpoint, were caught in a carefully laid trap. They were invited to express their views in the columns of the *Moscow Literary Gazette*. Several of them took advantage of this seeming return to freedom of scientific discussion by restating the case for genetics. Lysenko and Present thereupon replied in their characteristic style. The discussion furnished an excuse for a new Soviet "conference" on genetics, held in Moscow this past July. Presumably this affair was Russia's substitute for the Eighth International Congress of Genetics in Stockholm. At Moscow last July the real and the spurious scientists debated once again. At length Lysenko announced that the Communist Central Committee had in fact prejudged the case, and had already decided in his own favor. This decision by a non-scientific political body of course settled the question.

Party members among the geneticists attending the conference hastened to recant their "heresies" publicly. The presidium of the Academy of Sciences, headed by the obedient physicist Sergei Ivanovitch Vavilov, brother of the great geneticist who had been done to death, toed the Party line by removing from their posts in utter disgrace the greatest Soviet physiologist, Orbeli, the greatest Soviet student of morphogenesis, Schmalhausen, and the best remaining Soviet geneticist, Dubinin. Dubinin's laboratory, long known for the admirable work done there by numerous careful investigators, was closed down.

It is significant that although Orbeli and Schmalhausen were biologists in fields other than genetics, they recognized the fundamental place genetic principles occupy in the biological sciences. Now that the real Russian geneticists are gone, scientists in kindred subjects are more open to attack. Indeed, the attack has already begun; recently *Pravda* reported that at the meeting of the Academy of Medical Sciences this September a whole group of leaders in physiology, microbiology, epidemiology, psychiatry, etc., were being severely criticized for "supporting Mendelian views."

Although it has been a long time since the teaching of genetics was permitted in the USSR, the Academy of Agricultural Sciences has ordered the revision of textbooks and courses in biology to remove all traces of genetic doctrines. In September the minister of higher education, Kaftanov, confessed that his department had been too lax in the past and promised that all university teachers and research workers infected with the "reactionary theory"—the phrases are his—of "Mendelism-Morganism" would be eradicated. The publishing houses were to be purged likewise.

These developments have been given wide publicity in the Soviet press, and popular feeling is being deliberately stirred against the scientists. At the same time, the scientific academies are making public obeisances to Stalin himself, thanking him for his direction and his "daily assistance to scientists," and pledging themselves to correct their errors. Malenkov, Deputy

Premier of the Soviet Union, and since Zhdanov's death widely considered as the most likely successor to Stalin, is now specifically mentioned in press dispatches as considering Lysenko one of his most important protégés.

Nowhere in the world today do laymen—either politicians or ordinary citizens—have the kind of education which would fit them to judge the merits of a theory in natural science. In appealing to them the anti-scientist has the advantage of being able to make whatever assertions he likes and to play upon emotion and prejudice. On the other hand, the scientist's meticulous statements of the details of his evidence and of the often intricate steps of his reasoning are likely to fall upon deaf ears. But if he simply resorts truthfully to calling his opponent an ignoramus or fakir he is himself suspected of prejudice.

It would be unfair to genetics to give the impression that we could state the case for that science in the space of a magazine article. However, certain of its cardinal accomplishments, which have been denied by the Lysenkoists, should be pointed out here so that we may understand the issues involved.

One of the fundamentals of the science of genetics is the demonstration of the existence in all forms of life of a specific genetic material, or material of heredity, which is separate from the other materials of the body. This genetic material is composed of thousands of different kinds of ultramicroscopic particles, called genes, of which each cell has two whole outfits (one derived from each parent). Most genes are contained in microscopically visible bodies, called chromosomes, and are inherited according to definite rules discovered in the last century by the Czech Mendel. The other materials, making up the body as we see it, have been developed as a result of the coordinated activity of the genes, and in this process of development, both in embryo and in adult, environmental influences play a very considerable role in helping to determine just what kind of product, i.e. what bodily traits, shall be formed. Moreover, the developmental reactions started and guided by the genes are so adjusted that, in many cases, a given kind of modification in the environment results in an especially suited, or "adaptive," modification of these other materials of the body, so as to cause it to function better under the given conditions.

The genes themselves, however, are not changed in any directed or adaptive way by influences outside of themselves. Although they are relatively stable, they do sometimes undergo sudden inner changes in their chemical composition, called mutations. These mutations occur as a result of ultramicroscopic accidents. But order does emerge from these accidents. For the relatively frequent individual who inherits a mutated gene that is detrimental to life tends to die out, whereas the rare one who inherits a gene that chanced to change in a beneficial way tends to live and multiply. Thus, under natural conditions, a population may, in the course of ages, become ever better adapted in its characteristics, *i.e.*, it may evolve. In this way has modern genetics implemented Darwin's theory of natural selection and given it a firm basis.

The gene theory, then, gives us a unit on a lower level than the cell, and in a sense more fundamental than the cell, and even more necessary for a comprehension of all biological sciences, including agriculture and medicine. It is indispensable for a rational interpretation of the origin of life, of the relation between inanimate and animate, of the way in which organisms have undergone change in the past, and of how they may become changed, either in the course of natural breeding or in response to artificial manipulations, in the future. Moreover, through analysis of the genes of an organism, and of how they operate, we may hope to unravel ever more of the tangled web of biochemical processes which constitute its development, its physiology, and its pathology—studies which are already well under way. Finally, this knowledge must affect our whole philosophical outlook, and many phases of the anthropological, psychological, and social sciences.

Lightly waving away the amassed evidence for this coherent modern conception of living things, Lysenko and Present deny the very existence of genes or of a separate genetic material, ignore the all-important distinction between heredity and individual development, and offer—in the name of Darwin!—a return to pre-Darwinian days that had been all but forgotten by modern biologists. They would have the heredity itself respond in a directly adaptive way to outside influences, and would also have it able to incorporate the directly adaptive changes which the body may have undergone in its development. Thus, instead of explaining in a rational way the origin of the body's adaptive structures and reactions, they force upon the germ cells themselves (1) the ability to give that type of response which is to be to the advantage of the future body, and (2) the ability somehow to mirror changes already incurred by the body that contains them. This leaves entirely unexplained the origin and the *modus operandi* of the germ cells' assumed ability to respond adaptively, and hence it also fails to explain the origin of the body's own adaptive abilities. The Lysenko-Present doctrine therefore implies a mystical, Aristotelian "perfecting principle," a kind of foresight, in the basic makeup of living things, despite the fact that it claims in the same breath not to be "idealistic" at all. And, though verbally accepting natural selection as playing some role, it fails to make use of it for the solution of the main problem, that of why organisms do have adaptability.

In support of these fantastic claims, Lysenko and his followers offer no properly documented, controlled, or repeatable factual evidence. Mainly they attempt to convince by citation of authority, and quote two in particular. The more important of these is Darwin. Under the influence of the current opinion of his day, Darwin accepted to some extent the old doctrine of inheritance of acquired characters, which had been brought into prominence not long before by Lamarck. However, Darwin ascribed to this now disproved doctrine only a secondary role. His own most distinctive contribution was the theory of evolution through the natural selection of accidental changes in heredity, and this has, as we have seen, been abundantly substantiated in the present century. Yet it is mainly the erroneous feature borrowed by Darwin from Lamarck which the Lysenko group insists upon as "Darwinism." Moreover, Lysen-koists rely heavily on the work of the old practical plant breeders, especially the Russian Michurin and the American Burbank, who produced new varieties by trial-and-error cross-ing and rule-of-thumb selection. Despite the usefulness of some of these varieties, however, the writings of these men contrib-uted nothing to our understanding of the biological principles concerned. On the contrary, they adopted the same grave the-oretical misconceptions as were usual among laymen of their day. Yet the importance of Michurin as a scientist has been insisted on by Stalin himself, so that the Lysenko group often refer to themselves as "Michurinists."

As this militant mysticism spreads, it is certain to have dire repercussions in every branch of intellectual activity within the USSR and the countries in its growing sphere of influence. This one important falsehood, persisted in, will poison more and more of the structure of knowledge, affecting its practice and theory.

One curious effect of the Lysenko doctrine has been on the Communist conception of the nature of man and of racial and class differences. In the official view, individuals or populations which have lived under unfavorable conditions and have there-fore been physically or mentally stunted in their development, would tend, through the inheritance of these acquired charac-teristics, to pass on to successive generations an ever poorer hereditary endowment; on the other hand, those living under favorable conditions would produce progressively better germ cells and so become innately superior.* In a word, we should have innate master and subject races and classes, as the Nazis so blatantly insisted.

True, the Russian theory differed from that of the Nazi in certain ways. For example, the stocks of supposedly inferior

---

* The writer was told in 1936 that this was the "official" doctrine of the Communist Party, *i.e.*, held by the Party peerage, by Yakovlev, head of agri-culture in the Party. Yakovlev was later purged, but this does not affect the validity of his testimony.

heredity would, according to the Russians, have become inferior because of their worse conditions of living, while according to the Nazis, their assumed hereditary inferiority was primary and their lower economic status was a result of this. Moreover, according to the Russians, but not the Nazis, this hereditary inferiority, although an accumulated effect of many generations of poorer conditions, would nevertheless be remedied by "two or three generations" of bettered conditions. No explanation is offered of why the improvement should occur so much more readily than the deterioration. Yet, on both views alike, genetics is so perverted as to make inevitable the conclusion that the races and classes of mankind today are arranged in hereditary hierarchies corresponding to the economic hierarchies. From this it would follow that if a child were transferred at birth from one group to another, its inborn biological handicap or advantage could not be cancelled in its generation.

Modern geneticists, on the other hand, realizing the tremendous role physical and social environment play in the development of human mental traits, would not assume that culturally or economically less developed peoples are *ipso facto* inherently less capable. Indeed, the non-inherited effects of cultural differences on mental *development*—as contrasted with innate *endowment*—are so great that no valid conclusions concerning hereditary differences in mentality between existing human populations may be drawn at all.

This similarity between the Nazi and Communist theories was of course the reason why the Russians were reluctant to allow Western geneticists to come to the 1937 International Genetics Congress to attack the Nazi racial fallacies. It explains why the Communists did not want to allow any discussions concerning man—or even evolution in general—to be held at that Congress. It shows why they expunged all mention of man from the published proceedings of their 1936 "genetics controversy."

In the light of modern scientific knowledge, Lysenkoism must be termed a superstition, as much a superstition as belief that the earth is flat. It is an exceedingly dangerous superstition, for it not only leads to an entirely false conception of the nature of living things and to erroneous methods in the attempt to control other organisms, but it leads to social and medical policies which would, in the end, degrade rather than advance humanity.

II

Abundant evidence is available that the Lysenko superstition is now spreading beyond the boundaries of the USSR. Nowadays one often hears the validity of the discoveries of genetics questioned in our country—and of course particularly in the sections where Communist influence is strong. This is happening not only in the conversation of laymen, but in the columns of supposedly reputable newspapers and magazines. The same thing is true in other non-Communist countries. For example, the British *New Statesman and Nation,* in its issue of September 25, 1948, published a letter in defense of Lysenkoism which represented, from a scientific viewpoint, the depth of illiteracy. Similar discussions have been going on in French journals (*e.g., Les Lettres Françaises*), and in German publications. Yet scientists undertaking to answer the Lysenko myth have had considerable difficulty getting their articles published, even in the USA and Britain.

Naturally the situation is even bleaker in Soviet-dominated countries. In Czechoslovakia, many months before the Communist coup, a Lysenkoist from the USSR was appointed to redirect ideological teachings at Charles University, and Lysenko himself was elected a member of the Czech Academy. The geneticist delegates from Poland, Bulgaria, Hungary, Jugoslavia, and Czechoslovakia to the Stockholm Congress last July felt it necessary, in self-protection, formally to protest the attack on Lysenkoism made by the writer. In the Soviet zone of Germany, Lysenkoist propaganda is being widely disseminated, and German geneticists of high standing who suffered under the Nazis are again under attack. The Soviet Embassy in

Venezuela is serving as the distributing center for South America for a Spanish translation of Lysenko's book "Heredity and Its Variability."

What causes the Communist officials to push Lysenkoism so strongly? To me, the answer is obvious: it is the type of mind that sees things as only black and white, yes and no, and so cannot admit the importance of *both* heredity and environment. Believing that it has found the complete answer to all the world's ills, through its particular way of manipulating environment, the Communist Party regards as a menace any concept that does not fit patly into its scheme for mankind. The genes do not fit into that concept, in its opinion, hence the existence of the genes must be denied. So narrowminded are the present leaders of Russia that they do not realize that, by their denial of the existence of genes, they have set up a doctrine according to which the peoples of the world would be saddled, biologically, with the accumulated incubi of their respective past misfortunes, and would therefore be very unequal in inherent capacities.

Because the Communists have organized all their political units, even those in scientific institutions, pyramidally, like an army, they have created conditions inimical to free-thought processes. Such organization places a premium on subservience to those above and on arbitrary domineering over those below. It creates conditions where men rise by intrigue and by denunciation of others, rather than by merit. It is conducive to the amazing campaigns of defamation constantly being conducted against the conscientious workers in scientific institutions by their jealous but less capable Party "comrades."

Another major factor in the Russian attack on scientific inquiry is the perennial existence within the USSR of an emotional state resembling war hysteria, which permits any idea or activity to be damned or glorified merely by describing it as subversive or patriotic. For example, Vavilov was charged with national sabotage because he had conscientiously asserted that it might take five or more years for geneticists to develop cer-

tain improved and needed varieties of wheat, while Lysenko
promised that, through direct modification of the development
of the plants by special treatments, followed by the immediate
stable inheritance of these developmental changes, he could
get as good results in a year and a half. Needless to say, Lysenko has not been able to make good his promise.

Yet another deterrent to genetics is the existence of the
mystical, pretentious state philosophy (which might better be
described as a religion), known as "dialectic materialism."
With this young and old are indoctrinated. All scientific work
must be conducted and all scientific conclusions reached according to the precepts of this religion, as interpreted by its
high priests. In this way the theory of the gene and of Mendelian chromosomal inheritance has been accused of being both
"idealistic" and "mechanistic." These two heresies are supposed
to be as opposite as the poles, yet both are anathema to the
Party creed.

Genetics is by no means the only science that has suffered in
the USSR. Psychology was similarly set upon during the Thirties and largely destroyed. The branch of psychology which
deals with the testing of aptitudes and abilities, in which considerable progress had been made in the USSR, was the special
object of attack. In the field of medicine, certain very poorly
supported theories—notably Speransky's theory, which attrib-
utes much of disease to the nutritional condition of nerve tissue
—have enjoyed official favor to the detriment of more scientific
approaches. In physics, the relativity theory narrowly escaped
being condemned on dialectic materialist grounds, but adroit
political maneuvering by the scientists finally saved it. Even
some distinguished astronomers have felt the consequences of
the system.

This situation is all the more tragic because in the first decade and a half after the Revolution, public interest in science
was great in the USSR; scientists enjoyed a high prestige, and
were accorded considerable material support. Freedom of discussion, so essential to scientific development, was permitted

in a high degree. In the last fifteen years, however, the politicians have tightened their grip on all phases of Russian life; as they intruded into intellectual activity, they cut off the creative imagination, interfered with communication and criticism and the scrupulous objectivity basic to scientific progress. A similar enfeeblement has of course taken place in the arts.

Although its accomplishments have been great, science as a widespread organized activity is exceedingly young in terms of human history. It is a tender plant, requiring a special soil; its growth is easily checked or destroyed by outside interference. Very few people appreciate its cardinal need: complete freedom of inquiry and of criticism. It is always being menaced by men who wish to inhibit or redirect it at vital points and to destroy its freedom. The conclusions it reaches often have the effect of overthrowing long-accepted dogmas; the established interests which depend on these dogmas are usually much more powerful than the scientists. While it must be left to find its ways, unhampered by interference on the part of those who do not understand it, it must be furnished the material support without which it would have neither personnel nor facilities for work. Yet funds and recruits are not enough if its soul— spontaneous and independent inquiry—has been put into shackles.

When we criticize the Soviet attack on science, let us not, however, neglect the motes in our own eyes, nor the lesson it holds for our own practices. Well within the memory of many of us is the assault on the teaching of evolution in Tennessee, conducted by the Fundamentalists led by the politician William Jennings Bryan. The Scopes trial was only the most publicized of the scandals that resulted. The writer well recalls a session of the Texas legislature at which a preacher by the name of Norris delivered, by special invitation, a fanatical two-hour harangue on the doctrine of biological evolution and its "dangers"—Bolshevism, "nigger-loving," and the anti-Christ. The legislators listened attentively and frequently applauded. No qualified person was allowed to state the case for science.

Subsequently the lower house passed a bill forbidding the teaching of evolution in elementary and high schools, and the state textbook commission ordered the removal of all mention of the subject from school textbooks, an order that was rigorously executed.

Fortunately the movement as such has died down, yet its benighted influence is still pervasive. It is doubtful whether, in many regions of this country, there has as yet been any real recovery in the teaching of biology. Thus a basis has been laid for a popular misunderstanding which has prevented research in biological fundamentals from receiving adequate support, has hindered the comprehension of important genetic principles even in medical circles, and may at some future time facilitate the rise of Lysenkoism and other dangerous anti-scientific movements.

Still another potential danger to science lies in the practice of having scientific research supported by private foundations interested in their own ends rather than that of science as a whole, and by public funds administered by groups chosen by politicians or military men. Research has become increasingly expensive, and much of it is now dependent on such sources of funds.

It has been claimed that in the case of public-supported research, democratic procedure demands that at least the head of the administrative board be politically chosen, so that he will be responsible to the people. This is a curious argument. If the people wish, they can just as well leave the guidance of their expenditures for research to persons chosen by trustworthy scientific groups as to persons chosen by unscientific men who were elected to public office primarily to deal with quite different matters. During the recent war the government entered into large contracts with private firms, through which it entrusted them with great sums of public money in return for various industrial and even scientific services. No exception was taken to this practice because the firms were supposed to be expert in their lines. Why should the scientist have less prestige than the businessman and be considered less qualified for handling funds in his own field?

But the gravest present danger to American science stems from the activity of the super-patriots who, on the plea that they are battling totalitarianism and defending democratic freedoms, are themselves attempting to fasten the very evils they warn against upon our own country. The Un-American Activities Committee is only the most glaring illustration of these practices. The hysteria it has helped to foment has already driven many of our better scientists out of their chosen work.

Even in my own field of genetics, which is relatively unconnected with national defense, this hysteria is having unfortunate consequences. For example, last summer one of the foremost and most respected American geneticists was prevented from attending the International Congress of Genetics in Stockholm when the government refused to issue him a passport. The reason given for this was that he had once been a member of "The American Committee to Save Refugees," an organization not on the list of those officially considered subversive. True, the USA prevented only one of its geneticists from attending, while the USSR did not allow any of its citizens to be present. But we cannot take the Soviet Union to task with a quite clear conscience.

When we criticize the shocking treatment accorded scientists in Nazi Germany and which is now being given them in the USSR, we must also exert ourselves to prevent the same thing from happening in our own midst. Otherwise, we shall gravitate back towards that state of stultifying intolerance which from time immemorial has been accepted as normal by barbaric societies.

Louis Budenz

COMMUNIST CONFESSIONS

Editor's Note

FEW phenomena are more in-
dicative of the servility that lies at the base of allegiance to the
Soviet state than the gymnastics required by a "change in line."
A war that on one day of the week is characterized by Communist followers as "imperialistic" becomes, as soon as the Soviet
Union is involved, holy. Adolf Hitler remains to most of us
innocents a monster; Communists are prepared to be more
understanding toward Nazism when a Hitler-Stalin pact is
signed. Heroes of yesterday, on the proper occasion, become
devils overnight; elevation from ignominy is no less sudden in
the minds of Stalinists if the Soviet Union so decrees. In this
selection we are afforded an unusually valuable close-up of
what happens in Communist *headquarters* when the line is
changed. The occasion is Moscow's deposition of Earl Browder from his "leadership" of the American Communist Party.
The sequence in this Stalinist version of Tinker-to-Evers-to-
Chance: Moscow to Communist spokesman Jacques Duclos in
France to the Communist parties of the world. Louis Budenz
takes up the story in Communist headquarters in New York
where this pathetic drama unfolds.

Louis Francis Budenz is the former managing editor of the
Daily Worker, official Communist New York daily. He was
born in Indianapolis on July 17, 1891. He attended St. Xavier's
College, Ohio, St. Mary's College, Kansas, and in 1912 was

admitted to the bar in Indiana. He has had a long career in the American labor movement; among other positions, he has held the editorship of the *Carpenter,* the organ of the AFL carpenters and joiners union, and that of *Labor Age.* He was arrested, and acquitted, twenty-one times in the course of his labor activity. In 1935, he joined the Communist Party and became the first labor editor of the *Daily Worker.* In time he rose to managing editor and president of the "Freedom of the Press, Co., Inc." which "took over the publication" of the Stalinist paper. He was also a member of the National Committee of the Communist Party for six years. On October 10, 1945, he reentered the Catholic church, from which he had earlier been excommunicated. At present he is a professor of economics at Fordham University. An account of his experiences in the Communist Party is recorded in his *This Is My Story* (1947), from which this selection is taken.

#

Communist Confessions by Louis Budenz

THE audience assembled for the "trial of Browder" at the specially called meeting of the National Committee in June, 1945, was a completely hostile one. Sixty members of that body and about twenty specially invited trade union leaders met for a three-day session at the Hank Forbes Auditorium in the headquarters building.

"This time," I resolved, "I will attend a National Committee meeting all the way through and really see just what makes these people tick." I made special arrangements to be present every hour and every minute of the proceedings. I wanted to get a final view of the Communist party before my departure, which I had by now firmly resolved upon.

The meeting was scheduled for ten o'clock in the morning

and was to open with a report—this time, of course, by Foster. Browder, for whom meetings had waited breathlessly in the past, arrived early and took a chair at the front of the hall. Of the eighty persons who entered the hall, only three greeted Browder with the traditional "Good morning." I was one of them, and the other two were Doxey A. Wilkerson, the Negro professor from Howard University whom the Communists had put in the managing editorship of Adam Powell's Harlem weekly, *The People's Voice*, and a trade unionist who was not supposed to be Red-tinted. The other seventy-seven, who had formerly stood up for half an hour on all occasions in the past to applaud, to cheer and shout for Browder, now contemptuously ignored him.

With a rage-contorted face, Foster arose to point out the slough of error into which all the Communists except himself and Darcy had fallen. The assembled eighty again heard the long-forgotten words: "blood-wrung profits." Again they were reminded of Bernstein, Legien and Gompers, whom the Bolsheviks had branded as "notorious revisionists." And so they still were, said Foster, but Browder was "more shamelessly bourgeois" than any one of them. That was casting him into the nethermost Communist hell, since no one could be lower than Bernstein, Legien and Gompers.

Not content to condemn the fallen Communist chief for recent "errors," Foster tried to trace his guilt far back in his leadership. He was charging that Browder's revisionism could be seen in the original withdrawal of the Communist party from the Communist International, when Stachel interrupted.

"We had better leave the C.I. alone," Stachel said dryly. "The decision to leave was for protective and political purposes agreeable to all parties concerned."

Thus reminded that in his Leftist fanaticism he had begun to trample on the toes of the Moscow masters, Foster dropped that subject like a hot iron. But he continued to denounce Browder's "enervating revisionism," his "dictatorship," his "chronic tailism," and his "magic reverence for the spoken word" which made him "a talker, not a mass fighter." Warming to his subject, Foster went on to condemn Browder's nursing of "corroding bureaucratism," his "lowering of the Party's prestige," his play for "infallibility," his "deep intoxication with unseemly adulation," his "opportunist practice of supporting Roosevelt without self-criticism," his "corrosive effects" on the Party and his "line which dovetails with the big capitalists' plan of imperialist expansion and world domination."

The entire utterance was one long tirade against the man whom Foster had hailed in 1941 as the "great tribune of the people," as one who had "distinguished himself" in all phases of the antiwar struggle. In 1941 it was Foster's opinion that "it is quite impossible to do justice to the work of Comrade Browder in the historic fight of the American people to keep the United States out of the war." But in the special National Committee meeting of June, 1945, he asserted: "Browder's policies have been a detriment to our Party for years." These contradictory views can be examined at leisure in such articles as "Earl Browder and the Fight for Peace," written by Foster for *The Communist* of June, 1941, and "The Struggle against Revisionism" by the same Foster for *Political Affairs* (successor to *The Communist*) for September, 1945. The latter article on revisionism is a watered-down version of the speech made at the National Committee meeting. But even the restrained version contains all the phrases quoted above.

In his eagerness to damn Browder forever, Foster gave the Red game away. The following was part of his speech and was published in the September, 1945, issue of *Political Affairs*: "How far Browder was prepared to go to prevent political discussion was shown by the way he suppressed my letter of January, 1944, to the National Committee. The only way I could have gotten this letter to the membership was by facing expulsion and a sure split in the Party." In his speech that June morning Foster was even more emphatic, saying that Browder was angling for his expulsion and would have acted on the slightest provocation.

COMMUNIST CONFESSIONS—*Louis Budenz*   597

When Foster sat down, up rose Gene Dennis to upbraid Browder still more. He who had hailed the man from Kansas as "the genius of American Communism" now berated him as having led everyone down a crooked path. As was seemly, Dennis mentioned his own "errors" a couple of times, but most of his blows were aimed at the bowed head of Browder. Then it was announced that "Comrade Browder will be given unlimited time" to state his case—a gesture at allowing free discussion before a jury that knew its verdict in advance.

When he stood up to speak, absolute silence greeted him. But there was a buzz among the auditors and a straining forward to hear what the "defense" would be. In his first talk to the Political Committee before this meeting was called, Browder had already charged that Foster's line was "predicated upon war between the United States and the Soviet Union." A watered-down but enlightening version of this view is indicated in his printed statement in the *Daily Worker* of June 10, 1945. In effect, it accused the Duclos-Foster leaders of promoting Soviet warfare against the United States. Trained as they were, the audience knew what these charges entailed and they were concerned about how far Browder would go.

While he again injected this thought into his remarks, he did so obliquely. Instead of a vigorous defense, for an hour and a half in a singsong voice—interlarded with occasional sarcastic digs at his auditors—he read extracts from his various writings. These were intended to prove that he did not advocate "signing away" the revolution to American big business. Since everyone present had read, studied and repeated these words at countless meetings, there was a form of insult in this method. So a number of subsequent speakers indignantly charged when they got the rostrum.

There was no madness in this method. An hour or two after Browder had finished we had a recess, and I was chatting with William L. Patterson, the Negro who had been associated with the *Midwest Daily Record* when I was editor. "Why do you think Earl resorted to such a peculiar tactic?" I asked. "It didn't give much hope to anyone who wanted to defend him." Patterson, it turned out, had a fine case of anger against his former chief. Shaking his head, he declared that "Earl has made no case at all; it has been a bankrupt performance." Then, answering my question, he said, "It's clear he is preparing an appeal to the East."

On one vital matter Browder was adamant. As he closed his monotonous talk he suggested that he would go along with the draft resolution before the National Committee if one addition were made. He had told me some days before that it was the key to the whole preservation of "the Teheran policy." That was a pledge to "support the development of American markets in the world scene." And he repeated it several times so that it would sink in.

The more he insisted upon the insertion of that phrase in the report, the clearer it became that the Foster-Dennis clique would reject it. Their pretensions of concern over possible unemployment were thereby demonstrated as bankrupt, for the expansion of American markets is essential to hold off joblessness. But to that inconsistency they paid not the slightest heed. And why? Because the adoption of such a pledge would have been a signal that the Soviet Union genuinely intended to cooperate with the United States instead of sabotaging and undermining it, as the new line intended. That is why Browder chose "American markets" as his battleground and why his opponents sought to cancel the real issue in a fog of "revisionism" charges.

Three days and nights (until midnight) of breast beating and bizarre confessions followed. Never in all my varied experiences have I beheld anything so like an Arabian Nights scene. Each member of the Committee seemed to outdo the others in striving to demonstrate that he was a dolt and a dupe of a "higher power."

Samples will suffice. Roy Hudson, who had long been dubbed "the Commissar of Labor," affirmed that he had "an inadequate grasp of Marxism" and that he had always surrendered to what he thought were "Browder's greater ability, superior experience and mastery of Marxism." Tall, rawboned and awkward in manner when speaking, Hudson made a ludicrous figure as he declared: "For years every instinct in me rebelled at certain methods of leadership," which he admitted, had been bureaucratic and autocratic. But, he said, his relation to Browder had been as "an employee to an employer," and the former chief had ordered him around as "though I were his employee." This last confession caused a gasp even among that crowd. However, when Hudson's speech was printed in the *Political Affairs* of July, 1945, these damning words were carefully deleted. The rank-and-file comrades were still to be deprived of knowledge of the full depths to which the "leaders" had sunk by their own admissions.

What made Hudson's words the more absurd was the statement to me a few days before by a person well known in the C.I.O. He had said, "Whenever I come to report to Hudson I quake in my boots, I fear so much his grim correctness and his grasp of Marxism."

Particularly pathetic was the case of the former famous cartoonist, Robert Minor, who "had been flaying around in all directions," as several comrades reported. Minor had been Browder's closest confidant, was Assistant Secretary of the Party and had prominently carried the ball for Browder in the *Daily Worker's* pages after the C.P.A. was formed. But overnight he somersaulted from out-Browdering Browder to uttering the most savage, extreme and ultra-revolutionary echoes of Foster and Duclos.

Groans of protest rose in the hall when Minor said that he had "waged a continual struggle" against Browder. He was to be reminded that he had, in fact, used Browder's "approval" as a bludgeon over everyone else. With a sickly and scared look on his face, he persisted in trying to prove that he had been wrestling against Browder's revisionist errors all along. He who had traveled jauntily to Spain as a sort of commissar in the civil war was now shakingly reporting that Browder "had gone to several Senators in Washington—or was about to go—to get their advice as to whether even the C.P.A. should be closed down."

There was a hum of anger at this revelation. Voices shouted: "Who are they? Name the Senators." Then Jack Stachel's harsh accents again cut in. "We have no reason to discuss this matter here in this semipublic way," he declared. "Drop it!" And dropped it—so much so that the Party members have never officially heard of the incident, even though it occurred in a session of their "own" National Committee.

Shortly afterward Elizabeth Gurley Flynn scathingly scored Minor for always having been "fastened to Comrade Browder's mental apron strings." Then she made some confessions on her own account. While everyone again gasped with surprise, she said that she had been "afraid of our own National Board and National Committee." She asserted that whenever she wanted to raise a question, she was hampered by being made to feel she knew nothing about "theory." Although a member of the Political Committee, by the grace of Browder, and therefore one of six people in the inner circle, she broke down and admitted that this "inferiority complex" had prevented her from doing anything about anything.

The drama moved from confession to confession. Comrade after comrade agreed that many speeches were written in approval of Browder's reports before anyone knew what was in them. Others said sarcastically that much had been made in the past of the "unanimous votes in the committees and other organs of the Party, but these had all been the fruits of hot-house forced unity." (Another "unanimous" or "*Ja*" vote of the National Committee was recorded in the May 24, 1946, issue of the *Daily Worker* for a Foster statement which said: "Any attempt to spread Browderism within the Party will be ruthlessly combatted." That meant, of course, that any show of real democracy would be wiped out.)

One small voice was heard for practical action in favor of a democratic regime within the organization. That came from me, who had resolved to make "the need for democracy" one of my final tests of the organization. When it was my time to talk I stressed the "lack of democracy" which the reports all demonstrated. I then presented a motion that "a special commission be created to forward the extension of democracy within the organization, such a commission to be permanent in character." The proposal was immediately seconded by the Negro educator and editor Doxey A. Wilkerson. But the indifferent faces before me as I made the motion and the lack of response to Wilkerson's second, gave a forewarning of the motion's fate. Quite visible on the countenances of my colleagues was the bored expression which said: "Another American-trained bit of nonsense." Democracy was no more wanted under Foster than it had been under Browder.

The motion, I may add, was never put. In the evening session of the last day, when motions were acted upon, I went to Charlie Krumbein who was the chairman. "Is my motion for a commission on democracy on the agenda?" I asked. "It is not," he replied, "and we can't get it on." Time was his excuse, but when I spoke to John Williamson, Party secretary in charge of the agenda, he said wearily that the motion was "implied in the other things we are doing." So all mention of the motion was suppressed and the Party members had no knowledge that it was ever put. And in Wilkerson's remarks, which were subsequently published in *Political Affairs*, that section is completely expunged.

While the speech making was waxing warm, Browder let it be known that he was actually appealing to "a higher court" by being conspicuously absent from the sessions. The second half of the first day and all the second day, he did not appear. But he was in the building, supposedly busy in his office on the ninth floor. When Committee members met him in the elevators only one or two exchanged greetings with him. The ancient stigma of "enemy of the working class" was already upon him. It was precisely the title he was to receive from the Foster-Dennis leadership and the *Daily Worker* later on.

Again "Blackie" Myers of the National Maritime Union tried to rescue "unity" by announcing to the second-day session that he had appealed to Browder to return. On the third day Browder heeded the appeal. Not only did he appear, but he made another and rather brief speech. He began by saying that he "apologized to anyone who felt insulted by his method of presenting his case." Some had thought him "arrogant" for staying away from the meeting, but he pleaded his health, which he had to guard carefully. He hesitated before continuing, and then once more made a short statement favoring the inclusion of "support of American markets" in the draft resolution, but his voice was not so firm as it had been.

For the remainder of the third day the former chief listened to a torrent of abusive oratory directed at himself. Slumped far down in his chair, he sometimes put his head between his hands as the flood of criticism poured out. It ended with Foster's "summary," in which denunciation of Browder was again the theme. Foster noted that some comrades had thought him too severe on Browder, but nothing could be too severe for the fallen chief. The high light of the "summary"—though it was hastily suppressed afterward—was Foster's slip in mentioning that he had refrained from expressing his opinion in 1944 because, as he said, "I had been told there were tips from abroad that we should stand by Browder's line." That was raising the iron curtain a little too far, and it was quickly pulled down again.

At the night session of the third day, the National Committee voted to hold a special convention the following month— July, 1945. Then the Communist party would again emerge from the ashes of the "Communist Political Association." The accompanying resolution breathed the up-and-doing spirit for "the revolutionary cause" which Foster wanted. Only one ballot—Browder's—was against the resolution. And the Browder amendment for the inclusion of "American markets" was voted down. As a parting guest, I considered myself a spectator and took no part in the voting. When my resolution for a "commission on democracy" was presented and defeated, I felt that my work there was finished.

Sidney Hook

THE LITERATURE OF DISILLUSIONMENT

"The history of the Russian Revolution has demonstrated that a minority one-party dictatorship has led to an increase of the power of man over man, to a power exercised more brutally and accompanied by greater servility than anywhere else in the world. There is every reason to believe on economic, psychological, and historic grounds that a one-party dictatorship would lead to similar results everywhere in the world today. The presence of a superior productive technique would confer no immunity; it would merely make the engines of repression more efficient. But for a political party to forego the chance to take power, comes the crushing retort, may mean a lost revolution! Yet some things are much worse than a lost revolution. A betrayed revolution! A lost revolution is a defeat in one battle of an enduring war: a betrayed revolution invalidates the fundamental principles in behalf of which the war is waged, dispirits and makes cynical an entire generation, and far from removing the arbitrary power of man over man secures it more firmly." Reason, Social Myths and Democracy (1940) by Sidney Hook.

Editor's Note

THIS essay, an attempt at an overall examination of the literature of disillusion of disaffected Communists, is written by a thoroughly informed and long-recognized authority on the intellectual and political problems to which the Russian Revolution has given birth.

"Whatever the responsibility of these writers for their own illusions," Professor Hook states in this essay, "the record of their disillusionment is a record of growing intellectual and emotional maturity. No one has a right to be censorious of them, and least of all those who complacently accept any social change, whose emotions of sympathy for their fellow-men are never engaged, and who leave all the risks of thought and action to others."

Sidney Hook was born in New York City on December 20, 1902. He received his B.S.S. from the College of the City of New York in 1923, and his Ph.D. from Columbia University in 1927. He joined the philosophy faculty of New York University in 1927 and has taught there since. At present he is professor of philosophy and chairman of the department. He has also been a lecturer at the New School for Social Research since 1931. He has gained a wide reputation and following as a philosopher, acute analyst of social problems, and scholar on Marxism and other subjects. His writings on Stalinism have consistently ranked high among the most brilliant discussions of that subject. In 1928-29 he held a Guggenheim fellowship in philosophy for study in Germany and Russia; in the latter country he did research at the Marx-Engels Institute in Moscow. In 1945 he was awarded the Butler Silver Medal for distinction in philosophy. Among his books are: *Towards the Understanding of Karl Marx; From Hegel to Marx; The Metaphysics of Pragmatism; Reason, Social Myths and Democracy; The Hero in History; Education for Modern Man;* and *John Dewey: An Intellectual Portrait.* This selection appeared in *The American Mercury* as "Communism and the Intellectuals," in February, 1949.

\#

The Literature of Disillusionment by Sidney Hook

THE enthusiasm generated by the Russian Revolution produced an impressive body of literature in affirmation of the philosophy, program and practices of the Soviet régime. This literature of affirmation was in no way unique (except in volume), for the American and French Revolutions, as well as the national upheavals in Italy and Germany during the nineteenth century, had also given rise to libraries of passionate and interpretive sympathetic studies. But what does seem to be truly unique about the cultural and literary phenomena associated with the Russian Revolution is the literature of disillusionment with which the spiritual Odyssey of so many converts to the Bolshevik faith has terminated, so that they now recognize with Auden:

> *O Freedom still is far from home*
> *For Moscow is as far as Rome*
> *Or Paris.*

This literature of disillusion constitutes a distinct genre of writing in contemporary letters if only because of its international character and the common pattern of rediscovery and rededication to certain values of the Western tradition that had not been so much denied as ignored. Russell, Auden, Spender and Orwell in England; André Gide, Souvarine and Serge in France and Belgium; Ignazio Silone in Italy; Panait Istrati in Greece; Arthur Koestler in Central Europe; Anton Ciliga in the Balkans; Eastman, Dos Passos, Wilson, Hicks and Farrell in the United States are among the more noteworthy figures who have contributed to this literature. The evolution of attitudes in most of these men differs from the apostasies of Wordsworth and Dostoyevsky; whose early revolutionary enthusiasm and doctrines became transformed into their polar opposites. We do not find in their works sentiments comparable to those expressed in Wordsworth's *Ecclesiastical Sketches* or *Devotional Incitements;* and if their writings do not reach the great artistic heights of Dostoyevsky's bitter legend of the *Grand Inquisitor,* neither do they celebrate the central rôle which Dostoyevsky assigned to miracle, mystery and authority in human life.

If we ask what led so many sensitive and generous spirits to ardent, and sometimes sacrificial, support of Soviet Communism, we find a mixture of motives inexplicable in terms of the hedonistic determinism of Bentham or the economic determinism of Marxian orthodoxy. Neither self-interest nor fear nor vanity moved them to break with the conventional pieties and allegiances of the world in which they had been nurtured. In almost equal measure, they were impelled by a revulsion against the dismal spectacle of the postwar West which tottered without faith and with little hope from one crisis to another, and by an enthusiasm for the ideals of equality and human liberation broadcast in the official decrees and laws of the early Soviet régime. Both the revulsion and enthusiasm were rooted in a moral sensibility whose fibres had been fed from sources deeply imbedded in the traditions of the West. Not one of the neophytes to the Communist faith was conscious of accepting an alien creed, no matter how foreign the idiom in which it was clothed. The words in which one English convert to the Soviet idea describes her road to the Kremlin holds true with minor variations for the entire band of fellow-pilgrims:

> I came to Communism *via* Greek history, the French revolutionary literature I had read in childhood, and the English nineteenth-century poets of freedom. . . . In my mind Pericles' funeral oration, Shelley's and Swinburne's poems, Marx's and Lenin's writings, were all part and parcel of the same striving for the emancipation of mankind from oppression. [*Lost Illusion*, by Freda Utley.]

Stephen Spender, another English poet, in an effort to show that there is a continuity between the liberal idealists and philosophical radicals of the past century, on the one hand, and the Communists of the present century, on the other, between Blake, Godwin and J. S. Mill and Lenin, Trotsky and Stalin, writes:

> I am a Communist because I am a liberal. Liberalism
> seems to me to be the creed of those who, as far as it is
> possible in human affairs, are disinterested, if by disin-
> terestedness one understands not mere passivity but a
> regard for objective truth, an active will towards poli-
> tical justice. During an era of peace and progress, the
> liberal spirit is identical not only with political discus-
> sion, but also with scientific inquiry, speculative thought
> and the disinterested creation of works of art. [*Forward
> from Liberalism*, 1937.]

What Spender was saying is that he was a Communist because he believed in disinterestedness, objective truth and justice, free political discussion and inquiry, and creative integrity
—a cluster of values every one of which, oddly enough, has
been vehemently denounced as bourgeois prejudice by the
pundits of dialectical materialism.

Compare these strains of rationalism and humanism with
the *motifs* in the apologies of those adherents to National Socialism like Rauschning, Thyssen and Strasser who renounced
the Nazi régime. What elements in the Nazi practice and doctrine magnetized *their* minds, emotions and wills? "A national
awakening," "a surface discipline and order," "a vast display
of energy and achievement" whose new tempos and accelerated rhythms lift men out of the "humdrum of daily life"—these
are some of the things of which they speak. No ideals continuous with the heritage of either secular or Christian humanism
moved these men and their fellows; there was only the pull
of the dynamism of power. Here was no attempt to achieve
either a revolution from within or a transformation of basic
institutions, but, in Rauschning's phrase, "a revolution of nihilism." Not principle—even mistaken principle—drew them on.
They were sucked into the movement by a frenetic national
enthusiasm, and a mysticism centered on the person of Hitler.
"I looked into his eyes and he into mine; and at that I had only
one desire, to be at home and alone with that great, overwhelm-

ing experience." This extravagant outburst, Rauschning tells us, came not from an hysterical woman "but from a judge in a high position, talking to his colleagues."

A candid appraisal of the literature of Nazi disillusion shows that it is qualitatively of an entirely different order from that of the erstwhile partisans of the Soviet idea. Those who broke with Hitler did so because their stomachs were not strong enough to assimilate, as a constant diet, the atrocities to which they had originally resigned themselves as incidental and temporary— like Rauschning; or because their private interests were jeopardized by someone they had thought would be their creature —like Thyssen; or because their personal ambitions were frustrated—like Strasser.

I have contrasted these two types of literature of disillusion to underscore how misleading is the simple equation often drawn between Bolshevism and Nazism. In respect to their repudiation of many features of the democratic process they are, of course, identical; but in respect to the power of the Soviet and Nazi myths to attract the liberal spirits of the West they are vastly different. One need not agree with Toynbee that Russian Bolshevism is a species of Christian heresy to recognize the seductive effect of its use of categories drawn from the Western culture it would destroy. Just as the early Christian used the temples of pagan worship to make the new religion more palatable to peoples whose rulers had been converted, so the ideology of Bolshevism parades with a vocabulary of freedoms and rights freighted with connotations precious to all genuine humanists. That is why it is a more formidable opponent of free cultures than movements openly dedicated to their destruction. It is especially formidable in drawing to itself politically innocent men and women of good will and strong emotions whose minds are unfortified with relevant information, and who have not yet learned that only an intelligence hardened by skepticism is a safeguard against the credulities born of hope.

II

It is worthy of note that most of those who succumbed to the Soviet myth were devoid of political experience. They were led to their first political affair by emotional compulsion rather than by sober computation of the consequences of adopting a given proposal and its alternatives, which constitutes the every-day life of rational politics. Just as the necessity for loving creates its own object, so the necessity for believing selects the myth that appears best fitted to one's need and hopes. And, given the cultural climate, what seemed more congenial than the Soviet idea, the apparent offspring of moral idealism and scientific law? It not only held out guarantees of fulfillment of their highest hopes but provided a metaphysics to give them cosmic support.

All the great myths of history, from Augustine's *City of God* to Sorel's *General Strike,* have been able to sustain themselves because nowhere could they be exemplified, lived with, tested in terms of their fruits in experience. The Soviet myth of a humane, rationally ordered, classless, democratic society, however, was glorified not as an other-worldly ideal but as an historical fact with a definite locus in space and time. In staking out a claim in history, it subjected not only its power but its intent to the logic of events. We have no way of knowing the actual extent to which those who are native to the Soviet Union believe in the Soviet myth, carefully inculcated as it is in every textbook from the kindergarten to the university, and reinforced by an omnipresent secret police. But we do know, judging by the literature under review, that the first doubts in the minds of the pilgrims from other countries arose when they actually lived in the land of their dreams or pondered on the critical reports of those who had.

Some day a psychologist or poet will do justice to the drama of doubt in the minds of these political believers. Few individuals ever surrendered their belief in God with more agony, soul-searching and inner resistance than these latter-day apostles of revolutionary brotherhood surrendered their belief in the monolithic validity of the monolithic Soviet system.

It is an elementary truth of the psychology of perception that what a man sees often depends upon his beliefs and expectations. The stronger the beliefs, the more they function like *a priori* notions whose validity is beyond the tests of experience. Hopes can be so all-consuming that they affect even the range and quality of feeling.

It was to be expected that the Western intellectuals who saw the Soviet Union first hand would screen their impressions through the closely knit frame of doctrinal abstractions. It took some time before the cumulative shock of events tore a hole in this frame through which the facts of experience could pour. Only then did the agony of self-doubt begin. With varying details each one tells the same story. Once the evils of the system were recognized as evils, it was hoped they would disappear in time. When they grew worse with time, they were justified as necessary elements of the future good. When this necessity was challenged, the mind dwelt upon worse evils that could be found in other countries. But this provoked two gnawing questions. Were the evils in other countries really worse? And in any case, in the countries they came from, could not evils be publicly criticized?

The process of disenchantment was all the harder because in the course of their original conversion so much tortured dialectic had been expended in defense of what now seemed to be indefensible. As a rule, it requires more intellectual courage to renounce an illusion than to espouse one. For others are usually involved in such renunciations. These men and women felt a moral responsibility for those, and to those, who had been influenced by their enthusiasms. They knew that they would be showered with abuse, defamed as turncoats, that their former friends would construe the avowal of any doubt as evidence of personal fear or self-seeking—this despite the overwhelming evidence that neither popular favor nor material goods ranked high in their scale of values. They knew they faced loneliness and isolation. Bertrand Russell, the first of this group, and, as one would expect, the quickest to see through the myth, once confessed that he lost more friends by his criticism of Soviet terror than by his absolute pacifism during a war in which his country was locked in a battle of life and death with Germany.

Much graver considerations kept their lips sealed. They shrank in dismay at the prospect that reactionaries would seize upon their criticisms for their own purposes. More important still, a substitute faith to which they could wholeheartedly dedicate themselves was not available to them. They had lost their belief but not their hunger for belief. The man who cried, "O! Lord I believe. Help thou my *unbelief*," is usually on the way to a belief in which he may find peace, but he into whose soul the more radical acids of *disbelief* have entered can never again find peace in returning to the now-corroded original belief. He has lost his innocence, and in the end can only be useful as a Party functionary.

III

But as excess followed excess in a bloody succession, as intolerance and internal coercion increased in direct proportion to the strength and stability of the Soviet State, they felt compelled to make public their disavowal of their former allegiance. In every case it is clear that the ultimate grounds for their disavowal were the very same moral sentiments which had originally led them to the Kremlin. It was not the State, they discovered, which had withered away, but every vestige of political freedom, and with it all the brave ideals of the heroic period of the October Revolution.

None of the writers of this school could honestly be called sentimental dreamers or utopians. Most of them considered themselves Marxists of a sort. They had been trained to take a long view toward the stern necessities of history. Without swallowing Hegel, they agreed with him that what appears evil is often the negative dialectical moment in a cycle of progress, or what Toynbee today calls the ever-renewed challenge, necessary for a creative response on a higher level at a later time. They therefore allowed many times over for the blunders and crudities and rough edges of a new social justice.

It is one thing, however, to explain a phenomenon historically; it is another thing to justify it. Where explanation and justification are confused, then whatever is, is right. But if whatever is, is right, condemnation of capitalism and fascism, too, becomes meaningless wherever *they* exist, and the nerve of moral indignation which led to Communism in the first place becomes paralyzed. If history not only raises moral problems but settles them, then Gletkin's train of thought as he argues with Rubashev in Koestler's *Darkness at Noon* becomes inescapable. A mistake is a crime; successful might is always right; the weak are *ipso facto* wrong; every lost cause is a bad cause. Such a philosophy may be professed in words but in experience no sensitive human being can consistently act on it. That is why, for all their historical naturalism and scientific determinism, these enthusiasts were compelled to recognize that *not* everything they saw was necessary, and that some things could have been *different*.

What, then, were the specific experiences which led to disenchantment with the Soviet myth? At the outset it must be declared that it was *not* the discovery of the miserable living conditions of the Russian masses. Although they had been sadly unprepared for what they found—they had read too many extravagant claims made by Soviet partisans abroad— they could at least find reassurance in the promises of future five-year plans. What struck them most forcibly was the *cruelty*, the unnecessary cruelty, which pervaded almost every aspect of Soviet administrative practice.

This cruelty was not sadistic or demonic as in some fascist countries; it was systematic, a matter of State policy, carried out to teach object lessons to those who could not possibly profit by it because they were destroyed in the process. The use of bread as a political weapon had not been unknown in the past, but its calculated withdrawal for purposes of insuring absolute conformity was something new. Similarly the use of correctional labor camps for political prisoners. Ciliga, Serge and others bitterly contrast the conditions in which political prisoners, including Lenin and his lieutenants, lived under the Tsar with the conditions under which those charged with political offences lived under Stalin. And in a nationalized economy under dictatorial controls almost any offence can be regarded as political. Even theft of a handful of grain from a collective farm, moving from one town to another, not to speak of crossing a border without proper papers, are crimes against the State and punishable as such.

This cruelty was manifest not only in bureaucratic indifference but in official reminders that mercy, charity or pity were evidence of bourgeois decadence. According to our informants there was a total absence of concern for the individual person, an attitude in high official quarters and low which regarded the lives of *human* beings as if they were so much raw material, like iron, coal and scrap, to be consumed in the fires of production in order to swell the figures of output.

Of course bureaucratic indifference to the individual case, to personal need and suffering is not a Soviet phenomenon. In some degree it is found everywhere, as these men well knew. And cruelty, where State interests appear to be genuinely threatened, could be extenuated as a necessity, even if it was harshly and mistakenly conceived. But when it was coupled with wholesale injustice, it became unendurable to those nurtured in Western traditions. Two examples of this injustice, judging by the literature, were found especially outrageous. The first was the charge of "ideological complicity" directed against anyone whose views were similar to an individual believed guilty of any offence against the régime. Thousands were in consequence punished, sometimes by liquidation, for "ideological complicity" in the alleged act of someone they had never known or heard of. The second example, which particularly exercised Koestler, was the practice of holding entire families hostage for the exemplary behavior of its members. One decree provided that in the case of an individual's flight from the Soviet Union even those members of his family who had no knowledge of his act were to be "deported for five years to the remote regions of Siberia." Such sentences are served in penal work camps and are renewable by administrative decision.

As if to put a doctrinal seal upon these moral outrages and answer the unuttered protests on the lips of sympathizers, the People's Commissar for Justice proclaimed in the official organ of the Soviet régime: "In the opinion of liberals and opportunists of all kinds—the stronger a country is, the more lenient it can be to its opponents. . . . No, and again no! The stronger the country is, the mightier it is . . . the more justified are we in taking stern measures against those who disturb our socialist construction." (*Izvestia,* No. 37, Feb. 12, 1936.) Not long after, *he* was liquidated for not being stern enough. If this was socialist humanism, those who in the name of humanism had fought against such practices in countries under the heel of fascism could not swallow it.

IV

Most of the excesses against which the disillusioned intellectuals of the West protested did not at first concern their own professional fields. They protested as *human beings* against the degradation imposed on other human beings; or as *socialists* against mounting inequalities of power and position which, in fact, produced new class distinctions; or as *Marxists* against the willful disregard of objective historical conditions, and the blindness to the limits of endurance of human flesh. To all such protests came the reply "reasons of State." Those who received this reply confess that although they could not *see* these "reasons of State," they were puzzled and confused by the retort. After all, there are so many variables in history, the future is so indeterminate, who knows with certainty what is necessary for what?

But there was one kind of persecution for which the excuse

"reasons of State" could not be offered with the slightest plausibility. This was the cultural terror which raged in every field of the arts and sciences. All of these Western intellectuals lived in countries in which the slightest attempt to suppress a book or painting or a piece of music was sure to meet with fierce public opposition, even when the censorship was tangential. And at the worst, restrictions affected sales, not one's freedom and not one's life. To undergo the experience of a *total* censorship and control shocked and stunned them. For it was a control not only over what was written but also over what was painted and sung, not only over political thought but over thought in philosophy and science, not only over *what* was created but also over *how* it was created—the style and manner as well as theme and content. Nothing like it had ever existed in the modern world. In making art and philosophy a matter for the police, it violated the sense of dignity and authenticity among these writers and artists and thinkers of the West. It also affronted their sense of integrity as craftsmen.

It had been hard enough for them to accept Stalin's description of the intellectual as "an engineer of the human soul." When the engineer was required, however, to build not only to another's specifications but according to technical rules and laws laid down by those who had never undergone the discipline and training of the craftsman, they felt that some kind of atavistic cultural barbarism was being forced upon them. When on top of this, the penalties and sanctions of refusing to knuckle under entailed, because of the State monopoly of all means of publication and communication, the withdrawal of the means of life from the independent thinker and writer and his family, and in stubborn cases, like that of Vavilov, deportation and death, mystification gave way to passionate revulsion.

They were mystified because of the demonstrable uselessness of these cultural purges to the declared objectives of the Soviet régime. What bearing, for example, on any declared social policy was involved in the purge of physicists and astronomers for expressing disbelief in absolute space and time, a corollary of the theory of relativity? Or the condemnation of abstractionism in modern art, romanticism in the novel, formalism in poetry, and atonality in music? The decrees laid down with the awful authority of the Central Committee of the Communist Party and specifying the correct line in these fields must be read in order to realize how minutely this control extended to the very details of the arts and sciences. Or one could cite the dogmas of "Soviet biology"—a phrase reminiscent of the late unlamented "Nazi biology"—which renders taboo the Mendelian-Morgan theory of gene transmission in favor of Engels' Lamarckian notion, already disproved in his day, concerning the inheritance of acquired characteristics.

Not even this theory has any logical consequences of a political nature. Professor H. J. Muller, the famous American geneticist and Nobel Prize winner, who witnessed at first hand the tragic purge of Russian biologists, has observed that one can just as well argue from the theory of inherited acquired characteristics that the children of the ruling classes, because of the advantages of their environment, become superior types of human beings in comparison with the children of the masses, as that any human being can be transformed by environmental changes into a genius. Needless to say, both inferences are false. In insisting that the truth of a scientific theory had to be judged by its alleged social or political consequences, the Soviet régime, to the amazement of the Western intellectuals, was challenging what had been axiomatic since Galileo's time.

There was another horrible consequence of the operation of the Party line in cultural matters reported by those who observed it. Inasmuch as the line was a function of changing domestic and international conditions, it took sharp turns and shifts. Those who administered the Party decrees often became the victims of subsequent decrees. Since there was a normal risk in any utterance, a greater risk in silence, and even a risk in ferreting out deviations, there resulted a frenzied effort to purchase immunity by professions of orthodoxy, displays of ferocity towards scapegoats, and glorifications of Stalin in language as extravagant as anything that can be found in the sacred literature of Byzantinism. Everyone was caught up in an ever-expanding spiral of adulation and fear. It was this which moved André Gide, who had braved contumely in denouncing Western colonial practices, to write after he returned from the Soviet Union: "I doubt whether in any country of the world, even Hitler's Germany, is thought less free, more bowed down, more terrorized."

There were other elements in the common saga of disenchantment which received varying emphasis in the accounts written by those who had awakened from their dream. Edmund Wilson felt that the apotheosis of Stalin had reached a point at which the Russian people could react to him only neurotically, both on a conscious and unconscious level.

One of the initial impulses which led these Western intellectuals to accept Communism was a strong feeling of internationalism. They thought of themselves as citizens of the world, dedicated to an ideal of a universal parliament of free peoples. They looked to the Soviet Union as a fortress of a world movement to achieve this ideal. But when they saw that the road to power in Russia was imposed as a pattern for every other country they were disturbed. When they realized that socialist movements elsewhere were regarded as expendable border guards of the Soviet Union, active doubt set in. When, finally, cultural signs multiplied on all sides of aggressive Russian nationalism and pan-Slavism, when even Ivan, the Terrible, and Peter, the Great, were venerated as precursors of national Bolshevism, they felt themselves once more spiritual aliens. And with this they experienced a new resurgence of kinship with the West and their own countries, which until now they had seen only through a thick ideological fog.

The decay of faith led rapidly to two discoveries. One was that the rough economic equality which both Marx and Lenin assumed as a principle of socialist distribution was as far distant in the Soviet Union—in some respects even farther away—than in the countries of the middle way. The other was a nausea, more acute for being so long delayed, at the falsity of Soviet propaganda, its employment of semantic corruption as a weapon, illustrated, *e.g.*, in the use of the term democracy for a system in which expression of dissent was a grave penal offence.

V

It would be inappropriate to conclude this survey of political disillusionment without some evaluation of the weaknesses in the outlook of these Western intellectuals which contributed to their tragic self-deception. Even granting the partial truth of their plea that it was not so much *they* who changed as the Soviet system, it still remains undeniable that they were at fault in not conceiving the possibilities of change. But much more than this can be said in criticism. Even when all allowances are made for human fallibility, their responsibility for their own illusions remains heavy.

First, they looked to politics for something politics alone can never bring to the life of men—that absolute certainty, that emotional "sumptuosity of security," to use James' phrase, which, if attainable at all, can be most easily reached through a revealed religion they had properly rejected. In identifying themselves with those in the seats of power, they abdicated their true functions as intellectuals—to be the critical conscience of the smug and contented; and to fulfill their mission as the creatively possessed, the eternal questers after truth under all conditions. There is no loyalty to any community or State or party or church which absolves the individual from loyalty to himself. Whatever good the "saving remnant" can bring to the world, it must at least save the purity of the enkindling flame which by accident of natural grace burns within them.

Second, in their zeal for salvation by total political faith, they forgot that politics is always made by men, and that no doctrine or institution is a safeguard against its own abuses. They were doomed to be disillusioned because they forgot that no social change can make gods or even angels out of men, that to be human is to be tempted, and that no one can be forever tempted without erring.

Third, they made the mistake of all the typically *religieuse* of forgetting that in the affairs of *this* world, at least, faith can never be a substitute for intelligence. The transformation of the economic order is not a single problem that can be settled by fiat, poetic or philosophical. It is a series of problems, all very difficult, requiring prolonged study, in the absence of which a talent with paint or words or tones is not a sufficient qualification. They were immature in imagining that the field of economic behavior, from which as a youth, the great physicist, Planck had withdrawn because of its difficulty, could be stormed with weapons of moral indignation.

Fourth, they had abandoned too soon their own heritage of political democracy. They grossly underestimated the power of the self-corrective procedures of democracy to remedy, and perhaps to remove, the major economic disabilities and injustices of our age. Intent upon viewing everything *else* in historical perspective, they refused to take an historical perspective to Western democracy, and to observe the substantial progress that had been made since the time Marx described the pitiful conditions of the English proletariat in *Capital*, a book so sacred to most of them that they never read it. They failed to see that so long as the processes of political democracy remained intact, it was possible to carry the moral imperatives of the democratic way of life just as far as our courage, effort and powers of persuasion reached.

Fifth, they did not understand the genuine sense in which the social problem is a moral problem, *i.e.*, that no social institution or system is an end in itself but a means for realizing the primary value of security, freedom, justice, knowledge and kindness. Since the world is just as much a consequence of the means we use as of the end we profess, the end that actually comes to be depends upon the moral qualities of the means used. They had often heard that the end justifies the means but they never stopped to examine the evidence, in order to see whether the means used were *actually* bringing the end-in-view closer or pushing it farther away.

Whatever the responsibility of these writers for their own illusions, the record of their disillusionment is a record of growing intellectual and emotional maturity. No one has a right to be censorious of them, and least of all those who complacently accept any social change, whose emotions of sympathy for their fellow-men are never engaged, and who leave all the risks of thought and action to others. The very existence of this literature is a challenge to subsequent generations of writers who feel called to enlist themselves as foot-soldiers in a political crusade. We should be grateful to them for providing texts not only in the costs of human folly but in the grandeur of human faith and humility.

So long as there are human beings there will always be ideals and illusions. They cannot be foresworn. But this literature demonstrates that good sense in the quest for the good life in the good society depends not so much on *what* ideals are held as on *how* they are held; not so much on the nature of our beliefs as on the methods by which they are reached.

Underlying all other differences among human beings is the difference between the absolutist and the experimental temper of mind. The first converts its unreflective prejudices into first principles, and its shifting certitudes into a fanaticism of virtue which closes the gates of mercy against all who disagree. The second, although resolute in action, knows that finality of judgment is not possible to men, and is therefore prepared to review the evidence on which it stakes its ultimate commitments. It is this willingness to reconsider first principles in the light of relevant evidence and other alternatives which is the sign of the liberal and mature mind.

INDEX

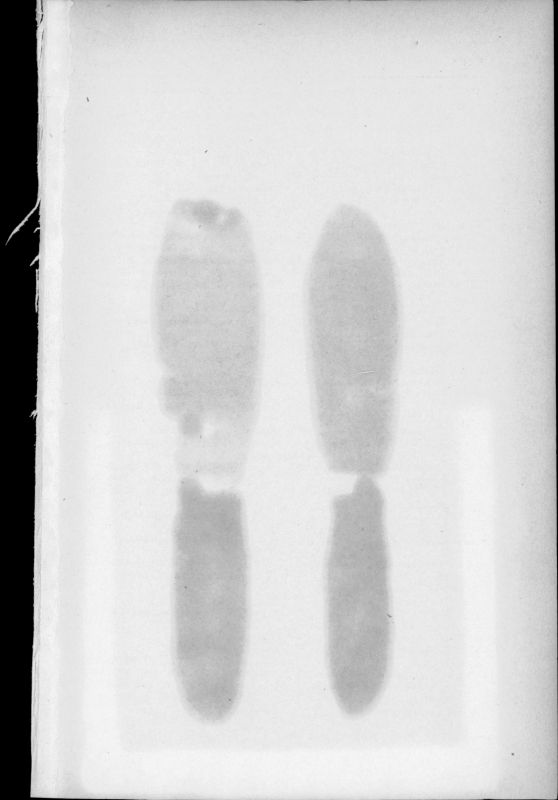